EXPERIENCING
THE WORD
NEW TESTAMENT

PRESENTED TO

_____

BY

_____

_____

DATE

_____

HOLMAN
CSB

EXPERIENCING
THE WORD
NEW TESTAMENT

HOLMAN
CSB

ISBN: 978-1-58640-482-6

Printed in the United States of America
1 2 3 4 5 6 12 11 10 09 08
RRD

Introducing

The Holman Christian Standard Bible

The Bible is God's revelation to man. It is the only book that gives us accurate information about God, man's need, and God's provision for that need. It provides us with guidance for life and tells us how to receive eternal life. The Bible can do these things because it is God's inspired Word, inerrant in the original manuscripts.

The Bible describes God's dealings with the ancient Jewish people and the early Christian church. It tells us about the great gift of God's Son, Jesus Christ, who fulfilled Jewish prophecies of the Messiah. It tells us about the salvation He accomplished through His death on the cross, His triumph over death in the resurrection, and His promised return to earth. It is the only book that gives us reliable information about the future, about what will happen to us when we die, and about where history is headed.

Bible translation is both a science and an art. It is a bridge that brings God's Word from the ancient world to the world today. In dependence on God to accomplish this sacred task, Holman Bible Publishers presents the Holman Christian Standard Bible, a new English translation of God's Word.

Textual Base of the Holman CSB®

The textual base for the New Testament [NT] is the Nestle-Aland *Novum Testamentum Graece,* 27th edition, and the United Bible Societies' *Greek New Testament,* 4th corrected edition. The text for the Old Testament [OT] is the *Biblia Hebraica Stuttgartensia,* 5th edition. At times, however, the translators have followed an alternative manuscript tradition, disagreeing with the editors of these texts about the original reading.

Where there are significant differences among Hebrew [Hb] and Aramaic [Aram] manuscripts of the OT or among Greek [Gk] manuscripts of the NT, the translators have followed what they believe is the original reading and have indicated the main alternative(s) in footnotes. In a few places in the NT, large square brackets indicate texts that the translation team and most biblical scholars today believe were not part of the original text. However, these texts have been retained in brackets in the Holman CSB because of their undeniable antiquity and their value for tradition and the history of NT interpretation in the church. The Holman CSB uses traditional verse divisions found in most Protestant Bibles.

Introducing

Goals of This Translation

The goals of this translation are:

- to provide English-speaking people across the world with an accurate, readable Bible in contemporary English

- to equip serious Bible students with an accurate translation for personal study, private devotions, and memorization

- to give those who love God's Word a text that has numerous reader helps, is visually attractive on the page, and is appealing when heard

- to affirm the authority of Scripture as God's Word and to champion its absolute truth against social or cultural agendas that would compromise its accuracy

The name, Holman Christian Standard Bible, captures these goals: *Holman* Bible Publishers presents a new *Bible* translation, for *Christian* and English-speaking communities, which will be a *standard* in Bible translations for years to come.

Why Is There a Need for Another English Translation of the Bible?

There are several good reasons why Holman Bible publishers invested its resources in a modern language translation of the Bible:

1. Each generation needs a fresh translation of the Bible in its own language.

The Bible is the world's most important book, confronting each individual and each culture with issues that affect life, both now and forever. Since each new generation must be introduced to God's Word in its own language, there will always be a need for new translations such as the Holman Christian Standard Bible. The majority of Bible translations on the market today are revisions of translations from previous generations. The Holman CSB is a new translation for today's generation.

2. English, one of the world's greatest languages, is rapidly changing, and Bible translations must keep in step with those changes.

English is the first truly global language in history. It is the language of education, business, medicine, travel, research, and the Internet. More than 1.3 billion people around the world speak or read English as a primary or secondary language. The Holman CSB seeks to serve many of those people with a translation they can easily use and understand.

English is also the world's most rapidly changing language. The Holman CSB seeks to reflect recent changes in English by using modern punctuation, formatting, and vocabulary, while avoiding slang, regionalisms, or changes made specifically for the sake of political or social agendas. Modern linguistic and semantic advances have been incorporated into the Holman CSB, including modern grammar.

3. Rapid advances in biblical research provide new data for Bible translators.

This has been called the "information age," a term that accurately describes the field of biblical research. Never before in history has there been as much information about the Bible as there is today—from archaeological discoveries to analysis of ancient manuscripts to years of study and statistical research on individual Bible books. Translations made as recently as 10 or 20 years ago do not reflect many of these advances in biblical research. The translators have taken into consideration as much of this new data as possible.

4. Advances in computer technology have opened a new door for Bible translation.

The Holman CSB has used computer technology and telecommunications in its creation perhaps more than any Bible translation in history. Electronic mail was used daily and sometimes hourly for communication and transmission of manuscripts. An advanced Bible software program, Accordance®, was used to create and revise the translation at each step in its production. A developmental copy of the translation itself was used within Accordance to facilitate cross-checking during the translation process—something never done before with a Bible translation.

Translation Philosophy of the Holman CSB

Most discussions of Bible translations speak of two opposite approaches: formal equivalence and dynamic equivalence. Although this terminology is meaningful, Bible translations cannot be neatly sorted into these two categories any more than people can be neatly sorted into two categories according to height or weight. Holman Bible Publishers is convinced there is room for another category of translation philosophies that capitalizes on the strengths of the other two.

1. Formal Equivalence:

Often called "word-for-word" (or "literal") translation, the principle of formal equivalence seeks as nearly as possible to preserve the structure of the original language. It seeks to represent each word of the original text with an exact equivalent word in the translation so that the reader can see word for word what the original human author wrote. The merits of this approach include its consistency with the conviction that the Holy Spirit did inspire the very words of Scripture in the original manuscripts. It also provides the English Bible student some access to the structure of the text in the original language. Formal equivalence can achieve accuracy to the degree that English has an exact equivalent for each word and that the grammatical patterns of the original language can be reproduced in understandable English. However, it can sometimes result in awkward, if not incomprehensible, English or in a misunderstanding of the author's intent. The literal rendering of ancient idioms is especially difficult.

2. <u>Dynamic or Functional Equivalence</u>:

Often called "thought-for-thought" translation, the principle of dynamic equivalence rejects as misguided the desire to preserve the structure of the original language. It proceeds by distinguishing the meaning of a text from its form and then translating the meaning so that it makes the same impact on modern readers that the ancient text made on its original readers. Strengths of this approach include a high degree of clarity and readability, especially in places where the original is difficult to render word for word. It also acknowledges that accurate and effective translation requires interpretation. However, the meaning of a text cannot always be neatly separated from its form, nor can it always be precisely determined. A biblical author may have intended multiple meanings. In striving for readability, dynamic equivalence also sometimes overlooks some of the less prominent elements of meaning. Furthermore, lack of formal correspondence to the original makes it difficult to verify accuracy and thus can affect the usefulness of the translation for in-depth Bible study.

3. <u>Optimal Equivalence</u>:

In practice, translations are seldom if ever purely formal or dynamic but favor one theory of Bible translation or the other to varying degrees. Optimal equivalence as a translation philosophy recognizes that form cannot be neatly separated from meaning and should not be changed (for example, nouns to verbs or third person "they" to second person "you") unless comprehension demands it. The primary goal of translation is to convey the sense of the original with as much clarity as the original text and the translation language permit. Optimal equivalence appreciates the goals of formal equivalence but also recognizes its limitations.

Optimal equivalence starts with an exhaustive analysis of the text at every level (word, phrase, clause, sentence, discourse) in the original language to determine its original meaning and intention (or purpose). Then relying on the latest and best language tools and experts, the nearest corresponding semantic and linguistic equivalents are used to convey as much of the information and intention of the original text with as much clarity and readability as possible. This process assures the maximum transfer of both the words and thoughts contained in the original.

The Holman CSB uses optimal equivalence as its translation philosophy. When a literal translation meets these criteria, it is used. When clarity and readability demand an idiomatic translation, the reader can still access the form of the original text by means of a footnote with the abbreviation "Lit."

Introducing

The Gender Language Policy in Bible translation

Some people today ignore the Bible's teachings on distinctive roles of men and women in family and church and have an agenda to eliminate those distinctions in every arena of life. These people have begun a program to engineer the removal of a perceived male bias in the English language. The targets of this program have been such traditional linguistic practices as the generic use of "man" or "men," as well as "he," "him," and "his."

A group of Bible scholars, translators, and other evangelical leaders met in 1997 to respond to this issue as it affects Bible translation. This group produced the "Guidelines for Translation of Gender-Related Language in Scripture" (adopted May 27, 1997 and revised Sept. 9, 1997). The Holman Christian Standard Bible was produced in accordance with these guidelines.

The goal of the translators has not been to promote a cultural ideology but to faithfully translate the Bible. While the Holman CSB avoids using "man" or "he" unnecessarily, the translation does not restructure sentences to avoid them when they are in the text. For example, the translators have not changed "him" to "you" or to "them," neither have they avoided other masculine words such as "father" or "son" by translating them in generic terms such as "parent" or "child."

History of the Holman Christian Standard Bible

After several years of preliminary development, Holman Bible Publishers, the oldest Bible publisher in America, assembled an international, interdenominational team of 100 scholars, editors, stylists, and proofreaders, all of whom were committed to biblical inerrancy. Outside consultants and reviewers contributed valuable suggestions from their areas of expertise. An executive team then edited, polished, and reviewed the final manuscripts.

Traditional Features Found in the Holman CSB

In keeping with a long line of Bible publications, the Holman Christian Standard Bible has retained a number of features found in traditional Bibles:

1. Traditional theological vocabulary (such as *justification, sanctification, redemption,* etc.) has been retained since such terms have no translation equivalent that adequately communicates their exact meaning.
2. Traditional spellings of names and places found in most Bibles have been used to make the Holman CSB compatible with most Bible study tools.
3. Some editions of the Holman CSB will print the words of Christ in red letters to help readers easily locate the spoken words of the Lord Jesus Christ.

4. Nouns and personal pronouns that clearly refer to any person of the Trinity are capitalized.
5. Descriptive headings, printed above each section of Scripture, help readers quickly identify the contents of that section.
6. Small lower corner brackets: ⌊ ⌋ indicate words supplied for clarity by the translators (but see below, under <u>Substitution of words in sentences</u>, for supplied words that are not bracketed).
7. Two common forms of punctuation are used in the Holman CSB to help with clarity and ease of reading: em dashes (a long dash —) are used to indicate sudden breaks in thought or to help clarify long or difficult sentences. Parentheses are used infrequently to indicate words that are parenthetical in the original languages.

How Certain Names and Terms Are Translated

<u>The names of God</u>

The Holman Christian Standard Bible OT consistently translates the Hebrew names for God as follows:

Holman CSB English:	**Hebrew original:**
God	*Elohim*
LORD	*YHWH (Yahweh)*
Lord	*Adonai*
Lord GOD	*Adonai Yahweh*
LORD of Hosts	*Yahweh Sabaoth*
God Almighty	*El Shaddai*

However, the Holman CSB OT uses Yahweh, the personal name of God in Hebrew, when a biblical text emphasizes Yahweh as a name: "His name is Yahweh" (Ps 68:4). Yahweh is used more often in the Holman CSB than in most Bible translations because the word LORD in English is a title of God and does not accurately convey to modern readers the emphasis on God's name in the original Hebrew.

<u>The uses of Christ and Messiah</u>

The Holman CSB translates the Greek word *Christos* ("anointed one") as either "Christ" or "Messiah" based on its use in different NT contexts. Where the NT emphasizes *Christos* as a name of our Lord or has a Gentile context, "Christ" is used (Eph 1:1 "Paul, an apostle of Christ Jesus . . ."). Where the NT *Christos* has a Jewish context, the title "Messiah" is used (Eph 1:12 ". . . we who had already put our hope in the Messiah"). The first use of "Messiah" in each chapter is also marked with a bullet referring readers to the Bullet Note at the back of most editions.

Place-names

In the original text of the Bible, particularly in the OT, a number of well-known places have names different from the ones familiar to contemporary readers. For example, "the Euphrates" often appears in the original text simply as "the River." In cases like this, the Holman Christian Standard Bible uses the modern name, "the Euphrates River," in the text without a footnote or lower corner brackets.

Substitution of words in sentences

A literal translation of the biblical text sometimes violates standard rules of English grammar, such as the agreement of subject and verb or person and number. In order to conform to standard usage, the Holman CSB has often made these kinds of grammatical constructions agree in English without footnotes or lower corner brackets.

In addition, the Greek or Hebrew texts sometimes seem redundant or ambiguous by repeating nouns where modern writing substitutes pronouns or by using pronouns where we would supply nouns for clarity and good style. When a literal translation of the original would make the English unclear, the Holman CSB sometimes changes a pronoun to its corresponding noun or a noun to its corresponding pronoun without a footnote or lower corner brackets. For example, Jn 1:42 reads: "And he brought Simon to Jesus . . ." The original Greek of this sentence reads: "And he brought him to Jesus."

Special Formatting Features

The Holman Christian Standard Bible has several distinctive formatting features:

1. OT passages quoted in the NT are set in boldface type. OT quotes consisting of two or more lines are block indented.
2. In dialogue, a new paragraph is used for each new speaker as in most modern publications.
3. Many passages, such as 1 Co 13, have been formatted as dynamic prose (separate block-indented lines like poetry) for ease in reading and comprehension. Special block-indented formatting has also been used extensively in both the OT and NT to increase readability and clarity in lists, series, genealogies and other parallel or repetitive texts.
4. Almost every Bible breaks lines in poetry using automatic typesetting programs with the result that words are haphazardly turned over to the next line. In the Holman CSB, special attention has been given to break every line in poetry and dynamic prose so that awkward or unsightly word wraps are avoided and complete units of thought turn over to the next line. The result is a Bible page that is much more readable and pleasing to the eye.

5. Certain foreign, geographical, cultural, or ancient words are preceded by a superscripted bullet (•*Abba*) at their first occurrence in each chapter. These words are listed in alphabetical order at the back of the Bible under the heading **Holman CSB Bullet Notes**. A few important or frequently misunderstood words (•slaves) are marked with a bullet more than one time per chapter.

6. Italics are used in the text for a transliteration of Greek and Hebrew words ("*Hosanna!*" in Jn 12:13) and in footnotes for direct quotations from the biblical text and for words in the original languages (the footnote at Jn 1:1 reads: "The *Word* (Gk *Logos*) is a title for Jesus . . .").

7. Since the majority of English readers do not need to have numbers and fractions spelled out in the text, the Holman CSB uses a similar style to that of modern newspapers in using Arabic numerals for the numbers 10 and above and in fractions, except in a small number of cases, such as when a number begins a sentence.

Footnotes

Footnotes are used to show readers how the original biblical language has been understood in the Holman Christian Standard Bible.

NT Textual Footnotes

NT textual notes indicate significant differences among Greek manuscripts (mss) and are normally indicated in one of three ways:

Other mss read _____
Other mss add _____
Other mss omit _____

In the NT, some textual footnotes that use the word "add" or "omit" also have square brackets before and after the corresponding verses in the biblical text (see the discussion above in the paragraph entitled "Textual Base of the Holman CSB"). Examples of this use of square brackets are Mk 16:9-20, Jn 5:3-4, and Jn 7:53–8:11.

OT Textual Footnotes

OT textual notes show important differences among Hebrew manuscripts and among ancient OT versions, such as the Septuagint and the Vulgate. See the list of abbreviations on page xxiv for a list of other ancient versions used.

Some OT textual notes (like NT textual notes) give only an alternate textual reading. However, other OT textual notes also give the support for the reading chosen by the editors as well as for the alternate textual reading. For example, the Holman CSB text of Ps 12:7 reads:

Introducing

You will protect us[a] from this generation forever.

The textual footnote for this verse reads:

[a]12:7 Some Hb mss, LXX; other Hb mss read *him*

The textual note in this example means that there are two different readings found in the Hebrew manuscripts: some manuscripts read *us* and others read *him*. The Holman CSB translators chose the reading *us*, which is also found in the Septuagint (LXX), and placed the other Hebrew reading *him* in the footnote.

Two other OT textual notes are:

Alt Hb tradition reads _____	a variation given by scribes in the Hebrew manuscript Tradition (known as *Kethiv/Qere* readings)
Hb uncertain	when it is uncertain what the original Hebrew text was

Other Kinds of Footnotes

Lit _____	a more literal rendering in English of the Hebrew, Aramaic, or Greek text
Or _____	an alternate or less likely English translation of the same Hebrew, Aramaic, or Greek text
=	an abbreviation for "it means" or "it is equivalent to"
Hb, Aram, Gk	the actual Hebrew, Aramaic, or Greek word is given using English letters
Hb obscure	the existing Hebrew text is especially difficult to translate
emend(ed) to _____	the original Hebrew text is so difficult to translate that competent scholars have conjectured or inferred a restoration of the original text based on the context, probable root meanings of the words, and uses incomparative languages

In some editions of the Holman Christian Standard Bible, additional footnotes clarify the meaning of certain biblical texts or explain biblical history, persons, customs, places, activities, and measurements. Cross-references are given for parallel passages or passages with similar wording, and in the NT, for passages quoted from the OT.

Word Studies

Located on the sidebar of many pages, word studies explain the meaning and usage of important Greek words. Each word study includes:

• the Greek word written in English letters
• an easy-to-use pronunciation guide for that word
• a frequent translation of that word in the HCSB NT
• the number of times that word is used by a NT writer and in the NT as a whole

Many word studies also contain historical background, theological significance, parallel passages, and cross references for the word.

Spiritual Insights by Dr. Henry Blackaby

A special feature of this edition of the HCSB are sidebars that contain devotional insights by Dr. Henry Blackaby. These comments offer applications of the biblical text for daily Christian living.

Henry Blackaby Presents

SEVEN STEPS TO
Experiencing the Word

Do your morning devotions ever seem disconnected from the rest of your day? Do familiar Scriptures feel at home in the context of a worship service, but sound like wishful thinking the rest of the week?

It's true, you can *read* the words without *experiencing* the Word. But it doesn't have to be that way. *Experiencing the Word* can be an everyday, anytime event.

Few people have been able to communicate this concept with as much power, clarity, and commitment as Henry Blackaby, best-selling author of the *Experiencing God* book and study course and numerous other titles and resources, now selling in the millions of copies. His methods for seeking God's will, listening for God's voice, and obeying God's teachings have helped many people begin experiencing God in their own lives on a daily basis.

Now he brings this same kind of spiritual depth to your study of the New Testament. As you travel these pages, as you interact with the Scriptures, as you sense God speaking through verses both comforting and confrontational, you'll be joined by Dr. Blackaby's wise counsel, awakening your heart to God's loving plan for your life, discovering His genuine desire to use you in helping others draw nearer to Him.

Be watching for Dr. Blackaby's godly advice around these overall themes:

1. Seek Relationship with God First
2. Tune Your Heart to Hear God's Voice
3. Live the Word Through Experience
4. Surrender Your Rights
5. Know God's Will by Knowing God's Heart
6. Obey, Obey, and Keep on Obeying
7. Relax—Let Your Witness Happen Naturally

Whether you catch them at random in your regular reading, or use the step-by-step outline on the following pages, you will come away with proven principles that will help you align yourself in harmony with God's will, becoming a person God can use to touch others with His love. Both relationships—both the vertical and horizontal—will be perfected as you let God's Word have its way in your life.

EXPERIENCING
THE WORD
NEW TESTAMENT

1. Seek Relationship with God First

Everything in your Christian life, everything about knowing Him and experiencing Him, everything about knowing His will depends on the quality of your love relationship with God.

Mt 5:23-24...... 11	Lk 12:34 167	Rm 6:13b...... 347	Heb 7:19....... 490
Mt 11:27 26	Lk 17:17 180	Rm 8:29........ 351	Heb 7:27....... 490
Mt 13:15-16...... 30	Lk 23:42-43..... 199	Rm 8:37........ 352	Heb 9:28....... 494
Mt 15:28 38	Lk 24:49,53 202	Rm 11:6........ 357	Heb 10:23 494
Mt 22:37-38...... 56	Jn 1:33-34 206	Rm 12:2........ 358	Heb 12:6 499
Mt 23:17 58	Jn 6:57 221	1 Co 4:7 373	2 Pt 2:9a 523
Mt 23:37 58	Jn 6:63 222	1 Co 11:1 382	1 Jn 3:21-22..... 529
Mt 24:35 61	Jn 11:42-43 237	1 Co 13:3 387	2 Jn 4.......... 534
Mt 25:8,10....... 63	Jn 12:3 238	2 Co 3:5 400	Jd 24-25........ 539
Mt 26:8b-10...... 66	Jn 14:10 244	2 Co 4:18 402	Rv 2:4 542
Mk 3:14-15 83	Jn 15:9 246	2 Co 6:16 405	Rv 7:15b 551
Mk 3:33,35 84	Jn 17:6 251	Gl 2:19b-20..... 419	Rv 7:17 551
Mk 6:46......... 93	Ac 2:28 268	Gl 3:3.......... 419	Rv 11:17 557
Mk 8:4.......... 96	Ac 7:20a 279	Eph 2:19 429	Rv 18:7 568
Mk 10:23....... 103	Ac 13:47 298	Php 4:12b 442	Rv 19:10 570
Mk 12:27a 110	Ac 16:33 305	Php 4:19 442	Rv 22:12 577
Mk 12:33....... 110	Ac 17:25 308	Col 1:17 445	
Mk 15:17-18 120	Ac 19:15 312	Col 3:1 447	
Lk 3:22......... 135	Ac 28:30-31..... 335	2 Tm 1:12b 471	
Lk 7:44......... 149	Rm 2:29........ 340	Ti 3:4-5a 477	
Lk 10:41-42..... 161	Rm 5:5......... 345	Heb 2:8b-9a 482	

2. Tune Your Heart to Hear God's Voice

You have to watch to see how God uniquely communicates with you. You will not have any other crutch. You will have to depend on God alone.

Mt 1:20 2	Lk 6:12 142	Ac 8:1b 283	1 Tm 2:1-2 461
Mt 2:13a 5	Lk 8:18 150	Ac 8:29 285	2 Tm 3:14-15 473
Mt 4:4 7	Lk 9:18 154	Ac 11:16 292	2 Tm 4:5 473
Mt 6:6 12	Lk 9:44 156	Ac 13:2 295	Heb 4:12 487
Mt 6:7-8 13	Lk 12:56 169	Ac 16:10 304	Heb 6:13,15 488
Mt 10:27 22	Lk 19:44 187	Ac 17:11b 307	Heb 8:10b 491
Mt 13:35b 32	Lk 20:39-40 189	Ac 20:7 314	Jms 1:21 504
Mt 13:52 34	Lk 24:6-8 201	Ac 24:25 325	Jms 5:16 509
Mt 18:20 44	Lk 24:45 202	Rm 3:4a 340	1 Pt 1:13 511
Mt 20:34 50	Jn 5:24 217	1 Co 11:31 385	2 Pt 1:19-21 521
Mt 22:37-38 56	Jn 7:47-48 225	1 Co 14:15 389	1 Jn 2:24 528
Mk 4:23 86	Jn 8:47a 228	1 Co 14:20 389	Rv 3:2 544
Mk 4:34 86	Jn 9:25 231	2 Co 1:20a 398	Rv 12:10 558
Mk 9:31b-32 100	Jn 10:27 233	2 Co 4:13-14 402	Rv 16:15 565
Mk 13:29 113	Jn 14:17 245	2 Co 11:3 411	Rv 19:7 570
Mk 13:33 114	Jn 18:37b 255	Gl 2:2a 417	Rv 21:5-6a 575
Lk 2:36-37 132	Jn 19:35 258	Eph 5:17 433	
Lk 3:21b 134	Jn 20:13 259	Col 4:2 449	
Lk 4:32 138	Ac 2:19a 267	1 Th 5:19 455	

3. Live the Word Through Experience

When you obey His Word, God accomplishes something through you only He can do. Then you come to know Him in a more intimate way by experiencing God at work through you.

Mt 6:14 13	Lk 11:13 162	Ac 23:23-24 323	Col 2:15 446
Mt 9:13 20	Lk 12:48b 168	Rm 2:6-7 339	2 Th 3:14-15 459
Mt 9:28-29 21	Lk 21:14-15 190	Rm 8:28 351	2 Tm 3:12 472
Mt 13:49-50 33	Lk 21:19 190	Rm 13:8 361	Phm 15-16a 480
Mt 17:20b 42	Lk 21:36 192	Rm 15:30 364	Heb 5:13-14 487
Mt 27:50-51 74	Jn 4:10 212	Rm 16:19 367	Heb 9:13-14 493
Mt 28:19-20 76	Jn 4:42 215	Rm 16:20 367	Heb 13:7 500
Mk 4:40-41 87	Jn 5:11 216	1 Co 15:10 391	Jms 2:15-17 505
Mk 6:5-6 90	Jn 8:12 226	1 Co 15:57 394	Jms 2:19 505
Mk 8:15 97	Jn 11:21-22 234	2 Co 13:2 415	1 Pt 4:8 517
Mk 11:24 106	Jn 16:21-22 249	Gl 5:6 423	2 Pt 1:3 521
Mk 12:24 109	Jn 18:26-27 254	Gl 6:8 425	2 Pt 3:11 524
Mk 14:28 116	Ac 4:31 273	Eph 3:16 430	Rv 18:14 568
Mk 16:7 123	Ac 5:41 276	Eph 4:1 431	
Lk 1:37 126	Ac 7:60 282	Eph 6:16 435	
Lk 4:18-19 137	Ac 16:25 305	Php 2:12b-13 439	
Lk 4:37 138	Ac 21:19 317	Php 3:10 440	
Lk 8:39 152	Ac 21:30-31 318	Php 3:16 440	
Lk 9:10 154	Ac 22:16 320	Col 2:6 445	

4. Surrender Your Rights

To live a God-centered life, you must focus your life on God's purposes, not your own plans. You must see things from God's perspective rather than your own.

Mt 3:8 5	Lk 20:18 188	Rm 12:9. 358	Heb 2:3 482
Mt 10:39 24	Jn 1:30 206	Rm 14:4. 361	Heb 3:13 484
Mt 19:21-22. 47	Jn 4:34. 214	Rm 16:2. 365	Heb 10:34 496
Mt 20:15a 48	Jn 6:38 221	Rm 16:3-4a 365	Heb 10:36 496
Mt 21:44 54	Jn 8:10-11 226	1 Co 4:5 373	Heb 11:24-25 . . . 498
Mt 27:32 73	Jn 12:26 239	1 Co 6:19-20. . . . 376	Heb 12:15 500
Mk 6:34 92	Ac 2:42 269	1 Co 7:22 377	1 Pt 2:16 513
Mk 8:38 99	Ac 7:34 280	1 Co 7:31 378	1 Pt 5:6-7 519
Mk 9:38 100	Ac 9:27 287	1 Co 8:9 378	1 Jn 2:9-10. 527
Mk 14:72 118	Ac 14:15a 299	1 Co 13:11 388	2 Jn 12 534
Lk 1:63. 128	Ac 14:19 299	1 Co 14:12 388	Rv 6:10 549
Lk 6:22. 143	Ac 15:36 303	2 Co 6:14 404	Rv 9:21 554
Lk 8:14. 150	Ac 19:18 312	2 Co 8:9 407	Rv 13:10 560
Lk 9:61. 158	Ac 21:11b 317	2 Co 11:29 412	
Lk 10:2. 158	Ac 23:16 322	Gl 4:19. 422	
Lk 11:2. 161	Rm 2:21a. 339	Gl 5:13. 423	
Lk 13:30 171	Rm 3:18. 341	Php 1:29 438	
Lk 14:11 173	Rm 7:18. 349	1 Th 3:9-10 453	
Lk 18:14 183	Rm 9:32. 354	1 Th 5:15 455	

5. Know God's Will by Knowing God's Heart

You never have to sense an emptiness or lack of purpose. God will always fill your life with Himself. When you have Him, you have everything there is.

Mt 8:21-22. 18	Lk 12:6-7 166	Ac 7:9-10a 278	Eph 4:11-12. 431
Mt 10:24-25a 22	Lk 12:32 167	Ac 7:32 280	Php 2:5-6. 438
Mt 14:17-18. 35	Lk 16:15 177	Ac 10:28 289	Col 2:20a. 446
Mt 17:16 42	Lk 19:5. 184	Ac 11:17b 292	1 Th 2:2. 451
Mt 18:3-4. 43	Lk 19:17 185	Ac 18:9-10. 309	2 Th 3:3. 458
Mt 21:6 50	Lk 22:31-32. 194	Ac 23:11 322	1 Tm 1:12 461
Mt 21:21 52	Lk 23:50-52. 201	Rm 3:11. 341	1 Tm 5:4 465
Mt 25:21 63	Jn 5:19 216	Rm 7:6. 349	Ti 3:14. 478
Mt 25:40 65	Jn 7:15-16 223	1 Co 1:28 369	Jms 5:17. 509
Mt 26:31-32. 67	Jn 9:4a 229	1 Co 9:19 381	1 Pt 5:10 519
Mt 26:39 68	Jn 9:33 231	1 Co 9:22b 381	3 Jn 11 536
Mk 1:38 79	Jn 12:27 239	1 Co 10:24 382	
Mk 5:28 89	Jn 12:42-43 241	1 Co 12:6-7. 385	
Mk 10:14 102	Jn 12:49 241	1 Co 15:49 393	
Mk 10:27 103	Jn 14:12 244	1 Co 15:51-52. . . 394	
Mk 10:29-30 104	Jn 17:21 251	2 Co 3:6 400	
Mk 14:35 116	Jn 17:25-26 252	2 Co 12:10 412	
Lk 1:45. 127	Jn 18:36 255	Gl 1:15-16. 417	
Lk 5:26. 140	Jn 19:10-11a 256	Gl 6:2. 425	
Lk 7:22-23 147	Jn 21:5-6 261	Eph 3:11 429	
Lk 7:39. 148	Jn 21:21-22 263	Eph 3:20-21a. . . . 430	

6. Obey, Obey, and Keep on Obeying

Adjust your life to God in the kind of relationship where you follow Him wherever He leads you—even if the assignment seems to be small or insignificant.

Mt 12:11-12......27	Lk 22:61-62.....196	I Co 14:15.....389	Heb 6:11-12.....488
Mt 14:28-29......37	Jn 6:9-10a......219	I Co 16:9......395	Heb 12:1......499
Mt 21:31b-32.....53	Jn 11:27........236	2 Co 6:10......404	Jms 1:22......504
Mt 24:45-46......62	Ac 5:3.........275	2 Co 7:1........405	Jms 4:17......508
Mt 26:69-70......70	Ac 7:51........281	2 Co 8:11......407	I Pt 1:15.......511
Mk 3:24-25......84	Ac 9:13........286	2 Co 11:14.....411	I Pt 4:3a,7......517
Mk 7:15.........95	Ac 9:20........286	Gl 4:16........422	2 Pt 2:19b......523
Mk 12:17.......108	Ac 9:39........287	Eph 5:11........433	2 Pt 3:17......524
Mk 14:16.......115	Ac 10:33.......290	I Th 4:2-3a.....453	I Jn 3:4-5......528
Mk 15:2-3......119	Ac 23:5........321	I Tm 3:10......463	Jd 23b.........539
Lk 2:15.........130	Ac 24:16.......325	I Tm 3:13......463	Rv 2:29.........544
Lk 2:27-28a.....131	Ac 26:19.......329	I Tm 5:25......466	Rv 11:18.......557
Lk 9:51.........157	Ac 26:25.......329	I Tm 6:12......466	Rv 18:2.........567
Lk 11:28.......163	Rm 6:6.........347	I Tm 6:20-21....468	Rv 18:4.........567
Lk 14:3-4.......172	I Co 3:3b.......371	2 Tm 2:16......471	Rv 20:4b.......572
Lk 17:10.......179	I Co 9:16......380	Ti 2:11-12......477	
Lk 22:10.......193	I Co 11:16.....384	Phm 21........480	

7. Relax—Let Your Witness Happen Naturally

When the world sees things happening through God's people that cannot be explained except that God Himself has done them, then the world will be drawn to the God they see.

Mt 8:13.........16	Lk 23:34-35a....198	Ac 27:35.......332	I Pt 3:15b......515
Mt 12:33........29	Jn 1:41-42a.....207	Ac 28:23.......334	I Jn 2:5b-6......527
Mt 12:36........29	Jn 7:17.........223	I Co 2:4.......371	I Jn 3:13.......529
Mt 13:54b-56.....34	Ac 2:37........268	I Co 7:16......377	I Jn 4:12.......531
Mt 22:3.........55	Ac 3:5.........269	2 Co 2:14......398	I Jn 4:15.......531
Mt 27:14........71	Ac 3:12........271	2 Co 13:3......415	3 Jn 5-6a.......536
Mk 1:36.........78	Ac 4:1-2........271	Eph 6:19.......435	Rv 16:10b-11.....565
Mk 1:45.........80	Ac 5:19-20......275	Php 2:15.......439	Rv 22:8.........577
Mk 5:31-33......89	Ac 5:32........276	Col 3:16.......447	
Lk 5:31-32......141	Ac 8:35........285	Col 4:6.......449	
Lk 6:37.........145	Ac 10:44-45....291	I Th 2:8........451	
Lk 6:41.........145	Ac 13:15.......296	2 Th 3:1........458	
Lk 10:22.......159	Ac 15:12.......301	I Tm 4:12......465	
Lk 16:31.......178	Ac 19:30.......313	2 Tm 2:24-25....472	
Lk 18:43.......184	Ac 25:19.......327	I Pt 2:12.......513	
Lk 23:5.........197	Ac 27:25.......331	I Pt 3:13.......514	

Greek Word Studies

TRANSLATION	GREEK WORD	PAGE	TRANSLATION	GREEK WORD	PAGE
Abba	ἀββά	117	Counselor	παράκλητος	247
abyss	ἄβυσσος	553	covenant	διαθήκη	492
accept	προσλαμβάνω	363	credit	λογίζομαι	343
adoption	υἱοθεσία	350	crown	στέφανος	452
again	ἄνωθεν	210	crucify	σταυρόω	72
Almighty	παντοκράτωρ	541	cure	θεραπεύω	333
Alpha	ἄλφα	574	custom	ἔθος	328
apostle	ἀπόστολος	82	deacon	διάκονος	462
appear	ὁράω	125	deceive	πλανάω	569
appearing	ἐπιφάνεια	467	deliver	σῴζω	112
assure	ἀμήν, ἀμήν	208	demon-possessed	δαιμονίζομαι	88
authority	ἐξουσία	107	descendant	σπέρμα	353
baptize	βαπτίζω	6	deserve	ἄξιος	564
beast	θηρίον	556	disciple	μαθητής	243
believe	πιστεύω	220	disciples (make)	μαθητεύω	75
betray	παραδίδωμι	69	divorce	ἀπολύω	46
blasphemy	βλασφημία	28	do	πράσσω	338
bless	εὐλογέω	203	elder	πρεσβύτερος	300
blessed	μακάριος	9	end	τέλος	355
body	σῶμα	386	engaged	μνηστεύομαι	129
boldness	παρρησία	272	epistle	ἐπιστολή	366
brother	ἀδελφός	15	eunuch	εὐνοῦχος	284
Caesar	Καῖσαρ	326	evangelist	εὐαγγελιστής	316
caught up	ἁρπάζω	454	exalt	ὑψόω	518
cause downfall	σκανδαλίζω	101	exorcist	ἐξορκιστής	311
centurion	ἑκατοντάρχης	330	faith	πίστις	497
Christian	Χριστιανός	293	fast	νηστεύω	81
church	ἐκκλησία	274	fear	φοβέω	23
circumcision	περιτομή	418	fellowship	κοινωνία	526
coming	παρουσία	457	finish	τελέω	257
commandment	ἐντολή	57	firstborn	πρωτότοκος	444
compassion	σπλαγχνίζομαι	39	firstfruits	ἀπαρχή	392
confess	ὁμολογέω	530	flesh	σάρξ	348
confirm	ἵστημι	414	forehead	μέτωπον	576
conscience	συνείδησις	379	foreknow	προγινώσκω	356
continue	προσκαρτερέω	265	forgive	ἀφίημι	45

Greek Word Studies

TRANSLATION	GREEK WORD	PAGE	TRANSLATION	GREEK WORD	PAGE
forsake	ἐγκαταλείπω	121	leper	λεπρός	146
foundation	καταβολή	164	life (*psuche*)	ψυχή	98
free	δικαιόω	346	life (*zoe*)	ζωή	213
fulfill	πληρόω	17	light	φῶς	227
Gentile	ἔθνος	297	live	κατοικέω	552
gentleness	πραΰτης	506	Lord	κύριος	186
ghost	φάντασμα	36	love (*agapao*)	ἀγαπάω	160
glory	δόξα	240	love (*phileo*)	φιλέω	262
gospel	εὐαγγέλιον	437	manager	οἰκονόμος	176
grace	χάρις	344	Maranatha	μαράνα θά	396
grief	λύπη	406	Master (*despotes*)	δεσπότης	538
Hades	ᾅδης	573	Master (*epistates*)	ἐπιστάτης	139
hate	μισέω	174	mercy	ἔλεος	19
head	κεφαλή	383	messenger	ἀγγελός	25
heart	καρδία	14	Messiah	Χριστός	40
heaven	οὐρανός	562	mind	νοῦ	359
heavenly	ἐπουράνιος	501	must	δεῖ	155
hell	γέεννα	165	name	ὄνομα	270
high priest	ἀρχιερεύς	486	offer defense	ἀπολογέομαι	324
holy	ἅγιος	546	only	μονογενής	211
Hosanna	Ὡσαννά	51	Originator	ἀρχή	545
hour	ὥρα	250	overseer	ἐπίσκοπος	476
humble	ταπεινός	409	owe	ὀφείλω	360
hypocrite	ὑποκριτής	59	parable	παραβολή	31
I am	ἐγώ εἰμί	253	paradise	παράδεισος	200
idol	εἴδωλον	532	patience	μακροθυμία	516
image	εἰκών	401	Pentecost	πεντηκοστή	266
immortality	ἀφθαρσία	470	perfect	τελειόω	483
inheritance	κληρονομία	448	persecute	διώκω	319
intention	νόημα	399	plan	βουλή	315
judge	κρίνω	375	power	δύναμις	337
kingdom	βασιλεία	8	praise	δόξα	240
know	ἐπίσταμαι	310	pray	προσεύχομαι	294
knowledge	γνῶσις	410	preach	κηρύσσω	91
language	γλῶσσα	390	predestine	προορίζω	427
law	νόμος	420	priesthood	ἱεράτευμα	512

Greek Word Studies

TRANSLATION	GREEK WORD	PAGE	TRANSLATION	GREEK WORD	PAGE
prophet	προφήτης	302	slave	δοῦλος	105
propitiation	ἱλαστήριον	342	Son, son	υἱός	421
proud	ὑπερήφανος	507	Spirit, spirit	πνεῦμα	424
rebuke	ἐπιτιμάω	474	suffer	πάσχω	181
reconcile	καταλλάσσω	403	synagogue	συναγωγή	111
redemption	ἀπολύτρωσις	432	talent	τάλαντον	64
rejoice	χαίρ	441	tax collector	τελώνης	182
repent	μετανοέω	175	Teacher	διδάσκαλος	242
rest	κατάπαυσις	485	temptation	πειρασμός	195
resurrect	ἐγείρω	49	testify	μαρτυρέω	218
resurrection	ἀνάστασις	235	throw down into		
revelation	ἀποκάλυψις	413	Tartarus	ταρταρόω	522
reward	μισθός	372	torment	βασανίζω	151
righteousness	δικαιοσύνη	10	tongue	γλῶσσα	390
Roman	Ῥωμαῖος	306	transform	μεταμορφόω	41
Sabbath	σάββατον	122	tribe	φυλή	550
sacrifice	θυσία	502	tribulation	θλῖψις	60
sanctify	ἁγιάζω	495	victorious	νικάω	543
sanctuary	ναός	563	vile	βδέλυγμα	566
Sanhedrin	συνέδριον	277	virgin	παρθένος	3
Satan	Σατανᾶς	170	visionary state	ἔκστασις	288
Savior	σωτήρ	464	voice	φωνή	555
scribe	γραμματεύς	94	water	ὕδωρ	224
scroll	βιβλίον	547	wisdom	σοφία	370
secret	μυστήριον	85	wise man	μάγος	4
seal	σφραγίς	548	without father	ἀπάτωρ	489
seed	σπέρμα	353	woe	οὐαί	144
send	πέμπω	260	word (rhema)	ῥήμα	434
sexual immorality	πορνεία	374	Word (logos)	λόγος	205
shepherd (poimaino)			work	ἔργον	428
	ποιμαίνω	571	world	κόσμος	248
shepherd (poimen)	ποιμήν	232	worship	προσκυνέω	136
sign	σημεῖον	209	wrath	ὀργή	191
sin	ἁμαρτία	362	write	γράφω	133
sinner	ἁμαρτωλός	230	zeal	ζῆλος	408
666	ἑξακόσιοι ἑξήκοντα ἕξ	561			

Transliteration Guide

GREEK LETTER	NAME	TRANSLITERATION INTO ENGLISH
α	alpha	a
β	beta	b
γ	gamma	g
δ	delta	d
ε	epsilon	e[1]
ζ	zeta	z
η	eta	e[1]
θ	theta	th
ι	iota	i
κ	kappa	k
λ	lambda	l
μ	mu	m
ν	nu	n
ξ	xi[2]	x
ο	omicron	o[1]
π	pi	p
ρ	rho	r
σ, ς	sigma	s[3]
τ	tau	t
υ	upsilon	u[4]
φ	phi	ph
χ	chi	ch
ψ	psi	ps
ω	omega	o[1]
ʽ	[rough breathing mark]	h

[1] No distinction is made in transliteration between the two *e* class vowels or between the two *o* class vowels. The distinction can be seen in the pronunciation guide: *epsilon* is a short *e* ("eh"); *eta* is a long *e* ("ay"); *omicron* is a short *o* ("ah"); and *omega* is a long *o* ("oh").

[2] Pronounced *ksee*

[3] There is no difference in sound between normal *sigma* (σ) and final *sigma* (ς).

[4] The vowel *upsilon* (υ) is often transliterated into English as *y* because Greek words containing an *upsilon* often come into English with a *y* (for example, English *dynamite* is a loan word from the Greek term *dunamis*). However, transliteration is primarily concerned with the proper sound, and *upsilon* never has the sound of the English *y*. *Upsilon* has the sound of a long *u* in English (as in the word *rule*), so we always use *u* to transliterate *upsilon*.

Pronunciation Guide
for Greek Words

CODE	EXAMPLE	CODE	EXAMPLE
a	HAT	oo	LOOK
ah	far, FAHR	<u>oo</u>	boot, B<u>OO</u>T
aw	call, KAWL		
ay	name, NAYM	ow	cow, KOW
b	BAD		out, OWT
ch	CHEW	oy	boil, BOYL
d	DAD	p	PAT
e, eh	met, MEHT	r	RAN
ee	sea, SEE	s	star, STAHR
	ski, SKEE		tsetse, SET see
ew	truth, TREWTH	sh	show, SHOH
f	FOOT		action, AK shuhn
	enough, ee NUHF		mission, MIH shuhn
g	GET		vicious, VIH shuhss
h	HIM	t	tie, TIGH
hw	whether, HWEH thuhr		Thomas, TAH muhss
i, ih	city, SIH tih	th	thin, THIHN, THIN
igh	sign, SIGHN	<u>th</u>	there, <u>TH</u>EHR
	eye, IGH	tw	TWIN
<u>igh</u>	lite, L<u>IGH</u>T	u, uh	tub, TUHB
ih	pin, PIHN, PIN		Joshua, JAHSH yew uh
j	jack, JAK		term TUHRM
	germ, JUHRM	v	veil, VAYL
k	KISS		of, AHV
	cow, KOW	w	WAY
ks	ox, AHKS		
kw	quail, KWAYL	wh	(whether) see *hw*
l	live, LIHV, LIGHV	y	year, YEER
m	more, MOHR	z	xerox, ZIHR ahks
n	note, NOHT		ZEE rahks
ng	ring, RING		his, HIHZ, HIZ
oh	go, GOH		zebra, ZEE bruh
	row, ROH (a boat)	zh	version, VUHR zhuhn

Taken from the book by W. Murray Severance, *That's Easy for You to Say: Your Quick Guide to Pronouncing Bible Names* (Nashville: Broadman & Holman Publishers, 1997). Used by permission of the author.

Bible Book Abbreviations

OLD TESTAMENT

Gn	Genesis
Ex	Exodus
Lv	Leviticus
Nm	Numbers
Dt	Deuteronomy
Jos	Joshua
Jdg	Judges
Ru	Ruth
1 Sm	1 Samuel
2 Sm	2 Samuel
1 Kg	1 Kings
2 Kg	2 Kings
1 Ch	1 Chronicles
2 Ch	2 Chronicles
Ezr	Ezra
Neh	Nehemiah
Est	Esther
Jb	Job
Ps	Psalms
Pr	Proverbs
Ec	Ecclesiastes
Sg	Song of Solomon
Is	Isaiah
Jr	Jeremiah
Lm	Lamentations
Ezk	Ezekiel
Dn	Daniel
Hs	Hosea
Jl	Joel
Am	Amos
Ob	Obadiah
Jnh	Jonah
Mc	Micah
Nah	Nahum
Hab	Habakkuk
Zph	Zephaniah
Hg	Haggai
Zch	Zechariah
Mal	Malachi

NEW TESTAMENT

Mt	Matthew
Mk	Mark
Lk	Luke
Jn	John
Ac	Acts
Rm	Romans
1 Co	1 Corinthians
2 Co	2 Corinthians
Gl	Galatians
Eph	Ephesians
Php	Philippians
Col	Colossians
1 Th	1 Thessalonians
2 Th	2 Thessalonians
1 Tm	1 Timothy
2 Tm	2 Timothy
Ti	Titus
Phm	Philemon
Heb	Hebrews
Jms	James
1 Pt	1 Peter
2 Pt	2 Peter
1 Jn	1 John
2 Jn	2 John
3 Jn	3 John
Jd	Jude
Rv	Revelation

Commonly Used Abbreviations in the Holman CSB

A.D.	in the year of our Lord
alt	alternate
a.m.	from midnight until noon
Aq	Aquila
Aram	Aramaic
B.C.	before Christ
c.	circa
chap	chapter
DSS	Dead Sea Scrolls
Eng	English
Gk	Greek
Hb	Hebrew
Lat	Latin
Lit	Literally
LXX	Septuagint—an ancient translation of the Old Testament into Greek
MT	Masoretic Text
NT	New Testament
ms(s)	manuscript(s)
OT	Old Testament
p.m.	from noon until midnight
pl	plural
Ps(s)	psalm(s)
Sam	Samaritan Pentateuch
sg	singular
syn.	synonym
Sym	Symmachus
Syr	Syriac
Tg	Targum
Theod	Theodotian
v., vv.	verse, verses
Vg	Vulgate—an ancient translation of the Bible into Latin
vol(s).	volume(s)

THE
NEW TESTAMENT

THE GOSPEL OF

MATTHEW

THE GENEALOGY OF JESUS CHRIST

1 The historical record[a] of Jesus Christ, the Son of David, the Son of Abraham:

FROM ABRAHAM TO DAVID

2 Abraham fathered[b] Isaac,
Isaac fathered Jacob,
Jacob fathered Judah and his brothers,
3 Judah fathered Perez and Zerah by Tamar,
Perez fathered Hezron,
Hezron fathered Aram,
4 Aram fathered Aminadab,
Aminadab fathered Nahshon,
Nahshon fathered Salmon,
5 Salmon fathered Boaz by Rahab,
Boaz fathered Obed by Ruth,
Obed fathered Jesse,
6 and Jesse fathered King David.

FROM DAVID TO THE BABYLONIAN EXILE

Then[c] David fathered Solomon by Uriah's wife,
7 Solomon fathered Rehoboam,
Rehoboam fathered Abijah,
Abijah fathered Asa,[d]
8 Asa[d] fathered Jehoshaphat,
Jehoshaphat fathered Joram,
Joram fathered Uzziah,

---

[a]1:1 Or *The book of the genealogy*
[b]1:2 In vv. 2-16 either a son, as here, or a later descendant, as in v. 8
[c]1:6 Other mss add *King*
[d]1:7,8 Other mss read *Asaph*

9 Uzziah fathered Jotham,
Jotham fathered Ahaz,
Ahaz fathered Hezekiah,
10 Hezekiah fathered Manasseh,
Manasseh fathered Amon,[a]
Amon[a] fathered Josiah,
11 and Josiah fathered Jechoniah and his brothers
at the time of the exile to Babylon.

FROM THE EXILE TO THE MESSIAH

12 Then after the exile to Babylon
Jechoniah fathered Salathiel,
Salathiel fathered Zerubbabel,
13 Zerubbabel fathered Abiud,
Abiud fathered Eliakim,
Eliakim fathered Azor,
14 Azor fathered Zadok,
Zadok fathered Achim,
Achim fathered Eliud,
15 Eliud fathered Eleazar,
Eleazar fathered Matthan,
Matthan fathered Jacob,
16 and Jacob fathered Joseph the husband of Mary,
who gave birth to[b] Jesus who is called
the •Messiah.

17 So all the generations from Abraham to David were 14 generations; and from David until the exile to Babylon, 14 generations; and from the exile to Babylon until the Messiah, 14 generations.

THE NATIVITY OF THE MESSIAH

18 The birth of Jesus Christ came about this way: After His mother Mary had been •engaged to Joseph, it was discovered before they came together that she was pregnant by the Holy Spirit. 19 So her husband Joseph, being a righteous man, and not wanting to disgrace her publicly, decided to divorce her secretly.

20 But after he had considered these things, an angel of the Lord suddenly appeared to him in a dream, saying, "Joseph, son of David, don't be afraid to take Mary

Unusual Times Call for Uncommon Faith

When you face confusing circumstances, don't start blaming God. Don't give up following Him. Go to God. Ask Him to reveal the truth of your circumstances. Ask Him to show you His perspective. Then wait on the Lord.

After he had considered these things, an angel of the Lord suddenly appeared to him in a dream, saying, "Joseph, son of David, don't be afraid to take Mary as your wife, because what has been conceived in her is by the Holy Spirit.
—Matthew 1:20

---

[a]1:10 Other mss read *Amos*   [b]1:16 Lit *Mary, from whom was born*

as your wife, because what has been conceived in her is by the Holy Spirit. ²¹ She will give birth to a son, and you are to name Him Jesus,ᵃ because He will save His people from their sins."

²² Now all this took place to fulfill what was spoken by the Lord through the prophet:

²³ **See, the virgin will become pregnant
    and give birth to a son,
    and they will name Him Immanuel,**ᵇ

which is translated "God is with us."

²⁴ When Joseph got up from sleeping, he did as the Lord's angel had commanded him. He married her ²⁵ but did not know her intimately until she gave birth to a son.ᶜ And he named Him Jesus.

WISE MEN SEEK THE KING

2 After Jesus was born in Bethlehem of Judea in the days of King •Herod, •wise men from the east arrived unexpectedly in Jerusalem, ² saying, "Where is He who has been born King of the Jews? For we saw His star in the eastᵈ and have come to worship Him."ᵉ

³ When King Herod heard this, he was deeply disturbed, and all Jerusalem with him. ⁴ So he assembled all the •chief priests and •scribes of the people and asked them where the •Messiah would be born.

⁵ "In Bethlehem of Judea," they told him, "because this is what was written by the prophet:

⁶ **And you, Bethlehem,** in the land of Judah,
    are by no means **least among the leaders
        of Judah:**
    **because out of you will come a leader
    who will shepherd My people Israel.**"ᶠ

⁷ Then Herod secretly summoned the wise men and asked them the exact time the star appeared. ⁸ He sent them to Bethlehem and said, "Go and search carefully for the child. When you find Him, report back to me so that I too can go and worship Him."ᵍ

ᵃ1:21 *Jesus* is the Gk form of the Hb name "Joshua," which = "The Lord saves" or "Yahweh saves."
ᵇ1:23 Is 7:14
ᶜ1:25 Other mss read *to her first-born son*

ᵈ2:2 Or *star at its rising*
ᵉ2:2 Or *to pay Him homage*
ᶠ2:6 Mc 5:2
ᵍ2:8 Or *and pay Him homage*

WORD STUDY

Greek word: ***magos***
[MAH gahss]
Translation: ***wise man, sorcerer***
Uses in Matthew's Gospel: **4**
Uses in the NT: **6**
Key passage: **Matthew 2:1,7,16**

In the Greek OT, *magos* occurs only in Daniel 2:2,10 and describes a group of people possessing knowledge of Babylonian religious and magical arts, whom Nebuchadnezzar summoned to interpret his dream. In Matthew 2:1,7,16, *magos* refers to those who have wisdom through investigation and interpretation of the movements of heavenly bodies (i.e., *wise men/astrologers*). It is likely (though not certain) these astrologers were from Babylon, since there they would have had contact with Jewish exiles and obtained an interest in the Jewish Messiah. The irony in the passage is difficult to miss: The Jewish King Herod in Jerusalem attempted to slaughter baby Jesus born in nearby Bethlehem, while pagan devotees of a foreign religion recognized Messiah's star, traveled a great distance to find Him, presented Him with valuable gifts, and paid homage to Him. Elsewhere in the NT, *magos* refers to Elymas the *sorcerer* (Ac 13:6,8).

⁹ After hearing the king, they went on their way. And there it was—the star they had seen in the east!ᵃ It led them until it came and stopped above the place where the child was. ¹⁰ When they saw the star, they were overjoyed beyond measure. ¹¹ Entering the house, they saw the child with Mary His mother, and falling to their knees, they worshiped Him.ᵇ Then they opened their treasures and presented Him with gifts: gold, frankincense, and myrrh. ¹² And being warned in a dream not to go back to Herod, they returned to their own country by another route.

THE FLIGHT INTO EGYPT

¹³ After they were gone, an angel of the Lord suddenly appeared to Joseph in a dream, saying, "Get up! Take the child and His mother, flee to Egypt, and stay there until I tell you. For Herod is about to search for the child to destroy Him." ¹⁴ So he got up, took the child and His mother during the night, and escaped to Egypt. ¹⁵ He stayed there until Herod's death, so that what was spoken by the Lord through the prophet might be fulfilled: **Out of Egypt I called My Son.**ᶜ

THE MASSACRE OF THE INNOCENTS

¹⁶ Then Herod, when he saw that he had been outwitted by the wise men, flew into a rage. He gave orders to massacre all the male children in and around Bethlehem who were two yearsᵈ old and under, in keeping with the time he had learned from the wise men. ¹⁷ Then what was spoken through Jeremiah the prophet was fulfilled:

> ¹⁸ **A voice was heard in Ramah,**
> **weeping,ᵉ and great mourning,**
> **Rachel weeping for her children;**
> **and she refused to be consoled,**
> **because they were no more.**ᶠ

ᵃ2:9 Or *star ... at its rising*
ᵇ2:11 Or *they paid Him homage*
ᶜ2:15 Hs 11:1
ᵈ2:16 Lit *were from two years*

ᵉ2:18 Other mss read *Ramah, lamentation, and weeping,*
ᶠ2:18 Jr 31:15

THE HOLY FAMILY IN NAZARETH

¹⁹ After Herod died, an angel of the Lord suddenly appeared in a dream to Joseph in Egypt, ²⁰ saying, "Get up! Take the child and His mother and go to the land of Israel, because those who sought the child's life are dead." ²¹ So he got up, took the child and His mother, and entered the land of Israel. ²² But when he heard that Archelausª was ruling over Judea in place of his father Herod, he was afraid to go there. And being warned in a dream, he withdrew to the region of Galilee. ²³ Then he went and settled in a town called Nazareth to fulfill what was spoken through the prophets, that He will be called a •Nazarene.

THE MESSIAH'S HERALD

3 In those days John the Baptist came, preaching in the Wilderness of Judea ² and saying, "Repent, because the kingdom of heaven has come near!" ³ For he is the one spoken of through the prophet Isaiah, who said:

A voice of one crying out
in the wilderness:
"Prepare the way for the Lord;
make His paths straight!"ᵇ

⁴ John himself had a camel-hair garment with a leather belt around his waist, and his food was locusts and wild honey. ⁵ Then ⌊people from⌋ Jerusalem, all Judea, and all the vicinity of the Jordan were flocking to him, ⁶ and they were baptized by him in the Jordan River as they confessed their sins.

⁷ When he saw many of the •Pharisees and •Sadducees coming to the place of his baptism,ᶜ he said to them, "Brood of vipers! Who warned you to flee from the coming wrath? ⁸ Therefore produce fruit consistent withᵈ repentance. ⁹ And don't presume to say to yourselves, 'We have Abraham as our father.' For I tell you that God is able to raise up children for Abraham from these stones! ¹⁰ Even now the ax is ready to strike

God's Voice Is Remarkably Clear

When God chose to speak to an individual in the Bible, the person had no doubt that it was God, and he knew what God was saying. When God speaks to you, you will be able to know He is the One speaking, and you will know clearly what He is saying to you.

After they were gone, an angel of the Lord suddenly appeared to Joseph in a dream, saying, "Get up! Take the child and His mother, flee to Egypt, and stay there until I tell you."
—Matthew 2:13a

Turn from Your Way and Walk God's Way

It is impossible to love anything else as much as you love God and still please Him.

"Therefore produce fruit consistent with repentance."
—Matthew 3:8

ª2:22 A son of Herod the Great who ruled a portion of his father's kingdom 4 B.C.–A.D. 6
ᵇ3:3 Is 40:3
ᶜ3:7 Lit *to his baptism*
ᵈ3:8 Lit *fruit worthy of*

WORD STUDY

Greek word: **baptizo**

[bap TIH dzoh]

Translation: **baptize**

Uses in Matthew's Gospel: **7**
(Mk, 13; Lk, 10; Jn, 13)

Uses in the NT: **77**

Key passage: **Matthew 3:11-17**

Baptizo is an intensive form of the verb *bapto* (*to immerse* or *dip*; Lk 16:24; Jn 13:26; Rv 19:13). *Baptizo* is common in the NT and always appears in a religious sense, referring to water baptism (Mt 3:13; 28:19; Ac 8:36-38), Spirit baptism (Mk 1:8; Ac 1:5; 1 Co 12:13), or baptism with fire (Mt 3:11 = Lk 3:16). Once Jesus used *baptizo* metaphorically to describe His suffering on the cross (Mk 10:38).

John used water to baptize those who identified with the kingdom community by confessing their sins (Mt 3:1-6 = Mk 1:4-6). Yet he indicated that Jesus Himself would also baptize, not "with water" (cf. Jn 4:1-2), but "with the Holy Spirit" and "with fire," the latter being a reference to final judgment (Mt 3:11-12).

While similar to John's baptism, Christian baptism identifies the believer with the Triune godhead (Mt 28:19) and symbolizes Jesus' death, burial, and resurrection (Rm 6:3-5).

the root of the trees! Therefore every tree that doesn't produce good fruit will be cut down and thrown into the fire.

¹¹ "I baptize you with[a] water for repentance,[b] but the One who is coming after me is more powerful than I. I am not worthy to take off[c] His sandals. He Himself will baptize you with[a] the Holy Spirit and fire. ¹² His winnowing shovel[d] is in His hand, and He will clear His threshing floor and gather His wheat into the barn. But the chaff He will burn up with fire that never goes out."

THE BAPTISM OF JESUS

¹³ Then Jesus came from Galilee to John at the Jordan, to be baptized by him. ¹⁴ But John tried to stop Him, saying, "I need to be baptized by You, and yet You come to me?"

¹⁵ Jesus answered him, "Allow it for now, because this is the way for us to fulfill all righteousness." Then he allowed Him ⌊to be baptized⌋.

¹⁶ After Jesus was baptized, He went up immediately from the water. The heavens suddenly opened for Him,[e] and He saw the Spirit of God descending like a dove and coming down on Him. ¹⁷ And there came a voice from heaven:

> This is My beloved Son.
> I take delight in Him!

THE TEMPTATION OF JESUS

4 Then Jesus was led up by the Spirit into the wilderness to be tempted by the Devil. ² After He had fasted 40 days and 40 nights, He was hungry. ³ Then the tempter approached Him and said, "If You are the Son of God, tell these stones to become bread."

⁴ But He answered, "It is written:

> **Man must not live on bread alone**
> **but on every word that comes**
> **from the mouth of God."[f]**

---

[a]**3:11** Or *in*
[b]**3:11** Baptism was the means by which repentance was expressed publicly.
[c]**3:11** Or *to carry*
[d]**3:12** A wooden farm implement

used to toss threshed grain into the wind so the lighter chaff would blow away and separate from the heavier grain
[e]**3:16** Other mss omit *for Him*
[f]**4:4** Dt 8:3

5 Then the Devil took Him to the holy city,ª had Him stand on the pinnacle of the temple, 6 and said to Him, "If You are the Son of God, throw Yourself down. For it is written:

> **He will give His angels orders**
> **concerning you, and**
> **they will support you with their hands**
> **so that you will not strike**
> **your foot against a stone."b**

7 Jesus told him, "It is also written: **Do not test the Lord your God."c**

8 Again, the Devil took Him to a very high mountain and showed Him all the kingdoms of the world and their splendor. 9 And he said to Him, "I will give You all these things if You will fall down and worship me."d

10 Then Jesus told him, "Go away,e Satan! For it is written:

> **Worship the Lord your God,**
> **and serve only Him."f**

11 Then the Devil left Him, and immediately angels came and began to serve Him.

MINISTRY IN GALILEE

12 When He heard that John had been arrested, He withdrew into Galilee. 13 He left Nazareth behind and went to live in Capernaum by the sea, in the region of Zebulun and Naphtali. 14 This was to fulfill what was spoken through the prophet Isaiah:

> 15 **Land of Zebulun and land of Naphtali,**
> **along the sea road, beyond the Jordan,**
> **Galilee of the Gentiles!**
> 16 **The people who live in darkness**
> **have seen a great light,**
> **and for those living in the shadowland**
> **of death,**
> **light has dawned.g h**

All Scripture Is Given for Your Inspiration

We usually want God to speak to us so He can give us a devotional thought to make us feel good all day. If you want the God of the universe to speak to you, you need to be open to every word He says.

He answered, "It is written: Man must not live on bread alone but on every word that comes from the mouth of God."
—Matthew 4:4

ª4:5 Jerusalem
b4:6 Ps 91:11-12
c4:7 Dt 6:16
d4:9 Or *and pay me homage*
e4:10 Other mss read *Get behind Me*
f4:10 Dt 6:13
g4:16 Lit *dawned on them*
h4:15-16 Is 9:1-2

7

WORD STUDY

Greek word: *basileia*
[bah sih LAY uh]

Translation: *kingdom*

Uses in Matthew's Gospel: **55**
(Mk, 20; Lk, 46; Jn, 5)

Uses in the NT: **162**

Key passage: **Matthew 4:17**

Jesus began His ministry by proclaiming, "Repent, because the *kingdom* (*basileia*) of heaven has come near" (Mt 4:17). Matthew alone records the phrase "*kingdom of heaven*" (32 times), while "*kingdom of God*" appears throughout the Gospels (Mt, 5 times; Mk, 14 times; Lk, 32 times; Jn, 2 times). The phrases are interchangeable (cf. Mt 8:11 & Lk 13:29; Mt 19:23-24; Mt 11:11 = Lk 7:28).

In the NT, *basileia* focuses upon the manifestation of God's sovereign authority and rule in human affairs. Jesus taught that the *kingdom* is a present reality with a fuller future manifestation (Mt 13:31-32 = Mk 4:30-32). He demonstrated the power of God's *kingdom* by casting out demons, healing the sick, and proclaiming the way to enter that *kingdom* (Mt 4:17,23; 11:2-15). Because of His resurrection, ascension, and enthronement, Jesus now reigns as King over God's *kingdom*, sitting on David's throne forever (Mt 28:18; Lk 1:32-33; Ac 2:24-36).

[17] From then on Jesus began to preach, "Repent, because the kingdom of heaven has come near!"

THE FIRST DISCIPLES

[18] As He was walking along the Sea of Galilee, He saw two brothers, Simon, who was called Peter, and his brother Andrew. They were casting a net into the sea, since they were fishermen. [19] "Follow Me," He told them, "and I will make you fish for[a] people!" [20] Immediately they left their nets and followed Him.

[21] Going on from there, He saw two other brothers, James the son of Zebedee, and his brother John. They were in a boat with Zebedee their father, mending their nets, and He called them. [22] Immediately they left the boat and their father and followed Him.

TEACHING, PREACHING, AND HEALING

[23] Jesus was going all over Galilee, teaching in their •synagogues, preaching the good news of the kingdom, and healing every[b] disease and sickness among the people. [24] Then the news about Him spread throughout Syria. So they brought to Him all those who were afflicted, those suffering from various diseases and intense pains, the demon-possessed, the epileptics, and the paralytics. And He healed them. [25] Large crowds followed Him from Galilee, •Decapolis, Jerusalem, Judea, and beyond the Jordan.

THE SERMON ON THE MOUNT

5 When He saw the crowds, He went up on the mountain, and after He sat down, His disciples came to Him. [2] Then[c] He began to teach them, saying:

THE BEATITUDES

[3] "Blessed are the poor in spirit,
because the kingdom of heaven is theirs.
[4] Blessed are those who mourn,
because they will be comforted.
[5] Blessed are the gentle,
because they will inherit the earth.

---

[a]4:19 Lit *you fishers of*
[b]4:23 Or *every kind of*

[c]5:2 Lit *Then opening His mouth*

⁶ Blessed are those who hunger
and thirst for righteousness,
because they will be filled.
⁷ Blessed are the merciful,
because they will be shown mercy.
⁸ Blessed are the pure in heart,
because they will see God.
⁹ Blessed are the peacemakers,
because they will be called sons of God.
¹⁰ Blessed are those who are persecuted
for righteousness,
because the kingdom of heaven is theirs.

¹¹ "Blessed are you when they insult you and persecute you and falsely say every kind of evil against you because of Me. ¹² Be glad and rejoice, because your reward is great in heaven. For that is how they persecuted the prophets who were before you.

BELIEVERS ARE SALT AND LIGHT

¹³ "You are the salt of the earth. But if the salt should lose its taste, how can it be made salty? It's no longer good for anything but to be thrown out and trampled on by men.
¹⁴ "You are the light of the world. A city situated on a hill cannot be hidden. ¹⁵ No one lights a lamp and puts it under a basket,[a] but rather on a lampstand, and it gives light for all who are in the house. ¹⁶ In the same way, let your light shine[b] before men, so that they may see your good works and give glory to your Father in heaven.

CHRIST FULFILLS THE LAW

¹⁷ "Don't assume that I came to destroy the Law or the Prophets. I did not come to destroy but to fulfill. ¹⁸ For •I assure you: Until heaven and earth pass away, not the smallest letter[c] or one stroke of a letter will pass from the law until all things are accomplished. ¹⁹ Therefore, whoever breaks one of the least of these commandments and teaches people to do so will be

WORD STUDY

Greek word: ***makarios***
[mah KAH ree ahss]
Translation: ***blessed***
Uses in Matthew's Gospel: **13**
(Lk, 15; Jn, 2)
Uses in the NT: **50**
Key passage: **Matthew 5:3-12**

Makarios occurs thirty times in the Gospels, all but two on the lips of Jesus (Lk 1:45; 11:27). The OT Hebrew term *ashrey* stands behind the NT usage of *makarios*. Both terms are normally translated "blessed" or "happy." *Makarios* has two main nuances in the NT. It predominantly refers to God's blessing upon His people, and secondarily to God's people blessing Him. In the latter sense, *makarios* is basically synonymous with *praise*. When one is blessed by God, he is approved by God. The opposite of *makarios* is "woe" (*ouai*), the status of one who is not approved by God and is thus the object of impending judgment (Mt 23:13-32; Lk 6:24-26). God's blessing does not necessarily include material prosperity in this life (Mt 19:23-24; Lk 6:24; 16:19-31)—the contrary is actually quite possible (Lk 6:20)—but it does anticipate full, uninterrupted prosperity in the future kingdom (Mt 5:4-9,11-12; 25:34).

---

[a]**5:15** A large basket used to measure grain
[b]**5:16** Or *way, your light must shine*
[c]**5:18** Or *not one iota; iota* is the *smallest letter* of the Gk alphabet.

WORD STUDY

Greek word: *dikaiosune*
[dih kigh ah SOO nay]

Translation: *righteousness*

Uses in Matthew's Gospel: **7**
(Lk, 1; Jn, 2)

Uses in the NT: **92**

Key passage: **Matthew 5:20**

In Pauline theology, *dikaiosune* (*righteousness*) often refers to a person's righteous standing before God (in a judicial sense), since God has accounted that person as righteous in His sight because of their faith in Christ (Rm 4:3,5-6; 5:17; cf. 3:26). God's *righteousness* leads Him to reward good, pardon sinners, and judge sin (Rm 3:5,25). Throughout the NT, *dikaiosune* emphasizes behavior that conforms to a divine standard (Lk 1:75; Eph 6:14; 2 Tm 3:16; 1 Pt 2:24; 3:14). In the Synoptic Gospels, *dikaiosune* frequently refers to the way a Christian disciple behaves, namely, in conformity with standards fit for God's kingdom (Mt 5:10,20). The hallmarks of a disciple are those qualities described by Jesus in the Sermon on the Mount (5:3–7:20). Additional hallmarks can be found elsewhere in Jesus' teachings (Mt 16:24-26; Lk 9:57-62; 14:25-35; Jn 13:34-35; 15:5,8,16) and in other NT passages as well (Ac 14:22; Eph 2:10; 2 Tm 3:12).

called least in the kingdom of heaven. But whoever practices and teaches ₍these commandments₎ will be called great in the kingdom of heaven. ²⁰ For I tell you, unless your righteousness surpasses that of the •scribes and •Pharisees, you will never enter the kingdom of heaven.

MURDER BEGINS IN THE HEART

²¹ "You have heard that it was said to our ancestors,[a] **Do not murder**,[b] and whoever murders will be subject to judgment. ²² But I tell you, everyone who is angry with his brother[c] will be subject to judgment. And whoever says to his brother, 'Fool!'[d] will be subject to the •Sanhedrin. But whoever says, 'You moron!' will be subject to •hellfire.[e] ²³ So if you are offering your gift on the altar, and there you remember that your brother has something against you, ²⁴ leave your gift there in front of the altar. First go and be reconciled with your brother, and then come and offer your gift. ²⁵ Reach a settlement quickly with your adversary while you're on the way with him, or your adversary will hand you over to the judge, the judge to[f] the officer, and you will be thrown into prison. ²⁶ I assure you: You will never get out of there until you have paid the last penny![g]

ADULTERY IN THE HEART

²⁷ "You have heard that it was said, **Do not commit adultery**.[h] ²⁸ But I tell you, everyone who looks at a woman to lust for her has already committed adultery with her in his heart. ²⁹ If your right eye •causes you to sin, gouge it out and throw it away. For it is better that you lose one of the parts of your body than for your whole body to be thrown into hell. ³⁰ And if your right hand causes you to sin, cut it off and throw it away. For it is better that you lose one of the parts of your body than for your whole body to go into hell!

---

[a]**5:21** Lit *to the ancients*
[b]**5:21** Ex 20:13; Dt 5:17
[c]**5:22** Other mss add *without a cause*
[d]**5:22** Lit *Raca*, an Aram term of abuse similar to "airhead"
[e]**5:22** Lit *the gehenna of fire*

[f]**5:25** Other mss read *judge will hand you over to*
[g]**5:26** Lit *quadrans*, the smallest and least valuable Roman coin, worth ¹⁄₆₄ of a daily wage
[h]**5:27** Ex 20:14; Dt 5:18

DIVORCE PRACTICES CENSURED

³¹ "It was also said, **Whoever divorces his wife must give her a written notice of divorce.**ᵃ ³² But I tell you, everyone who divorces his wife, except in a case of sexual immorality,ᵇ causes her to commit adultery. And whoever marries a divorced woman commits adultery.

TELL THE TRUTH

³³ "Again, you have heard that it was said to our ancestors,ᶜ **You must not break your oath, but you must keep your oaths to the Lord.**ᵈ ³⁴ But I tell you, don't take an oath at all: either by heaven, because it is God's throne; ³⁵ or by the earth, because it is His footstool; or by Jerusalem, because it is the city of the great King. ³⁶ Neither should you swear by your head, because you cannot make a single hair white or black. ³⁷ But let your word 'yes' be 'yes,' and your 'no' be 'no.'ᵉ Anything more than this is from the evil one.

GO THE SECOND MILE

³⁸ "You have heard that it was said, **An eye for an eye** and **a tooth for a tooth.**ᶠ ³⁹ But I tell you, don't resistᵍ an evildoer. On the contrary, if anyone slaps you on your right cheek, turn the other to him also. ⁴⁰ As for the one who wants to sue you and take away your shirt,ʰ let him have your coatⁱ as well. ⁴¹ And if anyone forcesʲ you to go one mile, go with him two. ⁴² Give to the one who asks you, and don't turn away from the one who wants to borrow from you.

LOVE YOUR ENEMIES

⁴³ "You have heard that it was said, **Love your neighbor**ᵏ and hate your enemy. ⁴⁴ But I tell you, love

Keep Your View of God Unobstructed

If your love relationship with God is not right, nothing else will be right.

"If you are offering your gift on the altar, and there you remember that your brother has something against you, leave your gift there in front of the altar. First go and be reconciled with your brother, and then come and offer your gift."
—Matthew 5:23-24

ᵃ**5:31** Dt 24:1
ᵇ**5:32** Gk *porneia* = fornication, or possibly a violation of Jewish marriage laws
ᶜ**5:33** Lit *to the ancients*
ᵈ**5:33** Lv 19:12; Nm 30:2; Dt 23:21
ᵉ**5:37** Say what you mean and mean what you say
ᶠ**5:38** Ex 21:24; Lv 24:20; Dt 19:21

ᵍ**5:39** Or *don't set yourself against,* or *don't retaliate against*
ʰ**5:40** Lit *tunic* = inner garment
ⁱ**5:40** Lit *robe,* or *garment* = outer garment
ʲ**5:41** Roman soldiers could require people to carry loads for them.
ᵏ**5:43** Lv 19:18

your enemies[a] and pray for those who[b] persecute you, [45] so that you may be[c] sons of your Father in heaven. For He causes His sun to rise on the evil and the good, and sends rain on the righteous and the unrighteous. [46] For if you love those who love you, what reward will you have? Don't even the tax collectors do the same? [47] And if you greet only your brothers, what are you doing out of the ordinary?[d] Don't even the Gentiles[e] do the same? [48] Be perfect, therefore, as your heavenly Father is perfect.

HOW TO GIVE

6 "Be careful not to practice your righteousness[f] in front of people, to be seen by them. Otherwise, you will have no reward from your Father in heaven. [2] So whenever you give to the poor, don't sound a trumpet before you, as the hypocrites do in the •synagogues and on the streets, to be applauded by people. •I assure you: They've got their reward! [3] But when you give to the poor, don't let your left hand know what your right hand is doing, [4] so that your giving may be in secret. And your Father who sees in secret will reward you.[g]

HOW TO PRAY

[5] "Whenever you pray, you must not be like the hypocrites, because they love to pray standing in the synagogues and on the street corners to be seen by people. I assure you: They've got their reward! [6] But when you pray, go into your private room, shut your door, and pray to your Father who is in secret. And your Father who sees in secret will reward you.[h] [7] When you pray, don't babble like the idolaters,[i] since they imagine they'll be heard for their many words. [8] Don't be like them, because your Father knows the things you need before you ask Him.

God's People Must Be Praying People

The greatest untapped resource that I know of is the united prayer of God's people.

"When you pray, go into your private room, shut your door, and pray to your Father who is in secret. And your Father who sees in secret will reward you."

—Matthew 6:6

---

[a]**5:44** Other mss add *bless those who curse you, do good to those who hate you,*
[b]**5:44** Other mss add *mistreat you and*
[c]**5:45** Or *may become,* or *may show yourselves to be*
[d]**5:47** Lit *doing more,* or *doing that is superior*

[e]**5:47** Other mss read *tax collectors*
[f]**6:1** Other mss read *charitable giving*
[g]**6:4** Other mss read *will Himself reward you openly*
[h]**6:6** Other mss add *openly*
[i]**6:7** Or *Gentiles,* or *nations,* or *heathen,* or *pagans*

THE MODEL PRAYER

9 "Therefore, you should pray like this:

> Our Father in heaven,
> Your name be honored as holy.
> 10 Your kingdom come.
> Your will be done
> on earth as it is in heaven.
> 11 Give us today our daily bread.[a]
> 12 And forgive us our debts,
> as we also have forgiven our debtors.
> 13 And do not bring us into[b] temptation,
> but deliver us from the evil one.[c]
> [For Yours is the kingdom and the power
> and the glory forever. •Amen.][d]

14 "For if you forgive people their wrongdoing,[e] your heavenly Father will forgive you as well. 15 But if you don't forgive people,[f] your Father will not forgive your wrongdoing.[e]

HOW TO FAST

16 "Whenever you fast, don't be sad-faced like the hypocrites. For they make their faces unattractive[g] so their fasting is obvious to people. I assure you: They've got their reward! 17 But when you fast, put oil on your head, and wash your face, 18 so that you don't show your fasting to people but to your Father who is in secret. And your Father who sees in secret will reward you.[h]

GOD AND POSSESSIONS

19 "Don't collect for yourselves treasures[i] on earth, where moth and rust destroy and where thieves break in and steal. 20 But collect for yourselves treasures in heaven, where neither moth nor rust destroys, and

Don't Just Pray to Hear Yourself Talk

When you begin asking questions to God in prayer, always check to see if you have asked the right question before you pursue the answer.

"When you pray, don't babble like the idolaters, since they imagine they'll be heard for their many words. Don't be like them, because your Father knows the things you need before you ask Him."

—Matthew 6:7-8

Share the Same Mercy You Have Received

When you consider the incredible, undeserved mercy you have been granted, how can you refuse to extend the same unconditional mercy to others?

"If you forgive people their wrongdoing, your heavenly Father will forgive you as well."

—Matthew 6:14

---

[a]6:11 Or *our necessary bread*, or *our bread for tomorrow*
[b]6:13 Or *do not cause us to come into*
[c]6:13 Or *from evil*
[d]6:13 Other mss omit bracketed text
[e]6:14,15 Or *trespasses*
[f]6:15 Other mss add *their wrongdoing*
[g]6:16 Or *unrecognizable*, or *disfigured*
[h]6:18 Other mss add *openly*
[i]6:19 Or *valuables*

WORD STUDY

Greek word: **kardia**
[kahr DEE uh]
Translation: **heart**
Uses in Matthew's Gospel: **16**
(Mk, 11; Lk, 22; Jn, 7)
Uses in the NT: **156**
Key passage: **Matthew 6:21**

The English word *heart* is used literally of the vital organ that pumps blood and figuratively of the inner person. The same was true for *kardia* (*heart*) in the ancient Greek-speaking world, but in the NT the literal sense of the term never occurs. As with the related OT Hebrew term for *heart* (*leb*), *kardia* can refer to the whole person (Lk 16:15; cf. 1 Ch 28:9) or to various aspects of a person's inner self: physical needs or wants (Ac 14:17; Jms 5:5; cf. Pr 15:15), thoughts or intellect (Lk 12:45; cf. Gn 6:5; Pr 23:7), values (Mt 6:21; cf. Jb 12:24), emotions (Ac 21:13; Phm 7; cf. Pr 31:11; Sg 8:6), volition (Lk 21:14; 2 Co 9:7; cf. Ex 7:22-23; Mal 4:6), and affections (Mt 22:37; cf. Dt 6:5; 30:6,10).

where thieves don't break in and steal. [21] For where your treasure is, there your heart will be also.

[22] "The eye is the lamp of the body. If your eye is good, your whole body will be full of light. [23] But if your eye is bad, your whole body will be full of darkness. So if the light within you is darkness—how deep is that darkness!

[24] "No one can be a slave of two masters, since either he will hate one and love the other, or be devoted to one and despise the other. You cannot be slaves of God and of money.

THE CURE FOR ANXIETY

[25] "This is why I tell you: Don't worry about your life, what you will eat or what you will drink; or about your body, what you will wear. Isn't life more than food and the body more than clothing? [26] Look at the birds of the sky: they don't sow or reap or gather into barns, yet your heavenly Father feeds them. Aren't you worth more than they? [27] Can any of you add a single •cubit to his height[a] by worrying? [28] And why do you worry about clothes? Learn how the wildflowers of the field grow: they don't labor or spin thread. [29] Yet I tell you that not even Solomon in all his splendor was adorned like one of these! [30] If that's how God clothes the grass of the field, which is here today and thrown into the furnace tomorrow, won't He do much more for you—you of little faith? [31] So don't worry, saying, 'What will we eat?' or 'What will we drink?' or 'What will we wear?' [32] For the idolaters[b] eagerly seek all these things, and your heavenly Father knows that you need them. [33] But seek first the kingdom of God[c] and His righteousness, and all these things will be provided for you. [34] Therefore don't worry about tomorrow, because tomorrow will worry about itself. Each day has enough trouble of its own.

DO NOT JUDGE

7 "Do not judge, so that you won't be judged. [2] For with the judgment you use,[d] you will be judged,

---

[a]**6:27** Or *add one moment to his life-span*
[b]**6:32** Or *Gentiles*, or *nations*, or *heathen*, or *pagans*
[c]**6:33** Other mss omit *of God*
[d]**7:2** Lit *you judge*

and with the measure you use,[a] it will be measured to you. ³ Why do you look at the speck in your brother's eye but don't notice the log in your own eye? ⁴ Or how can you say to your brother, 'Let me take the speck out of your eye,' and look, there's a log in your eye? ⁵ Hypocrite! First take the log out of your eye, and then you will see clearly to take the speck out of your brother's eye. ⁶ Don't give what is holy to dogs or toss your pearls before pigs, or they will trample them with their feet, turn, and tear you to pieces.

KEEP ASKING, SEARCHING, KNOCKING

⁷ "Keep asking,[b] and it will be given to you. Keep searching,[c] and you will find. Keep knocking,[d] and the door[e] will be opened to you. ⁸ For everyone who asks receives, and the one who searches finds, and to the one who knocks, the door[f] will be opened. ⁹ What man among you, if his son asks him for bread, will give him a stone? ¹⁰ Or if he asks for a fish, will give him a snake? ¹¹ If you then, who are evil, know how to give good gifts to your children, how much more will your Father in heaven give good things to those who ask Him! ¹² Therefore, whatever you want others to do for you, do also the same for them—this is the Law and the Prophets.[g]

ENTERING THE KINGDOM

¹³ "Enter through the narrow gate. For the gate is wide and the road is broad that leads to destruction, and there are many who go through it. ¹⁴ How narrow is the gate and difficult the road that leads to life, and few find it.

¹⁵ "Beware of false prophets who come to you in sheep's clothing but inwardly are ravaging wolves. ¹⁶ You'll recognize them by their fruit. Are grapes gathered from thornbushes or figs from thistles? ¹⁷ In the same way, every good tree produces good fruit, but a bad tree produces bad fruit. ¹⁸ A good tree can't

WORD STUDY

Greek word: **adelphos**
[ah dehl FAHSS]

Translation: **brother**

Uses in Matthew's Gospel: **39**
(Mk, 20; Lk, 24; Jn, 14)

Uses in the NT: **343**

Key passage: **Matthew 7:3-5**

Adelphos means *brother*, and the feminine *adelphe* means *sister*. The OT Hebrew term for brother (*'ach*) usually referred to a blood relative but could also refer by extension to a close companion (2 Sm 1:26) or those in Israel's covenant community (Lv 21:10; Dt 15:7,11). In the Gospels, *adelphos* usually refers to blood relative, but elsewhere in the NT it almost always refers metaphorically to the Christian community. Jesus established the precedent for this metaphorical use when He commanded that offenses be settled between *brothers* (Mt 5:21-24) and that we must judge ourselves rightly before judging a *brother* (Mt 7:3-5). He more clearly defined *adelphos* when He defined a true brother as anyone who does God's will (Mt 12:46-50). In the early church, *adelphos* became the common way to address other Christians (Ac 1:15-16; 21:17; Rm 1:13; Heb 3:1; Jms 1:2; 2 Pt 1:10; 1 Jn 3:13-17; Rv 1:9).

---

[a]7:2 Lit *you measure*
[b]7:7 Or *Ask*
[c]7:7 Or *Search*
[d]7:7 Or *Knock*
[e]7:7 Lit *and it*
[f]7:8 Lit *knocks, it*
[g]7:12 When capitalized, *the Law and the Prophets* = the OT

produce bad fruit; neither can a bad tree produce good fruit. ¹⁹ Every tree that doesn't produce good fruit is cut down and thrown into the fire. ²⁰ So you'll recognize them by their fruit.

²¹ "Not everyone who says to Me, 'Lord, Lord!' will enter the kingdom of heaven, but ⌊only⌋ the one who does the will of My Father in heaven. ²² On that day many will say to Me, 'Lord, Lord, didn't we prophesy in Your name, drive out demons in Your name, and do many miracles in Your name?' ²³ Then I will announce to them, 'I never knew you! **Depart from Me, you lawbreakers!**'ᵃ ᵇ

THE TWO FOUNDATIONS

²⁴ "Therefore, everyone who hears these words of Mine and acts on them will be like a sensible man who built his house on the rock. ²⁵ The rain fell, the rivers rose, and the winds blew and pounded that house. Yet it didn't collapse, because its foundation was on the rock. ²⁶ But everyone who hears these words of Mine and doesn't act on them will be like a foolish man who built his house on the sand. ²⁷ The rain fell, the rivers rose, the winds blew and pounded that house, and it collapsed. And its collapse was great!"

²⁸ When Jesus had finished this sermon,ᶜ the crowds were astonished at His teaching, ²⁹ because He was teaching them like one who had authority, and not like their •scribes.

CLEANSING A LEPER

8 When He came down from the mountain, large crowds followed Him. ² Right away a man with a serious skin disease came up and knelt before Him, saying, "Lord, if You are willing, You can make me clean."ᵈ

³ Reaching out His hand He touched him, saying, "I am willing; be made clean." Immediately his disease was healed.ᵉ ⁴ Then Jesus told him, "See that you don't tell anyone; but go, show yourself to the priest, and

---

Your Belief Can Make a Believer Out of Others

What does God want to do in the lives of those around you that waits upon your trust in Him and the removal of your doubts?

Jesus told the centurion, "Go. As you have believed, let it be done for you." And his servant was cured that very moment.
—Matthew 8:13

ᵃ**7:23** Lit *you who work lawlessness*
ᵇ**7:23** Ps 6:8
ᶜ**7:28** Lit *had ended these words*
ᵈ**8:2** In these vv. 2-3, *clean* includes healing, ceremonial purification, return to fellowship with people, and worship in the temple; Lv 14:1-32.
ᵉ**8:3** Lit *cleansed*

offer the gift that Moses prescribed, as a testimony to them."

A CENTURION'S FAITH

⁵ When He entered Capernaum, a •centurion came to Him, pleading with Him, ⁶ "Lord, my servant is lying at home paralyzed, in terrible agony!"

⁷ "I will come and heal him," He told him.

⁸ "Lord," the centurion replied, "I am not worthy to have You come under my roof. But only say the word, and my servant will be cured. ⁹ For I too am a man under authority, having soldiers under my command.ᵃ I say to this one, 'Go!' and he goes; and to another, 'Come!' and he comes; and to my slave, 'Do this!' and he does it."

¹⁰ Hearing this, Jesus was amazed and said to those following Him, "•I assure you: I have not found anyone in Israel with so great a faith! ¹¹ I tell you that many will come from east and west, and recline at the table with Abraham, Isaac, and Jacob in the kingdom of heaven. ¹² But the sons of the kingdom will be thrown into the outer darkness. In that place there will be weeping and gnashing of teeth." ¹³ Then Jesus told the centurion, "Go. As you have believed, let it be done for you." And his servant was cured that very moment.ᵇ

HEALINGS AT CAPERNAUM

¹⁴ When Jesus went into Peter's house, He saw his mother-in-law lying in bed with a fever. ¹⁵ So He touched her hand, and the fever left her. Then she got up and began to serve Him. ¹⁶ When evening came, they brought to Him many who were demon-possessed. He drove out the spirits with a word and healed all who were sick, ¹⁷ so that what was spoken through the prophet Isaiah might be fulfilled:

**He Himself took our weaknesses
and carried our diseases.**ᶜ

ᵃ8:9 Lit *under me*
ᵇ8:13 Or *that hour*; lit *very hour*
ᶜ8:17 Is 53:4

WORD STUDY

Greek word: *pleroo*
[play RAH oh]

Translation: *fulfill*

Uses in Matthew's Gospel: **16** (Mk, 2; Lk, 9; Jn, 15)

Uses in the NT: **86**

Key passage: **Matthew 8:17**

Pleroo (*to fill*) refers to the action of filling up an item with some object (Mt 13:48; Ac 2:2; 5:28), and metaphorically to the filling of persons with certain qualities or powers (Lk 2:40; Ac 2:28; Rm 15:13-14; 2 Tm 1:4), or to the completion (i.e., filling up) of some time period (Mk 1:15; Ac 9:23) or activity (Lk 7:1; Ac 12:25; 13:25). By extension, *pleroo* may also mean *to fulfill* and often indicates the fulfillment of OT prophecies. Prophecies may be directly prophetic (a predicted event is fulfilled; e.g., Jesus' Galilean ministry; Mt 4:13-16; cf. Is 9:1-7), or they may be indirectly fulfilled by the correspondence of two historical events (the first event foreshadows the second; Mt 27:9; cf. Jr 32:6-9; Zch 11:12-13), or they may be based on parallels between Israel's history and Jesus' life (Israel and Jesus being called out of Egypt; Mt 2:15; cf. Hs 11:1).

FOLLOWING JESUS

18 When Jesus saw large crowds[a] around Him, He gave the order to go to the other side ⌊of the sea⌋.[b] 19 A •scribe approached Him and said, "Teacher, I will follow You wherever You go!"

20 Jesus told him, "Foxes have dens and birds of the sky have nests, but the Son of Man has no place to lay His head."

21 "Lord," another of His disciples said, "first let me go bury my father."[c]

22 But Jesus told him, "Follow Me, and let the dead bury their own dead."

WIND AND WAVE OBEY THE MASTER

23 As He got into the[d] boat, His disciples followed Him. 24 Suddenly, a violent storm arose on the sea, so that the boat was being swamped by the waves. But He was sleeping. 25 So the disciples came and woke Him up, saying, "Lord, save ⌊us⌋! We're going to die!"

26 But He said to them, "Why are you fearful, you of little faith?" Then He got up and rebuked the winds and the sea. And there was a great calm.

27 The men were amazed and asked, "What kind of man is this?—even the winds and the sea obey Him!"

DEMONS DRIVEN OUT BY THE MASTER

28 When He had come to the other side, to the region of the Gadarenes,[e] two demon-possessed men met Him as they came out of the tombs. They were so violent that no one could pass that way. 29 Suddenly they shouted, "What do You have to do with us,[f] [g] Son of God? Have You come here to torment us before the time?"

30 Now a long way off from them, a large herd of pigs was feeding. 31 "If You drive us out," the demons begged Him, "send us into the herd of pigs."

32 "Go!" He told them. So when they had come out, they entered the pigs. And suddenly the whole herd rushed down the steep bank into the sea and perished

---

There's No Excuse for Doubting God

The moment you sense that God is moving in your life, you give Him a whole list of reasons why He has the wrong person or why the time is not right. When your focus is on yourself, you cannot see things from God's perspective.

"Lord," another of His disciples said, "first let me go bury my father." But Jesus told him, "Follow Me, and let the dead bury their own dead."

—Matthew 8:21-22

---

[a]8:18 Other mss read *saw a crowd*
[b]8:18 Sea of Galilee
[c]8:21 Not necessarily meaning his father was already dead
[d]8:23 Other mss read *to a*
[e]8:28 Other mss read *Gergesenes*
[f]8:29 Other mss add *Jesus*
[g]8:29 Lit *What to us and to You*

in the water. 33 Then the men who tended them fled. They went into the city and reported everything—especially what had happened to those who were demon-possessed. 34 At that, the whole town went out to meet Jesus. When they saw Him, they begged Him to leave their region.

THE SON OF MAN FORGIVES AND HEALS

9 So He got into a boat, crossed over, and came to His own town. 2 Just then some men[a] brought to Him a paralytic lying on a stretcher. Seeing their faith, Jesus told the paralytic, "Have courage, son, your sins are forgiven."

3 At this, some of the •scribes said among themselves, "He's blaspheming!"

4 But perceiving their thoughts, Jesus said, "Why are you thinking evil things in your hearts?[b] 5 For which is easier: to say, 'Your sins are forgiven,' or to say, 'Get up and walk'? 6 But so you may know that the •Son of Man has authority on earth to forgive sins"—then He told the paralytic, "Get up, pick up your stretcher, and go home." 7 And he got up and went home. 8 When the crowds saw this, they were awestruck[c] [d] and gave glory to God who had given such authority to men.

THE CALL OF MATTHEW

9 As Jesus went on from there, He saw a man named Matthew sitting at the tax office, and He said to him, "Follow Me!" So he got up and followed Him.

10 While He was reclining at the table in the house, many tax collectors and sinners came as guests to eat[e] with Jesus and His disciples. 11 When the •Pharisees saw this, they asked His disciples, "Why does your Teacher eat with tax collectors and sinners?"

12 But when He heard this, He said, "Those who are well don't need a doctor, but the sick do. 13 Go and learn what this means: **I desire mercy and not**

WORD STUDY

Greek word: **eleos**
[EH leh ahss]

Translation: **mercy**

Uses in Matthew's Gospel: **3** (Lk, 6)

Uses in the NT: **27**

Key passage: **Matthew 9:13**

Eleos is one of several NT words meaning *mercy*. Each of the three times that this word appears in Matthew, Jesus uses it to refer to principles established in the OT, where God clearly required that His people show mercy. Twice Jesus quotes Hosea 6:6, "I desire *mercy* and not sacrifice" (Mt 9:13; 12:7). The Hebrew term (*chesed*) underlying the Greek translation combines the ideas of love, mercy, and faithful loyalty. The Pharisees condemned Jesus for fraternizing with social outcasts (Mt 9:11), but He reminded them that God expected His people to show mercy before giving sacrifice. In Matthew 23 Jesus rebuked the Pharisees even more harshly, and one of His grievances was their neglect of the more important aspects of the law ("justice, *mercy*, and faith") even while they meticulously tithed their mint, dill, and cumin.

---

[a]9:2 Lit *then they*
[b]9:4 Or *minds*
[c]9:8 Other mss read *amazed*
[d]9:8 Lit *afraid*

[e]9:10 Lit *came, they were reclining* (at the table); at important meals the custom was to recline on a mat at a low table and lean on the left elbow.

sacrifice.[a] For I didn't come to call the righteous, but sinners."[b]

A QUESTION ABOUT FASTING

[14] Then John's disciples came to Him, saying, "Why do we and the Pharisees fast often, but Your disciples do not fast?"

[15] Jesus said to them, "Can the wedding guests[c] be sad while the groom is with them? The days will come when the groom will be taken away from them, and then they will fast. [16] No one patches an old garment with unshrunk cloth, because the patch pulls away from the garment and makes the tear worse. [17] And no one puts[d] new wine into old wineskins. Otherwise, the skins burst, the wine spills out, and the skins are ruined. But they put new wine into fresh wineskins, and both are preserved."

A GIRL RESTORED AND A WOMAN HEALED

[18] As He was telling them these things, suddenly one of the leaders[e] came and knelt down before Him, saying, "My daughter is near death,[f] but come and lay Your hand on her, and she will live." [19] So Jesus and His disciples got up and followed him.

[20] Just then, a woman who had suffered from bleeding for 12 years approached from behind and touched the •tassel on His robe, [21] for she said to herself, "If I can just touch His robe, I'll be made well!"[g]

[22] But Jesus turned and saw her. "Have courage, daughter," He said. "Your faith has made you well."[h] And the woman was made well from that moment.[i]

[23] When Jesus came to the leader's house, He saw the flute players and a crowd lamenting loudly. [24] "Leave," He said, "because the girl isn't dead, but sleeping." And they started laughing at Him. [25] But when the crowd had been put outside, He went in and took her by the

---

When Grace Found You, Sin Lost Forever

The wonder of salvation is that God has completely dealt with sin. He takes a life devastated by sin and makes it whole.

"Go and learn what this means: I desire mercy and not sacrifice. For I didn't come to call the righteous, but sinners."

—Matthew 9:13

---

[a]**9:13** Hs 6:6
[b]**9:13** Other mss add *to repentance*
[c]**9:15** Lit *the sons of the bridal chamber*
[d]**9:17** Lit *And they do not put*
[e]**9:18** A leader of a synagogue; Mk 5:22
[f]**9:18** Lit *daughter has now come to the end*
[g]**9:21** Or *be delivered*
[h]**9:22** Or *has saved you*
[i]**9:22** Lit *hour*

hand, and the girl got up. ²⁶ And this news spread throughout that whole area.

HEALING THE BLIND

²⁷ As Jesus went on from there, two blind men followed Him, shouting, "Have mercy on us, Son of David!"

²⁸ When He entered the house, the blind men approached Him, and Jesus said to them, "Do you believe that I can do this?"

"Yes, Lord," they answered Him.

²⁹ Then He touched their eyes, saying, "Let it be done for you according to your faith!" ³⁰ And their eyes were opened. Then Jesus warned them sternly, "Be sure that no one finds out!"ᵃ ³¹ But they went out and spread the news about Him throughout that whole area.

DRIVING OUT A DEMON

³² Just as they were going out, a demon-possessed man who was unable to speak was brought to Him. ³³ When the demon had been driven out, the manᵇ spoke. And the crowds were amazed, saying, "Nothing like this has ever been seen in Israel!"

³⁴ But the Pharisees said, "He drives out demons by the ruler of the demons!"

THE LORD OF THE HARVEST

³⁵ Then Jesus went to all the towns and villages, teaching in their •synagogues, preaching the good news of the kingdom, and healing everyᶜ disease and every sickness.ᵈ ³⁶ When He saw the crowds, He felt compassion for them, because they were weary and worn out, like sheep without a shepherd. ³⁷ Then He said to His disciples, "The harvest is abundant, but the workers are few. ³⁸ Therefore, pray to the Lord of the harvest to send out workers into His harvest."

COMMISSIONING THE TWELVE

10 Summoning His 12 disciples, He gave them authority over uncleanᵉ spirits, to drive them out

Belief Frees You to Experience God

When God lets you know what He wants to do through you, it will be something only God can do. If you have faith in the God who called you, you will obey Him, and He will bring to pass what He has purposed to do.

When He entered the house, the blind men approached Him, and Jesus said to them, "Do you believe that I can do this?" "Yes, Lord," they answered Him. Then He touched their eyes, saying, "Let it be done for you according to your faith!"
—Matthew 9:28-29

ᵃ9:30 Lit *no one knows*
ᵇ9:33 Lit *the man who was unable to speak*
ᶜ9:35 Or *every kind of*
ᵈ9:35 Other mss add *among the people*
ᵉ10:1 Morally or ceremonially impure

and to heal every[a] disease and sickness. ² These are the names of the 12 apostles:

First, Simon, who is called Peter,
and Andrew his brother;
James the son of Zebedee,
and John his brother;
³ Philip and Bartholomew;[b]
Thomas and Matthew the tax collector;
James the son of Alphaeus, and Thaddaeus;[c]
⁴ Simon the Zealot,[d] and Judas Iscariot,[e]
who also betrayed Him.

⁵ Jesus sent out these 12 after giving them instructions: "Don't take the road leading to other nations, and don't enter any •Samaritan town. ⁶ Instead, go to the lost sheep of the house of Israel. ⁷ As you go, announce this: 'The kingdom of heaven has come near.' ⁸ Heal the sick, raise the dead, cleanse those with skin diseases, drive out demons. You have received free of charge; give free of charge. ⁹ Don't take along gold, silver, or copper for your money-belts. ¹⁰ Don't take a traveling bag for the road, or an extra shirt, sandals, or a walking stick, for the worker is worthy of his food.

¹¹ "When you enter any town or village, find out who is worthy, and stay there until you leave. ¹² Greet a household when you enter it, ¹³ and if the household is worthy, let your peace be on it. But if it is unworthy, let your peace return to you. ¹⁴ If anyone will not welcome you or listen to your words, shake the dust off your feet when you leave that house or town. ¹⁵ •I assure you: It will be more tolerable on the day of judgment for the land of Sodom and Gomorrah than for that town.

PERSECUTIONS PREDICTED

¹⁶ "Look, I'm sending you out like sheep among wolves. Therefore be as shrewd as serpents and as harmless as doves. ¹⁷ Because people will hand you over to sanhedrins[f] and flog you in their •synagogues, beware of them. ¹⁸ You will even be brought before governors and kings because of Me, to bear witness

God's Business Is Now Your Occupation

Your job as a servant is to follow Jesus' example: Do what the Father is already doing—watch to see where God is at work and join Him!

"A disciple is not above his teacher, or a slave above his master. It is enough for a disciple to become like his teacher and a slave like his master."

—Matthew 10:24-25a

When God Speaks, That's the Time to Act

Unless God allows you to see where He is working, you will not see it. When God reveals to you what He is doing around you, that is your invitation to join Him.

"What I tell you in the dark, speak in the light. What you hear in a whisper, proclaim on the housetops."

—Matthew 10:27

---

[a]10:1 Or *every kind of*
[b]10:3 Probably the Nathanael of Jn 1:45-51
[c]10:3 Other mss read *and Lebbaeus, whose surname was Thaddaeus*
[d]10:4 Lit *the Cananaean*
[e]10:4 *Iscariot* probably = "a man of Kerioth," a town in Judea.
[f]10:17 Local Jewish courts or local councils

to them and to the nations. ¹⁹ But when they hand you over, don't worry about how or what you should speak. For you will be given what to say at that hour, ²⁰ because you are not speaking, but the Spirit of your Father is speaking through you.

²¹ "Brother will betray brother to death, and a father his child. Children will even rise up against their parents and have them put to death. ²² You will be hated by everyone because of My name. But the one who endures to the end will be delivered.ᵃ ²³ When they persecute you in one town, escape to another. For I assure you: You will not have covered the towns of Israel before the •Son of Man comes. ²⁴ A discipleᵇ is not above his teacher, or a slave above his master. ²⁵ It is enough for a disciple to become like his teacher and a slave like his master. If they called the head of the house '•Beelzebul,' how much more the members of his household!

FEAR GOD

²⁶ "Therefore, don't be afraid of them, since there is nothing covered that won't be uncovered, and nothing hidden that won't be made known. ²⁷ What I tell you in the dark, speak in the light. What you hear in a whisper,ᶜ proclaim on the housetops. ²⁸ Don't fear those who kill the body but are not able to kill the soul; rather, fear Him who is able to destroy both soul and body in •hell. ²⁹ Aren't two sparrows sold for a penny?ᵈ Yet not one of them falls to the ground without your Father's consent.ᵉ ³⁰ But even the hairs of your head have all been counted. ³¹ Don't be afraid therefore; you are worth more than many sparrows.

ACKNOWLEDGING CHRIST

³² "Therefore, everyone who will acknowledge Me before men, I will also acknowledge him before My Father in heaven. ³³ But whoever denies Me before men, I will also deny him before My Father in heaven. ³⁴ Don't assume that I came to bring peace on the earth. I did not come to bring peace, but a sword. ³⁵ For I came to turn

WORD STUDY

Greek word: *phobeo*
[fah BEH oh]

Translation: *fear*

Uses in Matthew's Gospel: **18**
(Mk, 12; Lk, 23; Jn, 5)

Uses in the NT: **95**

Key passage: **Matthew 10:28**

Like the English term *fear*, Greek *phobeo* covers a broad spectrum of meanings, including worry (Mt 1:20), discomfort at potential circumstances (Mt 2:22; 10:31; 14:5; 21:26,46), and feelings of awe and/or terror, especially in the presence of the supernatural (Mt 9:8; 10:28; 14:27; 17:6-7; 27:54; 28:5,10). *Phobeo* has two main applications in the NT: fear of God and fear of man or circumstances. In regard to the former, fear can be understood as a healthy understanding of who God is, His power, and what He demands from us (cf. Pr 1:7; 9:10). The unbeliever should tremble in terror before such a God, for He is the one who can "destroy both soul and body in hell" (Mt 10:28). For the believer, however, such fear is replaced by a relationship in which perfect love can flourish (1 Jn 4:18; cf. Rm 8:15), though awe of God's greatness remains (2 Co 5:11; 7:1).

ᵃ**10:22** Or *saved*
ᵇ**10:24** Or *student*
ᶜ**10:27** Lit *in the ear*
ᵈ**10:29** Gk *assarion*, a small copper coin
ᵉ**10:29** Lit *ground apart from your Father*

> a man against his father,
> a daughter against her mother,
> a daughter-in-law against her
>   mother-in-law;
> ³⁶ and a man's enemies will be
>   the members of his household.ᵃ

³⁷ The person who loves father or mother more than Me is not worthy of Me; the person who loves son or daughter more than Me is not worthy of Me. ³⁸ And whoever doesn't take up his cross and followᵇ Me is not worthy of Me. ³⁹ Anyone findingᶜ his life will lose it, and anyone losingᵈ his life because of Me will find it.

A CUP OF COLD WATER

⁴⁰ "The one who welcomes you welcomes Me, and the one who welcomes Me welcomes Him who sent Me. ⁴¹ Anyone whoᵉ welcomes a prophet because he is a prophetᶠ will receive a prophet's reward. And anyone whoᵍ welcomes a righteous person because he's righteousʰ will receive a righteous person's reward. ⁴² And whoever gives just a cup of cold water to one of these little ones because he is a discipleⁱ —I assure you: He will never lose his reward!"

IN PRAISE OF JOHN THE BAPTIST

11 When Jesus had finished giving orders to His 12 disciples, He moved on from there to teach and preach in their towns. ² When John heard in prison what the •Messiah was doing, he sent ₍a message₎ by his disciples ³ and asked Him, "Are You the One who is to come, or should we expect someone else?"

⁴ Jesus replied to them, "Go and report to John what you hear and see: ⁵ the blind see, the lame walk, those with skin diseases are healed,ʲ the deaf hear, the dead are raised, and the poor are told the good news. ⁶ And if anyone is not offended because of Me, he is blessed."

Yielding Control Yields Real Results

Oh, that we would discover the difference when we let God be the Head of the church. He will accomplish more in six months through a people yielded to Him than we could do in sixty years without Him.

"Anyone finding his life will lose it, and anyone losing his life because of Me will find it."
—Matthew 10:39

ᵃ10:35-36 Mc 7:6
ᵇ10:38 Lit *follow after*
ᶜ10:39 Or *The one who finds*
ᵈ10:41 Or *and the one who loses*
ᵉ10:41 Or *The one who*
ᶠ10:41 Lit *prophet in the name of a prophet*
ᵍ10:41 Or *And the one who*
ʰ10:41 Lit *person in the name of a righteous person*
ⁱ10:42 Lit *little ones in the name of a disciple*
ʲ11:5 Lit *cleansed*

⁷ As these men went away, Jesus began to speak to the crowds about John: "What did you go out into the wilderness to see? A reed swaying in the wind? ⁸ What then did you go out to see? A man dressed in soft clothes? Look, those who wear soft clothes are in kings' palaces. ⁹ But what did you go out to see? A prophet? Yes, I tell you, and far more than a prophet. ¹⁰ This is the one it is written about:

**Look, I am sending My messenger
ahead of You;ᵃ
he will prepare Your way before You.ᵇ**

¹¹ "•I assure you: Among those born of women no one greater than John the Baptist has appeared,ᶜ but the least in the kingdom of heaven is greater than he. ¹² From the days of John the Baptist until now, the kingdom of heaven has been suffering violence,ᵈ and the violent have been seizing it by force. ¹³ For all the prophets and the law prophesied until John; ¹⁴ if you're willing to accept it, he is the Elijah who is to come. ¹⁵ Anyone who has earsᵉ should listen!

AN UNRESPONSIVE GENERATION

¹⁶ "To what should I compare this generation? It's like children sitting in the marketplaces who call out to each other:

¹⁷ We played the flute for you,
but you didn't dance;
we sang a lament,
but you didn't mourn!ᶠ

¹⁸ For John did not come eating or drinking, and they say, 'He has a demon!' ¹⁹ The •Son of Man came eating and drinking, and they say, 'Look, a glutton and a drunkard, a friend of tax collectors and sinners!' Yet wisdom is vindicatedᵍ by her deeds."ʰ

²⁰ Then He proceeded to denounce the towns where most of His miracles were done, because they did not repent: ²¹ "Woe to you, Chorazin! Woe to you,

WORD STUDY

Greek word: **angelos**
[ahn geh LAHSS]

Translation: **messenger**

Uses in Matthew's Gospel: **20**
(Mk, 6; Lk, 25; Jn, 3)

Uses in the NT: **175**

Key passage: **Matthew 11:10**

The Greek noun *angelos* is related to the verb *angello*, which means *to proclaim* or *announce*. An *angelos* is *one who proclaims*, a *messenger*, and the term can refer to either human or celestial beings. In the vast majority of NT occurrences, *angelos* refers to a celestial being, an *angel*. A few times, however, human beings are in view (John the Baptist, Mt 11:10 = Mk 1:2 = Lk 7:27; his disciples, Lk 7:24; Jesus' disciples, Lk 9:52). Each reference to John the Baptist as an *angelos* follows the Greek OT, by quoting Malachi 3:1, where the Hb word *mal'ak* is used for messenger, a Hb term referring to humans much more often in the OT than *angelos* does in the NT. The final example in the NT of *angelos* used of men occurs in James 2:25 in reference to Joshua's spies (cf. Jos 6:25, where Hb *mal'ak* is used).

ᵃ11:10 Lit *messenger before Your face*
ᵇ11:10 Mal 3:1
ᶜ11:11 Lit *arisen*
ᵈ11:12 Or *has been forcefully advancing*

ᵉ11:15 Other mss add *to hear*
ᶠ11:17 Or *beat your breasts*
ᵍ11:19 Or *declared right*
ʰ11:19 Other mss read *children*

Bethsaida! For if the miracles that were done in you had been done in Tyre and Sidon, they would have repented in sackcloth and ashes long ago! ²² But I tell you, it will be more tolerable for Tyre and Sidon on the day of judgment than for you. ²³ And you, Capernaum, will you be exalted to heaven? You will go down to •Hades. For if the miracles that were done in you had been done in Sodom, it would have remained until today. ²⁴ But I tell you, it will be more tolerable for the land of Sodom on the day of judgment than for you."

THE SON GIVES KNOWLEDGE AND REST

²⁵ At that time Jesus said, "I praise[a] You, Father, Lord of heaven and earth, because You have hidden these things from the wise and learned and revealed them to infants. ²⁶ Yes, Father, because this was Your good pleasure.[b] ²⁷ All things have been entrusted to Me by My Father. No one knows[c] the Son except the Father, and no one knows the Father except the Son and anyone to whom the Son desires[d] to reveal Him.

²⁸ "Come to Me, all of you who are weary and burdened, and I will give you rest. ²⁹ All of you, take up My yoke and learn from Me, because I am gentle and humble in heart, and you will find rest for yourselves. ³⁰ For My yoke is easy and My burden is light."

LORD OF THE SABBATH

12 At that time Jesus passed through the grainfields on the Sabbath. His disciples were hungry and began to pick and eat some heads of grain. ² But when the •Pharisees saw it, they said to Him, "Look, Your disciples are doing what is not lawful to do on the Sabbath!"

³ He said to them, "Haven't you read what David did when he and those who were with him were hungry— ⁴ how he entered the house of God, and they ate[e] the •sacred bread, which is not lawful for him or for those with him to eat, but only for the priests? ⁵ Or haven't you

---

God Wants a Relationship with You

If we are to have any relationship with Him or His Son, God will have to take the initiative. This is exactly what He does. God draws us to Himself.

"All things have been entrusted to Me by My Father. No one knows the Son except the Father, and no one knows the Father except the Son and anyone to whom the Son desires to reveal Him."

—Matthew 11:27

---

[a]**11:25** Or *thank*
[b]**11:26** Lit *was well-pleasing in Your sight*
[c]**11:27** Or *knows exactly*
[d]**11:27** Or *wills,* or *chooses*
[e]**12:4** Other mss read *he ate*

read in the Law[a] that on Sabbath days the priests in the temple violate the Sabbath and are innocent? 6 But I tell you that something greater than the temple is here! 7 If you had known what this means: **I desire mercy and not sacrifice**,[b] you would not have condemned the innocent. 8 For the •Son of Man is Lord of the Sabbath."

THE MAN WITH THE PARALYZED HAND

9 Moving on from there, He entered their •synagogue. 10 There He saw a man who had a paralyzed hand. And in order to accuse Him they asked Him, "Is it lawful to heal on the Sabbath?"

11 But He said to them, "What man among you, if he had a sheep[c] that fell into a pit on the Sabbath, wouldn't take hold of it and lift it out? 12 A man is worth far more than a sheep, so it is lawful to do good on the Sabbath."

13 Then He told the man, "Stretch out your hand." So he stretched it out, and it was restored, as good as the other. 14 But the Pharisees went out and plotted against Him, how they might destroy Him.

THE SERVANT OF THE LORD

15 When Jesus became aware of this, He withdrew from there. Huge crowds[d] followed Him, and He healed them all. 16 He warned them not to make Him known, 17 so that what was spoken through the prophet Isaiah might be fulfilled:

18 **Here is My Servant whom I have chosen,**
My beloved in whom My soul delights;
I will put My Spirit on Him,
and He will proclaim justice to the nations.
19 **He will not argue or shout,**
and no one will hear His voice
in the streets.
20 **He will not break a bruised reed,**
and He will not put out a smoldering wick,
until He has led justice to victory.[e]

Take Your Obedience to the Next Level

God expects us to obey more than the letter of the law. When we follow the ways of God, He will take us far beyond the usual and expected.

He said to them, "What man among you, if he had a sheep that fell into a pit on the Sabbath, wouldn't take hold of it and lift it out? A man is worth far more than a sheep, so it is lawful to do good on the Sabbath."
—Matthew 12:11-12

---

[a]12:5 The Torah (the Pentateuch)
[b]12:7 Hs 6:6
[c]12:11 Or *had one sheep*
[d]12:15 Other mss read *Many*
[e]12:20 Or *until He has successfully put forth justice*

WORD STUDY

Greek word: *blasphemia*
[blahss fay MEE uh]

Translation: *blasphemy*

Uses in Matthew's Gospel: **4**
(Mk, 3; Lk, 1; Jn, 1)

Uses in the NT: **18**

Key passage: **Matthew 12:31**

The Greek noun *blasphemia* comes from a compound verb (*blasphemeo*) meaning *to speak evil against* (*blas*, *evil*; *phemi*, *to speak*), *slander*, or *revile*. In the NT, blasphemy is an extremely serious offense and primarily directed against God (Mt 9:3; 26:65), Christ (Lk 22:65), or anything related to either Person (1 Tm 6:1; Ti 2:5; Jms 2:7). Blasphemy can also be directed against angels (2 Pt 2:10; Jd 8) and human beings (Rm 3:8; 1 Co 4:13; 10:30; Ti 3:2). Jesus told the Jewish religious leaders that the most grievous sin, one that cannot be forgiven, is blasphemy against the Holy Spirit (Mt 12:31-32). Apparently, they were in danger of committing this sin, or perhaps already had, for Jesus' warning was in response to their claim that He cast out demons through the power of Satan (Mt 12:24) and that Jesus Himself was demon-possessed (Mk 3:30).

21 **The nations will put their hope in His name.**[a]

A HOUSE DIVIDED

22 Then a demon-possessed man who was blind and unable to speak was brought to Him. He healed him, so that the man[b] could both speak and see. **23** And all the crowds were astounded and said, "Perhaps this is the Son of David!"

24 When the Pharisees heard this, they said, "The man drives out demons only by •Beelzebul, the ruler of the demons."

25 Knowing their thoughts, He told them: "Every kingdom divided against itself is headed for destruction, and no city or house divided against itself will stand. **26** If Satan drives out Satan, he is divided against himself. How then will his kingdom stand? **27** And if I drive out demons by Beelzebul, who is it your sons drive them out by? For this reason they will be your judges. **28** If I drive out demons by the Spirit of God, then the kingdom of God has come to you. **29** How can someone enter a strong man's house and steal his possessions unless he first ties up the strong man? Then he can rob his house. **30** Anyone who is not with Me is against Me, and anyone who does not gather with Me scatters. **31** Because of this, I tell you, people will be forgiven every sin and blasphemy, but the blasphemy against[c] the Spirit will not be forgiven.[d] **32** Whoever speaks a word against the Son of Man, it will be forgiven him. But whoever speaks against the Holy Spirit, it will not be forgiven him, either in this age or in the one to come.

A TREE AND ITS FRUIT

33 "Either make the tree good and its fruit good, or make the tree bad[e] and its fruit bad; for a tree is known by its fruit. **34** Brood of vipers! How can you speak good things when you are evil? For the mouth speaks from the overflow of the heart. **35** A good man produces good things from his storeroom of good,[f] and an evil man

---

[a]**12:18-21** Is 42:1-4
[b]**12:22** Lit *mute*
[c]**12:31** Or *of*
[d]**12:31** Other mss add *people*

[e]**12:33** Lit *rotten*, or *decayed*
[f]**12:35** Other mss read *from the storehouse of his heart*

produces evil things from his storeroom of evil. 36 I tell you that on the day of judgment people will have to account for every careless word they speak.a 37 For by your words you will be acquitted, and by your words you will be condemned."

THE SIGN OF JONAH

38 Then some of the •scribes and Pharisees said to Him, "Teacher, we want to see a sign from You."
39 But He answered them, "An evil and adulterous generation demands a sign, but no sign will be given to it except the sign of the prophet Jonah. 40 For as Jonah was in the belly of the great fish three days and three nights, so the Son of Man will be in the heart of the earth three days and three nights. 41 The men of Nineveh will stand up at the judgment with this generation and condemn it, because they repented at Jonah's proclamation; and look—something greater than Jonah is here! 42 The queen of the south will rise up at the judgment with this generation and condemn it, because she came from the ends of the earth to hear the wisdom of Solomon; and look—something greater than Solomon is here!

AN UNCLEAN SPIRIT'S RETURN

43 "When an uncleanb spirit comes out of a man, it roams through waterless places looking for rest but doesn't find any. 44 Then it says, 'I'll go back to my house that I came from.' And when it arrives, it finds the house vacant, swept, and put in order. 45 Then off it goes and brings with it seven other spirits more evil than itself, and they enter and settle down there. As a result, that man's last condition is worse than the first. That's how it will also be with this evil generation."

TRUE RELATIONSHIPS

46 He was still speaking to the crowds when suddenly His mother and brothers were standing outside wanting to speak to Him. 47 Someone told Him, "Look, Your mother and Your brothers are standing outside, wanting to speak to You."c

Your Life Is a Walking Testimony

How you live your life is a testimony of what you believe about God.

"Either make the tree good and its fruit good, or make the tree bad and its fruit bad; for a tree is known by its fruit."
—Matthew 12:33

Discipline Yourself to Speak Careful Words

Think carefully about the words that come from your mouth. Christians should speak only words that uplift and bring grace to others.

"I tell you that on the day of judgment people will have to account for every careless word they speak."
—Matthew 12:36

---

a12:36 Lit *will speak*
b12:43 Morally or ceremonially impure
c12:47 Other mss omit this v.

48 But He replied to the one who told Him, "Who is My mother and who are My brothers?" 49 **And stretching out His hand toward His disciples, He said,** "Here are My mother and My brothers! 50 For whoever does the will of My Father in heaven, that person is My brother and sister and mother."

THE PARABLE OF THE SOWER

13 On that day Jesus went out of the house and was sitting by the sea. 2 Such large crowds gathered around Him that He got into a boat and sat down, while the whole crowd stood on the shore.

3 Then He told them many things in parables, saying: "Consider the sower who went out to sow. 4 As he was sowing, some seeds fell along the path, and the birds came and ate them up. 5 Others fell on rocky ground, where there wasn't much soil, and they sprang up quickly since the soil wasn't deep. 6 But when the sun came up they were scorched, and since they had no root, they withered. 7 Others fell among thorns, and the thorns came up and choked them. 8 Still others fell on good ground, and produced a crop: some 100, some 60, and some 30 times ˌwhat was sownˌ. 9 Anyone who has ears[a] should listen!"

WHY JESUS USED PARABLES

10 Then the disciples came up and asked Him, "Why do You speak to them in parables?"

11 He answered them, "Because the secrets[b] of the kingdom of heaven have been given for you to know, but it has not been given to them. 12 For whoever has, ˌmoreˌ will be given to him, and he will have more than enough. But whoever does not have, even what he has will be taken away from him. 13 For this reason I speak to them in parables, because looking they do not see, and hearing they do not listen or understand. 14 Isaiah's prophecy is fulfilled in them, which says:

> **You will listen and listen,**
> **yet never understand;**
> **and you will look and look,**
> **yet never perceive.**

Never Grow Tired of Walking with God

The constant presence of God is the most practical part of your life and ministry.

"This people's heart has grown callous; their ears are hard of hearing, and they have shut their eyes; otherwise they might see with their eyes and hear with their ears, understand with their hearts and turn back—and I would cure them. But your eyes are blessed because they do see, and your ears because they do hear!"

—Matthew 13:15-16

---

[a]13:9 Other mss add *to hear*
[b]13:11 The Gk word *mysteria* does not mean "mysteries" in the Eng sense; it means what we can know only by divine revelation.

¹⁵ **For this people's heart has grown callous;**
their ears are hard of hearing,
and they have shut their eyes;
otherwise they might see with their eyes
and hear with their ears,
understand with their hearts
and turn back—
and I would cure them.^a

¹⁶ "But your eyes are blessed because they do see, and your ears because they do hear! ¹⁷ For •I assure you: Many prophets and righteous people longed to see the things you see yet didn't see them; to hear the things you hear yet didn't hear them.

THE PARABLE OF THE SOWER EXPLAINED

¹⁸ "You, then, listen to the parable of the sower: ¹⁹ When anyone hears the word^b about the kingdom and doesn't understand it, the evil one comes and snatches away what was sown in his heart. This is the one sown along the path. ²⁰ And the one sown on rocky ground— this is one who hears the word and immediately receives it with joy. ²¹ Yet he has no root in himself, but is short-lived. When pressure or persecution comes because of the word, immediately he stumbles. ²² Now the one sown among the thorns—this is one who hears the word, but the worries of this age and the seduction^c of wealth choke the word, and it becomes unfruitful. ²³ But the one sown on the good ground—this is one who hears and understands the word, who does bear fruit and yields: some 100, some 60, some 30 times what was sown."

THE PARABLE OF THE WHEAT AND THE WEEDS

²⁴ He presented another parable to them: "The kingdom of heaven may be compared to a man who sowed good seed in his field. ²⁵ But while people were sleeping, his enemy came, sowed weeds^d among the wheat, and left.

WORD STUDY

Greek word: **parabole**
[pah rah bah LAY]

Translation: **parable**

Uses in Matthew's Gospel: **17** (Mk, 13; Lk, 18)

Uses in the NT: **50**

Key passage: **Matthew 13:3,10,13,18, etc.**

Outside of Hebrews 9:9 and 11:19, *parabole* (*parable*) occurs only in the Synoptic Gospels. The term may refer to a short saying combined with a figure of speech (Mt 15:15) or a proverbial saying (Lk 4:23), but it usually refers to a parable, an extended simile or metaphor, in which a simple comparison from a known experience, truth, or item (e.g., mustard seed, lamp, etc.) is turned into a story with setting, characters, and significant events in order to elaborate a spiritual truth. The parable was Jesus' most common method of teaching, and He alone used parables in the Gospels. The purpose of His parables was to reveal truth about Himself and God's kingdom to people of faith and at the same time to conceal these mysteries from people without faith (Mt 13:10-17).

---

^a13:14-15 Is 6:9-10
^b13:19 Gk *logos* = *word*, or *message*, or *saying*, or *thing*
^c13:22 Or *pleasure*, or *deceitfulness*

^d13:25 Or *darnel*, a weed similar in appearance to wheat in the early stages

²⁶ When the plants sprouted and produced grain, then the weeds also appeared. ²⁷ The landowner's slaves came to him and said, 'Master, didn't you sow good seed in your field? Then where did the weeds come from?'

²⁸ "'An enemy did this!' he told them.

"'So, do you want us to go and gather them up?' the slaves asked him.

²⁹ "'No,' he said. 'When you gather up the weeds, you might also uproot the wheat with them. ³⁰ Let both grow together until the harvest. At harvest time I'll tell the reapers: Gather the weeds first and tie them in bundles to burn them, but store the wheat in my barn.'"

THE PARABLES OF THE MUSTARD SEED AND OF THE YEAST

³¹ He presented another parable to them: "The kingdom of heaven is like a mustard seed that a man took and sowed in his field. ³² It's the smallest of all the seeds, but when grown, it's taller than the vegetables and becomes a tree, so that the birds of the sky come and nest in its branches."

³³ He told them another parable: "The kingdom of heaven is like yeast that a woman took and mixed into 50 pounds[a] of flour until it spread through all of it."[b]

USING PARABLES FULFILLS PROPHECY

³⁴ Jesus told the crowds all these things in parables, and He would not speak anything to them without a parable, ³⁵ so that what was spoken through the prophet might be fulfilled:

> I will open My mouth in parables;
> I will declare things kept secret
> from the foundation of the world.[c]

JESUS INTERPRETS THE WHEAT AND THE WEEDS

³⁶ Then He dismissed the crowds and went into the house. His disciples approached Him and said, "Explain the parable of the weeds in the field to us."

Expect a Word from the Lord

When God speaks to you by the Holy Spirit through the Bible, prayer, circumstances, and the church, you will know it is God, and you will know what He is saying.

"I will open My mouth in parables; I will declare things kept secret from the foundation of the world."

—Matthew 13:35b

---

[a]**13:33** Lit *3 sata*; about 40 quarts
[b]**13:33** Or *until all of it was leavened*
[c]**13:35** Ps 78:2

[37] **He replied:** "The One who sows the good seed is the •Son of Man; [38] the field is the world; and the good seed—these are the sons of the kingdom. The weeds are the sons of the evil one, and [39] the enemy who sowed them is the Devil. The harvest is the end of the age, and the harvesters are angels. [40] Therefore just as the weeds are gathered and burned in the fire, so it will be at the end of the age. [41] The Son of Man will send out His angels, and they will gather from His kingdom everything that causes sin[a] and those guilty of lawlessness.[b] [42] They will throw them into the blazing furnace where there will be weeping and gnashing of teeth. [43] Then the righteous will shine like the sun in their Father's kingdom. Anyone who has ears[c] should listen!

THE PARABLES OF THE HIDDEN TREASURE AND OF THE PRICELESS PEARL

[44] "The kingdom of heaven is like treasure, buried in a field, that a man found and reburied. Then in his joy he goes and sells everything he has and buys that field.

[45] "Again, the kingdom of heaven is like a merchant in search of fine pearls. [46] When he found one priceless[d] pearl, he went and sold everything he had, and bought it.

THE PARABLE OF THE NET

[47] "Again, the kingdom of heaven is like a large net thrown into the sea. It collected every kind ⌊of fish⌋, [48] and when it was full, they dragged it ashore, sat down, and gathered the good ⌊fish⌋ into containers, but threw out the worthless ones. [49] So it will be at the end of the age. The angels will go out, separate the evil people from the righteous, [50] and throw them into the blazing furnace. In that place there will be weeping and gnashing of teeth.

THE STOREHOUSE OF TRUTH

[51] "Have you understood all these things?"[e]

"Yes," they told Him.

The Heavenly Father Will Redeem The Righteous

God is pleased whenever He finds someone striving to live a righteous life and bring glory to Him. The world may not accord any special status to you, but at earth's end, God will welcome the righteous into His kingdom while the evil ones will be cast into eternal judgment.

"So it will be at the end of the age. The angels will go out, separate the evil people from the righteous, and throw them into the blazing furnace."
—Matthew 13:49-50

---

[a]13:41 Or *stumbling*
[b]13:41 Or *those who do lawlessness*
[c]13:43 Other mss add *to hear*
[d]13:46 Or *very precious*
[e]13:51 Other mss add *Jesus asked them*

52 "Therefore," He said to them, "every student of Scripture[a] instructed in the kingdom of heaven is like a landowner who brings out of his storeroom what is new and what is old." 53 When Jesus had finished these parables, He left there.

REJECTION AT NAZARETH

54 He went to His hometown and began to teach them in their •synagogue, so that they were astonished and said, "How did this wisdom and these miracles come to Him? 55 Isn't this the carpenter's son? Isn't His mother called Mary, and His brothers James, Joseph,[b] Simon, and Judas? 56 And His sisters, aren't they all with us? So where does He get all these things?" 57 And they were offended by Him.

But Jesus said to them, "A prophet is not without honor except in his hometown and in his household." 58 And He did not do many miracles there because of their unbelief.

JOHN THE BAPTIST BEHEADED

14 At that time •Herod the tetrarch heard the report about Jesus. 2 "This is John the Baptist!" he told his servants. "He has been raised from the dead, and that's why supernatural powers are at work in him." 3 For Herod had arrested John, chained[c] him, and put him in prison on account of Herodias, his brother Philip's wife, 4 since John had been telling him, "It's not lawful for you to have her!" 5 Though he wanted to kill him, he feared the crowd, since they regarded him as a prophet.

6 But when Herod's birthday celebration came, Herodias' daughter danced before them[d] and pleased Herod. 7 So he promised with an oath to give her whatever she might ask. 8 And prompted by her mother, she answered, "Give me John the Baptist's head here on a platter!" 9 Although the king regretted it, he commanded that it be granted because of his oaths and his guests. 10 So he sent orders and had John beheaded in the prison. 11 His head was brought on a platter and given to the girl, who carried it to her mother. 12 Then

God's Word Is Ever True, Ever Fresh

The Word of God is not merely a source of helpful suggestions, preventative warnings, or inspirational thoughts. It is life itself! To obey God's Word is the surest way to experience all that God has in store for us.

"Every student of Scripture instructed in the kingdom of heaven is like a landowner who brings out of his storeroom what is new and what is old."

—Matthew 13:52

People Will Notice God's Work in You

When God's people and the world see something happen that only God can do, they come to know God.

They were astonished and said, "How did this wisdom and these miracles come to Him? Isn't this the carpenter's son? Isn't His mother called Mary, and His brothers James, Joseph, Simon, and Judas? And His sisters, aren't they all with us? So where does He get all these things?"

—Matthew 13:54b-56

---

[a]13:52 Or *every scribe*
[b]13:55 Other mss read *Joses*; Mk 6:3
[c]14:3 Or *bound*
[d]14:6 Lit *danced in the middle*

his disciples came, removed the corpse,[a] buried it, and went and reported to Jesus.

FEEDING 5,000

[13] When Jesus heard about it, He withdrew from there by boat to a remote place to be alone. When the crowds heard this, they followed Him on foot from the towns. [14] As He stepped ashore,[b] He saw a huge crowd, felt compassion for them, and healed their sick.

[15] When evening came, the disciples approached Him and said, "This place is a wilderness, and it is already late.[c] Send the crowds away so they can go into the villages and buy food for themselves."

[16] "They don't need to go away," Jesus told them. "You give them something to eat."

[17] "But we only have five loaves and two fish here," they said to Him.

[18] "Bring them here to Me," He said. [19] Then He commanded the crowds to sit down[d] on the grass. He took the five loaves and the two fish, and looking up to heaven, He blessed them. He broke the loaves and gave them to the disciples, and the disciples ₍gave them₎ to the crowds. [20] Everyone ate and was filled. Then they picked up 12 baskets full of leftover pieces! [21] Now those who ate were about 5,000 men, besides women and children.

WALKING ON THE WATER

[22] Immediately He[e] made the disciples get into the boat and go ahead of Him to the other side, while He dismissed the crowds. [23] After dismissing the crowds, He went up on the mountain by Himself to pray. When evening came, He was there alone. [24] But the boat was already over a mile[f] from land,[g] battered by the waves, because the wind was against them. [25] Around three in the morning,[h] He came toward them walking on the sea. [26] When the disciples saw Him walking on the sea,

Don't Avoid the Impossible

Christ will lead you into many situations that will seem impossible. But stay in the middle of them, for that is where you will experience God.

"We only have five loaves and two fish here," they said to Him. "Bring them here to Me," He said.

—Matthew 14:17-18

---

[a]14:12 Other mss read *body*
[b]14:14 Lit *Coming out* (of the boat)
[c]14:15 Lit *and the time* (for the evening meal) *has already passed*
[d]14:19 Lit *to recline*
[e]14:22 Other mss read *Jesus*

[f]14:24 Lit *already many stadia*; 1 *stadion* = 600 feet
[g]14:24 Other mss read *already in the middle of the sea*
[h]14:25 Lit *fourth watch of the night* = 3 to 6 a.m.

WORD STUDY

Greek word: ***phantasma***
[FAN tahss mah]

Translation: ***ghost***

Uses in Matthew's Gospel: **1**
(Mk, 1)

Uses in the NT: **2**

Key passage: **Matthew 14:26**

Phantasma (*ghost*) is related to the verb *phantazo* meaning *to make visible* in the active sense and *to appear/become visible* in the passive sense. This word group normally refers to extraordinary events in nature or supernatural phenomena (cf. Heb 12:21). *Phantasma* occurs only twice in early Christian literature, both times in the NT parallel accounts of Jesus' walking on the water found in Matthew 14:26 and Mark 6:49. Luke does not record this miracle, and John only states that the disciples were frightened when they saw Jesus, believing Him to be a ghost. After He assured them that such was not the case, they worshiped Him. A similar incident occurred after Jesus' resurrection, where the term *pneuma* (*spirit, ghost*) was used to refer to this apparent apparition (Lk 24:37).

they were terrified. "It's a ghost!" they said, and cried out in fear.

²⁷ Immediately Jesus spoke to them. "Have courage! It is I. Don't be afraid."

²⁸ "Lord, if it's You," Peter answered Him, "command me to come to You on the water."

²⁹ "Come!" He said.

And climbing out of the boat, Peter started walking on the water and came toward Jesus. ³⁰ But when he saw the strength of the wind,ᵃ he was afraid. And beginning to sink he cried out, "Lord, save me!"

³¹ Immediately Jesus reached out His hand, caught hold of him, and said to him, "You of little faith, why did you doubt?" ³² When they got into the boat, the wind ceased. ³³ Then those in the boat worshiped Him and said, "Truly You are the Son of God!"

MIRACULOUS HEALINGS

³⁴ Once they crossed over, they came to land at Gennesaret. ³⁵ When the men of that place recognized Him, they alertedᵇ the whole vicinity and brought to Him all who were sick. ³⁶ They were begging Him that they might only touch the •tassel on His robe. And as many as touched it were made perfectly well.

THE TRADITION OF THE ELDERS

15 Then •Pharisees and •scribes came from Jerusalem to Jesus and asked, ² "Why do Your disciples break the tradition of the elders? For they don't wash their hands when they eat!"ᶜ

³ He answered them, "And why do you break God's commandment because of your tradition? ⁴ For God said:ᵈ

Honor your father and your mother;ᵉ and,
The one who speaks evil of father
or mother
must be put to death.ᶠ

⁵ But you say, 'Whoever tells his father or mother, "Whatever benefit you might have received from me is a

---

ᵃ**14:30** Other mss read *saw the wind*
ᵇ**14:35** Lit *sent into*
ᶜ**15:2** Lit *eat bread* = eat a meal
ᵈ**15:4** Other mss read *commanded, saying*
ᵉ**15:4** Ex 20:12; Dt 5:16
ᶠ**15:4** Ex 21:17; Lv 20:9

gift ⌊committed to the temple⌋"— ⁶ he does not have to honor his father.'ᵃ In this way, you have revoked God's wordᵇ because of your tradition. ⁷ Hypocrites! Isaiah prophesied correctly about you when he said:

⁸ **These peopleᶜ honor Me with their lips,**
    but their heart is far from Me.
⁹ **They worship Me in vain,**
    teaching as doctrines the commands
       of men."ᵈ

DEFILEMENT IS FROM WITHIN

¹⁰ Summoning the crowd, He told them, "Listen and understand: ¹¹ It's not what goes into the mouth that defiles a man, but what comes out of the mouth, this defiles a man."

¹² Then the disciples came up and told Him, "Do You know that the Pharisees took offense when they heard this statement?"

¹³ He replied, "Every plant that My heavenly Father didn't plant will be uprooted. ¹⁴ Leave them alone! They are blind guides.ᵉ And if the blind guide the blind, both will fall into a pit."

¹⁵ Then Peter replied to Him, "Explain this parable to us."

¹⁶ "Are even you still lacking in understanding?" Heᶠ asked. ¹⁷ "Don't you realizeᵍ that whatever goes into the mouth passes into the stomach and is eliminated?ʰ ¹⁸ But what comes out of the mouth comes from the heart, and this defiles a man. ¹⁹ For from the heart come evil thoughts, murders, adulteries, sexual immoralities, thefts, false testimonies, blasphemies. ²⁰ These are the things that defile a man, but eating with unwashed hands does not defile a man."

A GENTILE MOTHER'S FAITH

²¹ When Jesus left there, He withdrew to the area of Tyre and Sidon. ²² Just then a Canaanite woman from

Obedience Is a Step Toward the Impossible

When God calls a person to join Him in a God-sized task, faith is always required. Obedience indicates faith in God.

"Lord, if it's You," Peter answered Him, "command me to come to You on the water." "Come!" He said. And climbing out of the boat, Peter started walking on the water and came toward Jesus.
—Matthew 14:28-29

ᵃ**15:6** Other mss read *then he does not have to honor his father or mother*
ᵇ**15:6** Other mss read *commandment*
ᶜ**15:8** Other mss add *draws near to Me with their mouths, and*
ᵈ**15:8-9** Is 29:13 LXX
ᵉ**15:14** Other mss add *for the blind*
ᶠ**15:16** Other mss read *Jesus*
ᵍ**15:17** Other mss add *yet*
ʰ**15:17** Lit *and goes out into the toilet*

that region came and kept crying out,[a] "Have mercy on me, Lord, Son of David! My daughter is cruelly tormented by a demon."

23 Yet He did not say a word to her. So His disciples approached Him and urged Him, "Send her away because she cries out after us."[b]

24 He replied, "I was sent only to the lost sheep of the house of Israel."

25 But she came, knelt before Him, and said, "Lord, help me!"

26 He answered, "It isn't right to take the children's bread and throw it to their dogs."

27 "Yes, Lord," she said, "yet even the dogs eat the crumbs that fall from their masters' table!"

28 Then Jesus replied to her, "Woman, your faith is great. Let it be done for you as you want." And from that moment[c] her daughter was cured.

HEALING MANY PEOPLE

29 Moving on from there, Jesus passed along the Sea of Galilee. He went up on a mountain and sat there, 30 and large crowds came to Him, having with them the lame, the blind, the deformed, those unable to speak, and many others. They put them at His feet, and He healed them. 31 So the crowd was amazed when they saw those unable to speak talking, the deformed restored, the lame walking, and the blind seeing. And they gave glory to the God of Israel.

FEEDING 4,000

32 Now Jesus summoned His disciples and said, "I have compassion on the crowd, because they've already stayed with Me three days and have nothing to eat. I don't want to send them away hungry; otherwise they might collapse on the way."

33 The disciples said to Him, "Where could we get enough bread in this desolate place to fill such a crowd?"

34 "How many loaves do you have?" Jesus asked them. "Seven," they said, "and a few small fish."

Life Has Its Problems, Faith Has the Victory

Faith keeps you in a trusting relationship with God in the midst of your problems. Faith has to do with your relationship with God, not your circumstances.

Then Jesus replied to her, "Woman, your faith is great. Let it be done for you as you want." And from that moment her daughter was cured.

—Matthew 15:28

---

[a]**15:22** Other mss read *and cried out to Him*

[b]**15:23** Lit *she is yelling behind us* or *after us*

[c]**15:28** Lit *hour*

35 After commanding the crowd to sit down on the ground, 36 He took the seven loaves and the fish, and He gave thanks, broke them, and kept on giving them to the disciples, and the disciples ₁gave them₁ to the crowds. 37 They all ate and were filled. Then they collected the leftover pieces—seven large baskets full. 38 Now those who ate were 4,000 men, besides women and children. 39 After dismissing the crowds, He got into the boat and went to the region of Magadan.ᵃ

THE YEAST OF THE PHARISEES AND THE SADDUCEES

16 The •Pharisees and •Sadducees approached, and as a test, asked Him to show them a sign from heaven.

2 He answered them: "When evening comes you say, 'It will be good weather because the sky is red.' 3 And in the morning, 'Today will be stormy because the sky is red and threatening.' Youᵇ know how to read the appearance of the sky, but you can't read the signs of the times.ᶜ 4 An evil and adulterous generation wants a sign, but no sign will be given to it except the sign ofᵈ Jonah." Then He left them and went away.

5 The disciples reached the other shore,ᵉ and they had forgotten to take bread.

6 Then Jesus told them, "Watch out and beware of the yeastᶠ of the Pharisees and Sadducees."

7 And they discussed among themselves, "We didn't bring any bread."

8 Aware of this, Jesus said, "You of little faith! Why are you discussing among yourselves that you do not have bread? 9 Don't you understand yet? Don't you remember the five loaves for the 5,000 and how many baskets you collected? 10 Or the seven loaves for the 4,000 and how many large baskets you collected? 11 Why is it you don't understand that when I told you, 'Beware of the yeast of the Pharisees and Sadducees,' it wasn't about bread?" 12 Then they understood that He did not tell them to beware of the yeast in bread, but of the teaching of the Pharisees and Sadducees.

WORD STUDY

Greek word: *splanchnizomai*
[splahnk NIH zah migh]
Translation: *feel compassion for*
Uses in Matthew's Gospel: **5** (Mk, 4; Lk, 3)
Uses in the NT: **12**
Key passage: **Matthew 15:32**

Splanchnizomai (to feel compassion for) is related to the noun *splanchnon*, which in the plural literally means *bowels (insides;*Ac 1:18). In the ancient world, internal organs served as referents for psychological aspects (cf. modern English usage of *heart*). Thus, the *bowels* were considered the seat of love, sympathy, affection, and compassion (Lk 1:78; 2 Co 6:12; 7:15; Php 2:1; Col 3:12). By extension, *splanchnon* became synonymous with the feeling itself (i.e., *love, affection, compassion;* Php 1:8; Phm 12). The verb *splanchnizomai* occurs only in the Synoptic Gospels and apart from appearing in Jesus' parables (Mt 18:27; Lk 10:33; 15:20), the word refers to Jesus Himself. His compassion led Him to provide the crowds with leadership (Mt 9:36 = Mk 6:34), to feed people (Mt 15:32 = Mk 8:2), and to heal them (Mt 14:14; 20:34; Mk 1:41; Lk 7:13).

ᵃ15:39 Other mss read *Magdala*
ᵇ16:3 Other mss read *Hypocrites! You*
ᶜ16:2-3 Other mss omit *When* (v. 2) through end of v. 3
ᵈ16:4 Other mss add *the prophet*
ᵉ16:5 Lit *disciples went to the other side*
ᶠ16:6 Or *leaven*

39

WORD STUDY

Greek word: **christos**
[KRIHSS tahss]
Translation: **Messiah, Christ**

Uses in Matthew's Gospel: **16**
(Mk, 7; Lk, 12; Jn, 19)
Uses in the NT: **529**
Key passage: **Matthew 16:16**

Christos is related to the verb *chrio* (*to anoint*), which was utilized in the Greek OT to translate Hebrew *mashach* (*to anoint*). *Mashach* often referred to ceremonial anointing of those in a special office, such as a priest or king. It is related to the noun *mashiach* (*anointed one*), which was translated into Greek as *christos* (*Christ, Messiah*). In the Gospels and Acts, *christos* is usually best understood as a title representing one who fulfilled the role of Israel's expected deliverer (i.e., *Messiah*; Mt 16:16,20 = Mk 8:29-30; Jn 1:20, 25; Ac 2:31,36). As early Christians began applying *christos* to the person of Jesus, the word lost much of its force as a general reference to the Jewish Messiah and assumed a more specific status in the name Jesus *Christ* (Rm 1:7-8; Rv 1:1,2,5). While the Messianic implications of *christos* still remain outside of the Gospels and Acts, they are not as prominent.

PETER'S CONFESSION OF THE MESSIAH

13 When Jesus came to the region of Caesarea Philippi,[a] He asked His disciples, "Who do people say that the •Son of Man is?"[b]

14 And they said, "Some say John the Baptist; others, Elijah; still others, Jeremiah or one of the prophets."

15 "But you," He asked them, "who do you say that I am?"

16 Simon Peter answered, "You are the •Messiah, the Son of the living God!"

17 And Jesus responded, "Simon son of Jonah,[c] you are blessed because flesh and blood did not reveal this to you, but My Father in heaven. 18 And I also say to you that you are Peter,[d] and on this rock[e] I will build My church, and the forces[f] of •Hades will not overpower it. 19 I will give you the keys of the kingdom of heaven, and whatever you bind on earth is already bound[g] in heaven, and whatever you loose on earth is already loosed[h] in heaven."

20 And He gave the disciples orders to tell no one that He was[i] the Messiah.

HIS DEATH AND RESURRECTION PREDICTED

21 From then on Jesus began to point out to His disciples that He must go to Jerusalem and suffer many things from the elders, •chief priests, and •scribes, be killed, and be raised the third day. 22 Then Peter took Him aside and began to rebuke Him, "Oh no,[j] Lord! This will never happen to You!"

23 But He turned and told Peter, "Get behind Me, Satan! You are an offense to Me because you're not thinking about God's concerns,[k] but man's."

TAKE UP YOUR CROSS

24 Then Jesus said to His disciples, "If anyone wants to come with Me, he must deny himself, take up his cross, and follow Me. 25 For whoever wants to save his

---

[a]16:13 A town north of Galilee at the base of Mount Hermon
[b]16:13 Other mss read *that I, the Son of Man, am*
[c]16:17 Or *son of John*
[d]16:18 *Peter* (Gk *Petros*) = a specific stone or rock
[e]16:18 *Rock* (Gk *petra*) = a rocky crag or bedrock
[f]16:18 Lit *gates*
[g]16:19 Or *earth will be bound*
[h]16:19 Or *earth will be loosed*
[i]16:20 Other mss add *Jesus*
[j]16:22 Lit *Mercy to You = May God have mercy on You*
[k]16:23 Lit *about the things of God*

•life will lose it, but whoever loses his life because of Me will find it. ²⁶ What will it benefit a man if he gains the whole world yet loses his life? Or what will a man give in exchange for his life? ²⁷ For the Son of Man is going to come with His angels in the glory of His Father, and then He will reward each according to what he has done. ²⁸ •I assure you: There are some standing here who will not taste death until they see the Son of Man coming in His kingdom.''

THE TRANSFIGURATION

17 After six days Jesus took Peter, James, and his brother John, and led them up on a high mountain by themselves. ² He was transformedᵃ in front of them, and His face shone like the sun. Even His clothes became as white as the light. ³ Suddenly, Moses and Elijah appeared to them, talking with Him.

⁴ Then Peter said to Jesus, "Lord, it's good for us to be here! If You want, I will makeᵇ three •tabernacles here: one for You, one for Moses, and one for Elijah."

⁵ While he was still speaking, suddenly a bright cloud coveredᶜ them, and a voice from the cloud said:

This is My beloved Son.
I take delight in Him.
Listen to Him!

⁶ When the disciples heard it, they fell facedown and were terrified.

⁷ Then Jesus came up, touched them, and said, "Get up; don't be afraid." ⁸ When they looked up they saw no one except Himᵈ —Jesus alone. ⁹ As they were coming down from the mountain, Jesus commanded them, "Don't tell anyone about the vision until the •Son of Man is raisedᵉ from the dead."

¹⁰ So the disciples questioned Him, "Why then do the •scribes say that Elijah must come first?"

¹¹ "Elijah is comingᶠ and will restore everything," He replied.ᵍ ¹² "But I tell you: Elijah has already come, and

WORD STUDY

Greek word: **metamorphoo**
[meh tah mohr FAH oh]

Translation: **transform**

Uses in Matthew's Gospel: **1** (Mk, 1)

Uses in the NT: **4**

Key passage: **Matthew 17:2**

Metamorphoo means *to change* or *transform* and occurs only in the passive (*to be changed, transformed*, or *transfigured*) in the NT. *Metamorphoo* may refer to outward physical change (e.g., Jesus' *transfiguration*) or to an inward spiritual transformation.

Jesus was *transfigured* (Mt 17:1-2 = Mk 9:2) on the "holy mountain" (2 Pt 1:18) while Peter, James, and John looked on. He temporarily assumed the form of His heavenly glory, permitting His disciples to see Him as He will appear in His kingdom.

Paul employs *metamorphoo* in reference to the inward spiritual transformation occurring in Christians. As believers gaze upon the Lord's glory, they are transformed into His image through the work of the Spirit (2 Co 3:18), reattaining the fullness of the divine image, which they shared at creation. On the basis of their status in Christ, Paul commands believers to be inwardly *transformed* through the renewing of their minds (Rm 12:2).

ᵃ17:2 Or *transfigured*
ᵇ17:4 Other mss read *wish, let's make*
ᶜ17:5 Or *enveloped*; Ex 40:34-35
ᵈ17:8 Other mss omit *Him*
ᶜ17:9 Other mss read *Man has risen*
ᶠ17:11 Other mss add *first*
ᵍ17:11 Other mss read *Jesus said to them*

they didn't recognize him. On the contrary, they did whatever they pleased to him. In the same way the Son of Man is going to suffer at their hands."[a] [13] Then the disciples understood that He spoke to them about John the Baptist.

THE POWER OF FAITH OVER A DEMON

[14] When they reached the crowd, a man approached and knelt down before Him. [15] "Lord," he said, "have mercy on my son, because he has seizures[b] and suffers severely. He often falls into the fire and often into the water. [16] I brought him to Your disciples, but they couldn't heal him."

[17] Jesus replied, "You unbelieving and rebellious[c] generation! How long will I be with you? How long must I put up with you? Bring him here to Me." [18] Then Jesus rebuked the demon,[d] and it[e] came out of him, and from that moment[f] the boy was healed.

[19] Then the disciples approached Jesus privately and said, "Why couldn't we drive it out?"

[20] "Because of your little faith," He[g] told them. "For •I assure you: If you have faith the size of[h] a mustard seed, you will tell this mountain, 'Move from here to there,' and it will move. Nothing will be impossible for you. [[21] However, this kind does not come out except by prayer and fasting.]"[i]

THE SECOND PREDICTION OF HIS DEATH

[22] As they were meeting[j] in Galilee, Jesus told them, "The Son of Man is about to be betrayed into the hands of men. [23] They will kill Him, and on the third day He will be raised up." And they were deeply distressed.

Commit Yourself to Helping People

God ought to be able to send a hurting person to any of His children and expect that they will be helped. Be a faithful steward of every life God sends to you.

"I brought him to Your disciples, but they couldn't heal him."

—Matthew 17:16

A Little Faith Can Go a Long Way

Do you sense that God may be wanting to do far more through your life than what you have been experiencing? Ask God to show you what it is, then respond in faith.

"For I assure you: If you have faith the size of a mustard seed, you will tell this mountain, 'Move from here to there,' and it will move. Nothing will be impossible for you."

—Matthew 17:20b

---

[a]**17:12** Lit *suffer by them*
[b]**17:15** Lit *he is moonstruck*; thought to be a form of epilepsy
[c]**17:17** Or *corrupt*, or *perverted*, or *twisted*; Dt 32:5
[d]**17:18** Lit *rebuked him* or *it*
[e]**17:18** Lit *the demon*
[f]**17:18** Lit *hour*
[g]**17:20** Other mss read *your unbelief,"Jesus*
[h]**17:20** Lit *faith like*
[i]**17:21** Other mss omit bracketed text; Mk 9:29
[j]**17:22** Other mss read *were staying*

PAYING THE TEMPLE TAX

²⁴ When they came to Capernaum, those who collected the double-drachma tax[a] approached Peter and said, "Doesn't your Teacher pay the double-drachma tax?"
²⁵ "Yes," he said.

When he went into the house, Jesus spoke to him first,[b] "What do you think, Simon? Who do earthly kings collect tariffs or taxes from? From their sons or from strangers?"[c]
²⁶ "From strangers," he said.[d]

"Then the sons are free," Jesus told him. ²⁷ "But, so we won't offend them, go to the sea, cast in a fishhook, and catch the first fish that comes up. When you open its mouth you'll find a coin.[e] Take it and give it to them for Me and you."

WHO IS THE GREATEST?

18 At that time[f] the disciples came to Jesus and said, "Who is greatest in the kingdom of heaven?"
² Then He called a child to Him and had him stand among them. ³ "•I assure you," He said, "unless you are converted[g] and become like children, you will never enter the kingdom of heaven. ⁴ Therefore, whoever humbles himself like this child—this one is the greatest in the kingdom of heaven. ⁵ And whoever welcomes[h] one child like this in My name welcomes Me.

⁶ "But whoever •causes the downfall of one of these little ones who believe in Me—it would be better for him if a heavy millstone[i] were hung around his neck and he were drowned in the depths of the sea! ⁷ Woe to the world because of offenses.[j] For offenses must come, but woe to that man by whom the offense comes. ⁸ If your hand or your foot causes your downfall, cut it off and throw it away. It is better for you to enter life maimed or lame, than to have two hands or two feet

Give God Room to Work Through You

You must move from doing work for God according to your abilities, your gifts, your goals, your likes, and your dislikes, to being totally dependent on God, His working, and His resources.

"I assure you," He said, "unless you are converted and become like children, you will never enter the kingdom of heaven. Therefore, whoever humbles himself like this child—this one is the greatest in the kingdom of heaven."
—Matthew 18:3-4

---

[a]17:24 Jewish men paid this tax to support the temple; Ex 30:11-16. A double-drachma could purchase 2 sheep.
[b]17:25 Lit *Jesus anticipated him by saying*
[c]17:25 Or *foreigners*
[d]17:26 Other mss read *Peter said to Him*
[e]17:27 Gk *stater*, worth 2 double-drachmas
[f]18:1 Lit *hour*
[g]18:3 Or *are turned around*
[h]18:5 Or *receives*
[i]18:6 A millstone turned by a donkey
[j]18:7 Or *causes of stumbling*

and be thrown into the eternal fire. 9 And if your eye causes your downfall, gouge it out and throw it away. It is better for you to enter life with one eye, rather than to have two eyes and be thrown into •hellfire!ᵃ

THE PARABLE OF THE LOST SHEEP

10 "See that you don't look down on one of these little ones, because I tell you that in heaven their angels continually view the face of My Father in heaven. [11 For the •Son of Man has come to save the lost.]ᵇ 12 What do you think? If a man has 100 sheep, and one of them goes astray, won't he leave the 99 on the hillside and go and search for the stray? 13 And if he finds it, I assure you: He rejoices over that sheepᶜ more than over the 99 that did not go astray. 14 In the same way, it is not the will of your Father in heaven that one of these little ones perish.

RESTORING A BROTHER

15 "If your brother sins against you,ᵈ go and rebuke him in private.ᵉ If he listens to you, you have won your brother. 16 But if he won't listen, take one or two more with you, so that **by the testimonyᶠ of two or three witnesses every fact may be established.**ᵍ 17 If he pays no attention to them, tell the church.ʰ But if he doesn't pay attention even to the church, let him be like an unbelieverⁱ and a tax collector to you. 18 I assure you: Whatever you bind on earth is already boundʲ in heaven, and whatever you loose on earth is already loosedᵏ in heaven. 19 Again, I assure you: If two of you on earth agree about any matter that youˡ pray for, it will be done for youᵐ by My Father in heaven. 20 For where two or three are gathered together in My name, I am there among them."

God Speaks Through His Church

You can and should depend on God to speak through other believers and the church to help you know what assignment you are to carry out in the ministry of the kingdom.

"For where two or three are gathered together in My name, I am there among them."

—Matthew 18:20

ᵃ18:9 Lit *gehenna of fire*
ᵇ18:11 Other mss omit bracketed text
ᶜ18:13 Lit *over it*
ᵈ18:15 Other mss omit *against you*
ᵉ18:15 Lit *him between you and him alone*
ᶠ18:16 Lit *mouth*

ᵍ18:16 Dt 19:15
ʰ18:17 Or *congregation*
ⁱ18:17 Or *like a Gentile*
ʲ18:18 Or *earth will be bound*
ᵏ18:18 Or *earth will be loosed*
ˡ18:19 Lit *they*
ᵐ18:19 Lit *for them*

THE PARABLE OF THE UNFORGIVING SLAVE

21 Then Peter came to Him and said, "Lord, how many times could my brother sin against me and I forgive him? As many as seven times?"

22 "I tell you, not as many as seven," Jesus said to him, "but 70 times seven.ᵃ 23 For this reason, the kingdom of heaven can be compared to a king who wanted to settle accounts with his •slaves. 24 When he began to settle accounts, one who owed 10,000 talentsᵇ was brought before him. 25 Since he had no way to pay it back, his master commanded that he, his wife, his children, and everything he had be sold to pay the debt.

26 "At this, the •slave fell facedown before him and said, 'Be patient with me, and I will pay you everything!' 27 Then the master of that •slave had compassion, released him, and forgave him the loan.

28 "But that •slave went out and found one of his fellow slaves who owed him 100 •denarii.ᶜ He grabbed him, started choking him, and said, 'Pay what you owe!'

29 "At this, his fellow •slave fell downᵈ and began begging him, 'Be patient with me, and I will pay you back.' 30 But he wasn't willing. On the contrary, he went and threw him into prison until he could pay what was owed. 31 When the other slaves saw what had taken place, they were deeply distressed and went and reported to their master everything that had happened.

32 "Then, after he had summoned him, his master said to him, 'You wicked •slave! I forgave you all that debt because you begged me. 33 Shouldn't you also have had mercy on your fellow slave, as I had mercy on you?' 34 And his master got angry and handed him over to the jailersᵉ until he could pay everything that was owed. 35 So My heavenly Father will also do to you if each of you does not forgive his brotherᶠ from hisᵍ heart."

ᵃ18:22 Or *but 77 times*
ᵇ18:24 A huge sum of money that could never be repaid by a slave; a talent = 6,000 denarii
ᶜ18:28 A small sum compared to 10,000 talents
ᵈ18:29 Other mss add *at his feet*
ᵉ18:34 Or *torturers*
ᶠ18:35 Other mss add *his trespasses*
ᵍ18:35 Lit *your*

WORD STUDY

Greek word: **aphiemi**
[ah FEE ay mee]

Translation: **forgive**

Uses in Matthew's Gospel: **47** (Mk, 34; Lk 31; Jn 15)

Uses in the NT: **143**

Key passage: **Matthew 18:27**

Aphiemi exhibits a broad range of nuances in the NT. It can mean *to send away/dismiss* (Mt 13:36) and in a legal sense *to leave/divorce* (1 Co 7:11-13). It may also mean *to leave/depart* (Mk 1:20,31) or *to tolerate* (Rv 2:20). Another important meaning is *to pardon/forgive*. In this sense, *aphiemi* may describe the cancellation of a loan or debt (Mt 18:27,32), but it more commonly means *to forgive* sins (Mt 6:12,14-15; Mk 2:5,7,9-10; 3:28; Lk 7:47-49; Jn 20:23; Rm 4:7). The related noun *aphesis* almost always refers to God's *forgiveness* of human sins. The resurrected Lord told the disciples that this *forgiveness* would be preached in His name, and the apostles were the first to do exactly that (Ac 2:38; 5:31; 10:43; 13:38; 26:18). Paul employed *aphiemi* and *aphesis* to describe the cancellation of sin's infinite debt to God (Rm 4:7; Eph 1:7; Col 1:14).

WORD STUDY

Greek word: **apoluo**
[ah pah LOO oh]
Translation: **divorce**
Uses in Matthew's Gospel: **19**
(Mk, 12; Lk, 14; Jn, 5)
Uses in the NT: **66**
Key passage: **Matthew 19:3**

Apoluo predominantly means *to send away, let go*, or *release* in the NT (Mt 14:15; 18:27; 27:15). The term receives the more technical sense of *divorce* when a man releases or sends away his wife (Mt 5:31-32). This use of *apoluo* occurs fourteen times, all in the Synoptic Gospels. The term first occurs in the infancy narrative when Joseph decided to divorce Mary because he supposed that she had been unfaithful to him (Mt 1:19). *Apoluo* also occurs with this sense in the Sermon on the Mount (Mt 5:31-32), Jesus' dispute with the Pharisees over the issue of divorce (Mk 10:1-12), and a brief statement about divorce late in Jesus' ministry (Lk 16:18). Jesus condemned divorce but permitted it in cases of infidelity (Mt 19:8-9; cf. Dt 24:1-4)—a view the Pharisees hoped to use against Him (Mt 19:3,7).

THE QUESTION OF DIVORCE

19 When Jesus had finished this instruction, He departed from Galilee and went to the region of Judea across the Jordan. ² Large crowds followed Him, and He healed them there. ³ Some •Pharisees approached Him to test Him. They asked, "Is it lawful for a man to divorce his wife on any grounds?"

⁴ "Haven't you read," He replied, "that He who created[a] them in the beginning **made them male and female**,[b] ⁵ and He also said:

> **For this reason a man will leave**
> **his father and mother**
> **and be joined to his wife,**
> **and the two will become one flesh?**[c]

⁶ So they are no longer two, but one flesh. Therefore what God has joined together, man must not separate."

⁷ "Why then," they asked Him, "did Moses command ⌊us⌋ to give divorce papers and to send her away?"

⁸ He told them, "Moses permitted you to divorce your wives because of the hardness of your hearts. But it was not like that from the beginning. ⁹ And I tell you, whoever divorces his wife, except for sexual immorality, and marries another, commits adultery."[d]

¹⁰ His disciples said to Him, "If the relationship of a man with his wife is like this, it's better not to marry!"

¹¹ But He told them, "Not everyone can accept this saying, but only those it has been given to. ¹² For there are eunuchs who were born that way from their mother's womb, there are eunuchs who were made by men, and there are eunuchs who have made themselves that way because of the kingdom of heaven. Let anyone accept this who can."

BLESSING THE CHILDREN

¹³ Then children were brought to Him so He might put His hands on them and pray. But the disciples rebuked them. ¹⁴ Then Jesus said, "Leave the children alone, and don't try to keep them from coming to Me,

---

[a]**19:4** Other mss read *made*
[b]**19:4** Gn 1:27; 5:2
[c]**19:5** Gn 2:24

[d]**19:9** Other mss add *Also whoever marries a divorced woman commits adultery*; Mt 5:32

because the kingdom of heaven is made up of people like this."ᵃ ¹⁵ After putting His hands on them, He went on from there.

THE RICH YOUNG RULER

¹⁶ Just then someone came up and asked Him, "Teacher, what good must I do to have eternal life?"

¹⁷ "Why do you ask Me about what is good?"ᵇ He said to him. "There is only One who is good.ᶜ If you want to enter into life, keep the commandments."

¹⁸ "Which ones?" he asked Him.

Jesus answered,

> **Do not murder;**
> **do not commit adultery;**
> **do not steal;**
> **do not bear false witness;**
> ¹⁹ **honor your father and your mother;**
> **and love your neighbor as yourself.**ᵈ

²⁰ "I have kept all these,"ᵉ the young man told Him. "What do I still lack?"

²¹ "If you want to be perfect,"ᶠ Jesus said to him, "go, sell your belongings and give to the poor, and you will have treasure in heaven. Then come, follow Me."

²² When the young man heard that command, he went away grieving, because he had many possessions.

POSSESSIONS AND THE KINGDOM

²³ Then Jesus said to His disciples, "•I assure you: It will be hard for a rich person to enter the kingdom of heaven! ²⁴ Again I tell you, it is easier for a camel to go through the eye of a needle than for a rich person to enter the kingdom of God."

²⁵ When the disciples heard this, they were utterly astonished and asked, "Then who can be saved?"

²⁶ But Jesus looked at them and said, "With men this is impossible, but with God all things are possible."

Are You Willing to Give Your All to God?

When God asks you to do something that you cannot do, you will face a crisis of belief.

"If you want to be perfect," Jesus said to him, "go, sell your belongings and give to the poor, and you will have treasure in heaven. Then come, follow Me." When the young man heard that command, he went away grieving, because he had many possessions.

—Matthew 19:21-22

ᵃ**19:14** Lit *heaven is of such ones*
ᵇ**19:17** Other mss read *Why do you call Me good?*
ᶜ**19:17** Other mss read *No one is good but One—God*
ᵈ**19:18-19** Ex 20:12-16; Dt 5:16-20; Lv 19:18
ᵉ**19:20** Other mss add *from my youth*
ᶠ**19:21** Or *complete*

²⁷ Then Peter responded to Him, "Look, we have left everything and followed You. So what will there be for us?"

²⁸ Jesus said to them, "I assure you: In the Messianic Age,ᵃ when the •Son of Man sits on His glorious throne, you who have followed Me will also sit on 12 thrones, judging the 12 tribes of Israel. ²⁹ And everyone who has left houses, brothers or sisters, father or mother,ᵇ children, or fields because of My name will receive 100 times more and will inherit eternal life. ³⁰ But many who are first will be last, and the last first.

THE PARABLE OF THE VINEYARD WORKERS

20 "For the kingdom of heaven is like a landowner who went out early in the morning to hire workers for his vineyard. ² After agreeing with the workers on one •denarius for the day, he sent them into his vineyard. ³ When he went out about nine in the morning,ᶜ he saw others standing in the marketplace doing nothing. ⁴ To those men he said, 'You also go to my vineyard, and I'll give you whatever is right.' So off they went. ⁵ About noon and at three,ᵈ he went out again and did the same thing. ⁶ Then about fiveᵉ he went and found others standing around,ᶠ and said to them, 'Why have you been standing here all day doing nothing?'

⁷ "'Because no one hired us,' they said to him.

"'You also go to my vineyard,' he told them.ᵍ ⁸ When evening came, the owner of the vineyard told his foreman, 'Call the workers and give them their pay, starting with the last and ending with the first.'ʰ

⁹ "When those who were hired about fiveᵉ came, they each received one denarius. ¹⁰ So when the first ones came, they assumed they would get more, but they also received a denarius each. ¹¹ When they received it, they began to complain to the landowner: ¹² 'These last men

---

God Is in Charge; You Are in Submission

God has a right to interrupt your life. He is Lord. When you surrendered to Him as Lord, you gave Him the right to help Himself to your life anytime He wants.

"Don't I have the right to do what I want with my business?"
—Matthew 20:15a

ᵃ**19:28** Lit *the regeneration*
ᵇ**19:29** Other mss add *or wife*
ᶜ**20:3** Lit *about the third hour*
ᵈ**20:5** Lit *about the sixth hour and the ninth hour*
ᵉ**20:6,9** Lit *about the eleventh hour*
ᶠ**20:6** Other mss add *doing nothing*
ᵍ**20:7** Other mss add *'and you'll get whatever is right.'*
ʰ**20:8** Lit *starting from the last until the first*

put in one hour, and you made them equal to us who bore the burden of the day and the burning heat!'

¹³ "He replied to one of them, 'Friend, I'm doing you no wrong. Didn't you agree with me on a denarius? ¹⁴ Take what's yours and go. I want to give this last man the same as I gave you. ¹⁵ Don't I have the right to do what I want with my business?ᵃ Are you jealousᵇ because I'm generous?'ᶜ

¹⁶ "So the last will be first, and the first last."ᵈ

THE THIRD PREDICTION OF HIS DEATH

¹⁷ While going up to Jerusalem, Jesus took the 12 disciples aside privately and said to them on the way: ¹⁸ "Listen! We are going up to Jerusalem. The •Son of Man will be handed over to the •chief priests and •scribes, and they will condemn Him to death. ¹⁹ Then they will hand Him over to the Gentiles to be mocked, flogged,ᵉ and crucified, and He will be resurrectedᶠ on the third day."

SUFFERING AND SERVICE

²⁰ Then the mother of Zebedee's sons approached Him with her sons. She knelt down to ask Him for something. ²¹ "What do you want?" He asked her.

"Promise,"ᵍ she said to Him, "that these two sons of mine may sit, one on Your right and the other on Your left, in Your kingdom."

²² But Jesus answered, "You don't know what you're asking. Are you able to drink the cupʰ that I am about to drink?"ⁱ

"We are able," they said to Him.

²³ He told them, "You will indeed drink My cup.ʲ But to sit at My right and left is not Mine to give; instead, it belongs to those for whom it has been prepared by My Father." ²⁴ When the 10 ₗdisciplesⱼ heard this, they became

WORD STUDY

Greek word: **egeiro**
[eh GAY roh]

Translation: **resurrect, lift up**

Uses in Matthew's Gospel: **36** (Mk, 19; Lk, 18; Jn, 13)

Uses in the NT: **144**

Key passage: **Matthew 20:19**

In the NT, *egeiro* could mean *to get up* (Lk 11:8; Jn 11:29) or *to help somebody get up* (Mk 1:31; Ac 10:26). Further, it could mean *to wake up from sleep* (Mt 1:24; Mk 4:27) or *to wake someone from sleep* (Mt 8:25 = Mk 4:38; Ac 12:7). The comparison of death to sleep (Jn 11:11; 1 Co 15:20; 1 Th 4:13-14) brought *egeiro* into the theological vocabulary of the NT as the dominant verb used to describe the resurrection of believers and particularly that of Jesus (Ac 3:15; 4:10; 5:30; Rm 6:4; 1 Co 15:4; Eph 1:20; 2 Tm 2:8; 1 Pt 1:21). *Egeiro* was also used in reference to Jesus' acts of healing the lame and raising the dead (Mt 9:6 = Mk 2:9; Lk 7:14; 8:54; Jn 12:1), miracles which ultimately anticipate the greater and final resurrection of believers (Jn 5:28-29; cf. 11:23-26).

ᵃ**20:15** Lit *with what is mine*
ᵇ**20:15** Lit *Is your eye evil*; an idiom for jealousy or stinginess
ᶜ**20:15** Lit *good*
ᵈ**20:16** Other mss add *For many are called, but few are chosen.*
ᵉ**20:19** Or *scourged*
ᶠ**20:19** Other mss read *will rise again*
ᵍ**20:21** Lit *Say*

ʰ**20:22** Figurative language referring to His coming suffering; Mt 26:39; Jn 18:11
ⁱ**20:22** Other mss add *and (or) to be baptized with the baptism that I am baptized with*
ʲ**20:23** Other mss add *and be baptized with the baptism that I am baptized with*

indignant with the two brothers. ²⁵ But Jesus called them over and said, "You know that the rulers of the Gentiles dominate them, and the men of high position exercise power over them. ²⁶ It must not be like that among you. On the contrary, whoever wants to become great among you must be your servant, ²⁷ and whoever wants to be first among you must be your slave; ²⁸ just as the Son of Man did not come to be served, but to serve, and to give His life—a ransom for many."

Be Ready—God Could Call at Any Time

The next time you are in a crowd, listen to what the Holy Spirit is saying. You may discover that God has much on His heart for those people—and is waiting for one of His disciples to respond to His prompting.

Moved with compassion, Jesus touched their eyes. Immediately they could see, and they followed Him.

—Matthew 20:34

You Will Get All the Directions You Need

Your relationship with God is far more important to Him than any planning you can do. We cannot know the when, or where, or how of God's will until He tells us.

The disciples went and did just as Jesus directed them.

—Matthew 21:6

TWO BLIND MEN HEALED

²⁹ As they were leaving Jericho, a large crowd followed Him. ³⁰ There were two blind men sitting by the road. When they heard that Jesus was passing by, they cried out, "Lord, have mercy on us, Son of David!" ³¹ The crowd told them to keep quiet, but they cried out all the more, "Lord, have mercy on us, Son of David!"

³² Jesus stopped, called them, and said, "What do you want Me to do for you?"

³³ "Lord," they said to Him, "open our eyes!" ³⁴ Moved with compassion, Jesus touched their eyes. Immediately they could see, and they followed Him.

THE TRIUMPHAL ENTRY

21 When they approached Jerusalem and came to Bethphage at the •Mount of Olives, Jesus then sent two disciples, ² telling them, "Go into the village ahead of you. At once you will find a donkey tied there, and a colt with her. Untie them and bring them to Me. ³ If anyone says anything to you, you should say that the Lord needs them, and immediately he will send them."

⁴ This took place so that what was spoken through the prophet might be fulfilled:

⁵ **Tell Daughter Zion,**
   "See, your King is coming to you,
   gentle, and mounted on a donkey,
   even on a colt,
   the foal of a beast of burden."ᵃ

ᵃ**21:5** Is 62:11; Zch 9:9

6 The disciples went and did just as Jesus directed them. 7 They brought the donkey and the colt; then they laid their robes on them, and He sat on them. 8 A very large crowd spread their robes on the road; others were cutting branches from the trees and spreading them on the road. 9 Then the crowds who went ahead of Him and those who followed kept shouting:

> •*Hosanna* to the Son of David!
> **Blessed is He who comes**
> **in the name of the Lord!**[a]
> *Hosanna* in the highest heaven!

10 When He entered Jerusalem, the whole city was shaken, saying, "Who is this?" 11 And the crowds kept saying, "This is the prophet Jesus from Nazareth in Galilee!"

CLEANSING THE TEMPLE COMPLEX

12 Jesus went into the •temple complex[b] and drove out all those buying and selling in the temple. He overturned the money changers' tables and the chairs of those selling doves. 13 And He said to them, "It is written, **My house will be called a house of prayer.**[c] But you are making it **a den of thieves!**"[d]

CHILDREN CHEER JESUS

14 The blind and the lame came to Him in the temple complex, and He healed them. 15 When the •chief priests and the •scribes saw the wonders that He did and the children in the temple complex cheering, "*Hosanna* to the Son of David!" they were indignant 16 and said to Him, "Do You hear what these ₍children₎ are saying?"

"Yes," Jesus told them. "Have you never read:

> **You have prepared**[e] **praise**
> **from the mouths of children**
> **and nursing infants**"?[f]

17 Then He left them, went out of the city to Bethany, and spent the night there.

---

a21:9 Ps 118:25-26
b21:12 Other mss add *of God*
c21:13 Is 56:7
d21:13 Jr 7:11
e21:16 Or *restored*
f21:16 Ps 8:2

WORD STUDY

Greek word: *hosanna*
[hoh sahn NAH]

Translation: *Hosanna*

Uses in Matthew's Gospel: **3** (Mk, 2; Jn, 1)

Uses in the NT: **6**

Key passage: **Matthew 21:9,15**

Hosanna derives from two Hebrew words *hoshi'ah na'* via Aramaic *hosha' na'*, meaning "*Please save!*" The phrase first occurs in Psalm 118:25 (similar expressions occur in Ps 12:1; 20:9; 28:9; 60:5; 108:6), and by the time of Jesus it had become a fixed liturgical expression both as a prayer for help, an exclamation of praise, and a shout of celebration. Sometimes, the phrase was interpreted Messianically, and in this sense, the Gospels highlight Jesus' triumphal entry by noting the crowds' shouts of *Hosanna* (Mt 21:9 = Mk 11:9-10 = Lk 19:38 = Jn 12:13) as well as the cheering of the children in praise of Jesus (Mt 21:15).

THE BARREN FIG TREE

18 Early in the morning, as He was returning to the city, He was hungry. 19 Seeing a lone fig tree by the road, He went up to it and found nothing on it except leaves. And He said to it, "May no fruit ever come from you again!" At once the fig tree withered.

20 When the disciples saw it, they were amazed and said, "How did the fig tree wither so quickly?"

21 Jesus answered them, "•I assure you: If you have faith and do not doubt, you will not only do what was done to the fig tree, but even if you tell this mountain, 'Be lifted up and thrown into the sea,' it will be done. 22 And if you believe, you will receive whatever you ask for in prayer."

MESSIAH'S AUTHORITY CHALLENGED

23 When He entered the temple complex, the chief priests and the elders of the people came up to Him as He was teaching and said, "By what authority are You doing these things? Who gave You this authority?"

24 Jesus answered them, "I will also ask you one question, and if you answer it for Me, then I will tell you by what authority I do these things. 25 Where did John's baptism come from? From heaven or from men?"

They began to argue among themselves, "If we say, 'From heaven,' He will say to us, 'Then why didn't you believe him?' 26 But if we say, 'From men,' we're afraid of the crowd, because everyone thought John was a prophet." 27 So they answered Jesus, "We don't know."

And He said to them, "Neither will I tell you by what authority I do these things.

THE PARABLE OF THE TWO SONS

28 "But what do you think? A man had two sons. He went to the first and said, 'My son, go, work in the vineyard today.'

29 "He answered, 'I don't want to!' Yet later he changed his mind and went. 30 Then the man went to the other and said the same thing.

If It Seems Too Hard, It's Probably God

If you or your church are not responding to God by attempting things that only He can accomplish, then you are not exercising faith.

Jesus answered them, "I assure you: If you have faith and do not doubt, you will not only do what was done to the fig tree, but even if you tell this mountain, 'Be lifted up and thrown into the sea,' it will be done."

—Matthew 21:21

"'I will, sir,' he answered. But he didn't go.
31 "Which of the two did his father's will?"

"The first," they said.

Jesus said to them, "I assure you: Tax collectors
and prostitutes are entering the kingdom of God
before you! 32 For John came to you in the way of
righteousness,ª and you didn't believe him. Tax collectors and prostitutes did believe him, but you, when you
saw it, didn't even change your minds then and believe
him.

THE PARABLE OF THE
VINEYARD OWNER

33 "Listen to another parable: There was a man, a
landowner, who planted a vineyard, put a fence around
it, dug a winepress in it, and built a watchtower. He
leased it to tenant farmers and went away. 34 When
the grape harvestᵇ drew near, he sent his slaves to
the farmers to collect his fruit. 35 But the farmers
took his slaves, beat one, killed another, and stoned
a third. 36 Again, he sent other slaves, more than the
first group, and they did the same to them. 37 Finally,
he sent his son to them. 'They will respect my son,' he
said.

38 "But when the tenant farmers saw the son, they
said among themselves, 'This is the heir. Come, let's kill
him and take his inheritance!' 39 So they seized him and
threw him out of the vineyard, and killed him. 40 Therefore, when the owner of the vineyard comes, what will
he do to those farmers?"

41 "He will completely destroy those terrible men,"
they told Him, "and lease his vineyard to other farmers
who will give him his produce at the harvest."ᶜ

42 Jesus said to them, "Have you never read in the
Scriptures:

> The stone that the builders rejected
> has become the cornerstone.ᵈ
> This came from the Lord
> and is wonderful in our eyes?ᵉ

Sin Dies If You Give
It Too Much Light

We free ourselves from sin's bondage when we recognize it for the
evil it is. If we simply call our sin a
mistake, a bad habit, or a weakness, we will never escape its grasp.

*Jesus said to them, "I assure you:
Tax collectors and prostitutes
are entering the kingdom of God
before you! For John came to
you in the way of the righteousness . . . but you, when you
saw it, didn't even change your
minds then and believe him."*

—Matthew 21:31b-32

ª21:32 John came preaching and
practicing righteousness
ᵇ21:34 Lit *the season of fruits*

ᶜ21:41 Lit *him the fruits in their
seasons*
ᵈ21:42 Lit *the head of the corner*
ᵉ21:42 Ps 118:22-23

43 Therefore I tell you, the kingdom of God will be taken away from you and given to a nation producing its[a] fruit. [44 Whoever falls on this stone will be broken to pieces; but on whomever it falls, it will grind him to powder!"][b]

45 When the chief priests and the •Pharisees heard His parables, they knew He was speaking about them. 46 Although they were looking for a way to arrest Him, they feared the crowds, because they[c] regarded Him as a prophet.

THE PARABLE OF THE WEDDING BANQUET

22 Once more Jesus spoke to them in parables: 2 "The kingdom of heaven may be compared to a king who gave a wedding banquet for his son. 3 He sent out his •slaves to summon those invited to the banquet, but they didn't want to come. 4 Again, he sent out other slaves, and said, 'Tell those who are invited: Look, I've prepared my dinner; my oxen and fattened cattle have been slaughtered, and everything is ready. Come to the wedding banquet.'

5 "But they paid no attention and went away, one to his own farm, another to his business. 6 And the others seized his •slaves, treated them outrageously and killed them. 7 The king[d] was enraged, so he sent out his troops, destroyed those murderers, and burned down their city.

8 "Then he told his •slaves, 'The banquet is ready, but those who were invited were not worthy. 9 Therefore, go to where the roads exit the city and invite everyone you find to the banquet.' 10 So those slaves went out on the roads and gathered everyone they found, both evil and good. The wedding banquet was filled with guests.[e] 11 But when the king came in to view the guests, he saw a man there who was not dressed for a wedding. 12 So he said to him, 'Friend, how did you get in here without wedding clothes?' The man was speechless. 13 "Then the king told the attendants, 'Tie him up

---

He Is the Potter, You Are the Clay

If your tendency is to tell the Father what you can and cannot do for Him, submit to His agenda and allow Him to shape you into the person He wants you to be. Like clay.

"Whoever falls on this stone will be broken to pieces; but on whomever it falls, it will grind him to powder!"

—Matthew 21:44

---

[a]21:43 The word *its* refers back to *kingdom*.
[b]21:44 Other mss omit this v.
[c]21:46 The crowds

[d]22:7 Other mss read *But when the (that) king heard about it he*
[e]22:10 Lit *those reclining* (to eat)

hand and foot,[a] and throw him into the outer darkness, where there will be weeping and gnashing of teeth.'

[14] "For many are invited, but few are chosen."

GOD AND CAESAR

[15] Then the •Pharisees went and plotted how to trap Him by what He said.[b] [16] They sent their disciples to Him, with the •Herodians. "Teacher," they said, "we know that You are truthful and teach truthfully the way of God. You defer to no one, for You don't show partiality.[c] [17] Tell us, therefore, what You think. Is it lawful to pay taxes to Caesar or not?"

[18] But perceiving their malice, Jesus said, "Why are you testing Me, hypocrites? [19] Show Me the coin used for the tax." So they brought Him a •denarius. [20] "Whose image and inscription is this?" He asked them.

[21] "Caesar's," they said to Him.

Then He said to them, "Therefore, give back to Caesar the things that are Caesar's, and to God the things that are God's." [22] When they heard this, they were amazed. So they left Him and went away.

THE SADDUCEES AND THE RESURRECTION

[23] The same day some •Sadducees, who say there is no resurrection, came up to Him and questioned Him: [24] "Teacher, Moses said, **if a man dies, having no children, his brother is to marry his wife and raise up offspring for his brother.**[d] [25] Now there were seven brothers among us. The first got married and died. Having no offspring, he left his wife to his brother. [26] The same happened to the second also, and the third, and so to all seven.[e] [27] Then last of all the woman died. [28] Therefore, in the resurrection, whose wife will she be of the seven? For they all had married her."[f]

Don't Expect Everyone to Want Your Jesus

Many people are simply too busy to stop and too self-assured to realize that they have a need for a Savior. Don't take their rejection personally. They may be closer to responding than you think.

"He sent out his slaves to summon those invited to the banquet, but they didn't want to come."

—Matthew 22:3

---

[a]22:13 Other mss add *take him away*
[b]22:15 Lit *trap Him in [a] word*
[c]22:16 Lit *don't look on the face* of men; that is, on the outward appearance
[d]22:24 Dt 25:5
[e]22:26 Lit *so until the seven*
[f]22:28 Lit *all had her*

²⁹ Jesus answered them, "You are deceived, because you don't know the Scriptures or the power of God. ³⁰ For in the resurrection they neither marry nor are given in marriage but are likeᵃ angels in heaven. ³¹ Now concerning the resurrection of the dead, haven't you read what was spoken to you by God: ³² **I am the God of Abraham and the God of Isaac and the God of Jacob?**ᵇ Heᶜ is not the God of the dead, but of the living."

³³ And when the crowds heard this, they were astonished at His teaching.

THE PRIMARY COMMANDMENTS

³⁴ When the Pharisees heard that He had silenced the Sadducees, they came together in the same place. ³⁵ And one of them, an expert in the law, asked a question to test Him: ³⁶ "Teacher, which commandment in the law is the greatest?"ᵈ

³⁷ He said to him, **"Love the Lord your God with all your heart, with all your soul, and with all your mind.**ᵉ ³⁸ This is the greatest and most importantᶠ commandment. ³⁹ The second is like it: **Love your neighbor as yourself.**ᵍ ⁴⁰ All the Law and the Prophets dependʰ on these two commandments."

THE QUESTION ABOUT THE MESSIAH

⁴¹ While the Pharisees were together, Jesus questioned them, ⁴² "What do you think about the •Messiah? Whose Son is He?"

"David's," they told Him.

⁴³ He asked them, "How is it then that David, inspired by the Spirit,ⁱ calls Him 'Lord':

⁴⁴ **The Lord declared to my Lord,**
'Sit at My right hand
until I put Your enemies
under Your feet'?ʲ ᵏ

Loving God Is a Choice, Not a Feeling

More than anything else, God wants us to love Him with our total being.

He said to him, "Love the Lord your God with all your heart, with all your soul, and with all your mind. This is the greatest and most important commandment."

Matthew 22:37-38

ᵃ**22:30** Other mss add *God's*
ᵇ**22:32** Ex 3:6,15-16
ᶜ**22:32** Other mss read *God*
ᵈ**22:36** Lit *is great*
ᵉ**22:37** Dt 6:5
ᶠ**22:38** Lit *and first*
ᵍ**22:39** Lv 19:18
ʰ**22:40** Or *hang*
ⁱ**22:43** Lit *David in Spirit*
ʲ**22:44** Other mss read *until I make Your enemies Your footstool*
ᵏ**22:44** Ps 110:1

45 "If David calls Him 'Lord,' how then can the Messiah be his Son?" 46 No one was able to answer Him at all,a and from that day no one dared to question Him any more.

RELIGIOUS HYPOCRITES DENOUNCED

23 Then Jesus spoke to the crowds and to His disciples: 2 "The •scribes and the •Pharisees are seated in the chair of Moses.b 3 Therefore do whatever they tell you and observe [it]. But don't do what they do,c because they don't practice what they teach. 4 They tie up heavy loads that are hard to carryd and put them on people's shoulders, but they themselves aren't willing to lift a fingere to move them. 5 They do everythingf to be observed by others: They enlarge their phylacteriesg and lengthen their •tassels.h 6 They love the place of honor at banquets, the front seats in the •synagogues, 7 greetings in the marketplaces, and to be called '•Rabbi' by people.

8 "But as for you, do not be called 'Rabbi,' because you have one Teacher,i and you are all brothers. 9 Do not call anyone on earth your father, because you have one Father, who is in heaven. 10 And do not be called masters either, because you have one Master,j the •Messiah. 11 The greatest among you will be your servant. 12 Whoever exalts himself will be humbled, and whoever humbles himself will be exalted.

13 "But woe to you, scribes and Pharisees, hypocrites! You lock up the kingdom of heaven from people. For you don't go in, and you don't allow those entering to go in.

[14 "Woe to you, scribes and Pharisees, hypocrites! You devour widows' houses and make long prayers just for show.k This is why you will receive a harsher punishment.]l

15 "Woe to you, scribes and Pharisees, hypocrites! You travel over land and sea to make one •proselyte,

WORD STUDY

Greek word: **entole**
[ehn tah LAY]

Translation: **commandment**

Uses in Matthew's Gospel: **6**
(Mk, 6; Lk, 4; Jn, 10)

Uses in the NT: **67**

Key passage: **Matthew 22:35-40**

Entole (*commandment*) usually refers to specific demands from God to mankind, either those given in the OT (e.g., one of the Ten Commandments), OT teaching in general, or some other aspect of divine instruction (especially in John's writings). Despite the numerous commandments in the OT (over 600), Jesus stated that they all are summarized in the greatest command, that is, to love God with one's entire being (Mt 22:37), a truth already proclaimed in the OT (Dt 6:4-5). The second command is to love one's neighbors (Mt 22:38; cf. Lv 19:18). Every other commandment God has given relates directly to these two: we must first love God our Creator and Redeemer, and then we must love everyone else whom He created in His image and for whom He has provided redemption in Christ.

---

a22:46 Lit *answer Him a word*
b23:2 Perhaps a special chair for teaching in synagogues, or a metaphorical phrase for teaching with Moses' authority
c23:3 Lit *do according to their works*
d23:4 Other mss omit *that are hard to carry*
e23:4 Lit *lift with their finger*
f23:5 Lit *do all their works*
g23:5 Small leather boxes containing OT texts, worn by Jews on their arms and foreheads
h23:5 Other mss add *on their robes*
i23:8 Other mss add *the Messiah*
j23:10 Or *Teacher*
k23:14 Or *prayers with false motivation*
l23:14 Other mss omit bracketed text

and when he becomes one, you make him twice as fit for •hell[a] as you are!

16 "Woe to you, blind guides, who say, 'Whoever takes an oath by the sanctuary, it means nothing. But whoever takes an oath by the gold of the sanctuary is bound by his oath.'[b] 17 Blind fools![c] For which is greater, the gold or the sanctuary that sanctified the gold? 18 Also, 'Whoever takes an oath by the altar, it means nothing. But whoever takes an oath by the gift that is on it is bound by his oath.'[b] 19 Blind people![d] For which is greater, the gift or the altar that sanctifies the gift? 20 Therefore the one who takes an oath by the altar takes an oath by it and by everything on it. 21 The one who takes an oath by the sanctuary takes an oath by it and by Him who dwells in it. 22 And the one who takes an oath by heaven takes an oath by God's throne and by Him who sits on it.

23 "Woe to you, scribes and Pharisees, hypocrites! You pay a tenth of [e] mint, dill, and cumin,[f] yet you have neglected the more important matters of the law—justice, mercy, and faith. These things should have been done without neglecting the others. 24 Blind guides! You strain out a gnat, yet gulp down a camel!

25 "Woe to you, scribes and Pharisees, hypocrites! You clean the outside of the cup and dish, but inside they are full of greed[g] and self-indulgence! 26 Blind Pharisee! First clean the inside of the cup,[h] so the outside of it[i] may also become clean.

27 "Woe to you, scribes and Pharisees, hypocrites! You are like whitewashed tombs, which appear beautiful on the outside, but inside are full of dead men's bones and every impurity. 28 In the same way, on the outside you seem righteous to people, but inside you are full of hypocrisy and lawlessness.

29 "Woe to you, scribes and Pharisees, hypocrites! You build the tombs of the prophets and decorate the monuments of the righteous, 30 and you say, 'If we had lived in the days of our fathers, we wouldn't have

Does Your Faith Have Form But No Power?

Religious activity apart from fellowship with God is empty ritual. Don't settle for a religious life that lacks a vital relationship with Jesus Christ.

"Blind fools! For which is greater, the gold or the sanctuary that sanctified the gold?"
—Matthew 23:17

You Don't Know How Much God Loves You

God loves you, not because you deserve His love, but because His nature is love. His love for you gives you an inherent worth that nothing can diminish.

"Jerusalem, Jerusalem! The city who kills the prophets and stones those who are sent to her. How often I wanted to gather your children together, as a hen gathers her chicks under her wings, yet you were not willing!"
—Matthew 23:37

---

[a]23:15 Lit *twice the son of gehenna*
[b]23:16,18 Lit *is obligated*
[c]23:17 Lit *Fools and blind*
[d]23:19 Other mss read *Fools and blind*
[e]23:23 Or *You tithe*
[f]23:23 A plant whose seeds are used as a seasoning
[g]23:25 Or *full of violence*
[h]23:26 Other mss add *and dish*
[i]23:26 Other mss read *of them*

taken part with them in shedding the prophets' blood.'ᵃ ³¹ You therefore testify against yourselves that you are sons of those who murdered the prophets. ³² Fill up, then, the measure of your fathers' sins!ᵇ

³³ "Snakes! Brood of vipers! How can you escape being condemned to hell?ᶜ ³⁴ This is why I am sending you prophets, sages, and scribes. Some of them you will kill and crucify, and some of them you will flog in your synagogues and hound from town to town. ³⁵ So all the righteous blood shed on the earth will be charged to you,ᵈ from the blood of righteous Abel to the blood of Zechariah, son of Berechiah, whom you murdered between the sanctuary and the altar. ³⁶ •I assure you: All these things will come on this generation!

JESUS' LAMENTATION OVER JERUSALEM

³⁷ "Jerusalem, Jerusalem! The city who kills the prophets and stones those who are sent to her. How often I wanted to gather your children together, as a hen gathers her chicksᵉ under her wings, yet you were not willing! ³⁸ See, your house is left to you desolate. ³⁹ For I tell you, you will never see Me again until you say, **Blessed is He who comes in the name of the Lord!**"ᶠ

DESTRUCTION OF THE TEMPLE PREDICTED

24 As Jesus left and was going out of the •temple complex, His disciples came up and called His attention to the temple buildings. ² Then He replied to them, "Don't you see all these things? •I assure you: Not one stone will be left here on another that will not be thrown down!"

SIGNS OF THE END OF THE AGE

³ While He was sitting on the •Mount of Olives, the disciples approached Him privately and said, "Tell us,

WORD STUDY

Greek word: **hupokrites**
[hoo pah krih TAYSS]

Translation: **hypocrite**

Uses in Matthew's Gospel: **14** (Mk, 1; Lk, 3)

Uses in the NT: **18**

Key passage: **Matthew 23:13-36**

Hupokrites (hypocrite) is derived from the verb *hupokrinomai* meaning *to interpret* or *play the part. Hupokrinomai* was often used to describe what actors accomplished on stage, and *hupokrites* referred to an *actor*, as one who *interprets* the words of a poet and *plays a part*.Though not originally a negative term, *hupokrites* metaphorically assumed a negative sense in Jewish and Christian literature, referring to one who pretends or who misinterprets truth and subsequently plays a part contrary to reality (e.g., the Jewish leaders of Jesus' day misinterpreted the relationship between written Law and interpretive tradition and subsequently *played the part* of properly interpreting the Law when they were actually not properly interpreting it). Jesus uses *hupokrites* seventeen times to denounce the Jewish leaders' fraudulent claim to spirituality. Perhaps His most scorching declamation comes in Matthew 23:13-36.

ᵃ23:30 Lit *have been partakers with them in the blood of the prophets*
ᵇ23:32 Lit *the measure of your fathers*
ᶜ23:33 Lit *escape from the judgment of gehenna*
ᵈ23:35 Lit *will come on you*
ᵉ23:37 Or *as a mother bird gathers her young*
ᶠ23:39 Ps 118:26

WORD STUDY

Greek word: *thlipsis*
[THLIHP sihss]

Translation: *tribulation*

Uses in Matthew's Gospel: **4**
(Mk, 3; Jn, 2)

Uses in the NT: **45**

Key passage: **Matthew 24:21**

The noun *thlipsis* (*tribulation*) is related to the verb *thlibo*, which literally means *to press* or *crush* (Mk 3:9). This literal sense was figuratively expanded to mean *to oppress* or *afflict*. A link between this literal and figurative use appears in Matthew 7:14 ("[how] *difficult* the road"), where *thlibo* means *to cause difficulty* by making something (i.e., a road) narrow. In the NT, the noun *thlipsis* does not occur in the literal sense (*pressure*) but always takes the metaphorical sense of *affliction* or *tribulation*. In the Christian life, *thlipsis* refers to an *affliction* originating from an external source (Rm 5:3; 8:35; 12:12; 2 Co 1:4), though internal anguish can also be classed as *thlipsis* (2 Co 2:4; Php 1:17). Unbelievers can receive *afflictions* at God's hands (Rm 2:9). Four times, *thlipsis* occurs in the expression "great tribulation," two of which appear to refer to a future context (Mt 24:21; Rv 7:14).

when will these things happen? And what is the sign of Your coming and of the end of the age?"

⁴ Then Jesus replied to them: "Watch out that no one deceives you. ⁵ For many will come in My name, saying, 'I am the •Messiah,' and they will deceive many. ⁶ You are going to hear of wars and rumors of wars. See that you are not alarmed, because these things must take place, but the end is not yet. ⁷ For nation will rise up against nation, and kingdom against kingdom. There will be famines[a] and earthquakes in various places. ⁸ All these events are the beginning of birth pains.

PERSECUTIONS PREDICTED

⁹ "Then they will hand you over for persecution,[b] and they will kill you. You will be hated by all nations because of My name. ¹⁰ Then many will take offense, betray one another and hate one another. ¹¹ Many false prophets will rise up and deceive many. ¹² Because lawlessness will multiply, the love of many will grow cold. ¹³ But the one who endures to the end will be delivered.[c] ¹⁴ This good news of the kingdom will be proclaimed in all the world[d] as a testimony to all nations. And then the end will come.

THE GREAT TRIBULATION

¹⁵ "So when you see **the abomination that causes desolation**,[e] [f] spoken of by the prophet Daniel, standing in the holy place" (let the reader understand[g]), ¹⁶ "then those in Judea must flee to the mountains! ¹⁷ A man on the housetop[h] must not come down to get things out of his house. ¹⁸ And a man in the field must not go back to get his clothes. ¹⁹ Woe to pregnant women and nursing mothers in those days! ²⁰ Pray that your escape may not be in winter or on a Sabbath. ²¹ For at that time there will be great tribulation, the kind that hasn't taken place from the beginning of the world until now and never will again! ²² Unless those days were limited, no one would[i] survive.[j] But those days will be limited because of the elect.

---

[a]**24:7** Other mss add *epidemics*
[b]**24:9** Or *tribulation*, or *distress*
[c]**24:13** Or *be saved*
[d]**24:14** Or *in all the inhabited earth*
[e]**24:15** Or *abomination of desolation*, or *desolating sacrilege*

[f]**24:15** Dn 9:27
[g]**24:15** These are, most likely, Matthew's words to his readers.
[h]**24:17** Or *roof*
[i]**24:22** Lit *short, all flesh would not*
[j]**24:22** Or *be saved* or *delivered*

23 "If anyone tells you then, 'Look, here is the Messiah!' or, 'Over here!' do not believe it! 24 False messiahs[a] and false prophets will arise and perform great signs and wonders to lead astray, if possible, even the elect. 25 Take note: I have told you in advance. 26 So if they tell you, 'Look, he's in the wilderness!' don't go out; 'Look, he's in the inner rooms!' do not believe it. 27 For as the lightning comes from the east and flashes as far as the west, so will be the coming of the •Son of Man. 28 Wherever the carcass is, there the vultures[b] will gather.

THE COMING OF THE SON OF MAN

29 "Immediately after the tribulation of those days;

> The sun will be darkened,
> and the moon will not shed its light;
> the stars will fall from the sky,
> and the celestial powers will be shaken.

30 "Then the sign of the Son of Man will appear in the sky, and then all the peoples of the earth[c] will mourn;[d] and they will see the Son of Man coming on the clouds of heaven with power and great glory. 31 He will send out His angels with a loud trumpet, and they will gather His elect from the four winds, from one end of the sky to the other.

THE PARABLE OF THE FIG TREE

32 "Now learn this parable from the fig tree: As soon as its branch becomes tender and sprouts leaves, you know that summer is near. 33 In the same way, when you see all these things, recognize[e] that He[f] is near—at the door! 34 I assure you: This generation will certainly not pass away until all these things take place. 35 Heaven and earth will pass away, but My words will never pass away.

NO ONE KNOWS THE DAY OR HOUR

36 "Now concerning that day and hour no one knows—neither the angels in heaven, nor the Son[g]

**God's Way Is
the Only Way**

He did not say, "I will show you the way." He said, "I AM the way." Jesus knows the way; He is your way.

*"Heaven and earth will
pass away, but My words
will never pass away."*
—Matthew 24:35

---

[a]24:24 Or *False christs*
[b]24:28 Or *eagles*
[c]24:30 Or *all the tribes of the land*
[d]24:30 Lit *will beat*; = beat their breasts
[e]24:33 Or *things, you know*
[f]24:33 Or *it*; = summer
[g]24:36 Other mss omit *nor the Son*

—except the Father only. [37] As the days of Noah were, so the coming of the Son of Man will be. [38] For in those days before the flood they were eating and drinking, marrying and giving in marriage, until the day Noah boarded the ark. [39] They didn't know[a] until the flood came and swept them all away. So this is the way the coming of the Son of Man will be: [40] Then two men will be in the field: one will be taken and one left. [41] Two women will be grinding at the mill: one will be taken and one left. [42] Therefore be alert, since you don't know what day[b] your Lord is coming. [43] But know this: If the homeowner had known what time[c] the thief was coming, he would have stayed alert and not let his house be broken into. [44] This is why you also must be ready, because the Son of Man is coming at an hour you do not expect.

FAITHFUL SERVICE TO THE MESSIAH

[45] "Who then is a faithful and sensible slave, whom his master has put in charge of his household, to give them food at the proper time? [46] That slave whose master finds him working when he comes will be rewarded. [47] I assure you: He will put him in charge of all his possessions. [48] But if that wicked slave says in his heart, 'My master is delayed,' [49] and starts to beat his fellow slaves, and eats and drinks with drunkards, [50] that slave's master will come on a day he does not expect and at an hour he does not know. [51] He will cut him to pieces[d] and assign him a place with the hypocrites. In that place there will be weeping and gnashing of teeth.

THE PARABLE OF THE 10 VIRGINS

25 "Then the kingdom of heaven will be like 10 virgins[e] who took their lamps and went out to meet the groom. [2] Five of them were foolish and five were sensible. [3] When the foolish took their lamps, they didn't take oil with them. [4] But the sensible ones took

Obey Every Day

If you were to do everything that Jesus tells you one day at a time, you would always be right in the center of His will.

"Who then is a faithful and sensible slave, whom his master has put in charge of his household, to give them food at the proper time? That slave whose master finds him working when he comes will be rewarded."

—Matthew 24:45-46

[a]24:39 *They didn't know* the day and hour of the coming judgment
[b]24:42 Other mss read *hour*; = time
[c]24:43 Lit *watch*; a division of the night in ancient times
[d]24:51 Lit *him in two*
[e]25:1 Or *bridesmaids*

oil in their flasks with their lamps. [5] Since the groom was delayed, they all became drowsy and fell asleep.

[6] "In the middle of the night there was a shout: 'Here's the groom! Come out to meet him.'

[7] "Then all those virgins got up and trimmed their lamps. [8] But the foolish ones said to the sensible ones, 'Give us some of your oil, because our lamps are going out.'

[9] "The sensible ones answered, 'No, there won't be enough for us and for you. Go instead to those who sell, and buy oil for yourselves.'

[10] "When they had gone to buy some, the groom arrived. Then those who were ready went in with him to the wedding banquet, and the door was shut.

[11] "Later the rest of the virgins also came and said, 'Master, master, open up for us!'

[12] "But he replied, '•I assure you: I do not know you!'

[13] "Therefore be alert, because you don't know either the day or the hour.[a]

THE PARABLE OF THE TALENTS

[14] "For it is just like a man going on a journey. He called his own •slaves and turned over his possessions to them. [15] To one he gave five talents;[b] to another, two; and to another, one—to each according to his own ability. Then he went on a journey. Immediately [16] the man who had received five talents went, put them to work, and earned five more. [17] In the same way the man with two earned two more. [18] But the man who had received one talent went off, dug a hole in the ground, and hid his master's money.

[19] "After a long time the master of those •slaves came and settled accounts with them. [20] The man who had received five talents approached, presented five more talents, and said, 'Master, you gave me five talents. Look, I've earned five more talents.'

[21] "His master said to him, 'Well done, good and faithful •slave! You were faithful over a few things; I will put you in charge of many things. Share your master's joy!'

Stay Close, Very Close

Christians lose many opportunities to experience God's activity because they have not devoted enough time to their relationship with God.

"The foolish ones said to the sensible ones, 'Give us some of your oil, because our lamps are going out.'. . . When they had gone to buy some, the groom arrived. Then those who were ready went in with him to the wedding banquet, and the door was shut."
—Matthew 25:8,10

Be Faithful in the Small Things

Any assignment that comes from the Maker of the universe is an important assignment. Don't use human standards to measure the importance or value of an assignment.

"His master said to him, 'Well done, good and faithful slave! You were faithful over a few things; I will put you in charge of many things. Share your master's joy!'"
—Matthew 25:21

---

[a]25:13 Other mss add *in which the Son of Man is coming.*

[b]25:15 Worth a very large sum of money; a talent = 6,000 •denarii

WORD STUDY

Greek word: **talanton**
[TAL ahn tahn]

Translation: **talent**

Uses in Matthew's Gospel: **14**

Uses in the NT: **14**

Key passage: **Matthew 25:14-30**

———————————

A *talanton* (*talent*) was originally a unit of weight varying in size from 57 to 80 lbs. This weight eventually became a unit of coinage, whose value varied depending on whether it was determined on a gold, silver, or copper basis. A *talanton* of silver was equivalent to 6,000 *drachmas* (= 6,000 *denarii*), one *drachma* representing a worker's average daily wage during the third to second centuries B.C. (cf. Tobit 5:15).

Talanton occurs once in Jesus' parable about forgiveness (Mt 18:23-35). The 10,000 *talents* (Mt 18:24) owed by the slave to the king were equivalent to 60 million drachmas, a value well beyond the slave's ability to repay! The other thirteen occurrences of *talanton* occur in Mt 25:14-30. The *talents* distributed by the slaveowner in this passage represent no small amount. This last parable exhorts us to judiciously invest the gifts the Lord has given each of us.

²² "Then the man with two talents also approached. He said, 'Master, you gave me two talents. Look, I've earned two more talents.'

²³ "His master said to him, 'Well done, good and faithful •slave! You were faithful over a few things; I will put you in charge of many things. Share your master's joy!'

²⁴ "Then the man who had received one talent also approached and said, 'Master, I know you. You're a difficult man, reaping where you haven't sown and gathering where you haven't scattered seed. ²⁵ So I was afraid and went off and hid your talent in the ground. Look, you have what is yours.'

²⁶ "But his master replied to him, 'You evil, lazy •slave! If you knew that I reap where I haven't sown and gather where I haven't scattered, ²⁷ then[a] you should have deposited my money with the bankers. And when I returned I would have received my money[b] back with interest.

²⁸ "'So take the talent from him and give it to the one who has 10 talents. ²⁹ For to everyone who has, more will be given, and he will have more than enough. But from the one who does not have, even what he has will be taken away from him. ³⁰ And throw this good-for-nothing slave into the outer darkness. In that place there will be weeping and gnashing of teeth.'

THE SHEEP AND THE GOATS

³¹ "When the •Son of Man comes in His glory, and all the angels[c] with Him, then He will sit on the throne of His glory. ³² All the nations[d] will be gathered before Him, and He will separate them one from another, just as a shepherd separates the sheep from the goats. ³³ He will put the sheep on His right and the goats on the left. ³⁴ Then the King will say to those on His right, 'Come, you who are blessed by My Father, inherit the kingdom prepared for you from the foundation of the world.

³⁵ For I was hungry
and you gave Me something to eat;
I was thirsty
and you gave Me something to drink;

———————————

[a]25:26-27 Or *So you knew ... scattered? Then* (as a question)
[b]25:27 Lit *received what is mine*
[c]25:31 Other mss read *holy angels*
[d]25:32 Or *the Gentiles*

I was a stranger and you took Me in;
³⁶ I was naked and you clothed Me;
I was sick and you took care of Me;
I was in prison and you visited Me.'

³⁷ "Then the righteous will answer Him, 'Lord, when did we see You hungry and feed You, or thirsty and give You something to drink? ³⁸ When did we see You a stranger and take You in, or without clothes and clothe You? ³⁹ When did we see You sick, or in prison, and visit You?'

⁴⁰ "And the King will answer them, 'I assure you: Whatever you did for one of the least of these brothers of Mine, you did for Me.' ⁴¹ Then He will also say to those on the left, 'Depart from Me, you who are cursed, into the eternal fire prepared for the Devil and his angels!

⁴² For I was hungry
and you gave Me nothing to eat;
I was thirsty
and you gave Me nothing to drink;
⁴³ I was a stranger
and you didn't take Me in;
I was naked
and you didn't clothe Me,
sick and in prison
and you didn't take care of Me.'

⁴⁴ "Then they too will answer, 'Lord, when did we see You hungry, or thirsty, or a stranger, or without clothes, or sick, or in prison, and not help You?'

⁴⁵ "Then He will answer them, 'I assure you: Whatever you did not do for one of the least of these, you did not do for Me either.'

⁴⁶ "And they will go away into eternal punishment, but the righteous into eternal life."

THE PLOT TO KILL JESUS

26 When Jesus had finished saying all this, He told His disciples, ² "You know*a* that the •Passover takes place after two days, and the •Son of Man will be handed over to be crucified."

³ Then the •chief priests*b* and the elders of the people assembled in the palace of the high priest, who was called

Are You Ready to Go Where God Says?

Is your heart so filled with love for God that you are watching for the first opportunity to say, as Isaiah did, "Here am I. Send me!"?

"The King will answer them, 'I assure you: Whatever you did for one of the least of these brothers of Mine, you did for Me.'"

—Matthew 25:40

---

*a*26:2 Or *Know* (as a command)   *b*26:3 Other mss add *and the scribes*

Caiaphas, ⁴ and they conspired to arrest Jesus in a treacherous way and kill Him. ⁵ "Not during the festival," they said, "so there won't be rioting among the people."

THE ANOINTING AT BETHANY

⁶ While Jesus was in Bethany at the house of Simon, a man who had a serious skin disease, ⁷ a woman approached Him with an alabaster jar of very expensive fragrant oil. She poured it on His head as He was reclining at the table. ⁸ When the disciples saw it, they were indignant. "Why this waste?" they asked. ⁹ "This might have been sold for a great deal and given to the poor."

¹⁰ But Jesus, aware of this, said to them, "Why are you bothering this woman? She has done a noble thing for Me. ¹¹ You always have the poor with you, but you do not always have Me. ¹² By pouring this fragrant oil on My body, she has prepared Me for burial. ¹³ •I assure you: Wherever this gospel is proclaimed in the whole world, what this woman has done will also be told in memory of her."

¹⁴ Then one of the Twelve—the man called Judas Iscariot—went to the chief priests ¹⁵ and said, "What are you willing to give me if I hand Him over to you?" So they weighed out 30 pieces of silver for him. ¹⁶ And from that time he started looking for a good opportunity to betray Him.

BETRAYAL AT THE PASSOVER

¹⁷ On the first day of •Unleavened Bread the disciples came to Jesus and asked, "Where do You want us to prepare the Passover so You may eat it?"

¹⁸ "Go into the city to a certain man," He said, "and tell him, 'The Teacher says: My time is near; I am celebrating the Passover at your place[a] with My disciples.'"

¹⁹ So the disciples did as Jesus had directed them and prepared the Passover. ²⁰ When evening came, He was reclining at the table with the Twelve. ²¹ While they were eating, He said, "I assure you: One of you will betray Me."

²² Deeply distressed, each one began to say to Him, "Surely not I, Lord?"

Worship Is Not a Waste of Time

Jesus taught that our highest priority must be our relationship with Him. Have you been serving God so diligently that you have not had time to spend with Him?

"Why this waste?" they asked. "This might have been sold for a great deal and given to the poor. But Jesus, aware of this, said to them, "Why are you bothering this woman? She has done a noble thing for Me."

—Matthew 26:8b-10

---

[a]26:18 Lit *Passover with you*

23 He replied, "The one who dipped his hand with Me in the bowl—he will betray Me. 24 The Son of Man will go just as it is written about Him, but woe to that man by whom the Son of Man is betrayed! It would have been better for that man if he had not been born."

25 Then Judas, His betrayer, replied, "Surely not I, •Rabbi?"

"You have said it," He told him.

THE FIRST LORD'S SUPPER

26 As they were eating, Jesus took bread, blessed and broke it, gave it to the disciples, and said, "Take and eat it; this is My body." 27 Then He took a cup, and after giving thanks, He gave it to them and said, "Drink from it, all of you. 28 For this is My blood ⌊that establishes⌋ the covenant;[a] it is shed for many for the forgiveness of sins. 29 But I tell you, from this moment I will not drink of this fruit of the vine until that day when I drink it in a new way[b] in My Father's kingdom with you." 30 After singing psalms,[c] they went out to the •Mount of Olives.

PETER'S DENIAL PREDICTED

31 Then Jesus said to them, "Tonight all of you will run away[d] because of Me, for it is written:

> I will strike the shepherd,
> and the sheep of the flock
> will be scattered.[e]

32 But after I have been resurrected, I will go ahead of you to Galilee."

33 Peter told Him, "Even if everyone runs away because of You, I will never run away!"

34 "I assure you," Jesus said to him, "tonight—before the rooster crows, you will deny Me three times!"

35 "Even if I have to die with You," Peter told Him, "I will never deny You!" And all the disciples said the same thing.

God Wants to Use You—Warts and All

If you feel weak, limited, ordinary, you are the best material through which God can work!

Jesus said to them, "Tonight all of you will run away because of Me, for it is written: I will strike the shepherd, and the sheep of the flock will be scattered. But after I have been resurrected, I will go ahead of you to Galilee."

—Matthew 26:31-32

---

[a]26:28 Other mss read *new covenant*
[b]26:29 Or *drink new wine*; lit *drink it new*
[c]26:30 Pss 113–118 were sung during and after the Passover meal.
[d]26:31 Or •*stumble*
[e]26:31 Zch 13:7

THE PRAYER IN THE GARDEN

36 Then Jesus came with them to a place called Gethsemane,[a] and He told the disciples, "Sit here while I go over there and pray." 37 Taking along Peter and the two sons of Zebedee, He began to be sorrowful and deeply distressed. 38 Then He said to them, "My soul is swallowed up in sorrow[b]—to the point of death.[c] Remain here and stay awake with Me." 39 Going a little farther,[d] He fell facedown and prayed, "My Father! If it is possible, let this cup pass from Me. Yet not as I will, but as You will."

40 Then He came to the disciples and found them sleeping. He asked Peter, "So, couldn't you[e] stay awake with Me one hour? 41 Stay awake and pray, so that you won't enter into temptation. The spirit is willing, but the flesh is weak."

42 Again, a second time, He went away and prayed, "My Father, if this[f] cannot pass[g] unless I drink it, Your will be done." 43 And He came again and found them sleeping, because they could not keep their eyes open.[h]

44 After leaving them, He went away again and prayed a third time, saying the same thing once more. 45 Then He came to the disciples and said to them, "Are you still sleeping and resting?[i] Look, the time is near. The Son of Man is being betrayed into the hands of sinners. 46 Get up; let's go! See—My betrayer is near."

THE JUDAS KISS

47 While He was still speaking, Judas, one of the Twelve, suddenly arrived. A large mob, with swords and clubs, was with him from the chief priests and elders of the people. 48 His betrayer had given them a sign: "The One I kiss, He's the One; arrest Him!" 49 So he went right up to Jesus and said, "Greetings, Rabbi!"—and kissed Him.

Not My Will, But Yours Be Done

God's ways and thoughts are so different from yours and mine, they will often sound wrong, crazy, or impossible. When you recognize that the task is humanly impossible, you need to be ready to believe God and trust Him completely.

Going a little farther, He fell facedown and prayed, "My Father! If it is possible, let this cup pass from Me. Yet not as I will, but as You will."

—Matthew 26:39

[a]26:36 A garden east of Jerusalem at the base of the Mount of Olives; *Gethsemane* = olive oil press
[b]26:38 Or *I am deeply grieved*, or *I am overwhelmed by sorrow*; Ps 42:6,11; 43:5
[c]26:38 Lit *unto death*
[d]26:39 Other mss read *Drawing nearer*
[e]26:40 *You* = all 3 disciples because the verb in Gk is pl
[f]26:42 Other mss add *cup*
[g]26:42 Other mss add *from Me*
[h]26:43 Lit *because their eyes were weighed down*
[i]26:45 Or *Sleep on now and take your rest.*

⁵⁰ "Friend," Jesus asked him, "why have you come?"ᵃ Then they came up, took hold of Jesus, and arrested Him. ⁵¹ At that moment one of those with Jesus reached out his hand and drew his sword. He struck the high priest's slave and cut off his ear.

⁵² Then Jesus told him, "Put your sword back in place because all who take up a sword will perish by a sword. ⁵³ Or do you think that I cannot call on My Father, and He will provide Me at once with more than 12 legionsᵇ of angels? ⁵⁴ How, then, would the Scriptures be fulfilled that say it must happen this way?"

⁵⁵ At that time Jesus said to the crowds, "Have you come out with swords and clubs, as if I were a criminal,ᶜ to capture Me? Every day I used to sit, teaching in the •temple complex, and you didn't arrest Me. ⁵⁶ But all this has happened so that the prophetic Scripturesᵈ would be fulfilled." Then all the disciples deserted Him and ran away.

JESUS FACES THE SANHEDRIN

⁵⁷ Those who had arrested Jesus led Him away to Caiaphas the high priest, where the •scribes and the elders had convened. ⁵⁸ Meanwhile, Peter was following Him at a distance right to the high priest's courtyard.ᵉ He went in and was sitting with the temple policeᶠ to see the outcome.ᵍ

⁵⁹ The chief priests and the whole •Sanhedrin were looking for false testimony against Jesus so they could put Him to death. ⁶⁰ But they could not find any, even though many false witnesses came forward.ʰ Finally, twoⁱ who came forward ⁶¹ stated, "This man said, 'I can demolish God's sanctuary and rebuild it in three days.'"

⁶² The high priest then stood up and said to Him, "Don't You have an answer to what these men are testifying against You?" ⁶³ But Jesus kept silent. Then the high priest said to Him, "By the living God I place You under oath: tell us if You are the •Messiah, the Son of God!"

WORD STUDY

Greek word: **paradidomi**
[pah rah DIHD oh mee]

Translation: **betray, hand over, entrust**

Uses in Matthew's Gospel: **31** (Mk, 20; Lk, 17; Jn, 15)

Uses in the NT: **119**

Key passage: **Matthew 26:46**

In a positive sense, *paradidomi* (*entrust, hand down*) may describe commendation for service (Ac 14:26) or the passing on of traditions (Lk 1:2; Ac 6:14; Rm 6:17; 1 Co 11:2,23; 15:3; 2 Pt 2:21; Jd 3). It also describes the Father *entrusting* all things to the Son (Mt 11:27 = Lk 10:22) and the Son *handing over* all things to the Father (1 Co 15:24), as well as Jesus being *offered up* by the Father (Rm 8:32) and *giving* His own life as a sacrifice (Jn 19:30; Gl 2:20; Eph 5:2,25).

Negatively, *paradidomi* describes arrest and/or imprisonment (Mt 4:12; 10:19; 18:34; Ac 8:3; 22:4; 2 Pt 2:4); Jesus being *handed over* to death by His enemies (Mt 26:2; 27:2,26; Ac 3:13), believers being persecuted (Mt 10:21; 24:9; Ac 21:11), people being *turned over* to Satan (1 Co 5:5; 1 Tm 1:20), and God *delivering* people over to their sin (Rm 1:24,26,28).

ᵃ**26:50** Or *Jesus told him, "do what you have come for."* (as a statement)
ᵇ**26:53** A Roman legion contained up to 6,000 soldiers.
ᶜ**26:55** Lit *as against a criminal*
ᵈ**26:56** Or *the Scriptures of the prophets*

ᵉ**26:58** Or *high priest's palace*
ᶠ**26:58** Or *the officers*, or *the servants*
ᵍ**26:58** Lit *end*
ʰ**26:60** Other mss add *they found none*
ⁱ**26:60** Other mss add *false witnesses*

64 "You have said it,"ᵃ Jesus told him. "But I tell you, in the futureᵇ you will see **the Son of Man seated at the right hand** of the Power and **coming on the clouds of heaven**."ᶜ

65 Then the high priest tore his robes and said, "He has blasphemed! Why do we still need witnesses? Look, now you've heard the blasphemy! 66 What is your decision?"ᵈ

They answered, "He deserves death!" 67 Then they spit in His face and beat Him; others slapped Him 68 and said, "Prophesy to us, Messiah! Who hit You?"

PETER DENIES HIS LORD

69 Now Peter was sitting outside in the courtyard. A servant approached him and she said, "You were with Jesus the Galilean too."

70 But he denied it in front of everyone: "I don't know what you're talking about!"

71 When he had gone out to the gateway, another woman saw him and told those who were there, "This man was with Jesus the •Nazarene!"

72 And again he denied it with an oath, "I don't know the man!"

73 After a little while those standing there approached and said to Peter, "You certainly are one of them, since even your accentᵉ gives you away."

74 Then he started to curseᶠ and to swear with an oath, "I do not know the man!" Immediately a rooster crowed, 75 and Peter remembered the words Jesus had spoken, "Before the rooster crows, you will deny Me three times." And he went outside and wept bitterly.

JESUS HANDED OVER TO PILATE

27 When daybreak came, all the •chief priests and the elders of the people plotted against Jesus to put Him to death. 2 After tying Him up, they led

---

Never Be Ashamed to Be Called One of His

If we want to enjoy the blessings of God's presence, we must be willing to endure the costs and responsibilities of being known by His name.

Peter was sitting outside in the courtyard. A servant approached him and she said, "You were with Jesus the Galilean too." But he denied it in front of everyone: "I don't know what you're talking about!"

—Matthew 26:69-70

ᵃ26:64 Or *That is true*, an affirmative oath; Mt 27:11; Mk 15:2
ᵇ26:64 Lit *you, from now*
ᶜ26:64 Ps 110:1; Dn 7:13
ᵈ26:66 Lit *What does it seem to you?*
ᵉ26:73 Or *speech*
ᶠ26:74 To call down curses on himself if what he said weren't true

Him away and handed Him over to •Pilate,[a] the governor.

JUDAS HANGS HIMSELF

3 Then Judas, His betrayer, seeing that He had been condemned, was full of remorse and returned the 30 pieces of silver to the chief priests and elders. 4 "I have sinned by betraying innocent blood," he said.

"What's that to us?" they said. "See to it yourself!"

5 So he threw the silver into the sanctuary and departed. Then he went and hanged himself.

6 The chief priests took the silver and said, "It's not lawful to put it into the temple treasury,[b] since it is blood money."[c] 7 So they conferred together and bought the potter's field with it as a burial place for foreigners. 8 Therefore that field has been called "Blood Field" to this day. 9 Then what was spoken through the prophet Jeremiah was fulfilled:

They took the 30 pieces of silver, the price of Him whose price was set by the sons of Israel, 10 **and they gave them for the potter's field, as the Lord directed me.**[d]

JESUS FACES THE GOVERNOR

11 Now Jesus stood before the governor. "Are You the King of the Jews?" the governor asked Him.

Jesus answered, "You have said it."[e] 12 And while He was being accused by the chief priests and elders, He didn't answer.

13 Then Pilate said to Him, "Don't You hear how much they are testifying against You?" 14 But He didn't answer him on even one charge, so that the governor was greatly amazed.

JESUS OR BARABBAS

15 At the festival the governor's custom was to release to the crowd a prisoner they wanted. 16 At that time they

You Can Witness Without Saying a Word

The most compelling evidence that Christ is alive and triumphant is His activity in the lives of His people. Everywhere we go, our lives should demonstrate to others that Christ is victorious.

He didn't answer him on even one charge, so that the governor was greatly amazed.

—Matthew 27:14

---

[a]27:2 Other mss read *Pontius Pilate*
[b]27:6 See Mk 7:11 where the same Gk word used here (*Corban*) means a gift (pledged to the temple).
27:6 Lit *the price of blood*
[d]27:9-10 Jr 32:6-9; Zch 11:12-13
[e]27:11 Or *That is true*, an affirmative oath; Mt 26:64; Mk 15:2

WORD STUDY

Greek word: **stauroo**
[stow RAH oh]
Translation: **crucify**
Uses in Matthew's Gospel: **10**
(Mk, 8; Lk, 6; Jn, 11)
Uses in the NT: **46**
Key passage: **Matthew 27:31**

Stauroo originally referred to building a fence by driving stakes into the ground. Stakes could easily be used as instruments of death, and impalement became an early form of execution. Through the Roman practice of crucifixion, *stauroo* eventually came to refer primarily to the common form of execution—tying or nailing someone to a cross and leaving them hanging until they died. The vast majority of the occurrences of *stauroo* refer to the manner of Jesus' death, though the NT mentions others who died by crucifixion (Mt 23:34; 27:38). Crucifixion was occasionally used as a metaphor for the Christian life (Mt 16:24; Gl 5:24; 6:14), an image emphasizing the believers' identification with Christ and His suffering and death. It thus became a subject of boasting among Christians (Gl 6:14), for their crucified Savior was also the risen Lord and Messiah (Ac 2:36; 4:10; 1 Co 1:23; 2:2; 2 Co 13:4).

had a notorious prisoner called Barabbas.[a] 17 So when they had gathered together, Pilate said to them, "Who is it you want me to release for you—Barabbas,[a] or Jesus who is called •Messiah?" 18 For he knew they had handed Him over because of envy.

19 While he was sitting on the judge's bench, his wife sent word to him, "Have nothing to do with that righteous man, for today I've suffered terribly in a dream because of Him!"

20 The chief priests and the elders, however, persuaded the crowds to ask for Barabbas and to execute Jesus. 21 The governor asked them, "Which of the two do you want me to release for you?"

"Barabbas!" they answered.

22 Pilate asked them, "What should I do then with Jesus, who is called Messiah?"

They all answered, "Crucify Him!"[b]

23 Then he said, "Why? What has He done wrong?"

But they kept shouting, "Crucify Him!" all the more.

24 When Pilate saw that he was getting nowhere,[c] but that a riot was starting instead, he took some water, washed his hands in front of the crowd, and said, "I am innocent of this man's blood.[d] See to it yourselves!"

25 All the people answered, "His blood be on us and on our children!" 26 Then he released Barabbas to them. But after having Jesus flogged,[e] he handed Him over to be crucified.

MOCKED BY THE MILITARY

27 Then the governor's soldiers took Jesus into •headquarters and gathered the whole •company around Him. 28 They stripped Him and dressed Him in a scarlet robe. 29 They twisted together a crown of thorns, put it on His head, and placed a reed in His right hand. And they knelt down before Him and mocked Him: "Hail, King of the Jews!" 30 Then they spit at Him, took the reed, and kept hitting Him on the head. 31 When they

---

[a]27:16,17 Other mss read *Jesus Barabbas*
[b]27:22 Lit *"Him—be crucified!"*
[c]27:24 Lit *that it availed nothing*
[d]27:24 Other mss read *this righteous man's blood*

[e]27:26 Roman flogging was done with a whip made of leather strips embedded with pieces of bone or metal that brutally tore the flesh.

had mocked Him, they stripped Him of the robe, put His clothes on Him, and led Him away to crucify Him.

CRUCIFIED BETWEEN TWO CRIMINALS

32 As they were going out, they found a Cyrenian man named Simon. They forced this man to carry His cross. 33 When they came to a place called *Golgotha* (which means Skull Place), 34 they gave Him wine[a] mixed with gall to drink. But when He tasted it, He would not drink it. 35 After crucifying Him they divided His clothes by casting lots.[b] 36 Then they sat down and were guarding Him there. 37 Above His head they put up the charge against Him in writing:

THIS IS JESUS THE KING OF THE JEWS.

38 Then two criminals[c] were crucified with Him, one on the right and one on the left. 39 Those who passed by were yelling insults at[d] Him, shaking their heads 40 and saying, "The One who would demolish the sanctuary and rebuild it in three days, save Yourself! If You are the Son of God, come down from the cross!" 41 In the same way the chief priests, with the •scribes and elders,[e] mocked Him and said, 42 "He saved others, but He cannot save Himself! He is the King of Israel! Let Him[f] come down now from the cross, and we will believe in Him. 43 He has put His trust in God; let God rescue Him now—if He wants Him![g] For He said, 'I am God's Son.'" 44 In the same way even the criminals who were crucified with Him kept taunting Him.

THE DEATH OF JESUS

45 From noon until three in the afternoon[h] darkness came over the whole land.[i] 46 At about three in the

Your Service Should Be Free, Not by Force

God will often call us out of our comfort zones and use us to do things we would never undertake on our own. Our task is to follow Him willingly and to trust Him to know what is best.

As they were going out, they found a Cyrenian man named Simon. They forced this man to carry His cross.
—Matthew 27:32

---

[a]27:34 Other mss read *sour wine*
[b]27:35 Other mss add *that what was spoken by the prophet might be fulfilled:"They divided My clothes among them, and for My clothing they cast lots."*
[c]27:38 Or *revolutionaries*
[d]27:39 Lit *passed by blasphemed* or *were blaspheming*
[e]27:41 Other mss add *and Pharisees*
[f]27:42 Other mss read *If He ... Israel, let Him*
[g]27:43 Or *if He takes pleasure in Him*; Ps 22:8
[h]27:45 Lit *From the sixth hour to the ninth hour*
[i]27:45 Or *whole earth*

afternoon Jesus cried out with a loud voice, *"Elí, Elí, lemá sabachtháni?"* that is, **"My God, My God, why have You forsaken[a] Me?"[b]**

⁴⁷ When some of those standing there heard this, they said, "He's calling for Elijah!"

⁴⁸ Immediately one of them ran and got a sponge, filled it with sour wine, fixed it on a reed, and offered Him a drink. ⁴⁹ But the rest said, "Let's see if Elijah comes to save Him!"

⁵⁰ Jesus shouted again with a loud voice and gave up His spirit. ⁵¹ Suddenly, the curtain of the sanctuary[c] was split in two from top to bottom; the earth quaked and the rocks were split. ⁵² The tombs also were opened and many bodies of the saints who had gone to their rest[d] were raised. ⁵³ And they came out of the tombs after His resurrection, entered the holy city, and appeared to many.

⁵⁴ When the •centurion and those with him, who were guarding Jesus, saw the earthquake and the things that had happened, they were terrified and said, "This man really was God's Son!"[e]

⁵⁵ Many women who had followed Jesus from Galilee and ministered to Him were there, looking on from a distance. ⁵⁶ Among them were •Mary Magdalene, Mary the mother of James and Joseph, and the mother of Zebedee's sons.

THE BURIAL OF JESUS

⁵⁷ When it was evening, a rich man from Arimathea named Joseph came, who himself had also become a disciple of Jesus. ⁵⁸ He approached Pilate and asked for Jesus' body. Then Pilate ordered that it[f] be released. ⁵⁹ So Joseph took the body, wrapped it in clean, fine linen, ⁶⁰ and placed it in his new tomb, which he had cut into the rock. He left after rolling a great stone against the entrance of the tomb. ⁶¹ Mary Magdalene and the other Mary were seated there, facing the tomb.

There's Power in the Blood

Never forget the power of the cross. When you face challenging times in life, remember God's power, and let Him be your strength.

Jesus shouted again with a loud voice and gave up His spirit. Suddenly, the curtain of the sanctuary was split in two from top to bottom; the earth quaked and the rocks were split.

—Matthew 27:50-51

---

[a]**27:46** Or *abandoned*
[b]**27:46** Ps 22:1
[c]**27:51** A heavy curtain separated the inner room of the temple from the outer.
[d]**27:52** Lit *saints having fallen asleep*; that is, they had died
[e]**27:54** Or *the Son of God*
[f]**27:58** Other mss read *that the body*

THE CLOSELY GUARDED TOMB

⁶² The next day, which followed the preparation day, the chief priests and the •Pharisees gathered before Pilate ⁶³ and said, "Sir, we remember that while this deceiver was still alive, He said, 'After three days I will rise again.' ⁶⁴ Therefore give orders that the tomb be made secure until the third day. Otherwise, His disciples may come, steal Him, and tell the people, 'He has been raised from the dead.' Then the last deception will be worse than the first."

⁶⁵ "You haveᵃ a guard ₍of soldiers₎,"ᵇ Pilate told them. "Go and make it as secure as you know how." ⁶⁶ Then they went and made the tomb secure by sealing the stone and setting the guard.ᶜ

RESURRECTION MORNING

28 After the Sabbath, as the first day of the week was dawning, •Mary Magdalene and the other Mary went to view the tomb. ² Suddenly there was a violent earthquake, because an angel of the Lord descended from heaven and approached ₍the tomb₎. He rolled back the stone and was sitting on it. ³ His appearance was like lightning, and his robe was as white as snow. ⁴ The guards were so shaken from fear of him that they became like dead men.

⁵ But the angel told the women, "Don't be afraid, because I know you are looking for Jesus who was crucified. ⁶ He is not here! For He has been resurrected, just as He said. Come and see the place where He lay. ⁷ Then go quickly and tell His disciples, 'He has been raised from the dead. In fact, He is going ahead of you to Galilee; you will see Him there.' Listen, I have told you."

⁸ So, departing quickly from the tomb with fear and great joy, they ran to tell His disciples the news. ⁹ Just thenᵈ Jesus met them and said, "Good morning!" They came up, took hold of His feet, and worshiped Him. ¹⁰ Then Jesus told them, "Do not be afraid. Go and tell My brothers to leave for Galilee, and they will see Me there."

WORD STUDY

Greek word: **matheteuo**
[mah they TYOO oh]
Translation: **make disciples**
Uses in Matthew's Gospel: **3**
Uses in the NT: **4**
Key passage: **Matthew 28:19**

The verb *matheteuo* (*to make disciples*) is derived from the noun *mathetes*, which occurs over 250 times, entirely in the Gospels and Acts. *Mathetes* means *disciple, pupil, one who learns* from another, and typically indicates a person whose life is bound up with that of Jesus, his Master. *Matheteuo* means *to become a disciple* (Mt 27:57) or *to be instructed* (Mt 13:52). In another two occurrences it means *to make disciples* (Mt 28:19; Ac 14:21). In the Great Commission (Mt 28:18-20), the particular Greek construction (aorist participle followed by aorist imperative; this construction is relatively common in Matthew, Luke, and Acts) indicates that the primary weight of Jesus' command in the Great Commission is to make disciples, while the act of "going" is a necessary prerequisite to accomplishing this task.

ᵃ27:65 Or *"Take*
ᵇ27:65 It is uncertain whether this guard consisted of temple police or Roman soldiers.
ᶜ27:66 Lit *stone with the guard*
ᵈ28:9 Other mss add *as they were on their way to tell the news to His disciples*

THE SOLDIERS ARE BRIBED TO LIE

¹¹ As they were on their way, some of the guard came into the city and reported to the •chief priests everything that had happened. ¹² After the priests[a] had assembled with the elders and agreed on a plan, they gave the soldiers a large sum of money ¹³ and told them, "Say this, 'His disciples came during the night and stole Him while we were sleeping.' ¹⁴ If this reaches the governor's ears,[b] we will deal with[c] him and keep you out of trouble." ¹⁵ So they took the money and did as they were instructed. And this story has been spread among Jewish people to this day.

THE GREAT COMMISSION

¹⁶ The 11 disciples traveled to Galilee, to the mountain where Jesus had directed them. ¹⁷ When they saw Him, they worshiped,[d] but some doubted. ¹⁸ Then Jesus came near and said to them, "All authority has been given to Me in heaven and on earth. ¹⁹ Go, therefore, and make disciples of [e] all nations, baptizing them in the name of the Father and of the Son and of the Holy Spirit, ²⁰ teaching them to observe everything I have commanded you. And remember,[f] I am with you always,[g] to the end of the age."

Have You Decided to Follow Jesus?

Jesus never excused those who struggled to follow Him. He made it clear that to follow Him meant that He set the direction and they were to follow.

"Go, therefore, and make disciples of all nations, baptizing them in the name of the Father and of the Son and of the Holy Spirit, teaching them to observe everything I have commanded you. And remember, I am with you always, to the end of the age."

—Matthew 28:19-20

---

[a]28:12 Lit *After they*
[b]28:14 Lit *this is heard by the governor*
[c]28:14 Lit *will persuade*
[d]28:17 Other mss add *Him*

[e]28:19 Lit *and instruct*, or *and disciple* (as a verb)
[f]28:20 Lit *look*
[g]28:20 Lit *all the days*

THE GOSPEL OF

MARK

THE MESSIAH'S HERALD

1 The beginning of the gospel of Jesus Christ, the Son of God. ² As it is written in Isaiah the prophet:ᵃ

> **Look, I am sending My messenger ahead**
> **of You,**
> **who will prepare Your way.**ᵇ
> ³ **A voice of one crying out in the wilderness:**
> **"Prepare the way for the Lord;**
> **make His paths straight!"**ᶜ

⁴ John came baptizingᵈ in the wilderness and preaching a baptism of repentanceᵉ for the forgiveness of sins. ⁵ The whole Judean countryside and all the people of Jerusalem were flocking to him, and they were baptized by him in the Jordan River as they confessed their sins. ⁶ John wore a camel-hair garment with a leather belt around his waist and ate locusts and wild honey. ⁷ He was preaching: "Someone more powerful than I will come after me. I am not worthy to stoop down and untie the strap of His sandals. ⁸ I have baptized you withᶠ water, but He will baptize you withᶠ the Holy Spirit."

THE BAPTISM OF JESUS

⁹ In those days Jesus came from Nazareth in Galilee and was baptized in the Jordan by John. ¹⁰ As soon as He came up out of the water, He saw the heavens being torn open and the Spirit descending to Him like a dove. ¹¹ And a voice came from heaven:

ᵃ**1:2** Other mss read *in the prophets*
ᵇ**1:2** Other mss add *before You*
ᶜ**1:2-3** Mal 3:1; Is 40:3
ᵈ**1:4** Or *John the Baptist came*, or *John the Baptizer came*
ᵉ**1:4** Or *a baptism based on repentance*
ᶠ**1:8** Or *in*

You are My beloved Son;
I take delight in You![a]

THE TEMPTATION OF JESUS

[12] Immediately the Spirit drove Him into the wilderness. [13] He was in the wilderness 40 days, being tempted by Satan. He was with the wild animals, and the angels began to serve Him.

MINISTRY IN GALILEE

[14] After John was arrested, Jesus went to Galilee, preaching the good news[b] [c] of God:[d] [15] "The time is fulfilled, and the kingdom of God has come near. Repent and believe in the good news!"

THE FIRST DISCIPLES

Do People See You Seeking Jesus?

Whenever we see Peter coming to Jesus, he is always accompanied by others. Because Peter was seeking Jesus, others sought Him too.

Simon and his companions went searching for Him.

—Mark 1:36

[16] As He was passing along by the Sea of Galilee, He saw Simon and Andrew, Simon's brother. They were casting a net into the sea, since they were fishermen. [17] "Follow Me," Jesus told them, "and I will make you fish for[e] people!" [18] Immediately they left their nets and followed Him. [19] Going on a little farther, He saw James the son of Zebedee and his brother John. They were in their boat mending their nets. [20] Immediately He called them, and they left their father Zebedee in the boat with the hired men and followed Him.

DRIVING OUT AN UNCLEAN SPIRIT

[21] Then they went into Capernaum, and right away He entered the •synagogue on the Sabbath and began to teach. [22] They were astonished at His teaching because, unlike the •scribes, He was teaching them as one having authority.

[23] Just then a man with an unclean spirit was in their synagogue. He cried out,[f] [24] "What do You have to do with us,[g] Jesus—Nazarene? Have You come to destroy us? I know who You are—the Holy One of God!"

---

[a]1:11 Or *In You I am well pleased*
[b]1:14 Other mss add *of the kingdom*
[c]1:14 Or *gospel*
[d]1:14 Either *from God* or *about God*
[e]1:17 Lit *you to become fishers of*
[f]1:23 Other mss add to the beginning of v. 24: *"Leave us alone.*
[g]1:24 Lit *What to us and to You*

[25] But Jesus rebuked him and said, "Be quiet,[a] and come out of him!" [26] And the unclean spirit convulsed him, shouted with a loud voice, and came out of him.

[27] Then they were all amazed, so they began to argue with one another, saying, "What is this? A new teaching with authority![b] He commands even the unclean spirits, and they obey Him." [28] His fame then spread throughout the entire vicinity of Galilee.

HEALINGS AT CAPERNAUM

[29] As soon as they left the synagogue, they went into Simon and Andrew's house with James and John. [30] Simon's mother-in-law was lying in bed with a fever, and they told Him about her at once. [31] So He went to her, took her by the hand, and raised her up. The fever left her,[c] and she began to serve them.

[32] When evening came, after the sun had set, they began bringing to Him all those who were sick and those who were demon-possessed. [33] The whole town was assembled at the door, [34] and He healed many who were sick with various diseases and drove out many demons. But He would not permit the demons to speak, because they knew Him.

PREACHING IN GALILEE

[35] Very early in the morning, while it was still dark, He got up, went out, and made His way to a deserted place. And He was praying there. [36] Simon and his companions went searching for Him. [37] They found Him and said, "Everyone's looking for You!"

[38] And He said to them, "Let's go on to the neighboring villages so that I may preach there too. This is why I have come." [39] So He went into all of Galilee, preaching in their synagogues and driving out demons.

CLEANSING A LEPER

[40] Then a man with a serious skin disease came to Him and, on his knees,[d] begged Him: "If You are willing, You can make me clean."[e]

He Doesn't Expect You to Know It All

God does not ask us to dream our dreams for Him and then ask Him to bless our plans. He is already at work when He comes to us. His desire is to get us from where we are to where He is working.

He said to them, "Let's go on to the neighboring villages so that I may preach there too. This is why I have come."

—Mark 1:38

---

[a]1:25 Or *Be muzzled*
[b]1:27 Other mss read *What is this? What is this new teaching? For with authority*
[c]1:31 Other mss add *at once*
[d]1:40 Other mss omit *on his knees*
[e]1:40 In these vv., *clean* includes healing, ceremonial purification, return to fellowship with people, and worship in the temple; Lv 14:1-32.

⁴¹ Moved with compassion, Jesus reached out His hand and touched him. "I am willing," He told him. "Be made clean." ⁴² Immediately the disease left him, and he was healed.ᵃ ⁴³ Then He sternly warned him and sent him away at once, ⁴⁴ telling him, "See that you say nothing to anyone; but go and show yourself to the priest, and offer what Moses prescribed for your cleansing, as a testimony to them." ⁴⁵ Yet he went out and began to proclaim it widely and to spread the news, with the result that Jesus could no longer enter a town openly. But He was out in deserted places, and they would come to Him from everywhere.

THE SON OF MAN FORGIVES AND HEALS

2 When He entered Capernaum again after some days, it was reported that He was at home. ² So many people gathered together that there was no more room, not even in the doorway, and He was speaking the message to them. ³ Then they came to Him bringing a paralytic, carried by four men. ⁴ Since they were not able to bring him toᵇ Jesus because of the crowd, they removed the roof above where He was. And when they had broken through, they lowered the stretcher on which the paralytic was lying.

⁵ Seeing their faith, Jesus told the paralytic, "Son, your sins are forgiven."

⁶ But some of the •scribes were sitting there, thinking to themselves:ᶜ ⁷ "Why does He speak like this? He's blaspheming! Who can forgive sins but God alone?"

⁸ Right away Jesus understood in His spirit that they were reasoning like this within themselves and said to them, "Why are you reasoning these things in your hearts?ᵈ ⁹ Which is easier: to say to the paralytic, 'Your sins are forgiven,' or to say, 'Get up, pick up your stretcher, and walk'? ¹⁰ But so you may know that the •Son of Man has authority on earth to forgive sins," He told the paralytic, ¹¹ "I tell you: get up, pick up your stretcher, and go home."

Just Show People Jesus

Our job is not to transform people into Christians nor to convict them of their sin. Our task is to bring them to Jesus, and He will perform His divine work in their lives.

He went out and began to proclaim it widely and to spread the news, with the result that Jesus could no longer enter a town openly. But He was out in deserted places, and they would come to Him from everywhere.

—Mark 1:45

ᵃ**1:42** Lit *made clean*
ᵇ**2:4** Other mss read *able to get near*
ᶜ**2:6** Or *there, reasoning in their hearts*
ᵈ**2:8** Or *minds*

¹² Immediately he got up, picked up the stretcher, and went out in front of everyone. As a result, they were all astounded and gave glory to God, saying, "We have never seen anything like this!"

THE CALL OF MATTHEW

¹³ Then Jesus went out again beside the sea. The whole crowd was coming to Him, and He taught them. ¹⁴ Then, moving on, He saw Levi the son of Alphaeus sitting at the tax office, and He said to him, "Follow Me!" So he got up and followed Him.

DINING WITH SINNERS

¹⁵ While He was reclining at the table in Levi's house, many tax collectors and sinners were also guestsª with Jesus and His disciples, because there were many who were following Him. ¹⁶ When the scribes of the •Pharisees[b] saw that He was eating with sinners and tax collectors, they asked His disciples, "Why does He eat[c] with tax collectors and sinners?"

¹⁷ When Jesus heard this, He told them, "Those who are well don't need a doctor, but the sick ₎do need one₎. I didn't come to call the righteous, but sinners."

A QUESTION ABOUT FASTING

¹⁸ Now John's disciples and the Pharisees[d] were fasting. People came and asked Him, "Why do John's disciples and the Pharisees' disciples fast, but Your disciples do not fast?"

¹⁹ Jesus said to them, "The wedding guests[e] cannot fast while the groom is with them, can they? As long as they have the groom with them, they cannot fast. ²⁰ But the time[f] will come when the groom is taken away from them, and then they will fast in that day. ²¹ No one sews a patch of unshrunk cloth on an old garment. Otherwise, the new patch pulls away from the old cloth, and a worse tear is made. ²² And no one puts new wine into

---

ª**2:15** Lit *reclining* (at the table); at important meals the custom was to recline on a mat at a low table and lean on the left elbow.
ᵇ**2:16** Other mss read *scribes and Pharisees*
ᶜ**2:16** Other mss add *and drink*
ᵈ**2:18** Other mss read *the disciples of John and of the Pharisees*
ᵉ**2:19** Lit *The sons of the bridal chamber*
ᶠ**2:20** Lit *the days*

WORD STUDY

Greek word: ***nesteuo***
[nay STYOO oh]

Translation: ***fast***

Uses in Mark's Gospel: **6**
(Mt, 8; Lk, 4)

Uses in the NT: **20**

Key passage: **Mark 2:18**

The Greek verb *nesteuo* can mean *to be hungry* or *without food,* but most often it means *to fast* (that is, to purposely abstain from food). The related noun *nesteia* can mean *a fast* (Lk 2:37; Ac 14:23; 27:9) or simply *hunger* (2 Co 6:5; 11:27), which is also the meaning of another related term in both of its NT occurrences (*nestis;* Mt 15:32 = Mk 8:3).

In the law of Moses fasting was commanded only for the Day of Atonement (Lv 16:29, using the idiom "humble your souls"), but the OT records several other occasions of fasting by certain Israelites, particularly in times of physical or spiritual need (Dt 9:9,18; 1 Sm 1:7; 20:34; 2 Sm 12:21; Est 4:16; Ps 35:13; Dn 9:3; 10:2). The purpose of fasting was to set aside everyday and even necessary activities so that matters of great spiritual significance could receive a person's full attention.

By Jesus' time the Pharisees normally fasted twice a week, and His parable about the Pharisee and the tax collector includes a not-so-veiled reference to their surface spirituality in fasting this often (Lk 18:9-14). Every other occurrence of *nesteuo* in the Gospels refers either to Jesus' fasting (Mt 4:2), His warnings about hypocritical fasting (Mt 6:16-18), or His discussion about fasting with various disciples (Mt 9:14-15 = Mk 2:18-20 = Lk 5:33-35).

WORD STUDY

Greek word: **apostolos**
[ah PAHSS tah lahss]

Translation: **apostle**

Uses in Mark's Gospel: **2**
(Mt, 1; Lk, 6; Jn 1)

Uses in the NT: **80**

Key passage: **Mark 3:14**

The Greek noun *apostolos* comes from the common verb *apostello* and literally means *one sent forth with a message.* The noun did not attain the significance of being sent with authority, as the verb already had in the Greek-speaking world, until its adoption by Jesus and the NT writers. The original twelve disciples were chosen and named *apostles* by Jesus (Mt 10:2; Mk 3:14; Lk 6:13); they were trained by Him (see Ac 1:15-26) and invested with His authority to lead the church to accomplish the ongoing task He had given it (Mt 28:18-20). Apostles are referred to 28 times in Acts (most in the NT), which describes the growth and expansion of the church. Apostles had to be eyewitnesses of Jesus' resurrection (Ac 1:22; 1 Co 9:1; 15:8-9). Together with prophets, apostles were foundational for the early church (Eph 2:20), particularly in being responsible for giving divine revelation to God's people (Eph 3:5). Only fifteen people are *clearly* referred to as apostles in the NT: the original twelve (numerous times), Matthias (Ac 1:26), Paul (numerous times), and Barnabas (Ac 14:14).

old wineskins. Otherwise, the wine will burst the skins, and the wine is lost as well as the skins.[a] But new wine is for fresh wineskins."

LORD OF THE SABBATH

23 On the Sabbath He was going through the grain-fields, and His disciples began to make their way picking some heads of grain. 24 The Pharisees said to Him, "Look, why are they doing what is not lawful on the Sabbath?"

25 He said to them, "Have you never read what David and those who were with him did when he was in need and hungry— 26 how he entered the house of God in the time of Abiathar the high priest and ate the •sacred bread—which is not lawful for anyone to eat except the priests—and also gave some to his companions?" 27 Then He told them, "The Sabbath was made for[b] man and not man for[b] the Sabbath. 28 Therefore the Son of Man is Lord even of the Sabbath."

THE MAN WITH THE PARALYZED HAND

3 Now He entered the •synagogue again, and a man was there who had a paralyzed hand. 2 In order to accuse Him, they were watching Him closely to see whether He would heal him on the Sabbath. 3 He told the man with the paralyzed hand, "Stand before us."[c] 4 Then He said to them, "Is it lawful on the Sabbath to do good or to do evil, to save life or to kill?" But they were silent. 5 After looking around at them with anger and sorrow at the hardness of their hearts, He told the man, "Stretch out your hand." So he stretched it out, and his hand was restored. 6 Immediately the •Pharisees went out and started plotting with the •Herodians against Him, how they might destroy Him.

MINISTERING TO THE MULTITUDE

7 Jesus departed with His disciples to the sea, and a great multitude followed from Galilee, Judea, 8 Jerusalem, Idumea, beyond the Jordan, and around Tyre and Sidon. The great multitude came to Him because they

---

[a]2:22 Other mss read *the wine spills out and the skins will be ruined*

[b]2:27 Or *because of*

[c]3:3 Lit *Rise up in the middle*

heard about everything He was doing. ⁹ Then He told His disciples to have a small boat ready for Him, so the crowd would not crush Him. ¹⁰ Since He had healed many, all who had diseases were pressing toward Him to touch Him. ¹¹ Whenever the unclean spirits saw Him, those possessed fell down before Him and cried out, "You are the Son of God!" ¹² And He would strongly warn them not to make Him known.

THE 12 APOSTLES

¹³ Then He went up the mountain and summoned those He wanted, and they came to Him. ¹⁴ He also appointed 12—He also named them apostles[a] —to be with Him, to send them out to preach, ¹⁵ and to have authority to[b] drive out demons.

¹⁶ He appointed the Twelve:[c]

> To Simon, He gave the name Peter;
> ¹⁷ and to James the son of Zebedee,
> and to his brother John,
> He gave the name "Boanerges"
> (that is, "Sons of Thunder");
> ¹⁸ Andrew;
> Philip and Bartholomew;
> Matthew and Thomas;
> James the son of Alphaeus,
> and Thaddaeus;
> Simon the Zealot,[d]
> ¹⁹ and Judas Iscariot,[e]
> who also betrayed Him.

A HOUSE DIVIDED

²⁰ Then He went home, and the crowd gathered again so that they were not even able to eat.[f] ²¹ When His family heard this, they set out to restrain Him, because they said, "He's out of His mind."

²² The •scribes who had come down from Jerusalem said, "He has •Beelzebul in Him!" and, "He drives out demons by the ruler of the demons!"

Real, Personal, Practical Relationship

The apostles had a real, personal, and practical relationship with Jesus—the Son of God. Jesus had chosen them to be with Him. What a pleasure it must have been to have such an intimate relationship with Jesus! When they were given a very difficult assignment, Jesus did not send them out helpless. He gave them authority they had never known before over evil spirits.

He also appointed 12—He also named them apostles—to be with Him, to send them out to preach, and to have authority to drive out demons.

—Mark 3:14-15

---

[a]**3:14** Other mss omit *He also named them apostles*
[b]**3:15** Other mss add *heal diseases, and to*
[c]**3:16** Other mss omit *He appointed the Twelve*
[d]**3:18** Lit *the Cananaean*
[e]**3:19** *Iscariot* probably = "a man of Kerioth," a town in Judea.
[f]**3:20** Lit *eat bread*, or *eat a meal*

23 So He summoned them and spoke to them in parables: "How can Satan drive out Satan? 24 If a kingdom is divided against itself, that kingdom cannot stand. 25 If a house is divided against itself, that house cannot stand. 26 And if Satan rebels against himself and is divided, he cannot stand but is finished!ᵃ

27 "On the other hand, no one can enter a strong man's house and rob his possessions unless he first ties up the strong man. Then he will rob his house. 28 •I assure you: People will be forgiven for all sinsᵇ and whatever blasphemies they may blaspheme. 29 But whoever blasphemes against the Holy Spirit never has forgiveness, but is guilty of an eternal sin"ᶜ — 30 because they were saying, "He has an unclean spirit."

TRUE RELATIONSHIPS

31 Then His mother and His brothers came, and standing outside, they sent ⌊word⌋ to Him and called Him. 32 A crowd was sitting around Him and told Him, "Look, Your mother, Your brothers, and Your sistersᵈ are outside asking for You."

33 He replied to them, "Who are My mother and My brothers?" 34 And looking about at those who were sitting in a circle around Him, He said, "Here are My mother and My brothers! 35 Whoever does the will of God is My brother and sister and mother."

THE PARABLE OF THE SOWER

4 Again He began to teach by the sea, and a very large crowd gathered around Him. So He got into a boat on the sea and sat down, while the whole crowd was on the shore facing the sea. 2 He taught them many things in parables, and in His teaching He said to them: 3 "Listen! Consider the sower who went out to sow. 4 As he sowed, this occurred: Some seed fell along the path, and the birds came and ate it up. 5 Other seed fell on rocky ground where it didn't have much soil, and it sprang up right away, since it didn't have deep soil. 6 When the sun came up, it was scorched, and

---

Obedience Travels a One-Way Street

Sin robs you of the good things God has given. Diligently abstain from every form of evil, and you will be free to enjoy every good thing God has for you.

"If a kingdom is divided against itself, that kingdom cannot stand. If a house is divided against itself, that house cannot stand."

—Mark 3:24-25

Being His—What Else Could You Want?

A love relationship with God is more important than any other single factor in your life.

He replied to them, "Who are My mother and My brothers? . . . Whoever does the will of God is My brother and sister and mother."

—Mark 3:33,35

ᵃ3:26 Lit *but he has an end*
ᵇ3:28 Lit *All things will be forgiven the sons of men*
ᶜ3:29 Other mss read *is subject to eternal judgment*
ᵈ3:32 Other mss omit *and Your sisters*

since it didn't have a root, it withered. ⁷ Other seed fell among thorns, and the thorns came up and choked it, and it didn't produce a crop. ⁸ Still others fell on good ground and produced a crop that increased 30, 60, and 100 times ₍what was sown₎." ⁹ Then He said, "Anyone who has ears to hear should listen!"

WHY JESUS USED PARABLES

¹⁰ When He was alone with the Twelve, those who were around Him asked Him about the parables. ¹¹ He answered them, "The secretᵃ of the kingdom of God has been granted to you, but to those outside, everything comes in parables ¹² so that

> **they may look and look,**
> **yet not perceive;**
> **they may listen and listen,**
> **yet not understand;**
> **otherwise, they might turn back—**
> **and be forgiven."ᵇ ᶜ**

THE PARABLE OF THE SOWER EXPLAINED

¹³ Then He said to them: "Do you not understand this parable? How then will you understand any of the parables? ¹⁴ The sower sows the word. ¹⁵ Theseᵈ are the ones along the path where the word is sown: when they hear, immediately Satan comes and takes away the word sown in them.ᵉ ¹⁶ And these areᶠ the ones sown on rocky ground: when they hear the word, immediately they receive it with joy. ¹⁷ But they have no root in themselves; they are short-lived. When affliction or persecution comes because of the word, they immediately stumble. ¹⁸ Others are sown among thorns; these are the ones who hear the word, ¹⁹ but the worries of this age, the seductionᵍ of wealth, and the desires for other things enter in and choke the word, and it becomes unfruitful. ²⁰ But the ones sown on good ground are those

---

ᵃ**4:11** The Gk word *mysterion* does not mean "mystery" in the Eng sense; it means what we can know only by divine revelation.
ᵇ**4:12** Other mss read *and their sins be forgiven them*
ᶜ**4:12** Is 6:9-10
ᵈ**4:15** Some people
ᵉ**4:15** Other mss read *in their hearts*
ᶠ**4:16** Other mss read *are like*
ᵍ**4:19** Or *pleasure, or deceitfulness*

WORD STUDY

Greek word: ***mysterion***
[moo STAY ree ahn]

Translation: ***secret***

Uses in Mark's Gospel: **1**
(Mt, 1; Lk, 1)

Uses in the NT: **28**

Key passage: **Mark 4:11**

The English word *mystery* comes from the Greek noun *mysterion*, though our English word does not do it justice. A *mysterion* in the ancient world was any religious cult that demanded secrecy from its participants, who had to undergo sacred rites for membership. An element of this may lie behind *mysterion* in the NT, but the word normally translated "mystery" in Daniel is more likely the background for NT usage. In Daniel a mystery (Aramaic *raz*) was a revealed secret, something that could not be understood apart from divine revelation or explanation (Dn 2:17-47; 4:9); this is certainly the force of the numerous instances of *mysterion* in the NT. Jesus used *mysterion* only once, and this was in reference to the mysteries or secrets about the kingdom that He revealed and explained to His disciples (Mt 13:11 = Mk 4:11 = Lk 8:10). Paul used *mysterion* 21 times, and on each occasion the secret is already known from previous revelation (see Rm 16:25; Eph 1:9; 6:19; Col 2:2; 4:3; 1 Tm 3:16), or it is explained in the context (see Rm 11:25; 1 Co 15:51; Eph 3:1-13; 5:32; Col 1:25-27)—that is, it is no longer a secret! The final four uses of *mysterion* in the NT occur in Revelation, where the secret is a symbol that needs to be decoded (1:20; 10:7; 17:5,7).

who hear the word, welcome it, and produce a crop: 30, 60, and 100 times ₎what was sown₎."

USING YOUR LIGHT

²¹ He also said to them, "Is a lamp brought in to be put under a basket or under a bed? Isn't it to be put on a lampstand? ²² For nothing is concealed except to be revealed, and nothing hidden except to come to light. ²³ If anyone has ears to hear, he should listen!" ²⁴ Then He said to them, "Pay attention to what you hear. By the measure you use,ᵃ it will be measured and added to you. ²⁵ For to the one who has, it will be given, and from the one who does not have, even what he has will be taken away."

THE PARABLE OF THE GROWING SEED

²⁶ "The kingdom of God is like this," He said. "A man scatters seed on the ground; ²⁷ he sleeps and rises—night and day, and the seed sprouts and grows—he doesn't know how. ²⁸ The soil produces a crop by itself—first the blade, then the head, and then the ripe grain on the head. ²⁹ But as soon as the crop is ready, he sends for the sickle, because harvest has come."

THE PARABLE OF THE MUSTARD SEED

³⁰ And He said: "How can we illustrate the kingdom of God, or what parable can we use to describe it? ³¹ It's like a mustard seed that, when sown in the soil, is smaller than all the seeds on the ground. ³² And when sown, it comes up and grows taller than all the vegetables, and produces large branches, so that the birds of the sky can nest in its shade."

USING PARABLES

³³ He would speak the word to them with many parables like these, as they were able to understand. ³⁴ And He did not speak to them without a parable. Privately, however, He would explain everything to His own disciples.

Keep Your Ears Open, Your Calendar Clear

A tender and sensitive heart will be ready to respond to God at the slightest prompting. Then when God opens your spiritual eyes, you will know He is at work.

"If anyone has ears to hear, he should listen!"

—Mark 4:23

God Will Help You Understand His Word

God speaks by the Holy Spirit through the Bible, prayer, circumstances, and the church to reveal Himself, His purposes, and His ways.

He did not speak to them without a parable. Privately, however, He would explain everything to His own disciples.

—Mark 4:34

ᵃ4:24 Lit *you measure*

86

WIND AND WAVE OBEY THE MASTER

35 On that day, when evening had come, He told them, "Let's cross over to the other side ⌊of the lake⌋." 36 So they left the crowd and took Him along since He was ⌊already⌋ in the boat. And other boats were with Him. 37 A fierce windstorm arose, and the waves were breaking over the boat, so that the boat was already being swamped. 38 But He was in the stern, sleeping on the cushion. So they woke Him up and said to Him, "Teacher! Don't you care that we're going to die?"

39 He got up, rebuked the wind, and said to the sea, "Silence! Be still!" The wind ceased, and there was a great calm. 40 Then He said to them, "Why are you fearful? Do you still have no faith?"

41 And they were terrified and asked one another, "Who then is this? Even the wind and the sea obey Him!"

DEMONS DRIVEN OUT BY THE MASTER

5 Then they came to the other side of the sea, to the region of the Gerasenes.ᵃ 2 As soon as He got out of the boat, a man with an unclean spirit came out of the tombs and met Him. 3 He lived in the tombs. No one was able to restrain him any more—even with chains— 4 because he often had been bound with shackles and chains, but had snapped off the chains and smashed the shackles. No one was strong enough to subdue him. 5 And always, night and day, he was crying out among the tombs and in the mountains and cutting himself with stones.

6 When he saw Jesus from a distance, he ran and knelt down before Him. 7 And he cried out with a loud voice, "What do You have to do with me,ᵇ Jesus, Son of the Most High God? I begᶜ You before God, don't torment me!" 8 For He had told him, "Come out of the man, you unclean spirit!"

9 "What is your name?" He asked him.

"My name is Legion,"ᵈ he answered Him, "because we are many." 10 And he kept begging Him not to send them out of the region.

You Must Trust God, No Doubt About It

The fact that you have doubts indicates that you do not know God as you should.

He said to them, "Why are you fearful? Do you still have no faith?" And they were terrified and asked one another, "Who then is this? Even the wind and the sea obey Him!"

—Mark 4:40-41

ᵃ5:1 Other mss read *Gadarenes*; other mss read *Gergesenes*
ᵇ5:7 Lit *What to me and to You*
ᶜ5:7 Or *adjure*

ᵈ5:9 A Roman legion contained up to 6,000 soldiers; here *legion* indicates a large number.

WORD STUDY

Greek word: **daimonizomai**
[digh mah NEE zah migh]

Translation: **be demon-possessed**

Uses in Mark's Gospel: **4**
(Mt, 7; Lk, 1; Jn, 1)

Uses in the NT: **13**

Key passage: **Mark 5:1-20**

The Greek verb *daimonizomai* comes from the noun *daimonion,* meaning *demon,* an evil spirit. The verb literally means *to be demonized* and refers to the activities of demons in harassing, oppressing, and even possessing people. The phrase "to have a demon" occurs a few times in the NT with the same meaning. Though possession is not always in view when the NT mentions demonic activity, this is clearly the case in Mark 5 where a man is described with a "Legion" (v. 9) of demons that Jesus cast into a herd of pigs. (A legion in the Roman army was 6,000 soldiers.) The loss of 2,000 pigs (v. 13) strongly implies an incredibly high multiple possession in this instance, which explains the man's bizarre behavior and astounding strength. The word *daimonion* (and *daimonizomai* to a lesser extent) was used in the ancient world to refer to pagan gods and lesser deities (such as stars), but the NT reveals that they are actually Satan's followers. The verb is rare in the NT and occurs only in the Gospels; the noun *daimonion* occurs 63 times with 53 occurrences in the Gospels. The concentration of these terms in the Gospels demonstrates both the reality of the unseen world of spirit beings and Jesus' absolute power over demons, regardless of the evil they cause.

¹¹ Now a large herd of pigs was there, feeding on the hillside. ¹² The demons[a] begged Him, "Send us to the pigs, so we may enter them." ¹³ And He gave them permission. Then the unclean spirits came out and entered the pigs, and the herd of about 2,000 rushed down the steep bank into the sea and drowned there. ¹⁴ The men who tended them[b] ran off and reported it in the town and the countryside, and people went to see what had happened. ¹⁵ They came to Jesus and saw the man who had been demon-possessed by the legion, sitting there, dressed and in his right mind; and they were afraid. ¹⁶ The eyewitnesses described to them what had happened to the demon-possessed man and ₗtoldₗ about the pigs. ¹⁷ Then they began to beg Him to leave their region.

¹⁸ As He was getting into the boat, the man who had been demon-possessed kept begging Him to be with Him. ¹⁹ But He would not let him; instead, He told him, "Go back home to your own people, and report to them how much the Lord has done for you and how He has had mercy on you." ²⁰ So he went out and began to proclaim in the •Decapolis how much Jesus had done for him, and they were all amazed.

A GIRL RESTORED AND A WOMAN HEALED

²¹ When Jesus had crossed over again by boat to the other side, a large crowd gathered around Him while He was by the sea. ²² One of the •synagogue leaders, named Jairus, came, and when he saw Jesus, he fell at His feet ²³ and kept begging Him, "My little daughter is at death's door.[c] Come and lay Your hands on her so she can get well and live."

²⁴ So Jesus went with him, and a large crowd was following and pressing against Him. ²⁵ A woman suffering from bleeding for 12 years ²⁶ had endured much under many doctors. She had spent everything she had and was not helped at all. On the contrary, she became worse. ²⁷ Having heard about Jesus, she came behind Him in the crowd and touched His robe. ²⁸ For she said, "If I can just touch His robes, I'll be made well!"

---

[a]**5:12** Other mss read *All the demons*
[b]**5:14** Other mss read *tended the pigs*

[c]**5:23** Lit *My little daughter has it finally*; = to be at the end of life

²⁹ Instantly her flow of blood ceased, and she sensed in her body that she was cured of her affliction.

³⁰ At once Jesus realized in Himself that power had gone out from Him. He turned around in the crowd and said, "Who touched My robes?"

³¹ His disciples said to Him, "You see the crowd pressing against You, and You say, 'Who touched Me?'"

³² So He was looking around to see who had done this. ³³ Then the woman, knowing what had happened to her, came with fear and trembling, fell down before Him, and told Him the whole truth. ³⁴ "Daughter," He said to her, "your faith has made you well.ᵃ Go in peace and be freeᵇ from your affliction."

³⁵ While He was still speaking, people came from the synagogue leader's house and said, "Your daughter is dead. Why bother the Teacher any more?"

³⁶ But when Jesus overheard what was said, He told the synagogue leader, "Don't be afraid. Only believe." ³⁷ He did not let anyone accompany Him except Peter, James, and John, James' brother. ³⁸ They came to the leader's house, and He saw a commotion—people weeping and wailing loudly. ³⁹ He went in and said to them, "Why are you making a commotion and weeping? The child is not dead but asleep."

⁴⁰ They started laughing at Him, but He put them all outside. He took the child's father, mother, and those who were with Him, and entered the place where the child was. ⁴¹ Then He took the child by the hand and said to her, *"Talitha koum!"*ᶜ (which is translated, "Little girl, I say to you, get up!"). ⁴² Immediately the girl got up and began to walk. (She was 12 years old.) At this they were utterly astounded. ⁴³ Then He gave them strict orders that no one should know about this and said that she should be given something to eat.

REJECTION AT NAZARETH

6 He went away from there and came to His hometown, and His disciples followed Him. ² When the Sabbath came, He began to teach in the •synagogue, and many who heard Him were astonished. "Where did this man get these things?" they said. "What is this

Trust God to Do What You Cannot

We don't have to be able to accomplish the task within our limited ability or resources. With faith, we can proceed confidently, because we know that He is going to bring to pass what He purposes.

She said, "If I can just touch His robes, I'll be made well!"
—Mark 5:28

Watch for People Who Are Open to God

When Jesus passed through a crowd, He always looked for where the Father was at work. The crowd was not the harvest field. The harvest field was within the crowd.

His disciples said to Him, "You see the crowd pressing against You, and You say, 'Who touched Me?'" So He was looking around to see who had done this. Then the woman, knowing what had happened to her, came with fear and trembling, fell down before Him, and told Him the whole truth.
—Mark 5:31-33

ᵃ5:34 Or *has saved you*   ᶜ5:41 An Aram expression
ᵇ5:34 Lit *healthy*

wisdom given to Him, and how are these miracles performed by His hands? ³ Isn't this the carpenter, the son of Mary, and the brother of James, Joses, Judas, and Simon? And aren't His sisters here with us?" So they were offended by Him.

⁴ Then Jesus said to them, "A prophet is not without honor except in his hometown, among his relatives, and in his household." ⁵ So He was not able to do any miracles[a] there, except that He laid His hands on a few sick people and healed them. ⁶ And He was amazed at their unbelief.

COMMISSIONING THE TWELVE

Now He was going around the villages in a circuit, teaching. ⁷ He summoned the Twelve and began to send them out in pairs and gave them authority over unclean spirits. ⁸ He instructed them to take nothing for the road except a walking stick: no bread, no traveling bag, no money in their belts. ⁹ They were to wear sandals, but not put on an extra shirt. ¹⁰ Then He said to them, "Whenever you enter a house, stay there until you leave that place. ¹¹ If any place does not welcome you and people refuse to listen to you, when you leave there, shake the dust off your feet as a testimony against them."[b]

¹² So they went out and preached that people should repent. ¹³ And they were driving out many demons, anointing many sick people with oil, and healing.

JOHN THE BAPTIST BEHEADED

¹⁴ King •Herod heard of this, because Jesus' name had become well known. Some[c] said, "John the Baptist has been raised from the dead, and that's why supernatural powers are at work in him." ¹⁵ But others said, "He's Elijah." Still others said, "He's a prophet[d] —like one of the prophets."

¹⁶ When Herod heard of it, he said, "John, the one I beheaded, has been raised!" ¹⁷ For Herod himself had given orders to arrest John and to chain him in prison

Maybe You're Not Dreaming Big Enough

The reason much of the world is not being attracted to Christ and His church is that God's people lack the faith to attempt those things that only God can do.

He was not able to do any miracles there, except that He laid His hands on a few sick people and healed them. And He was amazed at their unbelief.

—Mark 6:5-6

[a]6:5 Lit miracle
[b]6:11 Other mss add I assure you, it will be more tolerable for Sodom or Gomorrah on judgment day than for that town.
[c]6:14 Other mss read He
[d]6:15 Lit Others said, "A prophet

on account of Herodias, his brother Philip's wife, whom he had married. ¹⁸ John had been telling Herod, "It is not lawful for you to have your brother's wife!" ¹⁹ So Herodias held a grudge against him and wanted to kill him. But she could not, ²⁰ because Herod was in awe of[a] John and was protecting him, knowing he was a righteous and holy man. When Herod heard him he would be very disturbed,[b] yet would hear him gladly.

²¹ Now an opportune time came on his birthday, when Herod gave a banquet for his nobles, military commanders, and the leading men of Galilee. ²² When Herodias' own daughter[c] came in and danced, she pleased Herod and his guests. The king said to the girl, "Ask me whatever you want, and I'll give it to you." ²³ So he swore oaths to her: "Whatever you ask me I will give you, up to half my kingdom."

²⁴ Then she went out and said to her mother, "What should I ask for?"

"John the Baptist's head!" she said.

²⁵ Immediately she hurried to the king and said, "I want you to give me John the Baptist's head on a platter—right now!"

²⁶ Though the king was deeply distressed, because of his oaths and the guests[d] he did not want to refuse her. ²⁷ The king immediately sent for an executioner and commanded him to bring John's head. So he went and beheaded him in prison, ²⁸ brought his head on a platter, and gave it to the girl. Then the girl gave it to her mother. ²⁹ When his disciples[e] heard about it, they came and removed his corpse and placed it in a tomb.

FEEDING 5,000

³⁰ The apostles gathered around Jesus and reported to Him all that they had done and taught. ³¹ He said to them, "Come away by yourselves to a remote place and rest a while." For many people were coming and going, and they did not even have time to eat. ³² So they went away in the boat by themselves to a remote place, ³³ but many saw them leaving and recognized them. People

WORD STUDY

Greek word: **kerusso**
[kay ROO soh]

Translation: **preach**

Uses in Mark's Gospel: **14**
(Mt, 9; Lk, 9)

Uses in the NT: **61**

Key passage: **Mark 6:12**

The Greek verb *kerusso* is one of the three main words in the NT for "proclamation"; the other two are *euangelizo* (the verb form of *euangelion*, which means *gospel* or *good news*), meaning *to evangelize* or *proclaim good news;* and *martureo*, which means *to witness or testify.* The noun *kerux*, meaning *herald* or *preacher*, was very important in the Greek world, for a herald often proclaimed important news and decrees from ruling authorities to the common people. Significantly, *kerux* occurs only three times in the NT (1 Tm 2:7; 2 Tm 1:11; 2 Pt 2:5), as opposed to sixty-one for the verb *kerusso*, for in preaching the gospel the emphasis is on the act of proclaiming the message or on the message itself and not on the person. The message proclaimed is called the *kerugma* in Greek (eight uses in the NT; see Mt 12:41 = Lk 11:32; Rm 16:25; 1 Co 1:21; 2:4; 15:14; 2 Tm 4:17; Ti 1:3), which in all six uses by Paul is a reference to the only message worth proclaiming to the world—the *euangelion*, that is, the gospel.

---

[a]**6:20** Or *Herod feared*
[b]**6:20** Other mss read *When he heard him, he did many things*
[c]**6:22** Other mss read *When his daughter Herodias*
[d]**6:26** Lit *and those reclining at the table*
[e]**6:29** John's disciples

ran there by land from all the towns and arrived ahead of them.[a] 34 So as He stepped ashore, He saw a huge crowd and had compassion on them, because they were like sheep without a shepherd. Then He began to teach them many things.

35 When it was already late, His disciples approached Him and said, "This place is a wilderness, and it is already late! 36 Send them away, so they can go into the surrounding countryside and villages to buy themselves something to eat."

37 "You give them something to eat," He responded.

They said to Him, "Should we go and buy 200 •denarii worth of bread and give them something to eat?"

38 And He asked them, "How many loaves do you have? Go look."

When they found out they said, "Five, and two fish."

39 Then He instructed them to have all the people sit down[b] in groups on the green grass. 40 So they sat down in ranks of hundreds and fifties. 41 Then He took the five loaves and the two fish, and looking up to heaven, He blessed and broke the loaves. He kept giving them to His disciples to set before the people. He also divided the two fish among them all. 42 Everyone ate and was filled. 43 Then they picked up 12 baskets full of pieces of bread and fish. 44 Now those who ate the loaves were 5,000 men.

WALKING ON THE WATER

45 Immediately He made His disciples get into the boat and go ahead of Him to the other side, to Bethsaida, while He dismissed the crowd. 46 After He said good-bye to them, He went away to the mountain to pray. 47 When evening came, the boat was in the middle of the sea, and He was alone on the land. 48 He saw them being battered as they rowed,[c] because the wind was against them. Around three in the morning[d] He came toward them walking on the sea and wanted to pass by them. 49 When they saw Him walking on the sea, they thought it was a ghost and cried out; 50 for

People Are Needing You to Notice Them

As long as you focus on yourself, you will be oblivious to the needs of others. Ask God to free you from selfishness so that your life is free to bless others

As He stepped ashore, He saw a huge crowd and had compassion on them, because they were like sheep without a shepherd. Then He began to teach them many things.

—Mark 6:34

---

[a]6:33 Other mss add *and gathered around Him*
[b]6:39 Lit *people recline*
[c]6:48 Or *them struggling as they rowed*
[d]6:48 Lit *Around the fourth watch of the night* = 3 to 6 a.m.

they all saw Him and were terrified. Immediately He spoke with them and said, "Have courage! It is I. Don't be afraid." ⁵¹ Then He got into the boat with them, and the wind ceased. They were completely astounded,ᵃ ⁵² because they had not understood about the loaves. Instead, their hearts were hardened.

MIRACULOUS HEALINGS

⁵³ When they had crossed over, they came to land at Gennesaret and beached the boat. ⁵⁴ As they got out of the boat, people immediately recognized Him. ⁵⁵ They hurried throughout that vicinity and began to carry the sick on stretchers to wherever they heard He was. ⁵⁶ Wherever He would go, into villages, towns, or the country, they laid the sick in the marketplaces and begged Him that they might touch just the •tassel of His robe. And everyone who touched it was made well.

THE TRADITIONS OF THE ELDERS

7 The •Pharisees and some of the •scribes who had come from Jerusalem gathered around Him. ² They observed that some of His disciples were eating their bread with unclean—that is, unwashed—hands. ³ (For the Pharisees, in fact all the Jews, will not eat unless they wash their hands ritually, keeping the tradition of the elders. ⁴ When they come from the marketplace, they do not eat unless they have washed. And there are many other customs they have received and keep, like the washing of cups, jugs, copper utensils, and dining couches.ᵇ) ⁵ Then the Pharisees and the scribes asked Him, "Why don't Your disciples live according to the tradition of the elders, instead of eating bread with ritually uncleanᶜ hands?"

⁶ He answered them, "Isaiah prophesied correctly about you hypocrites, as it is written:

> **These people honor Me with their lips,**
> **but their heart is far from Me.**
> ⁷ **They worship Me in vain,**

The Mountaintop Is for Praying

It is tempting to relax after a spiritual victory, but a crisis could follow at any time. You must stand your guard over your high points.

After He said good-bye to them, He went away to the mountain to pray.
—Mark 6:46

ᵃ**6:51** Lit *were astounded in themselves*

ᵇ**7:4** Other mss omit *and dining couches*

ᶜ**7:5** Other mss read *with unwashed*

WORD STUDY

Greek word: ***grammateus***
[grahm mah TOOSS]

Translation: **scribe**

Uses in Mark's Gospel: **21**
(Mt, 22; Lk, 14; Jn, 1)

Uses in the NT: **63**

Key passage: **Mark 7:5**

The Greek noun *grammateus* means *a secretary,* and the related noun *gramma* can mean *a letter of the alphabet* or *a letter* (that is, *an epistle* or *a document*). Both terms are derived from the verb *grapho,* meaning *to write.* In Jewish culture in NT times the *grammateus* was more than just a secretary. He was *a scribe* or *scholar,* a recognized expert in the law of Moses and the authoritative traditions related to it. Scribes could be Sadducees or Pharisees, and they are often mentioned in the same context as chief priests, elders, or Pharisees. These four influential groups of men made up the Sanhedrin, the ruling body of political and religious life for the Jewish people. All but six references to the scribes occur in the Synoptic Gospels, and the vast majority of the time they are antagonistic to Jesus. They questioned whom Jesus ate with (Mk 2:16) and how He ate (Mk 7:1-5), charged Jesus with being in league with Satan (Mk 3:22), challenged Jesus' views on the greatest commandment (Mk 12:28), and participated in Jesus' arrest, trial, and death (Mk 14:1,43,53; 15:1,31). Jesus in turn warned them about committing an unforgivable sin (Mk 3:23-30), rebuked them for hypocrisy (Mk 7:6-23; see Mt 23), and questioned their understanding of the Messiah, the Son of David (Mk 12:35-37)—a question that they could not answer despite their learning.

teaching as doctrines the commands of men.[a]

8 Disregarding the command of God, you keep the tradition of men."[b] 9 He also said to them, "You completely invalidate God's command in order to maintain[c] your tradition! 10 For Moses said:

Honor your father and your mother;[d] and, **Whoever speaks evil of father or mother must be put to death.**[e]

11 But you say, 'If a man tells his father or mother: Whatever benefit you might have received from me is Corban'" (that is, a gift ⌊committed to the temple⌋), 12 "you no longer let him do anything for his father or mother. 13 You revoke God's word by your tradition that you have handed down. And you do many other similar things." 14 Summoning the crowd again, He told them, "Listen to Me, all of you, and understand: 15 Nothing that goes into a person from outside can defile him, but the things that come out of a person are what defile him. 16 If anyone has ears to hear, he should listen!"[f]

17 When He went into the house away from the crowd, the disciples asked Him about the parable. 18 And He said to them, "Are you also as lacking in understanding? Don't you realize that nothing going into a man from the outside can defile him? 19 For it doesn't go into his heart but into the stomach and is eliminated."[g] (As a result, He made all foods clean.[h]) 20 Then He said, "What comes out of a person—that defiles him. 21 For from within, out of people's hearts, come evil thoughts, sexual immoralities, thefts, murders, 22 adulteries, greed, evil actions, deceit, lewdness, stinginess,[i] blasphemy, pride, and foolishness. 23 All these evil things come from within and defile a person."

A GENTILE MOTHER'S FAITH

24 He got up and departed from there to the region of Tyre and Sidon.[j] He entered a house and did not

---

[a]7:6-7 Is 29:13
[b]7:8 Other mss add *The washing of jugs, and cups, and many other similar things you practice.*
[c]7:9 Other mss read *to establish*
[d]7:10 Ex 20:12; Dt 5:16
[e]7:10 Ex 21:17; Lv 20:9

[f]7:16 Other mss omit this verse
[g]7:19 Lit *goes out into the toilet*
[h]7:19 Other mss read *is eliminated, making all foods clean."*
[i]7:22 Lit *evil eye*
[j]7:24 Other mss omit *and Sidon*

want anyone to know it, but He could not escape notice. 25 Instead, immediately after hearing about Him, a woman whose little daughter had an unclean spirit came and fell at His feet. 26 Now the woman was Greek, a Syrophoenician by birth, and she kept asking Him to drive the demon out of her daughter. 27 He said to her, "Allow the children to be satisfied first, because it isn't right to take the children's bread and throw it to the dogs."

28 But she replied to Him, "Lord, even the dogs under the table eat the children's crumbs."

29 Then He told her, "Because of this reply, you may go. The demon has gone out of your daughter." 30 When she went back to her home, she found her child lying on the bed, and the demon was gone.

JESUS DOES EVERYTHING WELL

31 Again, leaving the region of Tyre, He went by way of Sidon to the Sea of Galilee, through[a] the region of the •Decapolis. 32 They brought to Him a deaf man who also had a speech difficulty, and begged Jesus to lay His hand on him. 33 So He took him away from the crowd privately. After putting His fingers in the man's ears and spitting, He touched his tongue. 34 Then, looking up to heaven, He sighed deeply and said to him, *"Ephphatha!"*[b] (that is, "Be opened!"). 35 Immediately his ears were opened, his speech difficulty was removed,[c] and he began to speak clearly. 36 Then He ordered them to tell no one, but the more He would order them, the more they would proclaim it.

37 They were extremely astonished and said, "He has done everything well! He even makes deaf people hear, and people unable to speak, talk!"

FEEDING 4,000

8 In those days there was again a large crowd, and they had nothing to eat. He summoned the disciples and said to them, 2 "I have compassion on the crowd, because they've already stayed with Me three

Obedience Is More Than Skin-Deep

If you have an obedience problem, you have a love problem.

"Nothing that goes into a person from outside can defile him, but the things that come out of a person are what defile him."

—Mark 7:15

---

[a]7:31 Or *into*
[b]7:34 An Aram expression
[c]7:35 Lit *opened, the bond of his tongue was untied*

days and have nothing to eat. ³ If I send them home famished,ᵃ they will collapse on the way, and some of them have come a long distance."

⁴ His disciples answered Him, "Where can anyone get enough bread here in this desolate place to fill these people?"

⁵ "How many loaves do you have?" He asked them.

"Seven," they said. ⁶ Then He commanded the crowd to sit down on the ground. Taking the seven loaves, He gave thanks, broke the ⌊loaves⌋, and kept on giving ⌊them⌋ to His disciples to set before ⌊the people⌋. So they served the ⌊loaves⌋ to the crowd. ⁷ They also had a few small fish, and when He had blessed them, He said these were to be served as well. ⁸ They ate and were filled. Then they collected seven large baskets of leftover pieces. ⁹ About 4,000 ⌊men⌋ were there. He dismissed them ¹⁰ and immediately got into the boat with His disciples and went to the district of Dalmanutha.ᵇ

THE YEAST OF THE PHARISEES AND HEROD

¹¹ The •Pharisees came out and began to argue with Him, demanding of Him a sign from heaven to test Him. ¹² But sighing deeply in His spirit, He said, "Why does this generation demand a sign? •I assure you: No sign will be given to this generation!" ¹³ Then He left them, got on board ⌊the boat⌋ again, and went to the other side.

¹⁴ They had forgotten to take bread and had only one loaf with them in the boat. ¹⁵ Then He commanded them: "Watch out! Beware of the yeast of the Pharisees and the yeast of •Herod."

¹⁶ They were discussing among themselves that they did not have any bread. ¹⁷ Aware of this, He said to them, "Why are you discussing that you do not have any bread? Do you not yet understand or comprehend? Is your heart hardened? ¹⁸ **Do you have eyes, and not see, and do you have ears, and not hear?**ᶜ And do you not remember? ¹⁹ When I broke the five loaves for

---

Do You Need a Miracle—Or a Master?

At times we prefer the miracle over the miracle worker.

His disciples answered Him, "Where can anyone get enough bread here in this desolate place to fill these people?"

—Mark 8:4

ᵃ**8:3** Or *fasting*
ᵇ**8:10** Probably on the western shore of the Sea of Galilee

ᶜ**8:18** Jr 5:21; Ezk 12:2

the 5,000, how many baskets full of pieces of bread did you collect?"

"Twelve," they told Him.

20 "When I broke the seven loaves for the 4,000, how many large baskets full of pieces of bread did you collect?"

"Seven," they said.

21 And He said to them, "Don't you understand yet?"

HEALING A BLIND MAN

22 Then they came to Bethsaida. They brought a blind man to Him and begged Him to touch him. 23 He took the blind man by the hand and brought him out of the village. Spitting on his eyes and laying His hands on him, He asked him, "Do you see anything?"

24 He looked up and said, "I see people—they look to me like trees walking."

25 Again Jesus placed His hands on the man's eyes, and he saw distinctly. He was cured and could see everything clearly. 26 Then He sent him home, saying, "Don't even go into the village."[a]

PETER'S CONFESSION OF THE MESSIAH

27 Jesus went out with His disciples to the villages of Caesarea Philippi. And on the road He asked His disciples, "Who do people say that I am?"

28 They answered Him, "John the Baptist; others, Elijah; still others, one of the prophets."

29 "But you," He asked them again, "who do you say that I am?"

Peter answered Him, "You are the •Messiah!"

30 And He strictly warned them to tell no one about Him.

HIS DEATH AND RESURRECTION PREDICTED

31 Then He began to teach them that the •Son of Man must suffer many things, and be rejected by the elders, the •chief priests, and the •scribes, be killed, and rise

---

God's Word Shouldn't Freeze Us, But Free Us

If you serve the Lord out of duty and habit, but not out of joy and gratitude, you will envy those who are experiencing joy in the Lord and miss the abundant life the Father has planned for you.

He commanded them: "Watch out! Beware of the yeast of the Pharisees and the yeast of Herod,"
—Mark 8:15

---

[a]8:26 Other mss add *or tell anyone in the village*

WORD STUDY

Greek word: **psuche**
[psoo KAY]

Translation: *life*

Uses in Mark's Gospel: **8**
(Mt, 16; Lk, 14; Jn, 10)

Uses in the NT: **103**

Key passage: **Mark 8:35**

The Greek noun *psuche* comes from the verb *psucho,* meaning *to blow,* and then by extension *to become cold* (Mt 24:12). This is similar to the synonym *pneuma,* meaning *wind, breath, spirit* (or *Spirit*), which comes from the verb *pneo,* also meaning *to blow* (both *pneuma* and *pneo* are used in Jn 3:8). Overlap occurs between *psuche* and *soma* since both can refer to physical life or existence (Mt 2:20, *psuche;* Mt 27:52, *soma*), and both *psuche* and *pneuma* can refer to spiritual life or the inner self (Mk 8:36, *psuche;* Mk 14:38, *pneuma*). But no such overlap exists between *pneuma* and *soma* since the spirit and the body are distinguished in the NT. Sometimes both the physical and spiritual aspects of *psuche* are combined so that the whole person is in view, not just one aspect of his existence (Mk 8:35, used twice). An important synonym for *psuche* is *zoe,* another word meaning *life*.

after three days. ³² He was openly talking about this. So Peter took Him aside and began to rebuke Him.

³³ But turning around and looking at His disciples, He rebuked Peter and said, "Get behind Me, Satan, because you're not thinking about God's concerns,ª but man's!"

TAKE UP YOUR CROSS

³⁴ Summoning the crowd along with His disciples, He said to them, "If anyone wants to be My follower, he must deny himself, take up his cross, and follow Me. ³⁵ For whoever wants to save his •life will lose it, but whoever loses his life because of Me and the gospel will save it. ³⁶ For what does it benefit a man to gain the whole world yet lose his life? ³⁷ What can a man give in exchange for his life? ³⁸ For whoever is ashamed of Me and of My words in this adulterous and sinful generation, the Son of Man will also be ashamed of him when He comes in the glory of His Father with the holy angels."

9 Then He said to them, "•I assure you: There are some standing here who will not taste death until they see the kingdom of God come in power."

THE TRANSFIGURATION

² After six days Jesus took Peter, James, and John and led them up on a high mountain by themselves to be alone. He was transformedᵇ in front of them, ³ and His clothes became dazzling—extremely white as no launderer on earth could whiten them. ⁴ Elijah appeared to them with Moses, and they were talking with Jesus.

⁵ Then Peter said to Jesus, "•Rabbi, it is good for us to be here! Let us make three •tabernacles: one for You, one for Moses, and one for Elijah"— ⁶ because he did not know what he should say, since they were terrified.

⁷ A cloud appeared, overshadowing them, and a voice came from the cloud:

> This is My beloved Son;
> listen to Him!

ª**8:33** Lit *about the things of God*   ᵇ**9:2** Or *transfigured*

8 Then suddenly, looking around, they no longer saw anyone with them except Jesus alone.

9 As they were coming down from the mountain, He ordered them to tell no one what they had seen until the •Son of Man had risen from the dead. 10 They kept this word to themselves, discussing what "rising from the dead" meant.

11 Then they began to question Him, "Why do the •scribes say that Elijah must come first?"

12 "Elijah does come first and restores everything," He replied. "How then is it written about the Son of Man that He must suffer many things and be treated with contempt? 13 But I tell you that Elijah really has come, and they did to him whatever they wanted, just as it is written about him."

THE POWER OF FAITH OVER A DEMON

14 When they came to the disciples, they saw a large crowd around them and scribes disputing with them. 15 All of a sudden, when the whole crowd saw Him, they were amazed[a] and ran to greet Him. 16 Then He asked them, "What are you arguing with them about?"

17 Out of the crowd, one man answered Him, "Teacher, I brought my son to You. He has a spirit that makes him unable to speak. 18 Wherever it seizes him, it throws him down, and he foams at the mouth, grinds his teeth, and becomes rigid. So I asked Your disciples to drive it out, but they couldn't."

19 He replied to them, "You unbelieving generation! How long will I be with you? How long must I put up with you? Bring him to Me." 20 So they brought him to Him. When the spirit saw Him, it immediately convulsed the boy. He fell to the ground and rolled around, foaming at the mouth. 21 "How long has this been happening to him?" Jesus asked his father.

"From childhood," he said. 22 "And many times it has thrown him into fire or water to destroy him. But if You can do anything, have compassion on us and help us."

23 Then Jesus said to him, "'If You can?'[b] [c] Everything is possible to the one who believes."

Dying to Self Is the Only Way to Live

Self-centeredness is a subtle trap. God-centeredness requires a daily death to self and submission to God.

"Whoever is ashamed of Me and of My words in this adulterous and sinful generation, the Son of Man will also be ashamed of him when He comes in the glory of His Father with the holy angels."

—Mark 8:38

[a]9:15 Or *surprised*
[b]9:23 Other mss add *believe*
[c]9:23 Jesus appears to quote the father's words in v. 22 and then comment on them.

²⁴ Immediately the father of the boy cried out, "I do believe! Help my unbelief."

²⁵ When Jesus saw that a crowd was rapidly coming together, He rebuked the unclean spirit, saying to it, "You mute and deaf spirit,ᵃ I command you: come out of him and never enter him again!"

²⁶ Then it came out, shrieking and convulsing himᵇ violently. The boy became like a corpse, so that many said, "He's dead." ²⁷ But Jesus, taking him by the hand, raised him, and he stood up.

²⁸ After He went into a house, His disciples asked Him privately, "Why couldn't we drive it out?"

²⁹ And He told them, "This kind can come out by nothing but prayer [and fasting]."ᶜ

THE SECOND PREDICTION OF HIS DEATH

³⁰ Then they left that place and made their way through Galilee, but He did not want anyone to know it. ³¹ For He was teaching His disciples and telling them, "The Son of Man is being betrayedᵈ into the hands of men. They will kill Him, and after He is killed, He will rise three days later." ³² But they did not understand this statement, and they were afraid to ask Him.

WHO IS THE GREATEST?

³³ Then they came to Capernaum. When He was in the house, He asked them, "What were you arguing about on the way?" ³⁴ But they were silent, because on the way they had been arguing with one another about who was the greatest. ³⁵ Sitting down, He called the Twelve and said to them, "If anyone wants to be first, he must be last of all and servant of all." ³⁶ Then He took a child, had him stand among them, and taking him in His arms, He said to them, ³⁷ "Whoever welcomesᵉ one little child such as this in My name welcomes Me. And whoever welcomes Me does not welcome Me, but Him who sent Me."

Will You Believe When You Don't Understand?

An encounter with God requires us to adjust ourselves to the activity of God that has been revealed.

"The Son of Man is being betrayed into the hands of men. They will kill Him, and after He is killed, He will rise three days later." But they did not understand this statement, and they were afraid to ask Him.
—Mark 9:31b-32

Give Others Room to Serve God Their Way

Are you able to rejoice in the spiritual victories of others? Are you encouraging those who serve the Lord in a different way or who belong to a different group than you do?

John said to Him, "Teacher, we saw someone driving out demons in Your name, and we tried to stop him because he wasn't following us."
—Mark 9:38

ᵃ**9:25** A spirit that caused the boy to be deaf and unable to speak
ᵇ**9:26** Other mss omit *him*
ᶜ**9:29** Other mss omit bracketed text
ᵈ**9:31** Or *handed over*
ᵉ**9:37** Or *Whoever receives*

IN HIS NAME

³⁸ John said to Him, "Teacher, we saw someoneª driving out demons in Your name, and we tried to stop him because he wasn't following us."
³⁹ "Don't stop him," said Jesus, "because there is no one who will perform a miracle in My name who can soon afterwards speak evil of Me. ⁴⁰ For whoever is not against us is for us. ⁴¹ And whoever gives you a cup of water to drink because of My name,ᵇ since you belong to the •Messiah—I assure you: He will never lose his reward.

WARNINGS FROM JESUS

⁴² "But whoever •causes the downfall of one of these little ones who believe in Me—it would be better for him if a heavy millstoneᶜ were hung around his neck and he were thrown into the sea. ⁴³ And if your hand causes your downfall, cut it off. It is better for you to enter life maimed than to have two hands and go to •hell—the unquenchable fire, [⁴⁴ where

**Their worm does not die,
and the fire is not quenched.**]ᵈ ᵉ

⁴⁵ And if your foot causes your downfall, cut it off. It is better for you to enter life lame than to have two feet and be thrown into hell— [the unquenchable fire, ⁴⁶ where

**Their worm does not die,
and the fire is not quenched.**]ᵈ ᵉ

⁴⁷ And if your eye causes your downfall, gouge it out. It is better for you to enter the kingdom of God with one eye than to have two eyes and be thrown into hell, ⁴⁸ where

**Their worm does not die,
and the fire is not quenched.**ᵉ

⁴⁹ For everyone will be salted with fire.ᶠ ᵍ ⁵⁰ Salt is good, but if the salt should lose its flavor, how can you

WORD STUDY

Greek word: **skandalizo**
[skahn dah LEE zoh]

Translation: **cause the downfall of**

Uses in Mark's Gospel: **8**
(Mt, 14; Lk, 2; Jn, 2)

Uses in the NT: **29**

Key passage: **Mark 9:42-50**

The Greek verb *skandalizo* means *to entrap* and is related to the noun *skandalon*, meaning *trap* or *snare*. Metaphorically, *skandalizo* can mean *to cause [someone] to stumble* or (passively) *to take offense*. Similarly, the noun *skandalon* can mean *offense* or *stumbling block*. In the NT both *skandalizo* and *skandalon* always refer to offenses either given or taken in spiritual matters. Paul used *skandalizo* three times (1 Co 8:13 [twice]; 2 Co 11:29) and *skandalon* once (Rm 14:13) in connection with a Christian's responsibility to other Christians. Every other use of *skandalizo* occurs in the Gospels. Jesus often warns about offending people, that is, doing spiritual harm to others (Mk 9:42-50; see Jn 16:1). Incredibly, Jesus Himself is often the cause of offense, for those who did not believe in Him often misunderstood His words and actions (see Mt 11:6; 13:57; 15:12; 17:27; Mk 6:3; 14:27; Jn 6:61).

ª9:38 Other mss add *who didn't go along with us*
ᵇ9:41 Lit *drink in the name*; = Messiah
ᶜ9:42 A millstone turned by a donkey
ᵈ9:44,46 Other mss omit bracketed text
ᵉ9:44,46,48 Is 66:24
ᶠ9:49 Other mss add *and every sacrifice will be salted with salt*
ᵍ9:49 Lv 2:16; Ezk 43:24

make it salty? Have salt among yourselves and be at peace with one another."

THE QUESTION OF DIVORCE

10 He set out from there and went to the region of Judea and across the Jordan. Then crowds converged on Him again and, as He usually did, He began teaching them once more. ² Some •Pharisees approached Him to test Him. They asked, "Is it lawful for a man to divorce ⌊his⌋ wife?"

³ He replied to them, "What did Moses command you?"

⁴ They said, "Moses permitted us to write divorce papers and send her away."

⁵ But Jesus told them, "He wrote this commandment for you because of the hardness of your hearts. ⁶ But from the beginning of creation God^a **made them male and female.**^b

> ⁷ **For this reason a man will leave**
> **his father and mother**
> **[and be joined to his wife,]**^c
> ⁸ **and the two will become one flesh.**^d

So they are no longer two, but one flesh. ⁹ Therefore what God has joined together, man must not separate."

¹⁰ Now in the house the disciples questioned Him again about this matter. ¹¹ And He said to them, "Whoever divorces his wife and marries another commits adultery against her. ¹² Also, if she divorces her husband and marries another, she commits adultery."

BLESSING THE CHILDREN

¹³ Some people were bringing little children to Him so He might touch them, but His disciples rebuked them. ¹⁴ When Jesus saw it, He was indignant and said to them, "Let the little children come to Me. Don't stop them, for the kingdom of God belongs to such as these. ¹⁵ •I assure you: Whoever does not welcome^e the kingdom of God like a little child will never enter it." ¹⁶ Af-

---

Invest Your Life in Things That Last

The world will entice you to adopt its goals and to invest in temporal things. Rather, deny yourself and join the activity of God as He reveals it to you.

When Jesus saw it, He was indignant and said to them, "Let the little children come to Me. Don't stop them, for the kingdom of God belongs to such as these."

—Mark 10:14

---

^a**10:6** Other mss omit *God*
^b**10:6** Gn 1:27; 5:2
^c**10:7** Other mss omit bracketed text
^d**10:7-8** Gn 2:24
^e**10:15** Or *not receive*

ter taking them in His arms, He laid His hands on them and blessed them.

THE RICH YOUNG RULER

17 As He was setting out on a journey, a man ran up, knelt down before Him, and asked Him, "Good Teacher, what must I do to inherit eternal life?"
18 "Why do you call Me good?" Jesus asked him. "No one is good but One—God. 19 You know the commandments:

> Do not murder;
> do not commit adultery;
> do not steal;
> do not bear false witness;
> do not defraud;
> honor your father and mother."ª

20 He said to Him, "Teacher, I have kept all these from my youth."
21 Then, looking at him, Jesus loved him and said to him, "You lack one thing: Go, sell all you have and give to the poor, and you will have treasure in heaven. Then come,ᵇ follow Me." 22 But he was stunnedᶜ at this demand, and he went away grieving, because he had many possessions.

POSSESSIONS AND THE KINGDOM

23 Jesus looked around and said to His disciples, "How hard it is for those who have wealth to enter the kingdom of God!" 24 But the disciples were astonished at His words. Again Jesus said to them, "Children, how hard it isᵈ to enter the kingdom of God! 25 It is easier for a camel to go through the eye of a needle than for a rich person to enter the kingdom of God."
26 So they were even more astonished, saying to one another, "Then who can be saved?"
27 Looking at them, Jesus said, "With men it is impossible, but not with God, because all things are possible with God."

One Life, One Lord—No Two Ways About It

If you want to know God's will, you must respond to His invitation to love Him wholeheartedly.

Jesus looked around and said to His disciples, "How hard it is for those who have wealth to enter the kingdom of God!"
—Mark 10:23

God Is Not Bound by Your Limitations

The Christ who lived His life in complete obedience to the Father is fully present in you to enable you to know His will and accomplish it.

Looking at them, Jesus said, "With men it is impossible, but not with God, because all things are possible with God."
—Mark 10:27

ª10:19 Ex 20:12-16; Dt 5:16-20
ᵇ10:21 Other mss add *taking up the cross, and*
ᶜ10:22 Or *he became gloomy*
ᵈ10:24 Other mss add *for those trusting in wealth*

²⁸ Peter began to tell Him, "Look, we have left everything and followed You."

²⁹ "I assure you," **Jesus said,** "there is no one who has left house, brothers or sisters, mother or father,ᵃ children, or fields because of Me and the gospel, ³⁰ who will not receive 100 times more, now at this time—houses, brothers and sisters, mothers and children, and fields, with persecutions—and eternal life in the age to come. ³¹ But many who are first will be last, and the last first."

THE THIRD PREDICTION OF HIS DEATH

³² They were on the road, going up to Jerusalem, and Jesus was walking ahead of them. They were astonished, but those who followed Him were afraid. Taking the Twelve aside again, He began to tell them the things that would happen to Him.

³³ "Listen! We are going up to Jerusalem. The •Son of Man will be handed over to the •chief priests and the •scribes, and they will condemn Him to death. Then they will hand Him over to the Gentiles, ³⁴ and they will mock Him, spit on Him, flogᵇ Him, and kill Him, and He will rise after three days."

SUFFERING AND SERVICE

³⁵ Then James and John, the sons of Zebedee, approached Him and said, "Teacher, we want You to do something for us if we ask You."

³⁶ "What do you want Me to do for you?" He asked them.

³⁷ They answered Him, "Allow us to sit at Your right and at Your left in Your glory."

³⁸ But Jesus said to them, "You don't know what you're asking. Are you able to drink the cup I drink or to be baptized with the baptism I am baptized with?"

³⁹ "We are able," they told Him.

Jesus said to them, "You will drink the cup I drink, and you will be baptized with the baptism I am baptized with. ⁴⁰ But to sit at My right or left is not Mine to give; instead, it is for those it has been prepared for."

God's Way Can Be Trusted

You might like to wait until God tells you all the details before you start to follow Him. But that is not the pattern we see in Christ's life or in the Scriptures.

"I assure you," Jesus said, "there is no one who has left house, brothers or sisters, mother or father, children, or fields because of Me and the gospel, who will not receive 100 times more, now at this time . . . and eternal life in the age to come."

—Mark 10:29-30

ᵃ**10:29** Other mss add *or wife*   ᵇ**10:34** Or *scourge*

⁴¹ When the ⌊other⌋ 10 ⌊disciples⌋ heard this, they began to be indignant with James and John.

⁴² Jesus called them over and said to them, "You know that those who are regarded as rulers of the Gentiles dominate them, and their men of high positions exercise power over them. ⁴³ But it must not be like that among you. On the contrary, whoever wants to become great among you must be your servant, ⁴⁴ and whoever wants to be first among you must be a •slave to all. ⁴⁵ For even the Son of Man did not come to be served, but to serve, and to give His life—a ransom for many."ᵃ

A BLIND MAN HEALED

⁴⁶ They came to Jericho. And as He was leaving Jericho with His disciples and a large crowd, Bartimaeus (the son of Timaeus), a blind beggar, was sitting by the road. ⁴⁷ When he heard that it was Jesus the •Nazarene, he began to cry out, "Son of David, Jesus, have mercy on me!" ⁴⁸ Many people told him to keep quiet, but he was crying out all the more, "Have mercy on me, Son of David!"

⁴⁹ Jesus stopped and said, "Call him."

So they called the blind man and said to him, "Have courage! Get up; He's calling for you." ⁵⁰ He threw off his coat, jumped up, and came to Jesus.

⁵¹ Then Jesus answered him, "What do you want Me to do for you?"

"*Rabbouni*," ᵇ the blind man told Him, "I want to see!"

⁵² "Go your way," Jesus told him. "Your faith has healed you." Immediately he could see and began to follow Him on the road.

THE TRIUMPHAL ENTRY

11 When they approached Jerusalem, at Bethphage and Bethany near the •Mount of Olives, He sent two of His disciples ² and told them, "Go into the village ahead of you. As soon as you enter it, you will find a young donkey tied there, on which no one has ever sat. Untie it and bring it here. ³ If anyone says

---

WORD STUDY

Greek word: **doulos**
[DOO lahss]

Translation: *slave*

Uses in Mark's Gospel: **5**
(Mt, 30; Lk, 26; Jn, 11)

Uses in the NT: **126**

Key passage: **Mark 10:44**

Several Greek words in the NT convey the idea of one person being the servant of another. By far the most common is *doulos*, which is also the term of lowest rank and is best conveyed by the English word *slave*. Other types of servants had various responsibilities, privileges, and rights, but under Roman law the *doulos* had no rights. The slave was bought by the master from a slave auction or another slave owner (see 1 Co 7:21-23). He belonged completely to his master and had only those responsibilities and privileges granted by his master. In the NT *doulos* is normally used literally (Mt 8:9; Mk 14:47; Lk 17:7-10; Jn 13:16; Eph 6:5-9; Phm 16), but a figurative meaning describing someone who serves God and His people is also common (Mk 10:44; Ac 2:18; 4:29; Rm 1:1; 2 Co 4:5; 1 Pt 2:16; Rv 2:20). Paul has two very significant uses of *doulos*, one about Christ and the other about Christians. Philippians 2:6 refers to Jesus' condescension in the Incarnation, and Rm 6:16-18 refers to being slaves of righteousness instead of slaves of sin (see Jn 8:34).

ᵃ**10:45** Or *in the place of many*; Is 53:10-12   ᵇ**10:51** Hb for *my teacher*; Jn 20:16

to you, 'Why are you doing this?' say, 'The Lord needs it and will send it back here right away.'"

4 So they went and found a young donkey outside in the street, tied by a door. They untied it, 5 and some of those standing there said to them, "What are you doing, untying the donkey?" 6 They answered them just as Jesus had said, so they let them go. 7 Then they brought the donkey to Jesus and threw their robes on it, and He sat on it.

8 Many people spread their robes on the road, and others spread leafy branches cut from the fields.[a] 9 Then those who went ahead and those who followed kept shouting:

> •*Hosanna!*
> **Blessed is He who comes**
> **in the name of the Lord!**[b]
> 10 Blessed is the coming kingdom
> of our father David!
> *Hosanna* in the highest heaven!

11 And He went into Jerusalem and into the •temple complex. After looking around at everything, since it was already late, He went out to Bethany with the Twelve.

THE BARREN FIG TREE IS CURSED

12 The next day when they came out from Bethany, He was hungry. 13 After seeing in the distance a fig tree with leaves, He went to find out if there was anything on it. When He came to it, He found nothing but leaves, because it was not the season for figs. 14 He said to it, "May no one ever eat fruit from you again!" And His disciples heard it.

CLEANSING THE TEMPLE COMPLEX

15 They came to Jerusalem, and He went into the temple complex and began to throw out those buying and selling in the temple. He overturned the money changers' tables and the chairs of those selling doves,

---

Pray and Believe, and Watch for the Answer

Believe that He Himself will bring to pass what He has led you to pray. Then continue praying in faith and watching for it to come to pass.

"Therefore, I tell you, all the things you pray and ask for— believe that you have received them, and you will have them."

—Mark 11:24

---

[a]**11:8** Other mss read *others were cutting leafy branches from the trees and spreading them on the road*
[b]**11:9** Ps 118:26

¹⁶ and would not permit anyone to carry goods through the temple complex.

¹⁷ Then He began to teach them: "Is it not written, **My house will be called a house of prayer for all nations**?ᵃ But you have made it **a den of thieves**!"ᵇ ¹⁸ Then the •chief priests and the •scribes heard it and started looking for a way to destroy Him. For they were afraid of Him, because the whole crowd was astonished by His teaching.

¹⁹ And whenever evening came, they would go out of the city.

THE BARREN FIG TREE IS WITHERED

²⁰ Early in the morning, as they were passing by, they saw the fig tree withered from the roots up. ²¹ Then Peter remembered and said to Him, "•Rabbi, look! The fig tree that You cursed is withered."

²² Jesus replied to them, "Have faith in God. ²³ •I assure you: If anyone says to this mountain, 'Be lifted up and thrown into the sea,' and does not doubt in his heart, but believes that what he says will happen, it will be done for him. ²⁴ Therefore, I tell you, all the things you pray and ask for—believe that you have receivedᶜ them, and you will have them. ²⁵ And whenever you stand praying, if you have anything against anyone, forgive him, so that your Father in heaven will also forgive you your wrongdoing.ᵈ [²⁶ But if you don't forgive, neither will your Father in heaven forgive your wrongdoing."]ᵉ

MESSIAH'S AUTHORITY CHALLENGED

²⁷ They came again to Jerusalem. As He was walking in the temple complex, the chief priests, the scribes, and the elders came and asked Him, ²⁸ "By what authority are You doing these things? Who gave You this authority to do these things?"

²⁹ Jesus said to them, "I will ask you one question; then answer Me, and I will tell you by what authority

WORD STUDY

Greek word: *exousia*
[ehx oo SEE uh]

Translation: *authority*

Uses in Mark's Gospel: **10**
(Mt, 10; Lk, 16; Jn, 8)

Uses in the NT: **102**

Key passage: **Mark 11:27-33**

The Greek word *exousia* comes from the verb *exesti*, meaning *it is permissible, possible,* or *in one's power.* Thus, *exousia* can mean *authority* or *power.* The close synonym *dunamis* is normally translated *power.* (*Dynamite* comes from this term, though this is quite removed from the meaning of *dunamis.*) Ordinarily, *exousia* is used of authority or power derived from an external source, while *dunamis* is inherent to the one who possesses it—although this distinction can be pressed too far. In Matthew 7:29—the first instance of the word in Matthew's Gospel—*exousia* seems to refer to an inherent power that Jesus demonstrated by what He said. He did not rely on previous teachers to authenticate His message, a striking departure from the method of the rabbis. In Mark 11:27-33 *exousia* is used in its more normal sense of derived authority: the *exousia* of John the Baptist and Jesus came "from heaven," that is, from God the Father (although Jesus' enemies refused to admit this. Similarly, all *exousia* was given (by the Father) to the resurrected Lord, who then commissioned His disciples to make disciples of all nations (Mt 28:18-20).

ᵃ11:17 Is 56:7
ᵇ11:17 Jr 7:11
ᶜ11:24 Other mss read *you receive*; other mss read *you will receive*
ᵈ11:25 These are the only uses of this word in Mk. It means "the viola-tion of the Law" or "stepping over a boundary" or "departing from the path" or "trespass."
ᵉ11:26 Other mss omit bracketed text

I am doing these things. ³⁰ Was John's baptism from heaven or from men? Answer Me."

³¹ They began to argue among themselves: "If we say, 'From heaven,' He will say, 'Then why didn't you believe him?' ³² But if we say, 'From men'"—they were afraid of the crowd, because everyone thought that John was a genuine prophet. ³³ So they answered Jesus, "We don't know."

And Jesus said to them, "Neither will I tell you by what authority I do these things."

THE PARABLE OF THE VINEYARD OWNER

12 Then He began to speak to them in parables: "A man planted a vineyard, put a fence around it, dug out a pit for a winepress, and built a watchtower. Then he leased it to tenant farmers and went away. ² At harvest time he sent a •slave to the farmers to collect some of the fruit of the vineyard from the farmers. ³ But they took him, beat him, and sent him away empty-handed. ⁴ Again he sent another slave to them, and theyª hit him on the head and treated him shamefully.ᵇ ⁵ Then he sent another, and they killed that one. ⌊He⌋ also ⌊sent⌋ many others; they beat some and they killed some.

⁶ "He still had one to send, a beloved son. Finally he sent him to them, saying, 'They will respect my son.'

⁷ "But those tenant farmers said among themselves, 'This is the heir. Come, let's kill him, and the inheritance will be ours!' ⁸ So they seized him, killed him, and threw him out of the vineyard.

⁹ "Therefore, what will the ownerᶜ of the vineyard do? He will come and destroy the farmers and give the vineyard to others. ¹⁰ Haven't you read this Scripture:

> **The stone that the builders rejected**
> **has become the cornerstone.ᵈ**
> ¹¹ **This came from the Lord**
> **and is wonderful in our eyes?"ᵉ**

Obedience—Just Do It

When the Lord gives you instructions, obey immediately. Don't wait until you have figured it all out and everything makes perfect sense to you.

Jesus told them, "Give back to Caesar the things that are Caesar's, and to God the things that are God's." And they were amazed at Him.

—Mark 12:17

ª**12:4** Other mss add *threw stones and*
ᵇ**12:4** Other mss add *and sent him off*
ᶜ**12:9** Or *lord*
ᵈ**12:10** Lit *the head of the corner*
ᵉ**12:10-11** Ps 118:22-23

¹² Because they knew He had said this parable against them, they were looking for a way to arrest Him, but they were afraid of the crowd. So they left Him and went away.

GOD AND CAESAR

¹³ Then they sent some of the •Pharisees and the •Herodians to Him to trap Him by what He said.ᵃ ¹⁴ When they came, they said to Him, "Teacher, we know You are truthful and defer to no one, for You don't show partialityᵇ but teach truthfully the way of God. Is it lawful to pay taxes to Caesar or not? ¹⁵ Should we pay, or should we not pay?"

But knowing their hypocrisy, He said to them, "Why are you testing Me? Bring Me a •denarius to look at." ¹⁶ So they brought one. "Whose image and inscription is this?" He asked them.

"Caesar's," they said.

¹⁷ Then Jesus told them, "Give back to Caesar the things that are Caesar's, and to God the things that are God's." And they were amazed at Him.

THE SADDUCEES AND THE RESURRECTION

¹⁸ Some •Sadducees, who say there is no resurrection, came to Him and questioned Him: ¹⁹ "Teacher, Moses wrote for us that **if a man's brother dies**, leaves his wife behind, and **leaves no child, his brother should take the wife and produce •offspring for his brother.**ᶜ ²⁰ There were seven brothers. The first took a wife, and dying, left no offspring. ²¹ The second also took her, and he died, leaving no offspring. And the third likewise. ²² The seven alsoᵈ left no offspring. Last of all, the woman died too. ²³ In the resurrection, when they rise,ᵉ whose wife will she be, since the seven had married her?"ᶠ

²⁴ Jesus told them, "Are you not deceived because you don't know the Scriptures or the power of God?

ᵃ**12:13** Lit *trap Him in (a) word*
ᵇ**12:14** Lit *don't look on the face of men*; that is, on the outward appearance
ᶜ**12:19** Gn 38:8; Dt 25:5

ᵈ**12:22** Other mss add *had taken her and*
ᵉ**12:23** Other mss omit *when they rise*
ᶠ**12:23** Lit *the seven had her as a wife*

Obedience and Belief Go Hand in Hand

When you come to a moment of truth, you must choose whether or not to obey God. You cannot obey Him unless you believe and trust Him. You cannot believe and trust Him unless you love Him. You cannot love Him unless you know Him.

Jesus told them, "Are you not deceived because you don't know the Scriptures or the power of God?"

—Mark 12:24

25 For when they rise from the dead, they neither marry nor are given in marriage but are like angels in heaven. 26 Now concerning the dead being raised—haven't you read in the book of Moses, in the passage about the burning bush, how God spoke to him: **I am the God of Abraham and the God of Isaac and the God of Jacob?**[a] 27 He is not God of the dead but of the living. You are badly deceived."

THE PRIMARY COMMANDMENTS

28 One of the •scribes approached. When he heard them debating and saw that Jesus answered them well, he asked Him, "Which commandment is the most important of all?"[b]

29 "This is the most important,"[c] Jesus answered:

Listen, Israel! The Lord our God, the Lord is One.[d] 30 Love the Lord your God with all your heart, with all your soul, with all your mind, and with all your strength.[e] [f]

31 "The second is: **Love your neighbor as yourself.**[g] There is no other commandment greater than these."

32 Then the scribe said to Him, "You are right, Teacher! You have correctly said that He is One, and there is no one else except Him. 33 And to love Him with all your heart, with all your understanding,[h] and with all your strength, and to love your neighbor as yourself, is far more ⌊important⌋ than all the burnt offerings and sacrifices."

34 When Jesus saw that he answered intelligently, He said to him, "You are not far from the kingdom of God." And no one dared to question Him any longer.

THE QUESTION ABOUT THE MESSIAH

35 So Jesus asked this question as He taught in the •temple complex, "How can the scribes say that the

---

God Wants to Relate to You in Real Ways

A love relationship with God takes place between two real beings. A relationship with God is real and personal. He is a Person pouring His life into yours.

"He is not God of the dead but of the living."
—Mark 12:27a

Loving God Is Where Your Usefulness Starts

Focus your attention on your love relationship with God. He may be waiting until you respond to His loving invitation before entrusting an assignment to you.

"To love Him with all your heart, with all your understanding, and with all your strength, and to love your neighbor as yourself, is far more important than all the burnt offerings and sacrifices."
—Mark 12:33

---

[a]**12:26** Ex 3:6,15-16
[b]**12:28** Lit *Which commandment is first of all?*
[c]**12:29** Other mss add *of all the commandments*
[d]**12:29** Or *The Lord our God is one Lord.*
[e]**12:30** Dt 6:4-5; Jos 22:5
[f]**12:30** Other mss add *This is the first commandment.*
[g]**12:31** Lv 19:18
[h]**12:33** Other mss add *with all your soul*

•Messiah is the Son of David? [36] David himself says by the Holy Spirit:

> **The Lord declared to my Lord,**
> **'Sit at My right hand**
> **until I put Your enemies under Your feet.'**[a]

[37] David himself calls Him 'Lord'; how then can the Messiah be his Son?" And the large crowd was listening to Him with delight.

WARNING AGAINST THE SCRIBES

[38] He also said in His teaching, "Beware of the scribes, who want to go around in long robes, and who want greetings in the marketplaces, [39] the front seats in the •synagogues, and the places of honor at banquets. [40] They devour widows' houses and say long prayers just for show. These will receive harsher punishment."

THE WIDOW'S GIFT

[41] Sitting across from the temple treasury, He watched how the crowd dropped money into the treasury. Many rich people were putting in large sums. [42] And a poor widow came and dropped in two tiny coins worth very little.[b] [43] Summoning His disciples, He said to them, "•I assure you: This poor widow has put in more than all those giving to the temple treasury. [44] For they all gave out of their surplus, but she out of her poverty has put in everything she possessed—all she had to live on."

DESTRUCTION OF THE TEMPLE PREDICTED

13 As He was going out of the •temple complex, one of His disciples said to Him, "Teacher, look! What massive stones! What impressive buildings!"

[2] Jesus said to him, "Do you see these great buildings? Not one stone will be left here on another that will not be thrown down!"

---

[a]**12:36** Ps 110:1
[b]**12:42** Lit *dropped in two lepta, which is a quadrans*; the *lepton* was the smallest and least valuable

Gk coin in use. The *quadrans*, ¹⁄₆₄ of a daily wage, was the smallest Roman coin.

WORD STUDY

Greek word: **sunagoge**
[soon ah goh GAY]

Translation: **synagogue**

Uses in Mark's Gospel: **8**
(Mt, 9; Lk, 15; Jn, 2)

Uses in the NT: **56**

Key passage: **Mark 12:39**

The Greek noun *sunagoge* comes from the verb *sunago*, meaning *to bring* or *gather together*; thus, a *sunagoge* is *a gathering*, referring either to the place or the people (that is, an assembly or congregation). Among Greek speaking Jews, *sunagoge* was used for the Hebrew term *qahal* and the Aramaic *keneset*, both meaning *a gathering* and referring to either the place or the people.

The synagogue developed in Jewish life after the Babylonian exile and the destruction of Jerusalem and the temple (586 B.C.). After the exile ended, the temple was rebuilt and the sacrificial system resumed (515 B.C.), but by then synagogues were emerging as centralized places of worship emphasizing the study of the law of Moses in towns where they existed. Synagogues eventually replaced the temple as focal points of Jewish worship since they were more accessible to those not living near Jerusalem. Such a shift in worship patterns gave rise to rabbis and synagogue elders who challenged the established authority of the priesthood. By the time of Jesus, the lines of spiritual authority were drawn between the Sadducees, who controlled the priesthood and temple worship, and the Pharisees, who exercised influence over the synagogues, the rabbis and elders, and thus the common people.

WORD STUDY

Greek word: **SOZO**
[SOH zoh]

Translation: **deliver**

Uses in Mark's Gospel: **15**
(Mt, 15; Lk, 17; Jn, 6)

Uses in the NT: **106**

Key passage: **Mark 13:13**

The Greek verb *sozo* literally means *to preserve* or *keep safe* with an underlying idea of *making whole*. The term can refer to saving someone from physical harm (Mt 8:25) or death (Mt 14:30; Ac 27:20,31; Heb 5:7), healing (Mk 5:23,28,34; 6:56; Jms 5:15), exorcism (Lk 8:36), or deliverance from a severe ordeal (Jn 12:27; Jd 5). Of course, the most common use of *sozo* in the NT, especially in Acts and the Epistles, is to describe the various aspects of salvation.

Two important nouns are derived from *sozo:* (1) *soteria,* which means *salvation* (in the redemptive sense) or *deliverance* (from physical death or danger; see Ac 7:25; 27:34), the former being by far the more common; and (2) *soter,* which means *Savior* and is always a reference to either the Father or Jesus Christ in the work of redemption. A comparison of the NT uses of *sozo* and *soteria* indicates that salvation has three aspects. First, a person is saved from sin by grace through faith in Christ (Jn 3:17; Eph 2:5,8-9). Second, a believer is being saved as he matures in the Christian life (Php 2:12-13; 1 Tm 2:15; 4:16; Jms 1:21). Third, a believer will be saved from experiencing God's wrath in the end times (Mk 13:13; Rm 5:9-10; 13:11; 1 Th 5:9-10). The first happens at a specific moment in a person's life; the second is an ongoing process throughout a Christian's life; the third will not occur until Christ's return.

SIGNS OF THE END OF THE AGE

3 While He was sitting on the •Mount of Olives across from the temple complex, Peter, James, John, and Andrew asked Him privately, 4 "Tell us, when will these things happen? And what will be the sign when all these things are about to take place?"
5 Then Jesus began by telling them: "Watch out that no one deceives you. 6 Many will come in My name, saying, 'I am He,' and they will deceive many. 7 When you hear of wars and rumors of wars, don't be alarmed; these things must take place, but the end is not yet. 8 For nation will rise up against nation, and kingdom against kingdom. There will be earthquakes in various places, and famines.ª These are the beginning of birth pains.

PERSECUTIONS PREDICTED

9 "But you, be on your guard! They will hand you over to sanhedrins,ᵇ and you will be flogged in the •synagogues. You will stand before governors and kings because of Me, as a witness to them. 10 And the good newsᶜ must first be proclaimed to all nations. 11 So when they arrest you and hand you over, don't worry beforehand what you will say. On the contrary, whatever is given to you in that hour—say it. For it isn't you speaking, but the Holy Spirit. 12 Then brother will betray brother to death, and a father his child. Children will rise up against parents and put them to death. 13 And you will be hated by everyone because of My name. But the one who endures to the end will be delivered.ᵈ

THE GREAT TRIBULATION

14 "When you see the **abomination that causes desolation**ᵉ standing where it should not" (let the reader understand),ᶠ "then those in Judea must flee to the mountains! 15 A man on the housetop must not come down or go in to get anything out of his house.

ª**13:8** Other mss add *and disturbances*
ᵇ**13:9** Local Jewish courts or local councils
ᶜ**13:10** Or *the gospel*

ᵈ**13:13** Or *saved*
ᵉ**13:14** Dn 9:27
ᶠ**13:14** These are, most likely, Mark's words to his readers.

[16] And a man in the field must not go back to get his clothes. [17] Woe to pregnant women and nursing mothers in those days! [18] Pray it[a] won't happen in winter. [19] For those will be days of tribulation, the kind that hasn't been from the beginning of the world,[b] which God created, until now and never will be again! [20] Unless the Lord limited those days, no one would survive.[c] But He limited those days because of the elect, whom He chose.

[21] "Then if anyone tells you, 'Look, here is the •Messiah! Look—there!' do not believe it! [22] For false messiahs[d] and false prophets will rise up and will perform signs and wonders to lead astray, if possible, the elect. [23] And you must watch! I have told you everything in advance.

THE COMING OF THE SON OF MAN

[24] "But in those days, after that tribulation:

> The sun will be darkened,
> and the moon will not shed its light;
> [25] the stars will be falling from the sky,
> and the celestial powers will be shaken.

[26] Then they will see the •Son of Man coming in clouds with great power and glory. [27] He will send out the angels and gather His elect from the four winds, from the end of the earth to the end of the sky.

THE PARABLE OF THE FIG TREE

[28] "Learn this parable from the fig tree: As soon as its branch becomes tender and sprouts leaves, you know that summer is near. [29] In the same way, when you see these things happening, know[e] that He[f] is near—at the door! [30] •I assure you: This generation will certainly not pass away until all these things take place. [31] Heaven and earth will pass away, but My words will never pass away.

Watch for Things to Begin Lining Up

When God speaks—and what He is saying through the Bible, prayer, circumstances, and the church begin to line up to say the same thing—you can proceed with confidence to follow God's direction.

"In the same way, when you see these things happening, know that He is near—at the door!"

—Mark 13:29

---

[a]**13:18** Other mss read *pray that your escape*
[b]**13:19** Lit *creation*
[c]**13:20** Lit *days, all flesh would not survive*
[d]**13:22** Or *false christs*
[e]**13:29** Or *you know*
[f]**13:29** Or *it; = summer*

NO ONE KNOWS THE DAY OR HOUR

32 "Now concerning that day or hour no one knows—neither the angels in heaven nor the Son—except the Father. 33 Watch! Be alert![a] For you don't know when the time is ₍coming₎. 34 It is like a man on a journey, who left his house, gave authority to his •slaves, gave each one his work, and commanded the doorkeeper to be alert. 35 Therefore be alert, since you don't know when the master of the house is coming—whether in the evening or at midnight or at the crowing of the rooster or early in the morning. 36 Otherwise, he might come suddenly and find you sleeping. 37 And what I say to you, I say to everyone: Be alert!"

THE PLOT TO KILL JESUS

14 After two days it was the •Passover and the Festival of •Unleavened Bread. The •chief priests and the •scribes were looking for a treacherous way to arrest and kill Him. 2 "Not during the festival," they said, "or there may be rioting among the people."

THE ANOINTING AT BETHANY

3 While He was in Bethany at the house of Simon who had a serious skin disease, as He was reclining at the table, a woman came with an alabaster jar of pure and expensive fragrant oil of nard. She broke the jar and poured it on His head. 4 But some were expressing indignation to one another: "Why has this fragrant oil been wasted? 5 For this oil might have been sold for more than 300 •denarii and given to the poor." And they began to scold her.

6 Then Jesus said, "Leave her alone. Why are you bothering her? She has done a noble thing for Me. 7 You always have the poor with you, and you can do good for them whenever you want, but you do not always have Me. 8 She has done what she could; she has anointed My body in advance for burial. 9 •I assure you: Wherever the gospel is proclaimed in the whole world, what this woman has done will also be told in memory of her."

Wait with Your Eyes Wide Open

Waiting on the Lord is anything but inactive. While you wait on Him, you will be praying with a passion to know Him, His purposes, and His ways. You will be watching circumstances and asking God to interpret them by revealing to you His perspective. You will be sharing with other believers to find out what God is saying to them.

"Watch! Be alert! For you don't know when the time is coming."

—Mark 13:33

[a]13:33 Other mss add *and pray*

[10] Then Judas Iscariot, one of the Twelve, went to the chief priests to hand Him over to them. [11] And when they heard this, they were glad and promised to give him silver.[a] So he started looking for a good opportunity to betray Him.

PREPARATION FOR PASSOVER

[12] On the first day of Unleavened Bread, when they sacrifice the Passover lamb, His disciples asked Him, "Where do You want us to go and prepare the Passover so You may eat it?" [13] So He sent two of His disciples and told them, "Go into the city, and a man carrying a water jug will meet you. Follow him. [14] Wherever he enters, tell the owner of the house, 'The Teacher says, "Where is the guest room for Me to eat the Passover with My disciples?"' [15] He will show you a large room upstairs, furnished and ready. Make the preparations for us there." [16] So the disciples went out, entered the city, and found it just as He had told them, and they prepared the Passover.

BETRAYAL AT THE PASSOVER

[17] When evening came, He arrived with the Twelve. [18] While they were reclining and eating, Jesus said, "I assure you: One of you will betray Me—one who is eating with Me!"

[19] They began to be distressed and to say to Him one by one, "Surely not I?"

[20] He said to them, "[It is] one of the Twelve—the one who is dipping [bread] with Me in the bowl. [21] For the •Son of Man will go just as it is written about Him, but woe to that man by whom the Son of Man is betrayed! It would have been better for that man if he had not been born."

THE FIRST LORD'S SUPPER

[22] As they were eating, He took bread, blessed and broke it, gave it to them, and said, "Take [it];[b] this is My body."

Experience Comes from Obedience

To experience Him at work in and through you, you must obey Him. When you obey Him, He will accomplish His work through you, and you will come to know Him by experience.

The disciples went out, entered the city, and found it just as He had told them, and they prepared the Passover.
—Mark 14:16

---

[a]**14:11** Or *money*; in Mt 26:15 it is specified as 30 pieces of silver; see Zch 11:12-13

[b]**14:22** Other mss add *eat;*

23 Then He took a cup, and after giving thanks, He gave it to them, and so they all drank from it. 24 He said to them, "This is My blood ₁that establishes₁ the covenant;ᵃ it is shed for many. 25 I assure you: I will no longer drink of the fruit of the vine until that day when I drink it in a new wayᵇ in the kingdom of God." 26 After singing psalms,ᶜ they went out to the •Mount of Olives.

PETER'S DENIAL PREDICTED

27 Then Jesus said to them, "All of you will run away,ᵈ ᵉ because it is written:

**I will strike the shepherd,
and the sheep will be scattered.ᶠ**

28 But after I have been resurrected, I will go ahead of you to Galilee."

29 Peter told Him, "Even if everyone runs away, I will certainly not!"

30 "I assure you," Jesus said to him, "today, this very night, before the rooster crows twice, you will deny Me three times!"

31 But he kept insisting, "If I have to die with You, I will never deny You!" And they all said the same thing.

THE PRAYER IN THE GARDEN

32 Then they came to a place named Gethsemane, and He told His disciples, "Sit here while I pray." 33 He took Peter, James, and John with Him, and He began to be deeply distressed and horrified. 34 Then He said to them, "My soul is swallowed up in sorrowᵍ —to the point of death. Remain here and stay awake." 35 Then He went a little farther, fell to the ground, and began to pray that if it were possible, the hour might pass from Him. 36 And He said, "•*Abba*, Father! All things are possible for You. Take this cup away from Me. Nevertheless, not what I will, but what You will."

When in Doubt, Do What You Know

Whenever a silence comes, continue doing the last thing God told you and watch and wait for a fresh encounter with Him.

"After I have been resurrected, I will go ahead of you to Galilee."

—Mark 14:28

Is Your Faith Bigger than Your Questions?

Even when His will doesn't make sense from your human perspective, your obedience will reveal that His will was right.

He went a little farther, fell to the ground, and began to pray that if it were possible, the hour might pass from Him.

—Mark 14:35

ᵃ**14:24** Other mss read *the new covenant*
ᵇ**14:25** Or *drink new wine*; lit *drink it new*
ᶜ**14:26** Pss 113–118 were sung during and after the Passover meal.
ᵈ**14:27** Other mss add *because of Me this night*
ᵉ**14:27** Or *•stumble*
ᶠ**14:27** Zch 13:7
ᵍ**14:34** Or *I am deeply grieved*

37 Then He came and found them sleeping. "Simon, are you sleeping?" He asked Peter. "Couldn't you stay awake one hour? 38 Stay awake and pray so that you won't enter into temptation. The spirit is willing, but the flesh is weak."

39 Once again He went away and prayed, saying the same thing. 40 And He came again and found them sleeping, because they could not keep their eyes open.[a] They did not know what to say to Him. 41 Then He came a third time and said to them, "Are you still sleeping and resting? Enough! The time has come. Look, the Son of Man is being betrayed into the hands of sinners. 42 Get up; let's go! See—My betrayer is near."

THE JUDAS KISS

43 While He was still speaking, Judas, one of the Twelve, suddenly arrived. With him was a mob, with swords and clubs, from the chief priests, the scribes, and the elders. 44 His betrayer had given them a signal. "The One I kiss," he said, "He's the One; arrest Him and take Him away under guard." 45 So when he came, he went right up to Him and said, "•Rabbi!"—and kissed Him. 46 Then they took hold of Him and arrested Him. 47 And one of those who stood by drew his sword, struck the high priest's •slave, and cut off his ear.

48 But Jesus said to them, "Have you come out with swords and clubs, as though I were a criminal,[b] to capture Me? 49 Every day I was among you, teaching in the •temple complex, and you didn't arrest Me. But the Scriptures must be fulfilled." 50 Then they all deserted Him and ran away.

51 Now a certain young man,[c] having a linen cloth wrapped around his naked body, was following Him. They caught hold of him, 52 but he left the linen cloth behind and ran away naked.

JESUS FACES THE SANHEDRIN

53 They led Jesus away to the high priest, and all the chief priests, the elders, and the scribes convened.

WORD STUDY

Greek word: **abba** [ab bah]
Translation: **Abba**
Uses in Mark's Gospel: **1**
Uses in the NT: **3**
Key passage: **Mark 14:36**

In its original usage the Aramaic term *abba* was probably used by small children to address their father (*daddy*). By the 1st c. A.D., its usage had expanded and the single word *abba* could be substituted for the phrases "my father" and "our father," and older children used it to address their father as a term of endearment (*Father, Dad*). Because of the term's familiar nature (and perhaps because they believed it to be disrespectful when addressed to God), the Jews were probably shocked when Jesus used *abba* to address God (i.e., *Father, My Father, Our Father*).

In the Gospels, *abba* occurs only in Mk 14:36, however, the numerous occurrences of the Greek *pater* (*father*; cf. Mt 6:9; 11:25-27; 26:39,42; Jn 5:36; 11:41) probably indicate what was originally Aramaic speech (*abba*). Elsewhere, *abba* occurs only in Roman 8:15 and Galatians 4:6, indicating that Christians can use this term to refer to God.

---

[a]14:40 Lit *because their eyes were weighed down*
[b]14:48 Lit *as against a criminal*
[c]14:51 Perhaps John Mark who later wrote this Gospel

54 Peter followed Him at a distance, right into the high priest's courtyard. He was sitting with the temple police,[a] warming himself by the fire.[b]

55 The chief priests and the whole •Sanhedrin were looking for testimony against Jesus to put Him to death, but they could find none. 56 For many were giving false testimony against Him, but the testimonies did not agree. 57 Some stood up and were giving false testimony against Him, stating, 58 "We heard Him say, 'I will demolish this sanctuary made by ⌊human⌋ hands, and in three days I will build another not made by hands.'" 59 Yet their testimony did not agree even on this.

60 Then the high priest stood up before them all and questioned Jesus, "Don't You have an answer to what these men are testifying against You?" 61 But He kept silent and did not answer anything. Again the high priest questioned Him, "Are You the •Messiah, the Son of the Blessed One?"

62 "I am," said Jesus, "and all of you[c] will see **the Son of Man seated at the right hand** of the Power and **coming with the clouds of heaven**."[d]

63 Then the high priest tore his robes and said, "Why do we still need witnesses? 64 You have heard the blasphemy! What is your decision?"[e]

And they all condemned Him to be deserving of death. 65 Then some began to spit on Him, to blindfold Him, and to beat Him, saying, "Prophesy!" Even the temple police took Him and slapped Him.

PETER DENIES HIS LORD

66 While Peter was in the courtyard below, one of the high priest's servants came. 67 When she saw Peter warming himself, she looked at him and said, "You also were with that •Nazarene, Jesus."

68 But he denied it: "I don't know or understand what you're talking about!" Then he went out to the entryway, and a rooster crowed.[f]

69 When the servant saw him again she began to tell those standing nearby, "This man is one of them!"

Flesh vs. Spirit— Who's Going to Win?

Seek to bring every physical desire under the control of the Holy Spirit so that nothing will impede your accomplishing what Jesus asks of you.

Immediately a rooster crowed a second time, and Peter remembered when Jesus had spoken the word to him, "Before the rooster crows twice, you will deny Me three times." When he thought about it, he began to weep.
—Mark 14:72

[a]14:54 Or *the officers*; lit *the servants*
[b]14:54 Lit *light*
[c]14:62 Lit *and you* (pl in Gk)
[d]14:62 Ps 110:1; Dn 7:13
[e]14:64 Lit *How does it appear to you?*
[f]14:68 Other mss omit *and a rooster crowed*

[70] But again he denied it. After a little while those standing there said to Peter again, "You certainly are one of them, since you're also a Galilean!"[a]

[71] Then he started to curse[b] and to swear with an oath, "I don't know this man you're talking about!"

[72] Immediately a rooster crowed a second time, and Peter remembered when Jesus had spoken the word to him, "Before the rooster crows twice, you will deny Me three times." When he thought about it, he began to weep.[c]

JESUS FACES PILATE

15 As soon as it was morning, the •chief priests had a meeting with the elders, •scribes, and the whole •Sanhedrin. After tying Jesus up, they led Him away and handed Him over to •Pilate.

[2] So Pilate asked Him, "Are You the King of the Jews?" He answered him, "You have said it."[d]

[3] And the chief priests began to accuse Him of many things. [4] Then Pilate questioned Him again, "Are You not answering anything? Look how many things they are accusing You of!" [5] But Jesus still did not answer anything, so Pilate was amazed.

JESUS OR BARABBAS

[6] At the festival it was Pilate's custom to release for the people a prisoner they requested. [7] There was one named Barabbas, who was in prison with rebels who had committed murder during the rebellion. [8] The crowd came up and began to ask ⌊Pilate⌋ to do for them as was his custom. [9] So Pilate answered them, "Do you want me to release the King of the Jews for you?" [10] For he knew it was because of envy that the chief priests had handed Him over. [11] But the chief priests stirred up the crowd so that he would release Barabbas to them instead.

[12] Pilate asked them again, "Then what do you want me to do with the One you call the King of the Jews?"

Don't Be Surprised to Be Misunderstood

You will fail to follow Christ as you should if you let others' reaction determine your faithfulness.

Pilate asked Him, "Are You the King of the Jews?" He answered him, "You have said it." And the chief priests began to accuse Him of many things.

—Mark 15:2-3

---

[a]**14:70** Other mss add *and your speech shows it*
[b]**14:71** To call down curses on himself if what he said weren't true
[c]**14:72** Or *he burst into tears*, or *he broke down*
[d]**15:2** Or *That is true*, an affirmative oath; Mt 26:64; 27:11

¹³ Again they shouted, "Crucify Him!"
¹⁴ Then Pilate said to them, "Why? What has He done wrong?"

But they shouted, "Crucify Him!" all the more.
¹⁵ Then, willing to gratify the crowd, Pilate released Barabbas to them. And after having Jesus flogged,ᵃ he handed Him over to be crucified.

MOCKED BY THE MILITARY

¹⁶ Then the soldiers led Him away into the courtyard (that is, •headquarters) and called the whole •company together. ¹⁷ They dressed Him in a purple robe, twisted together a crown of thorns, and put it on Him. ¹⁸ And they began to salute Him, "Hail, King of the Jews!" ¹⁹ They kept hitting Him on the head with a reed and spitting on Him. Getting down on their knees, they were paying Him homage. ²⁰ When they had mocked Him, they stripped Him of the purple robe, put His clothes on Him, and led Him out to crucify Him.

CRUCIFIED BETWEEN TWO CRIMINALS

²¹ They forced a man coming in from the country, who was passing by, to carry Jesus' cross. He was Simon, a Cyrenian, the father of Alexander and Rufus. ²² And they brought Jesus to the place called *Golgotha* (which means Skull Place). ²³ They tried to give Him wine mixed with myrrh, but He did not take it. ²⁴ Then they crucified Him and divided His clothes, casting lots for them to decide what each would get. ²⁵ Now it was nine in the morningᵇ when they crucified Him. ²⁶ The inscription of the charge written against Him was

THE KING OF THE JEWS.

²⁷ They crucified two criminalsᶜ with Him, one on His right and one on His left. [²⁸ So the Scripture was fulfilled that says: **And He was counted among outlaws**.]ᵈ ᵉ
²⁹ Those who passed by were yelling insults atᶠ Him, shak-

See God's Love in the Suffering Christ

If you have lost your wonder at the incredible gift of salvation that has been given to you, you need to revisit the cross and witness your Savior suffering for you.

They dressed Him in a purple robe, twisted together a crown of thorns, and put it on Him. And they began to salute Him, "Hail, King of the Jews!"

—Mark 15:17-18

ᵃ**15:15** Roman flogging was done with a whip made of leather strips embedded with pieces of bone or metal that brutally tore the flesh.
ᵇ**15:25** Lit *was the third hour*

ᶜ**15:27** Or *revolutionaries*
ᵈ**15:28** Other mss omit bracketed text
ᵉ**15:28** Is 53:12
ᶠ**15:29** Lit *passed by blasphemed*

ing their heads, and saying, "Ha! The One who would demolish the sanctuary and build it in three days, ³⁰ save Yourself by coming down from the cross!" ³¹ In the same way, the chief priests with the scribes were mocking Him to one another and saying, "He saved others; He cannot save Himself! ³² Let the •Messiah, the King of Israel, come down now from the cross, so that we may see and believe." Even those who were crucified with Him were taunting Him.

THE DEATH OF JESUS

³³ When it was noon,ᵃ darkness came over the whole landᵇ until three in the afternoon.ᶜ ³⁴ And at threeᶜ Jesus cried out with a loud voice, *"Eloi, Eloi, lemá*ᵈ *sabachtháni?"* which is translated, **"My God, My God, why have You forsaken Me?"**ᵉ

³⁵ When some of those standing there heard this, they said, "Look, He's calling for Elijah!" ³⁶ Someone ran and filled a sponge with sour wine, fixed it on a reed, offered Him a drink, and said, "Let's see if Elijah comes to take Him down!"

³⁷ But Jesus let out a loud cry and breathed His last. ³⁸ Then the curtain of the sanctuaryᶠ was split in two from top to bottom. ³⁹ When the •centurion, who was standing opposite Him, saw the way Heᵍ breathed His last, he said, "This man really was God's Son!"ʰ

⁴⁰ There were also women looking on from a distance. Among them were •Mary Magdalene, Mary the mother of James the younger and of Joses, and Salome. ⁴¹ When He was in Galilee, they would follow Him and help Him. Many other women had come up with Him to Jerusalem.

THE BURIAL OF JESUS

⁴² When it was already evening, because it was preparation day (that is, the day before the Sabbath), ⁴³ Joseph of Arimathea, a prominent member of the

WORD STUDY

Greek word: **enkataleipo**
[en kah tah LIGH poh]

Translation: **forsake**

Uses in Mark's Gospel: **1** (Mt, 1)

Uses in the NT: **10**

Key passage: **Mark 15:34**

The Greek verb *enkataleipo* is a double compound that produces an intensive form of a verb meaning *to lack* or *leave (leipo)*. With one exception (Rm 9:29), each occurrence of the term in the NT means *forsake* or *abandon*. In Mark 15:34 and Matthew 27:46 *enkataleipo* is used to translate the Aramaic word *sabach*, which in turn translates the original Hebrew *'azab* in Psalm 22:1. Jesus' quote of this verse occurred toward the end of three hours of darkness (Mk 15:33) during which He endured God's wrath by being forsaken by the Father as payment for the sins of mankind. The word *enkataleipo* also occurs in Hebrews 13:5, "I will never forsake you." Since this promise is addressed to believers, it indicates that while God was willing to forsake Jesus on the cross in order to redeem us, He is not now willing to forsake those whom He has redeemed.

ᵃ**15:33** Lit *the sixth hour*
ᵇ**15:33** Or *whole earth*
ᶜ**15:33,34** Lit *the ninth hour*
ᵈ**15:34** Other mss read *lama*; other mss read *lima*
ᵉ**15:34** Ps 22:1

ᶠ**15:38** A heavy curtain separated the inner room of the temple from the outer.
ᵍ**15:39** Other mss read *saw that He cried out like this and*
ʰ**15:39** Or *the Son of God*; Mk 1:1

WORD STUDY

Greek word: **sabbaton**
[SAHB bah than]

Translation: **Sabbath**

Uses in Mark's Gospel: **12**
(Mt, 11; Lk, 20; Jn, 13)

Uses in the NT: **68**

Key passage: **Mark 16:1**

The Greek word *sabbaton* represents the Hebrew term *shabbat,* which comes from the Hebrew word for the number seven *(shabua).* The Fourth Commandment prohibited working on the Sabbath since it was a celebration of God's six days of work as Creator being finished (Ex 20:8-11; see Gn 2:1-3).

By NT times Jewish tradition had attempted to explain in detail exactly what constituted *work,* and in so doing the religious laws about keeping the Sabbath had enslaved the people instead of giving them rest. Jesus often addressed this problem, which was a constant source of antagonism between Him and the Jewish leaders (Mk 2:23-28; 3:1-5; Lk 13:10-17; 14:1-6; Jn 5:1-18; 7:22-23; 9:1-41).

One of the most significant aspects of Sabbath celebration in the NT involves establishing a chronology for Jesus' death and resurrection. The crucifixion of Jesus occurred on a Friday, the day before the weekly Sabbath (Lk 23:54,56; Jn 19:31). This was also the Sabbath of the week of Unleavened Bread (Lv 23:6-8; see vv. 4-5). Jesus arose from the dead on Sunday, the first day of the week, the day following the weekly Sabbath on Saturday (Mt 28:1; Mk 16:1; see Lk 24:1; Jn 20:1), which was also the day the Feast of Firstfruits was celebrated (Lv 23:9-14; see 1 Co 15:20).

Sanhedrin who was himself looking forward to the kingdom of God, came and boldly went in to Pilate and asked for Jesus' body. ⁴⁴ Pilate was surprised that He was already dead. Summoning the centurion, he asked him whether He had already died. ⁴⁵ When he found out from the centurion, he gave the corpse to Joseph. ⁴⁶ After he bought some fine linen, he took Him down and wrapped Him in the linen. Then he placed Him in a tomb cut out of the rock, and rolled a stone against the entrance to the tomb. ⁴⁷ Now Mary Magdalene and Mary the mother of Joses were watching where He was placed.

RESURRECTION MORNING

16 When the Sabbath was over, •Mary Magdalene, Mary the mother of James, and Salome bought spices, so they could go and anoint Him. ² Very early in the morning, on the first day of the week, they went to the tomb at sunrise. ³ They were saying to one another, "Who will roll away the stone from the entrance to the tomb for us?" ⁴ Looking up, they observed that the stone—which was very large—had been rolled away. ⁵ When they entered the tomb, they saw a young man[a] dressed in a long white robe sitting on the right side; they were amazed and alarmed.[b]

⁶ "Don't be alarmed," he told them. "You are looking for Jesus the •Nazarene, who was crucified. He has been resurrected! He is not here! See the place where they put Him. ⁷ But go, tell His disciples and Peter, 'He is going ahead of you to Galilee; you will see Him there just as He told you.'"

⁸ So they went out and started running from the tomb, because trembling and astonishment overwhelmed them. And they said nothing to anyone, since they were afraid.

APPEARANCES OF THE RISEN LORD

[⁹ Early on the first day of the week, after He had risen, He appeared first to Mary Magdalene, out of whom He had driven seven demons. ¹⁰ She went and

---

[a]**16:5** In Mt 28:2, the young man = an angel

[b]**16:5** *Amazed and alarmed* translate the idea of one Gk word.

reported to those who had been with Him, as they were mourning and weeping. [11] Yet, when they heard that He was alive and had been seen by her, they did not believe it. [12] Then after this, He appeared in a different form to two of them walking on their way into the country. [13] And they went and reported it to the rest, who did not believe them either.

THE GREAT COMMISSION

[14] Later, He appeared to the Eleven themselves as they were reclining at the table. He rebuked their unbelief and hardness of heart, because they did not believe those who saw Him after He had been resurrected. [15] Then He said to them, "Go into all the world and preach the gospel to the whole creation. [16] Whoever believes and is baptized will be saved, but whoever does not believe will be condemned. [17] And these signs will accompany those who believe: In My name they will drive out demons; they will speak in new languages; [18] they will pick up snakes;[a] if they should drink anything deadly, it will never harm them; they will lay hands on the sick, and they will get well."

THE ASCENSION

[19] Then after speaking to them, the Lord Jesus was taken up into heaven and sat down at the right hand of God. [20] And they went out and preached everywhere, the Lord working with them and confirming the word by the accompanying signs.][b]

God Does Give Second Chances

Don't give up if you've failed the Lord. Remember what happened to Peter. God has not yet finished developing you as a disciple.

"Go, tell His disciples and Peter, 'He is going ahead of you to Galilee; you will see Him there just as He told you.'"
—Mark 16:7

---

[a]**16:18** Other mss add *with their hands*

[b]**16:9-20** Other mss omit bracketed text

LUKE

THE DEDICATION TO THEOPHILUS

1 Many have undertaken to compile a narrative about the events that have been fulfilled[a] among us, ² just as the original eyewitnesses and servants of the word handed them down to us. ³ It also seemed good to me, since I have carefully investigated everything from the very first, to write to you in orderly sequence, most honorable Theophilus, ⁴ so that you may know the certainty of the things about which you have been instructed.[b]

GABRIEL PREDICTS JOHN'S BIRTH

⁵ In the days of King •Herod of Judea, there was a priest of Abijah's division[c] named Zechariah. His wife was from the daughters of Aaron, and her name was Elizabeth. ⁶ Both were righteous in God's sight, living without blame according to all the commandments and requirements of the Lord. ⁷ But they had no children[d] because Elizabeth could not conceive,[e] and both of them were well along in years.[f]

⁸ When his division was on duty and he was serving as priest before God, ⁹ it happened that he was chosen by lot, according to the custom of the priesthood, to enter the sanctuary of the Lord and burn incense. ¹⁰ At the hour of incense the whole assembly of the people was praying outside. ¹¹ An angel of the Lord appeared to him, standing to the right of the altar of incense.

---

[a]1:1 Or *events that have been accomplished*, or *events most surely believed*
[b]1:4 Or *informed*
[c]1:5 One of the 24 divisions of priests appointed by David for temple service; 1 Ch 24:10
[d]1:7 Lit *child*
[e]1:7 Lit *Elizabeth was sterile* or *barren*
[f]1:7 Lit *in their days*

12 When Zechariah saw him, he was startled and overcome with fear.ᵃ 13 But the angel said to him:

> Do not be afraid, Zechariah,
> because your prayer has been heard.
> Your wife Elizabeth will bear you a son,
> and you will name him John.
> 14 There will be joy and delight for you,
> and many will rejoice at his birth.
> 15 For he will be great in the sight of the Lord
> and will never drink wine or beer.
> He will be filled with the Holy Spirit
> while still in his mother's womb.
> 16 He will turn many of the sons of Israel
> to the Lord their God.
> 17 And he will go before Him
> in the spirit and power of Elijah,
> to turn the hearts of fathers
> to their children,
> and the disobedient
> to the understanding of the righteous,
> to make ready for the Lord
> a prepared people.

18 "How can I know this?" Zechariah asked the angel. "For I am an old man, and my wife is well along in
years."ᵇ

19 The angel answered him, "I am Gabriel, who
stands in the presence of God, and I was sent to speak
to you and tell you this good news. 20 Now listen! You
will become silent and unable to speak until the day
these things take place, because you did not believe my
words, which will be fulfilled in their proper time."

21 Meanwhile, the people were waiting for Zechariah,
amazed that he stayed so long in the sanctuary. 22 When
he did come out, he could not speak to them. Then
they realized that he had seen a vision in the sanctuary.
He kept making signs to them and remained speechless. 23 When the days of his ministry were completed,
he went back home.

24 After these days his wife Elizabeth conceived and
kept herself in seclusion for five months. She said,
25 "The Lord has done this for me. He has looked with

WORD STUDY

Greek word: **horao**
[horh RAH oh]

Translation: **appear**

Uses in Luke's Gospel: **81**
(Mt, 108; Mk, 50; Jn, 67)

Uses in Luke's Writings: **147**

Uses in the NT: **454**

Key passage: **Luke 1:11**

The Greek verb *horao* is one of
several NT words meaning *to see,
look, watch,* or the like. Most occurrences of *horao* mean *to see,
beware,* or *watch out.* A special
use of *horao* is in reference to appearances of supernatural beings
or entities that enter the physical
realm. In such cases *horao* means
appeared. Examples include Moses' and Elijah's appearance at
Jesus' transfiguration (Mt 17:3; Mk
9:4); God's appearance to Abraham (Ac 7:2) and then to Moses
(Ac 7:30); angelic appearances
to Zachariah (Lk 1:11) and Jesus
(Lk 22:43); and Paul's Macedonian
vision (Acts 16:9). This special
meaning of *horao* is also used for
Jesus' resurrection appearances,
both during the 40 days on earth
(Lk 24:34; Ac 13:31; 1 Co 15:5,6,7)
and after the ascension (Ac 26:16;
1 Co 15:8). Three apocalyptic appearances are recorded in Revelation: the ark in heaven (11:19),
and the woman (12:1) pursued
by the dragon (12:3).

ᵃ1:12 Lit *and fear fell on him*   ᵇ1:18 Lit *in her days*

favor in these days to take away my disgrace among the people."

GABRIEL PREDICTS JESUS' BIRTH

26 In the sixth month, the angel Gabriel was sent by God to a town in Galilee called Nazareth, 27 to a virgin •engaged to a man named Joseph, of the house of David. The virgin's name was Mary. 28 And ˻the angel˼ came to her and said, "Rejoice, favored woman! The Lord is with you."ᵃ 29 But she was deeply troubled by this statement, wondering what kind of greeting this could be. 30 Then the angel told her:

> Do not be afraid, Mary,
> for you have found favor with God.
> 31 Now listen:
> You will conceive and give birth to a son,
> and you will call His name JESUS.
> 32 He will be great
> and will be called the Son of the Most High,
> and the Lord God will give Him
> the throne of His father David.
> 33 He will reign over the house of Jacob forever,
> and His kingdom will have no end.

34 Mary asked the angel, "How can this be, since I have not been intimate with a man?"ᵇ
35 The angel replied to her:

> "The Holy Spirit will come upon you,
> and the power of the Most High
> will overshadow you.
> Therefore the holy One to be born
> will be called the Son of God.

36 And consider your relative Elizabeth—even she has conceived a son in her old age, and this is the sixth month for her who was called barren. 37 For nothing will be impossible with God."
38 "I am the Lord's •slave,"ᶜ said Mary. "May it be done to me according to your word." Then the angel left her.

Nothing Is Impossible with God

When God speaks of doing the impossible, it is no longer absurd. The miraculous should be a part of the Christian's experience.

"Nothing will be impossible with God."
—Luke 1:37

ᵃ1:28 Other mss add *blessed are you among women*
ᵇ1:34 Lit *since I do not know a man*
ᶜ1:38 Lit *Look, the Lord's slave*

MARY'S VISIT TO ELIZABETH

³⁹ In those days Mary set out and hurried to a town in the hill country of Judah ⁴⁰ where she entered Zechariah's house and greeted Elizabeth. ⁴¹ When Elizabeth heard Mary's greeting, the baby leaped inside her,ᵃ and Elizabeth was filled with the Holy Spirit. ⁴² Then she exclaimed with a loud cry:

"You are the most blessed of women,
and your child will be blessed!ᵇ

⁴³ How could this happen to me, that the mother of my Lord should come to me? ⁴⁴ For you see, when the sound of your greeting reached my ears, the baby leaped for joy inside me!ᶜ ⁴⁵ She who has believed is blessed because what was spoken to her by the Lord will be fulfilled!"

MARY'S PRAISE

⁴⁶ And Mary said:

My soul proclaims the greatness ofᵈ the Lord,
⁴⁷ and my spirit has rejoiced in God my Savior,
⁴⁸ because He has looked with favor
on the humble condition of His •slave.
Surely, from now on all generations
will call me blessed,
⁴⁹ because the Mighty One
has done great things for me,
and His name is holy.
⁵⁰ His mercy is from generation to generation
on those who fear Him.
⁵¹ He has done a mighty deed with His arm;
He has scattered the proud
because of the thoughts of their hearts;
⁵² He has toppled the mighty from their thrones
and exalted the lowly.
⁵³ He has satisfied the hungry with good things
and sent the rich away empty.
⁵⁴ He has helped His servant Israel,
mindful of His mercy,ᵉ

If God Says It, He Can Do It

No matter how big the assignment God gives you, He is able to accomplish His purposes through you.

"She who has believed is blessed because what was spoken to her by the Lord will be fulfilled!"
—Luke 1:45

ᵃ1:41 Lit *leaped in her abdomen* or *womb*
ᵇ1:42 Lit *and the fruit of your abdomen* (or *womb*) *is blessed*
ᶜ1:44 Lit *in my abdomen* or *womb*
ᵈ1:46 Or *soul magnifies*
ᵉ1:54 Because He remembered His mercy; see Ps 98:3

⁵⁵ just as He spoke to our ancestors,
to Abraham and his descendantsᵃ forever.

⁵⁶ And Mary stayed with her about three months; then she returned to her home.

THE BIRTH AND NAMING OF JOHN

⁵⁷ Now the time had come for Elizabeth to give birth, and she had a son. ⁵⁸ Then her neighbors and relatives heard that the Lord had shown her His great mercy,ᵇ and they rejoiced with her.

⁵⁹ When they came to circumcise the child on the eighth day, they were going to name him Zechariah, after his father. ⁶⁰ But his mother responded, "No! He will be called John."

⁶¹ Then they said to her, "None of your relatives has that name." ⁶² So they motioned to his father to find out what he wanted him to be called. ⁶³ He asked for a writing tablet and wrote:

HIS NAME IS JOHN.

And they were all amazed. ⁶⁴ Immediately his mouth was opened and his tongue ˌset freeˌ, and he began to speak, praising God. ⁶⁵ Fear came on all those who lived around them, and all these things were being talked about throughout the hill country of Judea. ⁶⁶ All who heard about ˌhimˌ took ˌitˌ to heart, saying, "What then will this child become?" For, indeed, the Lord's hand was with him.

ZECHARIAH'S PROPHECY

⁶⁷ Then his father Zechariah was filled with the Holy Spirit and prophesied:

⁶⁸ Praise the Lord, the God of Israel,
because He has visited
and provided redemption for His people.
⁶⁹ He has raised up a •horn of salvationᶜ for us
in the house of His servant David,
⁷⁰ just as He spoke by the mouth

Godly Thinking Is a Deliberate Decision

When God invites you to join Him, the first action will involve the adjustment of your life to God. The second action will be obedience to what God asks you to do. You cannot go on to obedience without first making the adjustments.

He asked for a writing tablet and wrote: HIS NAME IS JOHN. And they were all amazed.

—Luke 1:63

ᵃ**1:55** Or *offspring*; lit *seed*
ᵇ**1:58** Lit *the Lord magnified His mercy with her*

ᶜ**1:69** A strong Savior

of His holy prophets in ancient times;
71 salvation from our enemies
and from the clutches[a] of those who hate us.
72 He has dealt mercifully with our fathers
and remembered His holy covenant—
73 the oath that He swore to our father Abraham.
He has given us the privilege,
74 since we have been rescued
from our enemies' clutches,[b]
to serve Him without fear
75 in holiness and righteousness
in His presence all our days.
76 And child, you will be called
a prophet of the Most High,
for you will go before the Lord
to prepare His ways,
77 to give His people knowledge of salvation
through the forgiveness of their sins.
78 Because of our God's merciful compassion,
the Dawn from on high will visit us
79 to shine on those who live in darkness
and the shadow of death,
to guide our feet into the way of peace.

80 The child grew up and became spiritually strong, and he was in the wilderness until the day of his public appearance to Israel.

THE BIRTH OF JESUS

2 In those days a decree went out from Caesar Augustus[c] that the whole empire[d] should be registered. 2 This first registration took place while[e] Quirinius was governing Syria. 3 So everyone went to be registered, each to his own town.

4 And Joseph also went up from the town of Nazareth in Galilee, to Judea, to the city of David, which is called Bethlehem, because he was of the house and family line of David, 5 to be registered along with Mary, who was •engaged to him[f] and was pregnant. 6 While they

WORD STUDY

Greek word: **mnesteuo**
[mnay STYOO oh]

Translation: **engaged**

Uses in Luke's Gospel: **2**
(Mt, 1)

Uses in the NT: **3**

Key passage: **Luke 2:5**

The Greek verb *mnesteuo* is used only three times in the NT (Mt 1:18; Lk 1:27; 2:5), and each time it describes Mary who was "engaged" to Joseph. The word *mnesteuo* is roughly equivalent to the American concept of engagement, but the Jewish custom described by the term was much stronger. In Jewish culture in NT times, *mnesteuo* referred to a contractual arrangement that could only be broken by divorce. Joseph and Mary were legally considered husband and wife (Mt 1:19-20), although no wedding ceremony had been performed and they were neither living together nor having sexual relations (Mt 1:18; Lk 1:27,34). In obedience to the angel of the Lord, Joseph took Mary into his home as his wife (Mt 1:24). During this time Joseph and Mary made the trip together to Bethlehem (Lk 2:4-5). Both Matthew and Luke use the word *mnesteuo* to refer to this time period in light of the fact that Joseph and Mary refrained from sexual relations until after Jesus' birth (Mt 1:25; Lk 2:5).

---

a1:71 Lit *the hand*
b1:74 Lit *from the hand of enemies*
c2:1 Emperor who ruled the Roman Empire 27 B.C.–A.D. 14; also known as Octavian, he established the peaceful era known as the *Pax Romana*; Caesar was a title of Roman emperors.
d2:1 Or *the whole inhabited world*
e2:2 Or *This registration was the first while,* or *This registration was before*
f2:5 Other mss read *was his engaged wife*

were there, the time came for her to give birth. ⁷ Then she gave birth to her firstborn Son, and she wrapped Him snugly in cloth and laid Him in a feeding trough— because there was no room for them at the inn.

THE SHEPHERDS AND THE ANGELS

⁸ In the same region, shepherds were staying out in the fields and keeping watch at night over their flock. ⁹ Then an angel of the Lord stood before[a] them, and the glory of the Lord shone around them, and they were terrified.[b] ¹⁰ But the angel said to them, "Don't be afraid, for look, I proclaim to you good news of great joy that will be for all the people: ¹¹ today a Savior, who is •Messiah the Lord, was born for you in the city of David. ¹² This will be the sign for you: you will find a baby wrapped snugly in cloth and lying in a feeding trough."

¹³ Suddenly there was a multitude of the heavenly host with the angel, praising God and saying:

¹⁴ Glory to God in the highest heaven,
and peace on earth to people He favors![c] [d]

¹⁵ When the angels had left them and returned to heaven, the shepherds said to one another, "Let's go straight to Bethlehem and see what has happened, which the Lord has made known to us."

¹⁶ They hurried off and found both Mary and Joseph, and the baby who was lying in the feeding trough. ¹⁷ After seeing ₍them₎, they reported the message they were told about this child, ¹⁸ and all who heard it were amazed at what the shepherds said to them. ¹⁹ But Mary was treasuring up all these things[e] in her heart and meditating on them. ²⁰ The shepherds returned, glorifying and praising God for all they had seen and heard, just as they had been told.

THE CIRCUMCISION AND PRESENTATION OF JESUS

²¹ When the eight days were completed for His circumcision, He was named JESUS—the name given by

Obedience Will Draw You Closer to God

The reward for obedience and love is that He will show Himself to you.

When the angels had left them and returned to heaven, the shepherds said to one another, "Let's go straight to Bethlehem and see what has happened, which the Lord has made known to us."

—Luke 2:15

---

[a]2:9 Or *Lord appeared to*
[b]2:9 Lit *they feared a great fear*
[c]2:14 Other mss read *earth good will to people*
[d]2:14 Or *earth to men of good will*
[e]2:19 Lit *these words*

the angel before He was conceived.[a] ²² And when the days of their purification according to the law of Moses were finished, they brought Him up to Jerusalem to present Him to the Lord ²³ (just as it is written in the law of the Lord: **Every firstborn male[b] will be dedicated[c] to the Lord[d]**) ²⁴ and to offer a sacrifice (according to what is stated in the law of the Lord: **a pair of turtledoves or two young pigeons[e]**).

SIMEON'S PROPHETIC PRAISE

²⁵ There was a man in Jerusalem whose name was Simeon. This man was righteous and devout, looking forward to Israel's consolation,[f] and the Holy Spirit was on him. ²⁶ It had been revealed to him by the Holy Spirit that he would not see death before he saw the Lord's Messiah. ²⁷ Guided by the Spirit, he entered[g] the •temple complex. When the parents brought in the child Jesus to perform for Him what was customary under the law, ²⁸ Simeon took Him up in his arms, praised God, and said:

²⁹ Now, Master,
You can dismiss Your •slave in peace,
according to Your word.
³⁰ For my eyes have seen Your salvation.
³¹ You have prepared ⌊it⌋
in the presence of all peoples—
³² a light for revelation to the Gentiles[h]
and glory to Your people Israel.

³³ His father and mother[i] were amazed at what was being said about Him. ³⁴ Then Simeon blessed them and told His mother Mary: "Indeed, this child is destined to cause the fall and rise of many in Israel and to be a sign that will be opposed[j] — ³⁵ and a sword will pierce your own soul—that the thoughts[k] of many hearts may be revealed."

> **Stay on Task and You'll Be on Target**
>
> If you do everything He says, you will be in the center of His will when He wants to use you for a special assignment.
>
> ---
>
> *Guided by the Spirit, he entered the temple complex. When the parents brought in the child Jesus to perform for Him what was customary under the law, Simeon took Him up in his arms.*
>
> —Luke 2:27-28a

[a]2:21 Or *conceived in the womb*
[b]2:23 Lit *"Every male that opens a womb*
[c]2:23 Lit *be called holy*
[d]2:23 Ex 13:2,12
[e]2:24 Lv 5:11; 12:8
[f]2:25 The coming of the Messiah with His salvation for the nation; Lk 2:26,30; Is 40:1; 61:2
[g]2:27 Lit *And in the Spirit, he came into the*
[h]2:32 Or *the nations*
[i]2:33 Other mss read *But Joseph and His mother*
[j]2:34 Or *spoken against*
[k]2:35 Or *schemes*

ANNA'S TESTIMONY

³⁶ There was also a prophetess, Anna, a daughter of Phanuel, of the tribe of Asher. She was well along in years,ᵃ having lived with her husband seven years after her marriage,ᵇ ³⁷ and was a widow for 84 years.ᶜ She did not leave the temple complex, serving God night and day with fastings and prayers. ³⁸ At that very moment,ᵈ she came up and began to thank God and to speak about Him to all who were looking forward to the redemption of Jerusalem.ᵉ

THE FAMILY'S RETURN TO NAZARETH

³⁹ When they had completed everything according to the law of the Lord, they returned to Galilee, to their own town of Nazareth. ⁴⁰ The boy grew up and became strong, filled with wisdom, and God's grace was on Him.

IN HIS FATHER'S HOUSE

⁴¹ Every year His parents traveled to Jerusalem for the •Passover Festival. ⁴² When He was 12 years old, they went up according to the custom of the festival. ⁴³ After those days were over, as they were returning, the boy Jesus stayed behind in Jerusalem, but His parentsᶠ did not know it. ⁴⁴ Assuming He was in the traveling party, they went a day's journey. Then they began looking for Him among their relatives and friends. ⁴⁵ When they did not find Him, they returned to Jerusalem to search for Him. ⁴⁶ After three days, they found Him in the temple complex sitting among the teachers, listening to them and asking them questions. ⁴⁷ And all those who heard Him were astounded at His understanding and His answers. ⁴⁸ When His parents saw Him, they were astonished, and His mother said to Him, "Son, why have You treated us like this? Your father and I have been anxiously searching for You."

⁴⁹ "Why were you searching for Me?" He asked them. "Didn't you know that I had to be in My Father's

Loving God Is a Lifelong Habit

The key to knowing God's voice is not a formula. It is not a method you can follow. Knowing God's voice comes from an intimate love relationship with God.

There was also a prophetess, Anna, a daughter of Phanuel, of the tribe of Asher. She was well along in years, having lived with her husband seven years after her marriage, and was a widow for 84 years. She did not leave the temple complex, serving God night and day with fastings and prayers.

—Luke 2:36-37

ᵃ2:36 Lit *in many days*
ᵇ2:36 Lit *years from her virginity*
ᶜ2:37 Or *she was a widow until the age of 84*
ᵈ2:38 Lit *very hour*
ᵉ2:38 Other mss read *in Jerusalem*
ᶠ2:43 Other mss read *but Joseph and His mother*

house?"[a] 50 But they did not understand what He said to them.

IN FAVOR WITH GOD AND WITH PEOPLE

51 Then He went down with them and came to Nazareth and was obedient to them. His mother kept all these things in her heart. 52 And Jesus increased in wisdom and stature, and in favor with God and with people.

THE MESSIAH'S HERALD

3 In the fifteenth year of the reign of Tiberius Caesar,[b] while Pontius •Pilate was governor of Judea, •Herod was tetrarch[c] of Galilee, his brother Philip tetrarch of the region of Iturea[d] and Trachonitis,[d] and Lysanias tetrarch of Abilene,[e] 2 during the high priesthood of Annas and Caiaphas, God's word came to John the son of Zechariah in the wilderness. 3 He went into all the vicinity of the Jordan, preaching a baptism of repentance[f] for the forgiveness of sins, 4 as it is written in the book of the words of the prophet Isaiah:

> A voice of one crying out in the wilderness:
> "Prepare the way for the Lord;
> make His paths straight!
> 5 Every valley will be filled,
> and every mountain and hill will be
>   made low;[g]
> the crooked will become straight,
> the rough ways smooth,
> 6 and everyone[h] will see the salvation
>   of God."[i]

7 He then said to the crowds who came out to be baptized by him, "Brood of vipers! Who warned you to flee from the coming wrath? 8 Therefore produce fruit consistent with repentance. And don't start saying to

WORD STUDY

Greek word: **grapho**
[grah FOH]

Translation: **write**

Uses in Luke's Gospel: **20**
(Mt, 10; Mk, 10; Jn, 22)

Uses in Luke's Writings: **32**

Uses in the NT: **191**

Key passage: **Luke 3:4**

It is not surprising that *grapho* is a common word in the NT since the written word receives such high priority in the Bible. The word *grapho* was the basic Greek verb meaning *to write*. The corresponding noun *graphe* [grah PHAY], which literally means *a writing*, almost always refers to the OT (but see 2 Pt 3:16) and should be translated *Scripture*. (Another related noun, *grammateus*, means *scribe*.) Similarly, the verb *grapho* normally refers to an OT Scripture (Lk 3:4), a NT Scripture already written (2 Co 7:12; 2 Pt 3:15; 3 Jn 9), or a NT Scripture in the process of being written (Lk 1:3; Jn 20:30-31; 21:24-25; Rm 15:15; 16:22; 2 Co 13:10; Gl 1:20; 6:11; 2 Th 3:17; 1 Tm 3:14; Phm 19,21; 1 Pt 5:12; 2 Pt 3:1; 1 Jn 1:4; 5:13; 2 Jn 5; Jd 3; Rv 1:11). The most common use of the term *grapho* is as an introductory formula for OT quotations (over 60 times). The Greek verb tense that is normally used in this formula ("it is written" or perhaps "it stands written") emphasizes the permanence of God's written revelation.

---

[a]2:49 Or *be involved in My Father's interests* (or *things*), or *be among My Father's people*
[b]3:1 Emperor who ruled the Roman Empire A.D. 14–37
[c]3:1 Or *ruler*
[d]3:1 A small province northeast of Galilee
[e]3:1 A small Syrian province
[f]3:3 Or *baptism based on repentance*
[g]3:5 Lit *be humbled*
[h]3:6 Lit *all flesh*
[i]3:4-6 Is 40:3-5

yourselves, 'We have Abraham as our father,' for I tell you that God is able to raise up children for Abraham from these stones! 9 Even now the ax is ready to strike[a] the root of the trees! Therefore every tree that doesn't produce good fruit will be cut down and thrown into the fire."

10 "What then should we do?" the crowds were asking him.

11 He replied to them, "The one who has two shirts[b] must share with someone who has none, and the one who has food must do the same."

12 Tax collectors also came to be baptized, and they asked him, "Teacher, what should we do?"

13 He told them, "Don't collect any more than what you have been authorized."

14 Some soldiers also questioned him: "What should we do?"

He said to them, "Don't take money from anyone by force or false accusation; be satisfied with your wages."

15 Now the people were waiting expectantly, and all of them were debating in their minds[c] whether John might be the •Messiah. 16 John answered them all, "I baptize you with[d] water, but One is coming who is more powerful than I. I am not worthy to untie the strap of His sandals. He will baptize you with[d] the Holy Spirit and fire. 17 His winnowing shovel[e] is in His hand to clear His threshing floor and gather the wheat into His barn, but the chaff He will burn up with a fire that never goes out." 18 Then, along with many other exhortations, he proclaimed good news to the people. 19 But Herod the tetrarch, being rebuked by him about Herodias, his brother's wife, and about all the evil things Herod had done, 20 added this to everything else—he locked John up in prison.

THE BAPTISM OF JESUS

21 When all the people were baptized, Jesus also was baptized. As He was praying, heaven opened, 22 and the Holy Spirit descended on Him in a physical appearance like a dove. And a voice came from heaven:

Seek God in Prayer

Prayer is not a substitute for hard work—prayer is the work! God does things in and through our lives by prayer that He does in no other way.

As He was praying, heaven opened.
—Luke 3:21b

---

[a]3:9 Lit *the ax lies at*
[b]3:11 Lit *tunics*
[c]3:15 Or *hearts*
[d]3:16 Or *in*

[e]3:17 A wooden farm implement used to toss threshed grain into the wind so the lighter chaff would blow away and separate from the heavier grain

You are My beloved Son.
I take delight in You!

THE GENEALOGY OF JESUS CHRIST

²³ As He began ˌHis ministryˌ, Jesus was about 30 years old and was thought to beª the

son of Joseph, ˌsonˌᵇ of Heli,
²⁴ ˌsonˌ of Matthat, ˌsonˌ of Levi,
ˌsonˌ of Melchi, ˌsonˌ of Jannai,
ˌsonˌ of Joseph, ²⁵ ˌsonˌ of Mattathias,
ˌsonˌ of Amos, ˌsonˌ of Nahum,
ˌsonˌ of Esli, ˌsonˌ of Naggai,
²⁶ ˌsonˌ of Maath, ˌsonˌ of Mattathias,
ˌsonˌ of Semein, ˌsonˌ of Josech,
ˌsonˌ of Joda, ²⁷ ˌsonˌ of Joanan,
ˌsonˌ of Rhesa, ˌsonˌ of Zerubbabel,
ˌsonˌ of Shealtiel, ˌsonˌ of Neri,
²⁸ ˌsonˌ of Melchi, ˌsonˌ of Addi,
ˌsonˌ of Cosam, ˌsonˌ of Elmadam,
ˌsonˌ of Er, ²⁹ ˌsonˌ of Joshua,
ˌsonˌ of Eliezer, ˌsonˌ of Jorim,
ˌsonˌ of Matthat, ˌsonˌ of Levi,
³⁰ ˌsonˌ of Simeon, ˌsonˌ of Judah,
ˌsonˌ of Joseph, ˌsonˌ of Jonam,
ˌsonˌ of Eliakim, ³¹ ˌsonˌ of Melea,
ˌsonˌ of Menna, ˌsonˌ of Mattatha,
ˌsonˌ of Nathan, ˌsonˌ of David,
³² ˌsonˌ of Jesse, ˌsonˌ of Obed,
ˌsonˌ of Boaz, ˌsonˌ of Salmon,ᶜ
ˌsonˌ of Nahshon, ³³ ˌsonˌ of Amminadab,
ˌsonˌ of Ram,ᵈ ˌsonˌ of Hezron,
ˌsonˌ of Perez, ˌsonˌ of Judah,
³⁴ ˌsonˌ of Jacob, ˌsonˌ of Isaac,
ˌsonˌ of Abraham, ˌsonˌ of Terah,
ˌsonˌ of Nahor, ³⁵ ˌsonˌ of Serug,
ˌsonˌ of Reu, ˌsonˌ of Peleg,
ˌsonˌ of Eber, ˌsonˌ of Shelah,
³⁶ ˌsonˌ of Cainan, ˌsonˌ of Arphaxad,

God Wants to Be With His People

The heavenly Father's plan from the beginning of time was to place His eternal Son in every believer.

The Holy Spirit descended on Him in a physical appearance like a dove. And a voice came from heaven: "You are My beloved Son. I take delight in You!"

—Luke 3:22

ª**3:23** People did not know about His virgin birth; Lk 1:26-38; Mt 1:18-25
ᵇ**3:23** The relationship in some cases may be more distant than a son.
ᶜ**3:32** Other mss read *Sala*
ᵈ**3:33** Other mss read *Amminadab, son of Aram, son of Joram*; other mss read *Amminadab, son of Admin, son of Arni*

WORD STUDY

Greek word: **proskuneo**
[prahss koo NEH oh]

Translation: **worship**

Uses in Luke's Gospel: **3**
(Mt, 13; Mk, 2; Jn, 11)

Uses in Luke's Writings: **7**

Uses in the NT: **60**

Key passage: **Luke 4:7-8**

The Greek verb *proskuneo* is built from the words *pros,* meaning *toward,* and *kuneo,* meaning *kiss.* The term suggests the custom of falling to one's knees out of respect to someone superior in rank—normally rulers, royalty, or those considered divine. A few times in the NT *proskuneo* is used with the general meaning *bow down* (Mt 8:2; 9:18; Mk 15:19; Rv 3:9), and such homage to persons of great rank or power was common in the ancient world. But *proskuneo* in the sense of *worship* (that is, *show honor and reverence*) is reserved for God alone, as the term's use in the Greek OT (Ex 20:5; Dt 11:16; 26:10) and in the NT indicates (Jn 4:20-24; Rv 4:10; 7:11; 15:4; 19:10; 22:9). One of the strongest evidences in the NT for the deity of Christ is that *proskuneo* often refers to worshiping Him. If Christ is not God, this would violate the teachings of both Testaments to worship God alone (Dt 6:13-14; see Jesus' quote of this verse in response to one of Satan's temptations in Lk 4:7-8). Compare the reaction of Paul and Barnabas to being deified (Ac 14:11-18). People worshiped Christ when He was an infant (Mt 2:2,11), during His ministry (Mt 14:33; Jn 9:38), and after His resurrection (Mt 28:9,17; Lk 24:52).

ₗsonₗ of Shem, ₗsonₗ of Noah, ₗsonₗ of Lamech, ³⁷ ₗsonₗ of Methuselah, ₗsonₗ of Enoch, ₗsonₗ of Jared, ₗsonₗ of Mahalaleel, ₗsonₗ of Cainan, ³⁸ ₗsonₗ of Enos, ₗsonₗ of Seth, ₗsonₗ of Adam, ₗsonₗ of God.

THE TEMPTATION OF JESUS

4 Then Jesus returned from the Jordan, full of the Holy Spirit, and was led by the Spirit in the wilderness ² for 40 days to be tempted by the Devil. He ate nothing during those days, and when they were over,ᵃ He was hungry. ³ The Devil said to Him, "If You are the Son of God, tell this stone to become bread."

⁴ But Jesus answered him, "It is written: **Man must not live on bread alone.**"ᵇ ᶜ

⁵ So he took Him upᵈ and showed Him all the kingdoms of the world in a moment of time. ⁶ The Devil said to Him, "I will give You their splendor and all this authority, because it has been given over to me, and I can give it to anyone I want. ⁷ If You, then, will worship me,ᵉ all will be Yours."

⁸ And Jesus answered him,ᶠ "It is written:

**Worship the Lord your God,
and serve Him only.**"ᵍ

⁹ So he took Him to Jerusalem, had Him stand on the pinnacle of the temple, and said to Him, "If You are the Son of God, throw Yourself down from here. ¹⁰ For it is written:

**He will give His angels orders
    concerning you,
to protect you,**ʰ ¹¹ **and
they will support you with their hands,
so that you will not strike
your foot against a stone.**"ⁱ

ᵃ**4:2** Lit *were completed*
ᵇ**4:4** Other mss add *but on every word of God*
ᶜ**4:4** Dt 8:3
ᵈ**4:5** Other mss read *So the Devil took Him up on a high mountain*
ᵉ**4:7** Lit *will fall down before me*
ᶠ**4:8** Other mss add *"Get behind Me, Satan!*
ᵍ**4:8** Dt 6:13
ʰ**4:10** Ps 91:11
ⁱ**4:11** Ps 91:12

¹² And Jesus answered him, "It is said: **Do not test the Lord your God.**"ᵃ

¹³ After the Devil had finished every temptation, he departed from Him for a time.

MINISTRY IN GALILEE

¹⁴ Then Jesus returned to Galilee in the power of the Spirit, and news about Him spread throughout the entire vicinity. ¹⁵ He was teaching in their •synagogues, being acclaimedᵇ by everyone.

REJECTION AT NAZARETH

¹⁶ He came to Nazareth, where He had been brought up. As usual, He entered the synagogue on the Sabbath day and stood up to read. ¹⁷ The scroll of the prophet Isaiah was given to Him, and unrolling the scroll, He found the place where it was written:

¹⁸ **The Spirit of the Lord is on Me,**
   because He has anointed Me
   to preach good news to the poor.
   He has sent Meᶜ
   to proclaim freedomᵈ **to the captives**
   and recovery of sight to the blind,
   to set free the oppressed,
¹⁹ **to proclaim the year of the Lord's favor.**ᵉ ᶠ

²⁰ He then rolled up the scroll, gave it back to the attendant, and sat down. And the eyes of everyone in the synagogue were fixed on Him. ²¹ He began by saying to them, "Today as you listen, this Scripture has been fulfilled."

²² They were all speaking well of Himᵍ and were amazed by the gracious words that came from His mouth, yet they said, "Isn't this Joseph's son?"

²³ Then He said to them, "No doubt you will quote this proverbʰ to Me: 'Doctor, heal yourself.' 'All we've heard that took place in Capernaum, do here in Your hometown also.'"

God Will Use You to Meet Others' Needs

His whole plan for the advance of the kingdom depends on His working in real and practical ways through His relationship to His people.

"The Spirit of the Lord is on Me, because He has anointed Me to preach good news to the poor. He has sent Me to proclaim freedom to the captives and recovery of sight to the blind, to set free the oppressed, to proclaim the year of the Lord's favor."

—Luke 4:18-19

ᵃ4:12 Dt 6:16
ᵇ4:15 Or *glorified*
ᶜ4:18 Other mss add *to heal the brokenhearted,*
ᵈ4:18 Or *release,* or *forgiveness*
ᵉ4:19 The time of messianic grace
ᶠ4:18-19 Is 61:1-2
ᵍ4:22 Or *They were testifying against Him*
ʰ4:23 Or *parable*

24 He also said, "•I assure you: No prophet is accepted in his hometown. 25 But I say to you, there were certainly many widows in Israel in Elijah's days, when the sky was shut up for three years and six months while a great famine came over all the land. 26 Yet Elijah was not sent to any of them—but to a widow at Zarephath in Sidon. 27 And in the prophet Elisha's time, there were many in Israel who had serious skin diseases, yet not one of them was healed[a] —only Naaman the Syrian."

28 When they heard this, everyone in the synagogue was enraged. 29 They got up, drove Him out of town, and brought Him to the edge[b] of the hill their town was built on, intending to hurl Him over the cliff. 30 But He passed right through the crowd and went on His way.

DRIVING OUT AN UNCLEAN SPIRIT

31 Then He went down to Capernaum, a town in Galilee, and was teaching them on the Sabbath. 32 They were astonished at His teaching because His message had authority. 33 In the synagogue there was a man with an unclean demonic spirit who cried out with a loud voice, 34 "Leave us alone![c] What do You have to do with us,[d] Jesus—•Nazarene? Have You come to destroy us? I know who You are—the Holy One of God!"

35 But Jesus rebuked him and said, "Be quiet and come out of him!"

And throwing him down before them, the demon came out of him without hurting him at all. 36 They were all struck with amazement and kept saying to one another, "What is this message? For He commands the unclean spirits with authority and power, and they come out!" 37 And news about Him began to go out to every place in the vicinity.

HEALINGS AT CAPERNAUM

38 After He left the synagogue, He entered Simon's house. Simon's mother-in-law was suffering from a high fever, and they asked Him about her. 39 So He stood over her and rebuked the fever, and it left her. She got up immediately and began to serve them.

Hear His Voice in the Scriptures

Do you sense, as you read the Scripture, that God became real and personal to people? Your life also can reflect that kind of real, personal, and practical relationship as you respond to God's working in your life.

They were astonished at His teaching because His message had authority.

—Luke 4:32

Leave All the Results and Rewards to God

The working of God in you will bring a blessing. The blessing is a by-product of your obedience and the experience of God working in your midst.

News about Him began to go out to every place in the vicinity.

—Luke 4:37

---

[a]4:27 Lit cleansed
[b]4:29 Lit brow
[c]4:34 Or Ha!, or Ah!
[d]4:34 Lit What to us and to You

⁴⁰ When the sun was setting, all those who had anyone sick with various diseases brought them to Him. As He laid His hands on each one of them, He would heal them. ⁴¹ Also, demons were coming out of many, shouting and saying, "You are the Son of God!" But He rebuked them and would not allow them to speak, because they knew He was the •Messiah.

PREACHING IN GALILEE

⁴² When it was day, He went out and made His way to a deserted place. But the crowds were searching for Him. They came to Him and tried to keep Him from leaving them. ⁴³ But He said to them, "I must proclaim the good news about the kingdom of God to the other towns also, because I was sent for this purpose." ⁴⁴ And He was preaching in the synagogues of Galilee.ᵃ

THE FIRST DISCIPLES

5 As the crowd was pressing in on Jesus to hear God's word, He was standing by Lake Gennesaret.ᵇ ² He saw two boats at the edge of the lake;ᶜ the fishermen had left them and were washing their nets. ³ He got into one of the boats, which belonged to Simon, and asked him to put out a little from the land. Then He sat down and was teaching the crowds from the boat.

⁴ When He had finished speaking, He said to Simon, "Put out into deep water and let downᵈ your nets for a catch."

⁵ "Master," Simon replied, "we've worked hard all night long and caught nothing! But at Your word, I'll let down the nets."ᵉ

⁶ When they did this, they caught a great number of fish, and their netsᵉ began to tear. ⁷ So they signaled to their partners in the other boat to come and help them; they came and filled both boats so full that they began to sink.

⁸ When Simon Peter saw this, he fell at Jesus' knees and said, "Go away from me, because I'm a sinful man, Lord!" ⁹ For he and all those with him were amazedᶠ at

WORD STUDY

Greek word: **epistates**
[eh pee STAH tayss]
Translation: **Master**
Uses in Luke's Gospel: **7**
Uses in the NT: **7**
Key passage: **Luke 5:5**

The Greek noun *epistates* is related to a verb meaning *to place over* and refers to an *overseer* or *superintendent.* This word, a title of respect for someone in authority, occurs only in Luke's Gospel and was used as a term of respect for Jesus by His disciples (5:5; 8:24,45; 9:33,49; see also 17:13). Luke may have used the term *epistates* since He does not use *rabbi* (see note at Jn 1:38) and since in his Gospel only strangers address Jesus with the more common "Teacher" (*didaskalos*).

In Luke 5, Jesus' request that Simon Peter and the others let the nets down once again seemed quite unreasonable to the experienced fishermen in light of their hard but unproductive day at sea (vv. 4-5). But because Peter recognized Jesus' authority as *Master* (*epistates* in v. 5), he agreed to try again and caught more fish than the nets and boats could handle—little wonder that Peter then called Him "Lord" (v. 8). With this remarkable miracle, Peter's understanding of Jesus progressed from "Master" to "Lord" (*kurios*), and he and his partners became Jesus' disciples from that time forward (vv. 9-11).

ᵃ4:44 Other mss read *Judea*
ᵇ5:1 = Sea of Galilee
ᶜ5:2 Lit *boats standing by the lake*
ᵈ5:4 Lit *and you* (Gk pl) *let down*
ᵉ5:5,6 Other mss read *net* (Gk sg)
ᶠ5:9 Or *For amazement had seized him and all those with him*

the catch of fish they took, ¹⁰ and so were James and John, Zebedee's sons, who were Simon's partners.

"Don't be afraid," Jesus told Simon. "From now on you will be catching people!" ¹¹ Then they brought the boats to land, left everything, and followed Him.

CLEANSING A LEPER

¹² While He was in one of the towns, a man was there who had a serious skin disease all over him. He saw Jesus, fell facedown, and begged Him: "Lord, if You are willing, You can make me clean."ᵃ

¹³ Reaching out His hand, He touched him, saying, "I am willing; be made clean," and immediately the disease left him. ¹⁴ Then He ordered him to tell no one: "But go and show yourself to the priest, and offer what Moses prescribed for your cleansing as a testimony to them."

¹⁵ But the newsᵇ about Him spread even more, and large crowds would come together to hear Him and to be healed of their sicknesses. ¹⁶ Yet He often withdrew to deserted places and prayed.

THE SON OF MAN FORGIVES AND HEALS

¹⁷ On one of those days while He was teaching, •Pharisees and teachers of the law were sitting there who had come from every village of Galilee and Judea, and also from Jerusalem. And the Lord's power to heal was in Him. ¹⁸ Just then some men came, carrying on a stretcher a man who was paralyzed. They tried to bring him in and set him down before Him. ¹⁹ Since they could not find a way to bring him in because of the crowd, they went up on the roof and lowered him on the stretcher through the roof tiles into the middle of the crowd before Jesus.

²⁰ Seeing their faith He said, "Friend,ᶜ your sins are forgiven you."

²¹ Then the •scribes and the Pharisees began to reason: "Who is this man who speaks blasphemies? Who can forgive sins but God alone?"

God Makes You More Than You Can Be

All of the persons that you see in the Scriptures were ordinary people. Their relationship with God and the activity of God made them extraordinary.

Everyone was astounded, and they were giving glory to God. And they were filled with awe and said, "We have seen incredible things today!"

—Luke 5:26

ᵃ5:12 In these verses, *clean* includes healing, ceremonial purification, return to fellowship with people, and worship in the temple; Lv 14:1-32. ᵇ5:15 Lit *the word* ᶜ5:20 Lit *Man*

²² But perceiving their thoughts, Jesus replied to them, "Why are you reasoning this in your hearts?ᵃ ²³ Which is easier: to say, 'Your sins are forgiven you,' or to say, 'Get up and walk'? ²⁴ But so you may know that the •Son of Man has authority on earth to forgive sins"—He told the paralyzed man, "I tell you: get up, pick up your stretcher, and go home."

²⁵ Immediately he got up before them, picked up what he had been lying on, and went home glorifying God. ²⁶ Then everyone was astounded, and they were giving glory to God. And they were filled with awe and said, "We have seen incredible things today!"

THE CALL OF LEVI

²⁷ After this, Jesus went out and saw a tax collector named Levi sitting at the tax office, and He said to him, "Follow Me!" ²⁸ So, leaving everything behind, he got up and began to follow Him.

DINING WITH SINNERS

²⁹ Then Levi hosted a grand banquet for Him at his house. Now there was a large crowd of tax collectors and others who were guestsᵇ with them. ³⁰ But the Pharisees and their scribes were complaining to His disciples, "Why do you eat and drink with tax collectors and sinners?"

³¹ Jesus replied to them, "The healthy don't need a doctor, but the sick do. ³² I have not come to call the righteous, but sinners to repentance."

A QUESTION ABOUT FASTING

³³ Then they said to Him, "John's disciples fast often and say prayers, and those of the Pharisees do the same, but Yours eat and drink."ᶜ

³⁴ Jesus said to them, "You can't make the wedding guestsᵈ fast while the groom is with them, can you? ³⁵ But the days will come when the groom will be taken away from them—then they will fast in those days."

Be One Who Cares for Those Who Hurt

The world abounds with people whose sin has alienated them from God. And only Christ has the remedy. As His ambassadors, we are to take the message of reconciliation to a broken, divided world.

Jesus replied to them, "The healthy don't need a doctor, but the sick do. I have not come to call the righteous, but sinners to repentance."

—Luke 5:31-32

ᵃ5:22 Or *minds*
ᵇ5:29 Lit *were reclining* (at the table); at important meals the custom was to recline on a mat at a low table and lean on the left elbow.
ᶜ5:33 Other mss read *"Why do John's ... drink?"* (as a question)
ᵈ5:34 Or *the friends of the groom*; lit *sons of the bridal chamber*

³⁶ He also told them a parable: "No one tears a patch from a new garment and puts it on an old garment. Otherwise, not only will he tear the new, but also the piece from the new garment will not match the old. ³⁷ And no one puts new wine into old wineskins. Otherwise, the new wine will burst the skins, it will spill, and the skins will be ruined. ³⁸ But new wine should be put into fresh wineskins.ᵃ ³⁹ And no one, after drinking old wine, wants new, because he says, 'The old is better.'"ᵇ

LORD OF THE SABBATH

6 On a Sabbath,ᶜ He passed through the grainfields. His disciples were picking heads of grain, rubbing them in their hands, and eating them. ² But some of the •Pharisees said, "Why are you doing what is not lawful on the Sabbath?"

³ Jesus answered them, "Haven't you read what David and those who were with him did when he was hungry— ⁴ how he entered the house of God, and took and ate the •sacred bread, which is not lawful for any but the priests to eat? He even gave some to those who were with him." ⁵ Then He told them, "The •Son of Man is Lord of the Sabbath."

THE MAN WITH THE PARALYZED HAND

⁶ On another Sabbath He entered the •synagogue and was teaching. A man was there whose right hand was paralyzed. ⁷ The •scribes and Pharisees were watching Him closely, to see if He would heal on the Sabbath, so that they could find a charge against Him. ⁸ But He knew their thoughts and told the man with the paralyzed hand, "Get up and stand here."ᵈ So he got up and stood there. ⁹ Then Jesus said to them, "I ask you: is it lawful on the Sabbath to do good or to do evil, to save life or to destroy it?" ¹⁰ After looking around at them all, He told him, "Stretch out your hand." He did so, and his hand was restored.ᵉ ¹¹ They, however, were filled with rage and started discussing with one another what they might do to Jesus.

Even Jesus Depended on Prayer—Do You?

Becoming a person of prayer will require a major adjustment of your life to God. Prayer will always be a part of the obedience. It is in a prayer relationship that God gives further direction.

During those days He went out to the mountain to pray and spent all night in prayer to God.

—Luke 6:12

ᵃ**5:38** Other mss add *And so both are preserved.*
ᵇ**5:39** Other mss read *is good*
ᶜ**6:1** Other mss read *a second-first*
Sabbath; perhaps a special Sabbath
ᵈ**6:8** Lit *stand in the middle*
ᵉ**6:10** Other mss add *as sound as the other*

THE 12 APOSTLES

¹² During those days He went out to the mountain to pray and spent all night in prayer to God. ¹³ When daylight came, He summoned His disciples, and He chose 12 of them—He also named them apostles:

¹⁴ Simon, whom He also named Peter,
and Andrew his brother;
James and John;
Philip and Bartholomew;
¹⁵ Matthew and Thomas;
James the son of Alphaeus,
and Simon called the Zealot;
¹⁶ Judas the son of James,
and Judas Iscariot, who became a traitor.

TEACHING AND HEALING

¹⁷ After coming down with them, He stood on a level place with a large crowd of His disciples and a great multitude of people from all Judea and Jerusalem and from the seacoast of Tyre and Sidon. ¹⁸ They came to hear Him and to be healed of their diseases; and those tormented by unclean spirits were made well. ¹⁹ The whole crowd was trying to touch Him, because power was coming out from Him and healing them all.

THE BEATITUDES

²⁰ Then looking up at[a] His disciples, He said:

Blessed are you who are poor,
because the kingdom of God is yours.
²¹ Blessed are you who are hungry now,
because you will be filled.
Blessed are you who weep now,
because you will laugh.
²² Blessed are you when people hate you,
when they exclude you, insult you,
and slander your name as evil,
because of the Son of Man.

²³ "Rejoice in that day and leap for joy! Take note—your reward is great in heaven, because this is the way their ancestors used to treat the prophets.

[a]**6:20** Lit *Then lifting up His eyes to*

Friends of God Invite Enemies

Persecution may be the best evidence that your life is like that of Christ.

"Blessed are you when people hate you, when they exclude you, insult you, and slander your name as evil, because of the Son of Man."
—Luke 6:22

WORD STUDY

Greek word: ***ouai***
[oo IGH]

Translation: ***woe***

Uses in Luke's Gospel: **15**
(Mt, 13; Mk, 2)

Uses in the NT: **46**

Key passage: **Luke 6:24-26**

The Greek interjection *ouai* serves as a warning of impending disaster, pain, or suffering. All 30 uses of *ouai* in the Gospels are by Jesus, and His warnings often denounced the Jewish religious leaders for their hypocrisy (see Mt 23:13-36; Lk 11:42-52). In Luke 6 Jesus contrasted the blessings (*makarios*) of suffering for the kingdom of God with the disasters (*ouai*) that befall those who live in comfort now but do not care about the kingdom (vv. 20-26). Jesus warned about unbelief (Mt 11:21 = Lk 10:13; see Jd 11), stumbling blocks to faith (Mt 18:7 = Lk 17:1), and disasters associated with the end times (Mt 24:19 = Mk 13:17 = Lk 21:23), which is the context of the 14 uses of *ouai* in Revelation (8:13; 9:12; 11:14; 12:12; 18:10,16,19). All three Synoptic Gospels record Jesus' *ouai* against Judas (Mt 26:24 = Mk 14:21 = Lk 22:22). The only place the term occurs in a positive context is Paul's "Woe to me—if I do not preach the gospel!" (1 Co 9:16).

WOE TO THE SELF-SATISFIED

²⁴ But woe to you who are rich,
because you have received your comfort.
²⁵ Woe to you who are full now,
because you will be hungry.
Woe to youᵃ who are laughing now,
because you will mourn and weep.
²⁶ Woe to youᵃ
when all people speak well of you,
because this is the way their ancestors
used to treat the false prophets.

LOVE YOUR ENEMIES

²⁷ "But I say to you who listen: Love your enemies, do good to those who hate you, ²⁸ bless those who curse you, pray for those who mistreat you. ²⁹ If anyone hits you on the cheek, offer the other also. And if anyone takes away your coat, don't hold back your shirt either. ³⁰ Give to everyone who asks from you, and from one who takes away your things, don't ask for them back. ³¹ Just as you want others to do for you, do the same for them. ³² If you love those who love you, what credit is that to you? Even sinners love those who love them. ³³ If you do what is good to those who are good to you, what credit is that to you? Even sinners do that. ³⁴ And if you lend to those from whom you expect to receive, what credit is that to you? Even sinners lend to sinners to be repaid in full. ³⁵ But love your enemies, do what is good, and lend, expecting nothing in return. Then your reward will be great, and you will be sons of the Most High. For He is gracious to the ungrateful and evil. ³⁶ Be merciful, just as your Father also is merciful.

DO NOT JUDGE

³⁷ "Do not judge, and you will not be judged. Do not condemn, and you will not be condemned. Forgive, and you will be forgiven. ³⁸ Give, and it will be given to you; a good measure—pressed down, shaken together, and running over—will be poured into your lap. For with the measure you use,ᵇ it will be measured back to you."

ᵃ**6:25,26** Other mss omit *to you*   ᵇ**6:38** Lit *you measure*

39 He also told them a parable: "Can the blind guide the blind? Won't they both fall into a pit? 40 A disciple is not above his teacher, but everyone who is fully trained will be like his teacher.

41 "Why do you look at the speck in your brother's eye, but don't notice the log in your own eye? 42 Or how can you say to your brother, 'Brother, let me take out the speck that is in your eye,' when you yourself don't see the log in your eye? Hypocrite! First take the log out of your eye, and then you will see clearly to take out the speck in your brother's eye.

A TREE AND ITS FRUIT

43 "A good tree doesn't produce bad fruit; on the other hand, a bad tree doesn't produce good fruit. 44 For each tree is known by its own fruit. Figs aren't gathered from thornbushes, or grapes picked from a bramble bush. 45 A good man produces good out of the good storeroom of his heart. An evil man produces evil out of the evil storeroom, for his mouth speaks from the overflow of the heart.

THE TWO FOUNDATIONS

46 "Why do you call Me 'Lord, Lord,' and don't do the things I say? 47 I will show you what someone is like who comes to Me, hears My words, and acts on them: 48 He is like a man building a house, who dug deep[a] and laid the foundation on the rock. When the flood came, the river crashed against that house and couldn't shake it, because it was well built. 49 But the one who hears and does not act is like a man who built a house on the ground without a foundation. The river crashed against it, and immediately it collapsed. And the destruction of that house was great!"

A CENTURION'S FAITH

7 When He had concluded all His sayings in the hearing of the people, He entered Capernaum. 2 A •centurion's •slave, who was highly valued by him, was sick and about to die. 3 When the centurion

[a]**6:48** Lit *dug and went deep*

Love People, and You Will Win Their Hearts

You will be helpful to others only if you see them as God does. It is difficult to pray sincerely for someone while you are judging them.

"Do not judge, and you will not be judged. Do not condemn, and you will not be condemned. Forgive, and you will be forgiven."
—Luke 6:37

Write God's Love All Over Your Life

It is impossible to carry a message of love and yet be filled with hatred. In each of your relationships, make sure that your actions share the love and forgiveness that reflect what you have received from God.

"Why do you look at the speck in your brother's eye, but don't notice the log in your own eye?"
—Luke 6:41

WORD STUDY

Greek word: **lepros**
[leh PRAHSS]

Translation: **leper**

Uses in Luke's Gospel: **3**
(Mt, 4; Mk, 2)

Uses in the NT: **9**

Key passage: **Luke 7:22**

The Greek word *lepros* comes from a root meaning *scaly* or *rough,* such as the scales of a fish. Leprosy referred to various skin diseases that gave the skin a scaly texture and often included discoloring, most often white. The references to Jesus' healing of lepers in Luke 7:22 and elsewhere must be seen in the light of the law of Moses. Leviticus 13-14 is concerned with identifying, containing, and purifying leprosy and other skin diseases on someone in the covenant community. A leper was unclean (unfit to participate in worship rituals and ceremonies), and anyone or anything that came into contact with a leper became unclean also. Some cases of leprosy were mild (white patches or running sores on the skin), but others involved the loss of fingers and toes and could even result in death. If a leper were healed, he was to be examined by a priest and to offer the prescribed sacrifice. The priest would then pronounce the leper clean so that he could once again join community life. The healing of lepers is one of three instances of Jesus' overcoming something that the law pronounced unclean; healing the bleeding woman (Lk 8:43-44; see Lv 15:25-30) and raising the dead (Lk 8:54-55; see Nm 19:11) are the other two.

heard about Jesus, he sent some Jewish elders to Him, requesting Him to come and save the life of his slave. [4] When they reached Jesus, they pleaded with Him earnestly, saying, "He is worthy for You to grant this, [5] because he loves our nation and has built us a •synagogue." [6] Jesus went with them, and when He was not far from[a] the house, the centurion sent friends to tell Him, "Lord, don't trouble Yourself, since I am not worthy to have You come under my roof. [7] That is why I didn't even consider myself worthy to come to You. But say the word, and my servant will be cured.[b] [8] For I too am a man placed under authority, having soldiers under my command.[c] I say to this one, 'Go!' and he goes; and to another, 'Come!' and he comes; and to my slave, 'Do this!' and he does it."

[9] Jesus heard this and was amazed at him, and turning to the crowd following Him, He said, "I tell you, I have not found so great a faith even in Israel!" [10] When those who had been sent returned to the house, they found the •slave in good health.

A WIDOW'S SON RAISED TO LIFE

[11] Soon afterwards He was on His way to a town called Nain. His disciples and a large crowd were traveling with Him. [12] Just as He neared the gate of the town, a dead man was being carried out. He was his mother's only son, and she was a widow. A large crowd from the city was also with her. [13] When the Lord saw her, He had compassion on her and said, "Don't cry." [14] Then He came up and touched the open coffin,[d] and the pallbearers stopped. And He said, "Young man, I tell you, get up!"

[15] The dead man sat up and began to speak, and Jesus gave him to his mother. [16] Then fear[e] came over everyone, and they glorified God, saying, "A great prophet has risen among us," and "God has visited[f] His people." [17] This report about Him went throughout Judea and all the vicinity.

---

[a]7:6 Lit *and He already was not far from*
[b]7:7 Other mss read *and let my servant be cured*

[c]7:8 Lit *under me*
[d]7:14 Or *the bier*
[e]7:16 Or *awe*
[f]7:16 Or *come to help*

IN PRAISE OF JOHN THE BAPTIST

[18] Then John's disciples told him about all these things. So John summoned two of his disciples [19] and sent them to the Lord, asking, "Are You the One who is to come, or should we look for someone else?"

[20] When the men reached Him, they said, "John the Baptist sent us to ask You, 'Are You the One who is to come, or should we look for someone else?'"

[21] At that time Jesus healed many people of diseases, plagues, and evil spirits, and He granted sight to many blind people. [22] He replied to them, "Go and report to John the things you have seen and heard: The blind receive their sight, the lame walk, those with skin diseases are healed,[a] the deaf hear, the dead are raised, and the poor have the good news preached to them. [23] And anyone who is not offended because of Me is blessed." [24] After John's messengers left, He began to speak to the crowds about John: "What did you go out into the wilderness to see? A reed swaying in the wind? [25] What then did you go out to see? A man dressed in soft robes? Look, those who are splendidly dressed[b] and live in luxury are in royal palaces. [26] What then did you go out to see? A prophet? Yes, I tell you, and far more than a prophet. [27] This is the one it is written about:

> Look, I am sending My messenger
> ahead of You;[c]
> he will prepare Your way before You.[d]

[28] I tell you, among those born of women no one is greater than John,[e] but the least in the kingdom of God is greater than he."

[29] (And when all the people, including the tax collectors, heard this, they acknowledged God's way of righteousness,[f] because they had been baptized with John's baptism. [30] But since the •Pharisees and experts in the law had not been baptized by him, they rejected the plan of God for themselves.)

Concern Yourself with Kingdom Matters

His desire is for you to become involved in what He is doing. Finding out what He is doing helps you know what He will want to do through you.

He replied to them, "Go and report to John the things you have seen and heard: The blind receive their sight, the lame walk, those with skin diseases are healed, the deaf hear, the dead are raised, and the poor have the good news preached to them. And anyone who is not offended because of Me is blessed."

—Luke 7:22-23

---

[a]7:22 Lit cleansed
[b]7:25 Or who have glorious robes
[c]7:27 Lit messenger before Your face
[d]7:27 Mal 3:1
[e]7:28 Other mss read women is not a greater prophet than John the Baptist
[f]7:29 Lit they justified God

AN UNRESPONSIVE GENERATION

31 "To what then should I compare the people of this generation, and what are they like? 32 They are like children sitting in the marketplace and calling to each other:

> We played the flute for you,
> but you didn't dance;
> we sang a lament,
> but you didn't weep!

33 For John the Baptist did not come eating bread or drinking wine, and you say, 'He has a demon!' 34 The •Son of Man has come eating and drinking, and you say, 'Look, a glutton and a drunkard, a friend of tax collectors and sinners!' 35 Yet wisdom is vindicated[a] by all her children."

MUCH FORGIVENESS, MUCH LOVE

36 Then one of the Pharisees invited Him to eat with him. He entered the Pharisee's house and reclined at the table. 37 And a woman in the town who was a sinner found out that Jesus was reclining at the table in the Pharisee's house. She brought an alabaster flask of fragrant oil 38 and stood behind Him at His feet, weeping, and began to wash His feet with her tears. She wiped His feet with the hair of her head, kissing them and anointing them with the fragrant oil.

39 When the Pharisee who had invited Him saw this, he said to himself, "This man, if He were a prophet, would know who and what kind of woman this is who is touching Him—she's a sinner!"

40 Jesus replied to him, "Simon, I have something to say to you."

"Teacher," he said, "say it."

41 "A creditor had two debtors. One owed 500 •denarii, and the other 50. 42 Since they could not pay it back, he graciously forgave them both. So, which of them will love him more?"

43 Simon answered, "I suppose the one he forgave more."

God's Love Has No Limits

When the Father gave His precious Son to save the sinners of the world, He proved once and for all that His love is boundless.

When the Pharisee who had invited Him saw this, he said to himself, "This man, if He were a prophet, would know who and what kind of woman this is who is touching Him—she's a sinner!"

—Luke 7:39

---

e**7:35** Or *wisdom is declared right*

"You have judged correctly," He told him. [44] Turning to the woman, He said to Simon, "Do you see this woman? I entered your house; you gave Me no water for My feet, but she, with her tears, has washed My feet and wiped them with her hair. [45] You gave Me no kiss, but she hasn't stopped kissing My feet since I came in. [46] You didn't anoint My head with oil, but she has anointed My feet with fragrant oil. [47] Therefore I tell you, her many sins have been forgiven; that's why[a] she loved much. But the one who is forgiven little, loves little." [48] Then He said to her, "Your sins are forgiven."

[49] Those who were at the table with Him began to say among themselves, "Who is this man who even forgives sins?"

[50] And He said to the woman, "Your faith has saved you. Go in peace."

MANY WOMEN SUPPORT CHRIST'S WORK

8 Soon afterwards He was traveling from one town and village to another, preaching and telling the good news of the kingdom of God. The Twelve were with Him, [2] and also some women who had been healed of evil spirits and sicknesses: Mary, called •Magdalene (seven demons had come out of her); [3] Joanna the wife of Chuza, •Herod's steward; Susanna; and many others who were supporting them from their possessions.

THE PARABLE OF THE SOWER

[4] As a large crowd was gathering, and people were flocking to Him from every town, He said in a parable: [5] "A sower went out to sow his seed. As he was sowing, some fell along the path; it was trampled on, and the birds of the sky ate it up. [6] Other seed fell on the rock; when it sprang up, it withered, since it lacked moisture. [7] Other seed fell among thorns; the thorns sprang up with it and choked it. [8] Still other seed fell on good ground; when it sprang up, it produced a crop: 100 times ∟what was sown⌐." As He said this, He called out, "Anyone who has ears to hear should listen!"

To Love Him Is to Know Him

An intimate love relationship with God is the key to knowing God's voice, to hearing when God speaks.

Turning to the woman, He said to Simon, "Do you see this woman? I entered your house; you gave Me no water for My feet, but she, with her tears, has washed My feet and wiped them with her hair."

—Luke 7:44

---

[a]7:47 Her love shows that she has been forgiven

WHY JESUS USED PARABLES

9 Then His disciples asked Him, "What does this parable mean?" 10 So He said, "The secrets[a] of the kingdom of God have been given for you to know, but to the rest it is in parables, so that

**Looking they may not see,
and hearing they may not understand.**[b]

THE PARABLE OF THE SOWER EXPLAINED

11 "This is the meaning of the parable:[c] The seed is the word of God. 12 The seeds along the path are those who have heard. Then the Devil comes and takes away the word from their hearts, so that they may not believe and be saved. 13 And the seeds on the rock are those who, when they hear, welcome the word with joy. Having no root, these believe for a while and depart in a time of testing. 14 As for the seed that fell among thorns, these are the ones who, when they have heard, go on their way and are choked with worries, riches, and pleasures of life, and produce no mature fruit. 15 But the seed in the good ground—these are the ones who,[d] having heard the word with an honest and good heart, hold on to it and by enduring, bear fruit.

USING YOUR LIGHT

16 "No one, after lighting a lamp, covers it with a basket or puts it under a bed, but puts it on a lampstand so that those who come in may see the light. 17 For nothing is concealed that won't be revealed, and nothing hidden that won't be made known and come to light. 18 Therefore, take care how you listen. For whoever has, more will be given to him; and whoever does not have, even what he thinks he has will be taken away from him."

TRUE RELATIONSHIPS

19 Then His mother and brothers came to Him, but they could not meet with Him because of the crowd.

Going Our Way Is a Sure Way to Miss God

If we will not submit, God will let us follow our own devices. In following them, however, we will never experience what God is wanting to do for us and through us.

"As for the seed that fell among thorns, these are the ones who, when they have heard, go on their way and are choked with worries, riches, and pleasures of life, and produce no mature fruit."

—Luke 8:14

Stop, Look, and Listen

As you pray, watch to see how God uses His Word to confirm in your heart a word from Him. Watch what He is doing around you in circumstances. The God who is speaking to you as you pray and the God who is speaking to you in the Scriptures is the God who is working around you.

"Take care how you listen. For whoever has, more will be given to him; and whoever does not have, even what he thinks he has will be taken away from him."

—Luke 8:18

---

[a]**8:10** The Gk word *mysteria* does not mean "mysteries" in the Eng sense; it means what we can know only by divine revelation.
[b]**8:10** Is 6:9
[c]**8:11** Lit *But this is the parable:*
[d]**8:15** Or *these are the kind who*

20 He was told, "Your mother and Your brothers are standing outside, wanting to see You."

21 But He replied to them, "My mother and My brothers are those who hear and do the word of God."

WIND AND WAVE OBEY THE MASTER

22 One day He and His disciples got into a boat, and He told them, "Let's cross over to the other side of the lake." So they set out, 23 and as they were sailing He fell asleep. Then a fierce windstorm came down on the lake; they were being swamped and were in danger. 24 They came and woke Him up, saying, "Master, Master, we're going to die!" Then He got up and rebuked the wind and the raging waves. So they ceased, and there was a calm. 25 He said to them, "Where is your faith?"

They were fearful and amazed, asking one another, "Who can this be?a He commands even the winds and the waves, and they obey Him!"

DEMONS DRIVEN OUT BY THE MASTER

26 Then they sailed to the region of the Gerasenes,b which is opposite Galilee. 27 When He got out on land, a demon-possessed man from the town met Him. For a long time he had worn no clothes and did not stay in a house but in the tombs. 28 When he saw Jesus, he cried out, fell down before Him, and said in a loud voice, "What do You have to do with me,c Jesus, You Son of the Most High God? I beg You, don't torment me!" 29 For He had commanded the unclean spirit to come out of the man. Many times it had seized him, and although he was guarded, bound by chains and shackles, he would snap the restraints and be driven by the demon into deserted places.

30 "What is your name?" Jesus asked him.

"Legion," he said—because many demons had entered him. 31 And they begged Him not to banish them to the •abyss.

---

a8:25 Lit Who then is this?
b8:26 Other mss read the Gadarenes
c8:28 Lit What to me and to You

WORD STUDY

Greek word: **basanizo**
[bah sah NEE zoh]

Translation: **torment**

Uses in Luke's Gospel: **1**
(Mt, 3; Mk, 2)

Uses in the NT: **12**

Key passage: **Luke 8:28**

The Greek verb *basanizo* basically means *to torment* but has a wide range of uses in the NT. *Basanizo* is used literally in reference to the "terrible agony" caused by a disease (Mt 8:6; see 4:24 for the noun *basanos,* "intense pains") and the scorpion-like locusts that will torment the ungodly (Rv 9:5; see 11:10). The term also describes childbirth (Rv 12:2) and Lot's tormented soul regarding the evil he saw in Sodom and Gomorrah (2 Pt 2:8). *Basanizo* is used figuratively in Matthew's account of Jesus' walking on the water, where it refers to a boat being "battered" by waves from the sea (14:24; see Mk 6:48, where the disciples themselves are battered). *Basanizo* is also used in the account of numerous demons begging Jesus not to torment them (Mt 8:29 = Mk 5:7 = Lk 8:28—Luke explains this torment as the demons' fear of being sent into the abyss; v. 31); and of the torment of eternal punishment (Rv 14:10-11; 20:10). Related to the latter is the use of the word "torment" *(basanos)* by the rich man who was suffering in the flames to such a degree that he requested some relief from Abraham (Lk 16:23,28). Two other related nouns are *basanistes,* "jailers" who tortured prisoners (used only in Mt 18:34), and *basanismos,* which describes the torment of God's judgment and occurs only in Revelation (9:5 twice; 14:11; 18:7,10,15).

32 A large herd of pigs was there, feeding on the hillside. The demons begged Him to permit them to enter the pigs, and He gave them permission. 33 The demons came out of the man and entered the pigs, and the herd rushed down the steep bank into the lake and drowned. 34 When the men who tended them saw what had happened, they ran off and reported it in the town and in the countryside. 35 Then people went out to see what had happened. They came to Jesus and found the man the demons had departed from, sitting at Jesus' feet, dressed and in his right mind. And they were afraid. 36 Meanwhile the eyewitnesses reported to them how the demon-possessed man was delivered. 37 Then all the people of the Gerasene region[a] asked Him to leave them, because they were gripped by great fear. So getting into the boat, He returned. 38 The man from whom the demons had departed kept begging Him to be with Him. But He sent him away and said, 39 "Go back to your home, and tell all that God has done for you." And off he went, proclaiming throughout the town all that Jesus had done for him.

What Has God Done for You Lately?

Your responsibility is not to convince others of the reality of God, but simply to bear witness to what your Lord has said and done for you.

"Go back to your home, and tell all that God has done for you." And off he went, proclaiming throughout the town all that Jesus had done for him.

—Luke 8:39

A GIRL RESTORED AND A WOMAN HEALED

40 When Jesus returned, the crowd welcomed Him, for they were all expecting Him. 41 Just then, a man named Jairus came. He was a leader of the •synagogue. He fell down at Jesus' feet and pleaded with Him to come to his house, 42 because he had an only daughter about 12 years old, and she was at death's door.[b]

While He was going, the crowds were nearly crushing Him. 43 A woman suffering from bleeding for 12 years, who had spent all she had on doctors[c] yet could not be healed by any, 44 approached from behind and touched the •tassel of His robe. Instantly her bleeding stopped.

45 "Who touched Me?" Jesus asked.

When they all denied it, Peter[d] said, "Master, the crowds are hemming You in and pressing against You."[e]

---

[a]8:37 Other mss read *the Gadarenes*
[b]8:42 Lit *she was dying*
[c]8:43 Other mss omit *who had spent all she had on doctors*
[d]8:45 Other mss add *and those with him*
[e]8:45 Other mss add *and You say, 'Who touched Me?'*

⁴⁶ "Somebody did touch Me," said Jesus. "I know that power has gone out from Me." ⁴⁷ When the woman saw that she was discovered,ᵃ she came trembling and fell down before Him. In the presence of all the people, she declared the reason she had touched Him and how she was instantly cured. ⁴⁸ "Daughter," He said to her, "your faith has made you well.ᵇ Go in peace."

⁴⁹ While He was still speaking, someone came from the synagogue leader's ⌊house⌋, saying, "Your daughter is dead. Don't bother the Teacher anymore."

⁵⁰ When Jesus heard it, He answered him, "Don't be afraid. Only believe, and she will be made well."

⁵¹ After He came to the house, He let no one enter with Him except Peter, John, James, and the child's father and mother. ⁵² Everyone was crying and mourning for her. But He said, "Stop crying, for she is not dead but asleep."

⁵³ They started laughing at Him, because they knew she was dead. ⁵⁴ So Heᶜ took her by the hand and called out, "Child, get up!" ⁵⁵ Her spirit returned, and she got up at once. Then He gave orders that she be given something to eat. ⁵⁶ Her parents were astounded, but He instructed them to tell no one what had happened.

COMMISSIONING THE TWELVE

9 Summoning the Twelve, He gave them power and authority over all the demons, and ⌊power⌋ to healᵈ diseases. ² Then He sent them to proclaim the kingdom of God and to heal the sick.

³ "Take nothing for the road," He told them, "no walking stick, no traveling bag, no bread, no money; and don't take an extra shirt. ⁴ Whatever house you enter, stay there and leave from there. ⁵ If they do not welcome you, when you leave that town, shake off the dust from your feet as a testimony against them." ⁶ So they went out and traveled from village to village, proclaiming the good news and healing everywhere.

Walk by Faith, Not by Sight

Many people miss out on experiencing God's mighty power working through them. If they cannot see exactly how everything can be done, they will not proceed. They want to walk with God by sight. To follow God, you will have to walk by faith; and faith always requires action.

"Daughter," He said to her, "your faith has made you well. Go in peace."
—Luke 8:48

ᵃ8:47 Lit *she had not escaped notice*
ᵇ8:48 Or *has saved you*
ᶜ8:54 Other mss add *having put them all outside*
ᵈ9:1 In this passage, different Gk words are translated as *heal*. In Eng,

"to heal" or "to cure" are synonyms with little distinction in meaning. Technically, we do not heal or cure diseases. People are healed or cured from diseases.

HEROD'S DESIRE TO SEE JESUS

7 •Herod the tetrarch heard about everything that was going on. He was perplexed, because some said that John had been raised from the dead, 8 some that Elijah had appeared, and others that one of the ancient prophets had risen. 9 "I beheaded John," Herod said, "but who is this I hear such things about?" And he wanted to see Him.

Experience Soon Becomes Understanding

When you make the adjustments and start to obey Him, you come to know Him by experience. This is the goal of God's activity in your life—that you come to know Him.

When the apostles returned, they reported to Jesus all that they had done. He took them along and withdrew privately to a town called Bethsaida.

—Luke 9:10

Talk Up and Listen Up

Prayer is two-way fellowship and communication with God, not a one-way conversation. In fact, what God says in prayer is far more important than what you say. Prayer is designed more to adjust you to God than to adjust God to you.

While He was praying in private and His disciples were with Him, He asked them, "Who do the crowds say that I am?"

—Luke 9:18

FEEDING 5,000

10 When the apostles returned, they reported to Jesus all that they had done. He took them along and withdrew privately to aª town called Bethsaida. 11 When the crowds found out, they followed Him. He welcomed them, spoke to them about the kingdom of God, and curedᵇ those who needed healing.

12 Late in the day,ᶜ the Twelve approached and said to Him, "Send the crowd away, so they can go into the surrounding villages and countryside to find food and lodging, because we are in a deserted place here."

13 "You give them something to eat," He told them.

"We have no more than five loaves and two fish," they said, "unless we go and buy food for all these people." 14 (For about 5,000 men were there.)

Then He told His disciples, "Have them sit downᵈ in groups of about 50 each." 15 They did so, and had them all sit down. 16 Then He took the five loaves and the two fish, and looking up to heaven, He blessed and broke them. He kept giving them to the disciples to set before the crowd. 17 Everyone ate and was filled. Then they picked upᵉ 12 baskets of leftover pieces.

PETER'S CONFESSION OF THE MESSIAH

18 While He was praying in private and His disciples were with Him, He asked them, "Who do the crowds say that I am?"

ª**9:10** Other mss add *deserted place near a*
ᵇ**9:11** Or *healed*; in this passage, different Gk words are translated as *heal*. In Eng, "to heal" or "to cure" are synonyms with little distinction in meaning. Technically, we do not heal or cure diseases. People are healed or cured from diseases.
ᶜ**9:12** Lit *When the day began to decline*
ᵈ**9:14** Lit *them recline*
ᵉ**9:17** Lit *Then were picked up by them*

¹⁹ They answered, "John the Baptist; others, Elijah; still others, that one of the ancient prophets has come back."ᵃ

²⁰ "But you," He asked them, "who do you say that I am?"

Peter answered, "God's •Messiah!"

HIS DEATH AND RESURRECTION PREDICTED

²¹ But He strictly warned and instructed them to tell this to no one, ²² saying, "The •Son of Man must suffer many things and be rejected by the elders, •chief priests, and •scribes, be killed, and be raised the third day."

TAKE UP YOUR CROSS

²³ Then He said to ⌊them⌋ all, "If anyone wants to come withᵇ Me, he must deny himself, take up his cross daily,ᶜ and follow Me. ²⁴ For whoever wants to save his •life will lose it, but whoever loses his life because of Me will save it. ²⁵ What is a man benefited if he gains the whole world, yet loses or forfeits himself? ²⁶ For whoever is ashamed of Me and My words, the Son of Man will be ashamed of him when He comes in His glory and that of the Father and the holy angels. ²⁷ I tell you the truth: there are some standing here who will not taste death until they see the kingdom of God."

THE TRANSFIGURATION

²⁸ About eight days after these words, He took along Peter, John, and James, and went up on the mountain to pray. ²⁹ As He was praying, the appearance of His face changed, and His clothes became dazzling white. ³⁰ Suddenly, two men were talking with Him—Moses and Elijah. ³¹ They appeared in glory and were speaking of His death,ᵈ which He was about to accomplish in Jerusalem. ³² Peter and those with him were in a deep sleep,ᵉ and when they became fully awake, they saw His glory

---

ᵃ9:19 Lit *has risen*
ᵇ9:23 Lit *come after*
ᶜ9:23 Other mss omit *daily*
ᵈ9:31 Or *departure*; Gk *exodus*
ᵉ9:32 Lit *were weighed down with sleep*

WORD STUDY

Greek word: **dei** [DIGH]
Translation: **must**
Uses in Luke's Gospel: **18** (Mt, 8; Mk, 6; Jn, 10)
Uses in Luke's Writings: **40**
Uses in the NT: **101**
Key passage: **Luke 9:22**

The Greek word *dei* is a special form of the verb *deo*, meaning *to bind*, and refers to something that is a binding obligation upon someone. In the Gospels the term *dei* normally occurs in contexts related to some aspect of salvation, and the binding obligation comes from the decree of God—though this is not stated but is clearly implied. Thus, in Luke's Gospel *dei* indicates that Jesus must do the Father's will (2:49); preach (4:43); keep a divine appointment with a tax collector (19:5); suffer, die, and rise again (9:22; 17:25; 24:7,26; see Mt 16:21; Mk 8:31; Ac 17:3); and that the Scriptures must be fulfilled (Lk 24:44; see Jn 20:9; Ac 1:16). Luke continued the theme of divine necessity in Acts: Jesus must remain in heaven until the appointed time (Ac 3:21), everyone must believe in Jesus for salvation (Ac 4:12; 16:30-31), and believers must suffer for Jesus' sake (Ac 9:16; 14:22). Similarly, in John's Gospel *dei* refers to the necessity of the new birth (3:7), Jesus' appointment with the woman of Samaria (4:4), the obligation to worship God "in spirit and truth" (4:24), and Jesus' bringing all sheep into "one flock" (10:16). The term *dei* also describes the divine necessity of certain events in the end times that relate to final salvation (Mt 24:6 = Mk 13:7 = Lk 21:9; see 1 Co 15:25,53; 2 Co 5:10; Rv 1:1; 4:1; 11:5; 17:10; 20:3; 22:6).

and the two men who were standing with Him. [33] As the two men were departing from Him, Peter said to Jesus, "Master, it's good for us to be here! Let us make three •tabernacles: one for You, one for Moses, and one for Elijah"—not knowing what he said.

[34] While he was saying this, a cloud appeared and overshadowed them. They became afraid as they entered the cloud. [35] Then a voice came from the cloud, saying:

> This is My Son, the Chosen One;[a]
> listen to Him!

[36] After the voice had spoken, only Jesus was found. They kept silent, and in those days told no one what they had seen.

THE POWER OF FAITH OVER A DEMON

[37] The next day, when they came down from the mountain, a large crowd met Him. [38] Just then a man from the crowd cried out, "Teacher, I beg You to look at my son, because he's my only ₁child₁. [39] Often a spirit seizes him; suddenly he shrieks, and it throws him into convulsions until he foams at the mouth;[b] wounding[c] him, it hardly ever leaves him. [40] I begged Your disciples to drive it out, but they couldn't."

[41] Jesus replied, "You unbelieving and rebellious[d] generation! How long will I be with you and put up with you? Bring your son here."

[42] As the boy was still approaching, the demon knocked him down and threw him into severe convulsions. But Jesus rebuked the unclean spirit, cured the boy, and gave him back to his father. [43] And they were all astonished at the greatness of God.

THE SECOND PREDICTION OF HIS DEATH

While everyone was amazed at all the things He was doing, He told His disciples, [44] "Let these words sink in:[e] the Son of Man is about to be betrayed into the hands of men."

Maintain a Teachable Spirit

Don't allow the limited knowledge you have now to blind you to the great truths God still wants to reveal to you.

"Let these words sink in: the Son of Man is about to be betrayed into the hands of men."

—Luke 9:44

---

[a]9:35 Other mss read *the Beloved*
[b]9:39 Lit *convulsions with foam*
[c]9:39 Or *bruising*, or *mauling*
[d]9:41 Or *corrupt*, or *perverted*, or *twisted*; Dt 32:5
[e]9:44 Lit *Put these words in your ears*

45 But they did not understand this statement; it was concealed from them so that they could not grasp it, and they were afraid to ask Him about it.ᵃ

WHO IS THE GREATEST?

46 Then an argument started among them about who would be the greatest of them. 47 But Jesus, knowing the thoughts of their hearts, took a little child and had him stand next to Him. 48 He told them, "Whoever welcomesᵇ this little child in My name welcomes Me. And whoever welcomes Me welcomes Him who sent Me. For whoever is least among you—this one is great."

IN HIS NAME

49 John responded, "Master, we saw someone driving out demons in Your name, and we tried to stop him because he does not follow us."
50 "Don't stop him," Jesus told him, "because whoever is not against you is for you."ᶜ

THE JOURNEY TO JERUSALEM

51 When the days were coming to a close for Him to be taken up,ᵈ He determinedᵉ to journey to Jerusalem. 52 He sent messengers ahead of Him, and on the way they entered a village of the •Samaritans to make preparations for Him. 53 But they did not welcome Him, because He determined to journey to Jerusalem. 54 When the disciples James and John saw this, they said, "Lord, do You want us to call down fire from heaven to consume them?"ᶠ
55 But He turned and rebuked them,ᵍ 56 and they went to another village.

FOLLOWING JESUS

57 As they were traveling on the road someone said to Him, "I will follow You wherever You go!"

God Can Give You the Strength to Obey

As you obey Him, God will prepare you for the next assignment.

When the days were coming to a close for Him to be taken up, He determined to journey to Jerusalem.

—Luke 9:51

ᵃ9:45 Lit *about this statement*
ᵇ9:48 Or *receives* throughout the verse
ᶜ9:50 Other mss read *against us is for us*
ᵈ9:51 His ascension
ᵉ9:51 Lit *He stiffened His face to go*; Is 50:7

ᶠ9:54 Other mss add *as Elijah also did*
ᵍ9:55-56 Other mss add *and said, "You don't know what kind of spirit you belong to. 56 For the Son of Man did not come to destroy people's lives but to save them."*

⁵⁸ Jesus told him, "Foxes have dens, and birds of the sky ᵃ have nests, but the Son of Man has no place to lay His head." ⁵⁹ **Then He said to another,** "Follow Me."

"Lord," he said, "first let me go bury my father."ᵇ

⁶⁰ **But He told him,** "Let the dead bury their own dead, but you go and spread the news of the kingdom of God."

⁶¹ **Another also said,** "I will follow You, Lord, but first let me go and say good-bye to those at my house."

⁶² **But Jesus said to him,** "No one who puts his hand to the plow and looks back is fit for the kingdom of God."

SENDING OUT THE SEVENTY

10 After this, the Lord appointed 70ᶜ others, and He sent them ahead of Him in pairs to every town and place where He Himself was about to go. ² He told them: "The harvest is abundant, but the workers are few. Therefore, pray to the Lord of the harvest to send out workers into His harvest. ³ Now go; I'm sending you out like lambs among wolves. ⁴ Don't carry a money-bag, traveling bag, or sandals; don't greet anyone along the road. ⁵ Whatever house you enter, first say, 'Peace to this household.' ⁶ If a son of peaceᵈ is there, your peace will rest on him; but if not, it will return to you. ⁷ Remain in the same house, eating and drinking what they offer, for the worker is worthy of his wages. Don't be moving from house to house. ⁸ When you enter any town, and they welcome you, eat the things set before you. ⁹ Heal the sick who are there, and tell them, 'The kingdom of God has come near you.' ¹⁰ When you enter any town, and they don't welcome you, go out into its streets and say, ¹¹ 'We are wiping off ⌊as a witness⌋ against you even the dust of your town that clings to our feet. Know this for certain: the kingdom of God has come near.' ¹² I tell you, on that day it will be more tolerable for Sodom than for that town.

Be Prepared for God to Change You

Adjustments prepare you for obedience. You cannot continue life as usual, or stay where you are, and go with God at the same time.

Another also said, "I will follow You, Lord, but first let me go and say good-bye to those at my house."

—Luke 9:61

Are You Committed to God's Business?

Frequently, the reason we do not join Him is because we are not committed to Him. We are wanting God to bless us, not to work through us.

He told them: "The harvest is abundant, but the workers are few. Therefore, pray to the Lord of the harvest to send out workers into His harvest."

—Luke 10:2

ᵃ**9:58** Wild birds, as opposed to domestic birds
ᵇ**9:59** Not necessarily meaning his father was already dead

ᶜ**10:1** Other mss read *72*
ᵈ**10:6** A peaceful person; one open to the message of the kingdom

UNREPENTANT TOWNS

¹³ "Woe to you, Chorazin! Woe to you, Bethsaida! For if the miracles that were done in you had been done in Tyre and Sidon, they would have repented long ago, sitting in sackcloth and ashes! ¹⁴ But it will be more tolerable for Tyre and Sidon at the judgment than for you. ¹⁵ And you, Capernaum, will you be exalted to heaven? No, you will go down to •Hades! ¹⁶ Whoever listens to you listens to Me. Whoever rejects you rejects Me. And whoever rejects Me rejects the One who sent Me."

THE RETURN OF THE SEVENTY

¹⁷ The Seventy^a returned with joy, saying, "Lord, even the demons submit to us in Your name."
¹⁸ He said to them, "I watched Satan fall from heaven like a lightning flash. ¹⁹ Look, I have given you the authority to trample on snakes and scorpions and over all the power of the enemy; nothing will ever harm you. ²⁰ However, don't rejoice that^b the spirits submit to you, but rejoice that your names are written in heaven."

THE SON REVEALS THE FATHER

²¹ In that same hour He^c rejoiced in the Holy^d Spirit and said, "I praise^e You, Father, Lord of heaven and earth, because You have hidden these things from the wise and the learned and have revealed them to infants. Yes, Father, because this was Your good pleasure.^f ²² All things have^g been entrusted to Me by My Father. No one knows who the Son is except the Father, and who the Father is except the Son, and anyone to whom the Son desires^h to reveal Him."
²³ Then turning to His disciples He said privately, "The eyes that see the things you see are blessed! ²⁴ For I tell you that many prophets and kings wanted to see the things you see yet didn't see them; to hear the things you hear yet didn't hear them."

God Has Good Reason for Working in You

The Holy Spirit will manifest Himself through your life, not for your good alone, but for the benefit of those around you.

In that same hour He rejoiced in the Holy Spirit and said, "I praise You, Father, Lord of heaven and earth, because You have hidden these things from the wise and the learned and have revealed them to infants. Yes, Father, because this was Your good pleasure"
—Luke 10:21

---

^a**10:17** Other mss read *The Seventy-two*
^b**10:20** Lit *don't rejoice in this, that*
^c**10:21** Other mss read *Jesus*
^d**10:21** Other mss omit *Holy*
^e**10:21** Or *thank,* or *confess*
^f**10:21** Lit *was well-pleasing in Your sight*
^g**10:22** Other mss read *And turning to the disciples, He said, "Everything has*
^h**10:22** Or *wills,* or *chooses*

WORD STUDY

Greek word: **agapao**
[ah gah PAH oh]
Translation: **love**

Uses in Luke's Gospel: **13**
(Mt, 8; Mk, 5; Jn, 37)

Uses in the NT: **143**

Key passage: **Luke 10:27**

The most common Greek words for love in the NT are *agapao* (verb) and *agape* (noun). These two words are used to describe the purest and highest form of love, although they have other uses that are not as noble (see Lk 11:43). The synonymous verb *phileo* was also used in the noblest of senses on occasion, which reflects common Greek usage in the first century. However, *agapao* is used in the Greek OT regarding the two greatest commandments, which is what the expert in the Mosaic law quoted (Lk 10:27; see Dt 6:5; Lv 19:18). God demands that we love Him with our entire being—heart, soul, mind, and strength. Loving God means that we must also love those created in His image, even our enemies (Lk 6:27). Jesus' explanation of the two greatest commandments indicates that every sin violates one or both of the commands to love God and to love others (Mt 22:40).

THE PARABLE OF THE GOOD SAMARITAN

25 Just then an expert in the law stood up to test Him, saying, "Teacher, what must I do to inherit eternal life?" 26 "What is written in the law?" He asked him. "How do you read it?"

27 He answered:

Love the Lord your God with all your heart, with all your soul, with all your strength, and with all your mind; and your neighbor as yourself.[a]

28 "You've answered correctly," He told him. "Do this and you will live."

29 But wanting to justify himself, he asked Jesus, "And who is my neighbor?"

30 Jesus took up ⌊the question⌋ and said: "A man was going down from Jerusalem to Jericho and fell into the hands of robbers. They stripped him, beat him up, and fled, leaving him half dead. 31 A priest happened to be going down that road. When he saw him, he passed by on the other side. 32 In the same way, a Levite, when he arrived at the place and saw him, passed by on the other side. 33 But a •Samaritan on his journey came up to him, and when he saw ⌊the man⌋, he had compassion. 34 He went over to him and bandaged his wounds, pouring on oil and wine. Then he put him on his own animal, brought him to an inn, and took care of him. 35 The next day[b] he took out two •denarii, gave them to the innkeeper, and said, 'Take care of him. When I come back I'll reimburse you for whatever extra you spend.'

36 "Which of these three do you think proved to be a neighbor to the man who fell into the hands of the robbers?"

37 "The one who showed mercy to him," he said.
Then Jesus told him, "Go and do the same."

MARTHA AND MARY

38 While they were traveling, He entered a village, and a woman named Martha welcomed Him into her home.[c]

---

[a]**10:27** Dt 6:5; Lv 19:18
[b]**10:35** Other mss add *as he was leaving*

[c]**10:38** Other mss omit *into her home*

39 She had a sister named Mary, who also sat at the Lord's[a] feet and was listening to what He said.[b] 40 But Martha was distracted by her many tasks, and she came up and asked, "Lord, don't You care that my sister has left me to serve alone? So tell her to give me a hand."[c]

41 The Lord[d] answered her, "Martha, Martha, you are worried and upset about many things, 42 but one thing is necessary. Mary has made the right choice,[e] and it will not be taken away from her."

THE MODEL PRAYER

11 He was praying in a certain place, and when He finished, one of His disciples said to Him, "Lord, teach us to pray, just as John also taught his disciples."

2 He said to them, "Whenever you pray, say:

Father,[f]
Your name be honored as holy.
Your kingdom come.[g]
3 Give us each day our daily bread.[h]
4 And forgive us our sins,
for we ourselves also forgive everyone
in debt[i] to us.
And do not bring us into temptation."[j]

KEEP ASKING, SEARCHING, KNOCKING

5 He also said to them: "Suppose one of you[k] has a friend and goes to him at midnight and says to him, 'Friend, lend me three loaves of bread, 6 because a friend of mine on a journey has come to me, and I don't have anything to offer him.'[l] 7 Then he will answer from inside and say, 'Don't bother me! The door is already locked, and my children and I have gone to bed. I can't get up to give you anything.' 8 I tell you, even though he won't get up and give him anything because

When You Have God, You Have It All

You do not need to be doing something to feel fulfilled. You are fulfilled completely in a relationship with God. When you are filled with Him, what else do you need?

The Lord answered her, "Martha, Martha, you are worried and upset about many things, but one thing is necessary. Mary has made the right choice, and it will not be taken away from her."
—Luke 10:41-42

Make Sure He Is Lord No Matter What

He calls you to a relationship where He is Lord—where you are willing to do and be anything He chooses.

He said to them, "Whenever you pray, say: Father, Your name be honored as holy. Your kingdom come."
—Luke 11:2

---

a10:39 Other mss read *at Jesus'*
b10:39 Lit *to His word* or *message*
c10:40 Or *tell her to help me*
d10:41 Other mss read *Jesus*
e10:42 Lit *has chosen the good part*
f11:2 Other mss read *Our Father in heaven*
g11:2 Other mss add *Your will be* done on earth as it is in heaven
h11:3 Or *our bread for tomorrow*
i11:4 Or *everyone who wrongs us*
j11:4 Other mss add *But deliver us from the evil one*
k11:5 Lit *Who of you*
l11:6 Lit *I have nothing to set before him*

he is his friend, yet because of his persistence,[a] he will get up and give him as much as he needs.

⁹ "So I say to you, keep asking,[b] and it will be given to you. Keep searching,[c] and you will find. Keep knocking,[d] and the door will be opened to you. ¹⁰ For everyone who asks receives, and the one who searches finds, and to the one who knocks, the door will be opened. ¹¹ What father among you, if his son[e] asks for a fish, will give him a snake instead of a fish? ¹² Or if he asks for an egg, will give him a scorpion? ¹³ If you then, who are evil, know how to give good gifts to your children, how much more will the heavenly Father give[f] the Holy Spirit to those who ask Him?"

A HOUSE DIVIDED

¹⁴ Now He was driving out a demon that was mute.[g] When the demon came out, the man who had been mute, spoke, and the crowds were amazed. ¹⁵ But some of them said, "He drives out demons by •Beelzebul, the ruler of the demons!" ¹⁶ And others, as a test, were demanding of Him a sign from heaven.

¹⁷ Knowing their thoughts, He told them: "Every kingdom divided against itself is headed for destruction, and a house divided against itself falls. ¹⁸ If Satan also is divided against himself, how will his kingdom stand? For you say I drive out demons by Beelzebul. ¹⁹ And if I drive out demons by Beelzebul, who is it your sons[h] drive them out by? For this reason they will be your judges. ²⁰ If I drive out demons by the finger of God, then the kingdom of God has come to you. ²¹ When a strong man, fully armed, guards his estate, his possessions are secure.[i] ²² But when one stronger than he attacks and overpowers him, he takes from him all his weapons[j] he trusted in, and divides up his plunder. ²³ Anyone who is not with Me is against Me, and anyone who does not gather with Me scatters.

**God Is So Good,
So Good to Me**

He will always direct you in ways that are best for you and for the world into which He calls you.

"If you then, who are evil, know how to give good gifts to your children, how much more will the heavenly Father give the Holy Spirit to those who ask Him?"

—Luke 11:13

---

[a]**11:8** Or *annoying persistence*, or *shamelessness*
[b]**11:9** Or *you, ask*
[c]**11:9** Or *Search*
[d]**11:9** Or *Knock*
[e]**11:11** Other mss read *son asks for bread, would give him a stone? Or if he*

[f]**11:13** Lit *the Father from heaven will give*
[g]**11:14** A demon that caused the man to be mute
[h]**11:19** Your exorcists
[i]**11:21** Lit *his possessions are in peace*
[j]**11:22** Gk *panoplia*, the armor and weapons of a foot soldier; Eph 6:11, 13

AN UNCLEAN
SPIRIT'S RETURN

²⁴ "When an unclean spirit comes out of a man, it roams through waterless places looking for rest, and not finding rest, it then[a] says, 'I'll go back to my house where I came from.' ²⁵ And returning, it finds ⌞the house⌟ swept and put in order. ²⁶ Then it goes and brings seven other spirits more evil than itself, and they enter and settle down there. As a result, that man's last condition is worse than the first."

TRUE BLESSEDNESS

²⁷ As He was saying these things, a woman from the crowd raised her voice and said to Him, "The womb that bore You and the one who nursed You are blessed!"
²⁸ He said, "Even more, those who hear the word of God and keep it are blessed!"

THE SIGN OF JONAH

²⁹ As the crowds were increasing, He began saying: "This generation is an evil generation. It demands a sign, but no sign will be given to it except the sign of Jonah.[b] ³⁰ For just as Jonah became a sign to the people of Nineveh, so also the •Son of Man will be to this generation. ³¹ The queen of the south will rise up at the judgment with the men of this generation and condemn them, because she came from the ends of the earth to hear the wisdom of Solomon, and look—something greater than Solomon is here! ³² The men of Nineveh will rise up at the judgment with this generation and condemn it, because they repented at Jonah's proclamation, and look—something greater than Jonah is here!

THE LAMP OF THE BODY

³³ "No one lights a lamp and puts it in the cellar or under a basket,[c] but on a lampstand, so that those who come in may see its light. ³⁴ Your eye is the lamp of the

Let God's Word Lead You into Obedience

When you become bewildered by circumstances in your life, Jesus can reorient you to Himself through the Scriptures. Then you will be eager to join God in what He is doing around you.

He said, "Even more, those who hear the word of God and keep it are blessed!"
—Luke 11:28

---

[a]11:24 Other mss omit *then*
[b]11:29 Other mss add *the prophet*
[c]11:33 Other mss omit *or under a basket*

WORD STUDY

Greek word: **katabole**
[kah tah bah LAY]

Translation: **foundation**

Uses in Luke's Gospel: **1**
(Mt, 2; Jn, 1)

Uses in the NT: **11**

Key passage: **Luke 11:50**

The Greek noun *katabole* is related to the verb *kataballo* meaning *to throw* or *lay down* (used only in 2 Co 4:9; Heb 6:1). In the NT the term always refers to the beginning of something, making it somewhat synonymous with the more common Greek word that means *beginning (arche)*. An unusual use of the term *katabole* occurs in Hebrews 11:11, where the beginning of the promised seed through Abraham and Sarah is achieved by faith despite their advanced ages. All ten of the other uses of *katabole* are followed by the words "of the world" and are preceded by one of two prepositions: "from [Gk *apo*] the foundation of the world" refers to the time of creation (Mt 13:35; 25:34; Lk 11:50; Heb 4:3; 9:26; Rv 13:8; 17:8); and "before [Gk *pro*] the foundation of the world" refers to the eternal acts of God the Father in loving (Jn 17:24) and foreknowing (1 Pt 1:20) the Son, and in choosing believers (Eph 1:4).

body. When your eye is good, your whole body is also full of light. But when it is bad, your body is also full of darkness. [35] Take care then, that the light in you is not darkness. [36] If therefore your whole body is full of light, with no part of it in darkness, the whole body will be full of light, as when a lamp shines its light on you."[a]

RELIGIOUS HYPOCRISY DENOUNCED

[37] As He was speaking, a •Pharisee asked Him to dine with him. So He went in and reclined at the table. [38] When the Pharisee saw this, he was amazed that He did not first perform the ritual washing[b] before dinner. [39] But the Lord said to him: "Now you Pharisees clean the outside of the cup and dish, but inside you are full of greed and evil. [40] Fools! Didn't He who made the outside make the inside too? [41] But give to charity what is within,[c] and then everything is clean for you.

[42] "But woe to you Pharisees! You give a tenth[d] of mint, rue, and every kind of herb, and you bypass[e] justice and love for God.[f] These things you should have done without neglecting the others.

[43] "Woe to you Pharisees! You love the front seat in the •synagogues and greetings in the marketplaces.

[44] "Woe to you![g] You are like unmarked graves; the people who walk over them don't know it."

[45] One of the experts in the law answered Him, "Teacher, when You say these things You insult us too."

[46] Then He said: "Woe also to you experts in the law! You load people with burdens that are hard to carry, yet you yourselves don't touch these burdens with one of your fingers.

[47] "Woe to you! You build monuments[h] to the prophets, and your fathers killed them. [48] Therefore you are witnesses that you approve[i] the deeds of your fathers, for they killed them, and you build their monuments.[j]

---

[a]11:36 Or *shines on you with its rays*
[b]11:38 Lit *He did not first wash*
[c]11:41 Or *But donate from the heart as charity*
[d]11:42 Or *a tithe*
[e]11:42 Or *neglect*
[f]11:42 Lit *the justice and the love of God*

[g]11:44 Other mss read *you scribes and Pharisees, hypocrites!*
[h]11:47 Or *graves*
[i]11:48 Lit *witnesses and approve*
[j]11:48 Other mss omit *their monuments*

49 Because of this, the wisdom of God said, 'I will send them prophets and apostles, and some of them they will kill and persecute,' 50 so that this generation may be held responsible for the blood of all the prophets shed since the foundation of the world[a] — 51 from the blood of Abel to the blood of Zechariah, who perished between the altar and the sanctuary.

"Yes, I tell you, this generation will be held responsible.[b]

52 "Woe to you experts in the law! You have taken away the key of knowledge! You didn't go in yourselves, and you hindered those who were going in."

53 When He left there,[c] the •scribes and the Pharisees began to oppose Him fiercely and to cross-examine Him about many things; 54 they were lying in wait for Him to trap Him in something He said.[d]

BEWARE OF RELIGIOUS HYPOCRISY

12 In these circumstances,[e] a crowd of many thousands came together, so that they were trampling on one another. He began to say to His disciples first: "Be on your guard against the yeast[f] of the •Pharisees, which is hypocrisy. 2 There is nothing covered that won't be uncovered, nothing hidden that won't be made known. 3 Therefore whatever you have said in the dark will be heard in the light, and what you have whispered in an ear in private rooms will be proclaimed on the housetops.

FEAR GOD

4 "And I say to you, My friends, don't fear those who kill the body, and after that can do nothing more. 5 But I will show you the One to fear: Fear Him who has authority to throw ˌpeopleˌ into •hell after death. Yes, I say to you, this is the One to fear! 6 Aren't five sparrows sold for two pennies?[g] Yet not one of them is forgotten

WORD STUDY

Greek word: **geenna**
[GEH ehn nah]

Translation: **hell**

Uses in Luke's Gospel: **1**
(Mt, 7; Mk, 3)

Uses in the NT: **12**

Key passage: **Luke 12:5**

Geenna (*hell*) is the Greek form of Hb *gey'-hinnom* (*Valley of Hinnom*) via Aramaic *geyhinnam*, a valley located just south/southwest of Jerusalem's Old City. In the days of Ahaz and Manasseh, it was the location where children were dedicated and/or sacrificed to Molech (2 Kg 23:10; 2 Ch 28:3; 33:6; Jr 7:31), and by NT times it had become a place for burning trash. Because of its sordid history, the Hinnom valley became associated in Jewish thought with *hell*, the place of final punishment. *Geenna* is described primarily with images of fire (Mt 5:22; 18:9; Mk 9:43,45,48), and though the term does not occur in Revelation, it is a prominent theme there (cf. the lake of fire; Rv 19:20; 20:10,14-15; 21:8). At the final resurrection, the souls of the ungodly (in Hades) will be reunited with their resurrected bodies, and thrown into *Geenna* (Mt 10:28).

---

[a]11:50 Lit so that the blood of all ... world may be required of this generation,
[b]11:51 Lit you, it will be required of this generation
[c]11:53 Other mss read And as He was saying these things to them

[d]11:54 Other mss add so that they might bring charges against Him
[e]12:1 Or Meanwhile, or At this time, or During this period
[f]12:1 Or leaven
[g]12:6 Lit two assaria; the assarion (sg) was a small copper coin

in God's sight. 7 Indeed, the hairs of your head are all counted. Don't be afraid; you are worth more than many sparrows!

ACKNOWLEDGING CHRIST

8 "And I say to you, anyone who acknowledges Me before men, the •Son of Man will also acknowledge him before the angels of God, 9 but whoever denies Me before men will be denied before the angels of God. 10 Anyone who speaks a word against the Son of Man will be forgiven, but the one who blasphemes against the Holy Spirit will not be forgiven. 11 Whenever they bring you before •synagogues and rulers and authorities, don't worry about how you should defend yourselves or what you should say. 12 For the Holy Spirit will teach you at that very hour what must be said."

THE PARABLE OF THE RICH FOOL

13 Someone from the crowd said to Him, "Teacher, tell my brother to divide the inheritance with me."

14 "Friend,"a He said to him, "who appointed Me a judge or arbitrator over you?" 15 He then told them, "Watch out and be on guard against all greed because one's life is not in the abundance of his possessions."

16 Then He told them a parable: "A rich man's land was very productive. 17 He thought to himself, 'What should I do, since I don't have anywhere to store my crops? 18 I will do this,' he said. 'I'll tear down my barns and build bigger ones and store all my grain and my goods there. 19 Then I'll say to myself, "Youb have many goods stored up for many years. Take it easy; eat, drink, and enjoy yourself."'

20 "But God said to him, 'You fool! This very night your •life is demanded of you. And the things you have prepared—whose will they be?'

21 "That's how it is with the one who stores up treasure for himself and is not rich toward God."

THE CURE FOR ANXIETY

22 Then He said to His disciples: "Therefore I tell you, don't worry about your life, what you will eat; or about

---

He Cares About What Happens to You

Anything significant that happens in your life will be a result of God's activity in your life. He is infinitely more interested in your life than you or I could possibly be.

"Aren't five sparrows sold for two pennies? Yet not one of them is forgotten in God's sight. Indeed, the hairs of your head are all counted. Don't be afraid; you are worth more than many sparrows!"

—Luke 12:6-7

---

a**12:14** Lit *Man*   b**12:19** Lit *say to my soul, "Soul, you*

the body, what you will wear. ²³ For life is more than food and the body more than clothing. ²⁴ Consider the ravens: they don't sow or reap; they don't have a store-room or a barn; yet God feeds them. Aren't you worth much more than the birds? ²⁵ Can any of you add a •cu-bit to his height[a] by worrying? ²⁶ If then you're not able to do even a little thing, why worry about the rest?

²⁷ "Consider how the wildflowers grow: they don't labor or spin thread. Yet I tell you, not even Solomon in all his splendor was adorned like one of these! ²⁸ If that's how God clothes the grass, which is in the field today and is thrown into the furnace tomorrow, how much more will He do for you—you of little faith? ²⁹ Don't keep striving for what you should eat and what you should drink, and don't be anxious. ³⁰ For the Gentile world eagerly seeks all these things, and your Father knows that you need them.

³¹ "But seek His kingdom, and these things will be provided for you. ³² Don't be afraid, little flock, be-cause your Father delights to give you the kingdom. ³³ Sell your possessions and give to the poor. Make money-bags for yourselves that won't grow old, an in-exhaustible treasure in heaven, where no thief comes near and no moth destroys. ³⁴ For where your treasure is, there your heart will be also.

READY FOR THE MASTER'S RETURN

³⁵ "Be ready for service[b] and have your lamps lit. ³⁶ You must be like people waiting for their master to return[c] from the wedding banquet so that when he comes and knocks, they can open ⌊the door⌋ for him at once. ³⁷ Those •slaves the master will find alert when he comes will be blessed. •I assure you: He will get ready,[d] have them recline at the table, then come and serve them. ³⁸ If he comes in the middle of the night, or even near dawn,[e] and finds them alert, those slaves are blessed. ³⁹ But know this: if the homeowner had known at what hour the thief was coming, he would not

God Always Gives Good Directions

Because His nature is love, you can be confident that however He expresses Himself to you will always be what is best.

"Don't be afraid, little flock, because your Father delights to give you the kingdom."
—Luke 12:32

It's a Relationship, Not Just a Discipline

I hear many persons say, "I really struggle trying to have that time alone with God." If that is a problem you face, make the priority in your life to come to love Him with all your heart. That will solve most of your problem with your quiet time.

"For where your treasure is, there your heart will be also."
—Luke 12:34

ᵃ**12:25** Or *add one moment to his life-span*
ᵇ**12:35** Lit *Let your loins be girded*; an idiom for tying up loose outer clothing in preparation for action; Ex 12:11
ᶜ**12:36** Lit *master, when he should return*
ᵈ**12:37** Lit *will gird himself*
ᵉ**12:38** Lit *even in the second or third watch*

have let his house be broken into. [40] You also be ready, because the Son of Man is coming at an hour that you do not expect."

REWARDS AND PUNISHMENT

[41] "Lord," Peter asked, "are You telling this parable to us or to everyone?"

[42] The Lord said: "Who then is the faithful and sensible manager his master will put in charge of his household servants to give them their allotted food at the proper time? [43] That •slave whose master finds him working when he comes will be rewarded. [44] I tell you the truth: he will put him in charge of all his possessions. [45] But if that slave says in his heart, 'My master is delaying his coming,' and starts to beat the male and female slaves, and to eat and drink and get drunk, [46] that slave's master will come on a day he does not expect him and at an hour he does not know. He will cut him to pieces[a] and assign him a place with the unbelievers.[b] [47] And that slave who knew his master's will and didn't prepare himself or do it[c] will be severely beaten. [48] But the one who did not know and did things deserving of blows will be beaten lightly. Much will be required of everyone who has been given much. And even more will be expected of the one who has been entrusted with more.[d]

NOT PEACE BUT DIVISION

[49] "I came to bring fire on the earth, and how I wish it were already set ablaze! [50] But I have a baptism to be baptized with, and how it consumes Me until it is finished! [51] Do you think that I came here to give peace to the earth? No, I tell you, but rather division! [52] From now on, five in one household will be divided: three against two, and two against three.

[53] They will be divided, father against son,
    son against father,
    mother against daughter,
    daughter against mother,

God Gives So That You Can Pour Out

Are you trying to serve God and yet ignore something He has told you to do? Are you living your life as if God does not notice your disobedience? Do you apply God's standards to yourself as rigorously as you apply them to others?

"Much will be required of everyone who has been given much. And even more will be expected of the one who has been entrusted with more."

—Luke 12:48b

---

[a]12:46 Lit *him in two*
[b]12:46 Or *unfaithful*, or *untrustworthy*
[c]12:47 Lit *or do toward his will*
[d]12:48 Or *much*

mother-in-law against her daughter-in-law,
and daughter-in-law against
mother-in-law."ᵃ

INTERPRETING THE TIME

⁵⁴ He also said to the crowds: "When you see a cloud
rising in the west, right away you say, 'A storm is coming,' and so it does. ⁵⁵ And when the south wind is
blowing, you say, 'It's going to be a scorcher!' and it is.
⁵⁶ Hypocrites! You know how to interpret the appearance of the earth and the sky, but why don't you know
how to interpret this time?

SETTLING ACCOUNTS

⁵⁷ "Why don't you judge for yourselves what is right?
⁵⁸ As you are going with your adversary to the ruler,
make an effort to settle with him on the way. Then he
won't drag you before the judge, the judge hand you
over to the bailiff, and the bailiff throw you into prison.
⁵⁹ I tell you, you will never get out of there until you
have paid the last cent."ᵇ

REPEClarissN OR PERISH

13 At that time, some people came and reported
to Him about the Galileans whose blood •Pi-
late had mixed with their sacrifices. ² And Heᶜ responded to them, "Do you think that these Galileans were
more sinful than all Galileans because they suffered
these things? ³ No, I tell you; but unless you repent,
you will all perish as well! ⁴ Or those 18 that the tower
in Siloam fell on and killed—do you think they were
more sinful than all the people who live in Jerusalem?
⁵ No, I tell you; but unless you repent, you will all perish as well!"

THE PARABLE OF THE
BARREN FIG TREE

⁶ And He told this parable: "A man had a fig tree that
was planted in his vineyard. He came looking for fruit

**God Will Help You
Learn to Discern**

God does not want you merely
to gain intellectual knowledge of truth. He wants you
to experience His truth.

*"Hypocrites! You know how
to interpret the appearance
of the earth and the sky, but
why don't you know how
to interpret this time?"*
—Luke 12:56

ᵃ**12:53** Mc 7:6
ᵇ**12:59** Gk *lepton*, the smallest and least valuable copper coin in use
ᶜ**13:2** Other mss read *Jesus*

WORD STUDY

Greek word: **Satanas**
[sah tahn AHSS]

Translation: **Satan**

Uses in Luke's Gospel: **5**
(Mt, 4; Mk, 6; Jn, 1)

Uses in Luke's Writings: **7**

Uses in the NT: **36**

Key passage: **Luke 13:16**

The Greek word *satanas* comes from the Hebrew term *satan,* meaning *adversary, one who opposes another,* and the related Hebrew verb meaning *to withstand, accuse.* The Bible teaches that the adversary or arch enemy of God and His people is Satan, who is mentioned a few times in the OT (1 Ch 21:1; several times in Jb 1-2; Zch 3:1-2) but receives much greater prominence in the NT. The Greek word *diabolos,* meaning *slanderer,* is used 34 times in the NT to refer to this same spirit being as *the Devil.* (Three times *diabolos* is used in the plural with the general meaning *gossips* or *slanderers;* see 1 Tm 3:11; 2 Tm 3:3; Ti 2:3). Satan is the leader of the fallen angels or demons, who assist him in attempting to thwart and destroy God's plans and His people through tempting (Lk 4:1-13; 1 Co 7:5), possessing (Lk 4:31-37; 8:26-39; Jn 13:27), deceiving (Rv 12:9), and afflicting them with illness (Lk 11:14; 13:10-17). The final defeat and judgment of "the dragon, that ancient serpent, who is the Devil and Satan" is described in Revelation 20:1-10 (see v. 2).

on it and found none. 7 He told the vineyard worker, 'Listen, for three years I have come looking for fruit on this fig tree and haven't found any. Cut it down! Why should it even waste the soil?'

8 "But he replied to him, 'Sir,[a] leave it this year also, until I dig around it and fertilize it. 9 Perhaps it will bear fruit next year, but if not, you can cut it down.'"

HEALING A DAUGHTER OF ABRAHAM

10 As He was teaching in one of the •synagogues on the Sabbath, 11 a woman was there who had been disabled by a spirit[b] for over 18 years. She was bent over and could not straighten up at all.[c] 12 When Jesus saw her, He called out to her,[d] "Woman, you are free of your disability." 13 Then He laid His hands on her, and instantly she was restored and began to glorify God.

14 But the leader of the synagogue, indignant because Jesus had healed on the Sabbath, responded by telling the crowd, "There are six days when work should be done; therefore come on those days and be healed and not on the Sabbath day."

15 But the Lord answered him and said, "Hypocrites! Doesn't each one of you untie his ox or donkey from the feeding trough on the Sabbath and lead it to water? 16 Satan has bound this woman, a daughter of Abraham, for 18 years—shouldn't she be untied from this bondage on the Sabbath day?"

17 When He had said these things, all His adversaries were humiliated, but the whole crowd was rejoicing over all the glorious things He was doing.

THE PARABLES OF THE MUSTARD SEED AND OF THE YEAST

18 He said therefore, "What is the kingdom of God like, and what can I compare it to? 19 It's like a mustard seed that a man took and sowed in his garden. It grew and became a tree, and the birds of the sky nested in its branches."

20 Again He said, "What can I compare the kingdom of God to? 21 It's like yeast that a woman took and

---

[a]13:8 Or *Lord*
[b]13:11 Lit *had a spirit of disability*
[c]13:11 Or *straighten up completely*
[d]13:12 Or *He summoned her*

mixed into 50 pounds[a] of flour until it spread through the entire mixture."[b]

THE NARROW WAY

[22] He went through one town and village after another, teaching and making His way to Jerusalem. [23] "Lord," someone asked Him, "are there few being saved?"[c]

He said to them, [24] "Make every effort to enter through the narrow door, because I tell you, many will try to enter and won't be able [25] once the homeowner gets up and shuts the door. Then you will stand[d] outside and knock on the door, saying, 'Lord, open up for us!' He will answer you, 'I don't know you or where you're from.' [26] Then you will say,[e] 'We ate and drank in Your presence, and You taught in our streets!' [27] But He will say, 'I tell you, I don't know you or where you're from. Get away from Me, all you workers of unrighteousness!' [28] There will be weeping and gnashing of teeth in that place, when you see Abraham, Isaac, Jacob, and all the prophets in the kingdom of God but yourselves thrown out. [29] They will come from east and west, from north and south, and recline at the table in the kingdom of God. [30] Note this: some are last who will be first, and some are first who will be last."

JESUS AND HEROD ANTIPAS

[31] At that time some •Pharisees came and told Him, "Go, get out of here! •Herod wants to kill You!"

[32] He said to them, "Go tell that fox, 'Look! I'm driving out demons and performing healings today and tomorrow, and on the third day[f] I will complete My work.'[g] [33] Yet I must travel today, tomorrow, and the next day, because it is not possible for a prophet to perish outside of Jerusalem!

Learn the Everlasting Value of Service

The world will estimate your importance by the number of people serving you. God is more concerned with the number of people you are serving.

"Note this: some are last who will be first, and some are first who will be last."
—Luke 13:30

---

[a]**13:21** Lit *3 sata*; about 40 quarts
[b]**13:21** Or *until all of it was leavened*
[c]**13:23** Or *are the saved few?* (in number); lit *are those being saved few?*
[d]**13:25** Lit *you will begin to stand*
[e]**13:26** Lit *you will begin to say*
[f]**13:32** Very shortly
[g]**13:32** Lit *I will be finished*

JESUS' LAMENTATION OVER JERUSALEM

³⁴ "Jerusalem, Jerusalem! The city who kills the prophets and stones those who are sent to her. How often I wanted to gather your children together, as a hen gathers her chicks under her wings, but you were not willing! ³⁵ See, your house[a] is abandoned to you. And I tell you, you will not see Me until the time comes when you say, **Blessed is He who comes in the name of the Lord!**"[b]

A SABBATH CONTROVERSY

14 One Sabbath, when He went to eat[c] at the house of one of the leading •Pharisees, they were watching Him closely. ² There in front of Him was a man whose body was swollen with fluid.[d] ³ In response, Jesus asked the law experts and the Pharisees, "Is it lawful to heal on the Sabbath or not?" ⁴ But they kept silent. He took the man, healed him, and sent him away. ⁵ And to them, He said, "Which of you whose son or ox falls into a well, will not immediately pull him out on the Sabbath day?" ⁶ To this they could find no answer.

Don't Be Surprised to See God at Work

Unbelievers see God's activity and don't know what they see. But we should already be watching so we will know it is God at work and will be ready to respond.

Jesus asked the law experts and the Pharisees, "Is it lawful to heal on the Sabbath or not?" But they kept silent. He took the man, healed him, and sent him away.

—Luke 14:3-4

TEACHINGS ON HUMILITY

⁷ He told a parable to those who were invited, when He noticed how they would choose the best places for themselves: ⁸ "When you are invited by someone to a wedding banquet, don't recline at the best place, because a more distinguished person than you may have been invited by your host.[e] ⁹ The one who invited both of you may come and say to you, 'Give your place to this man,' and then in humiliation, you will proceed to take the lowest place.

¹⁰ "But when you are invited, go and recline in the lowest place, so that when the one who invited you comes, he will say to you, 'Friend, move up higher.' You will then be honored in the presence of all the

---

[a]**13:35** Probably the temple; Jr 12:7; 22:5
[b]**13:35** Ps 118:26
[c]**14:1** Lit *eat bread*; = eat a meal
[d]**14:2** Afflicted with dropsy or edema
[e]**14:8** Lit *by him*

other guests. ¹¹ For everyone who exalts himself will be humbled, and the one who humbles himself will be exalted."

¹² He also said to the one who had invited Him, "When you give a lunch or a dinner, don't invite your friends, your brothers, your relatives, or your rich neighbors, because they might invite you back, and you would be repaid. ¹³ On the contrary, when you host a banquet, invite those who are poor, maimed, lame, or blind. 14 And you will be blessed, because they cannot repay you; for you will be repaid at the resurrection of the righteous."

THE PARABLE OF THE LARGE BANQUET

¹⁵ When one of those who reclined at the table with Him heard these things, he said to Him, "The one who will eat bread in the kingdom of God is blessed!"

¹⁶ Then He told him: "A man was giving a large banquet and invited many. ¹⁷ At the time of the banquet, he sent his •slave to tell those who were invited, 'Come, because everything is now ready.'

¹⁸ "But without exceptionᵃ they all began to make excuses. The first one said to him, 'I have bought a field, and I must go out and see it. I ask you to excuse me.'

¹⁹ "Another said, 'I have bought five yoke of oxen, and I'm going to try them out. I ask you to excuse me.'

²⁰ "And another said, 'I just got married,ᵇ and therefore I'm unable to come.'

²¹ "So the slave came back and reported these things to his master. Then in anger, the master of the house told his slave, 'Go out quickly into the streets and alleys of the city, and bring in here the poor, maimed, blind, and lame!'

²² "'Master,' the slave said, 'what you ordered has been done, and there's still room.'

²³ "Then the master told the slave, 'Go out into the highways and lanes and make them come in, so that my house may be filled. ²⁴ For I tell you, not one of those men who were invited will enjoy my banquet!'"

You Need His Word Not Just His OK

Do not look for how God is going to bless your church. Look for how God is going to reveal Himself to accomplish His purposes.

"Everyone who exalts himself will be humbled, and the one who humbles himself will be exalted."
—Luke 14:11

ᵃ14:18 Lit *And from one* (voice)　　ᵇ14:20 Lit *I have married a woman*

WORD STUDY

Greek word: *miseo*
[mih SEH oh]

Translation: *hate*

Uses in Luke's Gospel: **7**
(Mt, 5; Mk, 1; Jn, 12)

Uses in the NT: **40**

Key passage: **Luke 14:26**

The Greek verb *miseo* is the basic word meaning *to hate*, the exact antonym of *love* (*agapao*). The essence of love is caring more about others than about self, even to the point of great sacrifice—including death (Jn 15:13). Hate, on the other hand, is the opposite; it cares little or nothing about others and actually wishes them harm or even death (Mt 24:9).

With only one exception (Lk 1:71), *miseo* in the Gospels is always used by Jesus. By far the most difficult occurrence of *miseo* is Luke 14:26—difficult both to understand and to practice. In this passage Jesus seems to demand hatred, even toward one's parents, wife, children, and siblings—those whom we are specifically told elsewhere in Scripture to honor, protect, and love! Jesus' statement is best understood as the willingness to choose Him above all else. The context is Jesus' challenge to measure the cost of being His disciple (see 14:26-35). He warned those who were following Him (see v. 25) that continuing to do so might cost them their lives (v. 27) or perhaps their possessions (v. 33; see Lk 16:13). Therefore, Jesus' disciples must be willing to give up their most important earthly relationships—their own families—if these relationships stand in the way of following Him.

THE COST OF FOLLOWING JESUS

25 Now great crowds were traveling with Him. So He turned and said to them: 26 "If anyone comes to Me and does not hate his own father and mother, wife and children, brothers and sisters—yes, and even his own life—he cannot be My disciple. 27 Whoever does not bear his own cross and come after Me cannot be My disciple.

28 "For which of you, wanting to build a tower, doesn't first sit down and calculate the cost to see if he has enough to complete it? 29 Otherwise, after he has laid the foundation and cannot finish it, all the onlookers will begin to make fun of him, 30 saying, 'This man started to build and wasn't able to finish.'

31 "Or what king, going to war against another king, will not first sit down and decide if he is able with 10,000 to oppose the one who comes against him with 20,000? 32 If not, while the other is still far off, he sends a delegation and asks for terms of peace. 33 In the same way, therefore, every one of you who does not say good-bye to[a] all his possessions cannot be My disciple.

34 "Now, salt is good, but if salt should lose its taste, how will it be made salty? 35 It isn't fit for the soil or for the manure pile; they throw it out. Anyone who has ears to hear should listen!"

THE PARABLE OF THE LOST SHEEP

15 All the tax collectors and sinners were approaching to listen to Him. 2 And the •Pharisees and •scribes were complaining, "This man welcomes sinners and eats with them!"

3 So He told them this parable: 4 "What man among you, who has 100 sheep and loses one of them, does not leave the 99 in the open field[b] and go after the lost one until he finds it? 5 When he has found it, he joyfully puts it on his shoulders, 6 and coming home, he calls his friends and neighbors together, saying to them, 'Rejoice with me, because I have found my lost sheep!' 7 I tell you, in the same way, there will be more joy in

---

[a]14:33 Or *does not renounce* or *leave*   [b]15:4 Or *the wilderness*

heaven over one sinner who repents than over 99 righteous people who don't need repentance.

THE PARABLE OF THE LOST COIN

8 "Or what woman who has 10 silver coins,a if she loses one coin, does not light a lamp, sweep the house, and search carefully until she finds it? 9 When she finds it, she calls her women friends and neighbors together, saying, 'Rejoice with me, because I have found the silver coin I lost!' 10 I tell you, in the same way, there is joy in the presence of God's angels over one sinner who repents."

THE PARABLE OF THE LOST SON

11 He also said: "A man had two sons. 12 The younger of them said to his father, 'Father, give me the share of the estate I have coming to me.' So he distributed the assetsb to them. 13 Not many days later, the younger son gathered together all he had and traveled to a distant country, where he squandered his estate in foolish living. 14 After he had spent everything, a severe famine struck that country, and he had nothing.c 15 Then he went to work ford one of the citizens of that country, who sent him into his fields to feed pigs. 16 He longed to eat his fill frome the carob podsf the pigs were eating, but no one would give him any. 17 When he came to his senses,g he said, 'How many of my father's hired hands have more than enough food, and here I am dyingh of hunger!i 18 I'll get up, go to my father, and say to him, Father, I have sinned against heaven and in your sight. 19 I'm no longer worthy to be called your son. Make me like one of your hired hands.' 20 So he got up and went to his father. But while the son was still a long way off, his father saw him and was filled with compassion. He ran, threw his arms around his neck,j and kissed him. 21 The son said to him, 'Father, I have

WORD STUDY

Greek word: **metanoeo**
[meh tuh nah EH oh]

Translation: **repent**

Uses in Luke's Gospel: **9**
(Mt, 5; Mk, 2)

Uses in Luke's writings: **14**

Uses in the NT: **34**

Key passage: **Luke 15:7**

The Greek verb for *repent (metanoeo)* and the related noun for *repentance (metanoia)* signify *a change of mind (meta*, meaning *after* or *change;* and *nous*, meaning *mind*). More than just an intellectual change of mind is in view; rather, both terms refer to a change in one's way of thinking that results in different beliefs and a change in the direction of one's life. The verb *pisteuo* (meaning *believe*) is much more common than *metanoeo*, though both words refer to concepts foundational to salvation (Mt 4:17; Lk 15:7,10; Jn 3:16). *Repent* and *believe* may be understood as opposite sides of the same coin. *Repent* means to turn from one's allegiance to sin and unbelief, whereas *believe* means to place one's trust in Christ. Thus, when one is mentioned the other is implied. John's Gospel and his three Epistles never use *repent* or *repentance*, but *believe* occurs numerous times. On one occasion in the NT, *repent* and *believe* are used together for emphasis (Mk 1:15); similarly, *repentance* and *faith* occur together only once (Ac 20:21).

---

a15:8 Gk *10 drachmas;* a *drachma* was a silver coin = a · denarius.
b15:12 Lit *livelihood*, or *living*
c15:14 Lit *and he began to be in need*
d15:15 Lit *went and joined with*
e15:16 Other mss read *to fill his stomach with*

e15:16 Seed casings of a tree used as food for cattle, pigs, and sometimes the poor
g15:17 Lit *to himself*
h15:17 The word *dying* is translated *lost* in vv. 4-9 and vv. 24,32.
i15:17 Or *dying in the famine;* v. 14
j15:20 Lit *He ran, fell on his neck*

WORD STUDY

Greek word: **oikonomos**
[oy kah NAH mahss]

Translation: **manager**

Uses in Luke's Gospel: **4**

Uses in the NT: **10**

Key passage: **Luke 16:1-8**

The noun *oikonomos* is one of several Greek words for a servant, but this term describes someone with significant prestige and responsibility (by contrast, see the word study on *doulos*). The term is a compound of two Greek words, *oikos,* meaning *house,* and *nomos,* meaning *law;* thus, an *oikonomos* is *the law of the house,* a manager, one who runs a household. The related noun *oikonomia* (English *economy*) means *stewardship, administration,* or *dispensation.*

An *oikonomos* was given responsibility to run certain affairs of the household for the master (*kurios*) and his duties could include cooking, housekeeping, accounting, estate management, or supervising children (see Gl 4:2), depending on the needs of the master. In both contexts that Jesus used the term *oikonomos,* the steward is specifically an accountant or treasurer (Lk 12:42; 16:1-8). On one occasion the term was used by Paul to describe a city official (Rm 16:23), but he also used it metaphorically in reference to those with responsibility in God's kingdom (1 Co 4:1-2; Ti 1:7; see 1 Pt 4:10).

sinned against heaven and in your sight. I'm no longer worthy to be called your son.'

²² "But the father told his •slaves, 'Quick! Bring out the best robe and put it on him; put a ring on his finger[a] and sandals on his feet. ²³ Then bring the fattened calf and slaughter it, and let's celebrate with a feast, ²⁴ because this son of mine was dead and is alive again; he was lost and is found!' So they began to celebrate.

²⁵ "Now his older son was in the field; as he came near the house, he heard music and dancing. ²⁶ So he summoned one of the servants and asked what these things meant. ²⁷ 'Your brother is here,' he told him, 'and your father has slaughtered the fattened calf because he has him back safe and sound.'[b]

²⁸ "Then he became angry and didn't want to go in. So his father came out and pleaded with him. ²⁹ But he replied to his father, 'Look, I have been slaving many years for you, and I have never disobeyed your orders, yet you never gave me a young goat so I could celebrate with my friends. ³⁰ But when this son of yours came, who has devoured your assets[c] with prostitutes, you slaughtered the fattened calf for him.'

³¹ "'Son,'[d] he said to him, 'you are always with me, and everything I have is yours. ³² But we had to celebrate and rejoice, because this brother of yours was dead and is alive again; he was lost and is found.'"

THE PARABLE OF THE DISHONEST MANAGER

16 He also said to the disciples: "There was a rich man who received an accusation that his manager was squandering his possessions. ² So he called the manager in and asked, 'What is this I hear about you? Give an account of your management, because you can no longer be ⌊my⌋ manager.'

³ "Then the manager said to himself, 'What should I do, since my master is taking the management away from me? I'm not strong enough to dig; I'm ashamed to beg. ⁴ I know what I'll do so that when I'm removed from management, people will welcome me into their homes.'

---

[a]**15:22** Lit *hand*
[b]**15:27** Lit *him back healthy*
[c]**15:30** Lit *livelihood,* or *living*
[d]**15:31** Or *Child*

5 "So he summoned each one of his master's debtors. 'How much do you owe my master?' he asked the first one.

6 "'A hundred measures of oil,' he said.

"'Take your invoice,' he told him, 'sit down quickly, and write 50.'

7 "Next he asked another, 'How much do you owe?'

"'A hundred measures of wheat,' he said.

"'Take your invoice,' he told him, 'and write 80.'

8 "The master praised the unrighteous manager because he had acted astutely. For the sons of this age are more astute than the sons of light ⌊in dealing⌋ with their own people.[a] 9 And I tell you, make friends for yourselves by means of the unrighteous money so that when it fails,[b] they may welcome you into eternal dwellings. 10 Whoever is faithful in very little is also faithful in much, and whoever is unrighteous in very little is also unrighteous in much. 11 So if you have not been faithful with the unrighteous money, who will trust you with what is genuine? 12 And if you have not been faithful with what belongs to someone else, who will give you what is your own? 13 No household slave can be the •slave of two masters, since either he will hate one and love the other, or he will be devoted to one and despise the other. You can't be slaves to both God and money."

KINGDOM VALUES

14 The •Pharisees, who were lovers of money, were listening to all these things and scoffing at Him. 15 And He told them: "You are the ones who justify yourselves in the sight of others, but God knows your hearts. For what is highly admired by people is revolting in God's sight.

16 "The Law and the Prophets were[c] until John; since then, the good news of the kingdom of God has been proclaimed, and everyone is strongly urged to enter it.[d] 17 But it is easier for heaven and earth to pass away than for one stroke of a letter in the law to drop out.

God Only Blesses What He Begins

We do not sit down and dream what we want to do for God and then call God in to help us accomplish it. The pattern in the Scripture is that we submit ourselves to God and wait until He shows us what He is about to do, or we watch to see what God is doing around us and join Him.

He told them: "You are the ones who justify yourselves in the sight of others, but God knows your hearts. For what is highly admired by people is revolting in God's sight."

—Luke 16:15

---

[a]16:8 Lit *own generation*
[b]16:9 Other mss read *when you fail* or *pass away*

[c]16:16 Perhaps *were proclaimed*, or *were in effect*
[d]16:16 Or *everyone is forcing his way into it*

¹⁸ "Everyone who divorces his wife and marries another woman commits adultery, and everyone who marries a woman divorced from her husband commits adultery.

THE RICH MAN
AND LAZARUS

¹⁹ "There was a rich man who would dress in purple and fine linen, feasting lavishly every day. ²⁰ But a poor man named Lazarus, covered with sores, was left at his gate. ²¹ He longed to be filled with what fell from the rich man's table, but instead the dogs would come and lick his sores. ²² One day the poor man died and was carried away by the angels to Abraham's side.ᵃ The rich man also died and was buried. ²³ And being in torment in •Hades, he looked up and saw Abraham a long way off, with Lazarus at his side. ²⁴ 'Father Abraham!' he called out, 'Have mercy on me and send Lazarus to dip the tip of his finger in water and cool my tongue, because I am in agony in this flame!'

²⁵ "'Son,'ᵇ Abraham said, 'remember that during your life you received your good things, just as Lazarus received bad things, but now he is comforted here, while you are in agony. ²⁶ Besides all this, a great chasm has been fixed between us and you, so that those who want to pass over from here to you cannot; neither can those from there cross over to us.'

²⁷ "'Father,' he said, 'then I beg you to send him to my father's house— ²⁸ because I have five brothers—to warn them, so they won't also come to this place of torment.'

²⁹ "But Abraham said, 'They have Moses and the prophets; they should listen to them.'

³⁰ "'No, father Abraham,' he said. 'But if someone from the dead goes to them, they will repent.'

³¹ "But he told him, 'If they don't listen to Moses and the prophets, they will not be persuaded if someone rises from the dead.'"

Better to Have a Sensitive Heart Than the Art of Persuasion

People do not naturally seek God or pursue righteousness. Only as the Spirit awakens their hearts to the Person of Christ are they able to see God.

"He told him, 'If they don't listen to Moses and the prophets, they will not be persuaded if someone rises from the dead.'"

—Luke 16:31

ᵃ**16:22** Lit *to the fold of Abraham's robe*, or *to Abraham's bosom*; see Jn 13:23 ᵇ**16:25** Lit *Child*

WARNINGS FROM JESUS

17 He said to His disciples, "Offenses[a] will certainly come,[b] but woe to the one they come through! [2] It would be better for him if a millstone[c] were hung around his neck and he were thrown into the sea than for him to cause one of these little ones to •stumble. [3] Be on your guard. If your brother sins,[d] rebuke him, and if he repents, forgive him. [4] And if he sins against you seven times in a day, and comes back to you seven times, saying, 'I repent,' you must forgive him."

FAITH AND DUTY

[5] The apostles said to the Lord, "Increase our faith."
[6] "If you have faith the size of[e] a mustard seed," the Lord said, "you can say to this mulberry tree, 'Be uprooted and planted in the sea,' and it will obey you.

[7] "Which one of you having a •slave plowing or tending sheep, will say to him when he comes in from the field, 'Come at once and sit down to eat'? [8] Instead, will he not tell him, 'Prepare something for me to eat, get ready,[f] and serve me while I eat and drink; later you can eat and drink'? [9] Does he thank that slave because he did what was commanded?[g] [10] In the same way, when you have done all that you were commanded, you should say, 'We are good-for-nothing slaves; we've only done our duty.'"

THE 10 LEPERS

[11] While traveling to Jerusalem, He passed between[h] Samaria and Galilee. [12] As He entered a village, 10 men with serious skin diseases met Him. They stood at a distance [13] and raised their voices, saying, "Jesus, Master, have mercy on us!"
[14] When He saw them, He told them, "Go and show yourselves to the priests." And while they were going, they were healed.[i]

Remember Who's In Charge Here

Adjusting your mind to the truth God has revealed to you is one step short of completion. You must also respond to the truth in obedience. Then you are free to experience a more complete relationship with God.

"In the same way, when you have done all that you were commanded, you should say, 'We are good-for-nothing slaves; we've only done our duty.'"
—Luke 17:10

---

[a]**17:1** Or *Traps*, or *Bait-sticks*, or *Causes of stumbling*, or *Causes of sin*
[b]**17:1** Lit *It is impossible for offenses not to come*
[c]**17:2** Large stone used for grinding grains into flour
[d]**17:3** Other mss add *against you*
[e]**17:6** Lit *faith like*
[f]**17:8** Lit *eat, tuck in your robe*, or *eat, gird yourself*
[g]**17:9** Other mss add *I don't think so*
[h]**17:11** Or *through the middle of*
[i]**17:14** Lit *cleansed*

¹⁵ But one of them, seeing that he was healed, returned and, with a loud voice, gave glory to God. ¹⁶ He fell facedown at His feet, thanking Him. And he was a •Samaritan.

¹⁷ Then Jesus said, "Were not 10 cleansed? Where are the nine? ¹⁸ Didn't any return[a] to give glory to God except this foreigner?" ¹⁹ **And He told him,** "Get up and go on your way. Your faith has made you well."[b]

THE COMING OF THE KINGDOM

²⁰ Being asked by the •Pharisees when the kingdom of God will come, He answered them, "The kingdom of God is not coming with something observable; ²¹ no one will say,[c] 'Look here!' or 'There!' For you see, the kingdom of God is among you."

²² Then He told the disciples: "The days are coming when you will long to see one of the days of the •Son of Man, but you won't see it. ²³ They will say to you, 'Look there!' or 'Look here!' Don't follow or run after them. ²⁴ For as the lightning flashes from horizon to horizon and lights up the sky, so the Son of Man will be in His day. ²⁵ But first He must suffer many things and be rejected by this generation.

²⁶ "Just as it was in the days of Noah, so it will be in the days of the Son of Man: ²⁷ people went on eating, drinking, marrying and giving in marriage until the day Noah boarded the ark, and the flood came and destroyed them all. ²⁸ It will be the same as it was in the days of Lot: people went on eating, drinking, buying, selling, planting, building. ²⁹ But on the day Lot left Sodom, fire and sulfur rained from heaven and destroyed them all. ³⁰ It will be like that on the day the Son of Man is revealed. ³¹ On that day, a man on the housetop, whose belongings are in the house, must not come down to get them. Likewise the man who is in the field must not turn back. ³² Remember Lot's wife! ³³ Whoever tries to make his •life secured[d] [e] will lose it, and whoever loses his life will preserve it. ³⁴ I tell you, on that night two will be in one bed: one will be taken

---

Always Be Quick to Say "Thank You, God"

Thankfulness is foundational to the Christian life. Thankfulness is a conscious response that comes from looking beyond our blessings to their source.

Jesus said, "Were not 10 cleansed? Where are the nine?"

—Luke 17:17

---

[a]**17:18** Lit *Were they not found returning*
[b]**17:19** Or *faith has saved you*
[c]**17:21** Lit *they will not say*

[d]**17:33** Other mss read *to save his life*
[e]**17:33** Or *tries to retain his life*

and the other will be left. ³⁵ Two women will be grinding grain together: one will be taken and the other left. [³⁶ Two will be in a field: one will be taken, and the other will be left."]ᵃ

³⁷ "Where, Lord?" they asked Him.

He said to them, "Where the corpse is, there also the vultures will be gathered."

THE PARABLE OF THE PERSISTENT WIDOW

18 He then told them a parable on the need for them to pray always and not become discouraged: ² "There was a judge in one town who didn't fear God or respect man. ³ And a widow in that town kept coming to him, saying, 'Give me justice against my adversary.'

⁴ "For a while he was unwilling, but later he said to himself, 'Even though I don't fear God or respect man, ⁵ yet because this widow keeps pestering me,ᵇ I will give her justice, so she doesn't wear me outᶜ by her persistent coming.'"

⁶ Then the Lord said, "Listen to what the unjust judge says. ⁷ Will not God grant justice to His elect who cry out to Him day and night? Will He delay ⌊to help⌋ them?ᵈ ⁸ I tell you that He will swiftly grant them justice. Nevertheless, when the •Son of Man comes, will He find that faithᵉ on earth?"

THE PARABLE OF THE PHARISEE AND THE TAX COLLECTOR

⁹ He also told this parable to some who trusted in themselves that they were righteous and looked down on everyone else: ¹⁰ "Two men went up to the •temple complex to pray, one a •Pharisee and the other a tax collector. ¹¹ The Pharisee took his standᶠ and was praying like this: 'God, I thank You that I'm not like other peopleᵍ —greedy, unrighteous, adulterers, or even like

WORD STUDY

Greek word: *pascho*
[PAHSS koh]

Translation: *suffer*

Uses in Luke's Gospel: **6**
(Mt, 4; Mk, 3)

Uses in Luke's Writings: **11**

Uses in the NT: **42**

Key passage: **Luke 17:25**

The Greek verb *pascho* was originally used in reference to experiencing something from an external source, whether good or bad. In the NT it is always used of negative experiences and thus means *to suffer.*

The sufferings of Jesus are prominent in the Gospels, Acts, and Hebrews; and in each case *pascho* refers to Jesus' Passion—His arrest, trial, and crucifixion (Mt 16:21 = Mk 8:31 = Lk 9:22; 17:25; 22:15; 24:26,46; Ac 1:3; 3:18; 17:3; Heb 2:18; 5:8; 9:26; 13:12). In the rest of the NT, believers are the ones who suffer (2 Co 1:6; Php 1:29; 1 Th 2:14; 2 Th 1:5; 2 Tm 1:12; 1 Pt 4:19; 5:10; Rv 2:10), but they do so for Jesus' sake and with His example in mind (1 Pt 2:19-23; 3:14-18; 4:1).

ᵃ**17:36** Other mss omit bracketed text
ᵇ**18:5** Lit *widow causes me trouble*
ᶜ**18:5** Or *doesn't give me a black eye,* or *doesn't ruin my reputation*
ᵈ**18:7** Or *Will He put up with them?*

ᵉ**18:8** Or *faith,* or *that kind of faith,* or *any faith,* or *the faith,* or *faithfulness;* the faith that persists in prayer for God's vindication
ᶠ**18:11** Or *Pharisee stood by himself*
ᵍ**18:11** Or *like the rest of men*

WORD STUDY

Greek word: **telones**
[teh LOH nayss]

Translation: **tax collector**

Uses in Luke's Gospel: **10**
(Mt, 8; Mk, 3)

Uses in the NT: **21**

Key passage: **Luke 18:9-14**

The Greek noun *telones* was used in reference to various levels of tax collecting personnel. A similar term, *architelones,* meaning *chief tax collector,* is used only in Lk 19:2 in the NT and probably indicates that several lesser *telones* reported to Zacchaeus.

Since collecting taxes often involved working for the Romans, such tax collectors were regarded as traitors by the common Jewish people in Israel. Also, tax collectors of all kinds could take advantage of their position to accumulate wealth at the people's expense. For these reasons tax collectors were so despised that in the NT they are often juxtaposed with sinners (Mt 9:10,11; 11:19; Mk 2:15,16; Lk 5:30; 7:34; 15:1; 18:11; see also the word study on *sinner*), unbelievers (Mt 18:17), and prostitutes (Mt 21:31,32)—those considered at the lowest level of society. Jesus challenged this line of thinking, and especially the thinking of the Jewish religious leaders, when He told the parable of the Pharisee and the tax collector (Lk 18:9-14). In this parable Jesus taught that God will save anyone who humbly casts himself on His mercy but that the self-righteous will not receive His mercy. By God's grace, society's outcasts can become kingdom citizens (see Mt 21:31-32).

this tax collector. [12] I fast twice a week; I give a tenth[a] of everything I get.'

[13] "But the tax collector, standing far off, would not even raise his eyes to heaven but kept striking his chest[b] and saying, 'God, turn Your wrath from me[c] —a sinner!' [14] I tell you, this one went down to his house justified rather than the other; because everyone who exalts himself will be humbled, but the one who humbles himself will be exalted."

BLESSING THE CHILDREN

[15] Some people were even bringing infants to Him so He might touch them, but when the disciples saw it, they rebuked them. [16] Jesus, however, invited them: "Let the little children come to Me, and don't stop them, because the kingdom of God belongs to such as these. [17] •I assure you: Whoever does not welcome the kingdom of God like a little child will never enter it."

THE RICH YOUNG RULER

[18] A ruler asked Him, "Good Teacher, what must I do to inherit eternal life?"

[19] "Why do you call Me good?" Jesus asked him. "No one is good but One—God. [20] You know the commandments:

> **Do not commit adultery;**
> **do not murder;**
> **do not steal;**
> **do not bear false witness;**
> **honor your father and mother.**"[d]

[21] "I have kept all these from my youth," he said.

[22] When Jesus heard this, He told him, "You still lack one thing: sell all that you have and distribute it to the poor, and you will have treasure in heaven. Then come, follow Me."

[23] After he heard this, he became extremely sad, because he was very rich.

---

[a]**18:12** Or *give tithes*
[b]**18:13** Mourning
[c]**18:13** Lit *God, be propitious*; = May

Your wrath be turned aside by the sacrifice
[d]**18:20** Ex 20:12-16; Dt 5:16-20

POSSESSIONS AND THE KINGDOM

24 Seeing that he became sad,[a] Jesus said, "How hard it is for those who have wealth to enter the kingdom of God! 25 For it is easier for a camel to go through the eye of a needle than for a rich person to enter the kingdom of God."

26 Those who heard this asked, "Then who can be saved?"

27 He replied, "What is impossible with men is possible with God."

28 Then Peter said, "Look, we have left what we had and followed You."

29 So He said to them, "I assure you: There is no one who has left a house, wife or brothers, parents or children because of the kingdom of God, 30 who will not receive many times more at this time, and eternal life in the age to come."

THE THIRD PREDICTION OF HIS DEATH

31 Then He took the Twelve aside and told them, "Listen! We are going up to Jerusalem. Everything that is written through the prophets about the Son of Man will be accomplished. 32 For He will be handed over to the Gentiles, and He will be mocked, insulted, spit on; 33 and after they flog Him, they will kill Him, and He will rise on the third day."

34 They understood none of these things. This saying[b] was hidden from them, and they did not grasp what was said.

A BLIND MAN RECEIVES HIS SIGHT

35 As He drew near Jericho, a blind man was sitting by the road begging. 36 Hearing a crowd passing by, he inquired what this meant. 37 "Jesus the •Nazarene is passing by," they told him.

38 So he called out, "Jesus, Son of David, have mercy on me!" 39 Then those in front told him to keep quiet,[c] but he kept crying out all the more, "Son of David, have mercy on me!"

Humble Yourself— He Will Lift You Up

God wants us to adjust our lives to Him so He can do through us what He wants to do.

"I tell you, this one went down to his house justified rather than the other; because everyone who exalts himself will be humbled, but the one who humbles himself will be exalted."

—Luke 18:14

---

[a]18:24 Other mss omit *he became sad*
[b]18:34 The meaning of the saying
[c]18:39 Or *those in front rebuked him*

40 Jesus stopped and commanded that he be brought to Him. When he drew near, He asked him, 41 "What do you want Me to do for you?"

"Lord," he said, "I want to see!"

42 "Receive your sight!" Jesus told him. "Your faith has healed you."a 43 Instantly he could see, and he began to follow Him, glorifying God. All the people, when they saw it, gave praise to God.

JESUS VISITS ZACCHAEUS

19 He entered Jericho and was passing through. 2 There was a man named Zacchaeus who was a chief tax collector, and he was rich. 3 He was trying to see who Jesus was, but he was not able because of the crowd, since he was a short man. 4 So running ahead, he climbed up a sycamore tree to see Jesus, since He was about to pass that way. 5 When Jesus came to the place, He looked up and said to him, "Zacchaeus, hurry and come down, because today I must stay at your house."

6 So he quickly came down and welcomed Him joyfully. 7 All who saw it began to complain, "He's gone to lodge with a sinful man!"

8 But Zacchaeus stood there and said to the Lord, "Look, I'll giveb half of my possessions to the poor, Lord! And if I have extorted anything from anyone, I'll payc back four times as much!"

9 "Today salvation has come to this house," Jesus told him, "because he too is a son of Abraham. 10 For the •Son of Man has come to seek and to save the lost."d

THE PARABLE OF THE 10 MINAS

11 As they were listening to this, He went on to tell a parable because He was near Jerusalem, and they thought the kingdom of God was going to appear right away.

12 Therefore He said: "A nobleman traveled to a far country to receive for himself authority to be kinge and then return. 13 He called 10 of his •slaves, gave them

---

God's Work Will Get the World's Attention

The only way people will know what God is like is when they see Him at work.

Instantly he could see, and he began to follow Him, glorifying God. All the people, when they saw it, gave praise to God.

—Luke 18:43

You're Not Capable, You're Chosen

An ordinary person is the one God most likes to use.

When Jesus came to the place, He looked up and said to him, "Zacchaeus, hurry and come down, because today I must stay at your house."

—Luke 19:5

---

a18:42 Or *has saved you*
b19:8 Or *I give*
c19:8 Or *I pay*
d19:10 Or *save what was lost*
e19:12 Lit *to receive for himself a kingdom* or *sovereignty*

10 minas,[a] and told them, 'Engage in business until I come back.'

¹⁴ "But his subjects hated him and sent a delegation after him, saying, 'We don't want this man to rule over us!'

¹⁵ "At his return, having received the authority to be king,[b] he summoned those •slaves he had given the money to so he could find out how much they had made in business. ¹⁶ The first came forward and said, 'Master, your mina has earned 10 more minas.'

¹⁷ "'Well done, good[c] •slave!' he told him. 'Because you have been faithful in a very small matter, have authority over 10 towns.'

¹⁸ "The second came and said, 'Master, your mina has made five minas.'

¹⁹ "So he said to him, 'You will be over five towns.'

²⁰ "And another came and said, 'Master, here is your mina. I have kept it hidden away in a cloth ²¹ because I was afraid of you, for you're a tough man: you collect what you didn't deposit and reap what you didn't sow.'

²² "He told him, 'I will judge you by what you have said,[d] you evil •slave! ₗIfₗ you knew I was a tough man, collecting what I didn't deposit and reaping what I didn't sow, ²³ why didn't you put my money in the bank? And when I returned, I would have collected it with interest!' ²⁴ So he said to those standing there, 'Take the mina away from him and give it to the one who has 10 minas.'

²⁵ "But they said to him, 'Master, he has 10 minas.'

²⁶ "'I tell you, that to everyone who has, more will be given; and from the one who does not have, even what he does have will be taken away. ²⁷ But bring here these enemies of mine, who did not want me to rule over them, and slaughter[e] them in my presence.'"

THE TRIUMPHAL ENTRY

²⁸ When He had said these things, He went on ahead, going up to Jerusalem. ²⁹ As He approached Bethphage and Bethany, at the place called the •Mount of Olives,

Always Be Willing to Start Small

Smaller assignments are always used by God to develop character. If God has a great assignment for you, He has to develop a great character to match.

"'Well done, good slave!' he told him. 'Because you have been faithful in a very small matter, have authority over 10 towns.'"

—Luke 19:17

---

[a]19:13 = Gk coin worth 100 drachmas or about 100 days' wages
[b]19:15 Lit *to receive for himself a kingdom* or *sovereignty*
[c]19:17 Or *capable*
[d]19:22 Lit *you out of your mouth*
[e]19:27 Or *execute*

WORD STUDY

Greek word: *kurios*
[KUHR ee ahss]

Translation: **Lord**

Uses in Luke's Gospel: **104**
(Mt, 80; Mk, 18; Jn, 52)

Uses in Luke's Writings: **211**

Uses in the NT: **717**

Key passage: **Luke 19:30-34**

The word *kurios* is the twenty-second most common word in the Greek NT and the third most common noun (after the words for "God" and "Jesus"). *Kurios* can mean *lord, master* (both with reference to either deity or humans), and even *sir* (see Jn 4:11; 5:7). In the Greek OT, however, *kurios* was used to translate two significant Hebrew words: *Yahweh* (over six thousand times), the personal name for God (normally translated LORD or GOD); and *adonai* (over seven hundred times; over three hundred in reference to God), a title of respect and honor (normally translated *Lord/lord* or *Master/master*).

Thus, two important ideas from the OT carry over into the NT's use of *kurios:* deity and lordship. *Yahweh* is God and demands absolute loyalty to Himself as Master. The NT teaches that Jesus, God's Son, is deity and demands loyalty to Himself as absolute Lord—His deity being the basis of His lordship. Therefore, in the NT *kurios* emphasizes either the deity of Christ (Rm 10:9-13; see Jl 2:32) or His lordship (Mt 7:21-23; Lk 19:30-34; notice also the OT quotation in v. 38 using *kurios,* referring to deity). It is likely that the two ideas of deity and lordship are so closely intertwined that the NT writers often intended both of them (for example, see Php 2:11).

He sent two of the disciples ³⁰ and said, "Go into the village ahead of you. As you enter it, you will find a young donkey tied there, on which no one has ever sat. Untie it and bring it here. ³¹ If anyone asks you, 'Why are you untying it?' say this: 'The Lord needs it.'"

³² So those who were sent left and found it just as He had told them. ³³ As they were untying the young donkey, its owners said to them, "Why are you untying the donkey?"

³⁴ "The Lord needs it," they said. ³⁵ Then they brought it to Jesus, and after throwing their robes on the donkey, they helped Jesus get on it. ³⁶ As He was going along, they were spreading their robes on the road. ³⁷ Now He came near the path down the Mount of Olives, and the whole crowd of the disciples began to praise God joyfully with a loud voice for all the miracles they had seen:

> ³⁸ **Blessed is the King**
> **who comes in the name of the Lord.**ᵃ ᵇ
> Peace in heaven
> and glory in the highest heaven!

³⁹ Some of the •Pharisees from the crowd told Him, "Teacher, rebuke Your disciples."

⁴⁰ He answered, "I tell you, if they were to keep silent, the stones would cry out!"

JESUS' LOVE FOR JERUSALEM

⁴¹ As He approached and saw the city, He wept over it, ⁴² saying, "If you knew this day what ⌊would bring⌋ peace—but now it is hidden from your eyes. ⁴³ For the days will come on you when your enemies will build an embankment against you, surround you, and hem you in on every side. ⁴⁴ They will crush you and your children within you to the ground, and they will not leave one stone on another in you, because you did not recognize the time of your visitation."

CLEANSING THE TEMPLE COMPLEX

⁴⁵ He went into the •temple complex and began to throw out those who were selling,ᶜ ⁴⁶ and He said, "It is

---

ᵃ**19:38** The words *the King* are substituted for *He* in Ps 118:26.
ᵇ**19:38** Ps 118:26

ᶜ**19:45** Other mss add *and buying in it*

written, **My house will be a house of prayer,** but you have made it **a den of thieves!**"ᵃ

⁴⁷ Every day He was teaching in the temple complex. The •chief priests, the •scribes, and the leaders of the people were looking for a way to destroy Him, ⁴⁸ but they could not find a way to do it, because all the people were captivated by what they heard.ᵇ

THE AUTHORITY OF JESUS CHALLENGED

20 One dayᶜ as He was teaching the people in the •temple complex and proclaiming the good news, the •chief priests and the •scribes, with the elders, came up ² and said to Him: "Tell us, by what authority are You doing these things? Who is it who gave You this authority?"

³ He answered them, "I will also ask you a question. Tell Me, ⁴ was the baptism of John from heaven or from men?"

⁵ They discussed it among themselves: "If we say, 'From heaven,' He will say, 'Why didn't you believe him?' ⁶ But if we say, 'From men,' all the people will stone us, because they are convinced that John was a prophet."

⁷ So they answered that they did not know its origin.ᵈ

⁸ And Jesus said to them, "Neither will I tell you by what authority I do these things."

THE PARABLE OF THE VINEYARD OWNER

⁹ Then He began to tell the people this parable: "A man planted a vineyard, leased it to tenant farmers, and went away for a long time. ¹⁰ At harvest time he sent a •slave to the farmers so that they might give him some fruit from the vineyard. But the farmers beat him and sent him away empty-handed. ¹¹ He sent yet another slave, but they beat that one too, treated him shamefully, and sent him away empty-handed. ¹² And he sent yet a third, but they wounded this one too and threw him out.

Be Ready to Act at a Moment's Notice

As you follow Him, the time may come that your life and future may depend on your adjusting quickly to God's directives.

"They will crush you and your children within you to the ground, and they will not leave one stone on another in you, because you did not recognize the time of your visitation."
—Luke 19:44

ᵃ**19:46** Is 56:7; Jr 7:11
ᵇ**19:48** Lit *people hung on what they heard*
ᶜ**20:1** Lit *It happened on one of the days*
ᵈ**20:7** Or *know where it was from*

13 "Then the owner of the vineyard said, 'What should I do? I will send my beloved son. Perhaps[a] they will respect him.'

14 "But when the tenant farmers saw him, they discussed it among themselves and said, 'This is the heir. Let's kill him, so the inheritance will be ours!' 15 So they threw him out of the vineyard and killed him.

"Therefore, what will the owner of the vineyard do to them? 16 He will come and destroy those farmers and give the vineyard to others."

But when they heard this they said, "No—never!"

17 But He looked at them and said, "Then what is the meaning of this Scripture:[b]

> **The stone that the builders rejected—**
> **this has become the cornerstone?**[c] [d]

18 Everyone who falls on that stone will be broken to pieces, and if it falls on anyone, it will grind him to powder!"

19 Then the scribes and the chief priests looked for a way to get their hands on Him that very hour, because they knew He had told this parable against them, but they feared the people.

GOD AND CAESAR

20 They[e] watched closely and sent spies who pretended to be righteous,[f] so they could catch Him in what He said,[g] to hand Him over to the governor's rule and authority. 21 They questioned Him, "Teacher, we know that You speak and teach correctly, and You don't show partiality,[h] but teach truthfully the way of God. 22 Is it lawful for us to pay taxes to Caesar or not?"

23 But detecting their craftiness, He said to them,[i] 24 "Show Me a •denarius. Whose image and inscription does it have?"

"Caesar's," they said.

When God Breaks You, You Are Truly Whole

Righteousness is not to be taken lightly, nor is it easily attained. God does not give it to people indiscriminately. He gives it to those who know they cannot live without it.

"Everyone who falls on that stone will be broken to pieces, and if it falls on anyone, it will grind him to powder!"

—Luke 20:18

---

[a]**20:13** Other mss add *when they see him*
[b]**20:17** Lit *What then is this that is written*
[c]**20:17** Lit *the head of the corner*
[d]**20:17** Ps 118:22
[e]**20:20** The scribes and chief priests of v. 19
[f]**20:20** Or *upright*; that is, loyal to God's law
[g]**20:20** Lit *catch Him in [a] word*
[h]**20:21** Lit *You don't receive a face*
[i]**20:23** Other mss add *"Why are you testing Me?*

25 "Well then," He told them, "give back to Caesar the things that are Caesar's and to God the things that are God's."

26 They were not able to catch Him in what He said[a] in public,[b] and being amazed at His answer, they became silent.

THE SADDUCEES AND THE RESURRECTION

27 Some of the •Sadducees, who say there is no resurrection, came up and questioned Him: 28 "Teacher, Moses wrote for us that **if a man's brother** has a wife, and **dies childless, his brother should take the wife and produce •offspring for his brother.**[c] 29 Now there were seven brothers. The first took a wife and died without children. 30 Also the second[d] 31 and the third took her. In the same way, all seven died and left no children. 32 Finally, the woman died too. 33 Therefore, in the resurrection, whose wife will the woman be? For all seven had married her."[e]

34 Jesus told them, "The sons of this age marry and are given in marriage. 35 But those who are counted worthy to take part in that age and in the resurrection from the dead neither marry nor are given in marriage. 36 For they cannot die anymore, because they are like angels and are sons of God, since they are sons of the resurrection. 37 Moses even indicated ⌊in the passage⌋ about the burning bush that the dead are raised, where he calls the Lord **the God of Abraham and the God of Isaac and the God of Jacob.**[f] 38 He is not God of the dead but of the living, because all are living to[g] Him."

39 Some of the scribes answered, "Teacher, You have spoken well." 40 And they no longer dared to ask Him anything.

THE QUESTION ABOUT THE MESSIAH

41 Then He said to them, "How can they say that the •Messiah is the Son of David? 42 For David himself says in the Book of Psalms:

God's Word Is All We Really Need to Hear

God always finishes what He begins. Even with the extremely complex assignment Jesus received from His Father, He could shout triumphantly from the cross, "It is finished!" When it's all said and done, God has the last word.

Some of the scribes answered, "Teacher, You have spoken well." And they no longer dared to ask Him anything.
—Luke 20:39-40

---

[a]**20:26** Lit *catch Him in [a] word*
[b]**20:26** Lit *in front of the people*
[c]**20:28** Dt 25:5
[d]**20:30** Other mss add *took her as wife, and he died without children*
[e]**20:33** Lit *had her as wife*
[f]**20:37** Ex 3:6,15
[g]**20:38** Or *with*

> The Lord declared to my Lord,
> 'Sit at My right hand
> [43] until I make Your enemies Your footstool.'[a]

[44] David calls Him 'Lord'; how then can the Messiah be his Son?"

WARNING AGAINST THE SCRIBES

[45] While all the people were listening, He said to His disciples, [46] "Beware of the scribes, who want to go around in long robes and who love greetings in the marketplaces, the front seats in the •synagogues, and the places of honor at banquets. [47] They devour widows' houses and say long prayers just for show. These will receive greater punishment."[b]

THE WIDOW'S GIFT

21 He looked up and saw the rich dropping their offerings into the temple treasury. [2] He also saw a poor widow dropping in two tiny coins.[c] [3] "I tell you the truth," He said. "This poor widow has put in more than all of them. [4] For all these people have put in gifts out of their surplus, but she out of her poverty has put in all she had to live on."

DESTRUCTION OF THE TEMPLE PREDICTED

[5] As some were talking about the •temple complex, how it was adorned with beautiful stones and gifts dedicated to God,[d] He said, [6] "These things that you see— the days will come when not one stone will be left on another that will not be thrown down!"

SIGNS OF THE END OF THE AGE

[7] "Teacher," they asked Him, "so when will these things be? And what will be the sign when these things are about to take place?"

[8] Then He said, "Watch out that you are not deceived. For many will come in My name, saying, 'I am He,' and,

---

Just Watch God Work. It'll Truly Amaze You.

He does not simply wait around in order to help us achieve our goals for Him! He comes to accomplish His own goals through us—and in His own way.

"Make up your minds not to prepare your defense ahead of time, for I will give you such words and a wisdom that none of your adversaries will be able to resist or contradict."

—Luke 21:14-15

Be Willing to Wait, Eager to Learn

Waiting on Him is always worth the wait. You must depend on Him to guide you in His way and in His timing to accomplish His purpose.

"By your endurance gain your lives."

—Luke 21:19

---

[a]20:42-43 Ps 110:1
[b]20:47 Or *judgment*
[c]21:2 Lit *two lepta*; the *lepton* was the smallest and least valuable Gk coin in use.
[d]21:5 Gifts given to the temple in fulfillment of vows to God

'The time is near.' Don't follow them. ⁹ When you hear of wars and rebellions,ª don't be alarmed. Indeed, these things must take place first, but the end won't come right away."

¹⁰ Then He told them: "Nation will be raised up against nation, and kingdom against kingdom. ¹¹ There will be violent earthquakes, and famines and plagues in various places, and there will be terrifying sights and great signs from heaven. ¹² But before all these things, they will lay their hands on you and persecute you. They will hand you over to the •synagogues and prisons, and you will be brought before kings and governors because of My name. ¹³ It will lead to an opportunity for you to witness.ᵇ ¹⁴ Therefore make up your mindsᶜ not to prepare your defense ahead of time, ¹⁵ for I will give you such wordsᵈ and a wisdom that none of your adversaries will be able to resist or contradict. ¹⁶ You will even be betrayed by parents, brothers, relatives, and friends. They will kill some of you. ¹⁷ You will be hated by everyone because of My name, ¹⁸ but not a hair of your head will be lost. ¹⁹ By your enduance gainᵉ your •lives.

THE DESTRUCTION OF JERUSALEM

²⁰ "When you see Jerusalem surrounded by armies, then recognize that its desolation has come near. ²¹ Then those in Judea must flee to the mountains! Those inside the cityᶠ must leave it, and those who are in the country must not enter it, ²² because these are days of vengeance to fulfill all the things that are written. ²³ Woe to pregnant women and nursing mothers in those days, for there will be great distress in the landᵍ and wrath against this people. ²⁴ They will fall by the edge of the sword and be led captive into all the nations, and Jerusalem will be trampled by the Gentilesʰ until the times of the Gentiles are fulfilled.

ª**21:9** Or *insurrections*, or *revolutions*
ᵇ**21:13** Lit *lead to a testimony for you*
ᶜ**21:14** Lit *Therefore place* (determine) *in your hearts*
ᵈ**21:15** Lit *you a mouth*
ᵉ**21:19** Other mss read *endurance you will gain*
ᶠ**21:21** Lit *inside her*
ᵍ**21:23** Or *the earth*
ʰ**21:24** Or *nations*

WORD STUDY

Greek word: **orge**
[ohr GAY]

Translation: **wrath**

Uses in Luke's Gospel: **2**
(Mt, 1; Mk, 1; Jn, 1)

Uses in the NT: **36**

Key passage: **Luke 21:23**

The most common Greek word in the NT to describe God's wrath is *orge,* normally translated *wrath* or *anger.* Only five occurrences of *orge* in the NT do not refer to God's wrath (Eph 4:31; Col 3:8; 1 Tm 2:8; Jms 1:19,20). Mark alone refers specifically to the *orge* ("anger") of Jesus (3:5); Matthew refers to God's *orge* once (3:7); and Luke does so twice (3:7; 21:23).

A three-fold dynamic exists as an expression of God's *orge:*

(1) His wrath is a present reality for everyone who does not believe in His Son (Jn 3:36; Rm 1:18-32), but unbelievers do not recognize God's wrath when they see it; (2) His wrath on unbelievers will intensify as the day of Christ's return approaches (1 Th 5:9; Rv 6:16,17; 11:18; 16:19); and (3) the complete and final demonstration of His wrath is reserved for the time of Christ's personal presence on earth as King and Judge (Rv 14:10; 19:15).

While *orge* is an attribute of God, man's *orge* is rarely appropriate. (Eph 4:26 uses words related to *orge.*) Although Paul referred to the *orge* of God in Colossians 3:6, he followed this immediately with a command to rid ourselves of such things (v. 8). The reason for this is given in James—"human anger does not accomplish God's righteousness" (1:20). Only God's wrath is always righteous.

THE COMING OF THE SON OF MAN

25 "Then there will be signs in the sun, moon, and stars; and there will be anguish on the earth among nations bewildered by the roaring sea and waves. 26 People will faint from fear and expectation of the things that are coming on the world, because the celestial powers will be shaken. 27 Then they will see the •Son of Man coming in a cloud with power and great glory. 28 But when these things begin to take place, stand up and lift up your heads, because your redemption is near!"

THE PARABLE OF THE FIG TREE

29 Then He told them a parable: "Look at the fig tree, and all the trees. 30 As soon as they put out ⌊leaves⌋ you can see for yourselves and recognize that summer is already near. 31 In the same way, when you see these things happening, recognize[a] that the kingdom of God is near. 32 •I assure you: This generation will certainly not pass away until all things take place. 33 Heaven and earth will pass away, but My words will never pass away.

THE NEED FOR WATCHFULNESS

34 "Be on your guard, so that your minds are not dulled[b] from carousing,[c] drunkenness, and worries of life, or that day will come on you unexpectedly 35 like a trap. For it will come on all who live on the face of the whole earth. 36 But be alert at all times, praying that you may have strength[d] to escape all these things that are going to take place and to stand before the Son of Man."

37 During the day, He was teaching in the temple complex, but in the evening He would go out and spend the night on what is called the •Mount of Olives. 38 Then all the people would come early in the morning to hear Him in the temple complex.

THE PLOT TO KILL JESUS

22 The Festival of •Unleavened Bread, which is called •Passover, was drawing near. 2 The

---

God's Strength Will Keep You Standing

God's presence lights your path so that you can see impending danger, but the god of this age can distort your spiritual vision. Ask Christ to illuminate your life and let you clearly see the state of your spiritual condition.

"Be alert at all times, praying that you may have strength to escape all these things that are going to take place and to stand before the Son of Man."

—Luke 21:36

---

[a]21:31 Or *you know*
[b]21:34 Lit *your hearts are not weighed down*
[c]21:34 Or *hangovers*
[d]21:36 Other mss read *you may be counted worthy*

•chief priests and the •scribes were looking for a way to put Him to death, because they were afraid of the people.

³ Then Satan entered Judas, called Iscariot, who was numbered among the Twelve. ⁴ He went away and discussed with the chief priests and temple police how he could hand Him over to them. ⁵ They were glad and agreed to give him silver.ᵃ ⁶ So he accepted ₗthe offer₎ and started looking for a good opportunity to betray Him to them when the crowd was not present.

PREPARATION FOR PASSOVER

⁷ Then the Day of Unleavened Bread came when the Passover lamb had to be sacrificed. ⁸ Jesus sent Peter and John, saying, "Go and prepare the Passover meal for us, so we can eat it."

⁹ "Where do You want us to prepare it?" they asked Him.

¹⁰ "Listen," He said to them, "when you've entered the city, a man carrying a water jug will meet you. Follow him into the house he enters. ¹¹ Tell the owner of the house, 'The Teacher asks you, "Where is the guest room where I can eat the Passover with My disciples?"'" ¹² Then he will show you a large, furnished room upstairs. Make the preparations there."

¹³ So they went and found it just as He had told them, and they prepared the Passover.

THE FIRST LORD'S SUPPER

¹⁴ When the hour came, He reclined at the table, and the apostles with Him. ¹⁵ Then He said to them, "I have fervently desired to eat this Passover with you before I suffer. ¹⁶ For I tell you, I will not eat it againᵇ until it is fulfilled in the kingdom of God." ¹⁷ Then He took a cup, and after giving thanks, He said, "Take this and share it among yourselves. ¹⁸ For I tell you, from now on I will not drink of the fruit of the vine until the kingdom of God comes."

¹⁹ And He took bread, gave thanks, broke it, gave it to them, and said, "This is My body, which is given for you. Do this in remembrance of Me."

Take What He Gives and Go with That

God does not usually reveal all the details of His will at once. Instead, He tells you enough so you can implement what He said. You must continue to rely on His guidance.

"Listen," He said to them, "when you've entered the city, a man carrying a water jug will meet you. Follow him into the house he enters."

—Luke 22:10

ᵃ22:5 Or *money*; Mt 26:15 specifies 30 pieces of silver; Zch 11:12-13   ᵇ22:16 Other mss omit *again*

²⁰ In the same way He also took the cup after supper and said, "This cup is the new covenant ⌊established by⌋ My blood; it is shed for you.ᵃ ²¹ But look, the hand of the one betraying Me is at the table with Me! ²² For the •Son of Man will go away as it has been determined, but woe to that man by whom He is betrayed!"

²³ So they began to argue among themselves which of them it could be who was going to do this thing.

THE DISPUTE OVER GREATNESS

²⁴ Then a dispute also arose among them about who should be considered the greatest. ²⁵ But He said to them, "The kings of the Gentiles dominate them, and those who have authority over them are calledᵇ 'Benefactors.'ᶜ ²⁶ But it must not be like that among you. On the contrary, whoever is greatest among you must become like the youngest, and whoever leads, like the one serving. ²⁷ For who is greater, the one at the table or the one serving? Isn't it the one at the table? But I am among you as the One who serves. ²⁸ You are the ones who stood by Me in My trials. ²⁹ I bestow on you a kingdom, just as My Father bestowed one on Me, ³⁰ so that you may eat and drink at My table in My kingdom. And you will sit on thrones judging the 12 tribes of Israel.

PETER'S DENIAL PREDICTED

³¹ "Simon, Simon,ᵈ look out! Satan has asked to sift youᵉ like wheat. ³² But I have prayed for youᶠ that your faith may not fail. And you, when you have turned back, strengthen your brothers."

³³ "Lord," he told Him, "I'm ready to go with You both to prison and to death!"

³⁴ "I tell you, Peter," He said, "the rooster will not crow today untilᵍ you deny three times that you know Me!"

Today Is Preparation Day for Tomorrow

Your life as a child of God ought to be shaped by the future (what you will be one day). God uses your present time to mold and shape your future here on earth and in eternity.

"Simon, Simon, look out! Satan has asked to sift you like wheat. But I have prayed for you that your faith may not fail. And you, when you have turned back, strengthen your brothers."

—Luke 22:31-32

ᵃ**22:19-20** Other mss omit *which is given for you* (v. 19) through the end of v. 20
ᵇ**22:25** Or *them call themselves*
ᶜ**22:25** Title of honor given to those who benefited the public good
ᵈ**22:31** Other mss read *Then the Lord said, "Simon, Simon*
ᵉ**22:31** *you* (pl in Gk)
ᶠ**22:32** *you* (sg in Gk)
ᵍ**22:34** Other mss read *before*

MONEY-BAG, BACKPACK, AND SWORD

³⁵ He also said to them, "When I sent you out without money-bag, traveling bag, or sandals, did you lack anything?"

"Not a thing," they said.

³⁶ Then He said to them, "But now, whoever has a money-bag should take it, and also a traveling bag. And whoever doesn't have a sword should sell his robe and buy one. ³⁷ For I tell you, what is written must be fulfilled in Me: **And He was counted among the outlaws.**ᵃ Yes, what is written about Me is coming to its fulfillment."

³⁸ "Lord," they said, "look, here are two swords."

"Enough of that!"ᵇ He told them.

THE PRAYER IN THE GARDEN

³⁹ He went out and made His way as usual to the •Mount of Olives, and the disciples followed Him. ⁴⁰ When He reached the place, He told them, "Pray that you may not enter into temptation." ⁴¹ Then He withdrew from them about a stone's throw, knelt down, and began to pray, ⁴² "Father, if You are willing, take this cup away from Me—nevertheless, not My will, but Yours, be done."

[⁴³ Then an angel from heaven appeared to Him, strengthening Him. ⁴⁴ Being in anguish, He prayed more fervently, and His sweat became like drops of blood falling to the ground.]ᶜ ⁴⁵ When He got up from prayer and came to the disciples, He found them sleeping, exhausted from their grief.ᵈ ⁴⁶ "Why are you sleeping?" He asked them. "Get up and pray, so that you won't enter into temptation."

THE JUDAS KISS

⁴⁷ While He was still speaking, suddenly a mob was there, and one of the Twelve named Judas was leading them. He came near Jesus to kiss Him, ⁴⁸ but Jesus said to him, "Judas, are you betraying the Son of Man with a kiss?"

WORD STUDY

Greek word: **peirasmos**
[pigh rahss MAHSS]

Translation: **temptation**

Uses in Luke's Gospel: **6**
(Mt, 2; Mk, 1)

Uses in Luke's Writings: **7**

Uses in the NT: **21**

Key passage: **Luke 22:28-46**

The Greek noun *peirasmos* means *temptation* or *trial* and is related to the verb *peirazo,* which means *to tempt.* In the NT these two terms are normally used in a negative sense, indicating that the temptation would be spiritually harmful if not resisted, though there are exceptions (see Heb 11:17; Rv 2:2). Twice the verb is used to describe Satan as "the tempter" (Mt 4:3; 1 Th 3:5), and Jesus was tempted by Satan (Lk 4:2) and by His enemies (Mt 19:3; 22:18,35; Lk 11:16; see Heb 2:18; 4:15) on several occasions. The verb *dokimazo* means *to test, prove,* or *approve,* and is similar to *peirazo* but normally has a positive connotation.

Jesus used the term *peirasmos* three times in Luke 22:28-46. In v. 28 Jesus commended His disciples for staying with Him during His various "trials," probably a reference to various attacks by Satan and the religious leaders during His ministry. In vv. 40,46 Jesus told the disciples to pray that they "may not enter into temptation." The time for Jesus' arrest, trial, and crucifixion had come, and the disciples' conduct during this crisis would reveal their spiritual maturity. The context indicates that two of the disciples in particular, Judas (vv. 47-53) and Peter (vv. 54-62), failed miserably.

ᵃ22:37 Is 53:12
ᵇ22:38 Or *It is enough!*

ᶜ22:43-44 Other mss omit bracketed text
ᵈ22:45 Lit *sleeping from grief*

49 When those around Him saw what was going to happen, they asked, "Lord, should we strike with the sword?" 50 Then one of them struck the high priest's •slave and cut off his right ear.

51 But Jesus responded, "No more of this!"[a] And touching his ear, He healed him. 52 Then Jesus said to the chief priests, temple police, and the elders who had come for Him, "Have you come out with swords and clubs as if I were a criminal?[b] 53 Every day while I was with you in the •temple complex, you never laid a hand on Me. But this is your hour—and the dominion of darkness."

PETER DENIES HIS LORD

54 They seized Him, led Him away, and brought Him into the high priest's house. Meanwhile Peter was following at a distance. 55 They lit a fire in the middle of the courtyard and sat down together, and Peter sat among them. 56 When a servant saw him sitting in the firelight, and looked closely at him, she said, "This man was with Him too."

57 But he denied it: "Woman, I don't know Him!"

58 After a little while, someone else saw him and said, "You're one of them too!"

"Man, I am not!" Peter said.

59 About an hour later, another kept insisting, "This man was certainly with Him, since he's also a Galilean."

60 But Peter said, "Man, I don't know what you're talking about!" Immediately, while he was still speaking, a rooster crowed. 61 Then the Lord turned and looked at Peter. So Peter remembered the word of the Lord, how He had said to him, "Before the rooster crows today, you will deny Me three times." 62 And he went outside and wept bitterly.

JESUS MOCKED AND BEATEN

63 The men who were holding Jesus started mocking and beating Him. 64 After blindfolding Him, they kept[c] asking, "Prophesy! Who hit You?" 65 And they were saying many other blasphemous things against Him.

Sin Never Escapes God's Attention

God never conceals His expectations from us. We never have to guess how we should live.

Then the Lord turned and looked at Peter. So Peter remembered the word of the Lord, how He had said to him, "Before the rooster crows today, you will deny Me three times." And he went outside and wept bitterly.

—Luke 22:61-62

---

[a]22:51 Lit *Permit as far as this*
[b]22:52 Lit *as against a criminal*
[c]22:64 Other mss add *striking Him on the face and*

196

JESUS FACES THE SANHEDRIN

66 When daylight came, the elders[a] of the people, both the chief priests and the scribes, convened and brought Him before their •Sanhedrin. 67 They said, "If You are the •Messiah, tell us."

But He said to them, "If I do tell you, you will not believe. 68 And if I ask you, you will not answer. 69 But from now on, the Son of Man will be seated at the right hand of the Power of God."

70 They all asked, "Are You, then, the Son of God?"

And He said to them, "You say that I am."

71 "Why do we need any more testimony," they said, "since we've heard it ourselves from His mouth?"

JESUS FACES PILATE

23 Then their whole assembly rose up and brought Him before •Pilate. 2 They began to accuse Him, saying, "We found this man subverting our nation, opposing payment of taxes to Caesar, and saying that He Himself is the •Messiah, a King."

3 So Pilate asked Him, "Are You the King of the Jews?"

He answered him, "You have said it."[b]

4 Pilate then told the •chief priests and the crowds, "I find no grounds for charging this man."

5 But they kept insisting, "He stirs up the people, teaching throughout all Judea, from Galilee where He started even to here."

God Desires to Get People's Attention

People may choose to receive Christ or reject Him. But one thing is for sure: they cannot ignore Him forever.

They kept insisting, "He stirs up the people, teaching throughout all Judea, from Galilee where He started even to here."

—Luke 23:5

JESUS FACES HEROD ANTIPAS

6 When Pilate heard this,[c] he asked if the man was a Galilean. 7 Finding that He was under •Herod's jurisdiction, he sent Him to Herod, who was also in Jerusalem during those days. 8 Herod was very glad to see Jesus; for a long time he had wanted to see Him, because he had heard about Him and was hoping to see some miracle[d] performed by Him. 9 So he kept asking Him questions, but Jesus did not answer him. 10 The chief priests and the •scribes stood by, vehemently accusing Him. 11 Then Herod, with his soldiers, treated Him

---

[a]22:66 Or *council of elders*
[b]23:3 Or *That is true*; an affirmative oath
[c]23:6 Other mss read *heard "Galilee"*
[d]23:8 Or *sign*

with contempt, mocked Him, dressed Him in a brilliant robe, and sent Him back to Pilate. ¹² That very day Herod and Pilate became friends.ᵃ Previously, they had been hostile toward each other.

JESUS OR BARABBAS

¹³ Pilate called together the chief priests, the leaders, and the people, ¹⁴ and said to them, "You have brought me this man as one who subverts the people. But in fact, after examining Him in your presence, I have found no grounds to charge this man with those things you accuse Him of. ¹⁵ Neither has Herod, because he sent Him back to us. Clearly, He has done nothing to deserve death. ¹⁶ Therefore I will have Him whippedᵇ and ⌊then⌋ release Him." [¹⁷ For according to the festival he had to release someone to them.]ᶜ

¹⁸ Then they all cried out together, "Take this man away! Release Barabbas to us!" ¹⁹ (He had been thrown into prison for a rebellion that had taken place in the city, and for murder.)

²⁰ Pilate, wanting to release Jesus, addressed them again, ²¹ but they kept shouting, "Crucify! Crucify Him!"

²² A third time he said to them, "Why? What has this man done wrong? I have found in Him no grounds for the death penalty. Therefore I will have Him whipped and ⌊then⌋ release Him."

²³ But they kept up the pressure, demanding with loud voices that He be crucified. And their voicesᵈ won out. ²⁴ So Pilate decided to grant their demand ²⁵ and released the one they were asking for, who had been thrown into prison for rebellion and murder. But he handed Jesus over to their will.

THE WAY TO THE CROSS

²⁶ As they led Him away, they seized Simon, a Cyrenian, who was coming in from the country, and laid the cross on him to carry behind Jesus. ²⁷ A great multitude of the people followed Him, including women who were

---

Living God's Way Will Bring God Glory

When God accomplishes His purposes in His ways through us, people will come to know God. They will recognize that what has happened can only be explained by God. He will get glory to Himself!

Jesus said, "Father, forgive them, because they do not know what they are doing." And they divided His clothes and cast lots. The people stood watching.

—Luke 23:34-35a

ᵃ**23:12** Lit *friends with one another*
ᵇ**23:16** Gk *paideuo*; to discipline or "teach a lesson"; 1 Kg 12:11,14 LXX; 2 Ch 10:11,14; perhaps a way of referring to the Roman scourging; Lat *flagellatio*
ᶜ**23:17** Other mss omit bracketed text
ᵈ**23:23** Other mss add *and those of the chief priests*

mourning and lamenting Him. 28 But turning to them, Jesus said, "Daughters of Jerusalem, do not weep for Me, but weep for yourselves and your children. 29 Look, the days are coming when they will say, 'Blessed are the barren, the wombs that never bore, and the breasts that never nursed!' 30 Then they will begin **to say to the mountains, 'Fall on us!' and to the hills, 'Cover us!'**a 31 For if they do these things when the wood is green, what will happen when it is dry?"

CRUCIFIED BETWEEN TWO CRIMINALS

32 Two others—criminals—were also led away to be executed with Him. 33 When they arrived at the place called The Skull, they crucified Him there, along with the criminals, one on the right and one on the left. [34 Then Jesus said, "Father, forgive them, because they do not know what they are doing."]b And they divided His clothes and cast lots.

35 The people stood watching, and even the leaders kept scoffing: "He saved others; let Him save Himself if this is God's Messiah, the Chosen One!" 36 The soldiers also mocked Him. They came offering Him sour wine 37 and said, "If You are the King of the Jews, save Yourself!"

38 An inscription was above Him:c

THIS IS THE
KING OF THE JEWS.

39 Then one of the criminals hanging there began to yell insults atd Him: "Aren't You the Messiah? Save Yourself and us!"

40 But the other answered, rebuking him: "Don't you even fear God, since you are undergoing the same punishment? 41 We are punished justly, because we're getting back what we deserve for the things we did, but this man has done nothing wrong." 42 Then he said, "Jesus, remember mee when You come into Your kingdom!"

Always Keep the Cross in Mind

I never look at circumstances without seeing them on the backdrop of the cross. That is where God clearly demonstrated once and for all time His deep love for me.

He said, "Jesus, remember me when You come into Your kingdom!" And He said to him, "I assure you: Today you will be with Me in paradise."
—Luke 23:42-43

---

a**23:30** Hs 10:8
b**23:34** Other mss omit bracketed text
c**23:38** Other mss add *written in Greek, Latin, and Hebrew letters*

d**23:39** Or *began to blaspheme*
e**23:42** Other mss add *Lord*

WORD STUDY

Greek word: **paradeisos**
[pah RAH digh sahss]

Translation: **paradise**

Uses in Luke's Gospel: **1**

Uses in the NT: **3**

Key passage: **Luke 23:43**

The word "paradise" in Luke 23:43 is transliterated directly from the Greek word *paradeisos,* which occurs in only two other places in the NT. In the Greek world *paradeisos* could refer to a garden, a grove, or a park; thus, it is the word found in the Greek OT for the Garden of Eden (11 times in Gn 2–3). Luke 23:43 and 2 Corinthians 12:4 use *paradeisos* to refer to the place where God especially manifests His presence, which we call *heaven.* Revelation 2:7 refers to *paradeisos* as the place where believers (those who "conquer") eat from "the tree of life," which is in the new Jerusalem (see Rv 22:2,14,19).

43 And He said to him, "•I assure you: Today you will be with Me in paradise."

THE DEATH OF JESUS

44 It was now about noon,a and darkness came over the whole landb until three,c 45 because the sun's light failed.d The curtain of the sanctuary was split down the middle. 46 And Jesus called out with a loud voice, "Father, **into Your hands I entrust My spirit.**"e Saying this, He breathed His last.

47 When the •centurion saw what happened, he began to glorify God, saying, "This man really was righteous!" 48 All the crowds that had gathered for this spectacle, when they saw what had taken place, went home, striking their chests.f 49 But all who knew Him, including the women who had followed Him from Galilee, stood at a distance, watching these things.

THE BURIAL OF JESUS

50 There was a good and righteous man named Joseph, a member of the •Sanhedrin, 51 who had not agreed with their plan and action. He was from Arimathea, a Judean town, and was looking forward to the kingdom of God. 52 He approached Pilate and asked for Jesus' body. 53 Taking it down, he wrapped it in fine linen and placed it in a tomb cut into the rock, where no one had ever been placed.g 54 It was preparation day, and the Sabbath was about to begin.h 55 The women who had come with Him from Galilee followed along and observed the tomb and how His body was placed. 56 Then they returned and prepared spices and perfumes. And they rested on the Sabbath according to the commandment.

RESURRECTION MORNING

24 On the first day of the week, very early in the morning, theyi came to the tomb, bringing the

---

a**23:44** Lit *about the sixth hour*
b**23:44** Or *whole earth*
c**23:44** Lit *the ninth hour*
d**23:45** Other mss read *three, and the sun was darkened*
e**23:46** Ps 31:5
f**23:48** Mourning
g**23:53** Or *interred,* or *laid*
h**23:54** Lit *was dawning;* not in the morning but at sundown Friday
i**24:1** Other mss add *and other women with them*

spices they had prepared. ² They found the stone rolled away from the tomb. ³ They went in but did not find the body of the Lord Jesus. ⁴ While they were perplexed about this, suddenly two men stood by them in dazzling clothes. ⁵ So the women were terrified and bowed down to the ground.ᵃ

"Why are you looking for the living among the dead?" asked the men. ⁶ "He is not here, but He has been resurrected! Remember how He spoke to you when He was still in Galilee, ⁷ saying, 'The •Son of Man must be betrayed into the hands of sinful men, be crucified, and rise on the third day'?" ⁸ And they remembered His words.

⁹ Returning from the tomb, they reported all these things to the Eleven and to all the rest. ¹⁰ •Mary Magdalene, Joanna, Mary the mother of James, and the other women with them were telling the apostles these things. ¹¹ But these words seemed like nonsense to them, and they did not believe the women. ¹² Peter, however, got up and ran to the tomb. When he stooped to look in, he saw only the linen cloths.ᵇ So he went home, amazed at what had happened.

THE EMMAUS DISCIPLES

¹³ Now that same day two of them were on their way to a village calledᶜ Emmaus, which was about seven milesᵈ from Jerusalem. ¹⁴ Together they were discussing everything that had taken place. ¹⁵ And while they were discussing and arguing, Jesus Himself came near and began to walk along with them. ¹⁶ But theyᵉ were prevented from recognizing Him. ¹⁷ Then He asked them, "What is this dispute that you're havingᶠ with each other as you are walking?" And they stopped ₗwalking and lookedⱼ discouraged.

¹⁸ The one named Cleopas answered Him, "Are You the only visitor in Jerusalem who doesn't know the things that happened there in these days?"

¹⁹ "What things?" He asked them.

You Never Know What God Will Do Through You Next

If you will respond to Him as Lord, He may lead you to do and be things you would never have dreamed.

There was a good and righteous man named Joseph, a member of the Sanhedrin, who had not agreed with their plan and action. He was from Arimathea, a Judean town, and was looking forward to the kingdom of God. He approached Pilate and asked for Jesus' body.
—Luke 23:50-52

Examine the Prevailing Patterns in Your Life

When God gets ready for you to take a new step or direction in His activity, it will be in sequence with what He has already been doing in your life.

"He is not here, but He has been resurrected! Remember how He spoke to you when He was still in Galilee, saying, 'The Son of Man must be betrayed into the hands of sinful men, be crucified, and rise on the third day'?" And they remembered His words.
—Luke 24:6-8

ᵃ24:5 Lit *and inclined their faces to the ground*
ᵇ24:12 Other mss add *lying there*
ᶜ24:13 Lit *village, which name is*
ᵈ24:13 Lit *about 60 stadia*; 1 *stadion* = 600 feet
ᵉ24:16 Lit *their eyes*
ᶠ24:17 Lit *What are these words that you are exchanging*

So they said to Him, "The things concerning Jesus the •Nazarene, who was a Prophet powerful in action and speech before God and all the people, 20 and how our •chief priests and leaders handed Him over to be sentenced to death, and they crucified Him. 21 But we were hoping that He was the One who was about to redeem Israel. Besides all this, it's the third day since these things happened. 22 Moreover, some women from our group astounded us. They arrived early at the tomb, 23 and when they didn't find His body, they came and reported that they had seen a vision of angels who said He was alive. 24 Some of those who were with us went to the tomb and found it just as the women had said, but they didn't see Him."

25 He said to them, "How unwise and slow you are to believe in your hearts all that the prophets have spoken! 26 Didn't the •Messiah have to suffer these things and enter into His glory?" 27 Then beginning with Moses and all the Prophets, He interpreted for them the things concerning Himself in all the Scriptures.

28 They came near the village where they were going, and He gave the impression that He was going farther. 29 But they urged Him: "Stay with us, because it's almost evening, and now the day is almost over." So He went in to stay with them.

30 It was as He reclined at the table with them that He took the bread, blessed and broke it, and gave it to them. 31 Then their eyes were opened, and they recognized Him, but He disappeared from their sight. 32 So they said to each other, "Weren't our hearts ablaze within us while He was talking with us on the road and explaining the Scriptures to us?" 33 That very hour they got up and returned to Jerusalem. They found the Eleven and those with them gathered together, 34 who said,[a] "The Lord has certainly been raised, and has appeared to Simon!" 35 Then they began to describe what had happened on the road and how He was made known to them in the breaking of the bread.

THE REALITY OF THE RISEN JESUS

36 And as they were saying these things, He Himself stood among them. He said to them, "Peace to you!"

---

[a]24:34 Gk is specific that this refers to the Eleven and those with them.

God's Word Reveals God's Ways

The Bible is designed to help you understand the ways of God. Then, when God starts to act in your life, you will recognize that it is God.

He opened their minds to understand the Scriptures.

—Luke 24:45

Worship While You Wait

Whenever you do not seem to be receiving assignments from God, focus on the love relationship and stay there until the assignment comes.

"Look, I am sending you what My Father promised. As for you, stay in the city until you are empowered from on high."... And they were continually in the temple complex blessing God.

—Luke 24:49,53

37 But they were startled and terrified and thought they were seeing a ghost. 38 "Why are you troubled?" He asked them. "And why do doubts arise in your hearts? 39 Look at My hands and My feet, that it is I Myself! Touch Me and see, because a ghost does not have flesh and bones as you can see I have." 40 Having said this, He showed them His hands and feet. 41 But while they still could not believe[a] because of ₗtheirↃ joy and were amazed, He asked them, "Do you have anything here to eat?" 42 So they gave Him a piece of a broiled fish,[b] 43 and He took it and ate in their presence.

44 Then He told them, "These are My words that I spoke to you while I was still with you—that everything written about Me in the Law of Moses, the Prophets, and the Psalms must be fulfilled." 45 Then He opened their minds to understand the Scriptures. 46 He also said to them, "This is what is written:[c] the Messiah would suffer and rise from the dead the third day, 47 and repentance for[d] forgiveness of sins would be proclaimed in His name to all the nations, beginning at Jerusalem. 48 You are witnesses of these things. 49 And look, I am sending you[e] what My Father promised. As for you, stay in the city[f] until you are empowered[g] from on high."

THE ASCENSION OF JESUS

50 Then He led them out as far as Bethany, and lifting up His hands He blessed them. 51 And while He was blessing them, He left them and was carried up into heaven. 52 After worshiping Him, they returned to Jerusalem with great joy. 53 And they were continually in the •temple complex blessing God.[h]

---

[a]24:41 Or *they still disbelieved*
[b]24:42 Other mss add *and some honeycomb*
[c]24:46 Other mss add *and thus it was necessary that*
[d]24:47 Other mss read *repentance and*

[e]24:49 Lit *upon you*
[f]24:49 Other mss add *of Jerusalem*
[g]24:49 Lit *clothed with power*
[h]24:53 Other mss read *praising and blessing God. Amen.*

WORD STUDY

Greek word: **eulogeo**
[yoo lah GEH oh]

Translation: **bless**

Uses in Luke's Gospel: **13**
(Mt, 5; Mk, 5; Jn, 1)

Uses in Luke's Writings: **15**

Uses in the NT: **42**

Key passage: **Luke 24:50-53**

The English word *eulogy* comes from the Greek verb *eulogeo*, meaning *to bless* or *praise*. The term literally means *to speak well of* someone or something and was commonly used with the meaning *to extol*, especially of pagan gods in secular literature. In the NT, however, *eulogeo* has a distinct OT flavor, for behind it is the Hebrew term *barak*, a verb also meaning *to bless*. Thus, NT usage follows the OT precedent and has two main ideas: first, to speak well of someone by calling on God to bless that person or by recognizing that He has already done so; and second, to speak well of God, that is, to praise or thank Him.

In Luke's Gospel various people call on God to bless others (1:42; 2:34) and to praise or thank God as well (1:64; 2:28; 9:16; 24:30). Jesus called on His disciples to bless those who curse them (6:28; see Rm 12:14). Luke's Gospel ends with a threefold use of *eulogeo*: Jesus blessed the disciples at the Ascension (Lk 24:50-51—which is reminiscent of Jacob's blessing of his sons just before his death, Gn 49:28), and as a result of all they had witnessed, the disciples praised God (v. 53).

THE GOSPEL OF

JOHN

PROLOGUE

1 In the beginning was the Word,[a]
and the Word was with God,
and the Word was God.
[2] He was with God in the beginning.
[3] All things were created through Him,
and apart from Him not one thing
   was created
that has been created.
[4] Life was in Him,[b]
and that life was the light of men.
[5] That light shines in the darkness,
yet the darkness did not overcome[c] it.

[6] There was a man named John
who was sent from God.
[7] He came as a witness
to testify about the light,
so that all might believe through him.[d]
[8] He was not the light,
but he came to testify about the light.
[9] The true light, who gives light to everyone,
was coming into the world.[e]

[10] He was in the world,
and the world was created through Him,
yet the world did not recognize Him.

---

[a]**1:1** The *Word* (Gk *Logos*) is a title for Jesus as the communication and the revealer of God the Father; Jn 1:14,18; Rv 19:13.
[b]**1:3-4** Other punctuation is possible: ... *not one thing was created. What was created in Him was life*
[c]**1:5** Or *grasp,* or *comprehend,* or *overtake*; Jn 12:35
[d]**1:7** Or *through it* (the light)
[e]**1:9** Or *The true light who comes into the world gives light to everyone,* or *The true light enlightens everyone coming into the world.*

11 He came to His own,[a]
and His own people[a] did not receive Him.
12 But to all who did receive Him,
He gave them the right to be[b] children of God,
to those who believe in His name,
13 who were born,
not of blood,[c]
or of the will of the flesh,
or of the will of man,[d]
but of God.

14 The Word became flesh[e]
and took up residence[f] among us.
We observed His glory,
the glory as the •One and Only Son[g]
from the Father,
full of grace and truth.
15 (John testified concerning Him
and exclaimed,
"This was the One of whom I said,
'The One coming after me has surpassed me,
because He existed before me.'")
16 Indeed, we have all received grace after grace
from His fullness,
17 for although the law was given
through Moses,
grace and truth came through Jesus Christ.
18 No one has ever seen God.[h]
The One and Only Son[i] —
the One who is at the Father's side[j] —
He has revealed Him.

WORD STUDY

Greek word: **logos** [LAH gahss]

Translation: **Word**

Uses in John's Gospel: **40**
(Mt, 33; Mk, 24; Lk, 32)

Uses in John's writings: **65**

Uses in the NT: **330**

Key passages: **John 1:1,14**

Like the related verb *lego (to speak)*, the noun *logos* most often refers to either oral or written communication. It means *statement* or *report* in some contexts, but most often in John's Gospel (and in the NT in general) *logos* refers to God's Word (that is, the Old Testament) or to Jesus' words. Thus, the primary use of *logos* is to denote divine revelation in some form or another. John used the term in its most exalted sense when he personified *logos* to refer to Christ. The *Logos* eternally existed as God (the Son) and with God (the Father)—He was in fact the Creator (Jn 1:1-3)—but He became a human being (v. 14), Jesus of Nazareth, so that He could reveal the Father and His will for humanity (v. 18).

---

[a]1:11 The same Gk adjective is used twice in this verse: the first refers to all that Jesus owned as Creator (*to His own*); the second refers to the Jews (*His own people*).
[b]1:12 Or *become*
[c]1:13 Lit *bloods*; the pl form of *blood* occurs only here in the NT. It may refer either to lineal descent (that is, blood from one's father and mother) or to the OT sacrificial system (that is, the various blood sacrifices). Neither is the basis for birth into the family of God.
[d]1:13 Or *not of human lineage, or of human capacity, or of human volition*

[e]1:14 The eternally existent Word (vv. 1-2) took on full humanity, but without sin; Heb 4:15.
[f]1:14 Lit *and tabernacled*, or *and dwelt in a tent*; this word occurs only here in John. A related word, referring to the Festival of Tabernacles, occurs only in 7:2; Ex 40:34-38.
[g]1:14 *Son* is implied from the reference to the Father and from Gk usage.
[h]1:18 Since God is an infinite being, no one can see Him in His absolute essential nature; Ex 33:18-23.
[i]1:18 Other mss read *God*
[j]1:18 Lit *is in the bosom of the Father*

JOHN THE BAPTIST'S TESTIMONY

¹⁹ This is John's testimony when the •Jews from Jerusalem sent priests and Levites to ask him, "Who are you?"

²⁰ He did not refuse to answer, but he declared: "I am not the •Messiah."

²¹ "What then?" they asked him. "Are you Elijah?"

"I am not," he said.

"Are you the Prophet?"[a]

"No," he answered.

²² "Who are you, then?" they asked. "We need to give an answer to those who sent us. What can you tell us about yourself?"

²³ He said, "I am a **voice of one crying out in the wilderness: Make straight the way of the Lord**[b] —just as Isaiah the prophet said."

²⁴ Now they had been sent from the •Pharisees. ²⁵ So they asked him, "Why then do you baptize if you aren't the Messiah, or Elijah, or the Prophet?"

²⁶ "I baptize with[c] water," John answered them. "Someone stands among you, but you don't know ⌊Him⌋. ²⁷ He is the One coming after me,[d] whose sandal strap I'm not worthy to untie."

²⁸ All this happened in Bethany[e] across the Jordan,[f] where John was baptizing.

THE LAMB OF GOD

²⁹ The next day John saw Jesus coming toward him and said, "Here is the Lamb of God, who takes away the sin of the world! ³⁰ This is the One I told you about: 'After me comes a man who has surpassed me, because He existed before me.' ³¹ I didn't know Him, but I came baptizing with[c] water so He might be revealed to Israel."

³² And John testified, "I watched the Spirit descending from heaven like a dove, and He rested on Him.

He Must Increase, We Must Decrease

The call to salvation is a call to be on mission with Him. In this new relationship you move into a servant role with God as your Lord and Master.

"This is the One I told you about: 'After me comes a man who has surpassed me, because He existed before me.'"

—John 1:30

The Way to God's Will Is Through God's Son

Knowing God does not come through a program, a study, or a method. Knowing God comes through a relationship with a Person.

"I didn't know Him, but He who sent me to baptize with water told me, 'The One you see the Spirit descending and resting on—He is the One who baptizes with the Holy Spirit.' I have seen and testified that He is the Son of God!"

—John 1:33-34

---

[a]**1:21** Probably = the Prophet in Dt 18:15
[b]**1:23** Is 40:3
[c]**1:26,31** Or *in*
[d]**1:27** Other mss add *who came before me*
[e]**1:28** Other mss read *in Bethabara*
[f]**1:28** Another Bethany, near Jerusalem, was the home of Lazarus, Martha, and Mary; Jn 11:1.

[33] I didn't know Him, but He[a] who sent me to baptize with[b] water told me, 'The One you see the Spirit descending and resting on—He is the One who baptizes with[b] the Holy Spirit.' [34] I have seen and testified that He is the Son of God!"[c]

[35] Again the next day, John was standing with two of his disciples. [36] When he saw Jesus passing by, he said, "Look! The Lamb of God!"

[37] The two disciples heard him say this and followed Jesus. [38] When Jesus turned and noticed them following Him, He asked them, "What are you looking for?"

They said to Him, "•Rabbi" (which means "Teacher"), "where are You staying?"

[39] "Come and you'll see," He replied. So they went and saw where He was staying, and they stayed with Him that day. It was about 10 in the morning.[d]

[40] Andrew, Simon Peter's brother, was one of the two who heard John and followed Him. [41] He first found his own brother Simon and told him, "We have found the Messiah!"[e] (which means "Anointed One"), [42] and he brought ₍Simon₎ to Jesus.

When Jesus saw him, He said, "You are Simon, son of John.[f] You will be called •Cephas" (which means "Rock").

PHILIP AND NATHANAEL

[43] The next day He[g] decided to leave for Galilee. Jesus found Philip and told him, "Follow Me!"

[44] Now Philip was from Bethsaida, the hometown of Andrew and Peter. [45] Philip found Nathanael[h] and told him, "We have found the One Moses wrote about in the

By Knowing God, You Can Help Others Know Him

People know us. They know what we can do. When they see things happen that can only be explained by God's involvement, they will come to know Him.

He first found his own brother Simon and told him, "We have found the Messiah!" (which means "Anointed One"), and he brought Simon to Jesus.

—John 1:41-42a

[a]1:33 *He* refers to God the Father, who gave John a sign to help him identify the Messiah. Vv. 32-34 indicate that John did not know that Jesus was the Messiah until the Spirit descended upon Him at His baptism.
[b]1:33 Or *in*
[c]1:34 Other mss read *is the Chosen One of God*
[d]1:39 Lit *about the tenth hour*. Various methods of reckoning time were used in the ancient world. John probably used a different method from the other 3 Gospels. If John used the same method of time reckoning as the other 3 Gospels, the translation would be: *It was about four in the afternoon.*
[e]1:41 In the NT, the word Messiah translates the Gk word *Christos* ("Anointed One"), except here and in Jn 4:25 where it translates *Messias*.
[f]1:42 Other mss read *Simon, son of Jonah*
[g]1:43 Or *he*, referring either to Peter (v. 42) or Andrew (vv. 40-41)
[h]1:45 Probably the Bartholomew of the other Gospels and Acts

WORD STUDY

Greek word: **amen**
[ah MAYN]

Translation: **assure**

Uses in John's Gospel: **50**
(Mt, 31; Mk, 14; Lk, 6)

Uses in John's writings: **58**

Uses in the NT: **129**

Key passage: **John 1:51**

The English word *amen* comes from a Hebrew verb meaning *to trust, believe,* which is related to the noun for *truth, faith,* or *faithfulness.* It is common for Christians to end a prayer with the word *amen;* this occurs often in the Bible also. But Jesus used *amen* as part of a formula to introduce certain statements that He considered especially important (literally, *amen, I say to you*). This occurs 31 times in Matthew, 14 times in Mark, and six times in Luke. The emphasis in Jesus' use of this term was on the certainty of what He was about to say. In John's Gospel all 25 sayings have the double *amen* (literally, *amen, amen, I say to you*), which seems to add a tone of seriousness to His statements. Jesus normally used these special formulae to introduce truths about God, Jesus, the Spirit, or some aspect of salvation.

Law (and so did the prophets): Jesus the son of Joseph, from Nazareth!"

46 "Can anything good come out of Nazareth?" Nathanael asked him.

"Come and see," Philip answered.

47 Then Jesus saw Nathanael coming toward Him and said about him, "Here is a true Israelite; no deceit is in him."

48 "How do you know me?" Nathanael asked.

"Before Philip called you, when you were under the fig tree, I saw you," Jesus answered.

49 "Rabbi," Nathanael replied, "You are the Son of God! You are the King of Israel!"

50 Jesus responded to him, "Do you believe ⌐only⌐ because I told you I saw you under the fig tree? You[a] will see greater things than this." 51 Then He said, "•I assure you: You[b] will see heaven opened and the angels of God ascending and descending on the •Son of Man."

THE FIRST SIGN: TURNING WATER INTO WINE

2 On the third day a wedding took place in Cana of Galilee. Jesus' mother was there, and 2 Jesus and His disciples were invited to the wedding as well. 3 When the wine ran out, Jesus' mother told Him, "They don't have any wine."

4 "What has this concern of yours to do with Me,[c] •woman?" Jesus asked. "My hour[d] has not yet come."

5 "Do whatever He tells you," His mother told the servants.

6 Now six stone water jars had been set there for Jewish purification. Each contained 20 or 30 gallons.[e]

7 "Fill the jars with water," Jesus told them. So they filled them to the brim. 8 Then He said to them, "Now draw some out and take it to the chief servant."[f] And they did.

9 When the chief servant tasted the water (after it had

---

[a]**1:50** *You* (sg in Gk) refers to Nathanael.
[b]**1:51** *You* is pl in Gk and refers to Nathanael and the other disciples.
[c]**2:4** Or *You and I see things differently;* lit *What to Me and to you;* Mt 8:29; Mk 1:24; 5:7; Lk 8:28

[d]**2:4** The time of His sacrificial death and exaltation; Jn 7:30; 8:20; 12:23,27; 13:1; 17:1
[e]**2:6** Lit *2 or 3 measures*
[f]**2:8** Lit *ruler of the table;* perhaps *master of the feast,* or *headwaiter*

become wine), he did not know where it came from—though the servants who had drawn the water knew. He called the groom ¹⁰ and told him, "Everybody sets out the fine wine first, then, after people have drunk freely, the inferior. But you have kept the fine wine until now."

¹¹ Jesus performed this first sign[a] in Cana of Galilee. He displayed His glory, and His disciples believed in Him.

¹² After this, He went down to Capernaum, together with His mother, His brothers, and His disciples, and they stayed there only a few days.

CLEANSING THE TEMPLE COMPLEX

¹³ The Jewish •Passover was near, so Jesus went up to Jerusalem. ¹⁴ In the •temple complex He found people selling oxen, sheep, and doves, and ⌊He also found⌋ the money changers sitting there. ¹⁵ After making a whip out of cords, He drove everyone out of the temple complex with their sheep and oxen. He also poured out the money changers' coins and overturned the tables. ¹⁶ He told those who were selling doves, "Get these things out of here! Stop turning My Father's house into a marketplace!"[b]

¹⁷ And His disciples remembered that it is written:
Zeal for Your house will consume Me.[c]

¹⁸ So the Jews replied to Him, "What sign ⌊of authority⌋ will You show us for doing these things?"

¹⁹ Jesus answered, "Destroy this sanctuary, and I will raise it up in three days."

²⁰ Therefore the Jews said, "This sanctuary took 46 years to build, and will You raise it up in three days?"

²¹ But He was speaking about the sanctuary of His body. ²² So when He was raised from the dead, His disciples remembered that He had said this. And they believed the Scripture and the statement Jesus had made.

²³ While He was in Jerusalem at the Passover Festival, many trusted in His name when they saw the signs He was doing. ²⁴ Jesus, however, would not entrust Himself to them, since He knew them all ²⁵ and because He did

WORD STUDY

Greek word: **semeion**
say MIGH ahn]

Translation: **sign**

Uses in John's Gospel: **17**
(Mt, 13; Mk, 7; Lk, 11)

Uses in John's writings: **24**

Uses in the NT: **77**

Key passage: **John 2:11**

The three main terms that describe miracles in the NT are *semeion (sign), dunamis (power),* and *teras (wonder).* One problem in studying these three words is that some English versions use the term "miracle" to translate all three words, at least in some contexts. The word *teras* is the least common of the three (16 times) and always refers to miracles; *dunamis* and *semeion* occur numerous times and refer to other phenomena besides miracles. The word *teras* is always accompanied by *semeion* and sometimes by *dunamis* also (Ac 2:22; 2 Co 12:12; 2 Th 2:9; Heb 2:4). The distinction between the three terms is one of emphasis: *semeion* refers to the purpose of the miracle; *dunamis* refers to the source that enables someone to perform a miracle; and *teras* refers to the reaction of the crowd when a miracle was performed. John's favorite term for Jesus' miracles was *semeion* (*dunamis* does not occur in John's Gospel and *teras* occurs only once, John 4:48), for he emphasized the purpose for these miracles: they revealed who Jesus was so that people would believe in Him (20:30-31). In contrast to the other Gospels, John's Gospel provides only seven signs (the first two are numbered, 2:11; 4:54), but he reminds us that Jesus performed many others (20:30).

---

[a]2:11 Lit *this beginning of the signs;* Jn 4:54; 20:30. Seven miraculous signs occur in John's Gospel and are so noted in the headings.

[b]2:16 Lit *a house of business*
[c]2:17 Ps 69:9

WORD STUDY

Greek word: **anothen**
[AH noh thuhn]

Translation: **again**

Uses in John's Gospel: **5**
(Mt, 1; Mk, 1; Lk, 1)

Uses in John's writings: **5**

Uses in the NT: **13**

Key passages: **John 3:3,7**

The expression *born again* comes from John 3:3, where Jesus tells Nicodemus that he must be born (*gennao,* the term used for the genealogy in Mt 1:1-17) again (*anothen*). The term *anothen* can mean *again* or *from above.* The meaning *again* for *anothen* occurs in Galatians 4:9, which is the only clear instance of this meaning in the NT. All other uses of the term mean *from above* (see Jn 3:31; 19:11; Jms 1:17; 3:15,17) or something similar (such as *top* in Mt 27:51; Mk 15:38; Jn 19:23). It is likely that Nicodemus misunderstood Jesus' use of *anothen,* thinking He meant *again* as in a second time. This is why Nicodemus responded the way he did, by a reference to physical birth (v. 4). But Jesus went on to indicate that He was referring to the other meaning of *anothen,* a birth *from above,* a birth from the Spirit (Jn 3:5,6,8).

not need anyone to testify about man; for He Himself knew what was in man.

JESUS AND NICODEMUS

3 There was a man from the •Pharisees named Nicodemus, a ruler of the Jews. ² This man came to Him at night and said, "•Rabbi, we know that You have come from God as a teacher, for no one could perform these signs You do unless God were with him."

³ Jesus replied, "•I assure you: Unless someone is born again,ᵃ he cannot see the kingdom of God."

⁴ "But how can anyone be born when he is old?" Nicodemus asked Him. "Can he enter his mother's womb a second time and be born?"

⁵ Jesus answered, "I assure you: Unless someone is born of water and the Spirit,ᵇ he cannot enter the kingdom of God. ⁶ Whatever is born of the flesh is flesh, and whatever is born of the Spirit is spirit. ⁷ Do not be amazed that I told you that youᶜ must be born again. ⁸ The windᵈ blows where it pleases, and you hear its sound, but you don't know where it comes from or where it is going. So it is with everyone born of the Spirit."

⁹ "How can these things be?" asked Nicodemus.

¹⁰ "Are you a teacherᵉ of Israel and don't know these things?" Jesus replied. ¹¹ "I assure you: We speak what We know and We testify to what We have seen, but youᶠ do not accept Our testimony.ᵍ ¹² If I have told you about things that happen on earth and you don't believe, how will you believe if I tell you about things of heaven? ¹³ No one has ascended into heaven except the One who descended from heaven—the •Son of Man.ʰ ¹⁴ Just as Moses lifted up the snake in the wilderness, so the Son of Man must be lifted up, ¹⁵ so that everyone who believes in Him willⁱ have eternal life.

ᵃ3:3 The same Gk word can mean *again* or *from above* (also in v. 7).
ᵇ3:5 Or *spirit,* or *wind;* the Gk word *pneuma* can mean *wind, spirit,* or *Spirit,* each of which occurs in this context.
ᶜ3:7 The pronoun is pl in Gk.
ᵈ3:8 The Gk word *pneuma* can mean *wind, spirit,* or *Spirit,* each of which occurs in this context.

ᵉ3:10 Or *the teacher*
ᶠ3:11 The word *you* in Gk is pl here and throughout v. 12.
ᵍ3:11 The pl forms (*We, Our*) refer to Jesus and His authority to speak for the Father.
ʰ3:13 Other mss add *who is in heaven*
ⁱ3:15 Other mss add *not perish, but*

16 "For God loved the world in this way: He gave His •One and Only Son, so that everyone who believes in Him will not perish but have eternal life. 17 For God did not send His Son into the world that He might condemn the world, but that the world might be saved through Him. 18 Anyone who believes in Him is not condemned, but anyone who does not believe is already condemned, because he has not believed in the name of the One and Only Son of God.

19 "This, then, is the judgment: the light has come into the world, and people loved darkness rather than the light because their deeds were evil. 20 For everyone who practices wicked things hates the light and avoids it,[a] so that his deeds may not be exposed. 21 But anyone who lives by[b] the truth comes to the light, so that his works may be shown to be accomplished by God."[c]

JESUS AND JOHN THE BAPTIST

22 After this, Jesus and His disciples went to the Judean countryside, where He spent time with them and baptized. 23 John also was baptizing in Aenon near Salim, because there was plenty of water there. People were coming and being baptized, 24 since John had not yet been thrown into prison.

25 Then a dispute arose between John's disciples and a •Jew[d] about purification. 26 So they came to John and told him, "Rabbi, the One you testified about, and who was with you across the Jordan, is baptizing—and everyone is flocking to Him."

27 John responded, "No one can receive a single thing unless it's given to him from heaven. 28 You yourselves can testify that I said, 'I am not the •Messiah, but I've been sent ahead of Him.' 29 He who has the bride is the groom. But the groom's friend, who stands by and listens for him, rejoices greatly[e] at the groom's voice. So this joy of mine is complete. 30 He must increase, but I must decrease."

WORD STUDY

Greek word: **monogenes**
[mah nah gehn AYSS]

Translation: **only**

Uses in John's Gospel: **4**
(Lk, 3)

Uses in John's writings: **5**

Uses in the NT: **9**

Key passages: **John 3:16,18**

English translations have traditionally understood *monogenes* to be from *monos (only)* and *gennao (beget)*, thus following the Latin Vulgate *(unigenitus)* and translating the word *only begotten*. This has caused great misunderstanding since God the Son did not have an origin and was not created by God. He is Himself an eternal being. It is best to understand *monogenes* to be from *monos (only)* and *genos (kind,* Latin *genus),* meaning *the only one of its kind.* This view is more consistent with John's five uses of the word, and support for this translation is found in Hebrews 11:17 where Isaac is called Abraham's *monogenes.* Isaac was not Abraham's only-begotten son (Ishmael was his firstborn and there were other sons through Keturah), but Isaac was the only one of his kind—the son of promise. In the Old Latin translation, *monogenes* was translated as *unicus,* from which we get our word *unique.* This is what is meant by *monogenes* in John's writings (Jn 1:14,18; 3:16,18; 1 Jn 4:9): Jesus is God's unique Son in that His essential nature is the same as the Father's. There are many children of God (see Jn 1:12-13), but there is only one Son of God.

---

[a]3:20 Lit *and does not come to the light*
[b]3:21 Lit *who does*
[c]3:21 It is possible that Jesus' words end at v. 15. Ancient Gk did not have quotation marks.
[d]3:25 Other mss read *and the Jews*
[e]3:29 Lit *with joy rejoices*

THE ONE FROM HEAVEN

[31] The One who comes from above is above all. The one who is from the earth is earthly and speaks in earthly terms.[a] The One who comes from heaven is above all. [32] He testifies to what He has seen and heard, yet no one accepts His testimony. [33] The one who has accepted His testimony has affirmed that God is true. [34] For God sent Him, and He speaks God's words, since He[b] gives the Spirit without measure. [35] The Father loves the Son and has given all things into His hands. [36] The one who believes in the Son has eternal life, but the one who refuses to believe in the Son will not see life; instead, the wrath of God remains on him.

JESUS AND THE SAMARITAN WOMAN

4 When Jesus[c] knew that the •Pharisees heard He was making and baptizing more disciples than John [2] (though Jesus Himself was not baptizing, but His disciples were), [3] He left Judea and went again to Galilee. [4] He had to travel through Samaria, [5] so He came to a town of Samaria called Sychar near the property[d] that Jacob had given his son Joseph. [6] Jacob's well was there, and Jesus, worn out from His journey, sat down at the well. It was about six in the evening.[e]

[7] A woman of Samaria came to draw water.

"Give Me a drink," Jesus said to her, [8] for His disciples had gone into town to buy food.

[9] "How is it that You, a Jew, ask for a drink from me, a •Samaritan woman?" she asked Him. For Jews do not associate with[f] Samaritans.[g]

[10] Jesus answered, "If you knew the gift of God, and who is saying to you, 'Give Me a drink,' you would ask Him, and He would give you living water."

[11] "Sir," said the woman, "You don't even have a bucket, and the well is deep. So where do You get this 'living water'? [12] You aren't greater than our father Jacob, are You? He gave us the well and drank from it himself, as did his sons and livestock."

Give God Room to Prove Himself to You

We come to know God as we experience Him. We can know about God as a Provider, but we really come to know God as Provider when we experience Him providing something for our lives.

Jesus answered, "If you knew the gift of God, and who is saying to you, 'Give Me a drink,' you would ask Him, and He would give you living water."

—John 4:10

---

[a]**3:31** Or *of earthly things*
[b]**3:34** Other mss read *since God*
[c]**4:1** Other mss read *the Lord*
[d]**4:5** Lit *piece of land*
[e]**4:6** Lit *the sixth hour;* see note at

Jn 1:39; an alternate time reckoning would be *noon*
[f]**4:9** Or *do not share vessels with*
[g]**4:9** Other mss omit *For Jews do not associate with Samaritans.*

¹³ Jesus said, "Everyone who drinks from this water will get thirsty again. ¹⁴ But whoever drinks from the water that I will give him will never get thirsty again—ever! In fact, the water I will give him will become a well[a] of water springing up within him for eternal life."

¹⁵ "Sir," the woman said to Him, "give me this water so I won't get thirsty and come here to draw water."

¹⁶ "Go call your husband," He told her, "and come back here."

¹⁷ "I don't have a husband," she answered.

"You have correctly said, 'I don't have a husband,'" Jesus said. ¹⁸ "For you've had five husbands, and the man you now have is not your husband. What you have said is true."

¹⁹ "Sir," the woman replied, "I see that You are a prophet. ²⁰ Our fathers worshiped on this mountain,[b] yet you ⌊Jews⌋ say that the place to worship is in Jerusalem."

²¹ Jesus told her, "Believe Me, •woman, an hour is coming when you will worship the Father neither on this mountain nor in Jerusalem. ²² You Samaritans[c] worship what you do not know. We worship what we do know, because salvation is from the Jews. ²³ But an hour is coming, and is now here, when the true worshipers will worship the Father in spirit and truth. Yes, the Father wants such people to worship Him. ²⁴ God is spirit, and those who worship Him must worship in spirit and truth."

²⁵ The woman said to Him, "I know that •Messiah[d] is coming" (who is called Christ). "When He comes, He will explain everything to us."

²⁶ "I am ⌊He⌋," Jesus told her, "the One speaking to you."

THE RIPENED HARVEST

²⁷ Just then His disciples arrived, and they were amazed that He was talking with a woman. Yet no one

---

[a]4:14 Or *spring*
[b]4:20 Mount Gerizim, where there had been a Samaritan temple that rivaled Jerusalem's
[c]4:22 *Samaritans* is implied since the Gk verb and pronoun are pl.

[d]4:25 In the NT, the word Messiah translates the Gk word *Christos* ("Anointed One"), except here and in Jn 1:41 where it translates *Messias*.

WORD STUDY

Greek word: **zoe** [zoh AY]

Translation: *life*

Uses in John's Gospel: **36** (Mt, 7; Mk, 4; Lk, 5)

Uses in John's writings: **66**

Uses in the NT: **135**

Key passage: **John 4:14**

The Greek noun *zoe* means *life* and is related to the verb *zao*, which means to live. In the NT both words can be used for physical or spiritual life, though the latter is more common. The most important aspect of life is a relationship with God. The essence of life is union; the essence of death is separation. Physical life is the union of body and spirit; physical death is the separation of the body and spirit. Spiritual life is union or oneness with God through faith in Christ; spiritual death is separation from God. Life—spiritual life— means more than mere existence. It refers to a relationship with God. This is the life that Jesus came to give us, and He intended us to enjoy the blessings of that life, that relationship,"in abundance" (Jn 10:10).

Therefore, everyone will exist forever, but not everyone will *live* forever. Unbelievers will experience death forever, "the second death" (Rv 20:14), eternal separation from God in the lake of fire. But by God's grace Christians have "eternal redemption" (Heb 9:12) or "eternal life" (Jn 3:15-16; 4:14). The phrase "eternal life" occurs 43 times in the NT—23 of them in John and 1 John—and refers to the permanence of the relationship believers have with God even now. Eternal life is knowing the Father and the Son (Jn 17:2-3). This is God's never-ending gift to those who trust in Christ (Rm 6:23).

said, "What do You want?" or "Why are You talking with her?"

28 Then the woman left her water jar, went into town, and told the men, 29 "Come, see a man who told me everything I ever did! Could this be the Messiah?" 30 They left the town and made their way to Him.

31 In the meantime the disciples kept urging Him, "•Rabbi, eat something."

32 But He said, "I have food to eat that you don't know about."

33 The disciples said to one another, "Could someone have brought Him something to eat?"

34 "My food is to do the will of Him who sent Me and to finish His work," Jesus told them. 35 "Don't you say, 'There are still four more months, then comes the harvest'? Listen ⌊to what⌋ I'm telling you: Open[a] your eyes and look at the fields, for they are ready[b] for harvest. 36 The reaper is already receiving pay and gathering fruit for eternal life, so the sower and reaper can rejoice together. 37 For in this case the saying is true: 'One sows and another reaps.' 38 I sent you to reap what you didn't labor for; others have labored, and you have benefited from[c] their labor."

THE SAVIOR OF THE WORLD

39 Now many Samaritans from that town believed in Him because of what the woman said[d] when she testified, "He told me everything I ever did." 40 Therefore, when the Samaritans came to Him, they asked Him to stay with them, and He stayed there two days. 41 Many more believed because of what He said.[e] 42 And they told the woman, "We no longer believe because of what you said, for we have heard for ourselves and know that this really is the Savior of the world."[f]

A GALILEAN WELCOME

43 After two days He left there for Galilee. 44 Jesus Himself testified that a prophet has no honor in his own country. 45 When they entered Galilee, the Galileans

---

His Plan Takes Precedence Over Yours

God is far more interested in accomplishing His kingdom purposes than you are. He will move you into every assignment for which He knows you are ready.

"My food is to do the will of Him who sent Me and to finish His work," Jesus told them.

—John 4:34

---

[a]4:35 Lit *Raise*
[b]4:35 Lit *white*
[c]4:38 Lit *you have entered into*

[d]4:39 Lit *because of the woman's word*
[e]4:41 Lit *because of His word*
[f]4:42 Other mss add *the Messiah*

welcomed Him because they had seen everything He did in Jerusalem during the festival. For they also had gone to the festival.

THE SECOND SIGN: HEALING AN OFFICIAL'S SON

46 Then He went again to Cana of Galilee, where He had turned the water into wine. There was a certain royal official whose son was ill at Capernaum. 47 When this man heard that Jesus had come from Judea into Galilee, he went to Him and pleaded with Him to come down and heal his son, for he was about to die.

48 Jesus told him, "Unless you ₗpeopleᵣ see signs and wonders, you will not believe."

49 "Sir," the official said to Him, "come down before my boy dies!"

50 "Go," Jesus told him, "your son will live." The man believed whatᵃ Jesus said to him and departed.

51 While he was still going down, his •slaves met him saying that his boy was alive. 52 He asked them at what time he got better. "Yesterday at seven in the morningᵇ the fever left him," they answered. 53 The father realized this was the very hour at which Jesus had told him, "Your son will live." Then he himself believed, along with his whole household.

54 This therefore was the second sign Jesus performed after He came from Judea to Galilee.

THE THIRD SIGN: HEALING THE SICK

5 After this, a Jewish festival took place, and Jesus went up to Jerusalem. 2 By the Sheep Gate in Jerusalem there is a pool, called Bethesdaᶜ in Hebrew, which has five colonnades.ᵈ 3 Within these lay a multitude of the sick—blind, lame, and paralyzed [—waiting for the moving of the water, 4 because an angel would go down into the pool from time to time and stir up the water. Then the first one who got in after the water was stirred up recovered from whatever ailment he had].ᵉ

You Believe by Faith, Know by Experience

Knowledge of God comes through experience. We come to know God as we experience Him in and around our lives.

They told the woman, "We no longer believe because of what you said, for we have heard for ourselves and know that this really is the Savior of the world."
—John 4:42

ᵃ4:50 Lit *the word*
ᵇ4:52 Or *seven in the evening;* lit *at the seventh hour;* see note at Jn 1:39; an alternate time reckoning would be *at one in the afternoon*
ᶜ5:2 Other mss read *Bethzatha;* other mss read *Bethsaida*
ᵈ5:2 Rows of columns supporting a roof
ᵉ5:3-4 Other mss omit bracketed text

5 One man was there who had been sick for 38 years. 6 When Jesus saw him lying there and knew he had already been there a long time, He said to him, "Do you want to get well?"

7 "Sir," the sick man answered, "I don't have a man to put me into the pool when the water is stirred up, but while I'm coming, someone goes down ahead of me."

8 "Get up," Jesus told him, "pick up your bedroll and walk!" 9 Instantly the man got well, picked up his bedroll, and started to walk.

Now that day was the Sabbath, 10 so the •Jews said to the man who had been healed, "This is the Sabbath! It's illegal for you to pick up your bedroll."

11 He replied, "The man who made me well told me, 'Pick up your bedroll and walk.'"

12 "Who is this man who told you, 'Pick up ˪your bedroll˩ and walk?'" they asked. 13 But the man who was cured did not know who it was, because Jesus had slipped away into the crowd that was there.ᵃ

14 After this, Jesus found him in the •temple complex and said to him, "See, you are well. Do not sin any more, so that something worse doesn't happen to you." 15 The man went and reported to the Jews that it was Jesus who had made him well.

HONORING THE FATHER AND THE SON

16 Therefore, the Jews began persecuting Jesusᵇ because He was doing these things on the Sabbath. 17 But Jesus responded to them, "My Father is still working, and I am working also." 18 This is why the Jews began trying all the more to kill Him: not only was He breaking the Sabbath, but He was even calling God His own Father, making Himself equal with God.

19 Then Jesus replied, "•I assure you: The Son is not able to do anything on His own, but only what He sees the Father doing. For whatever the Fatherᶜ does, the Son also does these things in the same way. 20 For the

---

Trust and Obey

When you are convinced of His love, you can believe Him and trust Him. When you trust Him, you can obey Him.

He replied, "The man who made me well told me, 'Pick up your bedroll and walk.'"

—John 5:11

Make Sure You're Asking the Right Questions

"What is God's will for my life?" is not the best question to ask. I think the right question is simply, "What is God's will?" The focus needs to be on God and His purposes, not my life.

Jesus replied, "I assure you: The Son is not able to do anything on His own, but only what He sees the Father doing. For whatever the Father does, the Son also does these things in the same way."

—John 5:19

ᵃ5:13 Lit *slipped away, there being a crowd in that place*
ᵇ5:16 Other mss add *and trying to kill Him*
ᶜ5:19 Lit *whatever that One*

Father loves the Son and shows Him everything He is doing, and He will show Him greater works than these so that you will be amazed. ²¹ And just as the Father raises the dead and gives them life, so the Son also gives life to anyone He wants to. ²² The Father, in fact, judges no one but has given all judgment to the Son, ²³ so that all people will honor the Son just as they honor the Father. Anyone who does not honor the Son does not honor the Father who sent Him.

LIFE AND JUDGMENT

²⁴ "I assure you: Anyone who hears My word and believes Him who sent Me has eternal life and will not come under judgment but has passed from death to life. ²⁵ "I assure you: An hour is coming, and is now here, when the dead will hear the voice of the Son of God, and those who hear will live. ²⁶ For just as the Father has life in Himself, so also He has granted to the Son to have life in Himself. ²⁷ And He has granted Him the right to pass judgment, because He is the •Son of Man. ²⁸ Do not be amazed at this, because a time is coming when all who are in the graves will hear His voice ²⁹ and come out—those who have done good things, to the resurrection of life, but those who have done wicked things, to the resurrection of judgment.

³⁰ "I can do nothing on My own. I judge only as I hear, and My judgment is righteous, because I do not seek My own will, but the will of Him who sent Me.

FOUR WITNESSES TO JESUS

³¹ "If I testify about Myself, My testimony is not valid.[a] ³² There is Another who testifies about Me, and I know that the testimony He gives about Me is valid.[b] ³³ You have sent ˌmessengersˌ to John, and he has testified to the truth. ³⁴ I don't receive man's testimony, but I say these things so that you may be saved. ³⁵ John[c] was a burning and shining lamp, and for a time you were willing to enjoy his light.

³⁶ "But I have a greater testimony than John's because of the works that the Father has given Me to

Stay in the Word and Know What God Says

When you come to understand the spiritual meaning and application of a Scripture passage, God's Spirit has been at work. This does not *lead* you to an encounter with God. That *is* the encounter with God. When God speaks to you through the Bible, He is relating to you in a personal and real way.

"I assure you: Anyone who hears My word and believes Him who sent Me has eternal life and will not come under judgment but has passed from death to life."

—John 5:24

---

[a]5:31 Or *not true*
[b]5:32 Or *true*
[c]5:35 Lit *That man*

WORD STUDY

Greek word: *martureo*
[mahr tew REH oh]

Translation: **testify**

Uses in John's Gospel: **33**
(Mt, 1; Lk, 1)

Uses in John's writings: **47**

Uses in the NT: **76**

Key passage: **John 5:31-39**

The Greek verb *martureo* was a legal term in the ancient world, just as *testify* is in English today. The same is true of other related Greek words, such as *marturia* and *marturion* (both meaning *testimony* or *witness* with an emphasis on that which is stated), and *martus* (*witness,* the person testifying). The English word *martyr* is derived from *martus.* The legal concept was not always in view for these words in Greek usage, and in fact the court setting is rarely involved in the NT. The general ideas implied by testifying and witnessing are always there, however, such as persons declaring certain things to be factual and providing evidence to validate their claims. John 5 is not a legal setting, but Jesus used *martureo* seven times and *marturia* four times to provide four evidences that validate His claims about Himself and His relationship to the Father (vv. 17-30): John the Baptist (vv. 31-35); the works Christ performed (v. 36); the Father (vv. 37-38); and the Scriptures (vv. 39-47).

accomplish. These very works I am doing testify about Me that the Father has sent Me. [37] The Father who sent Me has Himself testified about Me. You have not heard His voice at any time, and you haven't seen His form. [38] You don't have His word living in you, because you don't believe the One He sent. [39] You pore over[a] the Scriptures because you think you have eternal life in them, yet they testify about Me. [40] And you are not willing to come to Me that you may have life.

[41] "I do not accept glory from men, [42] but I know you—that you have no love for God within you. [43] I have come in My Father's name, yet you don't accept Me. If someone else comes in his own name, you will accept him. [44] How can you believe? While accepting glory from one another, you don't seek the glory that comes from the only God. [45] Do not think that I will accuse you to the Father. Your accuser is Moses, on whom you have set your hope. [46] For if you believed Moses, you would believe Me, because he wrote about Me. [47] But if you don't believe his writings, how will you believe My words?"

THE FOURTH SIGN:
FEEDING 5,000

6 After this, Jesus crossed the Sea of Galilee (or Tiberias). [2] And a huge crowd was following Him because they saw the signs that He was performing on the sick. [3] So Jesus went up a mountain and sat down there with His disciples.

[4] Now the •Passover, a Jewish festival, was near. [5] Therefore, when Jesus looked up and noticed a huge crowd coming toward Him, He asked Philip, "Where will we buy bread so these people can eat?" [6] He asked this to test him, for He Himself knew what He was going to do.

[7] Philip answered, "Two hundred •denarii worth of bread wouldn't be enough for each of them to have a little."

[8] One of His disciples, Andrew, Simon Peter's brother, said to Him, [9] "There's a boy here who has five barley loaves and two fish—but what are they for so many?"

---

[a]5:39 In Gk this could be a command: *Pore over . . .*

10 Then Jesus said, "Have the people sit down."

There was plenty of grass in that place, so they sat down. The men numbered about 5,000. 11 Then Jesus took the loaves, and after giving thanks He distributed them to those who were seated—so also with the fish, as much as they wanted.

12 When they were full, He told His disciples, "Collect the leftovers so that nothing is wasted." 13 So they collected them and filled 12 baskets with the pieces from the five barley loaves that were left over by those who had eaten.

14 When the people saw the sign[a] He had done, they said, "This really is the Prophet who was to come into the world!" 15 Therefore, when Jesus knew that they were about to come and take Him by force to make Him king, He withdrew again[b] to the mountain by Himself.

THE FIFTH SIGN: WALKING ON WATER

16 When evening came, His disciples went down to the sea, 17 got into a boat, and started across the sea to Capernaum. Darkness had already set in, but Jesus had not yet come to them. 18 Then a high wind arose, and the sea began to churn. 19 After they had rowed about three or four miles,[c] they saw Jesus walking on the sea. He was coming near the boat, and they were afraid.

20 But He said to them, "It is I.[d] Don't be afraid!" 21 Then they were willing to take Him on board, and at once the boat was at the shore where they were heading.

THE BREAD OF LIFE

22 The next day, the crowd that had stayed on the other side of the sea knew there had been only one boat.[e] ⌊They also knew⌋ that Jesus had not boarded the boat with His disciples, but that His disciples had gone off alone. 23 Some boats from Tiberias came near the place

Take Faithfulness Over Success

A faithful servant is one that does what his Master tells him whatever the outcome may be.

"There's a boy here who has five barley loaves and two fish—but what are they for so many?" Then Jesus said, "Have the people sit down."

—John 6:9-10a

---

a6:14 Other mss read *signs*
b6:15 A previous withdrawal is mentioned in Mk 6:31-32, an event that occurred just before the feeding of the 5,000.
c6:19 Lit *25 or 30 stadia*; 1 *stadion* = 600 feet
d6:20 Lit *I am*
e6:22 Other mss add *into which His disciples had entered*

WORD STUDY

Greek word: *pisteuo*
[pihss TYEW oh]

Translation: *believe*

Uses in John's Gospel: **98**
(Mt, 11; Mk, 14; Lk, 9)

Uses in John's writings: **107**

Uses in the NT: **241**

Key passage: **John 6:29-47**

The Greek word *pisteuo* means *to believe, trust, rely upon,* and its related noun is *pistis (faith).* In his Gospel, John never used the words *repent, repentance,* or *faith* to describe the way people are saved. Instead, he used *believe* since this term included all these ideas. John preferred the verb form to emphasize the act that is necessary for someone to be saved—total dependence on the work of Another. John did indicate, however, that believing can be superficial; that is, it can be merely intellectual without resulting in true salvation (Jn 2:23-24; 12:42-43; see Jms 2:19). But John's main point is that complete reliance upon Jesus, the Messiah and Son of God (20:31), for salvation gives eternal life to the person who believes (3:16; 6:47). Jesus used a wordplay when He said that people must do "the work of God" for salvation, for His point was that we must not try to work for it at all. We must simply "believe in the One He has sent" (6:29).

where they ate the bread after the Lord gave thanks. ²⁴ When the crowd saw that neither Jesus nor His disciples were there, they got into the boats and went to Capernaum looking for Jesus.

²⁵ When they found Him on the other side of the sea, they said to Him, "•Rabbi, when did You get here?"

²⁶ Jesus answered, "•I assure you: You are looking for Me, not because you saw the signs, but because you ate the loaves and were filled. ²⁷ Don't work for the food that perishes but for the food that lasts for eternal life, which the •Son of Man will give you, because God the Father has set His seal of approval on Him."

²⁸ "What can we do to perform the works of God?" they asked.

²⁹ Jesus replied, "This is the work of God: that you believe in the One He has sent."

³⁰ "What sign then are You going to do so we may see and believe You?" they asked. "What are You going to perform? ³¹ Our fathers ate the manna in the wilderness, just as it is written: **He gave them bread from heaven to eat.**"ᵃ ᵇ

³² Jesus said to them, "I assure you: Moses didn't give you the bread from heaven, but My Father gives you the real bread from heaven. ³³ For the bread of God is the One who comes down from heaven and gives life to the world."

³⁴ Then they said, "Sir, give us this bread always!"

³⁵ "I am the bread of life," Jesus told them. "No one who comes to Me will ever be hungry, and no one who believes in Me will ever be thirsty again. ³⁶ But as I told you, you've seen Me,ᶜ and yet you do not believe. ³⁷ Everyone the Father gives Me will come to Me, and the one who comes to Me I will never cast out. ³⁸ For I have come down from heaven, not to do My will, but the will of Him who sent Me. ³⁹ This is the will of Him who sent Me: that I should lose none of those He has given Me but should raise them up on the last day. ⁴⁰ For this is the will of My Father: that everyone who sees the Son and believes in Him may have eternal life, and I will raise him up on the last day."

⁴¹ Therefore the Jews started complaining about Him,

ᵃ**6:31** Bread miraculously provided by God for the Israelites   ᵇ**6:31** Ex 16:4; Ps 78:24   ᶜ**6:36** Other mss omit *Me* because He said, "I am the bread that came down from heaven." ⁴² They were saying, "Isn't this Jesus the son of Joseph, whose father and mother we know? How can He now say, 'I have come down from heaven'?"

⁴³ Jesus answered them, "Stop complaining among yourselves. ⁴⁴ No one can come to Me unless the Father who sent Me draws ᵃ him, and I will raise him up on the last day. ⁴⁵ It is written in the Prophets: **And they will all be taught by God.** ᵇ Everyone who has listened to and learned from the Father comes to Me— ⁴⁶ not that anyone has seen the Father except the One who is from God. He has seen the Father.

⁴⁷ "I assure you: Anyone who believes ᶜ has eternal life. ⁴⁸ I am the bread of life. ⁴⁹ Your fathers ate the manna in the wilderness, and they died. ⁵⁰ This is the bread that comes down from heaven so that anyone may eat of it and not die. ⁵¹ I am the living bread that came down from heaven. If anyone eats of this bread he will live forever. The bread that I will give for the life of the world is My flesh."

⁵² At that, the Jews argued among themselves, "How can this man give us His flesh to eat?"

⁵³ So Jesus said to them, "I assure you: Unless you eat the flesh of the Son of Man and drink His blood, you do not have life in yourselves. ⁵⁴ Anyone who eats My flesh and drinks My blood has eternal life, and I will raise him up on the last day, ⁵⁵ because My flesh is real food and My blood is real drink. ⁵⁶ The one who eats My flesh and drinks My blood lives in Me, and I in him. ⁵⁷ Just as the living Father sent Me and I live because of the Father, so the one who feeds on Me will live because of Me. ⁵⁸ This is the bread that came down from heaven; it is not like the manna ᵈ your fathers ate—and they died. The one who eats this bread will live forever."

⁵⁹ He said these things while teaching in the •synagogue in Capernaum.

MANY DISCIPLES DESERT JESUS

⁶⁰ Therefore, when many of His disciples heard this, they said, "This teaching is hard! Who can accept ᵉ it?"

Live in a Constant State of Availability

Lord, if You want to meet a need through my life, I am Your servant; and I will do whatever is required.

"For I have come down from heaven, not to do My will, but the will of Him who sent Me."

—John 6:38

Depend on God for Everything

Do you realize that the Lord does not just give you life—He is your life?

"Just as the living Father sent Me and I live because of the Father, so the one who feeds on Me will live because of Me."

—John 6:57

ᵃ**6:44** Or *brings*, or *leads*; see the use of this Gk verb in Jn 12:32; 21:6; Ac 16:19; Jms 2:6.
ᵇ**6:45** Is 54:13
ᶜ**6:47** Other mss add *in Me*
ᵈ**6:58** Other mss omit *the manna*
ᵉ**6:60** Lit *hear*

⁶¹ Jesus, knowing in Himself that His disciples were complaining about this, asked them, "Does this offend you? ⁶² Then what if you were to observe the Son of Man ascending to where He was before? ⁶³ The Spirit is the One who gives life. The flesh doesn't help at all. The words that I have spoken to you are spirit and are life. ⁶⁴ But there are some among you who don't believe." (For Jesus knew from the beginning those who would notᵃ believe and the one who would betray Him.) ⁶⁵ He said, "This is why I told you that no one can come to Me unless it is granted to him by the Father."

⁶⁶ From that moment many of His disciples turned back and no longer accompanied Him. ⁶⁷ Therefore Jesus said to the Twelve, "You don't want to go away too, do you?"

⁶⁸ Simon Peter answered, "Lord, who will we go to? You have the words of eternal life. ⁶⁹ We have come to believe and know that You are the Holy One of God!"ᵇ

⁷⁰ Jesus replied to them, "Didn't I choose you, the Twelve? Yet one of you is the Devil!" ⁷¹ He was referring to Judas, Simon Iscariot's son,ᶜ ᵈ one of the Twelve, because he was going to betray Him.

THE UNBELIEF OF JESUS' BROTHERS

7 After this, Jesus traveled in Galilee, since He did not want to travel in Judea because the •Jews were trying to kill Him. ² The Jewish Festival of Tabernaclesᵉ ᶠ was near, ³ so His brothers said to Him, "Leave here and go to Judea so Your disciples can see Your works that You are doing. ⁴ For no one does anything in secret while he's seeking public recognition. If You do these things, show Yourself to the world." ⁵ (For not even His brothers believed in Him.)

⁶ Jesus told them, "My time has not yet arrived, but your time is always at hand. ⁷ The world cannot hate you, but it does hate Me because I testify about it—that its deeds are evil. ⁸ Go up to the festival yourselves. I'm

You Run on God's Power, Not Manpower

You do not get orders, then go out and carry them out on your own. You relate to God, respond to Him, and adjust your life so that He can do what He wants through you.

"The Spirit is the One who gives life. The flesh doesn't help at all. The words that I have spoken to you are spirit and are life."

—John 6:63

ᵃ6:64 Other mss omit *not*
ᵇ6:69 Other mss read *You are the Messiah, the Son of the Living God*
ᶜ6:71 Other mss read *Judas Iscariot, Simon's son*
ᵈ6:71 Lit *Judas, of Simon Iscariot*
ᵉ7:2 Or *Booths*
ᶠ7:2 One of 3 great Jewish religious festivals, along with Passover and Pentecost; Ex 23:14; Dt 16:16

not going up to the festival yet,[a] because My time has not yet fully come." ⁹ After He had said these things, He stayed in Galilee.

JESUS AT THE FESTIVAL OF TABERNACLES

¹⁰ After His brothers had gone up to the festival, then He also went up, not openly but secretly. ¹¹ The Jews were looking for Him at the festival and saying, "Where is He?" ¹² And there was a lot of discussion about Him among the crowds. Some were saying, "He's a good man." Others were saying, "No, on the contrary, He's deceiving the people." ¹³ Still, nobody was talking publicly about Him because they feared the Jews.

¹⁴ When the festival was already half over, Jesus went up into the •temple complex and began to teach. ¹⁵ Then the Jews were amazed and said, "How does He know the Scriptures, since He hasn't been trained?"

¹⁶ Jesus answered them, "My teaching isn't Mine but is from the One who sent Me. ¹⁷ If anyone wants to do His will, he will understand whether the teaching is from God or if I am speaking on My own. ¹⁸ The one who speaks for himself seeks his own glory. But He who seeks the glory of the One who sent Him is true, and there is no unrighteousness in Him. ¹⁹ Didn't Moses give you the law? Yet none of you keeps the law! Why do you want to kill Me?"

²⁰ "You have a demon!" the crowd responded. "Who wants to kill You?"

²¹ "I did one work, and you are all amazed," Jesus answered. ²² "Consider this: Moses has given you circumcision—not that it comes from Moses but from the fathers—and you circumcise a man on the Sabbath. ²³ If a man receives circumcision on the Sabbath so that the law of Moses won't be broken, are you angry at Me because I made a man entirely well on the Sabbath? ²⁴ Stop judging according to outward appearances; rather judge according to righteous judgment."

THE IDENTITY OF THE MESSIAH

²⁵ Some of the people of Jerusalem were saying, "Isn't this the man they want to kill? ²⁶ Yet, look! He's

---

His Calling Will Be Bigger Than You Are

The kind of assignments God gives in the Bible are always God-sized. They are always beyond what people can do because He wants to demonstrate His nature, His strength, His provision, and His kindness to His people and to a watching world. That is the only way the world will come to know Him.

The Jews were amazed and said, "How does He know the Scriptures, since He hasn't been trained?" Jesus answered them, "My teaching isn't Mine but is from the One who sent Me."

—John 7:15-16

Let Others See Jesus in You

Let the world see God at work and He will attract people to Himself. Let Christ be lifted up—not in words, but in life.

"If anyone wants to do His will, he will understand whether the teaching is from God or if I am speaking on My own."

—John 7:17

---

[a]7:8 Other mss omit *yet*

WORD STUDY

Greek word: **hudor**
[HOO dohr]

Translation: **water**

Uses in John's Gospel: **21**
(Mt, 7; Mk, 5; Lk, 6)

Uses in John's writings: **43**

Uses in the NT: **76**

Key passage: **John 7:38**

The English prefix *hydr-* (as in *hydraulic*) comes from the Greek word for water, *hudor.* This word often refers to literal water, of course, but *water* often has a symbolic or supernatural connotation in the Bible. This is particularly true in John's Gospel: Jesus changed water into wine as His first sign (2:1-11); Jesus offered the woman at the well "living water," which referred to Himself as the giver and sustainer of eternal life (4:7-26); the water in the pool of Bethesda was associated with healing (5:2-7); Jesus washed the disciples feet to symbolize their relationship to Him and mutual servanthood (13:1-16); and when the soldier pierced Jesus' side after His death, "blood and water" came forth (19:34), symbolizing death ("blood," Jesus really died) and life ("water," Jesus will rise from the dead; see 1 Jn 5:6-8). Twice water is used as a symbol of the Holy Spirit: the Spirit effects the new birth ("born of water and Spirit"; see Jn 3:5-8), and the Spirit is the living water that Jesus promised to those who believe in Him (Jn 7:37-39; see Rv 22:1,17).

speaking publicly and they're saying nothing to Him. Can it be true that the authorities know He is the •Messiah? ²⁷ But we know where this man is from. When the Messiah comes, nobody will know where He is from."

²⁸ As He was teaching in the temple complex, Jesus cried out, "You know Me and you know where I am from. Yet I have not come on My own, but the One who sent Me is true. You don't know Him; ²⁹ I know Him because I am from Him, and He sent Me."

³⁰ Then they tried to seize Him. Yet no one laid a hand on Him because His hour[a] had not yet come. ³¹ However, many from the crowd believed in Him and said, "When the Messiah comes, He won't perform more signs than this man has done, will He?"

³² The •Pharisees heard the crowd muttering these things about Him, so the •chief priests and the Pharisees sent temple police to arrest Him.

³³ Then Jesus said, "I am only with you for a short time. Then I'm going to the One who sent Me. ³⁴ You will look for Me, but you will not find Me; and where I am, you cannot come."

³⁵ Then the Jews said to one another, "Where does He intend to go so we won't find Him? He doesn't intend to go to the Dispersion[b] among the Greeks and teach the Greeks, does He? ³⁶ What is this remark He made: 'You will look for Me, and you will not find Me; and where I am, you cannot come'?"

THE PROMISE OF THE SPIRIT

³⁷ On the last and most important day of the festival, Jesus stood up and cried out, "If anyone is thirsty, he should come to Me[c] and drink! ³⁸ The one who believes in Me, as the Scripture has said,[d] will have streams of living water flow from deep within him." ³⁹ He said this about the Spirit, whom those who believed in Him were going to receive, for the Spirit[e] had not yet been received,[f] [g] because Jesus had not yet been glorified.

---

[a]**7:30** The time of His sacrificial death and exaltation; Jn 2:4; 8:20; 12:23,27; 13:1; 17:1
[b]**7:35** Jewish people scattered throughout Gentile lands who spoke Gk and were influenced by Gk culture
[c]**7:37** Other mss omit *to Me*
[d]**7:38** Jesus may have had several

OT passages in mind; Is 58:11; Ezk 47:1-12; Zch 14:8
[e]**7:39** Other mss read *Holy Spirit*
[f]**7:39** Other mss read *had not yet been given*
[g]**7:39** Lit *the Spirit was not yet*; the word *received* is implied from the previous clause.

THE PEOPLE ARE DIVIDED OVER JESUS

40 When some from the crowd heard these words, they said, "This really is the Prophet!"a 41 Others said, "This is the Messiah!" But some said, "Surely the Messiah doesn't come from Galilee, does He? 42 Doesn't the Scripture say that the Messiah comes from David's offspringb and from the town of Bethlehem, where David once lived?" 43 So a division occurred among the crowd because of Him. 44 Some of them wanted to seize Him, but no one laid hands on Him.

DEBATE OVER JESUS' CLAIMS

45 Then the temple police came to the chief priests and Pharisees, who asked them, "Why haven't you brought Him?"

46 The police answered, "No man ever spoke like this!"c

47 Then the Pharisees responded to them: "Are you fooled too? 48 Have any of the rulers believed in Him? Or any of the Pharisees? 49 But this crowd, which doesn't know the law, is accursed!"

50 Nicodemus—the one who came to Him previously, being one of them—said to them, 51 "Our law doesn't judge a man before it hears from him and knows what he's doing, does it?"

52 "You aren't from Galilee too, are you?" they replied. "Investigate and you will see that no prophet arises from Galilee."d

8 [53 So each one went to his house. 1 But Jesus went to the •Mount of Olives.

AN ADULTERESS FORGIVEN

2 At dawn He went to the •temple complex again, and all the people were coming to Him. He sat down and began to teach them.

3 Then the •scribes and the •Pharisees brought a woman caught in adultery, making her stand in the

Knowing Christ Exceeds Knowledge of Scripture

The Pharisees in Jesus' day thought God would be pleased with their knowledge of His Word. Yet Jesus condemned them because, although they knew the Scriptures, they did not know God. They were proud of their Bible knowledge, but they rejected the invitation to know God's Son.

The Pharisees responded to them: "Are you fooled too? Have any of the rulers believed in Him? Or any of the Pharisees?"

—John 7:47-48

---

a7:40 Probably = the Prophet in Dt 18:15
b7:42 Lit *seed*
c7:46 Other mss read *like this man*

d7:52 Jonah and probably other prophets did come from Galilee; 2 Kg 14:25

center. ⁴ "Teacher," they said to Him, "this woman was caught in the act of committing adultery. ⁵ In the law Moses commanded us to stone such women. So what do You say?" ⁶ They asked this to trap Him, in order that they might have evidence to accuse Him.

Jesus stooped down and started writing on the ground with His finger. ⁷ When they persisted in questioning Him, He stood up and said to them, "The one without sin among you should be the first to throw a stone at her."

⁸ Then He stooped down again and continued writing on the ground. ⁹ When they heard this, they left one by one, starting with the older men. Only He was left, with the woman in the center. ¹⁰ When Jesus stood up, He said to her, "•Woman, where are they? Has no one condemned you?"

¹¹ "No one, Lord,"ᵃ she answered.

"Neither do I condemn you," said Jesus. "Go, and from now on do not sin any more."]ᵇ

THE LIGHT OF THE WORLD

¹² Then Jesus spoke to them again: "I am the light of the world. Anyone who follows Me will never walk in the darkness but will have the light of life."

¹³ So the Pharisees said to Him, "You are testifying about Yourself. Your testimony is not valid."ᶜ

¹⁴ "Even if I testify about Myself," Jesus replied, "My testimony is valid,ᵈ because I know where I came from and where I'm going. But you don't know where I come from or where I'm going. ¹⁵ You judge by human standards.ᵉ I judge no one. ¹⁶ And if I do judge, My judgment is true, because I am not alone, but I and the Father who sent Me ₗjudge together₎. ¹⁷ Even in your law it is written that the witness of two men is valid. ¹⁸ I am the One who testifies about Myself, and the Father who sent Me testifies about Me."

¹⁹ Then they asked Him, "Where is Your Father?"

"You know neither Me nor My Father," Jesus answered. "If you knew Me, you would also know My

---

Make the Sacrifices of Right Choices

Until you are ready to make any adjustment necessary to follow and obey what God has said, you will be of little use to God. Your greatest single difficulty in following God may come at the point of the adjustment.

When Jesus stood up, He said to her, "Woman, where are they? Has no one condemned you?" "No one, Lord," she answered. "Neither do I condemn you," said Jesus. "Go, and from now on do not sin any more."

—John 8:10-11

Come On In—The Water's Fine

Have you ever heard people say they are experiencing a dry spell in their Christian life? What are they saying? Are they saying that the Lord ran out of water?

Jesus spoke to them again: "I am the light of the world. Anyone who follows Me will never walk in the darkness but will have the light of life."

—John 8:12

ᵃ**8:11** Or *Sir*; Jn 4:15,49; 5:7; 6:34; 9:36
ᵇ**8:11** Other mss omit bracketed text
ᶜ**8:13** The law of Moses required at least 2 witnesses to make a claim legally valid (v. 17).
ᵈ**8:14** Or *true*
ᵉ**8:15** Lit *You judge according to the flesh*

Father." 20 He spoke these words by the treasury,[a] while teaching in the temple complex. But no one seized Him, because His hour[b] had not come.

JESUS PREDICTS HIS DEPARTURE

21 Then He said to them again, "I'm going away; you will look for Me, and you will die in your sin. Where I'm going, you cannot come."

22 So the Jews said again, "He won't kill Himself, will He, since He says, 'Where I'm going, you cannot come'?"

23 "You are from below," He told them, "I am from above. You are of this world; I am not of this world. 24 Therefore I told you that you will die in your sins. For if you do not believe that I am ˻He˼,[c] you will die in your sins."

25 "Who are You?" they questioned.

"Precisely what I've been telling you from the very beginning," Jesus told them. 26 "I have many things to say and to judge about you, but the One who sent Me is true, and what I have heard from Him—these things I tell the world."

27 They did not know He was speaking to them about the Father. 28 So Jesus said to them, "When you lift up the •Son of Man, then you will know that I am ˻He˼, and that I do nothing on My own. But just as the Father taught Me, I say these things. 29 The One who sent Me is with Me. He has not left Me alone, because I always do what pleases Him."

TRUTH AND FREEDOM

30 As He was saying these things, many believed in Him. 31 So Jesus said to the Jews who had believed Him, "If you continue in My word,[d] you really are My disciples. 32 You will know the truth, and the truth will set you free."

WORD STUDY

Greek word: **phos** [FOHSS]
Translation: **light**
Uses in John: **23**
(Mt, 7; Mk, 1; Lk, 7)
Uses in John's writings: **33**
Uses in the NT: **73**
Key passage: **John 8:12**

The word *phos* is seldom used in the literal sense in the NT. Most often it is a metaphor referring to holiness, purity, or godliness. Jesus used the term in the Sermon on the Mount to describe His disciples and the holy standard of conduct that He expected them to model to the world (Mt 5:14-16; 6:23). In John's Gospel, however, Jesus Himself is "the light," as stated in the Prologue (1:4-5) and in Jesus' own words (8:12; 9:5). In this case, the light is revelatory and reflects God's character or holiness. In other words, *the light* refers to God's revelation or disclosure of Himself to the world in the incarnation (1:4-9). Incredibly, those in darkness prefer the darkness, at least until they accept the truth of God's revelation in His Son and believe in the light (3:19-21; 8:12; 12:46).

---

[a]8:20 A place for offerings to be given, perhaps in the court of women
[b]8:20 The time of His sacrificial death and exaltation; Jn 2:4; 7:30; 12:23,27; 13:1; 17:1
[c]8:24 Jesus claimed to be deity, but the Pharisees didn't understand His meaning.
[d]8:31 Or *My teaching*, or *My message*

³³ "We are descendants[a] of Abraham," they answered Him, "and we have never been enslaved to anyone. How can You say, 'You will become free'?"

³⁴ Jesus responded, "•I assure you: Everyone who commits sin is a slave of sin. ³⁵ A slave does not remain in the household forever, but a son does remain forever. ³⁶ Therefore if the Son sets you free, you really will be free. ³⁷ I know you are descendants[a] of Abraham, but you are trying to kill Me because My word[b] is not welcome among you. ³⁸ I speak what I have seen in the presence of the Father,[c] and therefore you do what you have heard from your father."

³⁹ "Our father is Abraham!" they replied.

"If you were Abraham's children," Jesus told them, "you would do what Abraham did. ⁴⁰ But now you are trying to kill Me, a man who has told you the truth that I heard from God. Abraham did not do this! ⁴¹ You're doing what your father does."

"We weren't born of sexual immorality," they said. "We have one Father—God."

⁴² Jesus said to them, "If God were your Father, you would love Me, because I came from God and I am here. For I didn't come on My own, but He sent Me. ⁴³ Why don't you understand what I say? Because you cannot listen to[d] My word. ⁴⁴ You are of your father the Devil, and you want to carry out your father's desires. He was a murderer from the beginning and has not stood in the truth, because there is no truth in him. When he tells a lie, he speaks from his own nature,[e] because he is a liar and the father of liars.[f] ⁴⁵ Yet because I tell the truth, you do not believe Me. ⁴⁶ Who among you can convict Me of sin? If I tell the truth, why don't you believe Me? ⁴⁷ The one who is from God listens to God's words. This is why you don't listen, because you are not from God."

JESUS AND ABRAHAM

⁴⁸ The Jews responded to Him, "Aren't we right in saying that You're a •Samaritan and have a demon?"

⁴⁹ "I do not have a demon," Jesus answered. "On the contrary, I honor My Father and you dishonor Me. ⁵⁰ I

God Is Speaking— Are You Listening?

Does God really speak to His people in our day? Yes! Will He reveal to you where He is working when He wants to use you? Yes! God has not changed. He still speaks to His people.

"The one who is from God listens to God's words."

—John 8:47a

---

[a]8:33,37 Or *offspring*; lit *seed*; Jn 7:42
[b]8:37 Or *My teaching*, or *My message*
[c]8:38 Other mss read *of My Father*
[d]8:43 Or *cannot hear*
[e]8:44 Lit *from his own things*
[g]8:44 Lit *of it*

do not seek My glory; the One who seeks it also judges. [51] I assure you: If anyone keeps My word, he will never see death—ever!"

[52] Then the Jews said, "Now we know You have a demon. Abraham died and so did the prophets. You say, 'If anyone keeps My word, he will never taste death—ever!' [53] Are You greater than our father Abraham who died? Even the prophets died. Who do You pretend to be?"[a]

[54] "If I glorify Myself," Jesus answered, "My glory is nothing. My Father—you say about Him, 'He is our God'—He is the One who glorifies Me. [55] You've never known Him, but I know Him. If I were to say I don't know Him, I would be a liar like you. But I do know Him, and I keep His word. [56] Your father Abraham was overjoyed that he would see My day; he saw it and rejoiced."

[57] The Jews replied, "You aren't 50 years old yet, and You've seen Abraham?"[b]

[58] Jesus said to them, "I assure you: Before Abraham was, I am."[c]

[59] At that, they picked up stones to throw at Him. But Jesus was hidden[d] and went out of the temple complex.[e]

THE SIXTH SIGN: HEALING A MAN BORN BLIND

9 As He was passing by, He saw a man blind from birth. [2] His disciples questioned Him: "•Rabbi, who sinned, this man or his parents, that he was born blind?"

[3] "Neither this man nor his parents sinned," Jesus answered. "⌐This came about⌐ so that God's works might be displayed in him. [4] We[f] must do the works of Him who sent Me[g] while it is day. Night is coming when no one can work. [5] As long as I am in the world, I am the light of the world."

[6] After He said these things He spit on the ground, made some mud from the saliva, and spread the mud

Take Your Orders One Day at a Time

God doesn't usually give you a one time assignment and leave you there forever. Yes, you may be placed in one job at one place for a long time, but God's assignments come to you on a daily basis.

"We must do the works of Him who sent Me while it is day."

—John 9:4a

---

[a]8:53 Lit *Who do You make Yourself?*
[b]8:57 Other mss read *and Abraham has seen You?*
[c]8:58 *I AM* is the name God gave Himself at the burning bush; Ex 3:13-14; see note at Jn 8:24.
[d]8:59 Or *Jesus hid Himself*
[e]8:59 Other mss add *and having gone through their midst, He passed by*
[f]9:4 Other mss read *I*
[g]9:4 Other mss read *sent us*

WORD STUDY

Greek word: **hamartolos**
[hah mahr toh LAHSS]

Translation: **sinner**

Uses in John: **4**
(Mt, 5; Mk, 6; Lk, 18)

Uses in John's writings: **4**

Uses in the NT: **47**

Key passages: **John 9:16,24**

One of the key doctrines of the Christian faith is that every person is a sinner and must believe in Jesus as Savior to have eternal life. This teaching is consistent with the use of the word *hamartolos (sinner)* in several places and with other related passages about sin (Rm 3:9-23; 5:12). A special use of the term *hamartolos* occurs in the Gospels and refers to those who have a reputation for being guilty of grievous sins, such as tax collectors, prostitutes, and pagans (see Mt 9:10-11; Lk 6:32-34; 7:36-39). In the aftermath of Jesus' miracle of healing the man born blind (Jn 9), Jewish leaders used the term *sinner* in this especially derisive sense to describe Jesus (v. 24). In doing so they hoped to undermine the clear implication of this miracle—that Jesus was the Messiah—and to keep people from following Him.

on his eyes. 7 "Go," He told him, "wash in the pool of Siloam" (which means "Sent"). So he left, washed, and came back seeing.

8 His neighbors and those who formerly had seen him as a beggar said, "Isn't this the man who sat begging?" 9 Some said, "He's the one." "No," others were saying, "but he looks like him."

He kept saying, "I'm the one!"

10 Therefore they asked him, "Then how were your eyes opened?"

11 He answered, "The man called Jesus made mud, spread it on my eyes, and told me, 'Go to Siloam and wash.' So when I went and washed I received my sight."

12 "Where is He?" they asked.

"I don't know," he said.

THE HEALED MAN'S TESTIMONY

13 They brought the man who used to be blind to the •Pharisees. 14 The day that Jesus made the mud and opened his eyes was a Sabbath. 15 So again the Pharisees asked him how he received his sight.

"He put mud on my eyes," he told them. "I washed and I can see."

16 Therefore some of the Pharisees said, "This man is not from God, for He doesn't keep the Sabbath!" But others were saying, "How can a sinful man perform such signs?" And there was a division among them.

17 Again they asked the blind man,[a] "What do you say about Him, since He opened your eyes?"

"He's a prophet," he said.

18 The Jews did not believe this about him—that he was blind and received sight—until they summoned the parents of the one who had received his sight.

19 They asked them, "Is this your son, ⌊the one⌋ you say was born blind? How then does he now see?"

20 "We know this is our son and that he was born blind," his parents answered. 21 "But we don't know how he now sees, and we don't know who opened his eyes. Ask him; he's of age. He will speak for himself."

22 His parents said these things because they were afraid of the Jews, since the Jews had already agreed

---

[a]9:17 = the man who had been blind

that if anyone confessed Him as •Messiah, he would be banned from the •synagogue. 23 This is why his parents said, "He's of age; ask him."

24 So a second time they summoned the man who had been blind and told him, "Give glory to God.ᵃ We know that this man is a sinner!"

25 He answered, "Whether or not He's a sinner, I don't know. One thing I do know: I was blind, and now I can see!"

26 Then they asked him, "What did He do to you? How did He open your eyes?"

27 "I already told you," he said, "and you didn't listen. Why do you want to hear it again? You don't want to become His disciples too, do you?"

28 They ridiculed him: "You're that man's disciple, but we're Moses' disciples. 29 We know that God has spoken to Moses. But this man—we don't know where He's from!"

30 "This is an amazing thing," the man told them. "You don't know where He is from, yet He opened my eyes! 31 We know that God doesn't listen to sinners, but if anyone is God-fearing and does His will, He listens to him. 32 Throughout historyᵇ no one has ever heard of someone opening the eyes of a person born blind. 33 If this man were not from God, He wouldn't be able to do anything."

34 "You were born entirely in sin," they replied, "and are you trying to teach us?" Then they threw him out.ᶜ

THE BLIND MAN'S SIGHT AND THE PHARISEES' BLINDNESS

35 When Jesus heard that they had thrown the man out, He found him and asked, "Do you believe in the •Son of Man?"ᵈ

36 "Who is He, Sir, that I may believe in Him?" he asked.

37 Jesus answered, "You have seen Him; in fact, He is the One speaking with you."

38 "I believe, Lord!" he said, and he worshiped Him.

Look for More Than Circumstances

Never, ever determine the truth of a situation by looking at the circumstances. Don't evaluate your situation until you have heard from Jesus. He is the Truth of all your circumstances.

He answered, "Whether or not He's a sinner, I don't know. One thing I do know: I was blind, and now I can see!"
—John 9:25

God Will Give You Everything You Need

God will never give you an assignment that He will not, at the same time, enable you to complete. That is what a spiritual gift is—a supernatural empowering to accomplish the assignment God gives you.

"If this man were not from God, He wouldn't be able to do anything."
—John 9:33

ᵃ9:24 *Give glory to God* was a solemn charge to tell the truth; Jos 7:19.
ᵇ9:32 Lit *From the age*
ᶜ9:34 = they banned him from the synagogue; v. 22
ᵈ9:35 Other mss read *the Son of God*

WORD STUDY

Greek word: ***poimen***
[poy MAYN]

Translation: ***shepherd***

Uses in John: **6**
(Mt, 3; Mk, 2; Lk, 4)

Uses in John's writings: **6**

Uses in the NT: **18**

Key passage: **John 10:1-18**

The Greek word *poimen* occurs in John's Gospel only in John 10 where Jesus refers to Himself as "the good shepherd [who] lays down his life for the sheep" (v. 11). The sheep (believers) and the shepherd (Jesus) know each other, and the shepherd will bring all the sheep from the various folds (nations) into one flock (vv. 14-16).

The background for Jesus' use of the shepherd imagery is Ezekiel 34. God denounced the false shepherds (that is, false prophets) who led the sheep (the nation of Judah) astray (Jn 10:1-10). Then the Lord said, "I Myself will search for My flock, and look for them" from among the many places they are scattered (vv. 11-12). Finally, David will be the shepherd over God's people again (vv. 23-24). In using the shepherd/sheep imagery, Jesus was identifying Himself as the Shepherd of Israel, just as the Lord had done in this OT passage—a clear statement that Jesus claimed to be deity. Jesus also indicated that He would have the role of David as shepherd—a clear statement that Jesus claimed to be the Messiah. No wonder "a division took place among the Jews" (v. 19) at this time! Some even thought Jesus was demon-possessed, but others took Jesus' claim seriously since He had healed a blind man (vv. 20-21).

39 Jesus said, "I came into this world for judgment, in order that those who do not see will see and those who do see will become blind."

40 Some of the Pharisees who were with Him heard these things and asked Him, "We aren't blind too, are we?"

41 "If you were blind," Jesus told them, "you wouldn't have sin.[a] But now that you say, 'We see'—your sin remains.

THE IDEAL SHEPHERD

10 "•I assure you: Anyone who doesn't enter the sheep pen by the door but climbs in some other way, is a thief and a robber. **2** The one who enters by the door is the shepherd of the sheep. **3** The doorkeeper opens it for him, and the sheep hear his voice. He calls his own sheep by name and leads them out. **4** When he has brought all his own outside, he goes ahead of them. The sheep follow him because they recognize his voice. **5** They will never follow a stranger; instead they will run away from him, because they don't recognize the voice of strangers."

6 Jesus gave them this illustration, but they did not understand what He was telling them.

THE GOOD SHEPHERD

7 So Jesus said again, "I assure you: I am the door of the sheep. **8** All who came before Me[b] are thieves and robbers, but the sheep didn't listen to them. **9** I am the door. If anyone enters by Me, he will be saved and will come in and go out and find pasture. **10** A thief comes only to steal and to kill and to destroy. I have come that they may have life and have it in abundance.

11 "I am the good shepherd. The good shepherd lays down his life for the sheep. **12** The hired man, since he is not the shepherd and doesn't own the sheep, leaves them[c] and runs away when he sees a wolf coming. The wolf then snatches and scatters them. **13** ⌊This happens⌋ because he is a hired man and doesn't care about the sheep.

---

[a]**9:41** To *have sin* is an idiom that refers to guilt caused by sin.

[b]**10:8** Other mss omit *before Me*
[c]**10:12** Lit *leaves the sheep*

¹⁴ "I am the good shepherd. I know My own sheep, and they know Me, ¹⁵ as the Father knows Me, and I know the Father. I lay down My life for the sheep. ¹⁶ But I have other sheep that are not of this fold; I must bring them also, and they will listen to My voice. Then there will be one flock, one shepherd. ¹⁷ This is why the Father loves Me, because I am laying down My life so I may take it up again. ¹⁸ No one takes it from Me, but I lay it down on My own. I have the right to lay it down, and I have the right to take it up again. I have received this command from My Father."

¹⁹ Again a division took place among the Jews because of these words. ²⁰ Many of them were saying, "He has a demon and He's crazy! Why do you listen to Him?" ²¹ Others were saying, "These aren't the words of someone demon-possessed. Can a demon open the eyes of the blind?"

JESUS AT THE FESTIVAL OF DEDICATION

²² Then the Festival of Dedication[a] took place in Jerusalem, and it was winter. ²³ Jesus was walking in the •temple complex in Solomon's Colonnade.[b] ²⁴ Then the Jews surrounded Him and asked, "How long are You going to keep us in suspense?[c] If You are the •Messiah, tell us plainly."[d]

²⁵ "I did tell you and you don't believe," Jesus answered them. "The works that I do in My Father's name testify about Me. ²⁶ But you don't believe because you are not My sheep.[e] ²⁷ My sheep hear My voice, I know them, and they follow Me. ²⁸ I give them eternal life, and they will never perish—ever! No one will snatch them out of My hand. ²⁹ My Father, who has given them to Me, is greater than all. No one is able to snatch them out of the Father's hand. ³⁰ The Father and I are one."[f]

Trust Him to Speak Where You Can Hear

God speaks to individuals, and He can do it in any way He pleases. As you walk in an intimate love relationship with God, you will come to recognize His voice. You will know when God is speaking to you.

"My sheep hear My voice, I know them, and they follow Me."

—John 10:27

---

[a]10:22 Or *Hanukkah*, also called the *Feast of Lights*; this festival commemorated the rededication of the temple in 164 B.C.
[b]10:23 Rows of columns supporting a roof
[c]10:24 Lit *How long are you taking away our life?*
[d]10:24 Or *openly*, or *publicly*
[e]10:26 Other mss add *just as I told you*
[f]10:30 Lit *I and the Father—We are one.*

RENEWED EFFORTS
TO STONE JESUS

31 Again the Jews picked up rocks to stone Him.
32 Jesus replied, "I have shown you many good works from the Father. Which of these works are you stoning Me for?"
33 "We aren't stoning You for a good work," the Jews answered, "but for blasphemy, because You—being a man—make Yourself God."
34 Jesus answered them, "Isn't it written in your law,[a] **I said, you are gods**?[b] 35 If He called those whom the word of God came to 'gods'—and the Scripture cannot be broken— 36 do you say, 'You are blaspheming' to the One the Father set apart and sent into the world, because I said: I am the Son of God? 37 If I am not doing My Father's works, don't believe Me. 38 But if I am doing them and you don't believe Me, believe the works. This way you will know and understand[c] that the Father is in Me and I in the Father." 39 Then they were trying again to seize Him, yet He eluded their grasp.

MANY BEYOND THE JORDAN
BELIEVE IN JESUS

40 So He departed again across the Jordan to the place where John had been baptizing earlier, and He remained there. 41 Many came to Him and said, "John never did a sign, but everything John said about this man was true." 42 And many believed in Him there.

LAZARUS DIES AT BETHANY

11 Now a man was sick, Lazarus, from Bethany, the village of Mary and her sister Martha. 2 Mary was the one who anointed the Lord with fragrant oil and wiped His feet with her hair, and it was her brother Lazarus who was sick. 3 So the sisters sent a message to Him: "Lord, the one You love is sick."
4 When Jesus heard it, He said, "This sickness will not end in death but is for the glory of God, so that the Son of God may be glorified through it." 5 (Jesus loved Martha, her sister, and Lazarus.) 6 So when He heard

Pray Expectantly

When I pray, it never crosses my mind that God is not going to answer. Expect God to answer prayer, but stick around for the answer. His timing is always right and best.

Martha said to Jesus, "Lord, if You had been here, my brother wouldn't have died. Yet even now I know that whatever You ask from God, God will give You."

—John 11:21-22

---

[a]**10:34** Other mss read *in the law*
[b]**10:34** Ps 82:6
[c]**10:38** Other mss read *know and believe*

that he was sick, He stayed two more days in the place where He was. ⁷ Then after that, He said to the disciples, "Let's go to Judea again."

⁸ "•Rabbi," the disciples told Him, "just now the Jews tried to stone You, and You're going there again?"

⁹ "Aren't there 12 hours in a day?" Jesus answered. "If anyone walks during the day, he doesn't stumble, because he sees the light of this world. ¹⁰ If anyone walks during the night, he does stumble, because the light is not in him." ¹¹ He said this, and then He told them, "Our friend Lazarus has fallen •asleep, but I'm on My way to wake him up."

¹² Then the disciples said to Him, "Lord, if he has fallen asleep, he will get well."

¹³ Jesus, however, was speaking about his death, but they thought He was speaking about natural sleep. ¹⁴ So Jesus then told them plainly, "Lazarus has died. ¹⁵ I'm glad for you that I wasn't there so that you may believe. But let's go to him."

¹⁶ Then Thomas (called "Twin") said to his fellow disciples, "Let's go so that we may die with Him."

THE RESURRECTION
AND THE LIFE

¹⁷ When Jesus arrived, He found that Lazarus had already been in the tomb four days. ¹⁸ Bethany was near Jerusalem (about two milesᵃ away). ¹⁹ Many of the Jews had come to Martha and Mary to comfort them about their brother. ²⁰ As soon as Martha heard that Jesus was coming, she went to meet Him. But Mary remained seated in the house.

²¹ Then Martha said to Jesus, "Lord, if You had been here, my brother wouldn't have died. ²² Yet even now I know that whatever You ask from God, God will give You."

²³ "Your brother will rise again," Jesus told her.

²⁴ Martha said, "I know that he will rise again in the resurrection at the last day."

²⁵ Jesus said to her, "I am the resurrection and the life. The one who believes in Me, even if he dies, will

WORD STUDY

Greek word: **anastasis**
[ah NAH stah sihss]

Translation: **resurrection**

Uses in John's Gospel: **4**
(Mt, 4; Mk, 2; Lk, 6)

Uses in John's writings: **6**

Uses in the NT: **42**

Key passage: **John 11:24-25**

The Greek noun *anastasis* is derived from the verb *anistemi*, meaning literally *to stand up* and then by extension "to rise up." Both words could be used metaphorically. The word *anastasis* was common in the ancient Greek world; but it rarely referred to the resurrection of the dead, which was the dominant meaning of its occurrences in the NT. Two major events are described with the word *anastasis* in the NT: the physical, bodily resurrection of Jesus in the past (Rm 1:4; 1 Co 15:12-13), and the physical, bodily resurrection of believers in the future (Jn 5:29; 11:24-25; 1 Co 15:42; Php 3:11; Rv 20:5-6).

ᵃ11:18 Lit *15 stadia*; 1 *stadion* = 600 feet

live. ²⁶ Everyone who lives and believes in Me will never die—ever. Do you believe this?"

²⁷ "Yes, Lord," she told Him, "I believe You are the •Messiah, the Son of God, who was to come into the world."

JESUS SHARES
THE SORROW OF DEATH

²⁸ Having said this, she went back and called her sister Mary, saying in private, "The Teacher is here and is calling for you."

²⁹ As soon as she heard this, she got up quickly and went to Him. ³⁰ Jesus had not yet come into the village but was still in the place where Martha had met Him. ³¹ The Jews who were with her in the house consoling her saw that Mary got up quickly and went out. So they followed her, supposing that she was going to the tomb to cry there.

³² When Mary came to where Jesus was and saw Him, she fell at His feet and told Him, "Lord, if You had been here, my brother would not have died!"

³³ When Jesus saw her crying, and the Jews who had come with her crying, He was angry[a] in His spirit and deeply moved. ³⁴ "Where have you put him?" He asked.

"Lord," they told Him, "come and see."

³⁵ Jesus wept.

³⁶ So the Jews said, "See how He loved him!" ³⁷ But some of them said, "Couldn't He who opened the blind man's eyes also have kept this man from dying?"

THE SEVENTH SIGN:
RAISING LAZARUS FROM THE DEAD

³⁸ Then Jesus, angry in Himself again, came to the tomb. It was a cave, and a stone was lying against it. ³⁹ "Remove the stone," Jesus said.

Martha, the dead man's sister, told Him, "Lord, he already stinks. It's been four days."

⁴⁰ Jesus said to her, "Didn't I tell you that if you believed you would see the glory of God?"

⁴¹ So they removed the stone. Then Jesus raised His

**Repeat These Words:
"Yes, Lord."**

Two words in the Christian's language cannot go together: "No, Lord." If He really is your Lord, your answer must always be "Yes."

"Yes, Lord," she told Him, "I believe You are the Messiah, the Son of God, who was to come into the world."

—John 11:27

---

[a]**11:33** The Gk word is very strong and probably indicates Jesus' anger against sin's tyranny and death.

eyes and said, "Father, I thank You that You heard Me. [42] I know that You always hear Me, but because of the crowd standing here I said this, so they may believe You sent Me." [43] After He said this, He shouted with a loud voice, "Lazarus, come out!" [44] The dead man came out bound hand and foot with linen strips and with his face wrapped in a cloth. Jesus said to them, "Loose him and let him go."

THE PLOT TO KILL JESUS

[45] Therefore many of the Jews who came to Mary and saw what He did believed in Him. [46] But some of them went to the •Pharisees and told them what Jesus had done.

[47] So the •chief priests and the Pharisees convened the •Sanhedrin and said, "What are we going to do since this man does many signs? [48] If we let Him continue in this way, everybody will believe in Him! Then the Romans will come and remove both our place[a] and our nation."

[49] One of them, Caiaphas, who was high priest that year, said to them, "You know nothing at all! [50] You're not considering that it is to your[b] advantage that one man should die for the people rather than the whole nation perish." [51] He did not say this on his own, but being high priest that year he prophesied that Jesus was going to die for the nation, [52] and not for the nation only, but also to unite the scattered children of God. [53] So from that day on they plotted to kill Him. [54] Therefore Jesus no longer walked openly among the Jews but departed from there to the countryside near the wilderness, to a town called Ephraim. And He stayed there with the disciples.

[55] The Jewish •Passover was near, and many went up to Jerusalem from the country to purify[c] themselves before the Passover. [56] They were looking for Jesus and asking one another as they stood in the •temple complex: "What do you think? He won't come to the festival, will He?" [57] The chief priests and the Pharisees

When You Believe, God Makes Your Life Unbelievable

Anyone who will take the time to enter into an intimate relationship with God can see God do extraordinary things through his or her life.

"I know that You always hear Me, but because of the crowd standing here I said this, so they may believe You sent Me." After He said this, He shouted with a loud voice, "Lazarus, come out!"

—John 11:42-43

---

[a]11:48 The temple or possibly all of Jerusalem
[b]11:50 Other mss read *to our*
[c]11:55 The law of Moses required God's people to purify or cleanse themselves so they could celebrate the Passover. Jews often came to Jerusalem a week early to do this; Nm 9:4-11.

had given orders that if anyone knew where He was, he should report it so they could arrest Him.

THE ANOINTING AT BETHANY

12 Six days before the •Passover, Jesus came to Bethany where Lazarus[a] was, the one Jesus had raised from the dead. [2] So they gave a dinner for Him there; Martha was serving them, and Lazarus was one of those reclining at the table with Him. [3] Then Mary took a pound of fragrant oil—pure and expensive nard—anointed Jesus' feet, and wiped His feet with her hair. So the house was filled with the fragrance of the oil.

[4] Then one of His disciples, Judas Iscariot (who was about to betray Him), said, [5] "Why wasn't this fragrant oil sold for 300 •denarii[b] and given to the poor?" [6] He didn't say this because he cared about the poor but because he was a thief. He was in charge of the moneybag and would steal part of what was put in it.

[7] Jesus answered, "Leave her alone; she has kept it for the day of My burial. [8] For you always have the poor with you, but you do not always have Me."

THE DECISION TO KILL LAZARUS

[9] Then a large crowd of the Jews learned He was there. They came not only because of Jesus, but also to see Lazarus the one He had raised from the dead. [10] Therefore the •chief priests decided to also kill Lazarus, [11] because he was the reason many of the Jews were deserting them[c] and believing in Jesus.

THE TRIUMPHAL ENTRY

[12] The next day, when the large crowd that had come to the festival heard that Jesus was coming to Jerusalem, [13] they took palm branches and went out to meet Him. They kept shouting: "•*Hosanna!* **Blessed is He who comes in the name of the Lord**[d] —the King of Israel!"

Your First Priority: Love Him

Can you describe your relationship with God by sincerely saying, "I love Him with all my heart"?

Mary took a pound of fragrant oil—pure and expensive nard—anointed Jesus' feet, and wiped His feet with her hair. So the house was filled with the fragrance of the oil.

—John 12:3

---

[a]**12:1** Other mss read *Lazarus who died*
[b]**12:5** This amount was about a year's wages for a common worker.
[c]**12:11** Lit *going away*
[d]**12:13** Ps 118:25-26

[14] Jesus found a young donkey and sat on it, just as it is written: [15] **Fear no more, Daughter Zion; look! your King is coming, sitting on a donkey's colt.**[a]

[16] His disciples did not understand these things at first. However, when Jesus was glorified, then they remembered that these things had been written about Him and that they had done these things to Him. [17] Meanwhile the crowd, which had been with Him when He called Lazarus out of the tomb and raised him from the dead, continued to testify.[b] [18] This is also why the crowd met Him, because they heard He had done this sign.

[19] Then the •Pharisees said to one another, "You see? You've accomplished nothing. Look—the world has gone after Him!"

JESUS PREDICTS HIS CRUCIFIXION

[20] Now some Greeks were among those who went up to worship at the festival. [21] So they came to Philip, who was from Bethsaida in Galilee, and requested of him, "Sir, we want to see Jesus."

[22] Philip went and told Andrew; then Andrew and Philip went and told Jesus. [23] Jesus replied to them, "The hour has come for the •Son of Man to be glorified.

[24] "•I assure you: Unless a grain of wheat falls into the ground and dies, it remains by itself. But if it dies, it produces a large crop.[c] [25] The one who loves his life will lose it, and the one who hates his life in this world will keep it for eternal life. [26] If anyone serves Me, he must follow Me. Where I am, there My servant also will be. If anyone serves Me, the Father will honor him.

[27] "Now My soul is troubled. What should I say— Father, save Me from this hour? But that is why I came to this hour. [28] Father, glorify Your name!"[d]

Then a voice came from heaven: "I have glorified it, and I will glorify it again!"

[29] The crowd standing there heard it and said it was thunder. Others said, "An angel has spoken to Him!"

What You Do Will Reveal Who You Are

You cannot stay where you are and go with God. You cannot continue doing things your way and accomplish God's purposes in His ways.

"If anyone serves Me, he must follow Me. Where I am, there My servant also will be. If anyone serves Me, the Father will honor him."
—John 12:26

Keep Your Focus on Today

God always will give you enough specific directions to do *now* what He wants you to do. When you need more directions, He gives you more in His timing.

"Now My soul is troubled. What should I say—Father, save Me from this hour? But that is why I came to this hour."
—John 12:27

---

[a]**12:15** Zch 9:9
[b]**12:17** Other mss read *Meanwhile the crowd, which had been with Him, continued to testify that He* *had called Lazarus out of the tomb and raised him from the dead.*
[c]**12:24** Lit *produces much fruit*
[d]**12:28** Other mss read *Your Son*

WORD STUDY

Greek word: *doxa*
[DAHKS uh]

Translation: *glory, praise*

Uses in John's Gospel: **19**
(Mt, 7; Mk, 3; Lk, 13)

Uses in John's writings: **36**

Uses in the NT: **166**

Key passage: **John 12:41-43**

The use of *doxa (glory)* in the NT is shaped by the Hebrew word *kabod* that is so common in the OT. The noun *kabod* is derived from a Hebrew verb meaning *to be heavy*. (A related noun, *kebed*, means *liver,* the heavy organ.) Thus, to recognize the glory of something is to attach weight or importance to it. The glory of the Lord refers to His nature and holiness as manifested to His creatures, humans and angels, both of whom can share in that glory. Even in the incarnation, Jesus shared in the Father's glory and especially manifested His grace and truth (Jn 1:14; see 17:5). The greatest manifestation of God's glory happened at the cross (Jn 13:31-32; the related verb *doxazo [glorify]* is used here), for here God's greatest work occurred. We praise God when we give Him glory, acknowledging that He is of greatest importance to us. Thus, *doxa* may often mean *praise.* John 12 contains a wordplay with these two meanings. John stated that Isaiah saw God's glory, which refers to the prophet's vision of the Lord in the temple with the seraphs exclaiming: "Holy, Holy, Holy is the LORD of Hosts; His glory fills the whole earth" (Is 6:3). But according to John, Isaiah saw the glory *(doxa)* of Jesus (Jn 12:41). Those who refused to confess Him did so because "they loved praise *[doxa]* from men more than praise *[doxa]* from God" (v. 43).

³⁰ Jesus responded, "This voice came, not for Me, but for you. ³¹ Now is the judgment of this world. Now the ruler of this world will be cast out. ³² As for Me, if I am lifted up[a] from the earth I will draw all ₗpeopleⱼ to Myself." ³³ He said this to signify what kind of death He was about to die.

³⁴ Then the crowd replied to Him, "We have heard from the law that the •Messiah will remain forever. So how can You say, 'The Son of Man must be lifted up'?[a] Who is this Son of Man?"

³⁵ Jesus answered, "The light will be with you only a little longer. Walk while you have the light so that darkness doesn't overtake you. The one who walks in darkness doesn't know where he's going. ³⁶ While you have the light, believe in the light so that you may become sons of light." Jesus said this, then went away and hid from them.

ISAIAH'S PROPHECIES FULFILLED

³⁷ Even though He had performed so many signs in their presence, they did not believe in Him. ³⁸ But this was to fulfill the word of Isaiah the prophet, who said:[b]

> **Lord, who has believed our message?**
> **And who has the arm of the Lord been revealed to?[c]**

³⁹ This is why they were unable to believe, because Isaiah also said:

> ⁴⁰ **He has blinded their eyes**
> **and hardened their hearts,**
> **so that they would not see with their eyes**
> **or understand with their hearts,**
> **and be converted,**
> **and I would heal them.[d]**

⁴¹ Isaiah said these things because[e] he saw His glory and spoke about Him.

⁴² Nevertheless, many did believe in Him even among the rulers, but because of the Pharisees they did not confess Him, so they would not be banned from the

---

[a]12:32,34 Or *exalted*
[b]12:38 Lit *which he said*
[c]12:38 Is 53:1
[d]12:40 Is 6:10
[e]12:41 Other mss read *when*

•synagogue. ⁴³ For they loved praise from men more than praise from God.ᵃ

A SUMMARY OF JESUS' MISSION

⁴⁴ Then Jesus cried out, "The one who believes in Me believes not in Me, but in Him who sent Me. ⁴⁵ And the one who sees Me sees Him who sent Me. ⁴⁶ I have come as a light into the world, so that everyone who believes in Me would not remain in darkness. ⁴⁷ If anyone hears My words and doesn't keep them, I do not judge him; for I did not come to judge the world but to save the world. ⁴⁸ The one who rejects Me and doesn't accept My sayings has this as his judge:ᵇ the word I have spoken will judge him on the last day. ⁴⁹ For I have not spoken on My own, but the Father Himself who sent Me has given Me a command as to what I should say and what I should speak. ⁵⁰ I know that His command is eternal life. So the things that I speak, I speak just as the Father has told Me."

JESUS WASHES
HIS DISCIPLES' FEET

13 Before the •Passover Festival, Jesus knew that His hour had come to depart from this world to the Father. Having loved His own who were in the world, He loved them to the end.ᶜ

² Now by the time of supper, the Devil had already put it into the heart of Judas, Simon Iscariot's son, to betray Him. ³ Jesus knew that the Father had given everything into His hands, that He had come from God, and that He was going back to God. ⁴ So He got up from supper, laid aside His robe, took a towel, and tied it around Himself. ⁵ Next, He poured water into a basin and began to wash His disciples' feet and to dry them with the towel tied around Him.

⁶ He came to Simon Peter, who asked Him, "Lord, are You going to wash my feet?"

⁷ Jesus answered him, "What I'm doing you don't understand now, but afterwards you will know."

God's Will Is an Expensive Calling

You cannot know and do the will of God without paying the price of adjustment and obedience.

Many did believe in Him even among the rulers, but because of the Pharisees they did not confess Him, so they would not be banned from the synagogue. For they loved praise from men more than praise from God.

—John 12:42-43

God Has Put You Here for a Reason

What you plan to do for God is not important. What He plans to do where you are is very important.

"I have not spoken on My own, but the Father Himself who sent Me has given Me a command as to what I should say and what I should speak."

—John 12:49

ᵃ**12:43** Lit *loved glory of men more than glory of God*; v. 41; Jn 5:41
ᵇ**12:48** Lit *has the one judging him*
ᶜ**13:1** *to the end = completely* or *always*

WORD STUDY

Greek word: **didaskalos**
[dih DAHSS kuh lahss]

Translation: **Teacher**

Uses in John: **8**
(Mt, 12; Mk, 12; Lk, 17)

Uses in John's writings: **8**

Uses in the NT: **59**

Key passage: **John 13:13-14**

The Greek noun *didaskalos* refers to Jesus most of the time in the Gospels but never does outside the Gospels. In the Gospels the term is used of a recognized spiritual leader with a group of committed followers or disciples (see word study on *mathetes*). John used *didaskalos* as the Greek equivalent of the technical Hebrew term *rabbi* (see note at 1:38) and the similar term *rabbouni* (see note at 20:16). The teacher not only instructed people about the Word of God but in so doing challenged them to conform to its demands. Thus, the majority of times *didaskalos* refers to Jesus in the Gospels, it is used as a title ("Teacher"). So strong was the role of the teacher in the life of a disciple that Jesus connected it with His title as "Lord" (13:13-14).

8 "You will never wash my feet—ever!" Peter said.

Jesus replied, "If I don't wash you, you have no part with Me."

9 Simon Peter said to Him, "Lord, not only my feet, but also my hands and my head."

10 "One who has bathed," Jesus told him, "doesn't need to wash anything except his feet, but he is completely clean. You are clean, but not all of you." 11 For He knew who would betray Him. This is why He said, "You are not all clean."

THE MEANING OF FOOTWASHING

12 When Jesus had washed their feet and put on His robe, He reclined[a] again and said to them, "Do you know what I have done for you? 13 You call Me Teacher and Lord. This is well said, for I am. 14 So if I, your Lord and Teacher, have washed your feet, you also ought to wash one another's feet. 15 For I have given you an example that you also should do just as I have done for you.

16 "•I assure you: A slave is not greater than his master,[b] and a messenger is not greater than the one who sent him. 17 If you know these things, you are blessed if you do them. 18 I'm not speaking about all of you; I know those I have chosen. But the Scripture must be fulfilled: **The one who eats My bread[c] has raised his heel against Me.**[d]

19 "I am telling you now before it happens, so that when it does happen you will believe that I am ₍He₎. 20 I assure you: The one who receives whomever I send receives Me, and the one who receives Me receives Him who sent Me."

JUDAS' BETRAYAL PREDICTED

21 When Jesus had said this, He was troubled in His spirit and testified, "I assure you: One of you will betray Me!"

22 The disciples started looking at one another—uncertain which one He was speaking about. 23 One of

---

[a]13:12 At important meals the custom was to recline on a mat at a low table and lean on the left elbow.
[b]13:16 Or *lord*

[c]13:18 Other mss read *eats bread with Me*
[d]13:18 Ps 41:9

His disciples, the one Jesus loved, was reclining close beside Jesus.[a] [24] Simon Peter motioned to him to find out who it was He was talking about. [25] So he leaned back against Jesus and asked Him, "Lord, who is it?"

[26] Jesus replied, "He's the one I give the piece of bread to after I have dipped it." When He had dipped the bread, He gave it to Judas, Simon Iscariot's son.[b] [27] After ⌊Judas ate⌋ the piece of bread, Satan entered him. Therefore Jesus told him, "What you're doing, do quickly."

[28] None of those reclining at the table knew why He told him this. [29] Since Judas kept the money-bag, some thought that Jesus was telling him, "Buy what we need for the festival," or that he should give something to the poor. [30] After receiving the piece of bread, he went out immediately. And it was night.

THE NEW COMMANDMENT

[31] When he had gone out, Jesus said, "Now the •Son of Man is glorified, and God is glorified in Him. [32] If God is glorified in Him,[c] God will also glorify Him in Himself and will glorify Him at once.

[33] "Children, I am with you a little while longer. You will look for Me, and just as I told the Jews, 'Where I am going you cannot come,' so now I tell you.

[34] "I give you a new commandment: love one another. Just as I have loved you, you must also love one another. [35] By this all people will know that you are My disciples, if you have love for one another."

PETER'S DENIALS PREDICTED

[36] "Lord," Simon Peter said to Him, "where are You going?"

Jesus answered, "Where I am going you cannot follow Me now, but you will follow later."

[37] "Lord," Peter asked, "why can't I follow You now? I will lay down my life for You!"

[38] Jesus replied, "Will you lay down your life for Me? I assure you: A rooster will not crow until you have denied Me three times.

---

[a]**13:23** Lit *reclining at Jesus' breast*; that is, on His right; Jn 1:18
[b]**13:26** Other mss read *Judas Iscariot, Simon's son*
[c]**13:32** Other mss omit *If God is glorified in Him*

WORD STUDY

Greek word: **mathetes**
[mah thay TAYSS]

Translation: **disciple**

Uses in John: **78**
(Mt, 76; Mk, 42; Lk, 37)

Uses in John's writings: **78**

Uses in the NT: **261**

Key passage: **John 13:35**

The English word *disciple* basically means *follower*. The Greek noun *mathetes*, however, comes from the verb *manthano*, which means *to learn*. Thus, a *mathetes* is primarily a learner, though being a follower is certainly included. *Mathetes* occurs only in the Gospels and Acts and refers to disciples of various teachers or rabbis, such as the Pharisees (Mk 2:18) and John the Baptist (Jn 1:35). In Jewish life there was no such thing as a *mathetes* without a *didaskalos* (*teacher,* see word study on *didaskalos*), the person the disciple learned from. Most often in the NT *mathetes* refers to disciples of Jesus, sometimes in general (6:61,66) but most often to the Twelve. Jesus stated that the single attribute that characterizes His disciples is that they love one another (13:35).

THE WAY TO THE FATHER

14 "Your heart must not be troubled. Believe[a] in God; believe also in Me. ² In My Father's house are many dwelling places;[b] if not, I would have told you. I am going away to prepare a place for you. ³ If I go away and prepare a place for you, I will come back and receive you to Myself, so that where I am you may be also. ⁴ You know the way where I am going."[c]

⁵ "Lord," Thomas said, "we don't know where You're going. How can we know the way?"

⁶ Jesus told him, "I am the way, the truth, and the life. No one comes to the Father except through Me.

JESUS REVEALS THE FATHER

⁷ "If you know Me, you will also know[d] My Father. From now on you do know Him and have seen Him."

⁸ "Lord," said Philip, "show us the Father, and that's enough for us."

⁹ Jesus said to him, "Have I been among you all this time without your knowing Me, Philip? The one who has seen Me has seen the Father. How can you say, 'Show us the Father'? ¹⁰ Don't you believe that I am in the Father and the Father is in Me? The words I speak to you I do not speak on My own. The Father who lives in Me does His works. ¹¹ Believe Me that I am in the Father and the Father is in Me. Otherwise, believe[e] because of the works themselves.

PRAYING IN JESUS' NAME

¹² "•I assure you: The one who believes in Me will also do the works that I do. And he will do even greater works than these, because I am going to the Father. ¹³ Whatever you ask in My name, I will do it so that the Father may be glorified in the Son. ¹⁴ If you ask Me[f] anything in My name, I will do it.[g]

Remember Where Your Strength Lies

Jesus realized that He could do nothing by Himself. Yet with the Father at work in Him, He could do anything. If Jesus was that dependent on the Father, then you and I should realize we are even more dependent on God the Father to be working in and through us.

"Don't you believe that I am in the Father and the Father is in Me? The words I speak to you I do not speak on My own. The Father who lives in Me does His works."

—John 14:10

You'd Be Surprised What He Can Do Through You

I have come to the place in my life that, if the assignment I sense God is giving me is something that I know I can handle, I know it probably is not from God.

"I assure you: The one who believes in Me will also do the works that I do. And he will do even greater works than these, because I am going to the Father."

—John 14:12

---

[a]**14:1** Or *You believe*
[b]**14:2** The Vg used the Lat term *mansio,* a traveler's resting place. The Gk word is related to the verb *meno,* meaning *remain* or *stay,* which occurs 40 times in John.
[c]**14:4** Other mss read this verse: *And you know where I am going, and you know the way*
[d]**14:7** Other mss read *If you had known Me, you would have known*
[e]**14:11** Other mss read *believe Me*
[f]**14:14** Other mss omit *Me*
[g]**14:14** Other mss omit all of v. 14

ANOTHER COUNSELOR PROMISED

¹⁵ "If you love Me, you will keepᵃ My commandments. ¹⁶ And I will ask the Father, and He will give you another •Counselor to be with you forever. ¹⁷ He is the Spirit of truth. The world is unable to receive Him because it doesn't see Him or know Him. But you do know Him, because He remains with you and will beᵇ in you. ¹⁸ I will not leave you as orphans; I am coming to you.

THE FATHER, THE SON, AND THE HOLY SPIRIT

¹⁹ "In a little while the world will see Me no longer, but you will see Me. Because I live, you will live too. ²⁰ In that day you will know that I am in My Father, you are in Me, and I am in you. ²¹ The one who has My commands and keeps them is the one who loves Me. And the one who loves Me will be loved by My Father. I also will love him and will reveal Myself to him."

²² Judas (not Iscariot) said to Him, "Lord, how is it You're going to reveal Yourself to us and not to the world?"

²³ Jesus answered, "If anyone loves Me, he will keep My word. My Father will love him, and We will come to him and make Our home with him. ²⁴ The one who doesn't love Me will not keep My words. The word that you hear is not Mine but is from the Father who sent Me.

²⁵ "I have spoken these things to you while I remain with you. ²⁶ But the Counselor, the Holy Spirit—the Father will send Him in My name—will teach you all things and remind you of everything I have told you.

JESUS' GIFT OF PEACE

²⁷ "Peace I leave with you. My peace I give to you. I do not give to you as the world gives. Your heart must not be troubled or fearful. ²⁸ You have heard Me tell you, 'I am going away and I am coming to you.' If you loved Me, you would have rejoiced that I am going to the Father, because the Father is greater than I. ²⁹ I have told you now before it happens so that when it

The Holy Spirit Will Steer You Right

When the Holy Spirit reveals Truth, He is not teaching you a concept to be thought about. He is leading you to a relationship with a Person.

"He is the Spirit of truth. The world is unable to receive Him because it doesn't see Him or know Him. But you do know Him, because He remains with you and will be in you."
—John 14:17

ᵃ14:15 Other mss read *If you love Me, keep* (as a command)   ᵇ14:17 Other mss read *and is*

245

does happen you may believe. [30] I will not talk with you much longer, because the ruler of the world is coming. He has no power over Me.[a] [31] On the contrary, ₗI am going awayₗ[b] so that the world may know that I love the Father. Just as the Father commanded Me, so I do.

"Get up; let's leave this place."

THE VINE AND THE BRANCHES

15 "I am the true vine, and My Father is the vineyard keeper. [2] Every branch in Me that does not produce fruit He removes, and He prunes every branch that produces fruit so that it will produce more fruit. [3] You are already clean because of the word I have spoken to you. [4] Remain in Me, and I in you. Just as a branch is unable to produce fruit by itself unless it remains on the vine, so neither can you unless you remain in Me.

[5] "I am the vine; you are the branches. The one who remains in Me and I in him produces much fruit, because you can do nothing without Me. [6] If anyone does not remain in Me, he is thrown aside like a branch and he withers. They gather them, throw them into the fire, and they are burned. [7] If you remain in Me and My words remain in you, ask whatever you want and it will be done for you. [8] My Father is glorified by this: that you produce much fruit and prove to be[c] My disciples.

CHRISTLIKE LOVE

[9] "As the Father has loved Me, I have also loved you. Remain in My love. [10] If you keep My commands you will remain in My love, just as I have kept My Father's commands and remain in His love.

[11] "I have spoken these things to you so that My joy may be in you and your joy may be complete. [12] This is My command: love one another as I have loved you. [13] No one has greater love than this, that someone would lay down his life for his friends. [14] You are My friends if you do what I command you. [15] I do not call you slaves anymore, because a slave doesn't know what his master[d] is doing. I have called you friends, because

---

Do You Know How Much God Loves You?

God is far more interested in a love relationship with you than He is in what you can do for Him.

"As the Father has loved Me, I have also loved you. Remain in My love."

—John 15:9

---

[a]**14:30** Lit *He has nothing in Me*
[b]**14:31** Probably refers to the cross
[c]**15:8** Or *and become*
[d]**15:15** Or *lord*

I have made known to you everything I have heard from My Father. ¹⁶ You did not choose Me, but I chose you. I appointed you that you should go out and produce fruit and that your fruit should remain, so that whatever you ask the Father in My name, He will give you. ¹⁷ This is what I command you: love one another.

PERSECUTIONS PREDICTED

¹⁸ "If the world hates you, understand that it hated Me before it hated you. ¹⁹ If you were of the world, the world would love ₗyou as₎ its own. However, because you are not of the world, but I have chosen you out of it, the world hates you. ²⁰ Remember the word I spoke to you: 'A slave is not greater than his master.' If they persecuted Me, they will also persecute you. If they kept My word, they will also keep yours. ²¹ But they will do all these things to you on account of My name, because they don't know the One who sent Me. ²² If I had not come and spoken to them, they would not have sin.ᵃ Now they have no excuse for their sin. ²³ The one who hates Me also hates My Father. ²⁴ If I had not done the works among them that no one else has done, they would not have sin. Now they have seen and hated both Me and My Father. ²⁵ But ₗthis happened₎ so that the statement written in their law might be fulfilled: **They hated Me for no reason.**ᵇ

COMING TESTIMONY
AND REJECTION

²⁶ "When the •Counselor comes, the One I will send to you from the Father—the Spirit of truth who proceeds from the Father—He will testify about Me. ²⁷ You also will testify, because you have been with Me from the beginning.

16 "I have told you these things to keep you from stumbling. ² They will ban you from the •synagogues. In fact, a time is coming when anyone who kills you will think he is offering service to God. ³ They will do these things because they haven't known the Father or Me. ⁴ But I have told you these things so that when

---

ᵃ**15:22** To *have sin* is an idiom that refers to guilt caused by sin.   ᵇ**15:25** Ps 69:4

WORD STUDY

Greek word: ***parakletos***
[pah RAH klay tahss]

Translation: ***Counselor***

Uses in John: **4**

Uses in John's writings: **5**

Uses in the NT: **5**

Key passages: **John 14:16,26; 15:26**

The Greek word *parakletos* is derived from the verb *parakaleo* (literally *to call alongside;* basically *to comfort, counsel, exhort*). It is also related to the noun *paraklesis (comfort, exhortation)*. Both are much more common than *parakletos* but do not occur in John's writings, while *parakletos* occurs only in John's writings. In all four occurrences of *parakletos* in John's Gospel, Jesus used the term to refer to the Holy Spirit as our *Counselor*. The idea is that the Spirit comes alongside to aid us in the tasks Jesus gave us as His disciples.

WORD STUDY

Greek word: **kosmos**
[KAHZ mahss]

Translation: **world**

Uses in John's Gospel: **78**
(Mt, 9; Mk, 3; Lk, 3)

Uses in John's writings: **105**

Uses in the NT: **186**

Key passages: **John 16:11,28,33**

The noun *kosmos* (English *cosmos, cosmic*), is normally translated *world* and most often has negative connotations, especially in John's writings. John provides the foundational verse about the *kosmos* in 1:10—"He [the Word] was in the world [earth; see 16:28], and the world [the universe; see 17:5] was created through Him, yet the world [unbelieving humanity] did not recognize Him" (see 17:25). The *kosmos* is consistently described by John as hostile to Jesus and the things of God. The world needs the light (1:9; see 8:12) because it is in darkness (3:19). It is dead and needs life (6:33,51). The world hates Jesus (7:7) and His followers (15:18; 17:14), but it will be judged (9:39; 12:31), as will its prince (that is, Satan; 12:31; 16:11). But as "the Lamb of God, who takes away the sin of the world" (1:29), Jesus "conquered the world" (16:33). God loved the world (despite its sins) and gave His Son to redeem the world (3:16-17). John warned believers not to love the world, for it is contrary to the things of God and is destined to disappear (1 Jn 2:15-17). This will occur when Jesus returns and "the kingdom of the world has become the kingdom of our Lord and of His Messiah," who "will reign forever and ever" (Rv 11:15).

their time[a] comes you may remember I told them to you. I didn't tell you these things from the beginning, because I was with you.

THE COUNSELOR'S MINISTRY

5 "But now I am going away to Him who sent Me, and not one of you asks Me, 'Where are You going?' 6 Yet, because I have spoken these things to you, sorrow has filled your heart. 7 Nevertheless, I am telling you the truth. It is for your benefit that I go away, because if I don't go away the •Counselor will not come to you. If I go, I will send Him to you. 8 When He comes, He will convict the world about sin, righteousness, and judgment: 9 about sin, because they do not believe in Me; 10 about righteousness, because I am going to the Father and you will no longer see Me; 11 and about judgment, because the ruler of this world has been judged.

12 "I still have many things to tell you, but you can't bear them now. 13 When the Spirit of truth comes, He will guide you into all the truth. For He will not speak on His own, but He will speak whatever He hears. He will also declare to you what is to come. 14 He will glorify Me, because He will take from what is Mine and declare it to you. 15 Everything the Father has is Mine. This is why I told you that He takes from what is Mine and will declare it to you.

SORROW TURNED TO JOY

16 "A little while and you will no longer see Me; again a little while and you will see Me."[b]

17 Therefore some of His disciples said to one another, "What is this He tells us: 'A little while and you will not see Me; again a little while and you will see Me'; and, 'because I am going to the Father'?" 18 They said, "What is this He is saying,[c] 'A little while'? We don't know what He's talking about!"

19 Jesus knew they wanted to question Him, so He said to them, "Are you asking one another about what

---

[a]**16:4** Other mss read *when the time*
[b]**16:16** Other mss add *because I am going to the Father*
[c]**16:18** Other mss omit *He is saying*

I said, 'A little while and you will not see Me; again a little while and you will see Me'?
20 "•I assure you: You will weep and wail, but the world will rejoice. You will become sorrowful, but your sorrow will turn to joy. 21 When a woman is in labor she has pain because her time has come. But when she has given birth to a child, she no longer remembers the suffering because of the joy that a person has been born into the world. 22 So you also have sorrow a now. But I will see you again. Your hearts will rejoice, and no one will rob you of your joy. 23 In that day you will not ask Me anything.

"I assure you: Anything you ask the Father in My name, He will give you. 24 Until now you have asked for nothing in My name. Ask and you will receive, that your joy may be complete.

JESUS THE VICTOR

25 "I have spoken these things to you in figures of speech. A time is coming when I will no longer speak to you in figures, but I will tell you plainly about the Father. 26 In that day you will ask in My name. I am not telling you that I will make requests to the Father on your behalf. 27 For the Father Himself loves you, because you have loved Me and have believed that I came from God.b 28 I came from the Father and have come into the world. Again, I am leaving the world and going to the Father."

29 "Ah!" His disciples said. "Now You're speaking plainly and not using any figurative language. 30 Now we know that You know everything and don't need anyone to question You. By this we believe that You came from God."

31 Jesus responded to them, "Do you now believe? 32 Look: An hour is coming, and has come, when each of you will be scattered to his own home, and you will leave Me alone. Yet I am not alone, because the Father is with Me. 33 I have told you these things so that in Me you may have peace. You will have suffering in this world. Be courageous! I have conquered the world."

Expect Times of Testing and Stretching

Waiting on the Lord should not be an idle time for you. Let God use times of waiting to mold and shape your character. Let God use those times to purify your life and make you into a clean vessel for His service.

"When a woman is in labor she has pain because her time has come. But when she has given birth to a child, she no longer remembers the suffering because of the joy that a person has been born into the world. So you also have sorrow now. But I will see you again. Your hearts will rejoice, and no one will rob you of your joy."

—John 16:21-22

---

a16:22 Other mss read *will have sorrow*

b16:27 Other mss read *from the Father*

WORD STUDY

Greek word: **hora**
[HOH rah]

Translation: **hour**

Uses in John: **26**
(Mt, 21; Mk, 12; Lk, 17)

Uses in John's writings: **38**

Uses in the NT: **106**

Key passage: **John 17:1**

In the NT the Greek word *hora* seldom if ever refers to a period of sixty minutes. Even "one hour" in Revelation (17:12; 18:10,17,19) should be understood as an idiom meaning *quickly* or *suddenly.* In John's Gospel a special use of *hour* occurs several times and refers to Jesus' death, though His exaltation in glory is often in view also. This meaning of *hour* first occurs at Jesus' miracle of changing the water into wine (Jn 2:4), and the final one occurs at the beginning of Jesus' prayer to the Father (17:1) just before His arrest (18:12; for other occurrences during passion week, see 12:23,27; 13:1). In between these two events, John's Gospel states on two occasions that the hour of Jesus' death had not yet arrived (7:30; 8:20). The appointed moment for His death on our behalf was set in eternity past and could not have been changed by anyone, no matter how powerful.

JESUS PRAYS FOR HIMSELF

17 Jesus spoke these things, looked up to heaven, and said:

Father,
the hour has come.
Glorify Your Son
so that the Son may glorify You,
2 for You gave Him authority
over all flesh;[a]
so He may give eternal life
to all You have given Him.
3 This is eternal life:
that they may know You, the only true God,
and the One You have sent—Jesus Christ.
4 I have glorified You on the earth
by completing the work You gave Me to do.
5 Now, Father, glorify Me in Your presence
with that glory I had with You
before the world existed.

JESUS PRAYS FOR HIS DISCIPLES

6 I have revealed Your name
to the men You gave Me from the world.
They were Yours, You gave them to Me,
and they have kept Your word.
7 Now they know that all things
You have given to Me are from You,
8 because the words that You gave Me,
I have given them.
They have received them
and have known for certain
that I came from You.
They have believed that You sent Me.
9 I pray[b] for them.
I am not praying for the world
but for those You have given Me,
because they are Yours.
10 All My things are Yours,
and Yours are Mine,
and I have been glorified in them.

---

[a]17:2 Or *people*   [b]17:9 Lit *ask* (throughout this passage)

¹¹ I am no longer in the world,
   but they are in the world,
   and I am coming to You.
   Holy Father,
   protectᵃ them by Your name
   that You have given Me,
   so that they may be one as We are one.
¹² While I was with them,
   I was protecting them by Your name
   that You have given Me.
   I guarded them and not one of them is lost,
   except the son of destruction,ᵇ
   so that the Scripture may be fulfilled.
¹³ Now I am coming to You,
   and I speak these things in the world
   so that they may have My joy completed in them.
¹⁴ I have given them Your word.
   The world hated them
   because they are not of the world,
   as I am not of the world.
¹⁵ I am not praying
   that You take them out of the world
   but that You protect them from the evil one.
¹⁶ They are not of the world,
   as I am not of the world.
¹⁷ Sanctifyᶜ them by the truth;
   Your word is truth.
¹⁸ As You sent Me into the world,
   I also have sent them into the world.
¹⁹ I sanctify Myself for them,
   so they also may be sanctified by the truth.

JESUS PRAYS FOR ALL BELIEVERS

²⁰ I pray not only for these,
   but also for those who believe in Me
   through their message.
²¹ May they all be one,
   as You, Father, are in Me and I am in You.
   May they also be oneᵈ in Us,
   so the world may believe You sent Me.

Focus on Your Own Relationship with God

The Scripture leads us to understand that God is saying, "I want you to love Me above everything else. When you are in a relationship of love with Me, you have everything there is." To be loved by God is the highest relationship, the highest achievement, and the highest position in life.

"I have revealed Your name to the men You gave Me from the world. They were Yours, You gave them to Me, and they have kept Your word."
—John 17:6

Your Calling Is No Better, No Worse—It Is Your Part in the Body

All members of the body belong to each other, and they need each other.

"May they all be one, as You, Father, are in Me and I am in You. May they also be one in Us, so the world may believe You sent Me."
—John 17:21

ᵃ17:11 Lit *keep* (throughout this passage)
ᵇ17:12 The one destined for destruction, loss, or perdition
ᶜ17:17 Set apart for special use
ᵈ17:21 Other mss omit *one*

22 I have given them the glory You have given Me.
May they be one as We are one.
23 I am in them and You are in Me.
May they be made completely one,
so the world may know You have sent Me
and have loved them as You have loved Me.
24 Father,
I desire those You have given Me
to be with Me where I am.
Then they will see My glory,
which You have given Me
because You loved Me
before the world's foundation.
25 Righteous Father!
The world has not known You.
However, I have known You,
and these have known that You sent Me.
26 I made Your name known to them
and will make it known,
so the love You have loved Me with
may be in them and I may be in them.

Our Motivation Of Love

You will be incapable of ministering to everyone God sends you unless you have His love. Seek to know the Father and His immeasurable love; then allow His Son to love others through you.

"Righteous Father! The world has not known You. However, I have known You, and these have known that You sent Me. I made Your name known to them and will make it known, so the love You have loved Me with may be in them and I may be in them."

—John 17:25-26

JESUS BETRAYED

18 After Jesus had said these things, He went out with His disciples across the Kidron Valley, where there was a garden, and He and His disciples went into it. 2 Judas, who betrayed Him, also knew the place, because Jesus often met there with His disciples. 3 So Judas took a •company of soldiers and some temple police from the •chief priests and the •Pharisees and came there with lanterns, torches, and weapons.

4 Then Jesus, knowing everything that was about to happen to Him, went out and said to them, "Who is it you're looking for?"

5 "Jesus the •Nazarene," they answered.

"I am He,"[a] Jesus told them.

Judas, who betrayed Him, was also standing with them. 6 When He told them, "I am He," they stepped back and fell to the ground.

7 Then He asked them again, "Who is it you're looking for?"

[a]18:5 Lit *I am*; see note at Jn 8:58

"Jesus the Nazarene," they said.

⁸ "I told you I am ₍He₎," Jesus replied. "So if you're looking for Me, let these men go." ⁹ This was to fulfill the words He had said: "I have not lost one of those You have given Me."

¹⁰ Then Simon Peter, who had a sword, drew it, struck the high priest's slave, and cut off his right ear. (The slave's name was Malchus.)

¹¹ At that, Jesus said to Peter, "Sheathe your sword! Am I not to drink the cup the Father has given Me?"

JESUS ARRESTED AND TAKEN TO ANNAS

¹² Then the company of soldiers, the commander, and the Jewish temple police arrested Jesus and tied Him up. ¹³ First they led Him to Annas, for he was the father-in-law of Caiaphas, who was high priest that year. ¹⁴ Caiaphas was the one who had advised the Jews that it was advantageous that one man should die for the people.

PETER DENIES JESUS

¹⁵ Meanwhile Simon Peter was following Jesus, as was another disciple. That disciple was an acquaintance of the high priest; so he went with Jesus into the high priest's courtyard. ¹⁶ But Peter remained standing outside by the door. So the other disciple, the one known to the high priest, went out and spoke to the girl who was the doorkeeper and brought Peter in.

¹⁷ Then the slave girl who was the doorkeeper said to Peter, "You aren't one of this man's disciples too, are you?"

"I am not!" he said. ¹⁸ Now the slaves and the temple police had made a charcoal fire, because it was cold. They were standing there warming themselves, and Peter was standing with them, warming himself.

JESUS BEFORE ANNAS

¹⁹ The high priest questioned Jesus about His disciples and about His teaching.

²⁰ "I have spoken openly to the world," Jesus answered him. "I have always taught in the •synagogue

WORD STUDY

Greek words: *ego eimi*
[eh GOH igh MEE]

Translation: *I am*

Uses in John's Gospel: **76**

Uses in John's writings: **86**

Uses in the NT: **153**

Key passage: **John 18:5**

The words *ego eimi* occur numerous times in the NT, but in John's Gospel they have a special meaning with two related connotations. First, *I am* often refers to Jesus' claim to be the Messiah. This is clear in John 4 where the woman at the well referred to the coming Messiah (v. 25) and Jesus responded, "I am He [*ego eimi*]" (v. 26). This meaning of *ego eimi* also occurs in Jesus' words to the disciples, "I am telling you now before it [Judas' betrayal] happens, so that when it does happen you will believe that I am He [*ego eimi*]" (13:19). Jesus' foreknowledge of Judas' betrayal provided evidence for the other disciples that He was indeed the Messiah. Second, *ego eimi* often refers to Jesus' claim to deity and probably reflects the burning bush episode when God revealed Himself to Moses as "I am" (Ex 3:14). This meaning of *I am* occurs at Jesus' walking on the water (Jn 6:20; "It is I"; see Mk 6:50; Lk 21:8), in a conversation with the Jewish leaders when Jesus stated that He existed prior to Abraham (Jn 8:58; "Before Abraham was, I am"), and at Jesus' arrest when the soldiers attempting to find Him fell back to the ground on hearing Jesus say the words "I am He" (18:5). The words *ego eimi* are also used in John's Gospel to introduce seven special titles for Jesus: (6:48; 8:12; 10:7; 10:11; 11:25; 14:6; 15:1).

and in the •temple complex, where all the Jews congregate, and I haven't spoken anything in secret. ²¹ Why do you question Me? Question those who heard what I told them. Look, they know what I said."

²² When He had said these things, one of the temple police standing by slapped Jesus, saying, "Is this the way you answer the high priest?"

²³ "If I have spoken wrongly," Jesus answered him, "give evidenceᵃ about the wrong; but if rightly, why do you hit Me?"

²⁴ Then Annas sent Him bound to Caiaphas the high priest.

PETER DENIES JESUS TWICE MORE

²⁵ Now Simon Peter was standing and warming himself. They said to him, "You aren't one of His disciples too, are you?"

He denied it and said, "I am not!"

²⁶ One of the high priest's slaves, a relative of the man whose ear Peter had cut off, said, "Didn't I see you with Him in the garden?"

²⁷ Peter then denied it again. Immediately a rooster crowed.

JESUS BEFORE PILATE

²⁸ Then they took Jesus from Caiaphas to the governor's •headquarters. It was early morning. They did not enter the headquarters themselves; otherwise they would be defiled and unable to eat the •Passover.

²⁹ Then •Pilate came out to them and said, "What charge do you bring against this man?"

³⁰ They answered him, "If this man weren't a criminal,ᵇ we wouldn't have handed Him over to you."

³¹ So Pilate told them, "Take Him yourselves and judge Him according to your law."

"It's not legalᶜ for us to put anyone to death," the Jews declared. ³² They said this so that Jesus' words might be fulfilled signifying what sort of death He was going to die.

Submit Yourself Freely to His Correction

Disobedience is never taken lightly by God. At times He lets you proceed in your disobedience, but He will never let you go too far without discipline to bring you back.

One of the high priest's slaves, a relative of the man whose ear Peter had cut off, said, "Didn't I see you with Him in the garden?" Peter then denied it again. Immediately a rooster crowed.

—John 18:26-27

ᵃ18:23 Or *him, testify*
ᵇ18:30 Lit *an evil doer*

ᶜ18:31 According to Roman law

33 Then Pilate went back into the headquarters, summoned Jesus, and said to Him, "Are You the King of the Jews?"

34 Jesus answered, "Are you asking this on your own, or have others told you about Me?"

35 "I'm not a Jew, am I?" Pilate replied. "Your own nation and the chief priests handed You over to me. What have You done?"

36 "My kingdom is not of this world," said Jesus. "If My kingdom were of this world, My servants[a] would fight, so that I wouldn't be handed over to the Jews. As it is, My kingdom does not have its origin here."[b]

37 "You are a king then?" Pilate asked.

"You say that I'm a king," Jesus replied. "I was born for this, and I have come into the world for this: to testify to the truth. Everyone who is of the truth listens to My voice."

38 "What is truth?" said Pilate.

JESUS OR BARABBAS

After he had said this, he went out to the Jews again and told them, "I find no grounds for charging Him. 39 You have a custom that I release one ˌprisonerˌ to you at the Passover. So, do you want me to release to you the King of the Jews?"

40 They shouted back, "Not this man, but Barabbas!" Now Barabbas was a revolutionary.[c]

JESUS FLOGGED AND MOCKED

19 Then •Pilate took Jesus and had Him flogged. 2 The soldiers also twisted together a crown of thorns, put it on His head, and threw a purple robe around Him. 3 And they repeatedly came up to Him and said, "Hail, King of the Jews!" and were slapping His face.

4 Pilate went outside again and said to them, "Look, I'm bringing Him outside to you to let you know I find no grounds for charging Him."

Means Can Be More Important Than Ends

Being practical or getting results can become a Christian's primary focus. But actions that seem to make sense on the surface can often be at variance with the purposes of God.

"My kingdom is not of this world," said Jesus. "If My kingdom were of this world, My servants would fight, so that I wouldn't be handed over to the Jews. As it is, My kingdom does not have its origin here."

—John 18:36

He Will Show You What He Wants You to Do

Truth is not discovered; it is revealed. Only God can tell you what He is doing or is wanting to do through your life. You will not be able to figure that out on your own.

"I have come into the world for this: to testify to the truth. Everyone who is of the truth listens to My voice."

—John 18:37b

---

a**18:36** Or *attendants*, or *helpers*
b**18:36** Lit *My kingdom is not from here*
c**18:40** Or *robber*; see Jn 10:1,8 for the same Gk word used here

PILATE SENTENCES JESUS TO DEATH

⁵ Then Jesus came out wearing the crown of thorns and the purple robe. Pilate said to them, "Here is the man!"

⁶ When the •chief priests and the temple police saw Him, they shouted, "Crucify! Crucify!"

Pilate responded, "Take Him and crucify Him yourselves, for I find no grounds for charging Him."

⁷ "We have a law," the Jews replied to him, "and according to that law He must die, because He made Himselfᵃ the Son of God."

⁸ When Pilate heard this statement, he was more afraid than ever. ⁹ He went back into the •headquarters and asked Jesus, "Where are You from?" But Jesus did not give him an answer. ¹⁰ So Pilate said to Him, "You're not talking to me? Don't You know that I have the authority to release You and the authority to crucify You?"

¹¹ "You would have no authority over Me at all," Jesus answered him, "if it hadn't been given you from above. This is why the one who handed Me over to you has the greater sin."ᵇ

¹² From that moment Pilate made every effortᶜ to release Him. But the Jews shouted, "If you release this man, you are not Caesar's friend. Anyone who makes himself a king opposes Caesar!"

¹³ When Pilate heard these words, he brought Jesus outside. He sat down on the judge's bench in a place called the Stone Pavement (but in Hebrew *Gabbatha*). ¹⁴ It was the preparation day for the •Passover, and it was about six in the morning.ᵈ Then he told the Jews, "Here is your king!"

¹⁵ But they shouted, "Take Him away! Take Him away! Crucify Him!"

Pilate said to them, "Should I crucify your king?"

"We have no king but Caesar!" the chief priests answered.

¹⁶ So then, because of them, he handed Him over to be crucified.

Watch the Way Jesus Did It

When I want to learn how to know and do the will of God, I always look to Jesus. I can find no better model.

So Pilate said to Him, "You're not talking to me? Don't You know that I have the authority to release You and the authority to crucify You?" "You would have no authority over Me at all," Jesus answered him, "if it hadn't been given you from above."

—John 19:10-11a

ᵃ19:7 He claimed to be
ᵇ19:11 To *have sin* is an idiom that refers to guilt caused by sin.
ᶜ19:12 Lit *Pilate was trying*
ᵈ19:14 Lit *the sixth hour*; see note at Jn 1:39; an alternate time reckoning would be *about noon*

THE CRUCIFIXION

Therefore they took Jesus away.[a] 17 Carrying His own cross, He went out to what is called Skull Place, which in Hebrew is called *Golgotha*. 18 There they crucified Him and two others with Him, one on either side, with Jesus in the middle. 19 Pilate also had a sign lettered and put on the cross. The inscription was:

**JESUS THE NAZARENE
THE KING OF THE JEWS.**

20 Many of the Jews read this sign, because the place where Jesus was crucified was near the city, and it was written in Hebrew,[b] Latin, and Greek. 21 So the chief priests of the Jews said to Pilate, "Don't write, 'The King of the Jews,' but that He said, 'I am the King of the Jews.'"

22 Pilate replied, "What I have written, I have written."

23 When the soldiers crucified Jesus, they took His clothes and divided them into four parts, a part for each soldier. They also took the tunic, which was seamless, woven in one piece from the top. 24 So they said to one another, "Let's not tear it, but toss for it, to see who gets it." They did this, to fulfill the Scripture that says: **They divided My clothes among themselves, and they cast lots for My clothing.**[c] And this is what the soldiers did.

JESUS' PROVISION FOR HIS MOTHER

25 Standing by the cross of Jesus were His mother, His mother's sister, Mary the wife of Clopas, and •Mary Magdalene. 26 When Jesus saw His mother and the disciple He loved standing there, He said to His mother, "•Woman, here is your son." 27 Then He said to the disciple, "Here is your mother." And from that hour the disciple took her into his home.

THE FINISHED WORK OF JESUS

28 After this, when Jesus knew that everything was now accomplished that the Scripture might be fulfilled,

WORD STUDY

Greek word: **teleo** [tehl EH oh]
Translation: **finish**
Uses in John's Gospel: **2** (Mt, 7; Lk, 4)
Uses in John's writings: **10**
Uses in the NT: **28**
Key passage: **John 19:28-30**

Just before His death on the cross, Jesus uttered a single word of victory: *tetelestai* [teh TEHL ehs tigh], "It is finished!" (Jn 19:30). The verb *teleo* is related to several other Greek words that refer to something being finished, accomplished, completed, or coming to an end. (The same verb is translated "accomplished" in v. 28.) The perfect tense of the Greek verb Jesus used indicates that He understood His death at this point in time to have abiding or lasting results. Jesus' death on the cross on our behalf was His purpose for coming into the world. It is not surprising that Revelation uses the term eight times, more than any other NT book, to describe various events related to Jesus' second coming (10:7; 11:7; 15:1,8; 17:17; 20:3,5,7).

---

[a]19:16 Other mss add *and led Him out* [b]19:20 Or *Aramaic* [c]19:24 Ps 22:18

He said, "I'm thirsty!" ²⁹ A jar full of sour wine was sitting there; so they fixed a sponge full of sour wine on hyssopᵃ and held it up to His mouth.

³⁰ When Jesus had received the sour wine, He said, "It is finished!" Then bowing His head, He gave up His spirit.

JESUS' SIDE PIERCED

³¹ Since it was the preparation day, the Jews did not want the bodies to remain on the cross on the Sabbath (for that Sabbath was a specialᵇ day). They requested that Pilate have the men's legs broken and that ⌊their bodies⌋ be taken away. ³² So the soldiers came and broke the legs of the first man and of the other one who had been crucified with Him. ³³ When they came to Jesus, they did not break His legs since they saw that He was already dead. ³⁴ But one of the soldiers pierced His side with a spear, and at once blood and water came out. ³⁵ He who saw this has testified so that you also may believe. His testimony is true, and he knows he is telling the truth. ³⁶ For these things happened so that the Scripture would be fulfilled: **Not one of His bones will be broken.**ᶜ ³⁷ Also, another Scripture says: **They will look at the One they pierced.**ᵈ

JESUS' BURIAL

³⁸ After this, Joseph of Arimathea, who was a disciple of Jesus—but secretly because of his fear of the Jews—asked Pilate that he might remove Jesus' body. Pilate gave him permission, so he came and took His body away. ³⁹ Nicodemus (who had previously come to Him at night) also came, bringing a mixture of about 75 poundsᵉ of myrrh and aloes. ⁴⁰ Then they took Jesus' body and wrapped it in linen cloths with the aromatic spices, according to the burial custom of the Jews. ⁴¹ There was a garden in the place where He was crucified. A new tomb was in the garden; no one had yet been placed in it. ⁴² They placed Jesus there because of the Jewish preparation and since the tomb was nearby.

Seek the Advice of Trustworthy Believers

Trust God to provide you counsel through other believers. Turn to them for counsel on major decisions. Listen attentively to anything the church has to say to you. Then let God confirm what His message is for you.

He who saw this has testified so that you also may believe. His testimony is true, and he knows he is telling the truth.

—John 19:35

ᵃ19:29 Or *with hyssop*
ᵇ19:31 Lit *great*
ᶜ19:36 Ex 12:46; Nm 9:12; Ps 34:20
ᵈ19:37 Zch 12:10
ᵉ19:39 Lit *100 litrai*; a Roman *litrai* = 12 ounces

THE EMPTY TOMB

20 On the first day of the week •Mary Magdalene came to the tomb early, while it was still dark. She saw that the stone had been removed[a] from the tomb. 2 So she ran to Simon Peter and to the other disciple, the one Jesus loved, and said to them, "They have taken the Lord out of the tomb, and we don't know where they have put Him!"

3 At that, Peter and the other disciple went out, heading for the tomb. 4 The two were running together, but the other disciple outran Peter and got to the tomb first. 5 Stooping down, he saw the linen cloths lying there, yet he did not go in. 6 Then, following him, Simon Peter came also. He entered the tomb and saw the linen cloths lying there. 7 The wrapping that had been on His head was not lying with the linen cloths but was folded up in a separate place by itself. 8 The other disciple, who had reached the tomb first, then entered the tomb, saw, and believed. 9 For they still did not understand the Scripture that He must rise from the dead. 10 Then the disciples went home again.

MARY MAGDALENE SEES THE RISEN LORD

11 But Mary stood outside facing the tomb, crying. As she was crying, she stooped to look into the tomb. 12 She saw two angels in white sitting there, one at the head and one at the feet, where Jesus' body had been lying. 13 They said to her, "•Woman, why are you crying?"

"Because they've taken away my Lord," she told them, "and I don't know where they've put Him."
14 Having said this, she turned around and saw Jesus standing there, though she did not know it was Jesus.

15 "Woman," Jesus said to her, "why are you crying? Who is it you are looking for?"

Supposing He was the gardener, she replied, "Sir, if you've removed Him, tell me where you've put Him, and I will take Him away."

16 Jesus said, "Mary."

Turning around, she said to Him in Hebrew, "Rabbouni!"[b] —which means "Teacher."

When Nothing Makes Sense

There are joyful moments of walking with Jesus, but there are also times when nothing makes sense and your world seems to be crumbling. At those times, you need to peer into the empty tomb. It is what gives you hope, for it symbolizes the life that is yours from your risen Lord.

"Woman, why are you crying?"
—John 20:13

---

[a]20:1 Lit *She saw the stone removed*   [b]20:16 *Rabbouni* is also used in Mk 10:51

WORD STUDY

Greek word: **pempo**
[PEHM poh]

Translation: **send**

Uses in John's Gospel: **32**
(Mt, 4; Mk, 1; Lk, 10)

Uses in John's writings: **37**

Uses in the NT: **79**

Key passage: **John 20:21**

The Greek verb *pempo* is an old and common term meaning *to send*, reaching all the way back to the writings of Homer (eighth century B.C.). In John's Gospel, however, *pempo* emphasizes that someone is being sent by another of higher rank to perform a special task. Those who questioned John the Baptist had been sent (1:22) by the Pharisees (see v. 24), but John explained that he had been sent by God (v. 33). The Father will send the Holy Spirit (14:26), and so will Jesus (15:26; 16:7). On two occasions Jesus stated that He sends His disciples (13:20; 20:21). The dominant function of *pempo* is found in Jesus' use of the term to explain that the Father had sent Him. This aspect of *pempo* occurs 23 times in John's Gospel and has two connotations: first, to remind us of Jesus' divine origin, that He came from the Father (5:23; 6:38-39; 7:33; 8:16; 16:5); second, to emphasize that the Father gave Him a special task that only He could accomplish, the task of redemption (4:34; 6:44; 7:16,28). In the latter case, *pempo* takes on the meaning *commission* or *appoint*.

[17] "Don't cling to Me," Jesus told her, "for I have not yet ascended to the Father. But go to My brothers and tell them that I am ascending to My Father and your Father—to My God and your God."

[18] Mary Magdalene went and announced to the disciples, "I have seen the Lord!" And she told them what[a] He had said to her.

THE DISCIPLES COMMISSIONED

[19] In the evening of that first day of the week, the disciples were ₁gathered together₁ with the doors locked because of their fear of the Jews. Then Jesus came, stood among them, and said to them, "Peace to you!"

[20] Having said this, He showed them His hands and His side. So the disciples rejoiced when they saw the Lord.

[21] Jesus said to them again, "Peace to you! As the Father has sent Me, I also send you." [22] After saying this, He breathed on them and said,[b] "Receive the Holy Spirit. [23] If you forgive the sins of any, they are forgiven them; if you retain ₁the sins of₁ any, they are retained."

THOMAS SEES AND BELIEVES

[24] But one of the Twelve, Thomas (called "Twin"), was not with them when Jesus came. [25] So the other disciples kept telling him, "We have seen the Lord!"

But he said to them, "If I don't see the mark of the nails in His hands, put my finger into the mark of the nails, and put my hand into His side, I will never believe!"

[26] After eight days His disciples were indoors again, and Thomas was with them. Even though the doors were locked, Jesus came and stood among them. He said, "Peace to you!"

[27] Then He said to Thomas, "Put your finger here and observe My hands. Reach out your hand and put it into My side. Don't be an unbeliever, but a believer."

[28] Thomas responded to Him, "My Lord and my God!"

[29] Jesus said, "Because you have seen Me, you have believed.[c] Those who believe without seeing are blessed."

---

[a]**20:18** Lit *these things*
[b]**20:22** Lit *He breathed and said to them*

[c]**20:29** Or *have you believed?* (as a question)

THE PURPOSE OF THIS GOSPEL

30 Jesus performed many other signs in the presence of His disciples that are not written in this book. 31 But these are written so that you may believe Jesus is the •Messiah, the Son of God,[a] and by believing you may have life in His name.

JESUS' THIRD APPEARANCE TO THE DISCIPLES

21 After this, Jesus revealed Himself again to His disciples by the Sea of Tiberias.[b] He revealed Himself in this way:

2 Simon Peter, Thomas (called "Twin"), Nathanael from Cana of Galilee, Zebedee's sons, and two others of His disciples were together.

3 "I'm going fishing," Simon Peter said to them.

"We're coming with you," they told him. They went out and got into the boat, but that night they caught nothing.

4 When daybreak came, Jesus stood on the shore. However, the disciples did not know it was Jesus.

5 "Men,"[c] Jesus called to them, "you don't have any fish, do you?"

"No," they answered.

6 "Cast the net on the right side of the boat," He told them, "and you'll find some." So they did,[d] and they were unable to haul it in because of the large number of fish. 7 Therefore the disciple, the one Jesus loved, said to Peter, "It is the Lord!"

When Simon Peter heard that it was the Lord, he tied his outer garment around him[e] (for he was stripped) and plunged into the sea. 8 But since they were not far from land (about 100 yards[f] away), the other disciples came in the boat, dragging the net full of fish. 9 When they got out on land, they saw a charcoal fire there, with fish lying on it, and bread.

10 "Bring some of the fish you've just caught," Jesus told them. 11 So Simon Peter got up and hauled the net ashore, full of large fish—153 of them. Even though there were so many, the net was not torn.

God's Will Is Always Right, Though Not Always Reasonable

When you do what He tells you, no matter how senseless it may seem, God accomplishes what He purposed through you. Not only do you experience God's power and presence, but so do those who observe what you are doing.

"Men," Jesus called to them, "you don't have any fish, do you?" "No," they answered. "Cast the net on the right side of the boat," He told them, "and you'll find some." So they did, and they were unable to haul it in because of the large number of fish.

—John 21:5-6

---

[a]20:31 Or *that the Messiah, the Son of God, is Jesus*
[b]21:1 The Sea of Galilee; *Sea of Tiberias* is used only in John; Jn 6:1,23
[c]21:5 Lit *Children*
[d]21:6 Lit *they cast*
[e]21:7 Lit *he girded his garment*
[f]21:8 Lit *about 200 cubits*

WORD STUDY

Greek word: **phileo**
[fihl EH oh]

Translation: **love**

Uses in John's Gospel: **13**
(Mt, 5; Mk, 1; Lk, 2)

Uses in John's writings: **15**

Uses in the NT: **25**

Key passage: **John 21:15-17**

Although *agapao* (verb) and *agape* (noun) are normally considered the Greek words for divine love, the verb *phileo* can be used in the same way. The *phileo* word family has over 30 terms in the NT, including *philos (friend)*, *philadelphia (brotherly love)*, and *philema (kiss)*. The verb *phileo* can refer to the wrong kind of love (Mt 6:5; 10:37; 23:6 Lk 20:46; Jn 12:25; 15:19; Rv 22:15), as can *agapao* (Lk 11:43; Jn 3:19; 12:43; 2 Tm 4:10; 2 Pt 2:15; 1 Jn 2:15). But *phileo* is also used to describe the Father's love for the Son (Jn 5:20), the Father's love for believers (Jn 16:27), Jesus' love for believers (Jn 11:3; 20:2; Rv 3:19), and believers' love for the Lord (1 Co 16:22) and for each other (Ti 3:15). Both *agapao* (Jn 13:23; 19:26; 21:7,20) and *phileo* (Jn 20:2) are used to describe "the disciple Jesus loved," and the meaning is the same. Thus, it is better not to make a sharp distinction in John 21:15-17 between *agapao* (Jesus' term in vv. 15,16) and *phileo* (Jesus' term in v. 17 and all three times by Peter). This is especially true since three other pairs of synonyms occur in this passage with no significant difference in meaning. In this context, both *agapao* and *phileo* refer to love in its purest form. Thus Peter's threefold confession of his love for Jesus, which corresponds to his earlier threefold denial of Him, should not be understood as a secondary form of love.

[12] "Come and have breakfast," Jesus told them. None of the disciples dared ask Him, "Who are You?" because they knew it was the Lord. [13] Jesus came, took the bread, and gave it to them. He did the same with the fish.

[14] This was now the third time[a] Jesus appeared[b] to the disciples after He was raised from the dead.

JESUS' THREEFOLD RESTORATION OF PETER

[15] When they had eaten breakfast, Jesus asked Simon Peter, "Simon, son of John,[c] do you love[d] Me more than these?"

"Yes, Lord," he said to Him, "You know that I love You."

"Feed My lambs," He told him.

[16] A second time He asked him, "Simon, son of John, do you love Me?"

"Yes, Lord," he said to Him, "You know that I love You."

"Shepherd My sheep," He told him.

[17] He asked him the third time, "Simon, son of John, do you love Me?"

Peter was grieved that He asked him the third time, "Do you love Me?" He said, "Lord, You know everything! You know that I love You."

"Feed My sheep," Jesus said. [18] "•I assure you: When you were young, you would tie your belt and walk wherever you wanted. But when you grow old, you will stretch out your hands and someone else will tie you and carry you where you don't want to go." [19] He said this to signify by what kind of death he would glorify God.[e] After saying this, He told him, "Follow Me!"

---

[a] 21:14 The other two are in Jn 20:19-29.

[b] 21:14 Lit *was revealed* (see v. 1)

[c] 21:15-17 Other mss read *Simon, son of Jonah*; Jn 1:42; Mt 16:17

[d] 21:15-17 Two synonyms are translated *love* in this conversation: *agapao*, the first 2 times by Jesus (vv. 15-16); and *phileo*, the last time by Jesus (v. 17) and all 3 times by Peter (vv. 15-17). Peter's threefold confession of love for Jesus corresponds to his earlier threefold denial of Jesus; Jn 18:15-18,25-27.

[e] 21:19 Jesus predicts that Peter would be martyred. Church tradition says that Peter was crucified upside down.

CORRECTING A FALSE REPORT

²⁰ So Peter turned around and saw the disciple Jesus loved following them. ₍That disciple₎ was the one who had leaned back against Jesus at the supper and asked, "Lord, who is the one that's going to betray You?" ²¹ When Peter saw him, he said to Jesus, "Lord—what about him?"

²² "If I want him to remain until I come," Jesus answered, "what is that to you? As for you, follow Me."

²³ So this report[a] spread to the brothers[b] that this disciple would not die. Yet Jesus did not tell him that he would not die, but, "If I want him to remain until I come, what is that to you?"

EPILOGUE

²⁴ This is the disciple who testifies to these things and who wrote them down. We know that his testimony is true.

²⁵ And there are also many other things that Jesus did, which, if they were written one by one, I suppose not even the world itself could contain the books[c] that would be written.

Your Part in God's Will Is Simply to Follow It

The servant does not tell the Master what kind of assignments he needs. The servant waits on his Master for the assignment.

When Peter saw him, he said to Jesus, "Lord—what about him?" "If I want him to remain until I come," Jesus answered, "what is that to you? As for you, follow Me."

—John 21:21-22

---

[a]21:23 Lit *this word*
[b]21:23 The word *brothers* refers to the whole Christian community.

[c]21:25 Lit *scroll*

ACTS

OF THE APOSTLES

PROLOGUE

1 I wrote the first narrative, Theophilus, about all that Jesus began to do and teach ² until the day He was taken up, after He had given orders through the Holy Spirit to the apostles whom He had chosen. ³ After He had suffered, He also presented Himself alive to them by many convincing proofs, appearing to them during 40 days and speaking about the kingdom of God.

THE HOLY SPIRIT PROMISED

⁴ While He was together with them,ᵃ He commanded them not to leave Jerusalem, but to wait for the Father's promise. "This," ⌊He said, "is what⌋ you heard from Me; ⁵ for John baptized with water, but you will be baptized with the Holy Spirit not many days from now."

⁶ So when they had come together, they asked Him, "Lord, at this time are You restoring the kingdom to Israel?"

⁷ He said to them, "It is not for you to know times or periods that the Father has set by His own authority. ⁸ But you will receive power when the Holy Spirit has come upon you, and you will be My witnesses in Jerusalem, in all Judea and Samaria, and to the endsᵇ of the earth."

THE ASCENSION

⁹ After He had said this, He was taken up as they were watching, and a cloud received Him out of their sight. ¹⁰ While He was going, they were gazing into heaven, and suddenly two men in white clothes stood by them.

ᵃ1:4 Or *He was eating with them,* or *He was lodging with them*   ᵇ1:8 Lit *the end*

¹¹ They said, "Men of Galilee, why do you stand looking up into heaven? This Jesus, who has been taken from you into heaven, will come in the same way that you have seen Him going into heaven."

UNITED IN PRAYER

¹² Then they returned to Jerusalem from the mount called Olive Grove, which is near Jerusalem—a Sabbath day's journey away. ¹³ When they arrived, they went to the room upstairs where they were staying:

> Peter, John,
> James, Andrew,
> Philip, Thomas,
> Bartholomew, Matthew,
> James the son of Alphaeus,
> Simon the Zealot, and Judas the son of James.

¹⁴ All these were continually united in prayer,ᵃ along with the women, including Maryᵇ the mother of Jesus, and His brothers.

MATTHIAS CHOSEN

¹⁵ During these days Peter stood up among the brothersᶜ —the number of people who were together was about 120—and said: ¹⁶ "Brothers, the Scripture had to be fulfilled that the Holy Spirit through the mouth of David spoke in advance about Judas, who became a guide to those who arrested Jesus. ¹⁷ For he was one of our number and was allotted a share in this ministry." ¹⁸ Now this man acquired a field with his unrighteous wages; and falling headfirst, he burst open in the middle, and all his insides spilled out. ¹⁹ This became known to all the residents of Jerusalem, so that in their own language that field is called *Hakeldama*, that is, Field of Blood. ²⁰ "For it is written in the Book of Psalms:

> **Let his dwelling become desolate;**
> **let no one live in it;ᵈ and**
> **Let someone else take his position.ᵉ**

WORD STUDY

Greek word: ***proskartereo***
[prahss kahr teh REH oh]

Translation: ***continue***

Uses in Acts: **6**

Uses in the NT: **10**

Key passage: **Acts 1:14**

The Greek verb *proskartereo* means *to devote oneself to* or *to persevere*. It is a compound word from the preposition *pros*, meaning *to* or *toward*, and the verb *kartereo*, meaning *to endure* or *to be strong*, though it can also be used in the stronger sense of *to persevere* (as in Heb 11:27, its only occurrence in the NT). Paul used *proskartereo* to describe government servants who devote themselves to the public good (Rm 13:6). Most of the occurrences of *proskartereo* in the NT are used in the religious sense to indicate devotion to prayer (Ac 1:14; 2:42,46; 6:4; Rm 12:12; Col 4:2), though in Acts 2:42 devotion to the apostles' teaching, fellowship, and breaking bread is included.

ᵃ1:14 Other mss add *and petition*
ᵇ1:14 Or *prayer, with their wives and Mary*
ᶜ1:15 Other mss read *disciples*
ᵈ1:20 Ps 69:25
ᵉ1:20 Ps 109:8

WORD STUDY

Greek word: **pentecoste**
[pehn tay kahss TAY]

Translation: **Pentecost**

Uses in Acts: **2**

Uses in the NT: **3**

Key passage: **Acts 2:1**

The Greek word *pentecoste* means *fiftieth* [*day*] because this festival occurred fifty days after the Sabbath in the week of Unleavened Bread (see Lv 23:15-16). The word does not occur in the Greek OT. Instead, we find references to the Festival of Harvest, the Festival of Weeks (Ex 24:32), and the day of firstfruits (Nm 28:26; not the Festival of Firstfruits), which is then called "the day of Pentecost" in Acts 2:1 (also in 20:16; see 1 Co 16:8). The Festival of Harvest is first mentioned in Exodus 23:16 as one of the festivals requiring all Israelite males to appear before the Lord (vv. 14-17). Leviticus 23:15-22 refers to it as one of the seven great festivals of the Lord that the Israelites must observe every year. This festival marked the end of the grain harvest (Lv 23:15-16), and was the only festival during which the Israelites could eat bread containing leaven or yeast (v. 17). Unlike the other six festivals, however, this one received little attention in the rest of the OT (see Nm 28:26-31; Dt 16:9-12). It was not connected to the exodus event as was Passover, Unleavened Bread, and the Festival of Booths. Its significance was related only to the yearly time of harvest, although animal sacrifices were included (Nm 28:27-30). It was not until the Holy Spirit came, as recorded in Acts 2, that the full significance of this festival was realized. Just as the Festival of Firstfruits anticipated Jesus' resurrection, the Festival of Harvest anticipated the coming of the Spirit.

21 "Therefore, from among the men who have accompanied us during the whole time the Lord Jesus went in and out among us— 22 beginning from the baptism of John until the day He was taken up from us—from among these, it is necessary that one become a witness with us of His resurrection."

23 So they proposed two: Joseph, called Barsabbas, who was also known as Justus, and Matthias. 24 Then they prayed, "You, Lord, know the hearts of all; show which of these two You have chosen 25 to take the place[a] in this apostolic service that Judas left to go to his own place." 26 Then they cast lots for them, and the lot fell to Matthias. So he was numbered with the 11 apostles.

PENTECOST

2 When the day of Pentecost had arrived, they were all together in one place. 2 Suddenly a sound like that of a violent rushing wind came from heaven, and it filled the whole house where they were staying. 3 And tongues, like flames of fire that were divided, appeared to them and rested on each one of them. 4 Then they were all filled with the Holy Spirit and began to speak in different languages, as the Spirit gave them ability for speech.

5 There were Jews living in Jerusalem, devout men from every nation under heaven. 6 When this sound occurred, the multitude came together and was confused because each one heard them speaking in his own language. 7 And they were astounded and amazed, saying,[b] "Look, aren't all these who are speaking Galileans? 8 How is it that we hear, each of us, in our own native language? 9 Parthians, Medes, Elamites; those who live in Mesopotamia, in Judea and Cappadocia, Pontus and Asia, 10 Phrygia and Pamphylia, Egypt and the parts of Libya near Cyrene; visitors from Rome, both Jews and •proselytes, 11 Cretans and Arabs—we hear them speaking in our own languages the magnificent acts of God." 12 And they were all astounded and perplexed, saying to one another, "What could this be?" 13 But some sneered and said, "They're full of new wine!"

---

[a]1:25 Other mss read *to share*   [b]2:7 Other mss add *to one another*

PETER'S SERMON

14 But Peter stood up with the Eleven, raised his voice, and proclaimed to them: "Jewish men and all you residents of Jerusalem, let this be known to you and pay attention to my words. 15 For these people are not drunk, as you suppose, since it's only nine in the morning[a] 16 On the contrary, this is what was spoken through the prophet Joel:

> 17 **And it will be** in the last days, says God,
> that **I will pour out My Spirit**
> **on all humanity;**
> **then your sons and your daughters**
> **will prophesy,**
> **your young men will see visions,**
> **and your old men will dream dreams.**
> 18 **I will even pour out My Spirit**
> **on My male and female slaves**
> **in those days,**
> and they will prophesy.
> 19 **I will display wonders in the heaven** above
> **and signs on the earth** below:
> **blood and fire and a cloud of smoke.**
> 20 **The sun will be turned to darkness,**
> **and the moon to blood,**
> **before the great and remarkable**
> **day of the Lord comes;**
> 21 **then whoever calls on the name of the Lord**
> **will be saved.**[b]

22 "Men of Israel, listen to these words: This Jesus the •Nazarene was a man pointed out to you by God with miracles, wonders, and signs that God did among you through Him, just as you yourselves know. 23 Though He was delivered up according to God's determined plan and foreknowledge, you used[c] lawless people[d] to nail Him to a cross and kill Him. 24 God raised Him up, ending the pains of death, because it was not possible for Him to be held by it. 25 For David says of Him:

> **I saw the Lord ever before me;**
> **because He is at my right hand,**

Don't Be Surprised to See God at Work

Unbelievers see God's activity and don't know what they see. But we should already be watching so we will know it is God at work and will be ready to respond.

"I will display wonders in the heaven above and signs on the earth below."

—Acts 2:19a

---

[a]2:15 Lit *it's the third hour of the day*
[b]2:17-21 Jl 2:28-32
[c]2:23 Other mss read *you have taken*
[d]2:23 Or *used the hand of lawless ones*

I will not be shaken.
26 **Therefore my heart was glad,**
and my tongue rejoiced.
Moreover my flesh will rest in hope,
27 **because You will not leave my soul**
in •Hades,
or allow Your Holy One to see decay.
28 **You have revealed the paths of life to me;**
You will fill me with gladness
in Your presence.[a]

29 "Brothers, I can confidently speak to you about the patriarch David: he is both dead and buried, and his tomb is with us to this day. 30 Since he was a prophet, he knew that God had sworn an oath to him to seat one of his descendants[b] [c] on his throne. 31 Seeing this in advance, he spoke concerning the resurrection of the •Messiah:

He[d] was not left in Hades,
and His flesh **did not experience decay.**[e]

32 "God has resurrected this Jesus. We are all witnesses of this. 33 Therefore, since He has been exalted to the right hand of God and has received from the Father the promised Holy Spirit, He has poured out what you both see and hear. 34 For it was not David who ascended into the heavens, but he himself says:

The Lord said to my Lord,
'Sit at My right hand
35 **until I make Your enemies Your footstool.'**[f]

36 "Therefore let all the house of Israel know with certainty that God has made this Jesus, whom you crucified, both Lord and Messiah!"

FORGIVENESS THROUGH THE MESSIAH

37 When they heard this, they were pierced to the heart and said to Peter and the rest of the apostles: "Brothers, what must we do?"

A Joy-Filled Life Is Your Birthright

There can be in every Christian a deep, settled fullness of the joy of Christ that no circumstance of life can shake.

"You have revealed the paths of life to me; You will fill me with gladness in Your presence."

—Acts 2:28

People Don't Have to Be Coerced to Christ

If you're experiencing Christ as He wants you to, others won't be able to resist seeking Him too.

When they heard this, they were pierced to the heart and said to Peter and the rest of the apostles: "Brothers, what must we do?"

—Acts 2:37

---

[a]2:25-28 Ps 16:8-11
[b]2:30 Other mss add *according to the flesh to raise up the Messiah*
[c]2:30 Lit *one from the fruit of his loin*
[d]2:31 Other mss read *His soul*
[e]2:31 Ps 16:10
[f]2:34-35 Ps 110:1

[38] "Repent," Peter said to them, "and be baptized, each of you, in the name of Jesus the Messiah for the forgiveness of your sins, and you will receive the gift of the Holy Spirit. [39] For the promise is for you and for your children, and for all who are far off,[a] as many as the Lord our God will call." [40] And with many other words he testified and strongly urged them, saying, "Be saved from this corrupt[b] generation!"

A GENEROUS AND GROWING CHURCH

[41] So those who accepted his message were baptized, and that day about 3,000 people were added to them. [42] And they devoted themselves to the apostles' teaching, to fellowship, to the breaking of bread, and to prayers.

[43] Then fear came over everyone, and many wonders and signs were being performed through the apostles. [44] Now all the believers were together and had everything in common. [45] So they sold their possessions and property and distributed the proceeds to all, as anyone had a need.[c] [46] And every day they devoted themselves ⌊to meeting⌋ together in the •temple complex, and broke bread from house to house. They ate their food with gladness and simplicity of heart, [47] praising God and having favor with all the people. And every day the Lord added to them[d] those who were being saved.

HEALING OF A LAME MAN

3 Now Peter and John were going up together to the •temple complex at the hour of prayer at three in the afternoon.[e] [2] And a man who was lame from his mother's womb was carried there and placed every day at the temple gate called Beautiful, so he could beg from those entering the temple complex. [3] When he saw Peter and John about to enter the temple complex, he asked for help. [4] Peter, along with John, looked at him intently and said, "Look at us." [5] So he turned to them,[f] expecting to get something from them. [6] But Peter said, "I have neither silver nor gold, but what

Are You Living in a Healthy Body?

God didn't design the Christian life to be a solitary venture. We are designed for each other, and we work best when we are working together.

They devoted themselves to the apostles' teaching, to fellowship, to the breaking of bread, and to prayers.

—Acts 2:42

Do People Expect Much from You?

The more you allow Christ to make His presence known in your life, the more people will draw near you and find Him.

He turned to them, expecting to get something from them.

—Acts 3:5

---

[a]2:39 Remote in time or space
[b]2:40 Or *crooked,* or *twisted*
[c]2:45 Or *to all, according to one's needs*
[d]2:47 Other mss read *to the church*
[e]3:1 Lit *at the ninth hour*
[f]3:5 Or *he paid attention to them*

WORD STUDY

Greek word: **onoma**
[AH nah mah]
Translation: **name**
Uses in Acts: **60**
Uses in Luke's writings: **94**
Uses in the NT: **231**
Key passage: **Acts 3:6,16**

The Greek noun *onoma* means *name* and has several uses, such as the following: (1) Like *name* in English, the word *onoma* is used for proper names of persons and places, which is the most common use of the term. (2) In Revelation 3:1 *onoma* is best rendered "reputation," as in the English expression *he has made a name for himself* (see also Gn 6:4; 11:4). (3) It also occurs in the sense of *title*, as in Matthew 10:41 (the literal *in the name of a prophet* means "because he is a prophet" or "because he has the title *prophet*"). In Hebrews 1:4 *onoma* refers to "Son" as the name or title that is more excellent than the angels' (see vv. 2,5,8), and in Philippians 2:9 the "name that is above every name" is the title "Lord" (*kurios*), as explained in verse 11. (4) Finally, the NT often demands that believers act for, or in the name of, Jesus Christ. The phrase "in Jesus' name" is not a mystical formula that one simply attaches to the end of a prayer. Rather, this formula is an expression of faith that identifies the Person whom believers serve (Mt 18:20; Ac 2:38) and the basis of authority and power upon which they act (Mt 19:20; Ac 4:7). Peter healed the lame man at the temple complex "in the name of Jesus Christ" (3:6), which he explained later as a miracle that occurred through "faith in His name" (v. 16). Thus, the apostle acted on behalf of Jesus and called on all the authority that His name represents to heal this man.

I have, I give to you: In the name of Jesus Christ the •Nazarene, get up and walk!" 7 Then, taking him by the right hand he raised him up, and at once his feet and ankles became strong. 8 So he jumped up, stood, and started to walk, and he entered the temple complex with them—walking, leaping, and praising God. 9 All the people saw him walking and praising God, 10 and they recognized that he was the one who used to sit and beg at the Beautiful Gate of the temple complex. So they were filled with awe and astonishment at what had happened to him.

PREACHING IN SOLOMON'S COLONNADE

11 While he[a] was holding on to Peter and John, all the people, greatly amazed, ran toward them in what is called Solomon's Colonnade. 12 When Peter saw this, he addressed the people: "Men of Israel, why are you amazed at this? Or why do you stare at us, as though by our own power or godliness we had made him walk? 13 The God of Abraham, Isaac, and Jacob, the God of our fathers, has glorified His Servant Jesus, whom you handed over and denied in the presence of •Pilate, when he had decided to release Him. 14 But you denied the Holy and Righteous One, and asked to have a murderer given to you. 15 And you killed the source[b] of life, whom God raised from the dead; we are witnesses of this. 16 By faith in His name, His name has made this man strong, whom you see and know. So the faith that comes through Him has given him this perfect health in front of all of you.

17 "And now, brothers, I know that you did it in ignorance, just as your leaders also did. 18 But what God predicted through the mouth of all the prophets—that His •Messiah would suffer—He has fulfilled in this way. 19 Therefore repent and turn back, that your sins may be wiped out so that seasons of refreshing may come from the presence of the Lord, 20 and He may send Jesus, who has been appointed Messiah for you. 21 Heaven must welcome[c] Him until the times of the restoration of all

---

[a]3:11 Other mss read *the lame man who was healed*
[b]3:15 Or *the Prince*, or *the Ruler*
[c]3:21 Or *receive*, or *retain*

things, which God spoke about by the mouth of His holy prophets from the beginning. 22 Moses said:[a]

The Lord your God will raise up for you a Prophet like me from among your brothers. You must listen to Him in everything He will say to you. 23 **And it will be that everyone who will not listen to that Prophet will be completely cut off from the people.**[b]

24 "In addition, all the prophets who have spoken, from Samuel and those after him, have also announced these days. 25 You are the sons of the prophets and of the covenant that God made with your forefathers, saying to Abraham, **And in your seed all the families of the earth will be blessed.**[c] 26 God raised up His Servant[d] and sent Him first to you to bless you by turning each of you from your evil ways."

PETER AND JOHN ARRESTED

4 Now as they were speaking to the people, the priests, the commander of the temple guard, and the •Sadducees confronted them, 2 because they were provoked that they were teaching the people and proclaiming in the person of Jesus[e] the resurrection from the dead. 3 So they seized them and put them in custody until the next day, since it was already evening. 4 But many of those who heard the message believed, and the number of the men came to about 5,000.

PETER AND JOHN FACE THE JEWISH LEADERSHIP

5 The next day, their rulers, elders, and •scribes assembled in Jerusalem 6 with Annas the high priest, Caiaphas, John and Alexander, and all the members of the high-priestly family.[f] 7 After they had Peter and John stand[g] before them, they asked the question: "By what power or in what name have you done this?"

8 Then Peter was filled with the Holy Spirit and said to them, "Rulers of the people and elders:[h] 9 If we are

This Is Not About You, It's About Jesus

If you have to prove that God has changed you, perhaps He hasn't. Those around you will notice when your life has been transformed by your relationship with Jesus.

When Peter saw this, he addressed the people: "Men of Israel, why are you amazed at this? Or why do you stare at us, as though by our own power or godliness we had made him walk?"

—Acts 3:12

Tell Us What God Has Done for You Lately

Your responsibility is not to convince others of the reality of God, but simply to bear witness to what your Lord has said and done for you.

Now as they were speaking to the people, the priests, the commander of the temple guard, and the Sadducees confronted them, because they were provoked that they were teaching the people and proclaiming in the person of Jesus the resurrection from the dead.

—Acts 4:1-2

---

[a]3:22 Other mss add *to the fathers*
[b]3:22-23 Dt 18:15-19
[c]3:25 Gn 12:3; 18:18; 22:18; 26:4
[d]3:26 Other mss add *Jesus*
[e]4:2 Lit *proclaiming in Jesus*
[f]4:6 Or *high-priestly class*, or *high-priestly clan*
[g]4:7 Lit *had placed them*
[h]4:8 Other mss add *of Israel*

WORD STUDY

Greek word: **parresia**
[pahr ray SEE ah]
Translation: **boldness**
Uses in Acts: **5**
Uses in the NT: **31**
Key passage: **Acts 4:13,29,31**

The Greek noun *parresia* literally means *every word* and thus signifies the freedom to speak openly. Since such freedom of speech often provokes opposition, *parresia* also indicated fearlessness in speaking one's mind. Finally, *parresia* developed into a term meaning *boldness, openness,* or *confidence* (as an adverb, *openly* or *plainly*). The word was normally used in a positive sense, but a negative usage such as *bluntness* or *shamelessness* also occurs in ancient Greek literature.

All ten occurrences of *parresia* in the Gospels refer to speaking openly or plainly, either by Jesus or about Jesus (Mk 8:32; Jn 7:4,13,26; 10:24; 11:14,54; 16:25, 29; 18:20). The uses of the term in Acts refer to three instances of boldness on the part of the apostles in proclaiming the gospel (2:29; 4:13,29,31; 28:31), something Paul referred to in his letters (2 Co 3:12; Eph 6:19; Php 1:20). In 2 Corinthians 7:4 *parresia* refers to Paul's confidence in the believers there, and in Philemon 8 it describes his authority in Christ as an apostle. In several passages *parresia* is used to describe various aspects of salvation. We have boldness and access to the Father through Christ (Eph 3:12; Heb 4:16; 10:19); and because of Christ we can have confidence for godly living (1 Tm 3:13; Heb 3:6; 10:35; 1 Jn 3:21), confidence in prayer (1 Jn 5:14), and confidence of His coming (1 Jn 2:28; 4:17).

being examined today about a good deed done to a disabled man—by what means he was healed— [10] let it be known to all of you and to all the people of Israel, that by the name of Jesus Christ the •Nazarene—whom you crucified and whom God raised from the dead—by Him this man is standing here before you healthy. [11] This ⌊Jesus⌋ is

**The stone despised by you builders,
who has become the cornerstone.**[a]

[12] There is salvation in no one else, for there is no other name under heaven given to people by which we must be saved."

THE NAME FORBIDDEN

[13] When they observed the boldness of Peter and John and realized that they were uneducated and untrained men, they were amazed and knew that they had been with Jesus. [14] And since they saw the man who had been healed standing with them, they had nothing to say in response. [15] After they had ordered them to leave the •Sanhedrin, they conferred among themselves, [16] saying, "What should we do with these men? For an obvious sign, evident to all who live in Jerusalem, has been done through them, and we cannot deny it! [17] But so this does not spread any further among the people, let's threaten them against speaking to anyone in this name again." [18] So they called for them and ordered them not to preach or teach at all in the name of Jesus.

[19] But Peter and John answered them, "Whether it's right in the sight of God ⌊for us⌋ to listen to you rather than to God, you decide; [20] for we are unable to stop speaking about what we have seen and heard."

[21] After threatening them further, they released them. They found no way to punish them, because the people were all giving glory to God over what had been done; [22] for the man was over 40 years old on whom this sign of healing had been performed.

PRAYER FOR BOLDNESS

[23] After they were released, they went to their own fellowship[b] and reported all that the •chief priests and

---

[a]4:11 Ps 118:22   [b]4:23 Or *friends*, or *companions*

the elders had said to them. 24 When they heard this, they raised their voices to God unanimously and said, "Master, You are the One who made the heaven, the earth, and the sea, and everything in them. 25 You said through the Holy Spirit, by the mouth of our father David Your servant:[a]

> Why did the Gentiles rage,
>   and the peoples plot futile things?
> 26 The kings of the earth took their stand,
>   and the rulers assembled together
>   against the Lord and
>   against His •Messiah.[b]

27 "For, in fact, in this city both •Herod and Pontius •Pilate, with the Gentiles and the peoples of Israel, assembled together against Your holy Servant Jesus, whom You anointed, 28 to do whatever Your hand and Your plan had predestined to take place. 29 And now, Lord, consider their threats, and grant that Your slaves may speak Your message with complete boldness, 30 while You stretch out Your hand for healing, signs, and wonders to be performed through the name of Your holy Servant Jesus." 31 When they had prayed, the place where they were assembled was shaken, and they were all filled with the Holy Spirit and began to speak God's message with boldness.

BELIEVERS SHARING

32 Now the multitude of those who believed were of one heart and soul, and no one said that any of his possessions was his own, but instead they held everything in common. 33 And with great power the apostles were giving testimony to the resurrection of the Lord Jesus, and great grace was on all of them. 34 For there was not a needy person among them, because all those who owned lands or houses sold them, brought the proceeds of the things that were sold, 35 and laid them at the apostles' feet. This was then distributed to each person as anyone had a need.

36 Joseph, a Levite and a Cypriot by birth, whom the apostles named Barnabas, which is translated Son of

Are You Praying for Big Things?

We are usually far more likely to underestimate what God wants to do through us than to overestimate it.

When they had prayed, the place where they were assembled was shaken, and they were all filled with the Holy Spirit and began to speak God's message with boldness.

—Acts 4:31

---

[a]4:25 Other mss read *through the mouth of David Your servant*   [b]4:25-26 Ps 2:1-2

WORD STUDY

Greek word: **ekklesia**
[ehk lay SEE ah]

Translation: **church**

Uses in Acts: **23**

Uses in the NT: **114**

Key passage: **Acts 5:11**

The Greek noun *ekklesia* is a compound from the preposition *ek*, meaning *out of*, and the verb *kaleo*, meaning *to call*; thus, *ekklesia* literally means called out ones. Despite the origin of the term ekklesia, its emphasis is not on a people called out but on a people gathered together, that is, an assembly or congregation. In secular Greek, *ekklesia* was commonly used for the assembled citizens of a city (see Ac 19:32,39-40).

In the NT, *ekklesia* is found in the Gospels only three times, all in Matthew (16:18; 18:17). It occurs in Acts more than any other book, and sixty-two times in Paul's letters. Jesus stated that He would build the *ekklesia* (Mt 16:18) and that the *ekklesia* must exercise discipline on members who sin (Mt 18:15-17). In the former passage Jesus used *ekklesia* in a corporate sense (all believers), and in the latter passage in the local sense (believers in a specific assembly). These are the two main ways *ekklesia* is used in the NT, though the local sense is the more common. In Acts, the growth of the corporate church (see 2:47; 5:11; 8:3; 9:31) is described as numerous local churches (11:22,26; 13:1; 14:23,27; 15:41) are begun and prosper despite external and internal challenges. Paul referred to local assemblies many times since ten of his letters were written to them. Paul also used *ekklesia* in the corporate sense as the body of Christ, who is its head (Eph 1:22; 5:23-32; Col 1:18,24).

Encouragement, 37 sold a field he owned, brought the money, and laid it at the apostles' feet.

LYING TO THE HOLY SPIRIT

5 But a man named Ananias, with Sapphira his wife, sold a piece of property. 2 However, he kept back part of the proceeds with his wife's knowledge, and brought a portion of it and laid it at the apostles' feet. 3 Then Peter said, "Ananias, why has Satan filled your heart to lie to the Holy Spirit and keep back part of the proceeds from the field? 4 Wasn't it yours while you possessed it? And after it was sold, wasn't it at your disposal? Why is it that you planned this thing in your heart? You have not lied to men but to God!" 5 When he heard these words, Ananias dropped dead, and a great fear came on all who heard. 6 The young men got up, wrapped ⌊his body⌋, carried him out, and buried him.

7 There was an interval of about three hours; then his wife came in, not knowing what had happened. 8 "Tell me," Peter asked her, "did you sell the field for this price?"

"Yes," she said, "for that price."

9 Then Peter said to her, "Why did you agree to test the Spirit of the Lord? Look! The feet of those who have buried your husband are at the door, and they will carry you out!"

10 Instantly she dropped dead at his feet. When the young men came in, they found her dead, carried her out, and buried her beside her husband. 11 Then great fear came on the whole church and on all who heard these things.

APOSTOLIC SIGNS AND WONDERS

12 Many signs and wonders were being done among the people through the hands of the apostles. By common consent they would all meet in Solomon's Colonnade. 13 None of the rest dared to join them, but the people praised them highly. 14 Believers were added to the Lord in increasing numbers—crowds of both men and women. 15 As a result, they would carry the sick out into the streets and lay them on beds and pallets so that when Peter came by, at least his shadow might fall on some of them. 16 In addition, a multitude came to-

gether from the towns surrounding Jerusalem, bringing sick people and those who were tormented by unclean spirits, and they were all healed.

IN AND OUT OF PRISON

¹⁷ Then the high priest took action. He and all his colleagues, those who belonged to the party of the •Sadducees, were filled with jealousy. ¹⁸ So they arrested[a] the apostles and put them in the city jail. ¹⁹ But an angel of the Lord opened the doors of the jail during the night, brought them out, and said, ²⁰ "Go and stand in the •temple complex, and tell the people all about this life." ²¹ In obedience to this, they entered the temple complex at daybreak and began to teach.

THE APOSTLES ON TRIAL AGAIN

When the high priest and those who were with him arrived, they convened the •Sanhedrin—the full Senate of the sons of Israel—and sent ⌊orders⌋ to the jail to have them brought. ²² But when the temple police got there, they did not find them in the jail, so they returned and reported, ²³ "We found the jail securely locked, with the guards standing in front of the doors; but when we opened them, we found no one inside!" ²⁴ As[b] the captain of the temple police and the •chief priests heard these things, they were baffled about them, as to what could come of this.

²⁵ Someone came and reported to them, "Look! The men you put in jail are standing in the temple complex and teaching the people." ²⁶ Then the captain went with the temple police and brought them in without force, because they were afraid the people might stone them. ²⁷ When they had brought them in, they had them stand before the Sanhedrin, and the high priest asked, ²⁸ "Didn't we strictly order you not to teach in this name? And look, you have filled Jerusalem with your teaching and are determined to bring this man's blood on us!"

²⁹ But Peter and the apostles replied, "We must obey God rather than men. ³⁰ The God of our fathers raised up Jesus, whom you had murdered by hanging Him

[a]5:18 Lit laid hands on   [b]5:24 Other mss add the high priest and

Christian Love Doesn't Look the Other Way

Don't ever try to ease the discomfort of someone whom the Holy Spirit is making uncomfortable. Be careful not to communicate that you find their lack of faith acceptable.

Peter said, "Ananias, why has Satan filled your heart to lie to the Holy Spirit and keep back part of the proceeds from the field?"
—Acts 5:3

We're Talking About the God of All Power

Christianity is not moral platitudes, lofty intentions, and noble thoughts. The fundamental characteristic of God's kingdom is *power*.

An angel of the Lord opened the doors of the jail during the night, brought them out, and said, "Go and stand in the temple complex, and tell the people all about this life."
—Acts 5:19-20

on a tree. ³¹ God exalted this man to His right hand as ruler and Savior, to grant repentance to Israel, and forgiveness of sins. ³² We are witnesses of these things, and so is the Holy Spirit whom God has given to those who obey Him."

GAMALIEL'S ADVICE

³³ When they heard this, they were enraged and wanted to kill them. ³⁴ A •Pharisee named Gamaliel, a teacher of the law who was respected by all the people, stood up in the Sanhedrin and ordered the menᵃ to be taken outside for a little while. ³⁵ He said to them, "Men of Israel, be careful about what you're going to do to these men. ³⁶ Not long ago Theudas rose up, claiming to be somebody, and a group of about 400 men rallied to him. He was killed, and all his partisans were dispersed and came to nothing. ³⁷ After this man, Judas the Galilean rose up in the days of the census and attracted a following.ᵇ That man also perished, and all his partisans were scattered. ³⁸ And now, I tell you, stay away from these men and leave them alone. For if this plan or this work is of men, it will be overthrown; ³⁹ but if it is of God, you will not be able to overthrow them. You may even be found fighting against God." So they were persuaded by him. ⁴⁰ After they called in the apostles and had them flogged, they ordered them not to speak in the name of Jesus and released them. ⁴¹ Then they went out from the presence of the Sanhedrin, rejoicing that they were counted worthy to be dishonored on behalf of the name.ᶜ ⁴² Every day in the temple complex, and in various homes, they continued teaching and proclaiming the good news that the •Messiah is Jesus.ᵈ

SEVEN CHOSEN TO SERVE

6 In those days, as the number of the disciples was multiplying, there arose a complaint by the Hellenistic Jewsᵉ against the Hebraic Jewsᶠ that their widows

---

Check Your Words Against God's Word

Be very careful that the words you share are indeed from the Lord and not from your own thinking. God promises to stand by every word He has spoken.

"We are witnesses of these things, and so is the Holy Spirit whom God has given to those who obey Him."
—Acts 5:32

See the Blessing in Suffering for Christ

Live with the expectancy that Christ will fill you with His power and will stretch you to do things in His service that you have never done before.

They went out from the presence of the Sanhedrin, rejoicing that they were counted worthy to be dishonored on behalf of the name.
—Acts 5:41

ᵃ5:34 Other mss read *apostles*
ᵇ5:37 Lit *and drew people after him*
ᶜ5:41 Other mss add *of Jesus*, or *of Christ*
ᵈ5:42 Or *that Jesus is the Messiah*
ᵉ6:1 Jews of Gk language and culture
ᶠ6:1 Jews of Aram or Hb language and culture

were being overlooked in the daily distribution. ² Then the Twelve summoned the whole company of the disciples and said, "It would not be right for us to give up preaching about God to wait on tables. ³ Therefore, brothers, select from among you seven men of good reputation, full of the Spirit and wisdom, whom we can appoint to this duty. ⁴ But we will devote ourselves to prayer and to the preaching ministry." ⁵ The proposal pleased the whole company. So they chose Stephen, a man full of faith and the Holy Spirit, and Philip, Prochorus, Nicanor, Timon, Parmenas, and Nicolaus, a •proselyte from Antioch. ⁶ They had them stand before the apostles, who prayed and laid their hands on them.ᵃ

⁷ So the preaching about God flourished, the number of the disciples in Jerusalem multiplied greatly, and a large group of priests became obedient to the faith.

STEPHEN ACCUSED OF BLASPHEMY

⁸ Stephen, full of grace and power, was performing great wonders and signs among the people. ⁹ Then some from what is called the Freedmen's •Synagogue, composed of both Cyrenians and Alexandrians, and some from Cilicia and Asia, came forward and disputed with Stephen. ¹⁰ But they were unable to stand up against the wisdom and the Spirit by whom he spoke. ¹¹ Then they induced men to say, "We heard him speaking blasphemous words against Moses and God!" ¹² They stirred up the people, the elders, and the •scribes; so they came up, dragged him off, and took him to the •Sanhedrin. ¹³ They also presented false witnesses who said, "This man does not stop speaking blasphemous words against this holy place and the law. ¹⁴ For we heard him say that Jesus, this •Nazarene, will destroy this place and change the customs that Moses handed down to us." ¹⁵ And all who were sitting in the Sanhedrin looked intently at him and saw that his face was like the face of an angel.

ᵃ6:6 The laying on of hands signified the prayer of blessing for the beginning of a new ministry.

WORD STUDY

Greek word: **sunedrion**
[soon EH dree ahn]

Translation: **Sanhedrin**

Uses in Acts: **14**

Uses in Luke's writings: **15**

Uses in the NT: **22**

Key passage: **Acts 6:12,15**

The Greek word *sunedrion* means *a sitting together, an assembly*. In the NT the word occurs only in the Gospels (eight times) and Acts, and it can also be translated "council" (Mt 5:22; Ac 5:27). Though local courts were called "sanhedrins" on occasion (Mk 10:17; 13:9), the term normally refers to the national court in Jerusalem.

The Sanhedrin included the high priest as president and seventy men who governed Jewish political and religious life from 225 B.C. to A.D. 70. Mark 8:31; 14:43,53 refer to three groups in the Sanhedrin: "elders," older experienced judges from lower courts; "chief priests," Sadducees from the high priest's family and greatly influential; and "scribes," experts in the OT and oral traditions.

The exact proportion of Pharisees to Sadducees in the Sanhedrin at the time of Jesus and the early church is unknown since it fluctuated, but the Sadducees were usually in the majority. This was the case when Stephen faced the Sanhedrin in Acts 6–7 and when Paul did so in Acts 23, although in both cases the Sadducees faced a strong Pharisaic minority. The Sanhedrin was responsible for Stephen's execution on the charge of blasphemy (Ac 6:11-15; 7:54-60). Many years later, Paul was able to divide the Sanhedrin by referring to his belief in "the resurrection of the dead"— which the Pharisees affirmed but the Sadducees denied—and provoking a quarrel between the two (Ac 23:1-11; see Mt 22:23).

STEPHEN'S ADDRESS

7 "Is this true?"[a] the high priest asked. ² "Brothers and fathers," he said, "listen: The God of glory appeared to our father Abraham when he was in Mesopotamia, before he settled in Haran, ³ and said to him:

**Get out of your country and away from
    your relatives,
and come to the land that I will show you.[b]**

⁴ "Then he came out of the land of the Chaldeans and settled in Haran. And from there, after his father died, God had him move to this land in which you now live. ⁵ He didn't give him an inheritance in it, not even a foot of ground, but He promised to give it to him as a possession, and to his descendants after him, even though he was childless. ⁶ God spoke in this way:

**His descendants would be strangers
    in a foreign country,
and they would enslave and oppress them
    for 400 years.**
⁷ **I will judge the nation that they will serve
    as slaves,** God said.
**After this, they will come out
    and worship Me in this place.[c]**

⁸ Then He gave him the covenant of circumcision. This being so, he fathered Isaac and circumcised him on the eighth day; Isaac did the same with Jacob, and Jacob with the 12 patriarchs.

THE PATRIARCHS IN EGYPT

⁹ "The patriarchs became jealous of Joseph and sold him into Egypt, but God was with him ¹⁰ and rescued him out of all his troubles. He gave him favor and wisdom in the sight of Pharaoh, king of Egypt, who appointed him governor over Egypt and over his whole household. ¹¹ Then a famine came over all of Egypt and Canaan, with great suffering, and our forefathers could find no food. ¹² When Jacob heard there was grain in Egypt, he sent our forefathers the first time. ¹³ The

---

Remember That God Knows the Big Picture

Trust God to lead you through confusing circumstances. You will look back and realize that God was in control all the time, guiding you into His perfect will.

"The patriarchs became jealous of Joseph and sold him into Egypt, but God was with him and rescued him out of all his troubles."

—Acts 7:9-10a

---

[a]7:1 Lit *"Are these things so?"*
[b]7:3 Gn 12:1
[c]7:6-7 Gn 15:13-14

second time, Joseph was revealed to his brothers, and Joseph's family became known to Pharaoh. [14] Joseph then invited his father Jacob and all his relatives, 75 people in all, [15] and Jacob went down to Egypt. He and our forefathers died there, [16] were carried back to Shechem, and were placed in the tomb that Abraham had bought for a sum of silver from the sons of Hamor in Shechem.

MOSES, A REJECTED SAVIOR

[17] "As the time was drawing near to fulfill the promise that God had made to Abraham, the people flourished and multiplied in Egypt [18] until a different king ruled over Egypt[a] who did not know Joseph. [19] He dealt deceitfully with our race and oppressed our forefathers by making them leave their infants outside so they wouldn't survive.[b] [20] At this time Moses was born, and he was beautiful before God. He was nursed in his father's home three months, [21] and when he was left outside, Pharaoh's daughter adopted and raised him as her own son. [22] So Moses was educated in all the wisdom of the Egyptians, and was powerful in his speech and actions.

[23] "As he was approaching the age of 40, he decided[c] to visit his brothers, the sons of Israel. [24] When he saw one of them being mistreated, he came to his rescue and avenged the oppressed man by striking down the Egyptian. [25] He assumed his brothers would understand that God would give them deliverance through him, but they did not understand. [26] The next day he showed up while they were fighting and tried to reconcile them peacefully, saying, 'Men, you are brothers. Why are you mistreating each other?'

[27] "But the one who was mistreating his neighbor pushed him[d] away, saying:

Who appointed you a ruler and a judge over us? [28] Do you want to kill me, the same way you killed the Egyptian yesterday?[e]

[29] "At this disclosure, Moses fled and became an exile in the land of Midian, where he fathered two sons.

You Are Beautiful Before Your God

It's easy to let other people's view of us lower the way we perceive our worth as a person. But God's view is that we are highly valuable to Him, and that is all that matters.

"At this time Moses was born, and he was beautiful before God."

—Acts 7:20a

---

[a]7:18 Other mss omit *over Egypt*
[b]7:19 A common pagan practice of population control by leaving infants outside to die
[c]7:23 Lit *40, it came into his heart*
[d]7:27 Moses
[e]7:27-28 Ex 2:14

[30] After 40 years had passed, an angel[a] appeared to him in the desert of Mount Sinai, in the flame of a burning bush. [31] When Moses saw it, he was amazed at the sight. As he was approaching to look at it, the voice of the Lord came: [32] **I am the God of your forefathers—the God of Abraham, of Isaac, and of Jacob.**[b] So Moses began to tremble and did not dare to look.

[33] "Then the Lord said to him:

Take the sandals off your feet, because the place where you are standing is holy ground. [34] I have certainly seen the oppression of My people in Egypt; I have heard their groaning and have come down to rescue them. And now, come, I will send you to Egypt.[c]

[35] "This Moses, whom they rejected when they said, **Who appointed you a ruler and a judge?**[d] —this one God sent as a ruler and a redeemer by means of the angel who appeared to him in the bush. [36] This man led them out and performed wonders and signs in the land of Egypt, at the Red Sea, and in the desert for 40 years.

ISRAEL'S REBELLION AGAINST GOD

[37] "This is the Moses who said to the sons of Israel, **God**[e] **will raise up for you a Prophet like me from among your brothers.**[f] [38] He is the one who was in the congregation in the desert together with the angel who spoke to him on Mount Sinai, and with our forefathers. He received living oracles to give to us. [39] Our forefathers were unwilling to obey him, but pushed him away, and in their hearts turned back to Egypt. [40] They told Aaron:

Make us gods who will go before us. As for this Moses who brought us out of the land of Egypt, we don't know what's become of him.[g]

[41] They even made a calf in those days, offered sacrifice to the idol, and were celebrating what their hands had made. [42] Then God turned away and gave them up to

Your Life Is Part of God's Eternal Purpose

We tend to think only of the present. Moses' involvement in God's work was in the context of hundreds of years of divine activity.

"I am the God of your fore-fathers—the God of Abraham, of Isaac, and of Jacob. So Moses began to tremble and did not dare to look."

—Acts 7:32

Your Purpose Is to Show God's Power

God does not call you to get involved just so people see what you can do. He calls you to an assignment that you cannot do without Him.

"I have certainly seen the op-pression of My people in Egypt; I have heard their groan-ing and have come down to rescue them. And now, come, I will send you to Egypt."

—Acts 7:34

---

[a]**7:30** Other mss add *of the Lord*
[b]**7:32** Ex 3:6,15
[c]**7:33-34** Ex 3:5,7-8,10
[d]**7:35** Ex 2:14
[e]**7:37** Other mss read *'The Lord your God*
[f]**7:37** Dt 18:15
[g]**7:40** Ex 32:1,23

worship the host of heaven, as it is written in the book of the prophets:

> **Did you bring Me offerings and sacrifices**
> **for 40 years in the desert,**
> **O house of Israel?**
> 43 **No, you took up the tent of Moloch[a]**
> **and the star of your god Rephan,[b]**
> **the images that you made to worship.**
> **So I will deport you beyond Babylon![c]**

GOD'S REAL TABERNACLE

44 "Our forefathers had the tabernacle of the testimony in the desert, just as He who spoke to Moses commanded him to make it according to the pattern he had seen. 45 Our forefathers in turn received it and with Joshua brought it in when they dispossessed the nations that God drove out before our fathers, until the days of David. 46 He found favor in God's sight and asked that he might provide a dwelling place for the God[d] of Jacob. 47 But it was Solomon who built Him a house. 48 However, the Most High does not dwell in sanctuaries made with hands, as the prophet says:

> 49 **Heaven is My throne,**
> **and earth My footstool.**
> **What sort of house will you build for Me?**
> **says the Lord,**
> **or what is My resting place?**
> 50 **Did not My hand make all these things?[e]**

RESISTING THE HOLY SPIRIT

51 "You stiff-necked people with uncircumcised hearts and ears! You are always resisting the Holy Spirit; as your forefathers did, so do you. 52 Which of the prophets did your fathers not persecute? They even killed those who announced beforehand the coming of the Righteous One, whose betrayers and murderers you have now become. 53 You received the law under the direction of angels and yet have not kept it."

Obedience Cures Stiff Necks and Cold Hearts

We cannot prevent God from accomplishing His work in the world around us, but our disobedience can quench His Spirit in our lives.

"You stiff-necked people with uncircumcised hearts and ears! You are always resisting the Holy Spirit; as your forefathers did, so do you."

—Acts 7:51

---

[a]7:43 Canaanite or Phoenician sky or sun god
[b]7:43 Perhaps an Assyrian star god—the planet Saturn
[c]7:42-43 Am 5:25-27
[d]7:46 Other mss read *house*
[e]7:49-50 Is 66:1-2

THE FIRST CHRISTIAN MARTYR

⁵⁴ When they heard these things, they were enraged in their hearts[a] and gnashed their teeth at him. ⁵⁵ But Stephen, filled by the Holy Spirit, gazed into heaven. He saw God's glory, with[b] Jesus standing at the right hand of God, and he said, ⁵⁶ "Look! I see the heavens opened and the •Son of Man standing at the right hand of God!"

⁵⁷ Then they screamed at the top of their voices, stopped their ears, and rushed together against him. ⁵⁸ They threw him out of the city and began to stone him. And the witnesses laid their robes at the feet of a young man named Saul. ⁵⁹ They were stoning Stephen as he called out: "Lord Jesus, receive my spirit!" ⁶⁰ Then he knelt down and cried out with a loud voice, "Lord, do not charge them with this sin!" And saying this, he fell •asleep.[c]

Forgivers Can Live and Die in Freedom

Forgiveness is not a spiritual gift, a skill, or an inherited trait. Forgiveness is a deliberate choice.

Then he knelt down and cried out with a loud voice, "Lord, do not charge them with this sin!" And saying this, he fell asleep.

—Acts 7:60

SAUL THE PERSECUTOR

8 Saul agreed with putting him to death. On that day a severe persecution broke out against the church in Jerusalem, and all except the apostles were scattered throughout the land of Judea and Samaria. ² But devout men buried Stephen and mourned deeply over him. ³ Saul, however, was ravaging the church, and he would enter house after house, drag off men and women, and put them in prison.

PHILIP IN SAMARIA

⁴ So those who were scattered went on their way proclaiming the message of good news. ⁵ Philip went down to a[d] city in Samaria and preached the •Messiah to them. ⁶ The crowds paid attention with one mind to what Philip said, as they heard and saw the signs he was performing. ⁷ For unclean spirits, crying out with a loud voice, came out of many who were possessed, and many who were paralyzed and lame were healed. ⁸ So there was great joy in that city.

[a]7:54 Or *were cut to the quick*
[b]7:55 Lit *and*
[c]7:60 He died; see Jn 11:11; 1 Co 11:30; 1 Th 4:13-15
[d]8:5 Other mss read *the*

THE RESPONSE OF SIMON

⁹ A man named Simon had previously practiced sorcery in that city and astounded the •Samaritan people, while claiming to be somebody great. ¹⁰ They all paid attention to him, from the least of them to the greatest, and they said, "This man is called the Great Power of God!"ᵃ ¹¹ They were attentive to him because he had astounded them with his sorceries for a long time. ¹² But when they believed Philip, as he proclaimed the good news about the kingdom of God and the name of Jesus Christ, both men and women were baptized. ¹³ Then even Simon himself believed. And after he was baptized, he went around constantly withᵇ Philip and was astounded as he observed the signs and great miracles that were being performed.

SIMON'S SIN

¹⁴ When the apostles who were at Jerusalem heard that Samaria had welcomed God's message, they sent Peter and John to them. ¹⁵ After they went down there, they prayed for them, that they might receive the Holy Spirit. ¹⁶ For He had not yet come down onᶜ any of them; they had only been baptized in the name of the Lord Jesus. ¹⁷ Then Peter and John laid their hands on them, and they received the Holy Spirit.

¹⁸ When Simon saw that the Holyᵈ Spirit was given through the laying on of the apostles' hands, he offered them money, ¹⁹ saying, "Give me this power too, so that anyone I lay hands on may receive the Holy Spirit."

²⁰ But Peter told him, "May your silver be destroyed with you, because you thought the gift of God could be obtained with money! ²¹ You have no part or share in this matter, because your heart is not right before God. ²² Therefore repent of this wickedness of yours, and pray to the Lord that the intent of your heart may be forgiven you. ²³ For I see you are poisoned by bitterness and bound by iniquity."

²⁴ "Please prayᵉ to the Lord for me," Simon replied, "so that nothing youᵉ have said may happen to me."

God Turns Setbacks into Opportunities

Persecution of the early church merely expanded the reach of God's message. A heart tuned to God's ways can look at difficult times and see new opportunities.

On that day a severe persecution broke out against the church in Jerusalem, and all except the apostles were scattered throughout the land of Judea and Samaria.

—Acts 8:1b

ᵃ8:10 Or *This is the power of God called Great*
ᵇ8:13 Or *he kept close company with*
ᶜ8:16 Or *yet fallen on*
ᵈ8:18 Other mss omit *Holy*
ᵉ8:24 Gk words *you* and *pray* are plural

WORD STUDY

Greek word: **eunouchos**
[YOO noo kahss]

Translation: **eunuch**

Uses in Acts: **5**

Uses in the NT: **8**

Key passage: **Acts 8:27-39**

The Greek noun *eunouchos* literally means *one holding the bed* or *bedchamberlain*, since eunuchs often were in charge of household affairs such as the care of women in the home. The word *eunouchos* occurs in only two passages in the NT. In Matthew 19:12, Jesus referred to three types of eunuchs: those "born that way from their mother's womb" (birth defect); those "who were made by men" (castration; see Dt 23:1); and those "who have made themselves that way because of the kingdom of heaven" (willingly unmarried and celibate). The second of these types was common in the ancient world, since men of power and influence often wanted servants who could be trusted to manage household affairs but without the threat of sexual activity in their absence (see 2 Kg 9:32; Est 1:10,15; 2:3,14-15; 4:4-5; 6:14; 7:9). Since many of these eunuchs did achieve a high level of authority and respect, the term came to be used in yet another way without this negative connotation. The eunuch was often a term for an official in a royal or noble household (see Is 39:7). This may have been the kind of eunuch Philip led to Christ in Acts 8:27-39, for he is specifically described as "a eunuch and high official of Candace, queen of the Ethiopians, who was in charge of her entire treasury" (v. 27).

25 Then, after they had testified and spoken the message of the Lord, they traveled back to Jerusalem, evangelizing many villages of the Samaritans.

THE CONVERSION OF THE ETHIOPIAN OFFICIAL

26 An angel of the Lord spoke to Philip: "Get up and go south to the road that goes down from Jerusalem to desert Gaza."a 27 So he got up and went. There was an Ethiopian man, a eunuch and high official of Candace, queen of the Ethiopians, who was in charge of her entire treasury. He had come to worship in Jerusalem 28 and was sitting in his chariot on his way home, reading the prophet Isaiah aloud.

29 The Spirit told Philip, "Go and join that chariot."

30 When Philip ran up to it, he heard him reading the prophet Isaiah, and said, "Do you understand what you're reading?"

31 "How can I," he said, "unless someone guides me?" So he invited Philip to come up and sit with him. 32 Now the Scripture passage he was reading was this:

He was led like a sheep to the slaughter,
and as a lamb is silent before its shearer,
so He does not open His mouth.
33 **In His humiliation justice was denied Him.**
Who will describe His generation?
For His life is taken from the earth.b

34 The eunuch replied to Philip, "I ask you, who is the prophet saying this about—himself or another person?" 35 So Philip proceededc to tell him the good news about Jesus, beginning from that Scripture.

36 As they were traveling down the road, they came to some water. The eunuch said, "Look, there's water! What would keep me from being baptized?" [37 And Philip said, "If you believe with all your heart you may." And he replied, "I believe that Jesus Christ is the Son of God."]d 38 Then he ordered the chariot to stop, and both Philip and the eunuch went down into the water, and he baptized him. 39 When they came up out of the

---

a8:26 Perhaps old Gaza or the road near the desert
b8:32-33 Is 53:7-8
c8:35 Lit *Philip opened his mouth*
d8:37 Other mss omit bracketed text

water, the Spirit of the Lord carried Philip away, and the eunuch did not see him any longer. But he went on his way rejoicing. ⁴⁰ Philip appeared in^a Azotus,^b and passing through, he was evangelizing all the towns until he came to Caesarea.

THE DAMASCUS ROAD

9 Meanwhile Saul, still breathing threats and murder against the disciples of the Lord, went to the high priest ² and requested letters from him to the •synagogues in Damascus, so that if he found any who belonged to the Way, either men or women, he might bring them as prisoners to Jerusalem. ³ As he traveled and was nearing Damascus, a light from heaven suddenly flashed around him. ⁴ Falling to the ground, he heard a voice saying to him, "Saul, Saul, why are you persecuting Me?"

⁵ "Who are You, Lord?" he said.

"I am Jesus, whom you are persecuting," He replied. ⁶ "But get up and go into the city, and you will be told what you must do."

⁷ The men who were traveling with him stood speechless, hearing the sound but seeing no one. ⁸ Then Saul got up from the ground, and though his eyes were open, he could see nothing. So they took him by the hand and led him into Damascus. ⁹ He was unable to see for three days, and did not eat or drink.

SAUL'S BAPTISM

¹⁰ Now in Damascus there was a disciple named Ananias. And the Lord said to him in a vision, "Ananias!"

"Here I am, Lord!" he said.

¹¹ "Get up and go to the street called Straight," the Lord said to him, "to the house of Judas, and ask for a man from Tarsus named Saul, since he is praying there. ¹² In a vision^c he has seen a man named Ananias coming in and placing his hands on him so he may regain his sight."

Are You Open to a Change in Plans?

Nothing on your agenda, no matter how pressing, is reason enough to ignore the voice of God when He tells you to stop and help.

The Spirit told Philip, "Go and join that chariot."
—Acts 8:29

Know the Scripture, Share the Scripture

When you speak with hurting or searching people, think Scripture and share Scripture. We don't have the words people need—but God does.

Philip proceeded to tell him the good news about Jesus, beginning from that Scripture.
—Acts 8:35

---

^a8:40 Or *Philip was found at*, or *Philip found himself in*
^b8:40 Or *Ashdod*

^c9:12 Other mss omit *In a vision*

[13] "Lord," Ananias answered, "I have heard from many people about this man, how much harm he has done to Your saints in Jerusalem. [14] And he has authority here from the •chief priests to arrest all who call on Your name."

[15] But the Lord said to him, "Go! For this man is My chosen instrument to carry My name before Gentiles, kings, and the sons of Israel. [16] I will certainly show him how much he must suffer for My name!"

[17] So Ananias left and entered the house. Then he placed his hands on him and said, "Brother Saul, the Lord Jesus, who appeared to you on the road you were traveling, has sent me so you may regain your sight and be filled with the Holy Spirit."

[18] At once something like scales fell from his eyes, and he regained his sight. Then he got up and was baptized. [19] And after taking some food, he regained his strength.

SAUL PROCLAIMING THE MESSIAH

Saul[a] was with the disciples in Damascus for some days. [20] Immediately he began proclaiming Jesus in the synagogues: "He is the Son of God."

[21] But all who heard him were astounded and said, "Isn't this the man who, in Jerusalem, was destroying those who called on this name, and then came here for the purpose of taking them as prisoners to the chief priests?"

[22] But Saul grew more capable, and kept confounding the Jews who lived in Damascus by proving that this One is the •Messiah.

[23] After many days had passed, the Jews conspired to kill him, [24] but their plot became known to Saul. So they were watching the gates day and night intending to kill him, [25] but his disciples took him by night and lowered him in a large basket through ⌊an opening in⌋ the wall.

SAUL IN JERUSALEM

[26] When he arrived in Jerusalem, he tried to associate with the disciples, but they were all afraid of him, since

[a]9:19 Lit *He*

Obedience Should Be a Reflex, Not a Rethink

Our difficulty is not usually that we don't know God's will. Our discomfort comes from the fact that we don't want to do it.

"Lord," Ananias answered, "I have heard from many people about this man, how much harm he has done to Your saints in Jerusalem."

—Acts 9:13

When God Says It, Let's Go Do It

Often our struggle as Christians is not in deciding whether we should obey Christ but in not realizing we must obey *immediately*.

Immediately he began proclaiming Jesus in the synagogues: "He is the Son of God."

—Acts 9:20

they did not believe he was a disciple. ²⁷ Barnabas, however, took him and brought him to the apostles and explained to them how, on the road, Saulᵃ had seen the Lord, and that He had talked to him, and how in Damascus he had spoken boldly in the name of Jesus. ²⁸ Saulᵃ was coming and going with them in Jerusalem, speaking boldly in the name of the Lord. ²⁹ He conversed and debated with the Hellenistic Jews,ᵇ but they attempted to kill him. ³⁰ When the brothers found out, they took him down to Caesarea and sent him off to Tarsus.

³¹ So the church throughout all Judea, Galilee, and Samaria had peace, being built up and walking in the fear of the Lord and in the encouragement of the Holy Spirit, and it increased in numbers.

THE HEALING OF AENEAS

³² As Peter was traveling from place to place,ᶜ he also came down to the saintsᵈ who lived in Lydda. ³³ There he found a man named Aeneas, who was paralyzed and had been bedridden for eight years. ³⁴ Peter said to him, "Aeneas, Jesus Christ heals you. Get up and make your own bed,"ᵉ and immediately he got up. ³⁵ So all who lived in Lydda and Sharon saw him and turned to the Lord.

DORCAS RESTORED TO LIFE

³⁶ In Joppa there was a disciple named Tabitha, which is translated Dorcas.ᶠ She was always doing good works and acts of charity. ³⁷ In those days she became sick and died. After washing her, they placed her in a room upstairs. ³⁸ Since Lydda was near Joppa, the disciples heard that Peter was there and sent two men to him who begged him, "Don't delay in coming with us." ³⁹ So Peter got up and went with them. When he arrived, they led him to the room upstairs. And all the widows approached him, weeping and showing him the robes and clothes that Dorcas had made while she

Look for the Godly Potential in People

Don't give up on those around you. Look to see where God is working in their lives.

Barnabas, however, took him and brought him to the apostles and explained to them how, on the road, Saul had seen the Lord, and that He had talked to him, and how in Damascus he had spoken boldly in the name of Jesus.

—Acts 9:27

Your Obedience Is Noticed in High Places

We sometimes assume that our expressions of devotion to God and others are small and insignificant, but in God's eyes they hold much meaning.

Peter got up and went with them. When he arrived, they led him to the room upstairs. And all the widows approached him, weeping and showing him the robes and clothes that Dorcas had made while she was with them.

—Acts 9:39

ᵃ9:27,28 Lit *he*
ᵇ9:29 Lit *Hellenists*; that is, Gk-speaking Jews
ᶜ9:32 Lit *Peter was passing through all*
ᵈ9:32 The believers
ᵉ9:34 Or *and get ready to eat*
ᶠ9:36 *Dorcas* = Gazelle

WORD STUDY

Greek word: **ekstasis**
[EHK stah sihss]
Translation: **visionary state**
Uses in Acts: **4**
Uses in Luke's writings: **5**
Uses in the NT: **7**
Key passage: **Acts 10:10**

The English words *ecstasy* and *ecstatic* come from the Greek noun *ekstasis*, which literally means *to stand out from*. The term refers to a situation in which a person experiences a kind of displacement from reality. Such feelings of displacement are of two kinds in the NT. The term is used four times to describe the astonishment of a crowd that witnessed a miracle: Jesus forgiving and healing a paralytic (Lk 5:26); Jesus raising Jairus' daughter from the dead (Mk 5:42); Jesus' resurrection (Mk 16:8); and Peter healing a lame man (Ac 3:10). The other three uses of *ekstasis* refer to a revelatory trance. Through a trance, God showed Peter that there is to be no distinction between the clean and the unclean, between Jew and Gentile (Ac 10:10; 11:5). In this same way, Jesus showed Paul that he should leave Jerusalem because of the Jews' unbelief (Ac 22:17-18).

was with them. ⁴⁰ Then Peter sent them all out of the room. He knelt down, prayed, and turning toward the body said, "Tabitha, get up!" She opened her eyes, saw Peter, and sat up. ⁴¹ He gave her his hand and helped her stand up. Then he called the saints and widows and presented her alive. ⁴² This became known throughout all Joppa, and many believed in the Lord. ⁴³ And Peterᵃ stayed on many days in Joppa with Simon, a leather tanner.ᵇ

CORNELIUS' VISION

10 There was a man in Caesarea named Cornelius, a •centurion of what was called the Italian •Regiment. ² He was a devout man and feared God along with his whole household. He did many charitable deeds for the ₗJewishₗ people and always prayed to God. ³ At about three in the afternoonᶜ he distinctly saw in a vision an angel of God who came in and said to him, "Cornelius!"

⁴ Looking intently at him, he became afraid and said, "What is it, Lord?"

And he told him, "Your prayers and your acts of charity have come up as a memorial offering before God. ⁵ Now send men to Joppa and call for Simon, who is also named Peter. ⁶ He is lodging with Simon, a tanner, whose house is by the sea."

⁷ When the angel who spoke to him had gone, he called two of his household slaves and a devout soldier, who was one of those who attended him. ⁸ After explaining everything to them, he sent them to Joppa.

PETER'S VISION

⁹ The next day, as they were traveling and nearing the city, Peter went up to pray on the housetop at about noon.ᵈ ¹⁰ Then he became hungry and wanted to eat, but while they were preparing something he went into a visionary state. ¹¹ He saw heaven opened and an object coming down that resembled a large sheet being lowered to the earth by its four corners. ¹² In it were all

---

ᵃ9:43 Lit *he*
ᵇ9:43 Tanners were considered ritually unclean because of their occupation.

ᶜ10:3 Lit *about the ninth hour*
ᵈ10:9 Lit *about the sixth hour*

the four-footed animals and reptiles of the earth, and the birds of the sky. ¹³ Then a voice said to him, "Get up, Peter; kill and eat!"

¹⁴ "No, Lord!" Peter said. "For I have never eaten anything common[a] and unclean!"

¹⁵ Again, a second time, a voice said to him, "What God has made clean, you must not call common." ¹⁶ This happened three times, and then the object was taken up into heaven.

PETER VISITS CORNELIUS

¹⁷ While Peter was deeply perplexed about what the vision he had seen might mean, the men who had been sent by Cornelius, having asked directions to Simon's house, stood at the gate. ¹⁸ They called out, asking if Simon, who was also named Peter, was lodging there.

¹⁹ While Peter was thinking about the vision, the Spirit told him, "Three men are here looking for you. ²⁰ Get up, go downstairs, and accompany them with no doubts at all, because I have sent them."

²¹ Then Peter went down to the men and said, "Here I am, the one you're looking for. What is the reason you're here?"

²² They said, "Cornelius, a centurion, an upright and God-fearing man, who has a good reputation with the whole Jewish nation, was divinely directed by a holy angel to call you to his house and to hear a message from you." ²³ Peter[b] then invited them in and gave them lodging.

The next day he got up and set out with them, and some of the brothers from Joppa went with him. ²⁴ The following day he entered Caesarea. Now Cornelius was expecting them and had called together his relatives and close friends. ²⁵ When Peter entered, Cornelius met him, fell at his feet, and worshiped him.

²⁶ But Peter helped him up and said, "Stand up! I myself am also a man." ²⁷ While talking with him, he went on in and found that many had come together there. ²⁸ Peter[b] said to them, "You know it's forbidden for a Jewish man to associate with or visit a foreigner.

Let God Be the Judge, You Be the Servant

You will be helpful to others only if you see them as God does. You cannot be judgmental and redemptive at the same time.

Peter said to them, "You know it's forbidden for a Jewish man to associate with or visit a foreigner. But God has shown me that I must not call any person common or unclean."
—Acts 10:28

---

[a]**10:14** Perhaps *profane*, or *non-sacred*; Jews ate distinctive food according to OT law and their tradi- tions, similar to modern kosher or non-kosher foods. [b]**10:23,28** Lit *He*

289

But God has shown me that I must not call any person common or unclean. ²⁹ That's why I came without any objection when I was sent for. So I ask, 'Why did you send for me?'"

³⁰ Cornelius replied, "Four days ago at this hour, at three in the afternoon,ᵃ I wasᵇ praying in my house. Just then a man in a dazzling robe stood before me ³¹ and said, 'Cornelius, your prayer has been heard, and your acts of charity have been remembered in God's sight. ³² Therefore send someone to Joppa and invite Simon here, who is also named Peter. He is lodging in Simon the tanner's house by the sea.'ᶜ ³³ Therefore I immediately sent for you, and you did the right thing in coming. So we are all present before God, to hear everything you have been commanded by the Lord."

GOOD NEWS FOR GENTILES

³⁴ Then Peter began to speak: "In truth, I understand that God doesn't show favoritism, ³⁵ but in every nation the person who fears Him and does righteousness is acceptable to Him. ³⁶ He sent the message to the sons of Israel, proclaiming the good news of peace through Jesus Christ—He is Lord of all. ³⁷ You know the eventsᵈ that took place throughout all Judea, beginning from Galilee after the baptism that John preached: ³⁸ how God anointed Jesus of Nazareth with the Holy Spirit and with power, and how He went about doing good and curing all who were under the tyranny of the Devil, because God was with Him. ³⁹ We ourselves are witnesses of everything He did in both the Judean country and in Jerusalem; yet they killed Him by hanging Him on a tree. ⁴⁰ God raised up this man on the third day and permitted Him to be seen, ⁴¹ not by all the people, but by us, witnesses appointed beforehand by God, who ate and drank with Him after He rose from the dead. ⁴² He commanded us to preach to the people, and to solemnly testify that He is the One appointed by God to be the Judge of the living and the dead. ⁴³ All the prophets testify about Him that through His name everyone who believes in Him will receive forgiveness of sins."

You Learn About God While You Obey Him

You will always be one step of obedience away from the next truth God wants you to learn about Him.

"Therefore I immediately sent for you, and you did the right thing in coming. So we are all present before God, to hear everything you have been commanded by the Lord."

—Acts 10:33

ᵃ**10:30** Lit *at the ninth hour*
ᵇ**10:30** Other mss add *fasting and*
ᶜ**10:32** Other mss add *When he ar-* rives, he will speak to you.
ᵈ**10:37** Lit *thing,* or *word*

GENTILE CONVERSION AND BAPTISM

⁴⁴ While Peter was still speaking these words, the Holy Spirit came down on all those who heard the message. ⁴⁵ The circumcised believers[a] who had come with Peter were astounded, because the gift of the Holy Spirit had been poured out on the Gentiles also. ⁴⁶ For they heard them speaking in ⌊other⌋ languages and declaring the greatness of[b] God.

Then Peter responded, ⁴⁷ "Can anyone withhold water and prevent these from being baptized, who have received the Holy Spirit just as we have?" ⁴⁸ And he commanded them to be baptized in the name of Jesus Christ. Then they asked him to stay for a few days.

GENTILE SALVATION DEFENDED

11 The apostles and the brothers who were throughout Judea heard that the Gentiles had welcomed God's message also. ² When Peter went up to Jerusalem, those who stressed circumcision[c] argued with him, ³ saying, "You visited uncircumcised men and ate with them!"

⁴ Peter began to explain to them in an orderly sequence, saying: ⁵ "I was in the town of Joppa praying, and I saw, in a visionary state, an object coming down that resembled a large sheet being lowered from heaven by its four corners, and it came to me. ⁶ When I looked closely and considered it, I saw the four-footed animals of the earth, the wild beasts, the reptiles, and the birds of the sky. ⁷ Then I also heard a voice telling me, 'Get up, Peter; kill and eat!'

⁸ "'No, Lord!' I said. 'For nothing common or unclean has ever entered my mouth!' ⁹ But a voice answered from heaven a second time, 'What God has made clean, you must not call common.'

¹⁰ "Now this happened three times, and then everything was drawn up again into heaven. ¹¹ At that very moment, three men who had been sent to me from Caesarea arrived at the house where we were. ¹² Then the Spirit told me to go with them with no doubts at all. These six brothers accompanied me, and we went

If You'll Speak, God Will Help Them Hear

Don't assume God will only use you to reach people who are just like you. His Spirit will help you know how to share God's love even with those who are different from you.

While Peter was still speaking these words, the Holy Spirit came down on all those who heard the message. The circumcised believers who had come with Peter were astounded, because the gift of the Holy Spirit had been poured out on the Gentiles also.

—Acts 10:44-45

---

[a]**10:45** Jewish Christians who stressed circumcision;Ac 11:2; 15:5; Gl 2:12;Col 4:11;Ti 1:10
[b]**10:46** Or *and magnifying*
[c]**11:2** Lit *those of the circumcision*

into the man's house. [13] He reported to us how he had seen the angel standing in his house and saying, 'Send[a] to Joppa, and call for Simon, who is also named Peter. [14] He will speak words[b] to you by which you and all your household will be saved.'

[15] "As I began to speak, the Holy Spirit came down on them, just as on us at the beginning. [16] Then I remembered the word of the Lord, how He said, 'John baptized with water, but you will be baptized with the Holy Spirit.' [17] Therefore, if God gave them the same gift that He also gave to us when we believed on the Lord Jesus Christ, how could I possibly hinder God?"

[18] When they heard this they became silent. Then they glorified God, saying, "So God has granted repentance resulting in life[c] to even the Gentiles!"

THE CHURCH IN ANTIOCH

[19] Those who had been scattered as a result of the persecution that started because of Stephen made their way as far as Phoenicia, Cyprus, and Antioch, speaking the message to no one except Jews. [20] But there were some of them, Cypriot and Cyrenian men, who came to Antioch and began speaking to the Hellenists,[d] [e] proclaiming the good news about the Lord Jesus. [21] The Lord's hand was with them, and a large number who believed turned to the Lord. [22] Then the report about them reached the ears of the church in Jerusalem, and they sent out Barnabas to travel[f] as far as Antioch. [23] When he arrived and saw the grace of God, he was glad, and he encouraged all of them to remain true to the Lord with a firm resolve of the heart— [24] for he was a good man, full of the Holy Spirit and of faith— and large numbers of people were added to the Lord. [25] Then he[g] went to Tarsus to search for Saul, [26] and when he found him he brought him to Antioch. For a whole year they met with the church and taught large numbers, and the disciples were first called Christians in Antioch.

God's Word Will Keep You on the Right Track

There will be times when events around you will confuse you. Turn to the Scriptures and allow them to reorient you to God and His activity.

"Then I remembered the word of the Lord."

—Acts 11:16

Humility Keeps You in the Path of God's Plan

Your obedient response to a directive from God will affect what He does next in your life, and may also affect how those around you experience Him.

"How could I possibly hinder God?"

—Acts 11:17b

---

[a]11:13 Other mss add *men*
[b]11:14 Or *speak a message*
[c]11:18 Or *repentance to life*
[d]11:20 Other mss read *Greeks*
[e]11:20 In this context, a non-Jewish person who spoke Gk
[f]11:22 Other mss omit *to travel*
[g]11:25 Other mss read *Barnabas*

FAMINE RELIEF

[27] In those days some prophets came down from Jerusalem to Antioch. [28] Then one of them, named Agabus, stood up and predicted by the Spirit that there would be a severe famine throughout the Roman world[a] This took place during the time of Claudius.[b] [29] So each of the disciples, according to his ability, determined to send relief to the brothers who lived in Judea. [30] This they did, sending it to the elders by means of Barnabas and Saul.

JAMES MARTYRED AND PETER JAILED

12 About that time King •Herod cruelly attacked some who belonged to the church, [2] and he killed James, John's brother, with the sword. [3] When he saw that it pleased the Jews, he proceeded to arrest Peter too, during the days of •Unleavened Bread. [4] After the arrest, he put him in prison and assigned four squads of four soldiers each to guard him, intending to bring him out to the people after the •Passover. [5] So Peter was kept in prison, but prayer was being made earnestly to God for him by the church.

PETER RESCUED

[6] On the night before Herod was to bring him out ₗfor execution₎, Peter was sleeping between two soldiers, bound with two chains, while the sentries in front of the door guarded the prison. [7] Suddenly an angel of the Lord appeared, and a light shone in the cell. Striking Peter on the side, he woke him up and said, "Quick, get up!" Then the chains fell off his wrists. [8] "Get dressed," the angel told him, "and put on your sandals." And he did so. "Wrap your cloak around you," he told him, "and follow me." [9] So he went out and followed, and he did not know that what took place through the angel was real, but thought he was seeing a vision. [10] After they passed the first and second guard posts, they came to the iron gate that leads into the city, which opened to them by itself. They went outside and passed one street, and immediately the angel left him.

---

[a]11:28 Or *the whole world*   [b]11:28 Emperor A.D. 41–54; there was a famine A.D. 47–48.

WORD STUDY

Greek word: **Christianos**
[krihss tee ah NAHSS]
Translation: **Christian**
Uses in Acts: **2**
Uses in the NT: **3**
Key passage: **Acts 11:26**

From the Greek noun *Christos* (*Christ* or *Messiah*) comes the word *Christianos*, meaning *belonging to Christ*. The term occurs in only three places in the NT. Acts 11:26 explains that it was in Antioch that the disciples were "first called Christians." The famine mentioned in the following verses occurred in A.D. 46 and indicates the term's usage entered sacred vocabulary about that time. Since this new word for followers of Christ was coined in Antioch rather than Israel, it may indicate that the Christian movement was being recognized among Gentiles as something distinct from Judaism and not just another Jewish sect. In Acts 26:28, Agrippa referred to Paul's attempt to persuade the king to become a Christian—an attempt Paul admitted applied not only to Agrippa but to everyone who was listening to his words of testimony (v. 29). This occurred about A.D. 60. Peter used the term in reference to suffering "as a Christian" (1 Pt 4:16), and that epistle can be dated about A.D. 64. The term *Christianos* was used on several occasions by Ignatius, the bishop of the church at Antioch, who died about A.D. 110. Thus, it seems that the very early church initially used *Christianos* sparingly, preferring words like *disciples, believers, brothers,* and *saints* as designations for themselves. Thereafter, beginning with Ignatius, *Christianos* was a common way for Christians and non-Christians to refer to believers, though unbelievers often used the term with contempt.

293

WORD STUDY

Greek word: *proseuchomai*
[prahss YOO kah migh]
Translation: *pray*
Uses in Acts: **16**
Uses in Luke's writings: **35**
Uses in the NT: **85**
Key passage: **Acts 12:12**

The Greek verb *proseuchomai* literally means *to pray toward*. The related noun *proseuche* [prahss yoo KAY] is the common term meaning *prayer* (thirty-six occurrences, with twelve in Luke/Acts). The word *proseuchomai* is a compound from *pros*, meaning *toward*, and *euchomai* is another less common term meaning *to pray* (Ac 27:29; 2 Co 13:7,9; Jms 5:16; 3 Jn 2) or to wish (Ac 26:29; Rm 9:3).

There is little distinction between the two terms, for in the NT *proseuchomai* always means *to pray* and *euchomai* usually does (though *euchomai* could be translated this way in Ac 26:29 and Rm 9:3). Essentially, *proseuchomai* functions as a general term for talking to God, while other more specific terms are used in the NT for prayer. The term *proseuchomai* never occurs in John's writings and only occurs nineteen times in Paul's writings, eight of them in 1 Corinthians. Sixty occurrences of *proseuchomai* are found in the Synoptic Gospels and Acts. Luke is particularly fond of *proseuchomai*, and over a third of its uses in the NT are in Luke's Gospel and Acts. Luke's Gospel has a special emphasis on the prayer life of Jesus, while Acts does the same for the early church in general (12:12; 13:3; 20:36; 21:5) and the apostles in particular (1:24; 6:6; 8:15; 9:40; 10:9; 14:23; 16:25; 22:17; 28:8).

[11] Then Peter came to himself and said, "Now I know for certain that the Lord has sent His angel and rescued me from Herod's grasp and from all that the Jewish people expected." [12] When he realized this, he went to the house of Mary, the mother of John Mark,[a] where many had assembled and were praying. [13] He knocked at the door in the gateway, and a servant named Rhoda came to answer. [14] She recognized Peter's voice, and because of her joy she did not open the gate, but ran in and announced that Peter was standing at the gateway.

[15] "You're crazy!" they told her. But she kept insisting that it was true. Then they said, "It's his angel!" [16] Peter, however, kept on knocking, and when they opened the door and saw him, they were astounded.

[17] Motioning to them with his hand to be silent, he explained to them how the Lord had brought him out of the prison. "Report these things to James[b] and the brothers," he said. Then he departed and went to a different place.

[18] At daylight, there was a great commotion[c] among the soldiers as to what could have become of Peter. [19] After Herod had searched and did not find him, he interrogated the guards and ordered their execution. Then Herod went down from Judea to Caesarea and stayed there.

HEROD'S DEATH

[20] He had been very angry with the Tyrians and Sidonians.[d] Together they presented themselves before him, and having won over Blastus, who was in charge of the king's bedroom, they asked for peace, because their country was supplied with food from the king's country. [21] So on an appointed day, dressed in royal robes and seated on the throne, Herod delivered a public address to them. [22] The populace began to shout, "It's the voice of a god and not of a man!" [23] At once an angel of the Lord struck him because he did not give the glory to God, and he became infected with worms and died. [24] Then God's message flourished and multi-

---

[a]**12:12** Lit *John who was called Mark*
[b]**12:17** This was James, the Lord's brother; see Mk 6:3. This was not James the apostle; see Ac 12:2.
[c]**12:18** Or *was no small disturbance*
[d]**12:20** The people of the area of modern Lebanon

plied. ²⁵ And Barnabas and Saul returned to^a Jerusalem after they had completed their relief mission, on which they took John Mark.^b

PREPARING FOR THE MISSION FIELD

13 In the local church at Antioch there were prophets and teachers: Barnabas, Simeon who was called Niger, Lucius the Cyrenian, Manaen, a close friend of •Herod the tetrarch, and Saul. ² As they were ministering to^c the Lord and fasting, the Holy Spirit said, "Set apart for Me Barnabas and Saul for the work that I have called them to." ³ Then, after they had fasted, prayed, and laid hands on them,^d they sent them off.

THE MISSION TO CYPRUS

⁴ Being sent out by the Holy Spirit, they came down to Seleucia, and from there they sailed to Cyprus. ⁵ Arriving in Salamis, they proclaimed God's message in the Jewish •synagogues. They also had John as their assistant. ⁶ When they had gone through the whole island as far as Paphos, they came across a sorcerer, a Jewish false prophet named Bar-Jesus. ⁷ He was with the •proconsul, Sergius Paulus, an intelligent man. This man summoned Barnabas and Saul and desired to hear God's message. ⁸ But Elymas, the sorcerer, which is how his name is translated, opposed them and tried to turn the proconsul away from the faith.

⁹ Then Saul—also called Paul—filled with the Holy Spirit, stared straight at the sorcerer^e ¹⁰ and said, "You son of the Devil, full of all deceit and all fraud, enemy of all righteousness! Won't you ever stop perverting the straight paths of the Lord? ¹¹ Now, look! The Lord's hand is against you: you are going to be blind, and will not see the sun for a time." Suddenly a mist and darkness fell on him, and he went around seeking someone to lead him by the hand.

¹² Then the proconsul, seeing what happened, believed and was astonished at the teaching about the Lord.

---

^a12:25 Other mss read *from*
^b12:25 Lit *John who was called Mark*
^c13:2 Or *were worshiping*
^d13:3 See note at Ac 6:6
^e13:9 Lit *at him*

The Road to God's Will Comes Through Prayer

When you face an important decision, pray. Let your time alone with God set the agenda for your life.

As they were ministering to the Lord and fasting, the Holy Spirit said, "Set apart for Me Barnabas and Saul for the work that I have called them to."

—Acts 13:2

PAUL'S SERMON IN ANTIOCH OF PISIDIA

¹³ Paul and his companions set sail from Paphos and came to Perga in Pamphylia. John, however, left them and went back to Jerusalem. ¹⁴ They continued their journey from Perga and reached Antioch in Pisidia. On the Sabbath day they went into the synagogue and sat down. ¹⁵ After the reading of the Law and the Prophets, the leaders of the synagogue sent ₗwordₗ to them, saying, "Brothers, if you have any message of encouragement for the people, you can speak."

¹⁶ Then standing up, Paul motioned with his hand and spoke: "Men of Israel, and you who fear God, listen! ¹⁷ The God of this people Israel chose our forefathers, exalted the people during their stay in the land of Egypt, and led them out of it with a mighty[a] arm. ¹⁸ And for about 40 years He put up with them[b] in the desert; ¹⁹ then after destroying seven nations in the land of Canaan, He gave their land to them as an inheritance. ²⁰ This all took about 450 years. After this, He gave them judges until Samuel the prophet. ²¹ Then they asked for a king, so God gave them Saul the son of Kish, a man of the tribe of Benjamin, for 40 years. ²² After removing him, He raised up David as their king, of whom He testified: 'I have found David the son of Jesse, a man after My heart,[c] who will carry out all My will.'

²³ "From this man's descendants, according to the promise, God brought the Savior, Jesus,[d] to Israel. ²⁴ Before He came to public attention,[e] John had previously proclaimed a baptism of repentance to all the people of Israel. ²⁵ Then as John was completing his life work, he said, 'Who do you think I am? I am not the One. But look! Someone is coming after me, and I am not worthy to untie the sandals on His feet.'

²⁶ "Brothers, sons of Abraham's race, and those among you who fear God, the message of this salvation has been sent to us. ²⁷ For the residents of Jerusalem and their rulers, since they did not recognize Him or the voices of the prophets that are read every Sab-

Be Ready to Move When God Says Go

If you're watching for where God is working, you'll be ready to act and know what to say when He opens the door of opportunity.

After the reading of the Law and the Prophets, the leaders of the synagogue sent word to them, saying, "Brothers, if you have any message of encouragement for the people, you can speak."

—Acts 13:15

---

[a]13:17 Lit *with an uplifted*
[b]13:18 Other mss read *He cared for them*
[c]13:22 1 Sm 13:14; Ps 89:20
[d]13:23 Other mss read *brought salvation*
[e]13:24 Lit *Before the face of His entrance*

bath, have fulfilled their words[a] by condemning Him. [28] Though they found no grounds for the death penalty, they asked •Pilate to have Him killed. [29] When they had fulfilled all that had been written about Him, they took Him down from the tree and put Him in a tomb. [30] But God raised Him from the dead, [31] and He appeared for many days to those who came up with Him from Galilee to Jerusalem, who are now His witnesses to the people. [32] And we ourselves proclaim to you the good news of the promise that was made to our forefathers. [33] God has fulfilled this to us their children by raising up Jesus, as it is written in the second Psalm:

> **You are My Son;**
> **today I have become Your Father.**[b] [c]

[34] Since He raised Him from the dead, never to return to decay, He has spoken in this way, **I will grant you the faithful covenant blessings[d] made to David.**[e] [35] Therefore He also says in another passage, **You will not allow Your Holy One to see decay.**[f] [36] For David, after serving his own generation in God's plan, fell •asleep, was buried with his fathers, and decayed. [37] But the One whom God raised up did not decay. [38] Therefore, let it be known to you, brothers, that through this man forgiveness of sins is being proclaimed to you, [39] and everyone who believes in Him is justified from everything, which you could not be justified from through the law of Moses. [40] So beware that what is said in the prophets does not happen to you:

> [41] **Look, you scoffers,**
> **marvel and vanish away,**
> **because I am doing a work in your days,**
> **a work that you will never believe,**
> **even if someone were to explain it to you.**"[g]

PAUL AND BARNABAS IN ANTIOCH

[42] As they[h] were leaving, they[i] [j] begged that these matters be presented to them the following Sabbath. [43] After the synagogue had been dismissed, many of the

[a]13:27 Lit *fulfilled them*
[b]13:33 Or *I have begotten You*
[c]13:33 Ps 2:7
[d]13:34 Lit *faithful holy things*
[e]13:34 Is 55:3
[f]13:35 Ps 16:10
[g]13:41 Hab 1:5
[h]13:42 Paul and Barnabas
[i]13:42 Other mss read *they were leaving the synagogue of the Jews, the Gentiles*
[j]13:42 The people

WORD STUDY

Greek word: **ethnos**
[EHTH nahss]

Translation: **Gentile**

Uses in Acts: **43**

Uses in Luke's writings: **56**

Uses in the NT: **162**

Key passage: **Acts 13:42-50**

The English word *ethnic* comes from the Greek noun *ethnos*, which means *gentile* or *nation*. In the Greek OT ethnos translated the Hebrew term *goy* (plural *goyim*) hundreds of times, often referring to a non-Hebrew, one who is outside the covenant community of God's people and does not worship the one true God. Similarly, in the NT *ethnos* can be understood to mean *pagan* in many contexts, since the emphasis of the term is not simply on one's not being a Hebrew but on one's being a worshiper of false gods (see Mt 6:32; Ac 4:25,27; 1 Pt 4:3). This is particularly true in Paul's letters in passages that discuss matters related to the salvation of Jews and Gentiles (Rm 2:14,24; 3:29; 9:30; 11:11-13; 15:9-12; 1 Co 12:2; Gl 2:12; Eph 2:11; 3:6; 4:17; 1 Th 2:16; 4:5). Most of the time, however, *ethnos* is simply a cultural designation that identifies Gentiles as a people distinct from the Jews. The term is especially common in Luke's writings. The reason is that one of Luke's purposes in Acts was to document the growth of the church, which was a completely Jewish entity at the outset but eventually became a predominantly Gentile movement (see Ac 10:45; 11:1,18; 14:27; 15:1-21).

Jews and devout •proselytes followed Paul and Barnabas, who were speaking with them and persuading them to continue in the grace of God.

⁴⁴ The following Sabbath almost the whole town assembled to hear the message of the Lord.ᵃ ⁴⁵ But when the Jews saw the crowds, they were filled with jealousy and began to oppose what Paul was saying by insulting him.

⁴⁶ Then Paul and Barnabas boldly said: "It was necessary that God's message be spoken to you first. But since you reject it, and consider yourselves unworthy of eternal life, we now turn to the Gentiles! ⁴⁷ For this is what the Lord has commanded us:

> **I have appointed you as a light**
> **for the Gentiles,**
> **to bring salvation to the endsᵇ**
> **of the earth."ᶜ**

⁴⁸ When the Gentiles heard this, they rejoiced and glorified the message of the Lord, and all who had been appointed to eternal life believed. ⁴⁹ So the message of the Lord spread through the whole region. ⁵⁰ But the Jews incited the religious women of high standing and the leading men of the city. They stirred up persecution against Paul and Barnabas and expelled them from their district. ⁵¹ But shaking the dust off their feet against them, they proceeded to Iconium. ⁵² And the disciples were filled with joy and the Holy Spirit.

GROWTH AND PERSECUTION IN ICONIUM

14 The same thing happened in Iconium; they entered the Jewish •synagogue and spoke in such a way that a great number of both Jews and Greeks believed. ² But the Jews who refused to believe stirred up and poisoned the mindsᵈ of the Gentiles against the brothers. ³ So they stayed there for some time and spoke boldly, in reliance on the Lord, who testified to the message of His grace by granting that signs and wonders be performed through them. ⁴ But the people of the city were divided, some siding with the Jews and some with

---

Share the Wealth of Your Heavenly Reward

God saved us so we would have a relationship with Him, through which He could carry out His mission to redeem a lost world.

"This is what the Lord has commanded us: I have appointed you as a light for the Gentiles, to bring salvation to the ends of the earth."

—Acts 13:47

ᵃ13:44 Other mss read *of God*
ᵇ13:47 Lit *the end*
ᶜ13:47 Is 49:6
ᵈ14:2 Lit *and harmed the souls*

the apostles. 5 When an attempt was made by both the Gentiles and Jews, with their rulers, to assault and stone them, 6 they found out about it and fled to the Lycaonian towns called Lystra and Derbe, and to the surrounding countryside. 7 And there they kept evangelizing.

MISTAKEN FOR GODS IN LYSTRA

8 In Lystra a man without strength in his feet, lame from birth,[a] and who had never walked, sat 9 and heard Paul speaking. After observing him closely and seeing that he had faith to be healed, 10 ₗPaulₗ said in a loud voice, "Stand up straight on your feet!" And he jumped up and started to walk around.

11 When the crowds saw what Paul had done, they raised their voices, saying in the Lycaonian language, "The gods have come down to us in the form of men!" 12 And they started to call Barnabas, Zeus, and Paul, Hermes, because he was the main speaker. 13 Then the priest of Zeus, whose temple was just outside the town, brought oxen and garlands to the gates. He, with the crowds, intended to offer sacrifice.

14 The apostles Barnabas and Paul tore their robes when they heard this and rushed into the crowd, shouting: 15 "Men! Why are you doing these things? We are men also, with the same nature as you, and we are proclaiming good news to you, that you should turn from these worthless things to the living God, **who made the heaven, the earth, the sea, and everything in them.**[b] 16 In past generations He allowed all the nations to go their own way, 17 although He did not leave Himself without a witness, since He did good: giving you rain from heaven and fruitful seasons, and satisfying your[c] hearts with food and happiness." 18 Even though they said these things, they barely stopped the crowds from sacrificing to them.

19 Then some Jews came from Antioch and Iconium, and when they had won over the crowds and stoned Paul, they dragged him out of the city, thinking he was dead. 20 After the disciples surrounded him, he got up and went into the town. The next day he left with Barnabas for Derbe.

Just Be Yourself—Let God Do the Rest

Paul was never deceived into thinking that his own intelligence or personal drive compelled others to faith. He was just an ordinary man serving an extraordinary God.

"Men! Why are you doing these things? We are men also, with the same nature as you, and we are proclaiming good news to you."
—Acts 14:15a

You Can a Learn a Lot from the Rocky Spots

Was it coincidence that God allowed Paul to be stoned in the same manner as Stephen? Perhaps God allowed it to make sure Paul never forgot what pride and arrogance could do.

Some Jews came from Antioch and Iconium, and when they had won over the crowds and stoned Paul, they dragged him out of the city, thinking he was dead.
—Acts 14:19

---

[a]14:8 Lit *from his mother's womb* [c]14:17 Other mss read *our*
[b]14:15 Ex 20:11; Ps 146:6

WORD STUDY

Greek word: **presbuteros**
[prehss BOO teh rahss]
Translation: **elder**
Uses in Acts: **18**
Uses in Luke's writings: **23**
Uses in the NT: **66**
Key passage: **Acts 14:23**

The English word *presbyterian* comes from the Greek noun *presbuteros*. The Greek word means *an older man*, which included the ideas of honor and dignity. More generally, the word means *an elder*. The term *presbuteros* was used in the Greek OT to translate the Hebrew word *zeqan*, also meaning *an older man*. The law demanded that older men be held in high esteem (see Lv 19:32; compare 1 Tm 5:1-2). They often attained positions of leadership in their communities.

The early church used the word *presbuteros* as one of the terms for its leaders. In Titus 1:5,7 and Acts 20:17,28, Paul used *presbuteros* interchangeably with *episkopos* (meaning *overseer* or *bishop*; see 1 Tm 3:1-2), a government term borrowed from the ancient Greek city-states. While *episkopos* refers to the leaders' responsibility in watching over the spiritual welfare of God's people in the church, *presbuteros* emphasizes the maturity and wisdom that enables them to direct matters in the church. Elders who demonstrate great ability in leadership and in handling God's word should be given even greater honor (see 1 Tm 5:17).

CHURCH PLANTING

21 After they had evangelized that town and made many disciples, they returned to Lystra, to Iconium, and to Antioch, 22 strengthening the hearts[a] of the disciples by encouraging them to continue in the faith, and by telling them, "It is necessary to pass through many troubles on our way into the kingdom of God."

23 When they had appointed elders in every church and prayed with fasting, they committed them to the Lord in whom they had believed. 24 Then they passed through Pisidia and came to Pamphylia. 25 After they spoke the message in Perga, they went down to Attalia. 26 From there they sailed back to Antioch where they had been entrusted to the grace of God for the work they had completed. 27 After they arrived and gathered the church together, they reported everything God had done with them, and that He had opened the door of faith to the Gentiles. 28 And they spent a considerable time[b] with the disciples.

DISPUTE IN ANTIOCH

15 Some men came down from Judea and began to teach the brothers: "Unless you are circumcised according to the custom prescribed by Moses, you cannot be saved!" 2 But after Paul and Barnabas had engaged them in serious argument and debate, they arranged for Paul and Barnabas and some others of them to go up to the apostles and elders in Jerusalem concerning this controversy. 3 When they had been sent on their way by the church, they passed through both Phoenicia and Samaria, explaining in detail the conversion of the Gentiles, and they created great joy among all the brothers.

4 When they arrived at Jerusalem, they were welcomed by the church, the apostles, and the elders, and they reported all that God had done with them. 5 But some of the believers from the party of the •Pharisees stood up and said, "It is necessary to circumcise them and to command them to keep the law of Moses!"

---

[a]14:22 Lit *souls*   [b]14:28 Or *spent no little time*

THE JERUSALEM COUNCIL

6 Then the apostles and the elders assembled to consider this matter. 7 After there had been much debate, Peter stood up and said to them: "Brothers, you are aware that in the early days God made a choice among you,[a] that by my mouth the Gentiles would hear the gospel message and believe. 8 And God, who knows the heart, testified to them by giving[b] the Holy Spirit, just as He also did to us. 9 He made no distinction between us and them, cleansing their hearts by faith. 10 Why, then, are you now testing God by putting on the disciples' necks a yoke that neither our forefathers nor we have been able to bear? 11 On the contrary, we believe we are saved through the grace of the Lord Jesus, in the same way they are."

12 Then the whole assembly fell silent and listened to Barnabas and Paul describing all the signs and wonders God had done through them among the Gentiles. 13 After they stopped speaking, James responded: "Brothers, listen to me! 14 Simeon[c] has reported how God first intervened to take from the Gentiles a people for His name. 15 And the words of the prophets agree with this, as it is written:

16 **After these things I will return
 and will rebuild David's tent,
  which has fallen down.
 I will rebuild its ruins and will set it up
  again,**
17 **so that those who are left of mankind
  may seek the Lord—
 even all the Gentiles who are called
  by My name,
 says the Lord who does these things,**
18 **which have been known from long ago.[d] [e]**

19 Therefore, in my judgment, we should not cause difficulties for those who turn to God from among the Gentiles, 20 but instead we should write to them to abstain from things polluted by idols, from sexual immorality, from eating anything that has been strangled, and

Declaring What God Is Doing Is Contagious

Others need to hear from someone who has just come from a personal, life-changing encounter with the living Christ. Will that be you?

The whole assembly fell silent and listened to Barnabas and Paul describing all the signs and wonders God had done through them among the Gentiles.

—Acts 15:12

a15:7 Other mss read *us*
b15:8 Other mss add *them*
c15:14 Simon (Peter)
d15:17-18 Other mss read *says the Lord who does all these things. Known to God from long ago are all His works.*
e15:16-18 Am 9:11-12; Is 45:21

WORD STUDY

Greek word: ***prophetes***
[prah FAY tayss]

Translation: ***prophet***

Uses in Acts: **30**

Uses in Luke's writings: **59**

Uses in the NT: **144**

Key passage: **Acts 15:32**

The English word *prophet* comes directly from the Greek noun *prophetes*, which is a compound word from the preposition *pro*, meaning *before*, and the verb *phemi*, meaning *to speak*. Thus, a prophet is someone who speaks before others, basically in one of two ways: proclaiming truths in the presence of others; and predicting events.

In the Greek OT, *prophetes* occurs dozens of times, almost always to translate the Hebrew word *nabi'*. This term refers to one who served as the mouthpiece of the God of Israel by speaking and interpreting His will to the covenant people. Therefore, when a prophet was speaking, God was speaking.

In the Gospels *prophetes* follows OT usage, since it refers mainly to OT prophets (Mt 2:17; 3:3; 5:17; 22:40; Lk 4:27; 16:29), John the Baptist (Mt 11:9; 14:5; Lk 1:76), and Jesus (Mt 21:11,46; Lk 7:16; 24:19; Jn 4:19; 7:40; 9:17). As in OT times, the early church had prophets who functioned as mouthpieces for God; like OT prophets, their task was revelatory, that is, they spoke for God to His people. Paul linked prophets with apostles on two occasions and explained that both were foundational gifts for the church (Eph 2:20; 3:5; see 4:11; Lk 11:49).

from blood. ²¹ For since ancient times, Moses has had in every city those who proclaim him, and he is read aloud in the •synagogues every Sabbath day."

THE LETTER TO THE GENTILE BELIEVERS

²² Then the apostles and the elders, with the whole church, decided to select men from among them and to send them to Antioch with Paul and Barnabas: Judas, called Barsabbas, and Silas, both leading men among the brothers. ²³ They wrote this letter to be delivered by them:[a]

From the apostles and the elders, your brothers,
To the brothers from among the Gentiles in Antioch, Syria, and Cilicia:
Greetings.
²⁴ Because we have heard that some to whom we gave no authorization went out from us and troubled you with their words and unsettled your hearts,[b] ²⁵ we have unanimously decided to select men and send them to you along with our beloved Barnabas and Paul, ²⁶ who have risked their lives for the name of our Lord Jesus Christ. ²⁷ Therefore we have sent Judas and Silas, who will personally report the same things by word of mouth.[c] ²⁸ For it was the Holy Spirit's decision—and ours—to put no greater burden on you than these necessary things: ²⁹ that you abstain from food offered to idols, from blood, from eating anything that has been strangled, and from sexual immorality. If you keep yourselves from these things, you will do well. Farewell.

THE OUTCOME OF THE JERUSALEM LETTER

³⁰ Then, being sent off, they went down to Antioch, and after gathering the assembly, they delivered the letter. ³¹ When they read it, they rejoiced because of its encouragement. ³² Both Judas and Silas, who were also prophets themselves, encouraged the brothers and strengthened them with a

---

[a]15:23 Lit *Writing by their hand:*
[b]15:24 Other mss add *by saying,*

"Be circumcised and keep the law,"
[c]15:27 Lit *things through word*

long message. [33] After spending some time there, they were sent back in peace by the brothers to those who had sent them.[a] [b] [35] But Paul and Barnabas, along with many others, remained in Antioch teaching and proclaiming the message of the Lord.

PAUL AND BARNABAS PART COMPANY

[36] After some time had passed, Paul said to Barnabas, "Let's go back and visit the brothers in every town where we have preached the message of the Lord, and see how they're doing." [37] Barnabas wanted to take along John Mark.[c] [38] But Paul did not think it appropriate to take along this man who had deserted them in Pamphylia and had not gone on with them to the work. [39] There was such a sharp disagreement that they parted company, and Barnabas took Mark with him and sailed off to Cyprus. [40] Then Paul chose Silas and departed, after being commended to the grace of the Lord by the brothers. [41] He traveled through Syria and Cilicia, strengthening the churches.

PAUL SELECTS TIMOTHY

16 Then he went on to Derbe and Lystra, where there was a disciple named Timothy, the son of a believing Jewish woman, but his father was a Greek. [2] The brothers at Lystra and Iconium spoke highly of him. [3] Paul wanted Timothy[d] to go with him, so he took him and circumcised him because of the Jews who were in those places, since they all knew that his father was a Greek. [4] As they traveled through the towns, they delivered the decisions reached by the apostles and elders at Jerusalem for them to observe. [5] So the churches were strengthened in the faith and were increased in number daily.

EVANGELIZATION OF EUROPE

[6] They went through the region of Phrygia and Galatia and were prevented by the Holy Spirit from speaking the message in the province of Asia. [7] When they came

People Need You to Care About Them

Those who encourage and lovingly challenge us are precious gifts from God. Are you that kind of friend?

After some time had passed, Paul said to Barnabas, "Let's go back and visit the brothers in every town where we have preached the message of the Lord, and see how they're doing."

—Acts 15:36

---

[a]15:33 Other mss read *the brothers to the apostles*
[b]15:33 Other mss add v. 34: *But Silas decided to stay there.*

[c]15:37 Lit *John who was called Mark*
[d]16:3 Lit *wanted this one*

to Mysia, they tried to go into Bithynia, but the Spirit of Jesus did not allow them. [8] So, bypassing Mysia, they came down to Troas. [9] During the night a vision appeared to Paul: a Macedonian man was standing and pleading with him, "Cross over to Macedonia and help us!" [10] After he had seen the vision, we[a] immediately made efforts to set out for Macedonia, concluding that God had called us to evangelize them.

LYDIA'S CONVERSION

[11] Then, setting sail from Troas, we ran a straight course to Samothrace, the next day to Neapolis, [12] and from there to Philippi, a Roman colony, which is a leading city of that district of Macedonia. We stayed in that city for a number of days. [13] On the Sabbath day we went outside the city gate by the river, where we thought there was a place of prayer. We sat down and spoke to the women gathered there. [14] A woman named Lydia, a dealer in purple cloth from the city of Thyatira, who worshiped God, was listening. The Lord opened her heart to pay attention to what was spoken by Paul. [15] After she and her household were baptized, she urged us, "If you consider me a believer in the Lord, come and stay at my house." And she persuaded us.

PAUL AND SILAS IN PRISON

[16] Once, as we were on our way to prayer, a slave girl met us who had a spirit of prediction[b] and made a large profit for her owners by fortune-telling. [17] As she followed Paul and us she cried out, "These men are the slaves of the Most High God, who are proclaiming to you[c] the way of salvation." [18] And she did this for many days.

But Paul was greatly aggravated, and turning to the spirit, said, "I command you in the name of Jesus Christ to come out of her!" And it came out right away.[d]

[19] When her owners saw that their hope of profit was gone, they seized Paul and Silas and dragged them into the marketplace to the authorities. [20] And bringing

---

Listen Carefully, Follow Decisively

If you want to know God's will, take time to cultivate your relationship with Jesus and learn to identify His voice. He is more than willing to show you the way.

After he had seen the vision, we immediately made efforts to set out for Macedonia, concluding that God had called us to evangelize them.

—Acts 16:10

---

[a]**16:10** The use of *we* in this passage probably indicates that the author Luke is joining Paul's missionary team here.

[b]**16:16** Or *a spirit by which she predicted the future*

[c]**16:17** Other mss read *us*

[d]**16:18** Lit *out this hour*

them before the chief magistrates, they said, "These men are seriously disturbing our city. They are Jews, ²¹ and are promoting customs that are not legal for us as Romans to adopt or practice."

²² Then the mob joined in the attack against them, and the chief magistrates stripped off their clothes and ordered them to be beaten with rods. ²³ After they had inflicted many blows on them, they threw them in jail, ordering the jailer to keep them securely guarded. ²⁴ Receiving such an order, he put them into the inner prison and secured their feet in the stocks.

A MIDNIGHT DELIVERANCE

²⁵ About midnight Paul and Silas were praying and singing hymns to God, and the prisoners were listening to them. ²⁶ Suddenly there was such a violent earthquake that the foundations of the jail were shaken, and immediately all the doors were opened, and everyone's chains came loose. ²⁷ When the jailer woke up and saw the doors of the prison open, he drew his sword and was going to kill himself, since he thought the prisoners had escaped.

²⁸ But Paul called out in a loud voice, "Don't harm yourself, because all of us are here!"

²⁹ Then the jailer[a] called for lights, rushed in, and fell down trembling before Paul and Silas. ³⁰ Then he escorted them out and said, "Sirs, what must I do to be saved?"

³¹ So they said, "Believe on the Lord Jesus, and you will be saved—you and your household." ³² Then they spoke the message of the Lord to him along with everyone in his house. ³³ He took them the same hour of the night and washed their wounds. Right away he and all his family were baptized. ³⁴ He brought them up into his house, set a meal before them, and rejoiced because he had believed God with his entire household.

AN OFFICIAL APOLOGY

³⁵ When daylight came, the chief magistrates sent the police to say, "Release those men!"

Deep Trouble Is a Time for Deeper Joy

God's miracle would later release them from their chains, but perhaps the greater miracle was how the Holy Spirit enabled them to overflow with joy in their painful imprisonment.

About midnight Paul and Silas were praying and singing hymns to God, and the prisoners were listening to them.
—Acts 16:25

What Example Are You Setting at Home?

If you set your mind wholeheartedly on serving God, your example will bring a tremendous blessing to your family.

He took them the same hour of the night and washed their wounds. Right away he and all his family were baptized.
—Acts 16:33

---

[a]16:29 Lit *Then he*

WORD STUDY

Greek word: **Romaios**
[roh MIGH ahss]

Translation: **Roman**

Uses in Acts: **11**

Uses in the NT: **12**

Key passage: **Acts 16:37-40**

The Greek noun *Romaios* comes from the Latin term *Romanus*, which refers to things pertaining to the Roman Empire. Roman citizenship was highly coveted by those living in the empire. Citizenship could be attained by birth, through legislation, and for a brief time with money (see Ac 22:27-28). Citizens could not be tortured or imprisoned without a trial, and they had the option of appealing to Caesar for trial if they chose. Citizens could not be executed by crucifixion unless so ordered by Caesar himself. Violating someone's citizenship could have harsh consequences, and claiming citizenship falsely was punishable by death.

Paul's Roman citizenship was an important issue. During the years he served the Lord, he appealed to his status as a Roman citizen (and Silas') to gain release from jail in Philippi (Ac 16:35-40), and later he did so again to keep from being beaten by Roman officials in Jerusalem (Ac 22:22-29). After Jewish officials brought charges against Paul, he was imprisoned in Caesarea where he appealed to Caesar for trial (Ac 25:6-12; see vv. 21,25; 26:32; 28:19).

36 The jailer reported these words to Paul: "The magistrates have sent orders for you to be released. So come out now and go in peace."

37 But Paul said to them, "They beat us in public without a trial, although we are Roman citizens, and threw us in jail. And now are they going to smuggle us out secretly? Certainly not! On the contrary, let them come themselves and escort us out!"

38 Then the police reported these words to the magistrates. And they were afraid when they heard that Paul and Silas[a] were Roman citizens. 39 So they came and apologized to them, and escorting them out, they urged them to leave town. 40 After leaving the jail, they came to Lydia's house where they saw and encouraged the brothers, and departed.

A SHORT MINISTRY IN THESSALONICA

17 Then they traveled through Amphipolis and Apollonia and came to Thessalonica, where there was a Jewish •synagogue. 2 As usual, Paul went to them, and on three Sabbath days reasoned with them from the Scriptures, 3 explaining and showing that the •Messiah had to suffer and rise from the dead, and saying: "This is the Messiah, Jesus, whom I am proclaiming to you." 4 Then some of them were persuaded and joined Paul and Silas, including a great number of God-fearing Greeks, as well as a number[b] of the leading women.

THE ASSAULT ON JASON'S HOUSE

5 But the Jews became jealous, and when they had brought together some scoundrels from the marketplace and formed a mob, they set the city in an uproar. Attacking Jason's house, they searched for them to bring them out to the public assembly. 6 When they did not find them, they dragged Jason and some of the brothers before the city officials, shouting, "These men who have turned the world upside down have come here too, 7 and Jason has received them as guests! They are all acting contrary to Caesar's decrees, saying that there is another king—Jesus!" 8 The Jews[c] stirred up

---

[a]16:38 Lit *heard they*
[b]17:4 Lit *as well as not a few*
[c]17:8 Lit *They*

the crowd and the city officials who heard these things. [9] So taking a security bond from Jason and the others, they released them.

THE BEROEANS SEARCH THE SCRIPTURES

[10] As soon as it was night, the brothers sent Paul and Silas off to Beroea. On arrival, they went into the synagogue of the Jews. [11] The people here were more open-minded than those in Thessalonica, since they welcomed the message with eagerness and examined the Scriptures daily to see if these things were so. [12] Consequently, many of them believed, including a number of the prominent Greek women as well as men. [13] But when the Jews from Thessalonica found out that God's message had been proclaimed by Paul at Beroea, they came there too, agitating and disturbing[a] the crowds. [14] Then the brothers immediately sent Paul away to go to the sea, but Silas and Timothy stayed on there. [15] Those who escorted Paul brought him as far as Athens, and after receiving instructions for Silas and Timothy to come to him as quickly as possible, they departed.

PAUL IN ATHENS

[16] While Paul was waiting for them in Athens, his spirit was troubled within him when he saw that the city was full of idols. [17] So he reasoned in the synagogue with the Jews and with those who worshiped God, and in the marketplace every day with those who happened to be there. [18] Then also, some of the Epicurean and Stoic philosophers argued with him. Some said, "What is this pseudo-intellectual[b] trying to say?"

Others replied, "He seems to be a preacher of foreign deities"—because he was telling the good news about Jesus and the resurrection.

[19] They took him and brought him to the Areopagus,[c] and said, "May we learn about this new teaching you're speaking of? [20] For what you say sounds strange to us,

Maintain the Bible as Your Reference Point

The Scriptures keep everything in perspective. Even when others fail or disappoint you, the Scriptures are your guide to truth.

They welcomed the message with eagerness and examined the Scriptures daily to see if these things were so.

—Acts 17:11b

---

[a]17:13 Other mss omit *and disturbing*
[b]17:18 Lit *this seed picker*; that is, one who picks up scraps
[c]17:19 Or *Mars Hill*, the oldest and most famous court in Athens with jurisdiction in moral, religious, and civil matters

and we want to know what these ideas mean." ²¹ Now all the Athenians and the foreigners residing there spent their time on nothing else but telling or hearing something new.

THE AREOPAGUS ADDRESS

²² Then Paul stood in the middle of the Areopagus and said: "Men of Athens! I see that you are extremely religious in every respect. ²³ For as I was passing through and observing the objects of your worship, I even found an altar on which was inscribed:

TO AN UNKNOWN GOD.

Therefore, what you worship in ignorance, this I proclaim to you. ²⁴ The God who made the world and everything in it—He is Lord of heaven and earth and does not live in shrines made by hands. ²⁵ Neither is He served by human hands, as though He needed anything, since He Himself gives everyone life and breath and all things. ²⁶ From one manᵃ He has made every nation of men to live all over the earth and has determined their appointed times and the boundaries of where they live, ²⁷ so that they might seek God, and perhaps they might reach out and find Him, though He is not far from each one of us. ²⁸ For in Him we live and move and exist, as even some of your own poets have said, 'For we are also His offspring.'ᵇ ²⁹ Being God's offspring, then, we shouldn't think that the divine nature is like gold or silver or stone, an image fashioned by human art and imagination.

³⁰ "Therefore, having overlooked the times of ignorance, God now commands all people everywhere to repent, ³¹ because He has set a day on which He is going to judge the world in righteousness by the Man He has appointed. He has provided proof of this to everyone by raising Him from the dead."

³² When they heard about resurrection of the dead, some began to ridicule him. But others said, "We will hear you about this again." ³³ So Paul went out from their presence. ³⁴ However, some men joined him and

Always Think of God as Big and Boundless

The Christ we serve today is the Lord of all creation. He is vastly more awesome and powerful than we often imagine.

"Neither is He served by human hands, as though He needed anything, since He Himself gives everyone life and breath and all things."

—Acts 17:25

ᵃ**17:26** Other mss read *one blood* ᵇ**17:28** This citation is from Aratus, a third-century B.C. Gk poet.

believed, among whom were Dionysius the Areopagite, a woman named Damaris, and others with them.

FOUNDING THE CORINTHIAN CHURCH

18 After this, he[a] left from Athens and went to Corinth, 2 where he found a Jewish man named Aquila, a native of Pontus, who had recently come from Italy with his wife Priscilla because Claudius[b] had ordered all the Jews to leave Rome. Paul[c] came to them, 3 and being of the same occupation, stayed with them and worked, for they were tentmakers by trade. 4 He reasoned in the •synagogue every Sabbath and tried to persuade both Jews and Greeks.

5 When Silas and Timothy came down from Macedonia, Paul was occupied with preaching the message[d] and solemnly testified to the Jews that the •Messiah is Jesus. 6 But when they resisted and blasphemed, he shook out his clothes[e] and told them, "Your blood is on your own heads! I am clean. From now on I will go to the Gentiles." 7 So he left there and went to the house of a man named Titius Justus, a worshiper of God, whose house was next door to the synagogue. 8 Crispus, the leader of the synagogue, believed the Lord, along with his whole household; and many of the Corinthians, when they heard, believed and were baptized.

9 Then the Lord said to Paul in a night vision, "Don't be afraid, but keep on speaking and don't be silent. 10 For I am with you, and no one will lay a hand on you to hurt you, because I have many people in this city." 11 And he stayed there a year and six months, teaching the word of God among them.

12 While Gallio was •proconsul of Achaia, the Jews made a united attack against Paul and brought him to the judge's bench. 13 "This man," they said, "persuades people to worship God contrary to the law!"

14 And as Paul was about to open his mouth, Gallio said to the Jews, "If it were a matter of a crime or of moral evil, it would be reasonable for me to put up with you Jews. 15 But if these are questions about

Focus on Your Faith, Not on Your Fears

Our imaginations can magnify problems until they seem insurmountable. That's why God gave us His Holy Spirit, to enable us to see things as God sees them.

The Lord said to Paul in a night vision, "Don't be afraid, but keep on speaking and don't be silent. For I am with you, and no one will lay a hand on you to hurt you, because I have many people in this city."

—Acts 18:9-10

---

[a]18:1 Other mss read *Paul*
[b]18:2 Roman emperor A.D. 41-54; he expelled all Jews from Rome in A.D. 49.
[c]18:2 Lit *He*
[d]18:5 Other mss read *was urged by the Spirit*
[e]18:6 A symbolic display of protest; see Ac 13:51; Mt 10:14

WORD STUDY

Greek word: *epistamai*
[eh PIH stah migh]

Translation: *know*

Uses in Acts: **9**

Uses in the NT: **14**

Key passage: **Acts 18:25**

The Greek verb *epistamai* literally means *to stand upon* and is a compound word from the preposition *epi*, meaning *upon*, and the verb *histemi*, meaning *to stand*. The term means *to know* in a different sense than the more common words *ginosko* and *oida*, which emphasize intellectual knowledge and/or knowledge gained through experience. Both *ginosko* and *oida* are commonly used for knowing persons, including God, with varying degrees of intimacy. The word *epistamai*, on the other hand, is rarely used for knowing people and never for knowing God. The main idea behind *epistamai* is a thorough knowledge of facts, and often understanding the significance of such information is implied.

The difference between *ginosko* and *epistamai* is best demonstrated in the only verse where both verbs occur. In Acts 19 would-be exorcists attempted to cast out a demon "by the Jesus whom Paul preaches," but the demon responded, "Jesus I know [*ginosko*], and Paul I recognize [*epistamai*], but who are you?" (vv. 13,15). The demon knew Jesus intellectually (His identity) and experientially (His power over demons) but was aware only of certain facts about Paul. *Oida* and *epistamai* occur together twice (Mk 14:68; Jd 10). In both instances the two terms are used to make a distinction between intellectual knowledge (*oida*) and comprehension (*epistamai*).

words, names, and your own law, see to it yourselves. I don't want to be a judge of such things." [16] So he drove them from the judge's bench. [17] Then they all[a] seized Sosthenes, the leader of the synagogue, and beat him in front of the judge's bench. But none of these things concerned Gallio.

THE RETURN TRIP TO ANTIOCH

[18] So Paul, having stayed on for many days, said good-bye to the brothers and sailed away to Syria. Priscilla and Aquila were with him. He shaved his head at Cenchreae, because he had taken a vow. [19] When they reached Ephesus he left them there, but he himself entered the synagogue and engaged in discussion with[b] the Jews. [20] And though they asked him to stay for a longer time, he declined, [21] but said good-bye and stated,[c] "I'll come back to you again, if God wills." Then he set sail from Ephesus.

[22] On landing at Caesarea, he went up and greeted the church,[d] and went down to Antioch. [23] And ⌊after⌋ spending some time there, he set out, traveling through one place after another in the Galatian territory and Phrygia, strengthening all the disciples.

THE ELOQUENT APOLLOS

[24] A Jew named Apollos, a native Alexandrian, an eloquent man who was powerful in the Scriptures, arrived in Ephesus. [25] This man had been instructed in the way of the Lord; and being fervent in spirit,[e] he spoke and taught the things about Jesus accurately, although he knew only John's baptism. [26] He began to speak boldly in the synagogue. After Priscilla and Aquila heard him, they took him home[f] and explained the way of God to him more accurately. [27] When he wanted to cross over to Achaia, the brothers wrote to the disciples urging them to welcome him. After he arrived, he greatly helped those who had believed through grace. [28] For he vigorously refuted the Jews in public, demonstrating through the Scriptures that Jesus is the Messiah.

---

[a]18:17 Other mss read *Then all the Greeks*
[b]18:19 Or *and addressed*
[c]18:21 Other mss add *"By all means it is necessary to keep the coming festival in Jerusalem. But*
[d]18:22 The church in Jerusalem
[e]18:25 Or *in the Spirit*
[f]18:26 Lit *they received him*

TWELVE DISCIPLES OF JOHN THE BAPTIST

19 While Apollos was in Corinth, Paul traveled through the interior regions and came to Ephesus. He found some disciples ² and asked them, "Did you receive the Holy Spirit when you believed?"

"No," they told him, "we haven't even heard that there is a Holy Spirit."

³ "Then with what ˌbaptismˌ were you baptized?" he asked them.

"With John's baptism," they replied.

⁴ Paul said, "John baptized with a baptism of repentance, telling the people that they should believe in the One who would come after him, that is, in Jesus."

⁵ On hearing this, they were baptized in the name of the Lord Jesus. ⁶ And when Paul had laid his hands on them, the Holy Spirit came on them, and they began to speak with ˌotherˌ languages and to prophesy. ⁷ Now there were about 12 men in all.

IN THE LECTURE HALL OF TYRANNUS

⁸ Then he entered the •synagogue and spoke boldly over a period of three months, engaging in discussion and trying to persuade them about the things related to the kingdom of God. ⁹ But when some became hardened and would not believe, slandering the Way in front of the crowd, he withdrew from them and met separately with the disciples, conducting discussions every day in the lecture hall of Tyrannus. ¹⁰ And this went on for two years, so that all the inhabitants of the province of Asia, both Jews and Greeks, heard the word of the Lord.

DEMONISM DEFEATED AT EPHESUS

¹¹ God was performing extraordinary miracles by Paul's hands, ¹² so that even facecloths or work aprons[a] that had touched his skin were brought to the sick, and the diseases left them, and the evil spirits came out of them.

---

[a]19:12 Or *that also sweatbands and sweatcloths or handkerchiefs*

WORD STUDY

Greek word: **exorkistes**
[ex or keess TAYSS]
Translation: **exorcist**
Uses in Acts: **1**
Uses in the NT: **1**
Key passage: **Acts 19:13**

The English word *exorcist* comes from the Greek noun *exorkistes*, which is a compound from the preposition *ek*, meaning *out of*, and the verb *horkizo*, meaning *to implore, to entreat* or *to command*. The related verb *exorkizo* means *to place someone under oath*, or more strongly, *to place a curse on someone*. The noun does not occur in the Greek OT and the verb occurs only twice (Gn 24:3; Jdg 17:2). In the NT both *exorkistes* (Ac 19:13) and *exorkizo* (Mt 26:63) occur only once, though the simple form *horkizo* occurs twice— once as a strong request (Mk 5:7) and once as a command (Ac 19:13, the words spoken to the demon).

In the NT, expressions like *to cast out* [*ekballo*] *demons* and *to rebuke* [*epitimao*] *demons* are commonly used for exorcisms performed by Jesus and the apostles. Thus, it is interesting that the only occurrence of *exorkistes* in the NT describes charlatan exorcists who were not believers in Jesus but who tried to cast out a demon by using Jesus' name. Their attempt failed and they paid the price for misunderstanding the proper use of the name of Jesus (Ac 19:11-17). The NT writers may have avoided the term *exorkistes* since it would bring to mind the magical spells and incantations so common in pagan and even in Jewish acts of exorcism. Jesus' name could not be used as a magical formula to cast out demons.

¹³ Then some of the itinerant Jewish exorcists attempted to pronounce the name of the Lord Jesus over those who had evil spirits, saying, "I command you by the Jesus whom Paul preaches!" ¹⁴ Seven sons of Sceva, a Jewish •chief priest, were doing this. ¹⁵ The evil spirit answered them, "Jesus I know, and Paul I recognize— but who are you?" ¹⁶ Then the man who had the evil spirit leaped on them, overpowered them all, and prevailed against them, so that they ran out of that house naked and wounded. ¹⁷ This became known to everyone who lived in Ephesus, both Jews and Greeks. Then fear fell on all of them, and the name of the Lord Jesus was magnified. ¹⁸ And many who had become believers came confessing and disclosing their practices, ¹⁹ while many of those who had practiced magic collected their books and burned them in front of everyone. So they calculated their value, and found it to be 50,000 pieces of silver. ²⁰ In this way the Lord's message flourished and prevailed.

THE RIOT IN EPHESUS

²¹ When these events were over, Paul resolved in the Spirit to pass through Macedonia and Achaia and go to Jerusalem. "After I've been there," he said, "I must see Rome as well!" ²² So after sending two of those who assisted him, Timothy and Erastus, to Macedonia, he himself stayed in the province of Asia for a while.

²³ During that time there was a major[a] disturbance about the Way. ²⁴ For a person named Demetrius, a silversmith who made silver shrines of Artemis,[b] provided a great deal of[c] business for the craftsmen. ²⁵ When he had assembled them, as well as the workers engaged in this type of business, he said: "Men, you know that our prosperity is derived from this business. ²⁶ You both see and hear that not only in Ephesus, but in almost the whole province of Asia, this man Paul has persuaded and misled a considerable number of people by saying that gods made by hand are not gods! ²⁷ So not only do we run a risk that our business may be discredited, but also that the temple of the great goddess Artemis may

You Can't Live Off Others' Faith

There is no secondhand spirituality. No one else can develop Christian maturity on your behalf.

The evil spirit answered them, "Jesus I know, and Paul I recognize—but who are you?"

—Acts 19:15

Admit Your Mistakes, Commit to a Change

It is important to confess your sins specifically and not to hide behind generalities. It is one thing to pray, "Lord, forgive my sin." It's quite another to identify them in painful honesty.

Many who had become believers came confessing and disclosing their practices.

—Acts 19:18

---

[a]19:23 Lit *was not a little*
[b]19:24 Artemis was the ancient Gk

mother goddess believed to control all fertility.
[c]19:24 Lit *provided not a little*

be despised and her magnificence come to the verge of ruin—the very one whom the whole province of Asia and the world adore."

28 When they had heard this, they were filled with rage and began to cry out, "Great is Artemis of the Ephesians!" 29 So the city was filled with confusion; and they rushed all together into the amphitheater, dragging along Gaius and Aristarchus, Macedonians who were Paul's traveling companions. 30 Though Paul wanted to go in before the people, the disciples did not let him. 31 Even some of the provincial officials of Asia, who were his friends, sent word to him, pleading with him not to take a chance by going[a] into the amphitheater. 32 Meanwhile, some were shouting one thing and some another, because the assembly was in confusion, and most of them did not know why they had come together. 33 Then some of the crowd gave Alexander advice when the Jews pushed him to the front. So motioning with his hand, Alexander wanted to make his defense to the people. 34 But when they recognized that he was a Jew, a united cry went up from all of them for about two hours: "Great is Artemis of the Ephesians!"

35 However, when the city clerk had calmed the crowd down, he said, "Men of Ephesus! What man is there who doesn't know that the city of the Ephesians is the temple guardian of the great[b] Artemis, and of the image that fell from heaven? 36 Therefore, since these things are undeniable, you must keep calm and not do anything rash. 37 For you have brought these men here who are not temple robbers or blasphemers of our[c] goddess. 38 So if Demetrius and the craftsmen who are with him have a case against anyone, the courts are in session, and there are •proconsuls. Let them bring charges against one another. 39 But if you want something else, it must be decided in a legal assembly. 40 In fact, we run a risk of being charged with rioting for what happened today, since there is no justification that we can give as a reason for this disorderly gathering." 41 After saying this, he dismissed the assembly.

Do You Have Godly Friends to Walk With?

During difficult times, it is critical that we are walking with other Christians. When a crisis hits or a big decision must be made, it is overwhelming to have to face it alone.

Though Paul wanted to go in before the people, the disciples did not let him.

—Acts 19:30

---

[a]19:31 Lit *not to give himself*
[b]19:35 Other mss add *goddess*

[c]19:37 Other mss read *your*

313

PAUL IN MACEDONIA

20 After the uproar was over, Paul sent for the disciples, encouraged them, and after saying good-bye, departed to go to Macedonia. ² And when he had passed through those areas and exhorted them at length, he came to Greece ³ and stayed three months. When he was about to set sail for Syria, a plot was devised against him by the Jews, so a decision was made to go back through Macedonia. ⁴ He was accompanied[a] by Sopater, son of Pyrrhus,[b] from Beroea, Aristarchus and Secundus from Thessalonica, Gaius from Derbe, Timothy, and Tychicus and Trophimus from Asia. ⁵ These men went on ahead and waited for us in Troas, ⁶ but we sailed away from Philippi after the days of •Unleavened Bread. In five days we reached them at Troas, where we spent seven days.

EUTYCHUS REVIVED AT TROAS

⁷ On the first day of the week,[c] we[d] assembled to break bread. Paul spoke to them, and since he was about to depart the next day, he extended his message until midnight. ⁸ There were many lamps in the room upstairs where we were assembled, ⁹ and a young man named Eutychus was sitting on a window sill and sank into a deep sleep as Paul kept on speaking. When he was overcome by sleep he fell down from the third story, and was picked up dead. ¹⁰ But Paul went down, threw himself on him, embraced him, and said, "Don't be alarmed, for his •life is in him!" ¹¹ After going upstairs, breaking the bread, and eating, he conversed a considerable time until dawn. Then he left. ¹² They brought the boy home alive and were greatly comforted.

FROM TROAS TO MILETUS

¹³ Then we went on ahead to the ship and sailed for Assos, from there intending to take Paul on board. For these were his instructions, since he himself was going by land. ¹⁴ When he met us at Assos, we took him

---

Don't Get in a Hurry When God is Moving

There is no mistaking when God inhabits a place. God's glorious presence can fill a worship service, and it is impossible to carry on business as usual.

On the first day of the week, we assembled to break bread. Paul spoke to them, and since he was about to depart the next day, he extended his message until midnight.

—Acts 20:7

---

[a]20:4 Other mss add *to Asia*
[b]20:4 Other mss omit *son of Pyrrhus*
[c]20:7 Lit *On one between the Sabbaths*; that is, Sunday
[d]20:7 Other mss read *the disciples*

on board and came to Mitylene. ¹⁵ Sailing from there, the next day we arrived off Chios. The following day we crossed over to Samos, andᵃ the day after, we came to Miletus. ¹⁶ For Paul had decided to sail past Ephesus so he would not have to spend time in the province of Asia, because he was hurrying to be in Jerusalem, if possible, for the day of Pentecost.

FAREWELL ADDRESS TO THE EPHESIAN ELDERS

¹⁷ Now from Miletus, he sent to Ephesus and called for the elders of the church. ¹⁸ And when they came to him, he said to them: "You know, from the first day I set foot in Asia, how I was with you the whole time— ¹⁹ serving the Lord with all humility, with tears, and with the trials that came to me through the plots of the Jews— ²⁰ and that I did not shrink back from proclaiming to you anything that was profitable, or from teaching it to you in public and from house to house. ²¹ I testified to both Jews and Greeks about repentance toward God and faith in our Lord Jesus.

²² "And now I am on my way to Jerusalem, bound in my spirit, not knowing what I will encounter there, ²³ except that in town after town the Holy Spirit testifies to me that chains and afflictions are waiting for me. ²⁴ But I count my life of no value to myself, so that I may finish my courseᵇ and the ministry I received from the Lord Jesus, to testify to the gospel of God's grace.

²⁵ "And now I know that none of you, among whom I went about preaching the kingdom, will ever see my face again. ²⁶ Therefore I testify to you this day that I am innocentᶜ of everyone's blood, ²⁷ for I did not shrink back from declaring to you the whole plan of God. ²⁸ Be on guard for yourselves and for all the flock, among whom the Holy Spirit has appointed you as •overseers, to shepherd the church of God,ᵈ which He purchased with His own blood. ²⁹ I know that after my departure savage wolves will come in among you, not sparing the flock. ³⁰ And men from among yourselves will rise up with deviant doctrines to lure the disciples

WORD STUDY

Greek word: **boule** [boo LAY]

Translation: **plan**

Uses in Acts: **7**

Uses in Luke's writings: **9**

Uses in the NT: **12**

Key passage: **Acts 20:27**

The Greek noun *boule* can mean *counsel, will, plan,* or *purpose.* The related verb *boulomai* occurs 37 times in the NT (14 in Acts) and can mean *to will, purpose, plan,* or *come to a decision.* In Greek religion the term *boule* often referred to the will or plan of the gods.

In the Greek OT, *boule* normally refers to human plans or desires that may or may not occur (Ps 1:1; 14:6; 20:4; 21:11; Jb 5:12-13; Is 8:10; 19:3; 29:15; Jr 19:7), and in this sense *boule* is often advice given to royalty (2 Sm 15:31,34; 16:20,23; 1 Kg 12:8; 2 Ch 22:5). But it can also refer to God's purpose that cannot be thwarted (Jb 12:13; Ps 33:11; Pr 19:21; Is 19:17; 46:10; Jr 50:45; see Pr 21:30) and that guides His people (Ps 73:24; see Pr 1:25,30; Is 30:1).

The NT usage of *boule* is very similar to that of the Greek OT. Humans may or may not see their plans realized (Lk 7:30; 23:51; Ac 5:38; 27:12,42), but God's plans and purposes will not fail (Ac 2:23; 4:28; 13:36; Eph 1:11; Heb 6:17). Paul stated that human *boule* (desires and intentions) will be judged by God (1 Co 4:5). By contrast, Paul proclaimed God's *boule*, a reference to His revealed will and purposes for humanity which centers in Jesus Christ (Ac 20:27).

ᵃ**20:15** Other mss add *after staying at Trogyllium*
ᵇ**20:24** Other mss add *with joy*
ᶜ**20:26** Lit *clean*

ᵈ**20:28** Other mss read *church of the Lord*; other mss read *church of the Lord and God*

WORD STUDY

Greek word: **euangelistes**
[yoo ahn geh leess TAYSS]

Translation: **evangelist**

Uses in Acts: **1**

Uses in the NT: **3**

Key passage: **Acts 21:8**

The English word *evangelist* comes from the Greek noun *euangelistes*, which means *one who proclaims the gospel*. The related noun *euangelion* means *gospel* (literally *good news*), and the related verb *euaggelizo* means *to proclaim the gospel*.

In the NT, *euangelistes* occurs only three times, in sharp contract to *euangelion* (seventy-six times; two in Acts) and *euangelizo* (fifty-four times; fifteen in Acts). The word *euangelistes* has not been found in Greek literature written before the NT era, perhaps indicating that the early church coined the term and that Acts 21:8 is its earliest occurrence. Philip is called "the evangelist, who was one of the Seven" (see Ac 6:5) to distinguish him from Philip the apostle, who was one of the Twelve (Mt 10:2-4; Ac 1:13). His evangelistic activities in Samaria and Judea are recounted in Acts 8 (the verb *euangelizo* describes his work in v. 40). The other two uses of *euangelistes* are found in Paul's letters. Paul referred to "evangelists" as those who are especially gifted at sharing the gospel (Eph 4:11), and he commanded Timothy to "do the work of an evangelist" (2 Tm 4:5). The latter passage may be understood in one of two ways: (1) Timothy had the gift of evangelism and was being encouraged to keep using it; or (2) Timothy was not an evangelist, but like all Christians he had the privilege and the responsibility to evangelize or share the gospel with the lost.

into following them. ³¹ Therefore be on the alert, remembering that night and day for three years I did not stop warning each one of you with tears.

³² "And now[a] I commit you to God and to the message of His grace, which is able to build you up and to give you an inheritance among all who are sanctified. ³³ I have not coveted anyone's silver or gold or clothing. ³⁴ You yourselves know that these hands have provided for my needs, and for those who were with me. ³⁵ In every way I've shown you that by laboring like this, it is necessary to help the weak and to keep in mind the words of the Lord Jesus, for He said, 'It is more blessed to give than to receive.'"

³⁶ After he said this, he knelt down and prayed with all of them. ³⁷ There was a great deal of weeping by everyone. And embracing Paul, they kissed him, ³⁸ grieving most of all over his statement that they would never see his face again. Then they escorted him to the ship.

WARNINGS ON THE JOURNEY TO JERUSALEM

21 After we tore ourselves away from them and set sail, we came by a direct route to Cos, the next day to Rhodes, and from there to Patara. ² Finding a ship crossing over to Phoenicia, we boarded and set sail. ³ After we sighted Cyprus, leaving it on the left, we sailed on to Syria and arrived at Tyre, because the ship was to unload its cargo there. ⁴ So we found some disciples and stayed there seven days. They said to Paul through the Spirit not to go to Jerusalem. ⁵ When our days there were over, we left to continue our journey, while all of them, with their wives and children, escorted us out of the city. After kneeling down on the beach to pray, ⁶ we said good-bye to one another. Then we boarded the ship, and they returned home.

⁷ When we completed our voyage from Tyre, we reached Ptolemais, where we greeted the brothers and stayed with them one day. ⁸ The next day we left and came to Caesarea, where we entered the house of Philip the evangelist, who was one of the Seven, and stayed with him. ⁹ This man had four virgin daughters who prophesied.

---

[a]20:32 Other mss add *brothers,*

10 While we were staying there many days, a prophet named Agabus came down from Judea. 11 He came to us, took Paul's belt, tied his own feet and hands, and said, "This is what the Holy Spirit says: 'In this way the Jews in Jerusalem will bind the man who owns this belt, and deliver him into Gentile hands.'" 12 When we heard this, both we and the local people begged him not to go up to Jerusalem.

13 Then Paul replied, "What are you doing, weeping and breaking my heart? For I am ready not only to be bound, but also to die in Jerusalem for the name of the Lord Jesus."

14 Since he would not be persuaded, we stopped talking and simply said, "The Lord's will be done!"

CONFLICT OVER THE GENTILE MISSION

15 After these days we got ready and went up to Jerusalem. 16 Some of the disciples from Caesarea also went with us and brought us to Mnason, a Cypriot and an early disciple, with whom we were to stay.

17 When we reached Jerusalem, the brothers welcomed us gladly. 18 The following day Paul went in with us to James, and all the elders were present. 19 After greeting them, he related one by one what God did among the Gentiles through his ministry.

20 When they heard it, they glorified God and said, "You see, brother, how many thousands of Jews there are who have believed, and they are all zealous for the law. 21 But they have been told about you that you teach all the Jews who are among the Gentiles to abandon Moses, by telling them not to circumcise their children or to walk in our customs. 22 So what is to be done?a They will certainly hear that you've come. 23 Therefore do what we tell you: We have four men who have obligated themselves with a vow. 24 Take these men, purify yourself along with them, and pay for them to get their heads shaved. Then everyone will know that what they were told about you amounts to nothing, but that you yourself are also careful about observing the law. 25 With regard to the Gentiles who have believed, we have written a letter containing our decision thatb they should keep

We Must Often Press on Amid the Pressure

Paul could have concluded that it was best to serve in less hostile regions. Instead, he based his decisions on God's activity rather than on what people were doing.

"This is what the Holy Spirit says: 'In this way the Jews in Jerusalem will bind the man who owns this belt, and deliver him into Gentile hands.'"

—Acts 21:11b

God Can Make Your Life an Incredible Story

When Christ takes control, your life takes on dimensions you would never have known apart from Him.

After greeting them, he related one by one what God did among the Gentiles through his ministry.

—Acts 21:19

---

a21:22 Other mss add *A multitude has to come together, since*

b21:25 Other mss add *they should observe no such thing, except that*

themselves from food sacrificed to idols, from blood, from what is strangled, and from sexual immorality."

THE RIOT IN THE TEMPLE COMPLEX

26 Then the next day, Paul took the men, having purified himself along with them, and entered the temple, announcing the completion of the purification days when the offering for each of them would be made. 27 As the seven days were about to end, the Jews from the province of Asia saw him in the •temple complex, stirred up the whole crowd, and seized him, 28 shouting, "Men of Israel, help! This is the man who teaches everyone everywhere against our people, our law, and this place. What's more, he also brought Greeks into the temple and has profaned this holy place." 29 For they had previously seen Trophimus the Ephesian in the city with him, and they supposed that Paul had brought him into the temple complex.ᵃ

30 The whole city was stirred up, and the people rushed together. They seized Paul, dragged him out of the temple complex, and at once the gates were shut. 31 As they were trying to kill him, word went up to the commander of the •regiment that all Jerusalem was in chaos. 32 Taking along soldiers and •centurions, he immediately ran down to them. Seeing the commander and the soldiers, they stopped beating Paul. 33 Then the commander came up, took him into custody, and ordered him to be bound with two chains. He asked who he was and what he had done. 34 Some in the mob were shouting one thing and some another. Since he was not able to get reliable information because of the uproar, he ordered him to be taken into the barracks. 35 When Paulᵇ got to the steps, he had to be carried by the soldiers because of the mob's violence, 36 for the mass of people were following and yelling, "Kill him!"

PAUL'S DEFENSE BEFORE THE JERUSALEM MOB

37 As he was about to be brought into the barracks, Paul said to the commander, "Am I allowed to say something to you?"

God's Strength Can Lessen Your Stress

Choose to allow God's Spirit to fill you with His unquenchable joy, and your life will be a miracle to those who watch you face the trials that come.

The whole city was stirred up, and the people rushed together. They seized Paul, dragged him out of the temple complex, and at once the gates were shut. As they were trying to kill him, word went up to the commander of the regiment that all Jerusalem was in chaos.

—Acts 21:30-31

ᵃ21:29 The inner temple court for Jewish men   ᵇ21:35 Lit *he*

He replied, "Do you know Greek? [38] Aren't you the Egyptian who raised a rebellion some time ago and led 4,000 Assassins[a] into the desert?"

[39] Paul said, "I am a Jewish man from Tarsus of Cilicia, a citizen of an important city.[b] Now I ask you, let me speak to the people."

[40] After he had given permission, Paul stood on the steps and motioned with his hand to the people. When there was a great hush, he addressed them in the Hebrew language: **22** [1] "Brothers and fathers, listen now to my defense before you." [2] When they heard that he was addressing them in the Hebrew language, they became even quieter. [3] He continued, "I am a Jewish man, born in Tarsus of Cilicia, but brought up in this city[c] at the feet of Gamaliel, and educated according to the strict view of our patriarchal law. Being zealous for God, just as all of you are today, [4] I persecuted this Way to the death, binding and putting both men and women in jail, [5] as both the high priest and the whole council of elders can testify about me. Having received letters from them to the brothers, I was traveling to Damascus to bring those who were prisoners there to be punished in Jerusalem.

PAUL'S TESTIMONY

[6] "As I was traveling and near Damascus, about noon an intense light from heaven suddenly flashed around me. [7] I fell to the ground and heard a voice saying to me, 'Saul, Saul, why are you persecuting Me?'

[8] "I answered, 'Who are You, Lord?'

"He said to me, 'I am Jesus the •Nazarene, whom you are persecuting!' [9] Now those who were with me saw the light,[d] but they did not hear the voice of the One who was speaking to me.

[10] "Then I said, 'What should I do, Lord?'

"And the Lord told me, 'Get up and go into Damascus, and there you will be told about everything that is assigned for you to do.'

---

[a]21:38 Lit *4,000 men of the Assassins*; that is, *Sicarii,* a Lat loanword from *sica,* dagger; compare "cutthroats" or daggermen.
[b]21:39 Lit *of no insignificant city*

[c]22:3 Probably Jerusalem, but others think Tarsus
[d]22:9 Other mss add *and were afraid*

WORD STUDY

Greek word: *dioko*
[dee OH koh]

Translation: *persecute*

Uses in Acts: **9**

Uses in Luke's writings: **12**

Uses in the NT: **45**

Key passage: **Acts 22:4,7-8**

The Greek verb *dioko* basically means *to pursue.* In a literal sense *dioko* means *to chase* or *to hunt* (see Mt 23:34). Two related terms that do not occur very often in the NT are *diogmos* (meaning *persecution*) and *dioktes* (meaning *persecutor*). As a legal term in the ancient world, *dioko* meant *to prosecute,* and a certain form of the word meant *the prosecutor.*

In the NT, *dioko* is used in a positive sense for pursuing hospitality (Rm 12:13), peace (Rm 14:19; Heb 12:14; 1 Pt 3:11), love (1 Co 14:1), goodness (1 Th 5:15), righteousness (1 Tm 6:11), and for striving after Christian maturity (Php 3:12,14). The negative sense of *dioko* is by far the most common (thirty-two times), and it normally refers to the persecution of Jesus and God's people (see Mt 5:10-12,44; Jn 5:16,20; Rm 12:14; 1 Co 4:12; 2 Co 4:9; Gl 5:11; 2 Tm 3:12; Rv 12:13). In the book of Acts, every use of *dioko,* except one (7:52), refers to Paul's persecution of the church prior to his conversion (9:4-5; 22:4,7-8; 26:11,14-15), an aspect of Paul's pre-Christian life that he often referred to in his letters (1 Co 15:9; Gl 1:13,23; Php 3:6; see 1 Tm 1:13).

Jesus' question to Saul on the Damascus road—"why are you persecuting Me?"—indicates that He takes the persecution of His people personally (Ac 9:4-5; 22:7-8; 26:14-15).

¹¹ "Since I couldn't see because of the brightness of that light, I was led by the hand by those who were with me, and came into Damascus. ¹² Someone named Ananias, a devout man according to the law, having a good reputation with all the Jews residing there, ¹³ came to me, stood by me, and said, 'Brother Saul, regain your sight.' And in that very hour I looked up and saw him. ¹⁴ Then he said, 'The God of our fathers has appointed you to know His will, to see the Righteous One, and to hear the sound of His voice.ᵃ ¹⁵ For you will be a witness for Him to all people of what you have seen and heard. ¹⁶ And now, why delay? Get up and be baptized, and wash away your sins by calling on His name.'

¹⁷ "After I came back to Jerusalem and was praying in the •temple complex, I went into a visionary state ¹⁸ and saw Him telling me, 'Hurry and get out of Jerusalem quickly, because they will not accept your testimony about Me!'

¹⁹ "But I said, 'Lord, they know that in •synagogue after synagogue I had those who believed in You imprisoned and beaten. ²⁰ And when the blood of Your witness Stephen was being shed, I myself was standing by and approving,ᵇ and I guarded the clothes of those who killed him.'

²¹ "Then He said to me, 'Go, because I will send you far away to the Gentiles.'"

PAUL'S ROMAN PROTECTION

²² They listened to him up to this word. Then they raised their voices, shouting, "Wipe this person off the earth—it's a disgrace for him to live!"

²³ As they were yelling and flinging aside their robes and throwing dust into the air, ²⁴ the commander ordered him to be brought into the barracks, directing that he be examined with the scourge, so he could discover the reason they were shouting against him like this. ²⁵ As they stretched him out for the lash, Paul said to the •centurion standing by, "Is it legal for you to scourge a man who is a Roman citizen and is uncondemned?"

Faith Is Belief Set in Motion

There comes a time for each of us when merely talking about the Christian pilgrimage is not sufficient—we must actually set out on the journey.

"Why delay? Get up and be baptized, and wash away your sins by calling on His name."

—Acts 22:16

ᵃ22:14 Lit *to hear a voice from His mouth*   ᵇ22:20 Other mss add *of his murder*

26 When the centurion heard this, he went and reported to the commander, saying, "What are you going to do? For this man is a Roman citizen."

27 The commander came and said to him, "Tell me—are you a Roman citizen?"

"Yes," he said.

28 The commander replied, "I bought this citizenship for a large amount of money."

"But I myself was born a citizen," Paul said.

29 Therefore, those who were about to examine him withdrew from him at once. The commander too was alarmed when he realized Paul was a Roman citizen and he had bound him.

PAUL BEFORE THE SANHEDRIN

30 The next day, since he wanted to find out exactly why Paul was being accused by the Jews, he released him[a] and instructed the •chief priests and all the •Sanhedrin to convene. Then he brought Paul down and

23 placed him before them. 1 Paul looked intently at the •Sanhedrin and said, "Brothers, I have lived my life before God in all good conscience until this day." 2 But the high priest Ananias ordered those who were standing next to him to strike him on the mouth. 3 Then Paul said to him, "God is going to strike you, you whitewashed wall! You are sitting there judging me according to the law, and in violation of the law are you ordering me to be struck?"

4 And those standing nearby said, "Do you dare revile God's high priest?"

5 "I did not know, brothers," Paul said, "that it was the high priest. For it is written, **You must not speak evil of a ruler of your people.**"[b] 6 When Paul realized that one part of them were •Sadducees and the other part were •Pharisees, he cried out in the Sanhedrin, "Brothers, I am a Pharisee, a son of Pharisees! I am being judged because of the hope of the resurrection of the dead!" 7 When he said this, a dispute broke out between the Pharisees and the Sadducees, and the assembly was divided. 8 For the Sadducees say there is no

Stop Your Sins Before They Grow on You

Blameless does not mean perfect. It means that in every situation, you do the correct thing. If you sin against someone, confess it immediately and ask for forgiveness.

"I did not know, brothers," Paul said, "that it was the high priest. For it is written, You must not speak evil of a ruler of your people."
—Acts 23:5

---

[a]22:30 Other mss add *from his chains* [b]23:5 Ex 22:28

resurrection, and no angel or spirit, but the Pharisees affirm them all.

⁹ The shouting grew loud, and some of the •scribes of the Pharisees' party got up and argued vehemently: "We find nothing evil in this man. What if a spirit or an angel has spoken to him?"ᵃ ¹⁰ When the dispute became violent, the commander feared that Paul might be torn apart by them and ordered the troops to go down, rescue him from them, and bring him into the barracks.

THE PLOT AGAINST PAUL

¹¹ The following night, the Lord stood by him and said, "Have courage! For as you have testified about Me in Jerusalem, so you must also testify in Rome."

¹² When it was day, the Jews formed a conspiracy and bound themselves under a curse: neither to eat nor to drink until they had killed Paul. ¹³ There were more than 40 who had formed this plot. ¹⁴ These men went to the •chief priests and elders and said, "We have bound ourselves under a solemn curse that we won't eat anything until we have killed Paul. ¹⁵ So now you, along with the Sanhedrin, make a request to the commander that he bring him down to youᵇ as if you were going to investigate his case more thoroughly. However, before he gets near, we are ready to kill him."

¹⁶ But the son of Paul's sister, hearing about their ambush, came and entered the barracks and reported it to Paul. ¹⁷ Then Paul called one of the •centurions and said, "Take this young man to the commander, because he has something to report to him."

¹⁸ So he took him, brought him to the commander, and said, "The prisoner Paul called me and asked me to bring this young man to you, because he has something to tell you."

¹⁹ Then the commander took him by the hand, led him aside, and inquired privately, "What is it you have to report to me?"

²⁰ "The Jews," he said, "have agreed to ask you to bring Paul down to the Sanhedrin tomorrow, as though they are going to hold a somewhat more careful inquiry about him. ²¹ Don't let them persuade you, because there are more than 40 of them arranging to ambush

---

Your Rough Road May Be Right in God's Will

Don't get discouraged when you face opposition. It may indicate that you are acting in obedience to God.

The following night, the Lord stood by him and said, "Have courage! For as you have testified about Me in Jerusalem, so you must also testify in Rome."

—Acts 23:11

You Are Called to Help Those in Trouble

God did not create us as isolated individuals, each seeking to achieve his own goals. The success of our efforts depends upon our interdependence.

The son of Paul's sister, hearing about their ambush, came and entered the barracks and reported it to Paul.

—Acts 23:16

ᵃ23:9 Other mss add *Let us not fight God.*
ᵇ23:15 Other mss add *tomorrow*

him, men who have bound themselves under a curse not to eat or drink until they kill him. Now they are ready, waiting for a commitment from you."

22 So the commander dismissed the young man and instructed him, "Don't tell anyone that you have informed me about this."

TO CAESAREA BY NIGHT

23 He summoned two of his centurions and said, "Get 200 soldiers ready with 70 cavalry and 200 spearmen to go to Caesarea at nine tonight.ᵃ 24 Also provide mounts so they can put Paul on them and bring him safely to Felix the governor."

25 He wrote a letter of this kind:

26 Claudius Lysias,
To the most excellent governor Felix:
Greetings.
27 When this man had been seized by the Jews and was about to be killed by them, I arrived with my troops and rescued him because I learned that he is a Roman citizen. 28 Wanting to know the charge for which they were accusing him, I brought him down before their Sanhedrin. 29 I found out that the accusations were about disputed matters in their law, and that there was no charge that merited death or chains. 30 When I was informed that there was a plot against the man,ᵇ I sent him to you right away. I also ordered his accusers to state their case against him in your presence.ᶜ

31 Therefore, during the night, the soldiers took Paul and brought him to Antipatris as they were ordered. 32 The next day, they returned to the barracks, allowing the cavalry to go on with him. 33 When these men entered Caesarea and delivered the letter to the governor, they also presented Paul to him. 34 After heᵈ read it, he asked what province he was from. So when he learned he was from Cilicia, 35 he said, "I will give you a hearing whenever your accusers get here too." And he ordered that he be kept under guard in •Herod's palace.ᵉ

God Will Protect You in a Big Way

When you relate to God, you always deal with abundance, for God does nothing in half-measures. No one has ever exhausted God's supply of protection and provision.

He summoned two of his centurions and said, "Get 200 soldiers ready with 70 cavalry and 200 spearmen to go to Caesarea at nine tonight. Also provide mounts so they can put Paul on them and bring him safely to Felix the governor."
—Acts 23:23-24

ᵃ23:23 Lit *at the third hour tonight*
ᵇ23:30 Other mss add *by the Jews*
ᶜ23:30 Other mss add *Farewell*
ᵈ23:34 Other mss read *the governor*

ᵉ23:35 Lit *praetorium,* a Lat word that can also refer to a military headquarters, to the governor's palace, or to the emperor's imperial guard

WORD STUDY

Greek word: *apologeomai*
[ah pah lah GEH ah migh]
Translation: *offer defense*
Uses in Acts: **6**
Uses in Luke's writings: **8**
Uses in the NT: **10**
Key passage: **Acts 24:10**

The Greek verb *apologeomai* means *to speak in defense, to defend oneself.* The English word *apology* comes directly from the related Greek noun *apologia.* The term *apologia* in Greek means *defense,* not *apology.* Plato's famous work, *The Apology,* is a defense of Socrates, not an attempt to apologize for him.

In the NT, *apologia* can refer to a defense given through conduct (2 Co 7:11) or by speech (Php 1:7,16; 1 Pt 3:15)—often in a legal setting (Ac 22:1; 25:16; 2 Tm 4:16)—or in written form (1 Co 9:3). Similarly, the verb *apologeomai* normally refers to a verbal defense (Ac 19:33)—often also in a legal setting (Lk 12:11; 21:14; Ac 24:10; 25:8; 26:1-2,24)—though Paul used it once of the conscience defending itself (Rm 2:15) and once of a written defense (2 Co 12:19).

THE ACCUSATION AGAINST PAUL

24 After five days Ananias the high priest came down with some elders and a lawyer[a] named Tertullus. These men presented their case against Paul to the governor. ² When he was called in, Tertullus began to accuse him and said: "Since we enjoy great peace because of you, and reforms are taking place for the benefit of this nation by your foresight, ³ we gratefully receive them always and in all places, most excellent Felix, with all thankfulness. ⁴ However, so that I will not burden you any further, I beg you in your graciousness to give us a brief hearing. ⁵ For we have found this man to be a plague, an agitator among all the Jews throughout the Roman world, and a ringleader of the sect of the •Nazarenes! ⁶ He even tried to desecrate the temple, so we apprehended him [and wanted to judge him according to our law. ⁷ But Lysias the commander came and took him from our hands, commanding his accusers to come to you.][b] ⁸ By examining him yourself you will be able to discern all these things of which we accuse him." ⁹ The Jews also joined in the attack, alleging that these things were so.

PAUL'S DEFENSE BEFORE FELIX

¹⁰ When the governor motioned to him to speak, Paul replied: "Because I know you have been a judge of this nation for many years, I am glad to offer my defense in what concerns me. ¹¹ You are able to determine that it is no more than 12 days since I went up to worship in Jerusalem. ¹² And they didn't find me disputing with anyone or causing a disturbance among the crowd, either in the •temple complex or in the •synagogues, or anywhere in the city. ¹³ Neither can they provide evidence to you of what they now bring against me. ¹⁴ But I confess this to you: that according to the Way, which they call a sect, so I worship my fathers' God, believing all the things that are written in the Law and in the Prophets. ¹⁵ And I have a hope in God, which these men themselves also accept, that there is going to be

---

[a]**24:1** Gk *rhetor*; compare the Eng "rhetoric," "rhetorician"—an orator skilled in public speaking. In this situation, skill in the Gk language was needed.
[b]**24:6-7** Other mss omit bracketed text

a resurrection,[a] both of the righteous and the unrighteous. [16] I always do my best to have a clear conscience
toward God and men. [17] After many years, I came to
bring charitable gifts and offerings to my nation, [18] and
while I was doing this, some Jews from the province of
Asia found me ritually purified in the temple, without a
crowd and without any uproar. [19] It is they who ought
to be here before you to bring charges, if they have anything against me. [20] Either let these men here state what
wrongdoing they found in me when I stood before the
•Sanhedrin, [21] or about this one statement I cried out
while standing among them, 'Today I am being judged
before you concerning the resurrection of the dead.'"

THE VERDICT POSTPONED

[22] Since Felix was accurately informed about the
Way, he adjourned the hearing, saying, "When Lysias
the commander comes down, I will decide your case."
[23] He ordered that the •centurion keep Paul[b] under
guard, though he could have some freedom, and that
he should not prevent any of his friends from serving[c]
him.

[24] After some days, when Felix came with his wife
Drusilla, who was Jewish, he sent for Paul and listened
to him on the subject of faith in Christ Jesus. [25] Now
as he spoke about righteousness, self-control, and the
judgment to come, Felix became afraid and replied,
"Leave for now, but when I find time I'll call for you."
[26] At the same time he was also hoping that money
would be given to him by Paul.[d] For this reason he sent
for him quite often and conversed with him.

[27] After two years had passed, Felix received a successor, Porcius Festus, and because he wished to do a
favor for the Jews, Felix left Paul in prison.

APPEAL TO CAESAR

25 Three days after Festus arrived in the province,
he went up to Jerusalem from Caesarea. [2] Then
the •chief priests and the leaders of the Jews presented

A Life Without Secrets Ensures You Security

The road to peace, contentment,
and happiness is paved with truth,
honesty, and integrity—the humble,
warm realization that your life
can stand the scrutiny of God.

*"I always do my best to
have a clear conscience
toward God and men."*

—Acts 24:16

Hear God Out—He Has Your Life at Heart

The Word of God is alive and can
read your thoughts and judge your
intentions. Never try to escape the
discomfort of conviction by avoiding what God is saying to you.

*Now as he spoke about righ-
teousness, self-control, and
the judgment to come, Felix
became afraid and replied,
"Leave for now, but when I
find time I'll call for you."*

—Acts 24:25

---

[a]**24:15** Other mss add *of the dead*
[b]**24:23** Lit *him*
[c]**24:23** Other mss add *or visiting*
[d]**24:26** Other mss add *so that he
might release him*

WORD STUDY

Greek word: **Kaisar**
[KIGH sahr]
Translation: **Caesar**
Uses in Acts: **10**
Uses in Luke's writings: **17**
Uses in the NT: **29**
Key passage: **Acts 25:10**

The Greek noun *Kaisar* comes directly from the Latin word *Caesar*, the surname of the founder of the Roman Empire, Julius Caesar (ruled 60-44 B.C.). Julius Caesar's conquests and power so greatly influenced the empire that subsequent emperors took his surname as a title, starting with his successor, Gaius Octavius, better known as Caesar Augustus, who was also Julius Caesar's great nephew and adopted son.

In the NT, only three Caesars are mentioned by name: Augustus (Lk 2:1; ruled 31 B.C.-A.D. 14); Tiberius (Lk 3:1; ruled A.D. 14-37); and Claudius (Ac 11:28; 18:2; ruled A.D. 41-54). With the exception of Luke 2:1, the numerous occurrences of *Kaisar* in the Gospels are references to Tiberius, since Jesus' ministry, death, and resurrection occurred during his reign. The Caesar to whom Paul appealed for trial as a Roman citizen was Nero (Ac 25:10-12, 21; 26:32; 28:19; see Php 4:22). Paul did stand before Nero Caesar (Ac 27:24; ruled A.D. 54-68) and was eventually released. A second Roman imprisonment ended in Nero's ordering the apostle's execution about A.D. 67, just a short time before Nero himself committed suicide in A.D. 68.

their case against Paul to him; and they appealed, ³ asking him to do them a favor against Paul,[a] that he might summon him to Jerusalem. They were preparing an ambush along the road to kill him. ⁴ However, Festus answered that Paul should be kept at Caesarea, and that he himself was about to go there shortly. ⁵ "Therefore," he said, "let the men of authority among you go down with me and accuse him, if there is any wrong in this man."

⁶ When he had spent not more than eight or 10 days among them, he went down to Caesarea. The next day, seated at the judge's bench, he commanded Paul to be brought in. ⁷ When he arrived, the Jews who had come down from Jerusalem stood around him and brought many serious charges that they were not able to prove, ⁸ while Paul made the defense that, "Neither against the Jewish law, nor against the temple, nor against Caesar have I sinned at all."

⁹ Then Festus, wanting to do a favor for the Jews, replied to Paul, "Are you willing to go up to Jerusalem, there to be tried before me on these charges?"

¹⁰ But Paul said: "I am standing at Caesar's tribunal, where I ought to be tried. I have done no wrong to the Jews, as even you can see very well. ¹¹ If then I am doing wrong, or have done anything deserving of death, I do not refuse to die, but if there is nothing to what these men accuse me of, no one can give me up to them. I appeal to Caesar!"

¹² After Festus conferred with his council, he replied, "You have appealed to Caesar; to Caesar you will go!"

KING AGRIPPA AND BERNICE VISIT FESTUS

¹³ After some days had passed, King Agrippa[b] and Bernice arrived in Caesarea and paid a courtesy call on Festus. ¹⁴ Since they stayed there many days, Festus presented Paul's case to the king, saying, "There's a man who was left as a prisoner by Felix. ¹⁵ When I was in Jerusalem, the chief priests and the elders of the Jews presented their case and asked for a judgment against him. ¹⁶ I answered them that it's not the Romans' cus-

---

[a]25:3 Lit *asking a favor against him*

[b]25:13 Herod Agrippa II ruled Palestine A.D. 52-92.

tom to give any man up[a] before the accused confronts the accusers face to face and has an opportunity to give a defense concerning the charge. ¹⁷ Therefore, when they had assembled here, I did not delay. The next day I sat at the judge's bench and ordered the man to be brought in. ¹⁸ Concerning him, the accusers stood up and brought no charge of the sort I was expecting. ¹⁹ Instead they had some disagreements with him about their own religion and about a certain Jesus, a dead man whom Paul claimed to be alive. ²⁰ Since I was at a loss in a dispute over such things, I asked him if he wished to go to Jerusalem and be tried there concerning these matters. ²¹ But when Paul appealed to be held for trial by the Emperor, I ordered him to be kept in custody until I could send him to Caesar."

²² Then Agrippa said to Festus, "I would like to hear the man myself."

"Tomorrow," he said, "you will hear him."

PAUL BEFORE AGRIPPA

²³ So the next day, Agrippa and Bernice came with great pomp and entered the auditorium with the commanders and prominent men of the city. When Festus gave the command, Paul was brought in. ²⁴ Then Festus said: "King Agrippa and all men present with us, you see this man about whom the whole Jewish community has appealed to me, both in Jerusalem and here, shouting that he should not live any longer. ²⁵ Now I realized that he had not done anything deserving of death, but when he himself appealed to the Emperor, I decided to send him. ²⁶ I have nothing definite to write to the Emperor about him. Therefore, I have brought him before all of you, and especially before you, King Agrippa, so that after this examination is over, I may have something to write. ²⁷ For it seems unreasonable to me to send a prisoner and not to indicate the charges against him."

PAUL'S DEFENSE BEFORE AGRIPPA

26 Agrippa said to Paul, "It is permitted for you to speak for yourself." Then Paul stretched out

---

[a]**25:16** Other mss add *to destruction*

The Problem Is Sin, Not Side Issues

Others will often hide behind religious arguments to avoid dealing with their own sin and pride. Ask questions that get to the heart of the issue— their heart.

"Instead they had some disagreements with him about their own religion and about a certain Jesus, a dead man whom Paul claimed to be alive."
—Acts 25:19

WORD STUDY

Greek word: *ethos*
[EH thahss]

Translation: *custom*

Uses in Acts: **7**

Uses in Luke's writings: **10**

Uses in the NT: **12**

Key passage: **Acts 26:3**

The English word *ethos* comes directly from the Greek noun *ethos*, which means *custom, habit,* or *practice*. The related noun *ethikos* means *custom* or *tradition*; this term does not occur in the NT but is the basis of the English word *ethic*. The related verb *ethizo* means *to become accustomed* or *used to doing something* and occurs only in Luke 2:27.

In the NT, *ethos* has three main meanings or usages. (1) It can be equivalent to law, either the law of Moses (Ac 6:14; 15:1; 21:21) or Roman law (Ac 25:16). (2) It can refer to Jewish customs not directly addressed by the law of Moses but still meticulously followed by the Jewish people (Lk 1:9; 2:42; Jn 19:40; Ac 16:21; 26:3; 28:17). (3) It can refer to something habitual, the way things are usually done, for good or bad (Lk 22:39; Heb 10:25). In the opening words of his defense before King Agrippa, Paul may have included both the law of Moses and Jewish customs in the term *ethos* (Ac 26:3), since this king (who may have been of Jewish descent) would have been quite familiar with both.

his hand and began his defense: 2 "I consider myself fortunate, King Agrippa, that today I am going to make a defense before you about everything I am accused of by the Jews, 3 especially since you are an expert in all the Jewish customs and controversies. Therefore I beg you to listen to me patiently.

4 "All the Jews know my way of life from my youth, which was spent from the beginning among my own nation and in Jerusalem. 5 They had previously known me for quite some time, if they were willing to testify, that according to the strictest party of our religion I lived as a •Pharisee. 6 And now I stand on trial for the hope of the promise made by God to our fathers, 7 ⌊the promise⌋ our 12 tribes hope to attain as they earnestly serve Him night and day. Because of this hope I am being accused by the Jews, O king! 8 Why is it considered incredible by any of you that God raises the dead? 9 In fact, I myself supposed it was necessary to do many things in opposition to the name of Jesus the •Nazarene. 10 This I actually did in Jerusalem, and I locked up many of the saints in prison, since I had received authority for that from the •chief priests. When they were put to death, I cast my vote against them. 11 In all the •synagogues I often tried to make them blaspheme by punishing them. Being greatly enraged at them, I even pursued them to foreign cities.

PAUL'S ACCOUNT OF HIS CONVERSION AND COMMISSION

12 "Under these circumstances I was traveling to Damascus with authority and a commission from the chief priests. 13 At midday, while on the road, O king, I saw a light from heaven brighter than the sun, shining around me and those traveling with me. 14 When we had all fallen to the ground, I heard a voice speaking to me in the Hebrew language, 'Saul, Saul, why are you persecuting Me? It is hard for you to kick against the goads.'[a]

15 "But I said, 'Who are You, Lord?'

"And the Lord replied: 'I am Jesus, whom you are persecuting. 16 But get up and stand on your feet. For I have appeared to you for this purpose, to appoint you

---

[a]26:14 Sharp sticks used to prod animals, such as oxen in plowing

as a servant and a witness of things you have seen,[a] and of things in which I will appear to you. 17 I will rescue you from the people and from the Gentiles, to whom I now send you, 18 to open their eyes that they may turn from darkness to light and from the power of Satan to God, that they may receive forgiveness of sins and a share among those who are sanctified by faith in Me.'

19 "Therefore, King Agrippa, I was not disobedient to the heavenly vision. 20 Instead, I preached to those in Damascus first, and to those in Jerusalem and in all the region of Judea, and to the Gentiles, that they should repent and turn to God, and do works worthy of repentance. 21 For this reason the Jews seized me in the •temple complex and were trying to kill me. 22 Since I have obtained help that comes from God, to this day I stand and testify to both small and great, saying nothing else than what the prophets and Moses said would take place— 23 that the •Messiah must suffer, and that as the first to rise from the dead, He would proclaim light to our people and to the Gentiles."

NOT QUITE PERSUADED

24 As he was making his defense this way, Festus exclaimed in a loud voice, "You're out of your mind, Paul! Too much study is driving you mad!"

25 But Paul replied, "I'm not out of my mind, most excellent Festus. On the contrary, I'm speaking words of truth and good judgment. 26 For the king knows about these matters. It is to him I am actually speaking boldly. For I'm not convinced that any of these things escapes his notice, since this was not done in a corner! 27 King Agrippa, do you believe the prophets? I know you believe."

28 Then Agrippa said to Paul, "Are you going to persuade me to become a Christian so easily?"

29 "I wish before God," replied Paul, "that whether easily or with difficulty, not only you but all who listen to me today might become as I am—except for these chains."

30 So the king, the governor, Bernice, and those sitting with them got up, 31 and when they had left they

---

[a]26:16 Other mss read *things in which you have seen Me*

Can You Honestly Say That You've Obeyed?

Oh, to have Paul's tenacity and devotion to the Father's will! It is God's desire that each of us could say at the end of our lives, "I was not disobedient."

"King Agrippa, I was not disobedient to the heavenly vision."

—Acts 26:19

Is Faithful Obedience Considered Abnormal?

Have we sunk so far below God's standard that when someone does live as God intended, we consider that person fanatical or superspiritual?

Paul replied, "I'm not out of my mind, most excellent Festus. On the contrary, I'm speaking words of truth and good judgment."

—Acts 26:25

WORD STUDY

Greek word: *hekatontarches*
[heh kah tahn TAHR kayss]

Translation: *centurion*

Uses in Acts: **13**

Uses in Luke's writings: **16**

Uses in the NT: **20**

Key passages: **Acts 27:1,6,11,31,43**

The Greek noun *hekatontarches* literally means *leader of a hundred*. This is also the meaning of the equivalent Latin term *centurio*, which is the basis of the English word *centurion* (compare century, a hundred years, and cent, one hundredth of a dollar). The Greek form of the Latin word is *kenturion* and occurs only in Mark 15:39,44-45. All other references to centurions use the Greek term *hekatontarches*. Centurions are mentioned on two occasions in Jesus' life. When a centurion requested that Jesus heal his servant without going to his home, Jesus marveled at this Gentile's faith and healed the servant from a distance (Mt 8:5-13 = Lk 7:1-10). At the crucifixion, a centurion proclaimed Jesus to be God's Son (Mt 27:54 = Mk 15:39) and a righteous person (Lk 23:47), and later informed Pilate of His death (Mk 15:44-45). Acts records the conversion of a God-fearing centurion who became one of the first Gentile converts (Ac 10:1-8, 17-48). The other eleven references to centurions are in relation to Paul's arrest in Jerusalem and subsequent journey to Rome (Ac 21-28).

Centurions were non-commissioned officers in the Roman army. A Roman legion had 6,000 soldiers, which were divided into ten cohorts of 600 soldiers. Each cohort was also divided into six centuries (100 soldiers), each with its own centurion.

---

talked with each other and said, "This man is doing nothing that deserves death or chains."
32 Then Agrippa said to Festus, "This man could have been released if he had not appealed to Caesar."

SAILING FOR ROME

27 When it was decided that we were to sail to Italy, they handed over Paul and some other prisoners to a •centurion named Julius, of the Imperial •Regiment. 2 So when we had boarded a ship of Adramyttium, we put to sea, intending to sail to ports along the coast of the province of Asia. Aristarchus, a Macedonian of Thessalonica, was with us. 3 The next day we put in at Sidon, and Julius treated Paul kindly and allowed him to go to his friends to receive their care. 4 When we had put out to sea from there, we sailed along the northern coast[a] of Cyprus because the winds were against us. 5 After sailing through the open sea off Cilicia and Pamphylia, we reached Myra in Lycia. 6 There the centurion found an Alexandrian ship sailing for Italy and put us on board. 7 Sailing slowly for many days, we came with difficulty as far as Cnidus. But since the wind did not allow us to approach it, we sailed along the south side[a] of Crete off Salmone. 8 With yet more difficulty we sailed along the coast, and came to a place called Fair Havens near the city of Lasea.

PAUL'S ADVICE IGNORED

9 By now much time had passed, and the voyage was already dangerous. Since the Fast[b] was already over, Paul gave his advice 10 and told them, "Men, I can see that this voyage is headed toward damage and heavy loss, not only of the cargo and the ship, but also of our lives." 11 But the centurion paid attention to the captain and the owner of the ship rather than to what Paul said. 12 Since the harbor was unsuitable to winter in, the majority decided to set sail from there, hoping somehow to reach Phoenix, a harbor on Crete open to the southwest and northwest, and to winter there.

---

[a]27:4,7 Lit *sailed under the lee*   [b]27:9 The Day of Atonement

STORM-TOSSED VESSEL

13 When a gentle south wind sprang up, they thought they had achieved their purpose; they weighed anchor and sailed along the shore of Crete. 14 But not long afterwards, a fierce wind called the "northeaster"[a] rushed down from the island.[b] 15 Since the ship was caught and was unable to head into the wind, we gave way to it and were driven along. 16 After running under the shelter of a little island called Cauda,[c] we were barely able to get control of the skiff. 17 After hoisting it up, they used ropes and tackle and girded the ship. Then, fearing they would run aground on the Syrtis,[d] they lowered the drift-anchor, and in this way they were driven along. 18 Because we were being severely battered by the storm, they began to jettison the cargo the next day. 19 On the third day, they threw the ship's gear overboard with their own hands.

20 For many days neither sun nor stars appeared, and the severe storm kept raging; finally all hope that we would be saved was disappearing. 21 Since many were going without food, Paul stood up among them and said, "You men should have followed my advice not to sail from Crete and sustain this damage and loss. 22 Now I urge you to take courage, because there will be no loss of any of your lives, but only of the ship. 23 For this night an angel of the God I belong to and serve stood by me, 24 saying, 'Don't be afraid, Paul. You must stand before Caesar. And, look! God has graciously given you all those who are sailing with you.' 25 Therefore, take courage, men, because I believe God that it will be just the way it was told to me. 26 However, we must run aground on a certain island."

27 When the fourteenth night came, we were drifting in the Adriatic Sea,[e] and in the middle of the night the sailors thought they were approaching land.[f] 28 They took a sounding and found it to be 120 feet[g] deep; when they had sailed a little farther and sounded again, they found it to be 90 feet[h] deep. 29 Then, fearing we might

Pass Along the Good Word of God

Those who are sensitive to God's voice know just what to say and do to encourage others who are going through difficult times.

"Take courage, men, because I believe God that it will be just the way it was told to me."

—Acts 27:25

---

[a]27:14 Lit *Euraquilo,* a violent northeast wind
[b]27:14 Lit *from her*
[c]27:16 Or *Clauda*
[d]27:17 *Syrtis* = sand banks or bars near North Africa
[e]27:27 Part of the northern Mediterranean Sea; not the modern Adriatic Sea east of Italy
[f]27:27 Lit *thought there was land approaching them*
[g]27:28 Lit *20 fathoms*
[h]27:28 Lit *15 fathoms*

run aground in some rocky place, they dropped four anchors from the stern and prayed for daylight to come.

³⁰ Some sailors tried to escape from the ship; they had let down the skiff into the sea, pretending that they were going to put out anchors from the bow. ³¹ Paul said to the centurion and the soldiers, "Unless these men stay in the ship, you cannot be saved." ³² Then the soldiers cut the ropes holding the skiff and let it drop away.

³³ When it was just about daylight, Paul urged them all to take food, saying, "Today is the fourteenth day that you have been waiting and going without food, having eaten nothing. ³⁴ Therefore I urge you to take some food. For this has to do with your survival, since not a hair will be lost from the head of any of you." ³⁵ After he said these things and had taken some bread, he gave thanks to God in the presence of them all, and when he had broken it, he began to eat. ³⁶ They all became encouraged and took food themselves. ³⁷ In all there were 276 of us on the ship. ³⁸ And having eaten enough food, they began to lighten the ship by throwing the grain overboard into the sea.

SHIPWRECK

³⁹ When daylight came, they did not recognize the land, but sighted a bay with a beach. They planned to run the ship ashore if they could. ⁴⁰ After casting off the anchors, they left them in the sea, at the same time loosening the ropes that held the rudders. Then they hoisted the foresail to the wind and headed for the beach. ⁴¹ But they struck a sandbar and ran the ship aground. The bow jammed fast and remained immovable, but the stern began to break up with the pounding of the waves.

⁴² The soldiers' plan was to kill the prisoners so that no one could swim off and escape. ⁴³ But the centurion kept them from carrying out their plan because he wanted to save Paul, so he ordered those who could swim to jump overboard first and get to land. ⁴⁴ The rest were to follow, some on planks and some on debris from the ship. In this way, all got safely to land.

Every Experience Is an Opportunity to Witness

Regardless of his circumstance, Paul's concern was how he could use his current situation to show forth the goodness of God and the power of His salvation.

After he said these things and had taken some bread, he gave thanks to God in the presence of them all, and when he had broken it, he began to eat.

—Acts 27:35

MALTA'S HOSPITALITY

28 Safely ashore, we then learned that the island was called Malta. ² The local people showed us extraordinary kindness, for they lit a fire and took us all in, since rain was falling and it was cold. ³ As Paul gathered a bundle of brushwood and put it on the fire, a viper came out because of the heat and fastened itself to his hand. ⁴ When the local people saw the creature hanging from his hand, they said to one another, "This man is probably a murderer, and though he has escaped the sea, Justiceª does not allow him to live!" ⁵ However, he shook the creature off into the fire and suffered no harm. ⁶ They expected that he would swell up or suddenly drop dead. But after they waited a long time and saw nothing unusual happen to him, they changed their minds and said he was a god.

MINISTRY IN MALTA

⁷ Now in the area around that place was an estate belonging to the leading man of the island, named Publius, who welcomed us and entertained us hospitably for three days. ⁸ It happened that Publius' father was in bed suffering from fever and dysentery. Paul went to him, and praying and laying his hands on him, he healed him. ⁹ After this, the rest of those on the island who had diseases also came and were cured. ¹⁰ So they heaped many honors on us, and when we sailed, they gave us what we needed.

ROME AT LAST

¹¹ After three months we set sail in an Alexandrian ship that had wintered at the island, with the Twin Brothersᵇ as its figurehead. ¹² Putting in at Syracuse, we stayed three days. ¹³ From there, after making a circuit along the coast,ᶜ we reached Rhegium. After one day a south wind sprang up, and the second day we came to Puteoli. ¹⁴ There we found believersᵈ and were invited to stay with them for seven days.

ª**28:4** Gk *Dike*, a goddess of justice
ᵇ**28:11** Gk *Dioscuri*, twin sons of Zeus
ᶜ**28:13** Other mss read *From there, casting off,*
ᵈ**28:14** Lit *brothers*

WORD STUDY

Greek word: ***therapeuo***
[theh rah pyoo oh]

Translation: ***cure***

Uses in Acts: **5**

Uses in Luke's writings: **19**

Uses in the NT: **43**

Key passage: **Acts 28:9**

The English words *therapy* and *therapeutic* come from the Greek verb *therapeuo*. In ancient Greek, therapeuo had a variety of meanings, such as *to be an attendant*, *do service*, particularly to the gods, human masters, or one's parents; *to serve* or *to take care of*, particularly by the gods on behalf of humans; *to cultivate*, particularly of land; and *to heal* or *to cure*, particularly in a medical sense. In the Greek OT, *therapeuo* is rare and always means *to serve*, normally serving royalty; it never means *to heal*. Two related nouns that are rare both in the Greek OT and the NT are *therapeia*, meaning *healing* (Lk 9:11; Rv 22:2) or *a group of servants* (Lk 12:42), and *therapon*, meaning *servant* (Heb 3:5).

In the NT, *therapeuo* always means *to heal* or *to cure*, and the dominant use of the term is to describe miracles. The word occurs 36 times in the Gospels (Mt 16; Mk 5; Lk 14; Jn 1), and 28 of them are in reference to the miraculous power of Jesus to heal the sick or demon-possessed; five times it refers to the twelve disciples' ability to heal miraculously (Mt 10:1,8 = Mk 6:13 = Lk 9:1,6; once for the seventy, see Lk 10:9), and once to their inability (Mt 17:16). The book of Acts uses *therapeuo* to record four instances of miraculous healing by the disciples (Peter, 4:14; the twelve apostles, 5:16; Philip the deacon, 8:7; Paul, 28:9). Once *therapeuo* is used in its more common sense of *to serve* (Ac 17:25).

And so we came to Rome. [15] Now the believers[a] from there had heard the news about us and had come to meet us as far as Forum of Appius and Three Taverns. When Paul saw them, he thanked God and took courage. [16] And when we entered Rome,[b] Paul was permitted to stay by himself with the soldier who guarded him.

PAUL'S FIRST INTERVIEW WITH ROMAN JEWS

[17] After three days he called together the leaders of the Jews. And when they had gathered he said to them: "Brothers, although I have done nothing against our people or the customs of our forefathers, I was delivered as a prisoner from Jerusalem into the hands of the Romans [18] who, after examining me, wanted to release me, since I had not committed a capital offense. [19] Because the Jews objected, I was compelled to appeal to Caesar; it was not as though I had any accusation against my nation. [20] So, for this reason I've asked to see you and speak to you. In fact, it is for the hope of Israel that I'm wearing this chain."

[21] And they said to him, "We haven't received any letters about you from Judea; none of the brothers has come and reported or spoken anything evil about you. [22] But we consider it suitable to hear from you what you think. For concerning this sect, we are aware that it is spoken against everywhere."

THE RESPONSE TO PAUL'S MESSAGE

[23] After arranging a day with him, many came to him at his lodging. From dawn to dusk he expounded and witnessed about the kingdom of God. He persuaded them concerning Jesus from both the Law of Moses and the Prophets. [24] Some were persuaded by what he said, but others did not believe.

[25] Disagreeing among themselves, they began to leave after Paul made one statement: "The Holy Spirit correctly spoke through the prophet Isaiah to your[c] forefathers [26] when He said,

People Will Come to You to Find Jesus

People who walk in a dynamic relationship with Christ are able to witness by their very nature and draw other people to Him.

After arranging a day with him, many came to him at his lodging. From dawn to dusk he expounded and witnessed about the kingdom of God. He persuaded them concerning Jesus from both the Law of Moses and the Prophets.

—Acts 28:23

---

[a]**28:15** Lit *brothers*
[b]**28:16** Other mss add *the centurion turned the prisoners over to the military commander; but*
[c]**28:25** Other mss read *our*

Go to this people and say:
'You will listen and listen,
  yet never understand;
and you will look and look,
  yet never perceive.
27 For this people's heart has grown callous,
  their ears are hard of hearing,
and they have shut their eyes; otherwise
  they might see with their eyes
and hear with their ears,
  understand with their heart,
and be converted—and I would heal them.'a

28 Therefore, let it be known to you that this saving work of God has been sent to the Gentiles; they will listen!" [29 After he said these things, the Jews departed, while engaging in a prolonged debate among themselves.]b

PAUL'S MINISTRY UNHINDERED

30 Then he stayed two whole years in his own rented house. And he welcomed all who visited him, 31 proclaiming the kingdom of God and teaching the things concerning the Lord Jesus Christ with full boldness and without hindrance.

Walk with Jesus All the Way Home

Paul remained committed to the kingdom of God to the very end of his life. The person whose life has been transformed by Christ will belong to Christ alone.

He stayed two whole years in his own rented house. And he welcomed all who visited him, proclaiming the kingdom of God and teaching the things concerning the Lord Jesus Christ with full boldness and without hindrance.

—Acts 28:30-31

---

a28:26-27 Is 6:9-10   b28:29 Other mss omit bracketed text

THE APOSTLE PAUL'S
LETTER TO THE

ROMANS

GOD'S GOOD NEWS FOR ROME

1 Paul, a slave of Christ Jesus, called as an apostle[a] and singled out for God's good news— 2 which He promised long ago through His prophets in the Holy Scriptures— 3 concerning His Son, Jesus Christ our Lord, who was a descendant of David[b] according to the flesh 4 and was established as the powerful Son of God by the resurrection from the dead according to the Spirit of holiness.[c] 5 We have received grace and apostleship through Him to bring about[d] the obedience of faith[e] among all the nations,[f] on behalf of His name, 6 including yourselves who are also Jesus Christ's by calling:

7 To all who are in Rome, loved by God, called as saints.

Grace to you and peace from God our Father and the Lord Jesus Christ.

THE APOSTLE'S DESIRE TO VISIT ROME

8 First, I thank my God through Jesus Christ for all of you because the news of your faith[g] is being reported in all the world. 9 For God, whom I serve with my spirit in ⌊telling⌋ the good news about His Son, is my witness that I constantly mention you, 10 always asking in my prayers that if it is somehow in God's will, I may now at last succeed in coming to you. 11 For I want very much to see you, that I may impart to you some spiritual gift to

---

[a]1:1 Or *Jesus, a called apostle*
[b]1:3 Lit *was of the seed of David*
[c]1:4 Or *the spirit of holiness*, or *the Holy Spirit*
[d]1:5 Lit *Him into*, or *Him for*
[e]1:5 Or *the obedience that is faith*, or *the faithful obedience*, or *the obedience that comes from faith*
[f]1:5 Or *Gentiles*
[g]1:8 Or *because your faith*

strengthen you, [12] that is, to be mutually encouraged by each other's faith, both yours and mine.

[13] Now I want you to know,[a] brothers, that I often planned to come to you (but was prevented until now) in order that I might have a fruitful ministry[b] among you, just as among the rest of the Gentiles. [14] I am obligated both to Greeks and barbarians,[c] both to the wise and the foolish. [15] So I am eager to preach the good news to you also who are in Rome.

THE RIGHTEOUS WILL LIVE BY FAITH

[16] For I am not ashamed of the gospel,[d] because it is God's power for salvation to everyone who believes, first to the Jew, and also to the Greek. [17] For in it God's righteousness is revealed from faith to faith,[e] just as it is written: **The righteous will live by faith.**[f][g]

THE GUILT OF THE GENTILE WORLD

[18] For God's wrath is revealed from heaven against all godlessness and unrighteousness of people who by their unrighteousness suppress the truth, [19] since what can be known[h] about God is evident among them, because God has shown it to them. [20] From the creation of the world His invisible attributes, that is, His eternal power and divine nature, have been clearly seen, being understood through what He has made. As a result, people[i] are without excuse. [21] For though they knew God, they did not glorify Him as God or show gratitude. Instead, their thinking became nonsense, and their senseless minds[j] were darkened. [22] Claiming to be wise, they became fools [23] and exchanged the glory of the immortal God for images resembling mortal man, birds, four-footed animals, and reptiles.

[24] Therefore God delivered them over in the cravings of their hearts to sexual impurity, so that their bodies were degraded among themselves. [25] They exchanged the truth of God for a lie, and worshiped and

---

[a]1:13 Lit I don't want you to be unaware
[b]1:13 Lit have some fruit
[c]1:14 Or non-Greeks
[d]1:16 Other mss add of Christ
[e]1:17 Or revealed out of faith into faith

[f]1:17 Or The one who is righteous by faith will live
[g]1:17 Hab 2:4
[g]1:19 Or what is known
[i]1:20 Lit they
[j]1:21 Lit hearts

WORD STUDY

Greek word: **dunamis**
[DOO nah mihss]

Translation: **power**

Uses in Romans: **8**

Uses in Paul's writings: **49**

Uses in the NT: **119**

Key passage: **Romans 1:16**

The English words *dynamic* and *dynamite* come directly from the Greek noun *dunamis*, though *dynamite* is far removed from the meaning of *dunamis*. The term *dunamis* can mean *power*, *might*, *strength*, or *ability*; the related verb *dunamai* means *to be able* (210 uses in the NT), and the adjective *dunatos* means *possible*. The synonym *exousia* means *power* or *authority* and usually refers to derived authority, whereas *dunamis* normally refers to inherent power.

Various kinds of power are described by the term *dunamis*, and the eight occurrences of the term in Romans effectively demonstrate this flexibility. In 1:16 *dunamis* refers to the gospel that has been infused with God's power so people can be saved (see 1 Co 1:18). *Dunamis* is also used to refer to God's omnipotence (Rm 1:20; see also 9:17), to the Son's power (1:4; see Mk 5:30; 13:26), and to the Spirit's power (Rm 15:13,19; see Lk 4:14). In 8:38 *dunamis* is used as a way of referring to demons (as in Eph 6:12; see Mk 13:25). Finally, *dunamis* is used as one of the words for miracles (Rm 15:19; see Mt 7:22; 11:20-21; Mk 6:2; Lk 19:37; Ac 2:22; 8:13; 19:11; 1 Co 12:10; 2 Co 12:12). Other uses of *dunamis* in the NT are: a name for God ("the Power"; Mk 14:62); natural human ability (Mt 25:15); Satan's power (Lk 10:19; Satanic miracles in 2 Th 2:9); and God's power in believers (Lk 9:1; 24:49; Ac 1:8; 6:8; 1 Co 2:4; Eph 1:19; 3:20).

WORD STUDY

Greek word: *prasso*
[PRAHSS oh]

Translation: *do*

Uses in Romans: **10**

Uses in Paul's writings: **18**

Uses in the NT: **39**

Key passage: **Romans 2:1-3**

In ancient Greek, the verb *prasso* had a variety of meanings, such as *to practice, effect, transact, negotiate, manage, achieve, accomplish,* and *make*. The term could also mean *to mind one's own affairs or business,* and it often occurred in connection with collecting taxes. In general, *prasso* meant *to do* or *to act* and could refer to almost any action. The corresponding noun *praxis* means *deed, action,* or *practice;* the plural form of this term is the first word of the Greek name for the book of Acts (*Praxeis Apostolon,* literally, "Actions of [the] Apostles").

Prasso in the NT ordinarily follows standard Greek usage. The meaning *to do* or *to act* is best seen in the six contexts where it is parallel with *poieo,* the more common term for *to do* (Jn 5:29; Rm 1:32; 2:3; 7:15,19; 13:4). However, *prasso* can also refer to specific actions such as collecting taxes (Lk 3:13) or interest (Lk 19:33). The term commonly emphasizes the experience in an action rather than just the action itself. It can refer to doing good (Ac 26:20; Rm 2:25; Php 4:9; 1 Th 4:11), but most often it refers to habitual evil actions (Lk 22:23; 23:15,41; Jn 3:20; Ac 3:17; 19:19, 36; 2 Co 12:21; Gl 5:21), especially in Romans (1:32; 2:1-3; 7:15,19; 13:4).

served something created instead of the Creator, who is blessed forever. •Amen.

FROM IDOLATRY TO DEPRAVITY

[26] This is why God delivered them over to degrading passions. For even their females exchanged natural sexual intercourse[a] for what is unnatural. [27] The males in the same way also left natural sexual intercourse[a] with females and were inflamed in their lust for one another. Males committed shameless acts with males and received in their own persons[b] the appropriate penalty for their perversion.[c]

[28] And because they did not think it worthwhile to have God in their knowledge, God delivered them over to a worthless mind to do what is morally wrong. [29] They are filled with all unrighteousness,[d] evil, greed, and wickedness. They are full of envy, murder, disputes, deceit, and malice. They are gossips, [30] slanderers, God-haters, arrogant, proud, boastful, inventors of evil, disobedient to parents, [31] undiscerning, untrustworthy, unloving,[e] and unmerciful. [32] Although they know full well God's just sentence—that those who practice such things deserve to die[f]—they not only do them, but even applaud[g] others who practice them.

GOD'S RIGHTEOUS JUDGMENT

2 Therefore, anyone of you[h] who judges is without excuse. For when you judge another, you condemn yourself, since you, the judge, do the same things. [2] We know that God's judgment on those who do such things is based on the truth. [3] Do you really think—anyone of you who judges those who do such things yet do the same—that you will escape God's judgment? [4] Or do you despise the riches of His kindness, restraint, and patience, not recognizing[i] that God's kindness is intended to lead you to repentance? [5] But because of your hardness and unrepentant heart you are storing

---

[a]1:26,27 Lit *natural use*
[b]1:27 Or *in themselves*
[c]1:27 Or *error*
[d]1:29 Other mss add *sexual immorality*
[e]1:31 Other mss add *unforgiving*

[f]1:32 Lit *things are worthy of death*
[g]1:32 Lit *even take pleasure in*
[h]2:1 Lit *Therefore, O man, every one*
[i]2:4 Or *patience, because you do not recognize*

up wrath for yourself in the day of wrath, when God's righteous judgment is revealed. [6] He **will repay each one according to his works**:[a] [7] eternal life to those who by patiently doing good seek for glory, honor, and immortality; [8] but wrath and indignation to those who are self-seeking and disobey the truth, but are obeying unrighteousness; [9] affliction and distress for every human being who does evil, first to the Jew, and also to the Greek; [10] but glory, honor, and peace for everyone who does good, first to the Jew, and also to the Greek. [11] There is no favoritism with God.

[12] All those who sinned without the law will also perish without the law, and all those who sinned under the law will be judged by the law. [13] For the hearers of the law are not righteous before God, but the doers of the law will be declared righteous.[b] [14] So, when Gentiles, who do not have the law, instinctively do what the law demands, they are a law to themselves even though they do not have the law. [15] They show that the work of the law[c] is written on their hearts. Their consciences testify in support of this, and their competing thoughts either accuse or excuse them[d] [16] on the day when God judges what people have kept secret, according to my gospel through Christ Jesus.

JEWISH VIOLATION OF THE LAW

[17] Now if[e] you call yourself a Jew, and rest in the law, and boast in God, [18] and know His will, and approve the things that are superior, being instructed from the law, [19] and are convinced that you are a guide for the blind, a light to those in darkness, [20] an instructor of the ignorant, a teacher of the immature, having in the law the full expression[f] of knowledge and truth— [21] you then, who teach another, do you not teach yourself? You who preach, "You must not steal"— do you steal? [22] You who say, "You must not commit adultery"—do you commit adultery? You who detest idols, do you rob their temples? [23] You who boast in the law, do you dishonor God by breaking the law? [24] For,

Make Every Day a Step in God's Direction

The world is preoccupied with the past, focusing on what they are overcoming. But Christians keep their eyes on the future, and focus on what they are becoming.

He will repay each one according to his works: eternal life to those who by patiently doing good seek for glory, honor, and immortality.

—Romans 2:6-7

Do You Have a Teachable Spirit?

Religious people with the most knowledge are sometimes the ones least responsive to God's Word. Knowledge easily leads to pride, and pride impedes us from seeking God.

You then, who teach another, do you not teach yourself?

—Romans 2:21a

---

[a]**2:6** Ps 62:12; Pr 24:12
[b]**2:13** Or *will be justified* or *acquitted*
[c]**2:15** The code of conduct required by the law
[d]**2:15** Internal debate, either in a person or among the pagan moralists
[e]**2:17** Other mss read *Look—*
[f]**2:20** Or *the embodiment*

as it is written: **The name of God is blasphemed among the Gentiles because of you.**[a]

CIRCUMCISION OF THE HEART

25 For circumcision benefits you if you observe the law, but if you are a lawbreaker, your circumcision has become uncircumcision. 26 Therefore if an uncircumcised man keeps the law's requirements, will his uncircumcision not be counted as circumcision? 27 A man who is physically uncircumcised, but who fulfills the law, will judge you who are a lawbreaker in spite of having the letter ‚of the law‚ and circumcision. 28 For a person is not a Jew who is one outwardly, and ‚true‚ circumcision is not something visible in the flesh. 29 On the contrary, a person is a Jew who is one inwardly, and circumcision is of the heart—by the Spirit, not the letter.[b] His praise[c] is not from men but from God.

PAUL ANSWERS AN OBJECTION

3 So what advantage does the Jew have? Or what is the benefit of circumcision? 2 Considerable in every way. First, they were entrusted with the spoken words of God. 3 What then? If some did not believe, will their unbelief cancel God's faithfulness? 4 Absolutely not! God must be true, but everyone is a liar, as it is written:

That You may be justified in Your words and triumph when You judge.[d]

5 But if our unrighteousness highlights[e] God's righteousness, what are we to say? I use a human argument:[f] Is God unrighteous to inflict wrath? 6 Absolutely not! Otherwise, how will God judge the world? 7 But if by my lie God's truth is amplified to His glory, why am I also still judged as a sinner? 8 And why not say, just as some people slanderously claim we say, "Let us do evil so that good may come"? Their condemnation is deserved!

God's Smile Should Be Reward Enough

The pleasure that your life gives to God should be your motivation to live righteously.

On the contrary, a person is a Jew who is one inwardly, and circumcision is of the heart—by the Spirit, not the letter. His praise is not from men but from God.

—Romans 2:29

God's Way Is the Right Way

Much of the frustration we experience as Christians has nothing to do with what God does or doesn't do, but with our false assumptions about how we think God will and should act.

Absolutely not! God must be true, but everyone is a liar.

—Romans 3:4a

---

[a]2:24 Is 52:5
[b]2:29 Or *heart—spiritually, not literally*
[c]2:29 In Hb, the words *Jew, Judah,* and *praise* are related.
[d]3:4 Ps 51:4
[e]3:5 Or *shows,* or *demonstrates*
[f]3:5 Lit *I speak as a man*

THE WHOLE WORLD GUILTY BEFORE GOD

[9] What then? Are we any better?[a] Not at all! For we have previously charged that both Jews and Gentiles[b] are all under sin,[c] [10] as it is written:[d]

> There is no one righteous, not even one;
> [11] there is no one who understands,
>   there is no one who seeks God.
> [12] All have turned away,
>   together they have become useless;
>   there is no one who does good,
>   there is not even one.[e]
> [13] Their throat is an open grave;
>   they deceive with their tongues.[f]
>   Vipers' venom is under their lips.[g]
> [14] Their mouth is full of cursing
>   and bitterness.[h]
> [15] Their feet are swift to shed blood;
> [16] ruin and wretchedness are in their paths,
> [17] and the path of peace they have not known.[i]
> [18] There is no fear of God before their eyes.[j]

[19] Now we know that whatever the law says speaks to those who are subject to the law,[k] so that every mouth may be shut and the whole world may become subject to God's judgment.[l] [20] For no flesh will be justified[m] in His sight by the works of the law, for through the law ⌊comes⌋ the knowledge of sin.

GOD'S RIGHTEOUSNESS THROUGH FAITH

[21] But now, apart from the law, God's righteousness has been revealed—attested by the Law and the Prophets[n] [22] —that is, God's righteousness through

Seek Those Who Are Seeking God

No one is going to seek God on his own initiative. When you see someone seeking God or asking about spiritual matters, you are seeing God at work.

There is no one who understands, there is no one who seeks God.
—Romans 3:11

Where Is God in All Our Thinking?

If we treat our sin lightly, we demonstrate that we have no sense of the enormity of our offense against Almighty God.

There is no fear of God before their eyes.
—Romans 3:18

---

[a]3:9 Are we Jews any better than the Gentiles?
[b]3:9 Lit *Greeks*
[c]3:9 Under sin's power or dominion
[d]3:10 Paul constructs this charge from a chain of OT quotations, mainly from the Psalms.
[e]3:10-12 Ps 14:1-3; 53:1-3; see Ec 7:20
[f]3:13 Ps 5:9
[g]3:13 Ps 140:3
[h]3:14 Ps 10:7
[i]3:15-17 Is 59:7-8
[j]3:18 Ps 36:1
[k]3:19 Lit *those in the law*
[k]3:19 Or *become guilty before God*, or *may be accountable to God*
[m]3:20 Or *will be declared righteous*, or *will be acquitted*
[n]3:21 When capitalized, *the Law and the Prophets* = OT

WORD STUDY

Greek word: *hilasterion*
[hih lahss TAY ree ahn]

Translation: *propitiation*

Uses in Romans: **1**

Uses in the NT: **2**

Key passage: **Romans 3:25**

The Greek noun *hilasterion* in Rm 3:25 is rich with theological meaning, though the word family is rare in the NT. The only other place this term occurs in the NT is Hebrews 9:5, which says that the cherubim above the ark of the covenant in the Most Holy Place were "overshadowing the mercy seat." In the OT, the word is used for the lid of the ark of the covenant (traditionally called "the mercy seat"; see Ex 25:17-22; Lv 16:2,13-15). Another related word, *hilasmos,* occurs twice in the NT (1 Jn 2:2; 4:10). This word family refers to the turning away of God's wrath against sin by means of a sacrifice. The same concept also occurs in nonbiblical Greek literature, such as Homer and Plutarch, for appeasing the wrath of the gods through sacrifice.

The main ideas of this word group are *mercy* and *satisfactory sacrifice for sin.* The innermost part of the tabernacle was the place where mercy was found, but only through the proper sacrifice. The glory of God's presence dwelled in the Most Holy Place of the tabernacle. Inside were the ark of the covenant and its cover, and no one but the high priest could enter there. He could do so only at the proper time (the Day of Atonement) and with the proper sacrifice. Similarly, Jesus' death is the only place one can find mercy. God's wrath against sin was turned away by Christ's sacrificial death.

faith in Jesus Christ,[a] to all who believe, since there is no distinction. 23 For all have sinned and fall short of the[b] glory of God. 24 They are justified freely by His grace through the redemption that is in Christ Jesus. 25 God presented Him as a propitiation[c] through faith in His blood, to demonstrate His righteousness, because in His restraint God passed over the sins previously committed. 26 He presented Him to demonstrate His righteousness at the present time, so that He would be righteous and declare righteous[d] the one who has faith in Jesus.

BOASTING EXCLUDED

27 Where then is boasting? It is excluded. By what kind of law?[e] By one of works? No, on the contrary, by a law[f] of faith. 28 For we conclude that a man is justified by faith apart from works of law. 29 Or is God for Jews only? Is He not also for Gentiles? Yes, for Gentiles too, 30 since there is one God who will justify the circumcised by faith and the uncircumcised through faith. 31 Do we then cancel the law through faith? Absolutely not! On the contrary, we uphold the law.

ABRAHAM JUSTIFIED BY FAITH

4 What then can we say that Abraham, our forefather according to the flesh, has found? 2 If Abraham was justified[g] by works, then he has something to brag about—but not before God.[h] 3 For what does the Scripture say?

> **Abraham believed God,**
> **and it was credited to him**
> **for righteousness.**[i]

4 Now to the one who works, pay is not considered as a gift, but as something owed. 5 But to the one who does

---

[a]3:22 Or *through the faithfulness of Jesus Christ*
[b]3:23 Or *and lack the*
[c]3:25 Or *as a propitiatory sacrifice,* or *as an offering of atonement,* or *as a mercy seat;* see Heb 9:5. The word *propitiation* has to do with the removal of divine wrath. Jesus' death is the means that turns God's wrath from the sinner; see 2 Co 5:21.
[d]3:26 Or *and justify,* or *and acquit*
[e]3:27 Or *what principle?*
[f]3:27 Or *a principle*
[g]4:2 Or *was declared righteous,* or *was acquitted*
[h]4:2 He has no reason for boasting in God's presence
[i]4:3 Gn 15:6

not work, but believes on Him who declares righteous[a] the ungodly, his faith is credited for righteousness.

DAVID CELEBRATING THE SAME TRUTH

[6] Likewise, David also speaks of the blessing of the man to whom God credits righteousness apart from works:

[7] **How happy those whose lawless acts are forgiven**
and whose sins are covered!
[8] **How happy the man whom**
the Lord will never charge with sin![b]

ABRAHAM JUSTIFIED BEFORE CIRCUMCISION

[9] Is this blessing only for the circumcised, then? Or is it also for the uncircumcised? For we say, **Faith was credited to Abraham for righteousness.**[c] [10] How then was it credited—while he was circumcised, or uncircumcised? Not while he was circumcised, but uncircumcised. [11] And he received the sign of circumcision as a seal of the righteousness that he had by faith[d] while still uncircumcised. This was to make him the father of all who believe but are not circumcised, so that righteousness may be credited to them also. [12] And he became the father of the circumcised, not only to those who are circumcised, but also to those who follow in the footsteps of the faith our father Abraham had while still uncircumcised.

THE PROMISE GRANTED THROUGH FAITH

[13] For the promise to Abraham or to his descendants that he would inherit the world was not through the law, but through the righteousness that comes by faith.[d] [14] If those who are of the law are heirs, faith is made empty and the promise is canceled. [15] For the law

---

[a]4:5 Or *who acquits*, or *who justifies*
[b]4:7-8 Ps 32:1-2
[c]4:9, Gn 15:6
[d]4:11,13 Lit *righteousness of faith*

WORD STUDY

Greek word: **charis**
[KAH rihss]

Translation: **grace**

Uses in Romans: **24**

Uses in Paul's writings: **100**

Uses in the NT: **155**

Key passage: **Romans 5:2**

The Greek noun *charis* refers to a favorable disposition toward someone or something, with an emphasis on this favor being unmerited. In the NT, *charis* is commonly used in relation to salvation, especially in Paul's writings. Paul used *charis* to explain that salvation comes from God's own choice to show favor in redeeming lost persons through faith in Christ (see Rm 5:1; Eph 2:8-9; 2 Tm 1:9). However, God's undeserved favor is not toward those who are neutral in His eyes and have done nothing offensive; rather, God shows grace toward those who have sinned against Him and thus are actually His enemies.

In Romans 5, Paul explained that peace with God is an act of God's grace (vv. 1-2), and he went on to remind believers that at one time they were God's enemies (v. 10; see Eph 2:1-16; Col 1:21-22). Therefore, a better NT definition of *charis* would be *unmerited favor toward an enemy*—grace toward one who has forfeited any claim on God's favor because of sin and who deserves the opposite—God's judgment (v. 9). This understanding of grace permeates Paul's teachings on how to enter into a right relationship with God (Rm 3:21-26; 4:3-5,16; 5:15-21; 11:5-6; Gl 1:6,15; 2:21; 5:4; Eph 1:6-7; 2:5-9; Ti 2:11-14) and how to live the Christian life (Rm 6:1-15; 12:6; 1 Co 15:10; 2 Co 1:12; 6:1; 12:9; Eph 4:7,29; Col 1:6; 4:6; 2 Th 1:12; 2 Tm 2:1; Ti 3:7).

produces wrath; but where there is no law, there is no transgression.

16 This is why the promise is by faith, so that it may be according to grace, to guarantee it to all the descendants—not only to those who are of the law,[a] but also to those who are of Abraham's faith. He is the father of us all 17 in God's sight. As it is written: **I have made you the father of many nations.**[b] He believed in God, who gives life to the dead and calls things into existence that do not exist. 18 Against hope, with hope he believed, so that he became **the father of many nations,**[b] according to what had been spoken: **So will your descendants be.**[c] 19 He considered[d] his own body to be already dead (since he was about a hundred years old), and the deadness of Sarah's womb, without weakening in the faith. 20 He did not waver in unbelief at God's promise, but was strengthened in his faith and gave glory to God, 21 because he was fully convinced that what He had promised He was also able to perform. 22 Therefore, **it was credited to him for righteousness.**[e] 23 Now **it was credited to him** was not written for Abraham alone, 24 but also for us. It will be credited to us who believe in Him who raised Jesus our Lord from the dead. 25 He was delivered up for[f] our trespasses and raised for[f] our justification.[g]

FAITH TRIUMPHS

5 Therefore, since we have been declared righteous by faith, we have peace[h] with God through our Lord Jesus Christ. 2 Also through Him, we have obtained access by faith[i] into this grace in which we stand, and we rejoice in the hope of the glory of God. 3 And not only that, but we also rejoice in our afflictions, because we know that affliction produces endurance, 4 endurance produces proven character, and proven character produces hope. 5 This hope does not disappoint, because God's love has been poured out in our hearts through the Holy Spirit who was given to us.

---

[a]**4:16** Or *not to those who are of the law only*
[b]**4:17,18** Gn 17:5
[c]**4:18** Gn 15:5
[d]**4:19** Other mss read *He did not consider*
[e]**4:22** Gn 15:6

[f]**4:25** Or *because of*
[g]**4:25** Or *acquittal*
[h]**5:1** Other mss read *faith, let us have peace*, which can also be translated *faith, let us grasp the fact that we have peace*
[i]**5:2** Other mss omit *by faith*

THOSE DECLARED RIGHTEOUS ARE RECONCILED

⁶ For while we were still helpless, at the appointed moment, Christ died for the ungodly. ⁷ For rarely will someone die for a just person—though for a good person perhaps someone might even dare to die. ⁸ But God proves His own love for us in that while we were still sinners Christ died for us! ⁹ Much more then, since we have now been declared righteous by His blood, we will be saved through Him from wrath. ¹⁰ For if, while we were enemies, we were reconciled to God through the death of His Son, ⌊then how⌋ much more, having been reconciled, will we be saved by His life! ¹¹ And not only that, but we also rejoice in God through our Lord Jesus Christ, through whom we have now received reconciliation.

DEATH THROUGH ADAM AND LIFE THROUGH CHRIST

¹² Therefore, just as sin entered the world through one man, and death through sin, in this way death spread to all men, because all sinned.ᵃ ¹³ In fact, sin was in the world before the law, but sin is not charged to one's account when there is no law. ¹⁴ Nevertheless, death reigned from Adam to Moses, even over those who did not sin in the likeness of Adam's transgression. He is a prototype of the Coming One.

¹⁵ But the gift is not like the trespass. For if by the one man's trespass the many died, how much more have the grace of God and the gift overflowed to the many by the grace of the one man, Jesus Christ. ¹⁶ And the gift is not like the one man's sin, because from one sin came the judgment, resulting in condemnation, but from many trespasses came the gift, resulting in justification.ᵇ ¹⁷ Since by the one man's trespass, death reigned through that one man, how much more will those who receive the overflow of grace and the gift of righteousness reign in life through the one man, Jesus Christ.

¹⁸ So then, as through one trespass there is condemnation for everyone, so also through one righteous act there is life-giving justificationᶜ for everyone. ¹⁹ For

Your Hope Is in a Safe Place

The knowledge of God's presence prevents us from being discouraged or giving up. It is impossible to stand in the presence of God and be a pessimist.

This hope does not disappoint, because God's love has been poured out in our hearts through the Holy Spirit who was given to us.

—Romans 5:5

ᵃ5:12 Or *have sinned*
ᵇ5:16 Or *acquittal*
ᶜ5:18 Lit *is justification of life*

345

WORD STUDY

Greek word: **dikaioo**
[dih kigh AH oh]
Translation: **free**
Uses in Romans: **15**
Uses in Paul's writings: **27**
Uses in the NT: **39**
Key passage: **Romans 6:7**

The Greek verb *dikaioo* means *to justify* or *to declare righteous.* Two related words occur quite often in the NT: the noun *dikaiosune,* meaning *righteousness,* and the adjective *dikaios,* meaning *just* or *righteous.* The common thread in this word family is conformity to a standard, and the standard is primarily God's will. In the Greek OT *dikaioo* occurs thirty times, and most of these are in judicial contexts, both divine and human (either God is Judge or man is judge). Human judges are to "declare righteous the righteous" (Dt 25:1; 1 Kg 8:32; 2 Ch 6:23)—to pronounce the innocent to be so and free him legally. The legal aspect of these terms also involves relational concepts, for judges must promote an individual's relation to society by judging fairly.

These two concepts carry over into Paul's letters, especially Romans and Galatians, as he explains how to have a right relationship with God. Since humans are unrighteous as sinners, righteousness comes only by faith (Rm 3:2; 4:5,13; 9:30; 10:3-4; Gl 2:21; 5:5). At the point of faith God declares the believer to be righteous (Rm 3:30–4:9; 5:1; Gl 2:16-17; 3:8,11,24; 5:4), free from the penalty of sin and in a right relationship with God. This means that those who were unrighteous have Christ's righteousness credited to their accounts (see 2 Co 5:21), freeing and empowering them to live godly lives (Rm 6:1-14).

just as through one man's disobedience the many were made sinners, so also through the one man's obedience the many will be made righteous. ²⁰ The law came along to multiply the trespass. But where sin multiplied, grace multiplied even more, ²¹ so that, just as sin reigned in death, so also grace will reign through righteousness, resulting in eternal life through Jesus Christ our Lord.

THE NEW LIFE IN CHRIST

6 What should we say then? Should we continue in sin in order that grace may multiply? ² Absolutely not! How can we who died to sin still live in it? ³ Or are you unaware that all of us who were baptized into Christ Jesus were baptized into His death? ⁴ Therefore we were buried with Him by baptism into death, in order that, just as Christ was raised from the dead by the glory of the Father, so we too may •walk in a new way^a of life. ⁵ For if we have been joined with Him in the likeness of His death, we will certainly also be^b in the likeness of His resurrection. ⁶ For we know that our old self^c was crucified with Him in order that sin's dominion over the body^d may be abolished, so that we may no longer be enslaved to sin, ⁷ since a person who has died is freed^e from sin's claims.^f ⁸ Now if we died with Christ, we believe that we will also live with Him, ⁹ because we know that Christ, having been raised from the dead, no longer dies. Death no longer rules over Him. ¹⁰ For in that He died, He died to sin once for all; but in that He lives, He lives to God. ¹¹ So, you too consider yourselves dead to sin, but alive to God in Christ Jesus.^g

¹² Therefore do not let sin reign in your mortal body, so that you obey^h its desires. ¹³ And do not offer any parts^i of it to sin as weapons for unrighteousness. But as those who are alive from the dead, offer yourselves to God, and all the parts^i of yourselves to God as weap-

---

^a6:4 Or *in newness*
^b6:5 Be joined with Him
^c6:6 Lit *man*; that is, the person that one was in Adam
^d6:6 Lit *that the body of sin*
^e6:7 Lit *acquitted,* or *justified*

^f6:7 Lit *from sin*
^g6:11 Other mss add *our Lord*
^h6:12 Other mss add *sin* (lit *it*) *in*
^i6:13 Or *members*

ons for righteousness. ¹⁴ For sin will not rule over you, because you are not under law but under grace.

FROM SLAVES OF SIN TO SLAVES OF GOD

¹⁵ What then? Should we sin because we are not under law but under grace? Absolutely not! ¹⁶ Do you not know that if you offer yourselves to someoneᵃ as obedient slaves, you are slaves of that one you obey— either of sin leading to death or of obedience leading to righteousness? ¹⁷ But thank God that, although you used to be slaves of sin, you obeyed from the heart that pattern of teaching you were entrusted to, ¹⁸ and having been liberated from sin, you became enslaved to righteousness. ¹⁹ I am using a human analogyᵇ because of the weakness of your flesh.ᶜ For just as you offered the partsᵈ of yourselves as slaves to moral impurity, and to greater and greater lawlessness, so now offer them as slaves to righteousness, which results in sanctification. ²⁰ For when you were slaves of sin, you were free from allegiance to righteousness.ᵉ ²¹ And what fruit was produced ᶠ then from the things you are now ashamed of? For the end of those things is death. ²² But now, since you have been liberated from sin and become enslaved to God, you have your fruit, which results in sanctification ᵍ—and the end is eternal life! ²³ For the wages of sin is death, but the gift of God is eternal life in Christ Jesus our Lord.

AN ILLUSTRATION FROM MARRIAGE

7 Since I am speaking to those who understand law, brothers, are you unaware that the law has authority over someone as long as he lives? ² For example, a married woman is legally bound to her husband while he lives. But if her husband dies, she is released from the law regarding the husband. ³ So then, if she gives herself to another man while her husband is living, she

To Sin Is to Live Below Your Privilege

You can choose to sin, but you are no longer in sin's power. When you succumb to sin, you are rejecting the freedom from sin that Christ gained for you by His death.

We know that our old self was crucified with Him in order that sin's dominion over the body may be abolished, so that we may no longer be enslaved to sin.
—Romans 6:6

Does God Have You— Heart, Mind, and Body?

Every area of our lives should reflect the holiness of God that is ours by salvation, so that we constantly demonstrate to ourselves and to others the difference Christ makes in us.

As those who are alive from the dead, offer yourselves to God, and all the parts of yourselves to God as weapons for righteousness.
—Romans 6:13b

ᵃ6:16 Lit *that to whom you offer yourselves*
ᵇ6:19 Lit *I speak humanly*; Paul is personifying sin and righteousness as slave masters.
ᶜ6:19 Or *your human nature*
ᵈ6:19 Or *members*
ᵉ6:20 Lit *free to righteousness*
ᶠ6:21 Lit *what fruit do you have*
ᵍ6:22 Or *holiness*

WORD STUDY

Greek word: **sarx**
[SAHRX]
Translation: *flesh*
Uses in Romans: **26**
Uses in Paul's writings: **91**
Uses in the NT: **147**
Key passage: **Romans 7:5**

The Greek noun *sarx* literally means *flesh,* but it is used figuratively in several different ways. The term normally carries a negative sense, especially in Paul's writings. Jesus sometimes used *sarx* to describe the fallen, sinful aspect of a person (Mt 26:41 = Mk 14:38; Jn 6:63), and Paul developed this even more in his writings. Paul used *sarx* to emphasize the ineffectiveness of human effort in spiritual matters (Rm 2:28; 6:19; 8:3 [first occurrence]; 2 Co 1:17; 10:2-3; Php 3:2-3). This is particularly the case in Romans and Galatians where the term has a dual connotation: (1) indwelling sin (Rm 7:5; 8:3 [second occurrence]; 13:14; Gl 5:24; see Eph 2:3; Col 2:18,23; 2 Pt 2:10,18; 1 Jn 2:16) and (2) the desire for a law-based relationship with God (Rm 7:18; Gl 3:3; 6:12-13). Indwelling sin makes a relationship with God based on obedience to the law impossible since no one can meet the law's demands (Rm 3:19-21; 7:25; 8:4; Gl 6:23; see Jms 2:10).

Positive uses of *sarx* in the NT include the Incarnation (Jn 1:14; Rm 1:3; 8:3 [third occurrence]), sexual union between husband and wife (Mt 19:5-6 = Mk 10:8; Eph 5:31; see 1 Co 6:16), the physical body (Lk 24:39; Jn 6:51-56; Ac 2:31; 1 Co 5:5; 15:39; Jms 5:3; 1 Pt 3:18; 1 Jn 4:2; Rv 19:18), family and other human relationships (Rm 4:1; 9:3,5,8; Gl 4:23,29; Eph 6:5), and humanity in general (Mt 24:22; Lk 3:6; Jn 17:2; Ac 2:17; 1 Co 1:29; Gl 2:16).

will be called an adulteress. But if her husband dies, she is free from that law. Then, if she gives herself to another man, she is not an adulteress.

[4] Therefore, my brothers, you also were put to death in relation to the law through the ⌊crucified⌋ body of the •Messiah, so that you may belong to another—to Him who was raised from the dead—that we may bear fruit for God. [5] For when we were in the flesh,[a] the sinful passions operated through the law in every part of us[b] and bore fruit for death. [6] But now we have been released from the law, since we have died to what held us, so that we may serve in the new way[c] of the Spirit and not in the old letter of the law.

SIN'S USE OF THE LAW

[7] What should we say then? Is the law sin? Absolutely not! On the contrary, I would not have known sin if it were not for the law. For example, I would not have known what it is to covet if the law had not said, **Do not covet.**[d] [8] And sin, seizing an opportunity through the commandment, produced in me coveting of every kind. For apart from the law sin is dead. [9] Once I was alive apart from the law, but when the commandment came, sin sprang to life [10] and I died. The commandment that was meant for life resulted in death for me. [11] For sin, seizing an opportunity through the commandment, deceived me, and through it killed me. [12] So then, the law is holy, and the commandment is holy and just and good.

THE PROBLEM OF SIN IN US

[13] Therefore, did what is good cause my death?[e] Absolutely not! On the contrary, sin, in order to be recognized as sin, was producing death in me through what is good, so that through the commandment sin might become sinful beyond measure. [14] For we know that the law is spiritual; but I am made out of flesh,[f] sold into sin's power. [15] For I do not understand what I am doing, because I do not practice what I want to do, but I

---

[a]7:5 *in the flesh* = a person's life before accepting Christ
[b]7:5 Lit *of our members*
[c]7:6 Lit *in newness*
[d]7:7 Ex 20:17
[e]7:13 Lit *good become death to me?*
[f]7:14 Other mss read *I am carnal*

do what I hate. [16] And if I do what I do not want to do, I agree with the law that it is good. [17] So now I am no longer the one doing it, but it is sin living in me. [18] For I know that nothing good lives in me, that is, in my flesh. For the desire to do what is good is with me, but there is no ability to do it. [19] For I do not do the good that I want to do, but I practice the evil that I do not want to do. [20] Now if I do what I do not want, I am no longer the one doing it, but it is the sin that lives in me. [21] So I discover this principle:[a] when I want to do good, evil is with me. [22] For in my inner self[b] I joyfully agree with God's law. [23] But I see a different law in the parts of my body,[c] waging war against the law of my mind and taking me prisoner to the law of sin in the parts of my body.[c] [24] What a wretched man I am! Who will rescue me from this body of death? [25] I thank God through Jesus Christ our Lord![d] So then, with my mind I myself am a slave to the law of God, but with my flesh, to the law of sin.

THE LIFE-GIVING SPIRIT

8 Therefore, no condemnation now exists for those in Christ Jesus,[e] [2] because the Spirit's law of life in Christ Jesus has set you[f] free from the law of sin and of death. [3] What the law could not do since it was limited[g] by the flesh, God did. He condemned sin in the flesh by sending His own Son in flesh like ours under sin's domain,[h] and as a sin offering, [4] in order that the law's requirement would be accomplished in us who do not •walk according to the flesh but according to the Spirit. [5] For those whose lives are[i] according to the flesh think about the things of the flesh, but those whose lives are[i] according to the Spirit, about the things of the Spirit. [6] For the mind-set of the flesh is death, but the mind-set of the Spirit is life and peace. [7] For the mind-set of the flesh is hostile to God because it does not submit itself to God's law, for it is unable to do so. [8] Those whose lives are[j] in the flesh are unable to please God. [9] You,

It's a New Way of Looking at Life

It is tempting to try to do God's work for Him, but we serve Him in a different way. Allow Him to do what only He can do: live out His divine life through you.

We have been released from the law, since we have died to what held us, so that we may serve in the new way of the Spirit and not in the old letter of the law.

—Romans 7:6

Nobody Said This Was Going to Be Easy

Never assume that you are immune to temptation or able to defeat it through willpower alone. Don't underestimate the craftiness of the devil or the weakness of your own flesh.

I know that nothing good lives in me, that is, in my flesh. For the desire to do what is good is with me, but there is no ability to do it.

—Romans 7:18

---

[a]**7:21** Or *law*
[b]**7:22** Lit *inner man*
[c]**7:23** Lit *my members*
[d]**7:25** Or *Thanks be to God*—(it is done) *through Jesus Christ our Lord!*
[e]**8:1** Other mss add *who do not*
walk according to the flesh but according to the Spirit
[f]**8:2** Other mss read *me*
[g]**8:3** Or *weak*
[h]**8:3** Lit *in the likeness of sinful flesh*
[i]**8:5** Or *those who are*
[j]**8:8** Or *Those who are*

WORD STUDY

Greek word: *huiothesia*
[hwee ah theh SEE ah]

Translation: *adoption*

Uses in Romans: **3**

Uses in Paul's writings: **5**

Uses in the NT: **5**

Key passages: **Romans 8:15,23**

The Greek noun *huiothesia* literally means *a son placing* and comes from *huios (son)* and *tithemi (to place)*. The term refers to the legal act whereby a child is accepted into a family on an equal basis—including the same rights of inheritance—with any physical offspring of the parents. Although *huiothesia* was quite common in Greek literature and adoption was widely practiced in the Greco-Roman world, only Paul used *huiothesia* in the NT, and then only five times. Paul explained that to Israel belonged "the adoption" (Rm 9:4), which probably refers to the fact that God called Israel His son on occasion (Ex 4:22; Is 1:2; 43; 45:11; Jr 3:14,22; see 2 Sm 7:14; Ps 2:7; Mal 1:6; 3:17). While the term *huiothesia* never occurs in the Greek OT, the concept does occur, since *huios* is used in these verses. In the other four passages where Paul used *huiothesia*, the term refers to those who by faith in Christ have been accepted into God's family (Rm 8:15; Gl 4:5), which was His plan before creation (Eph 1:5). Believers do not receive their full inheritance as sons of God until final salvation, "the redemption of our bodies" at the resurrection (Rm 8:23).

however, are not in the flesh, but in the Spirit, since[a] the Spirit of God lives in you. But if anyone does not have the Spirit of Christ, he does not belong to Him. [10] Now if Christ is in you, the body is dead[b] because of sin, but the Spirit[c] is life because of righteousness. [11] And if the Spirit of Him who raised Jesus from the dead lives in you, then He who raised Christ from the dead will also bring your mortal bodies to life through[d] His Spirit who lives in you.

THE HOLY SPIRIT'S MINISTRIES

[12] So then, brothers, we are not obligated to the flesh to live according to the flesh, [13] for if you live according to the flesh, you are going to die. But if by the Spirit you put to death the deeds of the body, you will live. [14] All those led by God's Spirit are God's sons. [15] For you did not receive a spirit of slavery to fall back into fear, but you received the Spirit of adoption, by whom we cry out, "•*Abba*, Father!" [16] The Spirit Himself testifies together with our spirit that we are God's children, [17] and if children, also heirs—heirs of God and co-heirs with Christ—seeing that[a] we suffer with Him so that we may also be glorified with Him.

FROM GROANS TO GLORY

[18] For I consider that the sufferings of this present time are not worth comparing with the glory that is going to be revealed to us. [19] For the creation eagerly waits with anticipation for God's sons to be revealed. [20] For the creation was subjected to futility—not willingly, but because of Him who subjected it—in the hope [21] that the creation itself will also be set free from the bondage of corruption into the glorious freedom of God's children. [22] For we know that the whole creation has been groaning together with labor pains until now. [23] And not only that, but we ourselves who have the Spirit as the •firstfruits—we also groan within ourselves, eagerly waiting for adoption, the redemption of our bodies. [24] Now in this hope we were saved, yet

---

[a]**8:9,17** Or *provided that*
[b]**8:10** Or *the body will die*
[c]**8:10** Or *spirit*
[d]**8:11** Other mss read *because of*

hope that is seen is not hope, because who hopes for what he sees? ²⁵ But if we hope for what we do not see, we eagerly wait for it with patience.

²⁶ In the same way the Spirit also joins to help in our weakness, because we do not know what to pray for as we should, but the Spirit Himself intercedes for usᵃ with unspoken groanings. ²⁷ And He who searches the hearts knows the Spirit's mind-set, because He intercedes for the saints according to the will of God.

²⁸ We know that all things work togetherᵇ for the goodᶜ of those who love God: those who are called according to His purpose. ²⁹ For those He foreknewᵈ He also predestined to be conformed to the image of His Son, so that He would be the firstborn among many brothers. ³⁰ And those He predestined, He also called; and those He called, He also justified; and those He justified, He also glorified.

THE BELIEVER'S TRIUMPH

³¹ What then are we to say about these things?
If God is for us, who is against us?
³² He did not even spare His own Son,
but offered Him up for us all;
how will He not also with Him grant us everything?
³³ Who can bring an accusation against God's elect?
God is the One who justifies.
³⁴ Who is the one who condemns?
Christ Jesus is the One who died, but even more, has been raised;
He also is at the right hand of God
and intercedes for us.
³⁵ Who can separate us from the love of Christ?
Can affliction or anguish or persecution
or famine or nakedness or danger or sword?
³⁶ As it is written:
**Because of You we are being put to death all day long;
we are counted as sheep to be slaughtered.**ᵉ

In Christ, Something Good Always Awaits

Don't expect God to remove every difficult situation you're going through. Watch instead to see how He will use your tough times to bring about good in your life.

We know that all things work together for the good of those who love God: those who are called according to His purpose.
—Romans 8:28

Being More Like Jesus Is Your #1 Job

Every event God allows into your life is designed to make you more like Christ.

Those He foreknew He also predestined to be conformed to the image of His Son, so that He would be the firstborn among many brothers.
—Romans 8:29

ᵃ8:26 Some mss omit *for us*
ᵇ8:28 Other mss read *that God works together in all things*
ᶜ8:28 The ultimate good
ᵈ8:29 From eternity God knew His people and entered into a personal relationship with them
ᵉ8:36 Ps 44:22; see Is 53:7; Zch 11:4,7

37 No, in all these things we are
more than victorious
through Him who loved us.
38 For I am persuaded that neither death nor life,
nor angels nor rulers,
nor things present, nor things to come,
nor powers,
39 nor height, nor depth, nor any other
created thing
will have the power to separate us
from the love of God that is in Christ Jesus
our Lord!

ISRAEL'S REJECTION OF CHRIST

9 I speak the truth in Christ—I am not lying; my conscience is testifying to me with the Holy Spirit[a] — 2 that I have intense sorrow and continual anguish in my heart. 3 For I could wish that I myself were cursed and cut off[b] from the •Messiah for the benefit of my brothers, my countrymen by physical descent.[c] 4 They are Israelites, and to them belong the adoption, the glory, the covenants, the giving of the law, the temple service, and the promises. 5 The forefathers are theirs, and from them, by physical descent,[d] came the Messiah, who is God over all, blessed forever.[e] •Amen.

GOD'S GRACIOUS ELECTION OF ISRAEL

6 But it is not as though the word of God has failed. For not all who are descended from Israel are Israel. 7 Neither are they all children because they are Abraham's descendants.[f] On the contrary, **in Isaac your seed will be called.**[g] 8 That is, it is not the children by physical descent[h] who are God's children, but the children of the promise are considered seed. 9 For this is the statement of the promise: **At this time I will come,**

Nothing Can Defeat a Follower of Christ

When Christ lives in you, He brings every divine resource with Him. Every time you face a need, you meet it with the presence of the crucified, risen, and triumphant Lord of the universe inhabiting you.

No, in all these things we are more than victorious through Him who loved us.

—Romans 8:37

---

[a]9:1 Or *testifying with me by the Holy Spirit*
[b]9:3 Lit *were anathema*
[c]9:3 Lit *countrymen according to the flesh*
[d]9:5 Lit *them, according to the flesh*
[e]9:5 Or *the Messiah, the One who is over all, the God who is blessed forever,* or *Messiah. God, who is over all, be blessed forever*
[f]9:7 Lit *seed*
[g]9:7 Gn 21:12
[h]9:8 Lit *children of the flesh*

and **Sarah will have a son.**[a] [10] And not only that, but also when Rebekah became pregnant[b] by Isaac our forefather [11] (for though they had not been born yet or done anything good or bad, so that God's purpose according to election might stand, [12] not from works but from the One who calls) she was told: **The older will serve the younger.**[c] [13] As it is written: **Jacob I have loved, but Esau I have hated.**[d]

GOD'S SELECTION IS JUST

[14] What should we say then? Is there injustice with God? Absolutely not! [15] For He tells Moses:

I will show mercy to whom I show mercy,
and I will have compassion on whom
I have compassion.[e]

[16] So then it does not depend on human will or effort,[f] but on God who shows mercy. [17] For the Scripture tells Pharaoh:

For this reason I raised you up:
so that I may display My power in you,
and that My name may be proclaimed
in all the earth.[g]

[18] So then, He shows mercy to whom He wills, and He hardens whom He wills.

[19] You will say to me, therefore, "Why then does He still find fault? For who can resist His will?" [20] But who are you—anyone[h] who talks back to God? Will what is formed say to the one who formed it, "Why did you make me like this?" [21] Or has the potter no right over His clay, to make from the same lump one piece of pottery for honor and another for dishonor? [22] And what if God, desiring to display His wrath and to make His power known, endured with much patience objects of wrath ready for destruction? [23] And ₗwhat if₎ He did this to make known the riches of His glory on objects of mercy that He prepared beforehand for glory— [24] on

---

[a]**9:9** Gn 18:10,14
[b]**9:10** Or *Rebekah conceived by the one act of sexual intercourse*
[c]**9:12** Gn 25:23
[d]**9:13** Mal 1:2-3
[e]**9:15** Ex 33:19

[f]**9:16** Lit *on the one willing*, or *on the one running*
[g]**9:17** Ex 9:16
[h]**9:20** Lit *you, O man*

WORD STUDY

Greek word: ***sperma***
[SPUHR mah]
Translation: ***descendant, seed***
Uses in Romans: **9**
Uses in Paul's writings: **17**
Uses in the NT: **43**
Key passage: **Romans 9:7-8**

The English word *sperm* comes directly from the Greek noun *sperma*, which literally means *seed*. The term was often used for the seeds of plants (Mt 13:24-38; Mk 4:31) and sometimes even of animals (referring to reproduction as in humans). The term *sperma* could refer figuratively to origin but refers more often to descendants or offspring, which is the dominant meaning in Paul's writings. He develops the descendant/offspring meaning along three main lines.

(1) Jesus the Messiah came from the promised *sperma* or family line (Rm 1:3; 2 Tm 2:8; see Gl 3:16,19; compare Jn 8:33; Ac 13:23).

(2) Those who are the *sperma* or descendants of Abraham by physical descent, that is, the Hebrew race (Rm 9:7,29 [translated "descendants"]; 11:1; 2 Co 11:22; see Lk 1:55; Heb 2:16; Rv 12:17).

(3) Those who are the *sperma* or descendants of Abraham by faith, that is, believers in Christ (Rm 4:13,16,18; 9:7-8 [translated "seed"]; Gl 3:29). Through these various uses of *sperma*, Paul indicated that actual physical descent from Abraham is neither necessary nor sufficient for salvation; faith in Christ alone brings a person into God's family (compare Mt 3:9; Jn 8:31-59; Rm 3:9-21).

us whom He also called, not only from the Jews but also from the Gentiles? 25 As He also says in Hosea:

> I will call "Not-My-People," "My-People,"
> and she who is "Unloved," "Beloved."ᵃ
> 26 And it will be in the place where
> they were told,
> you are not My people,
> there they will be called
> sons of the living God.ᵇ

27 But Isaiah cries out concerning Israel:

> Though the number of Israel's sons is like
> the sand of the sea,
> only the remnant will be saved;
> 28 for the Lord will execute His sentence
> completely and decisively on the earth.ᶜ ᵈ

29 And just as Isaiah predicted:

> If the Lord of Hostsᵉ had not left us a seed,
> we would have become like Sodom,
> and we would have been made
> like Gomorrah.ᶠ

ISRAEL'S PRESENT STATE

30 What should we say then? Gentiles, who did not pursue righteousness, have obtained righteousness—namely the righteousness that comes from faith. 31 But Israel, pursuing the law for righteousness, has not achieved the law.ᵍ 32 Why is that? Because they did not pursue it by faith, but as if it were by works.ʰ They stumbled over the stumbling stone. 33 As it is written:

> Look! I am putting a stone in Zion
> to stumble over,
> and a rock to trip over,
> yet the one who believes on Him will not
> be put to shame.ⁱ

Never Put Faith in Your Own Goodness

Regardless of the morality of your life, the good works you perform, the words you speak, or the sacrifices you make, if you do not have faith, you will not please God.

Why is that? Because they did not pursue it by faith, but as if it were by works. They stumbled over the stumbling stone.

—Romans 9:32

ᵃ9:25 Hs 2:23
ᵇ9:26 Hs 1:10
ᶜ9:28 Or *land*
ᵈ9:27-28 Is 10:22-23; 28:22; Hs 1:10
ᵉ9:29 Gk *Sabaoth*; this word is a transliteration of the Hb word for *Hosts*, or *Armies*.

ᶠ9:29 Is 1:9
ᵍ9:31 Other mss read *the law for righteousness*
ʰ9:32 Other mss add *of the law*
ⁱ9:33 Is 8:14; 28:16

RIGHTEOUSNESS BY FAITH ALONE

10 Brothers, my heart's desire and prayer to God concerning them[a] is for their salvation! ² I can testify about them that they have zeal for God, but not according to knowledge. ³ Because they disregarded the righteousness from God and attempted to establish their own righteousness, they have not submitted to God's righteousness. ⁴ For Christ is the end[b] of the law for righteousness to everyone who believes. ⁵ For Moses writes about the righteousness that is from the law: **The one who does these things will live by them.**[c] ⁶ But the righteousness that comes from faith speaks like this: **Do not say in your heart, "Who will go up to heaven?"**[d] that is, to bring Christ down ⁷ or, **"Who will go down into the •abyss?"**[e] that is, to bring Christ up from the dead. ⁸ On the contrary, what does it say? **The message is near you, in your mouth and in your heart.**[f] This is the message of faith that we proclaim: ⁹ if you confess with your mouth, "Jesus is Lord," and believe in your heart that God raised Him from the dead, you will be saved. ¹⁰ With the heart one believes, resulting in righteousness, and with the mouth one confesses, resulting in salvation. ¹¹ Now the Scripture says, **No one who believes on Him will be put to shame,**[g] ¹² for there is no distinction between Jew and Greek, since the same Lord of all is rich to all who call on Him. ¹³ For **everyone who calls on the name of the Lord will be saved.**[h]

ISRAEL'S REJECTION OF THE MESSAGE

¹⁴ But how can they call on Him in whom they have not believed? And how can they believe without hearing about Him? And how can they hear without a preacher? ¹⁵ And how can they preach unless they are sent? As it is written: **How welcome**[i] **are the feet of those**[j] **who announce the gospel of good things!**[k] ¹⁶ But all did not obey the gospel. For Isaiah says, **Lord, who has**

---

[a]10:1 Other mss read *God for Israel*
[b]10:4 Or *goal*
[c]10:5 Lv 18:5
[d]10:6 Dt 9:4; 30:12
[e]10:7 Dt 30:13
[f]10:8 Dt 30:14
[g]10:11 Is 28:16

[h]10:13 Jl 2:32
[i]10:15 Or *timely*, or *beautiful*
[j]10:15 Other mss read *feet of those who announce the gospel of peace, of those*
[k]10:15 Is 52:7; Nah 1:15

WORD STUDY

Greek word: **telos**
[TEHL ahss]

Translation: **end**

Uses in Romans: **5**

Uses in Paul's writings: **14**

Uses in the NT: **40**

Key passage: **Romans 10:4**

The Greek noun *telos* is related to the verbs *teleo* and *teleioo*, both meaning *to complete, perfect, finish*, and to the adjective *teleion*, meaning *complete, perfect, whole*. The term *telos* refers to the consummation, completion, or fulfillment of something.

In the NT, *telos* is commonly used for the end of this life (Mt 10:22; Lk 18:5; 1 Co 1:8; Php 3:19; Heb 3:14; 6:11; 7:3; Rv 2:26) or for events related to the end times (Mt 24:6,13,14; Mk 13:7,13; Lk 1:33; 21:9; 1 Co 10:11; 15:24; 2 Co 11:15; 1 Pt 4:7,17). Three times it indicates the maximum limit (Jn 13:1; 2 Co 1:13; 1 Th 2:16); twice it refers to taxes (Mt 17:25; Rm 13:7); and once it means "fulfillment" (Lk 22:37). The term can also mean "aim" (1 Tm 1:5) or "goal" (1 Pt 1:9). Spiritual death and life are in view in Romans 6:21-22. In Revelation *telos* occurs twice in the formula "the Beginning and the End" as a title for deity (21:6; 22:13). In Romans 10:4 *telos* refers to Christ as "the end of the law," which is similar to Paul's statement that believers are no longer "under the law" (Rm 6:14). Christians do not relate to God through the old covenant God made with Israel at Mt. Sinai through Moses, but through the new covenant He made at the cross through Christ's blood (see Jr 31:31-34; Lk 22:20; Heb 8:8-12).

WORD STUDY

Greek word: ***proginosko***
[prah gih NOH skoh]
Translation: ***foreknow***
Uses in Romans: **2**
Uses in Paul's writings: **2**
Uses in the NT: **5**
Key passage: **Romans 11:2**

The Greek verb *proginosko* comes from the preposition *pro* (meaning *before*) and the verb *ginosko* (meaning *to know*); the compound term thus means *to know beforehand*. The related noun *prognosis* means *fore-knowledge* and is the basis for the English medical term *progno-sis* (it was also a medical term in ancient Greek). On two occasions in the NT, *proginosko* is used for knowledge obtained in advance by human beings (Ac 26:5; 2 Pt 3:17). However, when God is the one foreknowing, the emphasis is not on prior knowledge but on prior choice. The other three uses of this verb and both uses of the noun indicate that God foreknows people, not events. These terms refer to God's choice of His people and of Christ for a redemptive purpose. Since God chose Israel—not the other way around—He did not reject her (Rm 11:2). God chose Christ "before the foundation of the world" for the purpose of redemption (1 Pt 1:20; see Ac 2:23), and in keeping with this purpose He also chose those whom He would conform "to the image of His Son" (Rm 8:29; see 1 Pt 1:2).

believed our message?[a] [17] So faith comes from what is heard, and what is heard comes through the message about Christ.[b] [18] But I ask, "Did they not hear?" Yes, they did:

> **Their voice has gone out to all the earth,**
> **and their words to the ends**
> **of the inhabited world.**[c]

[19] But I ask, "Did Israel not understand?" First, Moses said:

> **I will make you jealous of those**
> **who are not a nation;**
> **I will make you angry by a nation that lacks**
> **understanding.**[d]

[20] And Isaiah says boldly:

> **I was found by those who were not looking**
> **for Me;**
> **I revealed Myself to those who were not**
> **asking for Me.**[e]

[21] But to Israel he says: **All day long I have spread out My hands to a disobedient and defiant people.**[f]

ISRAEL'S REJECTION NOT TOTAL

11 I ask, then, has God rejected His people? Absolutely not! For I too am an Israelite, a descendant of Abraham, from the tribe of Benjamin. [2] God has not rejected His people whom He foreknew. Or do you not know what the Scripture says in the Elijah section—how he pleads with God against Israel?

> [3] **Lord, they have killed Your prophets,**
> **torn down Your altars;**
> **and I am the only one left,**
> **and they are trying to take my life!**[g]

[4] But what was God's reply to him? **I have left 7,000 men for Myself who have not bowed down to Baal.**[h] [5] In the same way, then, there is also at the present time

---

[a]10:16 Is 53:1
[b]10:17 Other mss read *God*
[c]10:18 Ps 19:4
[d]10:19 Dt 32:21
[e]10:20 Is 65:1
[f]10:21 Is 65:2
[g]11:3 1 Kg 19:10,14
[h]11:4 1 Kg 19:18

a remnant chosen by grace. ⁶ Now if by grace, then it is not by works; otherwise grace ceases to be grace.ᵃ

⁷ What then? Israel did not find what it was looking for, but the elect did find it. The rest were hardened, ⁸ as it is written:

> **God gave them a spirit of stupor,**
> **eyes that cannot see and ears**
>   **that cannot hear, to this day.**ᵇ

⁹ And David says:

> **Let their feasting**ᶜ **become a snare**
>   **and a trap,**
> **a pitfall and a retribution to them.**
> ¹⁰ **Let their eyes be darkened**
>   **so they cannot see,**
> **and their backs be bent continually.**ᵈ

ISRAEL'S REJECTION NOT FINAL

¹¹ I ask, then, have they stumbled so as to fall? Absolutely not! On the contrary, by their stumbling,ᵉ salvation has come to the Gentiles to make Israelᶠ jealous. ¹² Now if their stumblingᵉ brings riches for the world, and their failure riches for the Gentiles, how much more will their full number bring!

¹³ Now I am speaking to you Gentiles. In view of the fact that I am an apostle to the Gentiles, I magnify my ministry, ¹⁴ if I can somehow make my own peopleᵍ jealous and save some of them. ¹⁵ For if their being rejected is world reconciliation, what will their acceptance mean but life from the dead? ¹⁶ Now if the •firstfruits offered up are holy, so is the whole batch. And if the root is holy, so are the branches.

¹⁷ Now if some of the branches were broken off, and you, though a wild olive branch, were grafted in among them, and have come to share in the rich rootʰ of the cultivated olive tree, ¹⁸ do not brag that you are better than those branches. But if you do brag—you do not

You Can't Work Your Way into God's Good Graces

God loves us with a perfect love and reaches out to us with salvation when we can offer Him nothing in return.

If by grace, then it is not by works; otherwise grace ceases to be grace.

—Romans 11:6

ᵃ**11:6** Other mss add *But if of works it is no longer grace; otherwise work is no longer work.*
ᵇ**11:8** Dt 29:4; Is 29:10
ᶜ**11:9** Lit *table*
ᵈ**11:9-10** Ps 69:22-23
ᵉ**11:11,12** Or *transgression*
ᶠ**11:11** Lit *them*
ᵍ**11:14** Lit *flesh*
ʰ**11:17** Other mss read *the root and the richness*

sustain the root, but the root sustains you. ¹⁹ Then you will say, "Branches were broken off so that I might be grafted in." ²⁰ True enough; they were broken off by unbelief, but you stand by faith. Do not be arrogant, but be afraid. ²¹ For if God did not spare the natural branches, He will not spare you either. ²² Therefore, consider God's kindness and severity: severity toward those who have fallen, but God's kindness toward you—if you remain in His kindness. Otherwise you too will be cut off. ²³ And even they, if they do not remain in unbelief, will be grafted in, because God has the power to graft them in again. ²⁴ For if you were cut off from your native wild olive, and against nature were grafted into a cultivated olive tree, how much more will these—the natural branches—be grafted into their own olive tree?

²⁵ So that you will not be conceited, brothers, I do not want you to be unaware of this •mystery: a partial hardening has come to Israel until the full number of the Gentiles has come in. ²⁶ And in this way all[a] Israel will be saved, as it is written:

> **The Liberator will come from Zion;**
> **He will turn away godlessness from Jacob.**
> ²⁷ **And this will be My covenant with them,[b]**
> **when I take away their sins.[c]**

²⁸ Regarding the gospel, they are enemies for your advantage, but regarding election, they are loved because of their forefathers, ²⁹ since God's gracious gifts and calling are irrevocable.[d] ³⁰ As you once disobeyed God, but now have received mercy through their disobedience, ³¹ so they too have now disobeyed, ⌊resulting⌋ in mercy to you, so that they also now[e] may receive mercy. ³² For God has imprisoned all in disobedience, so that He may have mercy on all.

A HYMN OF PRAISE

> ³³ Oh, the depth of the riches
> both of the wisdom and the knowledge of God!
> How unsearchable His judgments

A Mind Is a Terrible Thing to Waste

There is a way to prevent the world's thinking patterns from taking over your own: offer yourself every day to God.

Do not be conformed to this age, but be transformed by the renewing of your mind, so that you may discern what is the good, pleasing, and perfect will of God.

—Romans 12:2

Are You Sick of Sin and Its Side-Effects?

Have you become comfortable around sin and evil? Are you tolerating sin in your life? Ask God to give you a holy aversion to sin.

Love must be without hypocrisy. Detest evil; cling to what is good.

—Romans 12:9

---

[a]11:26 Or *And then all*
[b]11:26-27 Is 59:20-21
[c]11:27 Jr 31:31-34
[d]11:29 Or *are not taken back*
[e]11:31 Other mss omit *now*

and untraceable His ways!

34 **For who has known the mind of the Lord?
Or who has been His counselor?**

35 **Or who has ever first given to Him,
and has to be repaid?**ª

36 For from Him and through Him and to Him
are all things.
To Him be the glory forever. •Amen.

A LIVING SACRIFICE

12 Therefore, brothers, by the mercies of God, I urge you to present your bodies as a living sacrifice, holy and pleasing to God; this is your spiritual worship.ᵇ 2 Do not be conformed to this age, but be transformed by the renewing of your mind, so that you may discern what is the good, pleasing, and perfect will of God.

MANY GIFTS BUT ONE BODY

3 For by the grace given to me, I tell everyone among you not to think of himself more highly than he should think. Instead, think sensibly, as God has distributed a measure of faith to each one. 4 Now as we have many parts in one body, and all the parts do not have the same function, 5 in the same way we who are many are one body in Christ and individually members of one another. 6 According to the grace given to us, we have different gifts:

If prophecy, use it according to the standard
of faith;
7 if service, in service; if teaching, in teaching;
8 if exhorting, in exhortation; giving,
with generosity;
leading, with diligence; showing mercy,
with cheerfulness.

CHRISTIAN ETHICS

9 Love must be without hypocrisy. Detest evil; cling to what is good. 10 Show family affection to one another with brotherly love. Outdo one another in showing honor. 11 Do not lack diligence; be fervent in spirit; serve

ª**11:34-35** Is 40:13; Jb 41:11; Jr 23:18   ᵇ**12:1** Or *your reasonable service*

WORD STUDY

Greek word: *nous* [NOOSS]
Translation: *mind*
Uses in Romans: **6**
Uses in Paul's writings: **21**
Uses in the NT: **24**
Key passage: **Romans 12:1-2**

The Greek noun *nous* was a common term that referred to human intellectual perception and moral judgment, thus the *mind*. The related verb *noeo* means *to think, perceive, understand*. All but three NT occurrences of the word *nous* are in Paul's letters. Luke 24:25 refers to *nous* as the seat of understanding, and Revelation 13:18; 17:9 refer to *nous* as the seat of wisdom. Pauline usage is similar but emphasizes that the mind is the seat of the intellect and thus affects the will; that is, the mind controls what a person says and does, as can be seen in several passages in Paul's letters (Rm 1:28; 7:23; 14:5; 1 Co 14:19; Eph 4:17; Col 2:18; 2 Th 2:2; 1 Tm 6:5; 2 Tm 3:8; Ti 1:15). Therefore the apostle encouraged believers to be transformed by renewing their minds. This transformation comes through the study of God's Word and results in being able to "discern what is the good, pleasing, and perfect will of God" (Rm 12:2).

WORD STUDY

Greek word: **opheilo**
[ah FIGH loh]

Translation: **owe**

Uses in Romans: **3**

Uses in Paul's writings: **14**

Uses in the NT: **35**

Key passage: **Romans 13:8**

The Greek verb *opheilo* refers to an obligation that a person has to someone else. This obligation takes two main forms: (1) that someone ought to do a certain thing; and (2) that someone owes something (normally money) to someone else. In the NT, the first meaning involves a moral, legal, or ethical obligation a person has to act in a certain way, and this is by far the more common of the two (Mt 23:16,18; Jn 13:14; 19:7; Ac 17:29; Heb 5:3,12; 1 Jn 6; 3:16; 4:11; 3 Jn 8). The second meaning occurs several times in Jesus' parables (Mt 18:28,30,34; Lk 7:41; 16:5,7; 17:10); it also occurs in a metaphorical sense in Luke's version of the Lord's Prayer (Lk 11:4). One of the uses of *opheilo* in Hebrews refer to the divine obligation under which Jesus became a man so He could accomplish redemption for His people (2:17).

In Paul's letters, *opheilo* is used to emphasize the moral or ethical obligation of believers in their behavior (Rm 15:1; 1 Co 11:7,10; 2 Co 12:11,14; Eph 5:28; 2 Th 1:3; 2:13). The term involves owing money only twice (Rm 13:8; Phm 18). In Romans 13:8 it is doubtful that Paul intended to forbid believers from borrowing money under any circumstances. Paul emphasized that our greatest obligation as believers is to love others and thus fulfill the law (see vv. 9-10).

the Lord. [12] Rejoice in hope; be patient in affliction; be persistent in prayer. [13] Share with the saints in their needs; pursue hospitality. [14] Bless those who persecute you; bless and do not curse. [15] Rejoice with those who rejoice; weep with those who weep. [16] Be in agreement with one another. Do not be proud; instead, associate with the humble. Do not be wise in your own estimation. [17] Do not repay anyone evil for evil. Try to do what is honorable in everyone's eyes. [18] If possible, on your part, live at peace with everyone. [19] Friends, do not avenge yourselves; instead, leave room for His[a] wrath. For it is written: **Vengeance belongs to Me; I will repay,**[b] says the Lord. [20] But

> **If your enemy is hungry, feed him.**
> **If he is thirsty, give him something to drink.**
> **For in so doing you will be heaping**
> **fiery coals on his head.**[c]

[21] Do not be conquered by evil, but conquer evil with good.

A CHRISTIAN'S DUTIES TO THE STATE

13 Everyone must submit to the governing authorities, for there is no authority except from God, and those that exist are instituted by God. [2] So then, the one who resists the authority is opposing God's command, and those who oppose it will bring judgment on themselves. [3] For rulers are not a terror to good conduct, but to bad. Do you want to be unafraid of the authority? Do good and you will have its approval. [4] For government is God's servant to you for good. But if you do wrong, be afraid, because it does not carry the sword for no reason. For government is God's servant, an avenger that brings wrath on the one who does wrong. [5] Therefore, you must submit, not only because of wrath, but also because of your conscience. [6] And for this reason you pay taxes, since the ₌authorities₌ are God's public servants, continually attending to these tasks.[d] [7] Pay your obligations to everyone: taxes to those you owe taxes, tolls to those you owe tolls, respect to those you owe respect, and honor to those you owe honor.

---

[a]**12:19** Lit *the*
[b]**12:19** Dt 32:35
[c]**12:20** Pr 25:21-22
[d]**13:6** Lit *to this very thing*

LOVE OUR PRIMARY DUTY

[8] Do not owe anyone anything,[a] except to love one another, for the one who loves another has fulfilled the law. [9] The commandments:

**Do not commit adultery,
do not murder,
do not steal,[b]
do not covet,[c]**

and if there is any other commandment—all are summed up by this: **Love your neighbor as yourself.[d]**

[10] Love does no wrong to a neighbor. Love, therefore, is the fulfillment of the law.

PUT ON CHRIST

[11] Besides this, knowing the time, it is already the hour for you[e] to wake up from sleep, for now our salvation is nearer than when we first believed. [12] The night is nearly over, and the daylight is near, so let us discard the deeds of darkness and put on the armor of light. [13] Let us •walk with decency, as in the daylight; not in carousing and drunkenness; not in sexual impurity and promiscuity; not in quarreling and jealousy. [14] But put on the Lord Jesus Christ, and make no plans to satisfy the fleshly desires.

THE LAW OF LIBERTY

14 Accept anyone who is weak in faith,[f] but don't argue about doubtful issues. [2] One person believes he may eat anything, but one who is weak eats only vegetables. [3] One who eats must not look down on one who does not eat; and one who does not eat must not criticize one who does, because God has accepted him. [4] Who are you to criticize another's household slave? Before his own Lord he stands or falls. And stand he will! For the Lord is able[g] to make him stand.

[5] One person considers one day to be above another day. Someone else considers every day to be the same.

More Than Anything Else, I.O.U. Love

God looks beyond your godly habits, moral lifestyle, and church involvement, and focuses His penetrating gaze on your heart—to see if it's a heart that's filled with love.

Do not owe anyone anything, except to love one another, for the one who loves another has fulfilled the law.

—Romans 13:8

We Can Love People the Way God Does

We are deeply loved—God's priceless treasures. That is why we should have no cause for insecurity, and therefore no reason to tear down others in order to increase our value.

Who are you to criticize another's household slave? Before his own Lord he stands or falls. And stand he will! For the Lord is able to make him stand.

—Romans 14:4

---

[a]13:8 Or *Leave no debt outstanding to anyone*
[b]13:9 Other mss add *you shall not bear false witness*
[c]13:9 Ex 20:13-17; Dt 5:17-21
[d]13:9 Lv 19:18
[e]13:11 Other mss read *for us*
[f]14:1 Or *weak in the Faith*
[g]14:4 Other mss read *For God has the power*

WORD STUDY

Greek word: *hamartia*
[hah mahr TEE ah]
Translation: *sin*
Uses in Romans: **48**
Uses in Paul's writings: **64**
Uses in the NT: **173**
Key passage: **Romans 14:23**

The Greek noun *hamartia* is the most common term in the NT for human violation of God's moral standard. The related verb *hamartano* (43 uses in the NT, 17 in Paul) literally means *to miss the mark*, but the term eventually acquired the additional meanings *to fail* and *to do wrong*. Finally, *hamartano* came to include the idea *to sin*, which is the meaning of the verb in the NT. Not surprisingly, both *hamartano* and *hamartia* occur quite frequently in the Greek OT, mainly to translate the most common Hebrew words for sin. The root idea here is also *to miss the mark*, picturing human effort missing the target of God's standard. The standard being violated is God's revealed will.

In demonstrating the wickedness of the entire human race (Rm 1:18–3:20), Paul concluded that one function of the law was that "the whole world may become subject to God's judgment" (Rm 3:19) since "through the law comes the knowledge of sin" (v. 20; see v. 23). The law exposes human sin in order to drive people to God's gracious provision of salvation in Christ (vv. 21-26). Paul defined sin even more sharply in Romans 14 when he said, "Everything that is not from faith is sin" (v. 23). The essence of sin is unbelief, so every violation of God's standard is a lack of faith in Him. God doesn't want superficial obedience to a standard; He wants us to trust Him completely (see Heb 11:6).

Each one must be fully convinced in his own mind. ⁶ Whoever observes the day, observes it to the Lord.ᵃ Whoever eats, eats to the Lord, since he gives thanks to God; and whoever does not eat, it is to the Lord that he does not eat, yet he thanks God. ⁷ For none of us lives to himself, and no one dies to himself. ⁸ If we live, we live to the Lord; and if we die, we die to the Lord. Therefore, whether we live or die, we belong to the Lord. ⁹ Christ died and came to life for this: that He might rule over both the dead and the living. ¹⁰ But you, why do you criticize your brother? Or you, why do you look down on your brother? For we will all stand before the judgment seat of God.ᵇ ¹¹ For it is written:

> **As I live, says the Lord,**
> **every knee will bow to Me,**
> **and every tongue will give praise to God.**ᶜ

¹² So then, each of us will give an account of himself to God.

THE LAW OF LOVE

¹³ Therefore, let us no longer criticize one another, but instead decide not to put a stumbling block or pitfall in your brother's way. ¹⁴ (I know and am persuaded by the Lord Jesus that nothing is unclean in itself. Still, to someone who considers a thing to be unclean, to that one it is unclean.) ¹⁵ For if your brother is hurt by what you eat, you are no longer •walking according to love. By what you eat, do not destroy that one for whom Christ died. ¹⁶ Therefore, do not let your good be slandered, ¹⁷ for the kingdom of God is not eating and drinking, but righteousness, peace, and joy in the Holy Spirit. ¹⁸ Whoever serves the •Messiah in this way is acceptable to God and approved by men.

¹⁹ So then, we must pursue what promotes peace and what builds up one another. ²⁰ Do not tear down God's work because of food. Everything is clean, but it is wrong for a man to cause stumbling by what he eats. ²¹ It is a noble thing not to eat meat, or drink wine, or do anything that makes your brother stumble.ᵈ ²² Do

---

ᵃ**14:6** Other mss add *but whoever does not observe the day, it is to the Lord that he does not observe it*
ᵇ**14:10** Other mss read *of Christ*
ᶜ**14:11** Is 45:23; 49:18
ᵈ**14:21** Other mss add *or offended or weakened*

you have faith? Keep it to yourself before God. Blessed is the man who does not condemn himself by what he approves. 23 But whoever doubts stands condemned if he eats, because his eating is not from faith, and everything that is not from faith is sin.

PLEASING OTHERS, NOT OURSELVES

15 Now we who are strong have an obligation to bear the weaknesses of those without strength, and not to please ourselves. 2 Each one of us must please his neighbor for his good, in order to build him up. 3 For even the •Messiah did not please Himself. On the contrary, as it is written, **The insults of those who insult You have fallen on Me.**a 4 For whatever was written before was written for our instruction, so that through our endurance and through the encouragement of the Scriptures we may have hope. 5 Now may the God of endurance and encouragement grant you agreement with one another, according to Christ Jesus, 6 so that you may glorify the God and Father of our Lord Jesus Christ with a united mind and voice.

GLORIFYING GOD TOGETHER

7 Therefore accept one another, just as the Messiah also accepted you, to the glory of God. 8 Now I say that Christ has become a servant of the circumcisedb on behalf of the truth of God, to confirm the promises to the fathers, 9 and so that Gentiles may glorify God for His mercy. As it is written:

> **Therefore I will praise You**
> **among the Gentiles,**
> **and I will sing psalms to Your name.**c

10 Again it says: **Rejoice, you Gentiles, with His people!**d
11 And again:

> **Praise the Lord, all you Gentiles;**
> **all the peoples should praise Him!**e

---

a15:3 Ps 69:9
b15:8 The Jews
c15:9 2 Sm 22:50; Ps 18:49
d15:10 Dt 32:43
e15:11 Ps 117:1

WORD STUDY

Greek word: **proslambano**
[prahss lahm BAH noh]
Translation: **accept**
Uses in Romans: **4**
Uses in Paul's writings: **5**
Uses in the NT: **12**
Key passage: **Romans 15:7**

The Greek verb *proslambano* is a compound from the preposition *pros*, meaning *beside* or *alongside*, and the verb *lambano*, meaning *take* or *receive*. Thus, *proslambano* means *to take along* or *alongside*. After Jesus told the disciples about His coming death in Jerusalem, Peter took Jesus aside and rebuked Him (Mt 16:22 = Mk 8:32). Priscilla and Aquila took Apollos aside to explain the gospel to him more accurately (Ac 18:26). In Thessalonica, Paul's Jewish opponents took some men with them and formed a mob to harass Paul and his companions (Ac 17:5). On two occasions proslambano has essentially the same meaning as *lambano*, since it is used for taking or eating food (Ac 27:33,36).

The term *proslambano* was used in a personal or relational sense as well (*to receive to oneself*). Paul told Philemon how to respond to the return of his runaway slave Onesimus: "accept him as you would me" (Phm 17). All three uses of *proslambano* in Romans refer to believers who are in conflict with one another. The strong in faith must accept the weak (Rm 14:1) instead of being judgmental, for God accepts both of them (v. 3). Finally, Paul stated that believers must accept one another in the same way Christ accepted them (15:7). Since Christ did not put stipulations on those He would receive, believers must not do so.

[12] And again, Isaiah says:

The root of Jesse will appear,
the One who rises to rule the Gentiles;
in Him the Gentiles will hope.[a]

[13] Now may the God of hope fill you with all joy and peace in believing, so that you may overflow with hope by the power of the Holy Spirit.

FROM JERUSALEM TO ILLYRICUM

[14] Now, my brothers, I myself am convinced about you that you also are full of goodness, filled with all knowledge, and able to instruct one another. [15] Nevertheless, to remind you, I have written to you more boldly on some points[b] because of the grace given me by God [16] to be a minister of Christ Jesus to the Gentiles, serving as a priest of God's good news. My purpose is that the offering of the Gentiles may be acceptable, sanctified by the Holy Spirit. [17] Therefore I have reason to boast in Christ Jesus regarding what pertains to God. [18] For I would not dare say anything except what Christ has accomplished through me to make the Gentiles obedient by word and deed, [19] by the power of miraculous signs and wonders, and by the power of God's Spirit. As a result, I have fully proclaimed the good news about the Messiah from Jerusalem all the way around to Illyricum.[c] [20] So my aim is to evangelize where Christ has not been named, in order that I will not be building on someone else's foundation, [21] but, as it is written:

Those who had no report of Him will see,
and those who have not heard
will understand.[d]

PAUL'S TRAVEL PLANS

[22] That is why I have been prevented many times from coming to you. [23] But now I no longer have any work to do in these provinces,[e] and I have strongly desired

---

Are You Doing the Hard Work of Prayer?

You do not "organize" the kingdom of God; you "agonize" the kingdom of God.

I implore you, brothers, through the Lord Jesus Christ and through the love of the Spirit, to agonize together with me in your prayers to God on my behalf.

—Romans 15:30

---

[a]**15:12** Is 11:10
[b]**15:15** Other mss add *brothers*
[c]**15:19** A Roman province northwest of Greece on the eastern shore of the Adriatic Sea
[d]**15:21** Is 52:15
[e]**15:23** Lit *now, having no longer a place in these parts*

for many years to come to you [24] whenever I travel to Spain.[a] For I do hope to see you when I pass through, and to be sent on my way there by you, once I have first enjoyed your company for a while. [25] Now, however, I am traveling to Jerusalem to serve the saints; [26] for Macedonia and Achaia[b] were pleased to make a contribution to the poor among the saints in Jerusalem. [27] Yes, they were pleased, and they are indebted to them. For if the Gentiles have shared in their spiritual benefits, then they are obligated to minister to Jews[c] in material needs. [28] So when I have finished this and safely delivered the funds[d] to them, I will go by way of you to Spain. [29] But I know that when I come to you, I will come in the fullness of the blessing[e] of Christ.

[30] Now I implore you, brothers, through the Lord Jesus Christ and through the love of the Spirit, to agonize together with me in your prayers to God on my behalf: [31] that I may be rescued from the unbelievers in Judea, that my service for Jerusalem may be acceptable to the saints, [32] and that, by God's will, I may come to you with joy and be refreshed together with you. [33] The God of peace be with all of you. •Amen.

PAUL'S COMMENDATION OF PHOEBE

16 I commend to you our sister Phoebe, who is a servant[f] of the church in Cenchreae. [2] So you should welcome her in the Lord in a manner worthy of the saints, and assist her in whatever matter she may require your help. For indeed she has been a benefactor of many—and of me also.

GREETING TO ROMAN CHRISTIANS

[3] Give my greetings to Prisca[g] and Aquila, my co-workers in Christ Jesus, [4] who risked their own necks for my life. Not only do I thank them, but so do all the Gentile churches.

To Get or to Give— That Is the Question

When we decide to daily change our focus from *receiving* a blessing to *giving* a blessing, then we are able to affect others for Christ.

You should welcome her in the Lord in a manner worthy of the saints, and assist her in whatever matter she may require your help. For indeed she has been a benefactor of many—and of me also.
—Romans 16:2

A Little Help for a Fellow Teammate?

A mark of spiritual maturity is a willingness to sacrifice personal comfort in order to strengthen other believers.

Give my greetings to Prisca and Aquila, my co-workers in Christ Jesus, who risked their own necks for my life.
—Romans 16:3-4a

[a]**15:24** Other mss add *I will come to you.*
[b]**15:26** The churches of these provinces
[c]**15:27** Lit *to them*
[d]**15:28** Lit *delivered this fruit*

[e]**15:29** Other mss add *of the gospel*
[f]**16:1** Others interpret this term in a technical sense: *deacon,* or *deaconess,* or *minister*
[g]**16:3** Traditionally, *Priscilla,* as in Ac 18:2,18,26

WORD STUDY

Greek word: **epistole**
[eh pihst ah LAY]

Translation: **epistle**

Uses in Romans: **1**

Uses in Paul's writings: **17**

Uses in the NT: **24**

Key passage: **Romans 16:22**

The English word *epistle* comes directly from the Greek noun *epistole*, which in the era of classical Greek could mean *message*, *command*, or *commission*. Since such messages were often in written form, the term took on the meaning *epistle* or *letter*, which is always the idea in the NT.

The term is used figuratively in only one passage (2 Co 3:2-3). Sometimes *epistole* refers to a letter whose content is given in the text (Ac 15:22-30; 23:25-30,33), and several times it refers to letters that are now books of the NT (Rm 16:22; Col 4:16 [first occurrence]; 1 Th 5:27; 2 Th 2:15; 3:14,17; 2 Pt 3:1, possibly v. 16).

The reference to Tertius as the writer of Romans (16:22) does not mean that Paul did not write the book but that Tertius acted as the apostle's scribe or secretary during the writing of the book. Other companions of Paul—such as Mark, Luke, Timothy, Silas, and Sosthenes—may have played a similar role in recording other letters by Paul.

Greek manuscripts of the NT books often included the word *epistole* as part of a book's name. This tradition gave to the Christian community the full names that are still used for many books of the NT, such as "The Epistle of Paul the Apostle to the Romans."

---

⁵ Greet also the church that meets in their home. Greet my dear friend Epaenetus, who is the first convert[a] to Christ from Asia.[b]

⁶ Greet Mary,[c] who has worked very hard for you.[d]

⁷ Greet Andronicus and Junia,[e] my fellow countrymen and fellow prisoners. They are outstanding among the apostles, and they were also in Christ before me.

⁸ Greet Ampliatus, my dear friend in the Lord.

⁹ Greet Urbanus, our co-worker in Christ, and my dear friend Stachys.

¹⁰ Greet Apelles, who is approved in Christ. Greet those who belong to the household of Aristobulus.

¹¹ Greet Herodion, my fellow countryman. Greet those who belong to the household of Narcissus who are in the Lord.

¹² Greet Tryphaena and Tryphosa, who have worked hard in the Lord. Greet my dear friend Persis, who has worked very hard in the Lord.

¹³ Greet Rufus, chosen in the Lord; also his mother—and mine.

¹⁴ Greet Asyncritus, Phlegon, Hermes, Patrobas, Hermas, and the brothers who are with them.

¹⁵ Greet Philologus and Julia, Nereus and his sister, and Olympas, and all the saints who are with them.

¹⁶ Greet one another with a holy kiss. All the churches of Christ send you greetings.

WARNING AGAINST DIVISIVE PEOPLE

¹⁷ Now I implore you, brothers, watch out for those who cause dissensions and pitfalls contrary to the doctrine you have learned. Avoid them; ¹⁸ for such people do not serve our Lord Christ but their own appetites,[f] and by smooth talk and flattering words they deceive the hearts of the unsuspecting.

---

[a]16:5 Lit *the firstfruits*
[b]16:5 Other mss read *Achaia*
[c]16:6 Or *Maria*
[d]16:6 Other mss read *us*

[e]16:7 Either a feminine name or *Junias*, a masculine name
[f]16:18 Lit *belly*

PAUL'S GRACIOUS CONCLUSION

19 The report of your obedience has reached everyone. Therefore I rejoice over you. But I want you to be wise about what is good, yet innocent about what is evil. 20 The God of peace will soon crush Satan under your feet. The grace of our Lord Jesus be with you.

21 Timothy, my co-worker, and Lucius, Jason, and Sosipater, my fellow countrymen, greet you.

22 I Tertius, who penned this epistle in the Lord, greet you.

23 Gaius, who is host to me and to the whole church, greets you. Erastus, the city treasurer, and our brother Quartus greet you.

[24 The grace of our Lord Jesus Christ be with you all.]ᵃ

GLORY TO GOD

25 Now to Him who has power to strengthen you according to my gospel and the proclamation of Jesus Christ, according to the revelation of the sacred secret kept silent for long ages, 26 but now revealed and made known through the prophetic Scriptures, according to the command of the eternal God, to advance the obedience of faith among all nations— 27 to the only wise God, through Jesus Christ—to Him be the glory forever!ᵇ •Amen.

Keep Growing in Grace and Goodness

No matter how far we've come, we're never all the way there. There is always something to learn. It's crucial that Christians never stop growing in wisdom.

The report of your obedience has reached everyone. Therefore I rejoice over you. But I want you to be wise about what is good, yet innocent about what is evil.

—Romans 16:19

Live in Victory over Satan—Jesus' Victory

Christians can become preoccupied with battling Satan. Our assignment is to trust in the victory Christ has already achieved and to daily resist the devil, recognizing the reality of his defeat.

The God of peace will soon crush Satan under your feet. The grace of our Lord Jesus be with you.

—Romans 16:20

ᵃ16:24 Other mss omit bracketed text; see v. 20

ᵇ16:25-27 Other mss have these vv. at the end of chap 14 or 15.

CORINTHIANS

GREETING

1 Paul, called as an apostle of Christ Jesus by God's will, and our brother Sosthenes:

² To God's church at Corinth, to those who are sanctified in Christ Jesus and called as saints, with all those in every place who call on the name of Jesus Christ our Lord—theirs and ours.

³ Grace to you and peace from God our Father and the Lord Jesus Christ.

THANKSGIVING

⁴ I always thank my God for you because of God's grace given to you in Christ Jesus, ⁵ that by Him you were made rich in everything—in all speaking and all knowledge— ⁶ as the testimony about Christ was confirmed among you, ⁷ so that you do not lack any spiritual gift as you eagerly wait for the revelation of our Lord Jesus Christ. ⁸ He will also confirm you to the end, blameless in the day of our Lord Jesus Christ. ⁹ God is faithful; by Him you were called into fellowship with His Son, Jesus Christ our Lord.

DIVISIONS AT CORINTH

¹⁰ Now I urge you, brothers, in the name of our Lord Jesus Christ, that you all say the same thing, that there be no divisions among you, and that you be united with the same understanding and the same conviction. ¹¹ For it has been reported to me about you, my brothers, by members of Chloe's household, that there are quarrels among you. ¹² What I am saying is this: each of you says, "I'm with Paul," or "I'm with Apollos," or "I'm with •Cephas," or "I'm with Christ." ¹³ Is Christ

divided? Was it Paul who was crucified for you? Or were you baptized in Paul's name? [14] I thank God[a] [b] that I baptized none of you except Crispus and Gaius, [15] so that no one can say you had been baptized in my name. [16] I did, in fact, baptize the household of Stephanas; beyond that, I don't know if I baptized anyone else. [17] For Christ did not send me to baptize, but to preach the gospel—not with clever words, so that the cross of Christ will not be emptied ₍of its effect₎.

CHRIST THE POWER AND WISDOM OF GOD

[18] For to those who are perishing the message of the cross is foolishness, but to us who are being saved it is God's power. [19] For it is written:

**I will destroy the wisdom of the wise,
and I will set aside the understanding
of the experts.**[c]

[20] Where is the philosopher?[d] Where is the scholar? Where is the debater of this age? Hasn't God made the world's wisdom foolish? [21] For since, in God's wisdom, the world did not know God through wisdom, God was pleased to save those who believe through the foolishness of the message preached. [22] For the Jews ask for signs and the Greeks seek wisdom, [23] but we preach Christ crucified, a stumbling block to the Jews and foolishness to the Gentiles.[e] [24] Yet to those who are called, both Jews and Greeks, Christ is God's power and God's wisdom, [25] because God's foolishness is wiser than human wisdom, and God's weakness is stronger than human strength.

BOASTING ONLY IN THE LORD

[26] Brothers, consider your calling: not many are wise from a human perspective,[f] not many powerful, not many of noble birth. [27] Instead, God has chosen the world's foolish things to shame the wise, and God has chosen the world's weak things to shame the strong. [28] God has chosen the world's insignificant and

Better to Be Available Than Merely Capable

Talent and ability are not prerequisites to being used by God. He is known for taking the ordinary and making it extraordinary.

God has chosen the world's insignificant and despised things—the things viewed as nothing—so He might bring to nothing the things that are viewed as something.

—1 Corinthians 1:28

---

[a]1:14 Other mss omit *God*
[b]1:14 Or *I am thankful*
[c]1:19 Is 29:14
[d]1:20 Or *wise*
[e]1:23 Other mss read *Greeks*
[f]1:26 Lit *wise according to the flesh*

WORD STUDY

Greek word: **sophia**
[sah FEE ah]
Translation: **wisdom**
Uses in 1 Corinthians: **17**
Uses in Paul's writings: **28**
Uses in the NT: **51**
Key passage: **1 Corinthians 2:6**

The Greek noun *sophia* means *wisdom, intelligence,* or *knowledge,* but this intelligence and knowledge pertain more to skill in living than to attainment of facts. Related words are the verb *sophizo,* meaning *to make wise* (2 Tm 3:15; 2 Pt 1:16 only in the NT), and *sophos,* the adjective meaning *wise* or *clever.*

In the Old Testament, wisdom does not refer to intellectual ability but to one who looks to God for instruction in living. Solomon stated that "the fear of the Lord is the beginning of knowledge" (Pr 1:7), which implies that even a genius who does not fear God is a fool (see Ps 14:1).

In the NT, *sophia* must be understood primarily in the light of the OT. Paul saw worldly wisdom and God's wisdom as opposites (see 1 Co 2:1-9; Col 2:23). The Greeks depended on human mental prowess and insight to unravel the mysteries of life, but Paul relied on God's revelation in Christ (1 Co 1:30; Eph 1:8-9,17; 3:8-12). This is why Paul said that God's wisdom in Christ is not "of this age" (1 Co 2:6) and that "the wisdom of this world is foolishness with God" (1 Co 3:19; see 1:18-25). By contrast, God's wisdom is taught by the Spirit (1 Co 2:13). Paul explained that wisdom for godly living is found in God's revelation in Christ (1 Co 2:6; Col 1:9,28; 3:16; 4:5).

despised things—the things viewed as nothing—so He might bring to nothing the things that are viewed as something, ²⁹ so that no one[a] can boast in His presence. ³⁰ But from Him you are in Christ Jesus, who for us became wisdom from God, as well as righteousness, sanctification, and redemption, ³¹ in order that, as it is written: **The one who boasts must boast in the Lord.**[b]

PAUL'S PROCLAMATION

2 When I came to you, brothers, announcing the testimony[c] of God to you, I did not come with brilliance of speech or wisdom. ² For I determined to know nothing among you except Jesus Christ and Him crucified. ³ And I was with you in weakness, in fear, and in much trembling. ⁴ My speech and my proclamation were not with persuasive words of wisdom,[d] but with a demonstration of the Spirit and power, ⁵ so that your faith might not be based on men's wisdom but on God's power.

SPIRITUAL WISDOM

⁶ However, among the mature we do speak a wisdom, but not a wisdom of this age, or of the rulers of this age, who are coming to nothing. ⁷ On the contrary, we speak God's hidden wisdom in a •mystery, which God predestined before the ages for our glory. ⁸ None of the rulers of this age knew it, for if they had known it, they would not have crucified the Lord of glory. ⁹ But as it is written:

> **What no eye has seen and no ear**
> **has heard,**
> **and what has never come**
> **into man's heart,**
> **is what God has prepared for those**
> **who love Him.**[e]

¹⁰ Now God has revealed them to us by the Spirit, for the Spirit searches everything, even the deep things of God. ¹¹ For who among men knows the concerns[f] of a

---

[a]1:29 Lit *that not all flesh*
[b]1:31 Jr 9:24
[c]2:1 Other mss read *mystery*
[d]2:4 Other mss read *human wisdom*
[e]2:9 Is 52:15; 64:4
[f]2:11 Lit *things*

man except the spirit of the man that is in him? In the same way, no one knows the concerns[a] of God except the Spirit of God. [12] Now we have not received the spirit of the world, but the Spirit who is from God, in order to know what has been freely given to us by God. [13] We also speak these things, not in words taught by human wisdom, but in those taught by the Spirit, explaining spiritual things to spiritual people.[b] [14] But the natural man does not welcome what comes from God's Spirit, because it is foolishness to him; he is not able to know it since it is evaluated[c] spiritually. [15] The spiritual person, however, can evaluate[d] everything, yet he himself cannot be evaluated[c] by anyone. [16] For:

**who has known the Lord's mind,
that he may instruct Him?[e]**

But we have the mind of Christ.

THE PROBLEM OF IMMATURITY

3 Brothers, I was not able to speak to you as spiritual people but as people of the flesh, as babies in Christ. [2] I fed you milk, not solid food, because you were not yet able to receive it. In fact, you are still not able, [3] because you are still fleshly. For since there is envy and strife[f] among you, are you not fleshly and living like ordinary people?[g] [4] For whenever someone says, "I'm with Paul," and another, "I'm with Apollos," are you not ⌊typical⌋ men?[h]

THE ROLE OF GOD'S SERVANTS

[5] So, what is Apollos? And what is Paul? They are servants through whom you believed, and each has the role the Lord has given. [6] I planted, Apollos watered, but God gave the growth. [7] So then neither the one who plants nor the one who waters is anything, but only God who gives the growth. [8] Now the one who plants and the one who waters are equal, and each will receive his own reward according to his own labor. [9] For we are

The Holy Spirit Is the Ultimate Persuader

Know the Scriptures and share the Scriptures, letting the Holy Spirit guide you. The Spirit of God and the Word of God will do their own work in each person.

My speech and my proclamation were not with persuasive words of wisdom, but with a demonstration of the Spirit and power.
—1 Corinthians 2:4

Disciples Are Different Down to the Details

We expect a lot from God, but too often we do not take seriously what He expects of us.

Since there is envy and strife among you, are you not fleshly and living like ordinary people?
—1 Corinthians 3:3b

---

[a]2:11 Lit *things*
[b]2:13 Or *things with spiritual words*
[c]2:14,15 Or *judged*, or *discerned*
[d]2:15 Or *judge*, or *discern*
[e]2:16 Is 40:13

[f]3:3 Other mss add *and divisions*
[g]3:3 Lit *and walking according to man*
[h]3:4 Other mss read *are you not carnal*

WORD STUDY

Greek word: ***misthos***
[mihss THASS]
Translation: ***reward***
Uses in 1 Corinthians: **4**
Uses in Paul's writings: **6**
Uses in the NT: **29**
Key passage: **1 Corinthians 3:8,14**

The Greek noun *misthos* means *pay, wage, reward, recompense.* Other related terms are *misthios* (used only in Lk 15:17,19) and *misthotos* (used only in Mk 1:20; Jn 10:12-13), both meaning *hired hand; misthoo* (*to hire someone,* used only in Mt 20:1,7); *misthoma* (*something rented,* used only in Ac 28:30); *misthapodosia* (*reward* in Heb 10:35-36; *penalty* in Heb 2:2); and *misthapodotes* (*rewarder,* used only in Heb 11:6). The main idea in this word family is compensation for a task.

The term *misthos* often refers to monetary payment but its main use is to describe some aspect of divine evaluation of human activity. Jesus used *misthos* several times in the Sermon on the Mount in reference to rewards that the ungodly receive in this life (Mt 5:46; 6:2,5,16; see 2 Pt 2:13,15; Jd 11) in contrast to rewards that believers will receive in heaven (Mt 5:12; 6:1; see Mk 9:41; Lk 6:23,35; 2 Jn 8).

Paul used the term *misthos* four times in 1 Corinthians, and all four refer to the reward that comes from Christian ministry. At the day of judgment the Lord will test by fire the purity of everyone's ministry. Some will receive a reward, while others will endure loss, though not the loss of salvation (1 Co 3:10-15).

God's co-workers. You are God's field, God's building. [10] According to God's grace that was given to me, as a skilled master builder I have laid a foundation, and another builds on it. But each one must be careful how he builds on it, [11] because no one can lay any other foundation than what has been laid—that is, Jesus Christ. [12] If anyone builds on the foundation with gold, silver, costly stones, wood, hay, or straw, [13] each one's work will become obvious, for the day[a] will disclose it, because it will be revealed by fire; the fire will test the quality of each one's work. [14] If anyone's work that he has built survives, he will receive a reward. [15] If anyone's work is burned up, it will be lost, but he will be saved; yet it will be like an escape through fire.[b]

[16] Don't you know that you are God's sanctuary and that the Spirit of God lives in you? [17] If anyone ruins God's sanctuary, God will ruin him; for God's sanctuary is holy, and that is what you are.

THE FOLLY OF HUMAN WISDOM

[18] No one should deceive himself. If anyone among you thinks he is wise in this age, he must become foolish so that he can become wise. [19] For the wisdom of this world is foolishness with God, since it is written: **He catches the wise in their craftiness**[c] — [20] and again, **The Lord knows the reasonings of the wise, that they are futile.**[d] [21] So no one should boast in men, for all things are yours: [22] whether Paul or Apollos or •Cephas or the world or life or death or things present or things to come—all are yours, [23] and you belong to Christ, and Christ to God.

THE FAITHFUL MANAGER

4 A person should consider us in this way: as servants of Christ and managers of God's •mysteries. [2] In this regard, it is expected of managers that each one be found faithful. [3] It is of little importance that I should be evaluated by you or by a human court.[e] In fact, I don't even evaluate myself. [4] For I am not conscious of anything against myself, but I am not justified

---

[a]**3:13** The Day of Christ's judgment of believers
[b]**3:15** Lit *yet so as through fire*
[c]**3:19** Jb 5:13
[d]**3:20** Ps 94:11
[e]**4:3** Lit *a human day*

by this. The One who evaluates me is the Lord. [5] Therefore don't judge anything prematurely, before the Lord comes, who will both bring to light what is hidden in darkness and reveal the intentions of the hearts. And then praise will come to each one from God.

THE APOSTLES' EXAMPLE OF HUMILITY

[6] Now, brothers, I have applied these things to myself and Apollos for your benefit, so that you may learn from us the saying: "Nothing beyond what is written."[a] The purpose is that none of you will be inflated with pride in favor of one person over another. [7] For who makes you so superior? What do you have that you didn't receive? If, in fact, you did receive it, why do you boast as if you hadn't received it? [8] Already you are full! Already you are rich! You have begun to reign as kings without us—and I wish you did reign, so that we also could reign with you! [9] For I think God has displayed us, the apostles, in last place, like men condemned to die: we have become a spectacle to the world and to angels and to men. [10] We are fools for Christ, but you are wise in Christ! We are weak, but you are strong! You are distinguished, but we are dishonored! [11] Up to the present hour we are both hungry and thirsty; we are poorly clothed, roughly treated, homeless; [12] we labor, working with our own hands. When we are reviled, we bless; when we are persecuted, we endure it; [13] when we are slandered, we entreat. We are, even now, like the world's garbage, like the filth of all things.

PAUL'S FATHERLY CARE

[14] I'm not writing this to shame you, but to warn you as my dear children. [15] For you can have 10,000 instructors in Christ, but you can't have many fathers. Now I have fathered you in Christ Jesus through the gospel. [16] Therefore I urge you, be imitators of me. [17] This is why I have sent to you Timothy, who is my beloved and faithful child in the Lord. He will remind you about my ways in Christ Jesus, just as I teach everywhere in every church. [18] Now some are inflated with

[a]4:6 The words in quotation marks could refer to the OT, a Jewish maxim, or a popular proverb.

Live Your Own Life, Not Someone Else's

It's wiser to focus on your own character, working on the things you need to change, than to waste time worrying about others getting what they deserve.

Don't judge anything prematurely, before the Lord comes, who will both bring to light what is hidden in darkness and reveal the intentions of the hearts. And then praise will come to each one from God.

—1 Corinthians 4:5

Never Forget Who Got You This Far

If pride has crept into some area of your life, ask God to give you victory over it before it robs you of God's will for you.

Who makes you so superior? What do you have that you didn't receive? If, in fact, you did receive it, why do you boast as if you hadn't received it?

—1 Corinthians 4:7

WORD STUDY

Greek word: **porneia**
[pohr NIGH ah]
Translation: **sexual immorality**
Uses in 1 Corinthians: **5**
Uses in Paul's writings: **10**
Uses in the NT: **25**
Key passage: **1 Corinthians 5:1**

The Greek noun *porneia* was a general term for all sexual activity outside marriage, so the term can be translated *fornication* or *sexual immorality.* Related terms include *porneuo,* meaning *to commit sexual immorality* (see 1 Co 6:18; 10:18); *porne,* meaning *an immoral woman* or *a female prostitute* (see 1 Co 6:15-16); and *pornos,* meaning *an immoral person* or *a male prostitute* (1 Co 5:9-11; 6:9).

Paul condemned a case of incest in the church in Corinth, a sin he called *porneia* (1 Co 5:1). In chapter 6 he explained that the believer's body is for the Lord and not for *porneia* (v. 13). Then he commanded believers to flee *porneia* (v. 18). On the other hand, sexual union in marriage is commended, partly because it helps believers avoid *porneia* (7:2). It is likely that cult prostitution, in which the Corinthian people could indulge at the temple of Aphrodite, was a major threat to the Corinthian believers' spiritual growth.

pride, as though I were not coming to you. [19] But I will come to you soon, if the Lord wills, and I will know not the talk but the power of those who are inflated with pride. [20] For the kingdom of God is not in talk but in power. [21] What do you want? Should I come to you with a rod, or in love and a spirit of gentleness?

IMMORAL CHURCH MEMBERS

5 It is widely reported that there is sexual immorality among you, and the kind of sexual immorality that is not even condoned[a] among the Gentiles—a man is living with his father's wife. [2] And you are inflated with pride, instead of filled with grief so that he who has committed this act might be removed from among you. [3] For though absent in body but present in spirit, I have already decided about him who has done this thing as though I were present. [4] In the name of our Lord Jesus, when you are assembled, along with my spirit and with the power of our Lord Jesus, [5] turn that one over to Satan for the destruction of the flesh, so that his spirit may be saved in the Day of the Lord.

[6] Your boasting is not good. Don't you know that a little yeast permeates the whole batch of dough? [7] Clean out the old yeast so that you may be a new batch, since you are unleavened. For Christ our •Passover has been sacrificed.[b] [8] Therefore, let us observe the feast, not with old yeast, or with the yeast of malice and evil, but with the unleavened bread of sincerity and truth.

CHURCH DISCIPLINE

[9] I wrote to you in a letter not to associate with sexually immoral people— [10] by no means referring to this world's immoral people, or to the greedy and swindlers, or to idolaters; otherwise you would have to leave the world. [11] But now I am writing[c] you not to associate with anyone who bears the name of brother who is sexually immoral or greedy, an idolater or a reviler, a drunkard or a swindler. Do not even eat with such a person. [12] For what is it to me to judge outsiders? Do you not judge those who are inside? [13] But

---

[a]5:1 Other mss read *named*
[b]5:7 Other mss add *for us*
[c]5:11 Or *now I wrote*

God judges outsiders. **Put away the evil person from among yourselves.**[a]

LAWSUITS AMONG BELIEVERS

6 Does any of you who has a complaint against someone dare go to law before the unrighteous,[b] and not before the saints? [2] Or do you not know that the saints will judge the world? And if the world is judged by you, are you unworthy to judge the smallest cases? [3] Do you not know that we will judge angels—not to speak of things pertaining to this life? [4] So if you have cases pertaining to this life, do you select those[c] who have no standing in the church to judge? [5] I say this to your shame! Can it be that there is not one wise person among you who will be able to arbitrate between his brothers? [6] Instead, brother goes to law against brother, and that before unbelievers!

[7] Therefore, it is already a total defeat for you that you have lawsuits against one another. Why not rather put up with injustice? Why not rather be cheated? [8] Instead, you act unjustly and cheat—and this to brothers! [9] Do you not know that the unjust will not inherit God's kingdom? Do not be deceived: no sexually immoral people, idolaters, adulterers, male prostitutes, homosexuals, [10] thieves, greedy people, drunkards, revilers, or swindlers will inherit God's kingdom. [11] Some of you were like this; but you were washed, you were sanctified, you were justified in the name of the Lord Jesus Christ and by the Spirit of our God.

GLORIFYING GOD IN BODY AND SPIRIT

[12] "Everything is permissible for me,"[d] but not everything is helpful. "Everything is permissible for me,"[d] but I will not be brought under the control of anything. [13] "Foods for the stomach and the stomach for foods,"[d] but God will do away with both of them.[e] The body is not for sexual immorality but for the Lord, and the Lord for the body. [14] God raised up the Lord and will also raise us up by His power. [15] Do you not know that your

---

[a]5:13 Dt 17:7
[b]6:1 Unbelievers; see v. 6
[c]6:4 Or *life, appoint those* (as a command)
[d]6:12,13 The words in quotation

marks are most likely slogans used by some Corinthian Christians. Paul evaluates and corrects these slogans.
[e]6:13 Lit *both it and them*

WORD STUDY

Greek word: *krino*
[KRIH noh]
Translation: *judge*
Uses in 1 Corinthians: **17**
Uses in Paul's writings: **41**
Uses in the NT: **114**
Key passage: **1 Corinthians 6:1-6**

The Greek verb *krino* means *to judge* and always involves the process of thinking through a situation and coming to a conclusion. The term could be used in a narrowly judicial sense but it also has several nuances related to judging in a more general sense. In nonjudicial contexts, *krino* can mean *to select, prefer, decide, consider.* Thirty terms related to *krino* occur in the NT; the three most common are the verb *apokrinomai* (meaning *to answer*), the noun *krisis* (meaning *judgment*), and another noun *krima* (meaning *judgment* or *condemnation*).

In the NT, *krino* most often refers to judging something or someone in general. However, *krino* does occur in specific judicial settings several times, and the court can be human (Mt 5:40; Jn 7:51; 18:31; Ac 23:3; 24:21; 25:9-10,20; 26:6; 1 Co 6:1,6) or divine (Jn 5:22,30; 12:48; Ac 17:31; Rm 2:16; 3:4-7; 2 Tm 4:1; 1 Pt 4:5; Rv 20:12-13). In two passages, *krino* is used with the meaning *to rule.* Jesus said that the twelve apostles would judge the twelve tribes of Israel "in the Messianic Age" (Mt 19:28), and here *krino* likely means *to rule,* as the verse's reference to sitting on thrones would imply. Similarly, Paul's statement that the saints would judge the world and angels (1 Co 6:2-3) probably means that believers will rule over them both in the future kingdom (compare Rv 2:26-27).

bodies are the members of Christ? So should I take the members of Christ and make them members of a prostitute? Absolutely not! [16] Do you not know that anyone joined to a prostitute is one body with her? For it says, **The two will become one flesh.**[a] [17] But anyone joined to the Lord is one spirit with Him.

[18] Flee from sexual immorality! "Every sin a person can commit is outside the body,"[b] but the person who is sexually immoral sins against his own body. [19] Do you not know that your body is a sanctuary of the Holy Spirit who is in you, whom you have from God? You are not your own, [20] for you were bought at a price; therefore glorify God in your body.[c]

PRINCIPLES OF MARRIAGE

7 About the things you wrote:[d] "It is good for a man not to have relations with[e] a woman."[f] [2] But because of sexual immorality,[g] each man should have his own wife, and each woman should have her own husband. [3] A husband should fulfill his marital duty to his wife, and likewise a wife to her husband. [4] A wife does not have authority over her own body, but her husband does. Equally, a husband does not have authority over his own body, but his wife does. [5] Do not deprive one another—except when you agree, for a time, to devote yourselves to[h] prayer. Then come together again; otherwise, Satan may tempt you because of your lack of self-control. [6] I say this as a concession, not as a command. [7] I wish that all people were just like me. But each has his own gift from God, one this and another that.

A WORD TO THE UNMARRIED

[8] I say to the unmarried and to widows: It is good for them if they remain as I am. [9] But if they do not have self-control, they should marry, for it is better to marry than to burn with desire.

The Spirit Is Living Right There Inside You

God has chosen you as His dwelling place. So treat your body as the holy temple that it is, and use it to bring glory to God in all that you do.

Do you not know that your body is a sanctuary of the Holy Spirit who is in you, whom you are not your own, for you were bought at a price; therefore glorify God in your body.

—1 Corinthians 6:19-20

---

[a]**6:16** Gn 2:24
[b]**6:18** See note at 1 Co 6:12
[c]**6:20** Other mss add *and in your spirit, which belong to God.*
[d]**7:1** Other mss add *to me*
[e]**7:1** Lit *not to touch*

[f]**7:1** The words in quotation marks are a principle that the Corinthians wrote to Paul and asked for his view about.
[g]**7:2** Lit *immoralities*
[h]**7:5** Other mss add *fasting and to*

ADVICE TO MARRIED PEOPLE

¹⁰ I command the married—not I, but the Lord—a wife is not to leaveᵃ her husband. ¹¹ But if she does leave, she must remain unmarried or be reconciled to her husband—and a husband is not to leave his wife. ¹² But to the rest I, not the Lord, say: If any brother has an unbelieving wife, and she is willing to live with him, he must not leave her. ¹³ Also, if any woman has an unbelieving husband, and he is willing to live with her, she must not leave her husband. ¹⁴ For the unbelieving husband is sanctified by the wife, and the unbelieving wife is sanctified by the Christian husband. Otherwise your children would be unclean, but now they are holy. ¹⁵ But if the unbeliever leaves, let him leave.ᵃ A brother or a sister is not bound in such cases. God has called youᵇ to peace. ¹⁶ For you, wife, how do you know whether you will save your husband? Or you, husband, how do you know whether you will save your wife?

VARIOUS SITUATIONS OF LIFE

¹⁷ However, each one must live his life in the situation the Lord assigned when God called him.ᶜ This is what I command in all the churches. ¹⁸ Was anyone already circumcised when he was called? He should not undo his circumcision. Was anyone called while uncircumcised? He should not get circumcised. ¹⁹ Circumcision does not matter and uncircumcision does not matter, but keeping God's commandments does. ²⁰ Each person should remain in the life situationᵈ in which he was called. ²¹ Were you called while a slave? It should not be a concern to you. But if you can become free, by all means take the opportunity.ᵉ ²² For he who is called by the Lord as a slave is the Lord's freedman.ᶠ Likewise he who is called as a free manᵍ is Christ's slave. ²³ You were bought at a price; do not become slaves of men. ²⁴ Brothers, each person should remain with God in whatever situation he was called.

Be a Living Witness of the Living God

When the Spirit of Almighty God fills you, others will see Him in your life. Wait patiently, and watch Him draw them to Jesus.

You, wife, how do you know whether you will save your husband? Or you, husband, how do you know whether you will save your wife?

— 1 Corinthians 7:16

Where Does He Want You to Go Today?

If you are a Christian, your life is not your own. Every day, you are to offer your life to Him for His service.

He who is called by the Lord as a slave is the Lord's freedman. Likewise he who is called as a free man is Christ's slave.

—1 Corinthians 7:22

ᵃ7:10,15 Or *separate from*, or *divorce*
ᵇ7:15 Other mss read *us*
ᶜ7:17 Lit *called each*
ᵈ7:20 Lit *in the calling*

ᵉ7:21 Or *But even though you can become free, make the most of your position as a slave.*
ᶠ7:22 A former slave
ᵍ7:22 A man who was never a slave

ABOUT THE UNMARRIED AND WIDOWS

25 About virgins: I have no command from the Lord, but I do give an opinion as one who by the Lord's mercy is trustworthy. 26 Therefore I consider this to be good because of the present distress: it is fine for a man to stay as he is. 27 Are you bound to a wife? Do not seek to be loosed. Are you loosed from a wife? Do not seek a wife. 28 However, if you do get married, you have not sinned, and if a virgin marries, she has not sinned. But such people will have trouble in this life,[a] and I am trying to spare you. 29 And I say this, brothers: the time is limited, so from now on those who have wives should be as though they had none, 30 those who weep as though they did not weep, those who rejoice as though they did not rejoice, those who buy as though they did not possess, 31 and those who use the world as though they did not make full use of it. For this world in its current form is passing away.

32 I want you to be without concerns. An unmarried man is concerned about the things of the Lord—how he may please the Lord. 33 But a married man is concerned about the things of the world—how he may please his wife— 34 and he is divided. An unmarried woman or a virgin is concerned about the things of the Lord, so that she may be holy both in body and in spirit. But a married woman is concerned about the things of the world—how she may please her husband. 35 Now I am saying this for your own benefit, not to put a restraint on you, but because of what is proper, and so that you may be devoted to the Lord without distraction.

36 But if any man thinks he is acting improperly toward his virgin,[b] if she is past marriageable age,[c] and so it must be, he can do what he wants. He is not sinning; they can get married. 37 But he who stands firm in his heart (who is under no compulsion, but has control over his own will) and has decided in his heart to keep his own virgin, will do well. 38 So then he who marries[d] his virgin does well, but he who does not marry[e] will do better.

This World Is Not Your Home

Has the world convinced you that there are certain rights you must protect? Have you noticed that in so doing, you are actually losing the life God wants you to have?

Those who use the world [live] as though they did not make full use of it. For this world in its current form is passing away.

—1 Corinthians 7:31

Think of How Your Actions Might Appear

Is there something you are doing that other Christians find objectionable? Are you willing to give up some of your freedom in order to live in harmony with them?

But be careful that this right of yours in no way becomes a stumbling block to the weak.

—1 Corinthians 8:9

---

[a]7:28 Lit *in the flesh*
[b]7:36 (1) a man's fiancée, or (2) his daughter, or (3) his Levirate wife, or (4) a celibate companion
[c]7:36 Or *virgin, if his passions are strong,*
[d]7:38 Or *marries off*
[e]7:38 Or *marry her off*

39 A wife is bound[a] as long as her husband is living. But if her husband dies, she is free to be married to anyone she wants—only in the Lord.[b] **40** But she is happier if she remains as she is, in my opinion. And I think that I also have the Spirit of God.

FOOD OFFERED TO IDOLS

8 About food offered to idols: We know that "we all have knowledge."[c] Knowledge inflates with pride, but love builds up. **2** If anyone thinks he knows anything, he does not yet know it as he ought to know it. **3** But if anyone loves God, he is known by Him.

4 About eating food offered to idols, then, we know that "an idol is nothing in the world,"[c] and that "there is no God but one."[c] **5** For even if there are so-called gods, whether in heaven or on earth—as there are many "gods" and many "lords"—

> **6** yet for us there is one God, the Father,
> from whom are all things, and we for Him;
> and one Lord, Jesus Christ,
> through whom are all things, and we
> through Him.

7 However, not everyone has this knowledge. In fact, some have been so used to idolatry up until now, that when they eat food offered to an idol, their conscience, being weak, is defiled. **8** Food will not make us acceptable to God. We are not inferior if we don't eat, and we are not better if we do eat. **9** But be careful that this right of yours in no way becomes a stumbling block to the weak. **10** For if somebody sees you, the one who has this knowledge, dining in an idol's temple, won't his weak conscience be encouraged to eat food offered to idols? **11** Then the weak person, the brother for whom Christ died, is ruined by your knowledge. **12** Now when you sin like this against the brothers and wound their weak conscience, you are sinning against Christ. **13** Therefore, if food causes my brother to fall, I will never again eat meat, so that I won't cause my brother to fall.

WORD STUDY

Greek word: **suneidesis**
[soon IGH day sihss]
Translation: **conscience**
Uses in 1 Corinthians: **8**
Uses in Paul's writings: **20**
Uses in the NT: **30**
Key passage: **1 Corinthians 8:7-12**

———

The Greek noun *suneidesis* literally means *a seeing together* and refers to one's insight into self—that is, *conscience*. The word occurs only once in the Greek OT (Ec 10:20) and never in the Gospels. The term normally has a moral aspect to it, for a person's conscience recognizes an existing standard that he or she must follow (Ac 23:1; Rm 9:1; 2 Co 1:12; 1 Tm 1:5; 2 Tm 1:3; 1 Pt 2:19). In 1 Corinthians, however, Paul used *suneidesis* in an ethical—not moral—sense. The conscience may tell a certain believer one thing and another believer something else. Such situations fall into the area of Christian liberty. Some Christians in Corinth thought eating meat sacrificed to an idol was sinful, and Paul stated that they must follow their consciences and not eat the meat. However, other Christians realized that such meat was not really defiled, and Paul explained that they were at liberty to eat the meat with a clear conscience in certain situations (see 1 Co 8:1-13; 10:25-30). Paul's teaching here has a parallel in Romans 14, where Paul stated that "everything that is not from faith is sin" (v. 23; see also vv. 2-3,5-6,13-16,20-21).

---

[a]7:39 Other mss add *by law*   [c]8:1,4 See note at 1 Co 6:12
[b]7:39 Only a believer

PAUL'S EXAMPLE AS AN APOSTLE

9 Am I not free? Am I not an apostle? Have I not seen Jesus our Lord? Are you not my work in the Lord? ² If I am not an apostle to others, at least I am to you, for you are the seal of my apostleship in the Lord. ³ My defense to those who examine me is this: ⁴ Don't we have the right to eat and drink? ⁵ Don't we have the right to be accompanied by a Christian wife, like the other apostles, the Lord's brothers, and •Cephas? ⁶ Or is it only Barnabas and I who have no right to refrain from working? ⁷ Who ever goes to war at his own expense? Who plants a vineyard and does not eat its fruit? Or who shepherds a flock and does not drink the milk from the flock? ⁸ Am I saying this from a human perspective? Doesn't the law also say the same thing? ⁹ For it is written in the law of Moses, **Do not muzzle an ox while it treads out the grain.**ᵃ Is God really concerned with oxen? ¹⁰ Or isn't He really saying it for us? Yes, this is written for us, because he who plows ought to plow in hope, and he who threshes should do so in hope of sharing the crop. ¹¹ If we have sown spiritual things for you, is it too much if we reap material things from you? ¹² If others share this authority over you, don't we even more?

However, we have not used this authority; instead we endure everything so that we will not hinder the gospel of Christ. ¹³ Do you not know that those who perform the temple services eat the food from the temple, and those who serve at the altar share in the offerings of the altar? ¹⁴ In the same way, the Lord has commanded that those who preach the gospel should earn their living by the gospel.

¹⁵ But I have used none of these rights, and I have not written this to make it happen that way for me. For it would be better for me to die than for anyone to deprive me of my boast! ¹⁶ For if I preach the gospel, I have no reason to boast, because an obligation is placed on me. And woe to me if I do not preach the gospel! ¹⁷ For if I do this willingly, I have a reward; but if unwillingly, I am entrusted with a stewardship. ¹⁸ What then is my reward? To preach the gospel and

---

Your Calling Is a Command, Not a Good Suggestion

Once you have received a clear assignment from God, your response should be unwavering obedience.

If I preach the gospel, I have no reason to boast, because an obligation is placed on me. And woe to me if I do not preach the gospel!
— 1 Corinthians 9:16

ᵃ9:9 Dt 25:4

offer it free of charge, and not make full use of my authority in the gospel.

19 For although I am free from all people, I have made myself a slave to all, in order to win more people. 20 To the Jews I became like a Jew, to win Jews; to those under the law, like one under the law—though I myself am not under the law[a]—to win those under the law. 21 To those who are outside the law, like one outside the law—not being outside God's law, but under the law of Christ—to win those outside the law. 22 To the weak I became weak, in order to win the weak. I have become all things to all people, so that I may by all means save some. 23 Now I do all this because of the gospel, that I may become a partner in its benefits.[b]

24 Do you not know that the runners in a stadium all race, but only one receives the prize? Run in such a way that you may win. 25 Now everyone who competes exercises self-control in everything. However, they do it to receive a perishable crown, but we an imperishable one. 26 Therefore I do not run like one who runs aimlessly, or box like one who beats the air. 27 Instead, I discipline my body and bring it under strict control, so that after preaching to others, I myself will not be disqualified.

WARNINGS FROM ISRAEL'S PAST

10 Now I want you to know, brothers, that our fathers were all under the cloud, all passed through the sea, 2 and all were baptized into Moses in the cloud and in the sea. 3 They all ate the same spiritual food, 4 and all drank the same spiritual drink. For they drank from a spiritual rock that followed them, and that rock was Christ. 5 But God was not pleased with most of them, for they were struck down in the desert.

6 Now these things became examples for us, so that we will not desire evil as they did.[c] 7 Don't become idolaters as some of them were; as it is written, **The people sat down to eat and drink, and got up to play.**[d] [e] 8 Let us not commit sexual immorality as

My, My—We Tend to Be Self-Centered

It's easy for us to become so preoccupied with our own spiritual journey that we begin to ignore others. We need God to place a burden on our hearts for other people.

Although I am free from all people, I have made myself a slave to all, in order to win more people.

—1 Corinthians 9:19

Look for the Lost Outside Your Circle

Maybe you assume God wants you to befriend only those who have something in common with you. Isn't it a good thing Jesus didn't make that assumption about us?

I have become all things to all people, so that I may by all means save some.

— 1 Corinthians 9:22b

---

[a]9:20 Other mss omit *though I myself am not under law*
[b]9:23 Lit *partner of it*
[c]10:6 Lit *they desired*
[d]10:7 Or *to dance*
[e]10:7 Ex 32:6

some of them did,[a] and in a single day 23,000 people fell dead. [9] Let us not tempt Christ as some of them did,[b] and were destroyed by snakes. [10] Nor should we complain as some of them did,[c] and were killed by the destroyer.[d] [11] Now these things happened to them as examples, and they were written as a warning to us, on whom the ends of the ages have come. [12] Therefore, whoever thinks he stands must be careful not to fall! [13] No temptation has overtaken you except what is common to humanity. God is faithful and He will not allow you to be tempted beyond what you are able, but with the temptation He will also provide a way of escape, so that you are able to bear it.

WARNING AGAINST IDOLATRY

[14] Therefore, my dear friends, flee from idolatry. [15] I am speaking as to wise people. Judge for yourselves what I say. [16] The cup of blessing that we bless, is it not a sharing in the blood of Christ? The bread that we break, is it not a sharing in the body of Christ? [17] Because there is one bread, we who are many are one body, for all of us share that one bread. [18] Look at the people of Israel.[e] Are not those who eat the sacrifices partners in the altar? [19] What am I saying then? That food offered to idols is anything, or that an idol is anything? [20] No, but I do say that what they[f] sacrifice, they sacrifice to demons and not to God. I do not want you to be partners with demons! [21] You cannot drink the cup of the Lord and the cup of demons. You cannot share in the Lord's table and the table of demons. [22] Or are we provoking the Lord to jealousy? Are we stronger than He?

CHRISTIAN LIBERTY

[23] "Everything is permissible,"[g][h] but not everything is helpful. "Everything is permissible,"[g][h] but not everything builds up. [24] No one should seek his own ₍good₎, but ₍the good₎ of the other person.

Put Other People into Your Plans

If you have become too busy to minister to those around you, ask God to re-establish your priorities so that you don't miss opportunities to serve Him.

No one should seek his own good, but the good of the other person.

—1 Corinthians 10:24

Be Like Christ— Be Worth Copying

Paul understood that the only things in his life worth emulating were the things that were like Jesus. Our lives are the same way.

Be imitators of me, as I also am of Christ.

—1 Corinthians 11:1

---

[a]**10:8** Lit *them committed sexual immorality*
[b]**10:9** Lit *them tempted*
[c]**10:10** Lit *them complained*
[d]**10:10** Or *the destroying angel*
[e]**10:18** Lit *Look at Israel according to the flesh*
[f]**10:20** Other mss read *Gentiles*
[g]**10:23** Other mss add *for me*
[h]**10:23** See note at 1 Co 6:12

25 Eat everything that is sold in the meat market, asking no questions for conscience' sake, for 26 **the earth is the Lord's, and all that is in it.**[a] 27 If one of the unbelievers invites you over and you want to go, eat everything that is set before you, without raising questions of conscience. 28 But if someone says to you, "This is food offered to an idol," do not eat it, out of consideration for the one who told you, and for conscience' sake.[b] 29 I do not mean your own conscience, but the other person's. For why is my freedom judged by another person's conscience? 30 If I partake with thanks, why am I slandered because of something for which I give thanks?

31 Therefore, whether you eat or drink, or whatever you do, do everything for God's glory. 32 Give no offense to the Jews or the Greeks or the church of God, 33 just as I also try to please all people in all things, not seeking my own profit, but the profit of many, that they may be saved. 1 Be imitators of me, as I also am of Christ.

INSTRUCTIONS ABOUT HEAD COVERINGS

2 Now I praise you[c] because you remember me in all things and keep the traditions just as I delivered them to you. 3 But I want you to know that Christ is the head of every man, and the man is the head of the woman,[d] and God is the head of Christ. 4 Every man who prays or prophesies with something on his head dishonors his head. 5 But every woman who prays or prophesies with her head uncovered dishonors her head, since that is one and the same as having her head shaved. 6 So if a woman's head[e] is not covered, her hair should be cut off. But if it is disgraceful for a woman to have her hair cut off or her head shaved, she should be covered.

7 A man, in fact, should not cover his head, because he is God's image and glory, but woman is man's glory. 8 For man did not come from woman, but woman came from man; 9 and man was not created for woman, but

WORD STUDY

Greek word: *kephale*
[keh fah LAY]

Translation: *head*

Uses in 1 Corinthians: **10**

Uses in Paul's writings: **18**

Uses in the NT: **75**

Key passage: **1 Corinthians 11:3**

The Greek noun *kephale* means *head* and usually refers to that part of the body for humans or animals. In the NT, *kephale* is often used in its literal sense, but it is also used figuratively in several passages, especially in Paul's writings and Revelation.

Paul used the body as a metaphor for the church three times. In 1 Corinthians 12, Paul explained that unity in the church is promoted through mutual dependence and cooperation among the individual members who make up Christ's body (1 Co 12:12-27). This metaphor is modified in Ephesians and Colossians to emphasize the dependence that the body has on its head, who is Christ (Eph 1:22; 4:15; 5:23; Col 1:18; 2:19). Paul taught the husband's role as head or leader of the home in two passages. Just as Christ is the Head of His church, so the husband is the head of his wife (Eph 5:23). Divine and human headship are joined in Paul's hierarchy: God is the head of Christ; Christ is the head of man; man is the head of woman (1 Co 11:3). A wife's subordination to her husband does not mean that she is inferior to him, for Christ is subordinate to the Father but is also equal with Him (see Jn 5:18; 1 Co 15:27-28; Php 2:6).

---

[a]10:26 Ps 24:1
[b]10:28 Other mss add *"For the earth is the Lord's and all that is in it."*
[c]11:2 Other mss add *brothers,*

[d]11:3 Or *the husband is the head of the wife*
[e]11:6 Lit *a woman*

woman for man. ¹⁰ This is why a woman should have ₗa symbol ofₗ authority on her head: because of the angels. ¹¹ However, in the Lord, woman is not independent of man, and man is not independent of woman. ¹² For just as woman came from man, so man comes through woman, and all things come from God.

¹³ Judge for yourselves: Is it proper for a woman to pray to God with her head uncovered? ¹⁴ Does not even nature itself teach you that if a man has long hair it is a disgrace to him, ¹⁵ but that if a woman has long hair, it is her glory? For her hair is given to her[a] as a covering. ¹⁶ But if anyone wants to argue about this, we have no other[b] custom, nor do the churches of God.

THE LORD'S SUPPER

¹⁷ Now in giving the following instruction I do not praise you, since you come together not for the better but for the worse. ¹⁸ For, to begin with, I hear that when you come together as a church there are divisions among you, and in part I believe it. ¹⁹ There must, indeed, be factions among you, so that the approved among you may be recognized. ²⁰ Therefore when you come together in one place, it is not really to eat the Lord's Supper. ²¹ For in eating, each one takes his own supper ahead of others, and one person is hungry while another is drunk! ²² Don't you have houses to eat and drink in? Or do you look down on the church of God and embarrass those who have nothing? What should I say to you? Should I praise you? I do not praise you for this!

²³ For I received from the Lord what I also passed on to you: on the night when He was betrayed, the Lord Jesus took bread, ²⁴ gave thanks, broke it, and said,[c] "This is My body, which is[d] for you. Do this in remembrance of Me."

²⁵ In the same way ₗHeₗ also ₗtookₗ the cup, after supper, and said, "This cup is the new covenant in My blood. Do this, as often as you drink it, in remembrance of Me." ²⁶ For as often as you eat this bread and drink the cup, you proclaim the Lord's death until He comes.

Bucking the Bible Is a Sure Sign of Trouble

When you start to argue with a command from God's Word, you give evidence that your heart has shifted—that you don't love Him like you used to.

If anyone wants to argue about this, we have no other custom, nor do the churches of God.
—1 Corinthians 11:16

---

[a]11:15 Other mss omit *to her*
[b]11:16 Or *no such*

[c]11:24 Other mss add *"Take, eat.*
[d]11:24 Other mss add *broken*

SELF-EXAMINATION

27 Therefore, whoever eats the bread or drinks the cup of the Lord in an unworthy way will be guilty of sin against the body[a] and blood of the Lord. 28 So a man should examine himself; in this way he should eat of the bread and drink of the cup. 29 For whoever eats and drinks without recognizing the body,[b] eats and drinks judgment on himself. 30 This is why many are sick and ill among you, and many have fallen •asleep. 31 If we were properly evaluating ourselves, we would not be judged, 32 but when we are judged, we are disciplined by the Lord, so that we may not be condemned with the world.

33 Therefore, my brothers, when you come together to eat, wait for one another. 34 If anyone is hungry, he should eat at home, so that you can come together and not cause judgment. And I will give instructions about the other matters whenever I come.

DIVERSITY OF SPIRITUAL GIFTS

12 About matters of the spirit:[c] brothers, I do not want you to be unaware. 2 You know how, when you were pagans, you were led to dumb idols— being led astray. 3 Therefore I am informing you that no one speaking by the Spirit of God says, "Jesus is cursed," and no one can say, "Jesus is Lord," except by the Holy Spirit.

4 Now there are different gifts, but the same Spirit. 5 There are different ministries, but the same Lord. 6 And there are different activities, but the same God is active in everyone and everything.[d] 7 A manifestation of the Spirit is given to each person to produce what is beneficial:

8 to one is given a message of wisdom
    through the Spirit,
  to another, a message of knowledge
    by the same Spirit,
9 to another, faith by the same Spirit,
  to another, gifts of healing by the one Spirit,

Keep Your Heart Under Close Watch

If you will stay spiritually prepared, you won't have to try to develop instantly the quality of a vibrant relationship with Christ when trouble or ministry opportunities arise.

If we were properly evaluating ourselves, we would not be judged.

—1 Corinthians 11:31

Seek to Serve God Through Your Church

God brings into each church specific people who help the body more accurately reflect the character of Jesus. He has placed you in yours for a purpose.

And there are different activities, but the same God is active in everyone and everything. A manifestation of the Spirit is given to each person to produce what is beneficial.

—1 Corinthians 12:6-7

---

[a]11:27 Lit *be guilty of the body*
[b]11:29 Other mss read *drinks unworthily, not discerning the Lord's body*
[c]12:1 Lit *About things spiritual*
[d]12:6 Lit *God acts all things in all*

WORD STUDY

Greek word: **soma**
[SOH mah]

Translation: **body**

Uses in 1 Corinthians: **46**

Uses in Paul's writings: **91**

Uses in the NT: **142**

Key passage: **1 Corinthians 12:12-27**

The Greek noun *soma* means *body* and usually refers to the physical element of a person's existence; this is the sense of the term in the NT. The *soma* needs to be clothed (Mt 6:25), can be killed (Mt 10:28), can be thrown into hell (Mt 5:29-30), can experience resuscitation (Ac 9:40), and will experience resurrection (1 Co 15:35-44; see Mt 27:52; Jn 2:19-21). Paul often referred to the *soma* as the vehicle for sinful actions (Rm 1:24; 6:6,12; 8:10,13; 1 Co 6:18), but he also used the term figuratively. In Romans 12 the church is "one body in Christ" (v.5); in 1 Corinthians 12 the church is the body of Christ (v. 27); in Ephesians and Colossians, the church is the body with Christ as its Head (Eph 1:22-23; 5:23; Col 1:18; 2:19).

The disunity among the believers in Corinth forced Paul to deal with this problem by expanding at length on the body metaphor. In 1 Corinthians 12:12-27, Paul used the word *soma* eighteen times and *melos*, its counterpart meaning *parts*, thirteen times. Believers in the church are the individual parts that make up Christ's body (v. 27). All parts of Christ's body must work together for the body to function properly (vv. 14-21; see v. 11).

10 to another, the performing of miracles,
to another, prophecy,
to another, distinguishing between spirits,
to another, different kinds of languages,
to another, interpretation of languages.

11 But one and the same Spirit is active in all these, distributing to each one as He wills.

UNITY YET DIVERSITY IN THE BODY

12 For as the body is one and has many parts, and all the parts of that body, though many, are one body—so also is Christ. 13 For we were all baptized by one Spirit into one body—whether Jews or Greeks, whether slaves or free—and we were all made to drink of one Spirit. 14 So the body is not one part but many. 15 If the foot should say, "Because I'm not a hand, I don't belong to the body," in spite of this it still belongs to the body. 16 And if the ear should say, "Because I'm not an eye, I don't belong to the body," in spite of this it still belongs to the body. 17 If the whole body were an eye, where would the hearing be? If the whole were an ear, where would be the sense of smell? 18 But now God has placed the parts, each one of them, in the body just as He wanted. 19 And if they were all the same part, where would the body be? 20 Now there are many parts, yet one body.

21 So the eye cannot say to the hand, "I don't need you!" nor again the head to the feet, "I don't need you!" 22 On the contrary, all the more, those parts of the body that seem to be weaker are necessary. 23 And those parts of the body that we think to be less honorable, we clothe these with greater honor, and our unpresentable parts have a better presentation. 24 But our presentable parts have no need ₁of clothing₁. Instead, God has put the body together, giving greater honor to the less honorable, 25 so that there would be no division in the body, but that the members would have the same concern for each other. 26 So if one member suffers, all the members suffer with it; if one member is honored, all the members rejoice with it.

27 Now you are the body of Christ, and individual members of it. 28 And God has placed these in the church:

first apostles, second prophets, third teachers,
   next, miracles,
then gifts of healing, helping, managing,
   various kinds of languages.
29 Are all apostles? Are all prophets?
   Are all teachers? Do all do miracles?
30 Do all have gifts of healing?
   Do all speak in languages?
   Do all interpret?

31 But desire the greater gifts. And I will show you an even better way.

LOVE: THE SUPERIOR WAY

13 If I speak the languages of men and of angels,
   but do not have love,
   I am a sounding gong or a clanging cymbal.
2 If I have ⌊the gift of⌋ prophecy,
   and understand all •mysteries
     and all knowledge,
   and if I have all faith,
     so that I can move mountains,
   but do not have love, I am nothing.
3 And if I donate all my goods to feed the poor,
   and if I give my body to be burned,[a]
   but do not have love, I gain nothing.
4 Love is patient; love is kind.
   Love does not envy;
   is not boastful; is not conceited;
5 does not act improperly;
   is not selfish;
   is not provoked; does not keep
     a record of wrongs;
6 finds no joy in unrighteousness, but rejoices
   in the truth;
7 bears all things, believes all things,
   hopes all things, endures all things.

8 Love never ends.
   But as for prophecies, they will come to an end;
   as for languages, they will cease;
   as for knowledge, it will come to an end.
9 For we know in part, and we prophesy in part.

From Start to Finish, Love Is All That Lasts

Many Christians seek to cultivate spiritual disciplines in their lives to be more obedient to Christ. But disciplines can never replace love for God. Love *is* the discipline.

If I donate all my goods to feed the poor, and if I give my body to be burned, but do not have love, I gain nothing.

—1 Corinthians 13:3

---

[a]13:3 Other mss read *to boast*

10 But when the perfect comes,
   the partial will come to an end.
11 When I was a child, I spoke like a child,
   I thought like a child, I reasoned like a child.
   When I became a man, I put aside
   childish things.
12 For now we see indistinctly, as in a mirror,
   but then face to face.
   Now I know in part, but then I will know fully,
   as I am fully known.
13 Now these three remain: faith, hope, and love.
   But the greatest of these is love.

PROPHECY: A SUPERIOR GIFT

14 Pursue love and desire spiritual gifts, and above all that you may prophesy. 2 For the person who speaks in ˻another˼ language is not speaking to men but to God, since no one understands him; however, he speaks •mysteries in the Spirit.ᵃ 3 But the person who prophesies speaks to people for edification, encouragement, and consolation. 4 The person who speaks in ˻another˼ language builds himself up, but he who prophesies builds up the church. 5 I wish all of you spoke in other languages, but even more that you prophesied. The person who prophesies is greater than the person who speaks in languages, unless he interprets so that the church may be built up.

6 But now, brothers, if I come to you speaking in ˻other˼ languages, how will I benefit you unless I speak to you with a revelation or knowledge or prophecy or teaching? 7 Even inanimate things producing sounds— whether flute or harp—if they don't make a distinction in the notes, how will what is played on the flute or harp be recognized? 8 In fact, if the trumpet makes an unclear sound, who will prepare for battle? 9 In the same way, unless you use your tongue for intelligible speech, how will what is spoken be known? For you will be speaking into the air. 10 There are doubtless many different kinds of languages in the world, and all have meaning.ᵇ 11 Therefore, if I do not know the meaning of

---

You Never Win by Playing Christianity

Some people are satisfied being spiritually immature their entire lives. But growing as a Christian requires putting some things behind you.

When I was a child, I spoke like a child, I thought like a child, I reasoned like a child. When I became a man, I put aside childish things.

—1 Corinthians 13:11

Check Your Freedom by Your Responsibility

Christians do not live in isolation. We must do everything with our fellow believers in mind.

So also you—since you are zealous in matters of the spirit, seek to excel in building up the church.

—1 Corinthians 14:12

ᵃ14:2 Or *in spirit*, or *in his spirit*   ᵇ14:10 Lit *and none is without a sound*

the language, I will be a foreigner[a] to the speaker, and the speaker will be a foreigner to me. ¹² So also you— since you are zealous in matters of the spirit,[b] seek to excel in building up the church.

¹³ Therefore the person who speaks in ₗanotherₗ language should pray that he can interpret. ¹⁴ For if I pray in ₗanotherₗ language, my spirit prays, but my understanding is unfruitful. ¹⁵ What then? I will pray with the spirit, and I will also pray with my understanding. I will sing with the spirit, and I will also sing with my understanding. ¹⁶ Otherwise, if you bless with the spirit, how will the uninformed person[c] say "•Amen" at your giving of thanks, since he does not know what you are saying? ¹⁷ For you may very well be giving thanks, but the other person is not being built up. ¹⁸ I thank God that I speak in ₗotherₗ languages more than all of you; ¹⁹ yet in the church I would rather speak five words with my understanding, in order to teach others also, than 10,000 words in ₗanotherₗ language.

²⁰ Brothers, don't be childish in your thinking, but be infants in evil and adult in your thinking. ²¹ It is written in the law:

> **By people of other languages**
> **and by the lips of foreigners,**
> **I will speak to this people;**
> **and even then, they will not listen to Me,[d]**

says the Lord. ²² It follows that speaking in other languages is intended as a sign,[e] not to believers but to unbelievers. But prophecy is not for unbelievers but for believers. ²³ Therefore if the whole church assembles together, and all are speaking in ₗotherₗ languages, and people who are uninformed or unbelievers come in, will they not say that you are out of your minds? ²⁴ But if all are prophesying, and some unbeliever or uninformed person comes in, he is convicted by all and is judged by all. ²⁵ The secrets of his heart will be revealed, and as a result he will fall down on his face and worship God, proclaiming, "God is really among you."

Pay Attention to What You're Praying

Watch and take note of the direction the Spirit is leading you as you pray, and you will begin to get a clear indication of what God is trying to say to you.

What then? I will pray with the spirit, and I will also pray with my understanding. I will sing with the spirit, and I will also sing with my understanding.
—1 Corinthians 14:15

Keep Your Mind Clear of Evil and Clearly on Christ

God's most effective servants are those who discipline their minds for His service. Are you using your mind in ways that bring glory to God?

Brothers, don't be childish in your thinking, but be infants in evil and adult in your thinking.
—1 Corinthians 14:20

---

a14:11 Gk *barbaros* = in Eng *a barbarian*. To a Gk, a *barbaros* was anyone who did not speak Gk.
b14:12 Lit *zealous of spirits; spirits* = human spirits, spiritual gifts or powers, or the Holy Spirit
c14:16 Lit *the one filling the place of the uninformed*
d14:21 Is 28:11-12
e14:22 Lit *that tongues are for a sign*

WORD STUDY

Greek word: **glossa**
[GLOH sah]

Translation: **tongue, language**

Uses in 1 Corinthians: **21**

Uses in Paul's writings: **24**

Uses in the NT: **50**

Key passage: **1 Corinthians 14:2-39**

The Greek noun *glossa* can mean *tongue,* and it refers literally to the organ of speech in the mouth. In the NT, *glossa* does occur with the literal meaning *tongue* in several passages (Mk 7:33; Lk 1:64; 16:24; Rm 3:13; Rv 16:10), and the meaning *language* is common also (Ac 2:11; 1 Jn 3:18; Rv 5:9; 7:9; 10:11; 11:9; 13:7; 14:6; 17:15).

Glossa is the term used in Acts and 1 Corinthians referring to speaking in tongues. Luke explained this phenomenon as the apostles' ability to speak in languages spoken by Jews from numerous other countries (Ac 2:4-11; see especially vv. 6, 8, 11). These were languages that the apostles had not previously learned, which is why those who heard were so surprised (vv. 7-8). In two other passages in Acts, speaking in tongues refers to the same supernatural ability as described in chapter 2 (10:46; 19:6).

ORDER IN CHURCH MEETINGS

26 How is it then, brothers? Whenever you come together, each one[a] has a psalm, a teaching, a revelation, ₍another₎ language, or an interpretation. All things must be done for edification. 27 If any person speaks in ₍another₎ language, there should be only two, or at the most three, each in turn, and someone must interpret. 28 But if there is no interpreter, that person should keep silent in the church and speak to himself and to God. 29 Two or three prophets should speak, and the others should evaluate. 30 But if something has been revealed to another person sitting there, the first prophet should be silent. 31 For you can all prophesy one by one, so that everyone may learn and everyone may be encouraged. 32 And the prophets' spirits are under the control of the prophets, 33 since God is not a God of disorder but of peace.

As in all the churches of the saints, 34 the women[b] should be silent in the churches, for they are not permitted to speak, but should be submissive, as the law also says. 35 And if they want to learn something, they should ask their own husbands at home, for it is disgraceful for a woman to speak in the church meeting. 36 Did the word of God originate from you, or did it come to you only?

37 If anyone thinks he is a prophet or spiritual, he should recognize that what I write to you is the Lord's command. 38 But if anyone ignores this, he will be ignored.[c] 39 Therefore, my brothers, be eager to prophesy, and do not forbid speaking in ₍other₎ languages. 40 But everything must be done decently and in order.

RESURRECTION ESSENTIAL TO THE GOSPEL

15 Now brothers, I want to clarify[d] for you the gospel I proclaimed to you; you received it and have taken your stand on it. 2 You are also saved by it, if you hold to the message I proclaimed to you—unless

---

[a]**14:26** Other mss add *of you*
[b]**14:34** Other mss read *your women*
[c]**14:38** Other mss read *he should be ignored*
[d]**15:1** Or *I make known*

you believed to no purpose.[a] 3 For I passed on to you as most important what I also received:

> that Christ died for our sins
> according to the Scriptures,
> 4 that He was buried,
> that He was raised on the third day
> according to the Scriptures,
> 5 and that He appeared to •Cephas,
> then to the Twelve.
> 6 Then He appeared to over 500 brothers
> at one time,
> most of whom remain to the present,
> but some have fallen •asleep.
> 7 Then He appeared to James,
> then to all the apostles.
> 8 Last of all, as to one abnormally born,
> He also appeared to me.

9 For I am the least of the apostles, unworthy to be called an apostle, because I persecuted the church of God. 10 But by God's grace I am what I am, and His grace toward me was not ineffective. However, I worked more than any of them, yet not I, but God's grace that was with me. 11 Therefore, whether it is I or they, so we preach and so you have believed.

RESURRECTION ESSENTIAL TO THE FAITH

12 Now if Christ is preached as raised from the dead, how can some of you say, "There is no resurrection of the dead"? 13 But if there is no resurrection of the dead, then Christ has not been raised; 14 and if Christ has not been raised, then our preaching is without foundation, and so is your faith.[b] 15 In addition, we are found to be false witnesses about God, because we have testified about God that He raised up Christ—whom He did not raise up if in fact the dead are not raised. 16 For if the dead are not raised, Christ has not been raised. 17 And if Christ has not been raised, your faith is worthless; you are still in your sins. 18 Therefore those who have

God's Grace Inspires a Hardworking Heart

Our character is fully a result of God's grace and power. Yet growing in Christ is also a conscious decision to bring our mind, heart, and actions into line with God's will.

But by God's grace I am what I am, and His grace toward me was not ineffective. However, I worked more than any of them, yet not I, but God's grace that was with me.

—1 Corinthians 15:10

---

[a]15:2 Or *believed in vain*
[b]15:14 Or *preaching is useless, and your faith also is useless*, or *preaching is empty, and your faith also is empty*

WORD STUDY

Greek word: *aparche*
[ahp ahr KAY]

Translation: *firstfruits*

Uses in 1 Corinthians: 3

Uses in Paul's writings: 6

Uses in the NT: 8

Key passage: **1 Corinthians 15:20,23**

The Greek noun *aparche* comes from the preposition *apo*, meaning *from*, and *arche*, meaning *beginning* or *first*. In ancient Greek, *aparche* was often used in connection with the beginning of an event and was the formal term for *birth certificate*. In the Greek OT, *aparche* was the term for *firstfruits*. The Festival of Firstfruits (or Harvest) occurred the Sunday after Passover. The Israelites were to bring the firstfruits of their harvest to the priests to be presented before the Lord (Ex 23:16-29; Lv 23:9-14).

In the NT, *aparche* occurs in connection with the Festival of Firstfruits but never as a specific reference to it. Instead, *aparche* refers figuratively to people as firstfruits in seven of eight occurrences (Rm 11:16 excepted). Twice Paul used *aparche* in reference to the believers who were the first converts of a certain province (Rm 16:5; 1 Co 16:15). A special group of believers in the end times are also called firstfruits (Rv 14:4). Believers receive the Spirit as the firstfruits of salvation (Rm 8:23), and this occurs through the power of God's word (Jms 1:18). In discussing the resurrection, Paul referred to Christ as "the firstfruits of those who have fallen asleep" (1 Co 15:20). Since Christ was the first to arise from the dead (v. 23), His resurrection is the basis for the resurrection of all believers.

fallen asleep in Christ have also perished. ¹⁹ If we have placed our hope in Christ for this life only, we should be pitied more than anyone.

CHRIST'S RESURRECTION GUARANTEES OURS

²⁰ But now Christ has been raised from the dead, the •firstfruits of those who have fallen asleep. ²¹ For since death came through a man, the resurrection of the dead also comes through a man. ²² For just as in Adam all die, so also in Christ all will be made alive. ²³ But each in his own order: Christ, the firstfruits; afterward, at His coming, the people of Christ. ²⁴ Then comes the end, when He hands over the kingdom to God the Father, when He abolishes all rule and all authority and power. ²⁵ For He must reign until He puts all His enemies under His feet. ²⁶ The last enemy to be abolished is death. ²⁷ For **He has put everything under His feet.**[a] But when it says "everything" is put under Him, it is obvious that He who puts everything under Him is the exception. ²⁸ And when everything is subject to Him, then the Son Himself will also be subject to Him who subjected everything to Him, so that God may be all in all.

RESURRECTION SUPPORTED BY CHRISTIAN EXPERIENCE

²⁹ Otherwise what will they do who are being baptized for the dead? If the dead are not raised at all, then why are people[b] baptized for them?[c] ³⁰ Why are we in danger every hour? ³¹ I affirm by the pride in you that I have in Christ Jesus our Lord: I die every day! ³² If I fought wild animals in Ephesus with only human hope,[d] what good does that do me?[e] If the dead are not raised, **Let us eat and drink, for tomorrow we die.**[f] ³³ Do not be deceived: "Bad company corrupts good morals."[g] ³⁴ Become right-minded[h] and stop sinning, because some people are ignorant about God. I say this to your shame.

---

[a]15:27 Ps 8:6
[b]15:29 Lit *they*
[c]15:29 Other mss read *for the dead*
[d]15:32 Lit *Ephesus according to man*
[e]15:32 Lit *what to me the profit?*
[f]15:32 Is 22:13
[g]15:33 A quotation from the poet Menander, *Thais*, 218
[h]15:34 Lit *Sober up righteously*

THE NATURE OF THE RESURRECTION BODY

35 But someone will say, "How are the dead raised? What kind of body will they have when they come?" 36 Foolish one! What you sow does not come to life unless it dies. 37 And as for what you sow—you are not sowing the future body, but only a seed,ᵃ perhaps of wheat or another grain. 38 But God gives it a body as He wants, and to each of the seeds its own body. 39 Not all flesh is the same flesh; there is one flesh for humans, another for animals, another for birds, and another for fish. 40 There are heavenly bodies and earthly bodies, but the splendor of the heavenly bodies is different from that of the earthly ones. 41 There is a splendor of the sun, another of the moon, and another of the stars; for star differs from star in splendor. 42 So it is with the resurrection of the dead:

> Sown in corruption,
> raised in incorruption;
> 43 sown in dishonor, raised in glory;
> sown in weakness, raised in power;
> 44 sown a natural body,
> raised a spiritual body.

If there is a natural body, there is also a spiritual body. 45 So it is written: **The first man Adam became a living being;**ᵇ the last Adam became a life-giving Spirit. 46 However, the spiritual is not first, but the natural; then the spiritual.

> 47 The first man was from the earth
> and made of dust;
> the second man isᶜ from heaven.
> 48 Like the man made of dust,
> so are those who are made of dust;
> like the heavenly man,
> so are those who are heavenly.
> 49 And just as we have borne the image
> of the man made of dust,
> we will also bear the image
> of the heavenly man.

God Has Turned Your Past into Promise

If you are preoccupied with your past, ask God to open your eyes to who you really are in Him, and to the incredible future that awaits you.

Just as we have borne the image of the man made of dust, we will also bear the image of the heavenly man.

—1 Corinthians 15:49

ᵃ15:37 Lit *but a naked seed*
ᵇ15:45 Gn 2:7
ᶜ15:47 Other mss add *the Lord*

VICTORIOUS RESURRECTION

50 Brothers, I tell you this: flesh and blood cannot inherit the kingdom of God, and corruption cannot inherit incorruption. 51 Listen! I am telling you a •mystery:

> We will not all fall asleep,
>   but we will all be changed,
> 52 in a moment, in the twinkling of an eye,
>   at the last trumpet.
> For the trumpet will sound,
>   and the dead will be raised incorruptible,
>   and we will be changed.
> 53 Because this corruptible must be clothed
>   with incorruptibility,
> and this mortal must be clothed
>   with immortality.
> 54 Now when this corruptible is clothed
>   with incorruptibility,
> and this mortal is clothed
>   with immortality,
> then the saying that is written
>   will take place:
> **Death has been swallowed up in victory.**[a]
> 55 **O Death, where is your victory?**
>   **O Death, where is your sting?**[b]
> 56 Now the sting of death is sin,
>   and the power of sin is the law.
> 57 But thanks be to God,
>   who gives us the victory
>   through our Lord Jesus Christ!

58 Therefore, my dear brothers, be steadfast, immovable, always excelling in the Lord's work, knowing that your labor in the Lord is not in vain.

COLLECTION FOR THE JERUSALEM CHURCH

16 Now about the collection for the saints: you should do the same as I instructed the Galatian churches. 2 On the first day of the week, each of you

---

Your Future Body Will Last for Eternity

God did not create you for time; He created you for eternity. His purposes for you go far beyond the here and now.

Listen! I am telling you a mystery: We will not all fall asleep, but we will all be changed, in a moment, in the twinkling of an eye, at the last trumpet. For the trumpet will sound, and the dead will be raised incorruptible, and we will be changed.

—1 Corinthians 15:51-52

Your Life Will Come Out in God's Favor

When you obey God no matter what the cost, you already have your victory assured.

But thanks be to God, who gives us the victory through our Lord Jesus Christ!

—1 Corinthians 15:57

---

[a]**15:54** Is 25:8   [b]**15:55** Hs 13:14

is to set something aside and save to the extent that he prospers, so that no collections will need to be made when I come. 3 And when I arrive, I will send those whom you recommend by letter to carry your gracious gift to Jerusalem. 4 If it is also suitable for me to go, they will travel with me.

PAUL'S TRAVEL PLANS

5 I will come to you after I pass through Macedonia—for I will be traveling through Macedonia— 6 and perhaps I will remain with you, or even spend the winter, that you may send me on my way wherever I go. 7 I don't want to see you now just in passing, for I hope to spend some time with you, if the Lord allows. 8 But I will stay in Ephesus until Pentecost, 9 because a wide door for effective ministry has opened for me[a]— yet many oppose me. 10 If Timothy comes, see that he has nothing to fear from you, because he is doing the Lord's work, just as I am. 11 Therefore no one should look down on him; but you should send him on his way in peace so he can come to me, for I am expecting him with the brothers.[b]

12 About our brother Apollos: I strongly urged him to come to you with the brothers, but he was not at all willing to come now. However, when he has time, he will come.

FINAL EXHORTATION

13 Be alert, stand firm in the faith, be brave and strong. 14 Your every ₍action₎ must be done with love.

15 Brothers, you know the household of Stephanas: they are the •firstfruits of Achaia and have devoted themselves to serving the saints. I urge you 16 also to submit to such people, and to everyone who works and labors with them. 17 I am delighted over the presence of Stephanas, Fortunatus, and Achaicus, because these men have made up for your absence. 18 For they have refreshed my spirit and yours. Therefore recognize such people.

Be Faithful to Christ, Not Fearful of Critics

The most rewarding spiritual work is often done in the crucible of opposition. As you seek places of service, look beyond what people are saying to find what God is doing.

A wide door for effective ministry has opened for me—yet many oppose me.

—1 Corinthians 16:9

---

[a]16:9 Lit *for a door has opened to me, great and effective*   [b]16:11 *With the brothers* may connect with Paul or Timothy.

WORD STUDY

Greek word: ***marana tha***
[mah rah nah thah]

Translation: ***Maranatha***

Uses in 1 Corinthians: **1**

Uses in Paul's writings: **1**

Uses in the NT: **1**

Key passage: **1 Corinthians 16:22**

The word *Maranatha* is a transliteration of two Aramaic words. It can be understood in two ways: either *marana tha,* meaning *Our Lord, come!* or *marana tha,* meaning *Our Lord has come!* In the NT, this exclamation occurs only in 1 Corinthians 16:22. Since Paul had expounded on Christ's coming kingdom in chapter 15, it is likely that Paul meant *marana tha—Our Lord, come!*—as an expression of joy and hope regarding Christ's return.

CONCLUSION

[19] The churches of the Asian province greet you. Aquila and Priscilla greet you heartily in the Lord, along with the church that meets in their home. [20] All the brothers greet you. Greet one another with a holy kiss.

[21] This greeting is in my own hand[a] —Paul. [22] If anyone does not love the Lord, a curse be on him. *Maranatha!*[b] [23] The grace of the Lord Jesus be with you. [24] My love be with all of you in Christ Jesus.

---

[a]**16:21** Paul normally dictated his letters to a secretary, but signed the end of each letter himself; see Rm 16:22; Gl 6:11; Col 4:18; 2 Th 3:17.

[b]**16:22** Aram expression meaning *Our Lord come!,* or *Our Lord has come!*

CORINTHIANS

GREETING

1 Paul, an apostle of Christ Jesus by God's will, and
Timothy our[a] brother: To God's church at Corinth,
with all the saints who are throughout Achaia.

2 Grace to you and peace from God our Father and
the Lord Jesus Christ.

THE GOD OF COMFORT

3 Blessed be the God and Father of our Lord Jesus
Christ, the Father of mercies and the God of all comfort.
4 He comforts us in all our affliction,[b] so that we may be
able to comfort those who are in any kind of affliction,
through the comfort we ourselves receive from God.
5 For as the sufferings of Christ overflow to us, so our
comfort overflows through Christ. 6 If we are afflicted, it
is for your comfort and salvation; if we are comforted,
it is for your comfort, which is experienced in the endurance of the same sufferings that we suffer. 7 And our
hope for you is firm, because we know that as you share
in the sufferings, so you will share in the comfort.

8 For we don't want you to be unaware, brothers, of
our affliction that took place in the province of Asia: we
were completely overwhelmed—beyond our strength—
so that we even despaired of life. 9 However, we personally had a death sentence within ourselves so that we
would not trust in ourselves, but in God who raises the
dead. 10 He has delivered us from such a terrible death,
and He will deliver us; we have placed our hope in Him
that He will deliver us again. 11 And you can join in
helping with prayer for us, so that thanks may be given

---

[a]1:1 Lit *the*
[b]1:4 Or *trouble*, or *tribulation*, or *tri-* als, or *oppression*; the Gk word has a
lit meaning of being under pressure.

by many[a] on our[b] behalf for the gift that came to us through ˎthe prayers ofˏ many.

A CLEAR CONSCIENCE

[12] For our boast is this: the testimony of our conscience that we have conducted ourselves in the world, and especially toward you, with God-given sincerity and purity, not by fleshly[c] wisdom but by God's grace. [13] Now we are writing you nothing other than what you can read and also understand. I hope you will understand completely— [14] as you have partially understood us—that we are your reason for pride, as you are ours, in the day of our[d] Lord Jesus.

A VISIT POSTPONED

[15] In this confidence, I planned to come to you first, so you could have a double benefit,[e] [16] and to go on to Macedonia with your help, then come to you again from Macedonia and be given a start by you on my journey to Judea. [17] So when I planned this, was I irresponsible? Or what I plan, do I plan in a purely human[f] way so that I say "Yes, yes" and "No, no" ˎsimultaneouslyˏ? [18] As God is faithful, our message to you is not "Yes and no." [19] For the Son of God, Jesus Christ, who was preached among you by us—by me and Silvanus[g] and Timothy—did not become "Yes and no"; on the contrary, "Yes" has come about in Him. [20] For every one of God's promises is "Yes" in Him. Therefore the "•Amen" is also through Him for God's glory through us. [21] Now the One who confirms us with you in Christ, and has anointed us, is God; [22] He has also sealed us and given us the Spirit as a down payment in our hearts.

[23] I call on God as a witness against me:[h] it was to spare you that I did not come to Corinth. [24] Not that we have control of[i] your faith, but we are workers with

God's Promises Are Right under Your Nose

Since every promise God has made in Scripture is available to us, we should search each promise out in order to meditate on its potential for our lives.

Every one of God's promises is "Yes" in Him.
—2 Corinthians 1:20a

Does Your Life Remind People of Jesus?

Those around you can choose whether to accept God's love or reject it, but there should be no doubt by your example that it is available to them.

Thanks be to God, who always puts us on display in Christ, and spreads through us in every place the scent of knowing Him.
—2 Corinthians 2:14

---

[a]**1:11** Lit *by many faces*
[b]**1:11** Other mss read *your*
[c]**1:12** The word *fleshly* (characterized by flesh) indicates that the wisdom is natural rather than spiritual.
[d]**1:14** Other mss omit *our*
[e]**1:15** Other mss read *a second joy*
[f]**1:17** Or *a worldly*, or *a fleshly*, or *a selfish*
[g]**1:19** Or *Silas*; see Ac 15:22-32; 16:19-40; 17:1-16
[h]**1:23** Lit *against my soul*
[i]**1:24** Or *we lord it over*, or *we rule over*

2 you for your joy, because you stand by faith. ¹ In fact, I made up my mind about this:ᵃ not to come to you on another painful visit.ᵇ ² For if I cause you pain, then who will cheer me other than the one hurt?ᶜ ³ I wrote this very thing so that when I came I wouldn't have pain from those who ought to give me joy, because I am confident about all of you that my joy is yours.ᵈ ⁴ For out of an extremely troubled and anguished heart I wrote to you with many tears—not that you should be hurt, but that you should know the abundant love I have for you.

A SINNER FORGIVEN

⁵ If anyone has caused pain, he has not caused pain to me, but in some degree—not to exaggerate—to all of you. ⁶ The punishment by the majority is sufficient for such a person, ⁷ so now you should forgive and comfort him instead; otherwise, this one may be overwhelmed by excessive grief. ⁸ Therefore I urge you to confirm your love to him. ⁹ It was for this purpose I wrote: so I may know your proven character, if you are obedient in everything. ¹⁰ Now to whom you forgive anything, I do too. For what I have forgiven, if I have forgiven anything, it is for you in the presence of Christ, ¹¹ so that we may not be taken advantage of by Satan; for we are not ignorant of his intentions.ᵉ

A TRIP TO MACEDONIA

¹² When I came to Troas for the gospel of Christ, a door was opened to me by the Lord. ¹³ I had no rest in my spirit because I did not find my brother Titus, but I said good-bye to them and left for Macedonia.

A MINISTRY OF LIFE OR DEATH

¹⁴ But thanks be to God, who always puts us on displayᶠ in Christ,ᵍ and spreads through us in every place the scent of knowing Him. ¹⁵ For to God we are the

WORD STUDY

Greek word: **noema**
[NAH ay mah]
Translation: **intention**
Uses in 2 Corinthians: **5**
Uses in Paul's writings: **6**
Uses in the NT: **6**
Key passage: **2 Corinthians 2:11**

The Greek noun *noema* comes from the verb *noeo*, meaning *to think* or *to understand*. The *-ma* ending indicates the result of thinking, that is, the thought itself, perception, or understanding. Thus, *noema* can mean *mind*, *thought*, or *intention*. In the NT, the term occurs in a positive sense only in Philippians 4:7, where Paul stated that the peace of God guards believers' hearts and minds. Three times in 2 Corinthians Paul connected the work of Satan with the Christian's mind (*noema*): believers are not ignorant of Satan's intentions to destroy them (2:11); Satan blinds the minds of unbelievers so they cannot be saved (4:4); believers, like Eve, can have their minds corrupted by Satan (11:3). Paul's other two uses of *noema* in 2 Corinthians refer to the closed minds of the Israelites that keep them from believing in Christ (3:14) and to thoughts that keep believers from obeying Christ (10:5).

ᵃ2:1 Lit *I decided this for myself*
ᵇ2:1 Lit *not again in sorrow to come to you*
ᶜ2:2 Lit *the one pained*
ᵈ2:3 Lit *is of you all*
ᵉ2:11 Or *thoughts*

ᶠ2:14 Or *always leads us in a triumphal procession*, or less likely, *always causes us to triumph*
ᵍ2:14 Lit *in the Christ*, or *in the Messiah*; see 1 Co 15:22; Eph 1:10,12,20; 3:11

fragrance of Christ among those who are being saved and among those who are perishing. [16] To some we are a scent of death leading to death, but to others, a scent of life leading to life. And who is competent for this? [17] For we are not like the many[a] who make a trade in God's message ˌfor profitˌ, but as those with sincerity, we speak in Christ, as from God and before God.

LIVING LETTERS

3 Are we beginning to commend ourselves again? Or like some, do we need letters of recommendation to you or from you? [2] You yourselves are our letter, written on our hearts, recognized and read by everyone, [3] since it is plain that you are Christ's letter, produced[b] by us, not written with ink but with the Spirit of the living God; not on stone tablets but on tablets that are hearts of flesh.

PAUL'S COMPETENCE

[4] We have this kind of confidence toward God through Christ: [5] not that we are competent in[c] ourselves to consider anything as coming from ourselves, but our competence is from God. [6] He has made us competent to be ministers of a new covenant, not of the letter, but of the Spirit; for the letter kills, but the Spirit produces life.

NEW COVENANT MINISTRY

[7] Now if the ministry of death, chiseled in letters on stones, came with glory, so that the sons of Israel were not able to look directly at Moses' face because of the glory from his face—a fading ˌgloryˌ— [8] how will the ministry of the Spirit not be more glorious? [9] For if the ministry of condemnation had glory, the ministry of righteousness overflows with even more glory. [10] In fact, what had been glorious is not glorious in this case because of the glory that surpasses it. [11] For if what was fading away was glorious, what endures will be even more glorious.

Just in Case We Think We're So Great...

God is not interested in receiving secondhand glory from *our* activity. God receives glory from *His* activity in our lives.

Not that we are competent in ourselves to consider anything as coming from ourselves, but our competence is from God.

—2 Corinthians 3:5

Seek Your Life in the Only Place It's Found

If you are experiencing spiritual dryness right now, perhaps you've been trying to find refreshment from man-made sources, which will fail you every time.

He has made us competent to be ministers of a new covenant, not of the letter, but of the Spirit; for the letter kills, but the Spirit produces life.

—2 Corinthians 3:6

---

[a]**2:17** Other mss read *the rest*
[b]**3:3** Lit *ministered to*
[c]**3:5** Lit *from*

¹² Therefore having such a hope, we use great boldness— ¹³ not like Moses, who used to put a veil over his face so that the sons of Israel could not look at the end of what was fading away. ¹⁴ But their minds were closed.ᵃ For to this day, at the reading of the old covenant, the same veil remains; it is not lifted, because it is set aside ₗonlyⱼ in Christ. ¹⁵ However, to this day, whenever Moses is read, a veil lies over their hearts, ¹⁶ but whenever a person turns to the Lord, the veil is removed. ¹⁷ Now the Lord is the Spirit; and where the Spirit of the Lord is, there is freedom. ¹⁸ We all, with unveiled faces, are reflectingᵇ the glory of the Lord and are being transformed into the same image from glory to glory;ᶜ this is from the Lord who is the Spirit.ᵈ

THE LIGHT OF THE GOSPEL

4 Therefore, since we have this ministry, as we have received mercy, we do not give up. ² Instead, we have renounced shameful secret things, not •walking in deceit or distorting God's message, but in God's sight we commend ourselves to every person's conscience by an open display of the truth. ³ But if, in fact, our gospel is veiled, it is veiled to those who are perishing. ⁴ Regarding them: the god of this age has blinded the minds of the unbelievers so they cannot see the light of the gospel of the glory of Christ,ᵉ who is the image of God. ⁵ For we are not proclaiming ourselves but Jesus Christ as Lord, and ourselves as your slaves because of Jesus. ⁶ For God, who said, "Light shall shine out of darkness"—He has shone in our hearts to give the light of the knowledge of God's glory in the face of Jesus Christ.

TREASURE IN CLAY JARS

⁷ Now we have this treasure in clay jars, so that this extraordinary power may be from God and not from us. ⁸ We are pressured in every way but not crushed; we are perplexed but not in despair; ⁹ we are persecuted

ᵃ3:14 Lit *their thoughts were hardened*
ᵇ3:18 Or *are looking as in a mirror at*
ᶜ3:18 Progressive glorification or sanctification
ᵈ3:18 Or *from the Spirit of the Lord*, or *from the Lord, the Spirit*
ᵉ4:4 Or *the gospel of the glorious Christ*, or *the glorious gospel of Christ*

WORD STUDY

Greek word: **eikon**
[igh KOHN]
Translation: **image**
Uses in 2 Corinthians: **2**
Uses in Paul's writings: **9**
Uses in the NT: **23**
Key passage: **2 Corinthians 4:4**

The English word *icon* comes from the Greek noun *eikon*, which means *image, form,* or *statue*. In ancient Greek *eikon* could refer to an image such as a portrait, a reflection in a mirror, or a phantom.

In the NT *eikon* is used in seven ways. (1) A Roman coin bears the image of Caesar (Mt 22:20; Mk 12:16; Lk 20:24). (2) Unbelievers worship images of man and animals instead of God (Rm 1:23). (3) All humans bear the image of Adam (1 Co 15:49, first use), and (4) believers bear the image of Christ and God (Rm 8:29; 1 Co 15:49, second use; 2 Co 3:18; Col 3:10). (5) Christ is the image of God (2 Co 4:4; Col 1:15). (6) The law of Moses was only a shadowy image of what Christ's sacrifice provides (Heb 10:1). (7) In language reminiscent of Daniel 3, Revelation refers to the beast who demands that everyone on earth worship his image (probably a statue), and those who do so are judged by God (13:14-15, 14:9,11; 15:2; 16:2; 19:20; 20:4).

Two main ideas emerge from these uses of *eikon*: representation and manifestation. Caesar is represented by his image on a coin, and pagan gods are represented by images of them. Man was created to represent God and to manifest His presence in the world. However, Christ does not merely represent God; He is the full manifestation of God. Believers are being conformed to Christ's image and thus manifest God's presence as well.

but not abandoned; we are struck down but not destroyed. [10] We always carry the death of Jesus in our body, so that the life of Jesus may also be revealed in our body. [11] For we who live are always given over to death because of Jesus, so that Jesus' life may also be revealed in our mortal flesh. [12] So death works in us, but life in you. [13] And since we have the same spirit of faith in accordance with what is written, **I believed, therefore I spoke,**[a] we also believe, and therefore speak, [14] knowing that the One who raised the Lord Jesus will raise us also with Jesus, and present us with you. [15] For all this is because of you, so that grace, extended through more and more people, may cause thanksgiving to overflow to God's glory.

[16] Therefore we do not give up; even though our outer person is being destroyed, our inner person is being renewed day by day. [17] For our momentary light affliction[b] is producing for us an absolutely incomparable eternal weight of glory. [18] So we do not focus on what is seen, but on what is unseen; for what is seen is temporary, but what is unseen is eternal.

OUR FUTURE AFTER DEATH

5 For we know that if our earthly house, a tent,[c] is destroyed, we have a building from God, a house[d] not made with hands, eternal in the heavens. [2] And, in fact, we groan in this one, longing to put on our house from heaven, [3] since, when we are clothed,[e] we will not be found naked. [4] Indeed, we who are in this tent groan, burdened as we are, because we do not want to be unclothed but clothed, so that mortality may be swallowed up by life. [5] And the One who prepared us for this very thing is God, who gave us the Spirit as a down payment.

[6] Therefore, though we are always confident and know that while we are at home in the body we are away from the Lord— [7] for we •walk by faith, not by sight— [8] yet we are confident and satisfied to be out of the body and at home with the Lord. [9] Therefore, whether we are at home or away, we make it our aim

[a]4:13 Ps 116:10 LXX
[b]4:17 See note at 2 Co 1:4
[c]5:1 Our present physical body
[d]5:1 *a building ... a house* = our future body
[e]5:3 Other mss read *stripped*

to be pleasing to Him. ¹⁰ For we must all appear before the judgment seat of Christ, so that each may be repaid for what he has done in the body, whether good or bad.

¹¹ Knowing, then, the fear of the Lord, we persuade people. We are completely open before God, and I hope we are completely open to your consciences as well. ¹² We are not commending ourselves to you again, but giving you an opportunity to be proud of us, so that you may have a reply for those who take pride in the outward appearance[a] rather than in the heart. ¹³ For if we are out of our mind, it is for God; if we have a sound mind, it is for you. ¹⁴ For Christ's love compels[b] us, since we have reached this conclusion: if One died for all, then all died. ¹⁵ And He died for all so that those who live should no longer live for themselves, but for the One who died for them and was raised.

THE MINISTRY OF RECONCILIATION

¹⁶ From now on, then, we do not know[c] anyone in a purely human way.[d] Even if we have known[e] Christ in a purely human way,[f] yet now we no longer know[e] Him like that. ¹⁷ Therefore if anyone is in Christ, there is a new creation; old things have passed away, and look, new things[g] have come. ¹⁸ Now everything is from God, who reconciled us to Himself through Christ and gave us the ministry of reconciliation: ¹⁹ that is, in Christ, God was reconciling the world to Himself, not counting their trespasses against them, and He has committed the message of reconciliation to us. ²⁰ Therefore, we are ambassadors for Christ; certain that God is appealing through us, we plead on Christ's behalf, "Be reconciled to God." ²¹ He made the One who did not know sin to be sin for us, so that we might become the righteousness of God in Him.

6 Working together[h] with Him, we also appeal to you: "Don't receive God's grace in vain." ² For He says:

---

[a]5:12 Lit *in face*
[b]5:14 Or *For the love of Christ impels*, or *For the love of Christ controls*
[c]5:16 Or *regard*
[d]5:16 Lit *anyone according to the flesh*
[e]5:16 Or *have regarded*
[f]5:16 Lit *Christ according to the flesh*
[g]5:17 Other mss read *look, all new things*
[h]6:1 Or *As we work together*

WORD STUDY

Greek word: **katallasso**
[kah tahl LAHSS oh]

Translation: **reconcile**

Uses in 2 Corinthians: **3**

Uses in Paul's writings: **6**

Uses in the NT: **6**

Key passage: **2 Corinthians 5:18-20**

The Greek verb *katallasso* basically means *to change* or *exchange*. It was often used as a monetary term referring to changing or exchanging money, but in general it referred to exchanging one thing for another. A common use of *katallasso* was in reference to changing someone from an enemy into a friend, that is, bringing together or reconciling two people or parties that are at odds with each other. This is how *katallasso* is used all six times in the NT, as is also the case for all four uses of the related noun *katallage* (meaning *reconciliation*; see Rm 5:11; 11:15; 2 Co 5:18-19). These two words are found only in Paul's writings. The compound verb *apokatallasso* also means *to reconcile*, and it occurs only in Paul (Eph 2:16; Col 1:20,22). In 1 Corinthians 7:11, Paul used *katallasso* to describe the reconciliation of husband and wife. Paul's other five uses of the term explain that unbelievers can be reconciled to God through Christ. Because of sin, unbelievers are God's enemies (Rm 5:10), but they can be reconciled to God through faith in Christ (2 Co 5:18-19). Consequently, Christians are Christ's ambassadors who take God's message of reconciliation to the world (2 Co 5:19-20).

> **In an acceptable time, I heard you,**
> **and in the day of salvation, I helped you.**[a]

Look, now is the acceptable time; look, now is the day of salvation.

THE CHARACTER OF PAUL'S MINISTRY

³ We give no opportunity for stumbling to anyone, so that the ministry will not be blamed. ⁴ But in everything, as God's ministers, we commend ourselves:

> by great endurance, by afflictions, by hardship,
>   by pressures,
> ⁵ by beatings, by imprisonments, by riots,
>   by labors,
> by sleepless nights, by times of hunger,
> ⁶ by purity, by knowledge, by patience,
>   by kindness,
> by the Holy Spirit, by sincere love,
> ⁷ by the message of truth, by the power of God;
>   through weapons of righteousness
>   on the right hand and the left,
> ⁸ through glory and dishonor, through slander
>   and good report;
>   as deceivers yet true;
> ⁹ as unknown yet recognized; as dying and look—
>   we live;
>   as being chastened yet not killed;
> ¹⁰ as grieving yet always rejoicing; as poor
>   yet enriching many;
>   as having nothing yet possessing everything.

¹¹ We have spoken openly[b] to you, Corinthians; our heart has been opened wide. ¹² You are not limited by us, but you are limited by your own affections. ¹³ Now in like response—I speak as to children—you also should be open to us.

SEPARATION TO GOD

¹⁴ Do not be mismatched with unbelievers. For what partnership is there between righteousness and lawlessness? Or what fellowship does light have with dark-

God Will Keep Giving If You're Giving Out

The Lord is not miserly when it comes to providing grace to His servants. You will always find an ample supply of God's grace to sustain you in His work.

As grieving yet always rejoicing; as poor yet enriching many; as having nothing yet possessing everything.

—2 Corinthians 6:10

Is Your Faith at Risk in Your Relationships?

Don't link your life with anyone who will distract you from loving God.

Do not be mismatched with unbelievers. For what partnership is there between righteousness and lawlessness? Or what fellowship does light have with darkness?

—2 Corinthians 6:14

---

[a]**6:2** Is 49:8   [b]**6:11** Lit *Our mouths have been open*

ness? [15] What agreement does Christ have with Belial?[a] Or what does a believer have in common with an unbeliever? [16] And what agreement does God's sanctuary have with idols? For we[b] are the sanctuary of the living God, as God said:

> I will dwell among them and walk
>   among them,
> and I will be their God,
> and they will be My people.[c]
> [17] Therefore, come out from among them
>   and be separate, says the Lord;
> do not touch any unclean thing,
>   and I will welcome you.[d]
> [18] I will be a Father to you,
>   and you will be sons and daughters to Me,
>   says the Lord Almighty.[e]

7 Therefore dear friends, since we have such promises, we should wash ourselves clean from every impurity of the flesh and spirit, making our sanctification complete[f] in the fear of God.

JOY AND REPENTANCE

[2] Take us into your hearts.[g] We have wronged no one, corrupted no one, defrauded no one. [3] I don't say this to condemn you, for I have already said that you are in our hearts, to die together and to live together. [4] I have great confidence in you; I have great pride in you. I am filled with encouragement; I am overcome with joy in all our afflictions.

[5] In fact, when we came into Macedonia, we[h] had no rest. Instead, we were afflicted in every way: struggles on the outside, fears inside. [6] But God, who comforts the humble, comforted us by the coming of Titus, [7] and not only by his coming, but also by the comfort he received from you. He announced to us your deep longing, your sorrow,[i] your zeal for me, so that I rejoiced

---

God Just Wants You to Be His Child, OK?

We are so activity oriented, we wrongly assume that we were saved for a task we are to perform rather than for a relationship to enjoy.

We are the sanctuary of the living God, as God said: I will dwell among them and walk among them, and I will be their God, and they will be My people.

—2 Corinthians 6:16

One Thing for Sure— This Sin Has Got to Go

If you will not abstain from evil, it will rob you of the good that God has given.

Since we have such promises, we should wash ourselves clean from every impurity of the flesh and spirit, making our sanctification complete in the fear of God.

—2 Corinthians 7:1

---

[a]**6:15** Or *Beliar*, a name for the Devil or antichrist in extra-biblical Jewish writings
[b]**6:16** Other mss read *you*
[c]**6:16** Lv 26:12; Jr 31:33; 32:38; Ezk 37:26
[d]**6:17** Is 52:11
[e]**6:18** 2 Sm 7:14; Is 43:6; 49:22; 60:4; Hs 1:10
[f]**7:1** Or *spirit, perfecting holiness*
[g]**7:2** Lit *Make room for us.*
[h]**7:5** Lit *our flesh*
[i]**7:7** Or *lamentation*, or *mourning*

WORD STUDY

Greek word: *lupe*
[LOO pay]

Translation: *grief*

Uses in 2 Corinthians: **6**

Uses in Paul's writings: **9**

Uses in the NT: **16**

Key passage: **2 Corinthians
7:10**

The Greek noun *lupe* means *pain, grief,* or *sorrow.* The related verb *lupeo* means *to cause pain* or *to grieve* and occurs 26 times in the NT (15 of them in Paul's writings; 12 in 2 Corinthians). In ancient Greek both *lupe* and *lupeo* could refer to pain experienced by the physical body, but most of the time the terms were used figuratively for mental and emotional anguish. In the NT *lupe* is literal only once (Jn 16:21), and *lupeo* is always figurative.

Four times in Paul's writings *lupe* refers in a negative sense to his deep concern about spiritual matters, such as Israel's unbelief (Rm 9:2), the attitude of other Christians to his ministry (2 Co 2:1,3), and the near death of a fellow worker in the Lord (Php 2:27). Paul also used *lupe* to describe the grief caused by sin in the life of a Christian (2 Co 2:7) and to explain that Christian giving should not be motivated by "regret" (*lupe*) but by a cheerful heart (2 Co 9:7). In 2 Corinthians 7:10 Paul contrasted the false grief of the world with the "godly grief" that leads to repentance, warning against the notion that any form of repentance is genuine.

even more. ⁸ For although I grieved you with my letter, I do not regret it—even though I did regret it since I saw that the letter grieved you, though only for a little while. ⁹ Now I am rejoicing, not because you were grieved, but because your grief led to repentance. For you were grieved as God willed, so that you didn't experience any loss from us. ¹⁰ For godly grief produces a repentance not to be regretted and leading to salvation, but worldly grief produces death. ¹¹ For consider how much diligence this very thing—this grieving as God wills—has produced in you: what a desire to clear yourselves, what indignation, what fear, what deep longing, what zeal, what justice! In every way you have commended yourselves to be pure in this matter. ¹² So even though I wrote to you, it was not because of the one who did wrong, or because of the one who was wronged, but in order that your diligence for us might be made plain to you in the sight of God. ¹³ For this reason we have been comforted.

In addition to our comfort, we were made to rejoice even more over the joy Titus had,[a] because his spirit was refreshed by all of you. ¹⁴ For if I have made any boast to him about you, I have not been embarrassed; but as I have spoken everything to you in truth, so our boasting to Titus has also turned out to be the truth. ¹⁵ And his affection toward you is even greater as he remembers the obedience of all of you, and how you received him with fear and trembling. ¹⁶ I rejoice that I have complete confidence in you.

APPEAL TO COMPLETE
THE COLLECTION

8 We want you to know, brothers, about the grace of God granted to the churches of Macedonia: ² during a severe testing by affliction, their abundance of joy and their deep poverty overflowed into the wealth of their generosity. ³ I testify that, on their own, according to their ability and beyond their ability, ⁴ they begged us insistently for the privilege of sharing in the ministry to the saints, ⁵ and not just as we had hoped. Instead, they gave themselves especially to the Lord, then to us

---

[a]7:13 Lit *the joy of Titus*

by God's will. 6 So we urged Titus that, just as he had begun, so he should also complete this grace to you. 7 Now as you excel in everything—in faith, in speech, in knowledge, in all diligence, and in your love for us[a]—excel also in this grace.

8 I am not saying this as a command. Rather, by means of the diligence of others, I am testing the genuineness of your love. 9 For you know the grace of our Lord Jesus Christ: although He was rich, for your sake He became poor, so that by His poverty you might become rich. 10 Now I am giving an opinion on this because it is profitable for you, who a year ago began not only to do something but also to desire it.[b] 11 But now finish the task[c] as well, that just as there was eagerness to desire it, so there may also be a completion from what you have. 12 For if the eagerness is there, it is acceptable according to what one has, not according to what he does not have. 13 It is not that there may be relief for others and hardship for you, but it is a question of equality[d] — 14 at the present time your surplus is ₍available₎ for their need, so that their abundance may also become ₍available₎ for your need, that there may be equality. 15 As it has been written:

> The person who gathered much
>   did not have too much,
> and the person who gathered little
>   did not have too little.[e]

ADMINISTRATION OF THE COLLECTION

16 Thanks be to God who put the same diligence for you into the heart of Titus. 17 For he accepted our urging and, being very diligent, went out to you by his own choice. 18 With him we have sent the brother who is praised throughout the churches for his gospel ministry.[f] 19 And not only that, but he was also appointed by the churches to accompany us with this gift[g] that is being administered by us for the glory of the Lord Himself and to show our eagerness ₍to help₎. 20 We are taking this precaution so no one can find fault with us

Surely We Expect the Christian Life to Cost Us Something

The Father asked His Son to make radical adjustments in His life. Can we not expect that He will ask us to sacrifice privileges and comforts as well?

You know the grace of our Lord Jesus Christ: although He was rich, for your sake He became poor, so that by His poverty you might become rich.

—2 Corinthians 8:9

Deciding to Obey Is Not Equal to Obeying

When God gives us a direction, it is not enough to write it in our spiritual journal or tell our friends about it. God's call is not to make a decision, but to obey.

Finish the task as well, that just as there was eagerness to desire it, so there may also be a completion from what you have.

—2 Corinthians 8:11

---

[a]8:7 Other mss read *in our love for you*
[b]8:10 Lit *to will*
[c]8:11 Lit *finish the doing*
[d]8:13 Lit *but from equality*
[e]8:15 Ex 16:18
[f]8:18 Lit *churches, in the gospel*
[g]8:19 Or *grace*

WORD STUDY

Greek word: **zelos**
[ZAY lahss]
Translation: **zeal**
Uses in 2 Corinthians: **5**
Uses in Paul's writings: **10**
Uses in the NT: **16**
Key passage: **2 Corinthians 9:2**

The English word *zeal* comes from the Greek noun *zelos*, which means *zeal* or *jealousy*. The related verb *zeloo* means *to be zealous* or *jealous*, and occurs only eleven times in the NT (eight in Paul's writings). The related noun *zelotes* means *one who is zealous* and twice in the NT refers to Simon, one of the Twelve, who had been a member of the militaristic Jewish sect, the Zealots (Lk 6:15; Ac 1:13). In ancient Greek *zelos* could mean *rivalry, zeal, jealousy, desire, bliss*, or *extravagance*. The term *zelos* occurs 30 times in the Greek OT, most often in reference to the Lord's zeal or jealousy.

In the NT *zelos* occurs with many of the meanings found in ancient Greek and the Greek OT. King David's zeal for the Lord's house was epitomized in the life of Jesus (Jn 2:17; see Ps 69:9). The term *zelos* commonly means *zeal, envy*, or *jealousy* and is often used in a negative sense (Ac 5:17; 13:45; Rm 10:2; 13:13; 1 Co 3:3; 2 Co 12:20; Gl 5:20; Php 3:6; Jms 3:14,16). Four times in 2 Corinthians, however, Paul used *zelos* in a positive sense. It describes the eagerness of the Corinthian believers to serve Paul (2 Co 7:7,11; 9:2; 11:2); their desire to act righteously regarding a brother in sin (7:11); their eagerness to contribute to the needs of other believers (9:2); and Paul's jealousy to present the Corinthian believers to Christ "as a pure virgin" (11:2)—that they would remain faithful to the truth of the gospel.

concerning this large sum administered by us. [21] For we are making provision for what is honorable, not only before the Lord but also before men. [22] We have also sent with them our brother whom we have often tested, in many circumstances, and found diligent— and now even more diligent because of his great confidence in you. [23] As for Titus, he is my partner and co-worker serving you; as for our brothers, they are the messengers of the churches, the glory of Christ. [24] Therefore, before the churches, show them the proof of your love and of our boasting about you.

MOTIVATIONS FOR GIVING

9 Now concerning the ministry to the saints, it is unnecessary for me to write to you. [2] For I know your eagerness, and I brag about you to the Macedonians:[a] "Achaia[b] has been prepared since last year," and your zeal has stirred up most of them. [3] But I sent the brothers so our boasting about you in the matter would not prove empty, and so you would be prepared just as I said. [4] For if any Macedonians should come with me and find you unprepared, we, not to mention you, would be embarrassed in that situation.[c] [5] Therefore I considered it necessary to urge the brothers to go on ahead to you and arrange in advance the generous gift you promised, so that it will be ready as a gift and not an extortion.

[6] Remember this:[d] the person who sows sparingly will also reap sparingly, and the person who sows generously will also reap generously. [7] Each person should do as he has decided in his heart—not out of regret or out of necessity, for God loves a cheerful giver. [8] And God is able to make every grace overflow to you, so that in every way, always having everything you need, you may excel in every good work. [9] As it is written:

> **He has scattered;**
> **He has given to the poor;**
> **His righteousness endures forever.[e]**

[a]9:2 Macedonia was a Roman province in the northern area of modern Greece.
[b]9:2 Achaia was the Roman province, south of Macedonia, where Corinth was located.
[c]9:4 Or *in this confidence*
[d]9:6 Lit *And this*
[e]9:9 Ps 112:9

[10] Now the One who provides seed for the sower and bread for food will provide and multiply your seed and increase the harvest of your righteousness, [11] as you are enriched in every way for all generosity, which produces thanksgiving to God through us. [12] For the ministry of this service is not only supplying the needs of the saints, but is also overflowing in many acts of thanksgiving to God. [13] Through the proof of this service, they will glorify God for your obedience to the confession of[a] the gospel of Christ, and for your generosity in sharing with them and with others. [14] And in their prayers for you they will have deep affection for[b] you because of the surpassing grace of God on you. [15] Thanks be to God for His indescribable gift.

PAUL'S APOSTOLIC AUTHORITY

10 Now I, Paul, make a personal appeal to you by the gentleness and graciousness of Christ—I who am humble among you in person, but bold toward you when absent. [2] I beg you that when I am present I will not need to be bold with the confidence by which I plan to challenge certain people who think we are •walking in a fleshly way.[c] [3] For although we are walking in the flesh, we do not wage war in a fleshly way,[d] [4] since the weapons of our warfare are not fleshly, but are powerful through God for the demolition of strongholds. We demolish arguments [5] and every high-minded thing that is raised up against the knowledge of God, taking every thought captive to the obedience of Christ. [6] And we are ready to punish any disobedience, once your obedience is complete.

[7] Look at what is obvious.[e] If anyone is confident that he belongs to Christ, he should remind himself of this: just as he belongs to Christ, so do we. [8] For if I boast some more about our authority, which the Lord gave for building you up and not for tearing you down, I am not ashamed. [9] I don't want to seem as though I am trying to terrify you with my letters. [10] For it is said, "His letters are weighty and powerful, but his physical presence is weak, and his public speaking is despicable."

---

[a]9:13 Or *your obedient confession to*
[b]9:14 Or *will long for*
[c]10:2 Lit *walking according to flesh*
[d]10:3 Lit *war according to flesh*
[e]10:7 Or *You are looking at things outwardly*

WORD STUDY

Greek word: *tapeinos*
[tah pigh NAHSS]

Translation: *humble*

Uses in 2 Corinthians: **2**

Uses in Paul's writings: **3**

Uses in the NT: **8**

Key passage: **2 Corinthians 10:1**

The Greek adjective *tapeinos* means *humble, lowly,* or *downcast.* The related verb *tapeinoo* means *to humiliate, humble,* or *make ashamed,* and occurs 14 times in the NT (four in Paul's writings). The related noun *tapeinosis* means *humiliation* or *humble condition* and occurs four times in the NT (Lk 1:48; Ac 8:33; Php 3:21; Jms 1:10); another term, *tapeinophrosune,* means *humility* and occurs seven times (Ac 20:19; Eph 4:2; Php 2:3; Col 2:18,23, 3:12; 1 Pt 5:5).

The ancient Greeks so emphasized personal strength and self-sufficiency that *tapeinos* and its related words were almost always used in a negative sense. To be humble or lowly was considered a vice. However, Jesus elevated *tapeinos* to the status of a virtue when He said, "I am gentle and humble in heart" (Mt 11:29), and Paul used *tapeinoo* to describe the incarnation (Php 2:8). Jesus warned that those who promote themselves will be judged by God, but He also said that those who humble themselves will be rewarded (Mt 23:12; Luke 14:11; 18:14; see Mt 18:4; see 2 Co 11:7). True humility is the opposite of putting self first. Humility means that a person does not think of self at all but instead thinks of the needs of others and makes their needs a priority (see Php 2:3-4). God gives grace to those who practice such humility (Jms 4:6; 1 Pt 5:5).

409

WORD STUDY

Greek word: **gnosis**
[NOH sihss]

Translation: **knowledge**

Uses in 2 Corinthians: **6**

Uses in Paul's writings: **23**

Uses in the NT: **29**

Key passage: **2 Corinthians 11:6**

The Greek noun *gnosis* means *knowledge* or *understanding*, and the related verb *ginosko* means *to know, understand,* or *discern*. A similar verb *gnorizo* means *to make known* or *explain* and occurs 25 times in the NT. The verb *ginosko* is much more common than the other two terms and is especially prominent in John's writings (57 uses in John; 25 in 1 John), though Paul used it often as well (50). The noun *gnosis* never occurs in John's writings and is found primarily in Paul's writings, particularly 1 and 2 Corinthians (16 uses).

For Paul, *gnosis* refers mainly to the knowledge of God and the things of God, so it is a key term for him in describing various aspects of salvation (1 Co 1:5; 2 Co 2:14; 4:6; 6:6; 8:7; 10:5; Php 3:8; Col 2:3). In 1 Corinthians *gnosis* is listed as a spiritual gift, probably a revelatory one (12:8; 13:2,8; 14:6). Though knowledge can cause pride (1 Co 8:1), knowledge is also essential for Christians to enjoy their liberty in Christ (1 Co 8:7,10,11). Gnosis in its positive sense is never merely intellectual knowledge, one that has no affect on the way a person lives. Instead, it is experiential knowledge that changes a person's worldview and lifestyle. Thus, believers must guard against false knowledge (1 Tm 6:20).

[11] Such a person should consider this: what we are in the words of our letters when absent, we will be in actions when present.

[12] For we don't dare classify or compare ourselves with some who commend themselves. But in measuring themselves by themselves and comparing themselves to themselves, they lack understanding. [13] We, however, will not boast beyond measure, but according to the measure of the area ⌞of ministry⌟ that God has assigned to us, ⌞which⌟ reaches even to you. [14] For we are not overextending ourselves, as if we had not reached you, since we have come to you with the gospel of Christ. [15] We are not bragging beyond measure about other people's labors. But we have the hope that as your faith increases, our area ⌞of ministry⌟ will be greatly enlarged, [16] so that we may preach the gospel to the regions beyond you, not boasting about what has already been done in someone else's area ⌞of ministry⌟. [17] So **the one who boasts must boast in the Lord.**[a] [18] For it is not the one commending himself who is approved, but the one the Lord commends.

PAUL AND THE FALSE APOSTLES

11 I wish you would put up with a little foolishness from me. Yes, do put up with me.[b] [2] For I am jealous over you with a godly jealousy, because I have promised you in marriage to one husband—to present a pure virgin to Christ. [3] But I fear that, as the serpent deceived Eve by his cunning, your minds may be corrupted from a complete and pure[c] devotion to Christ. [4] For if a person comes and preaches another Jesus, whom we did not preach, or you receive a different spirit, which you had not received, or a different gospel, which you had not accepted, you put up with it splendidly!

[5] Now I consider myself in no way inferior to the "super-apostles." [6] Though untrained in public speaking, I am certainly not ⌞untrained⌟ in knowledge. Indeed, we have always made that clear to you in everything. [7] Or did I commit a sin by humbling myself so that you

---

[a]10:17 Jr 9:24
[b]11:1 Or *Yes, you are putting up with me*

[c]11:3 Other mss omit *and pure*

might be exalted, because I preached the gospel of God to you free of charge? [8] I robbed other churches by taking pay ⌊from them⌋ to minister to you. [9] When I was present with you and in need, I did not burden anyone, for the brothers who came from Macedonia supplied my needs. I have kept myself, and will keep myself, from burdening you in any way. [10] As the truth of Christ is in me, this boasting of mine will not be stopped[a] in the regions of Achaia. [11] Why? Because I don't love you? God knows I do!

[12] But I will continue to do what I am doing, in order to cut off the opportunity of those who want an opportunity to be regarded just as we are in what they are boasting about. [13] For such people are false apostles, deceitful workers, disguising themselves as apostles of Christ. [14] And no wonder! For Satan himself is disguised as an angel of light. [15] So it is no great thing if his servants also disguise themselves as servants of righteousness. Their destiny[b] will be according to their works.

PAUL'S SUFFERINGS FOR CHRIST

[16] I repeat: no one should consider me a fool. But if ⌊you do⌋, at least accept me as a fool, so I too may boast a little. [17] What I say in this matter[c] of boasting, I don't speak as the Lord would, but foolishly. [18] Since many boast from a human perspective,[d] I will also boast. [19] For you gladly put up with fools since you are so smart![e] [20] In fact, you put up with it if someone enslaves you, if someone devours you, if someone captures you, if someone dominates you, or if someone hits you in the face. [21] I say this to ⌊our⌋ shame: we have been weak.

But in whatever anyone dares ⌊to boast⌋—I am talking foolishly—I also dare:

[22] Are they Hebrews? So am I.
Are they Israelites? So am I.
Are they the seed of Abraham? So am I.
[23] Are they servants of Christ?
I'm talking like a madman—I'm a better one:

God's Thinking Can Be Trusted, But Not Yours

If you are not firmly grounded in the Word, you have no way to evaluate whether or not some doctrine or activity is from God.

I fear that, as the serpent deceived Eve by his cunning, your minds may be corrupted from a complete and pure devotion to Christ.

—2 Corinthians 11:3

Watch Your Step— The Devil Is Slick

Satan will try to convince you that obedience carries much too high a price, but he will never tell you the cost of *not* obeying God.

Satan himself is disguised as an angel of light.

—2 Corinthians 11:14

---

[a]11:10 Or *silenced*
[b]11:15 Lit *end*
[c]11:17 Or *business*, or *confidence*

[d]11:18 Lit *boast according to the flesh*
[e]11:19 Or *are wise*

with far more labors,
many more imprisonments,
far worse beatings, near death[a] many times.
24 Five times I received from the Jews 40 lashes
minus one.
25 Three times I was beaten with rods.[b]
Once I was stoned.[c]
Three times I was shipwrecked.
I have spent a night and a day in the depths
of the sea.
26 On frequent journeys, ⌊I faced⌋
dangers from rivers, dangers from robbers,
dangers from my own people,
dangers from the Gentiles,
dangers in the city, dangers in the open country,
dangers on the sea, and dangers
among false brothers;
27 labor and hardship,
many sleepless nights, hunger and thirst,
often without food, cold, and lacking clothing.

28 Not to mention[d] other things, there is the daily pressure on me: my care for all the churches. 29 Who is weak, and I am not weak? Who is made to stumble, and I do not burn with indignation? 30 If boasting is necessary, I will boast about my weaknesses. 31 The eternally blessed One, the God and Father of the Lord Jesus, knows I am not lying. 32 In Damascus, the governor under King Aretas[e] guarded the city of the Damascenes in order to arrest me, 33 so I was let down in a basket through a window in the wall and escaped his hands.

SUFFICIENT GRACE

12 It is necessary to boast; it is not helpful, but I will move on to visions and revelations of the Lord. 2 I know a man in Christ who was caught up into the third heaven 14 years ago. Whether he was in the body or out of the body, I don't know; God knows. 3 I know that this man—whether in the body or out of

---

We're All in This Thing Together

If other believers around you are rejoicing or hurting, and you are unaffected, you have become desensitized to the people of God.

Who is weak, and I am not weak? Who is made to stumble, and I do not burn with indignation?

—2 Corinthians 11:29

God Strengthens You Right Where It Hurts

At times you may not understand why a loving Father would allow you to suffer as you do. Have confidence that this same God is directing your path.

Because of Christ, I am pleased in weaknesses, in insults, in catastrophes, in persecutions, and in pressures. For when I am weak, then I am strong.

—2 Corinthians 12:10

---

[a]11:23 Lit *and in deaths*
[b]11:25 A specifically Roman punishment; see Ac 16:22
[c]11:25 A common Jewish method of capital punishment; see Ac 14:5
[d]11:28 Lit *Apart from*
[e]11:32 Aretus IV (9 B.C.–A.D. 40), a Nabatean Arab king

the body I do not know, God knows— [4] was caught up into paradise. He heard inexpressible words, which a man is not allowed to speak. [5] I will boast about this person, but not about myself, except of my weaknesses. [6] For if I want to boast, I will not be a fool, because I will be telling the truth. But I will spare you, so that no one can credit me with something beyond what he sees in me or hears from me, [7] especially because of the extraordinary revelations. Therefore, so that I would not exalt myself, a thorn in the flesh was given to me, a messenger[a] of Satan to torment me so I would not exalt myself. [8] Concerning this, I pleaded with the Lord three times to take it away from me. [9] But He said to me, "My grace is sufficient for you, for power[b] is perfected in weakness." Therefore, I will most gladly boast all the more about my weaknesses, so that Christ's power may reside in me. [10] So because of Christ, I am pleased in weaknesses, in insults, in catastrophes, in persecutions, and in pressures. For when I am weak, then I am strong.

SIGNS OF AN APOSTLE

[11] I have become a fool; you forced it on me. I ought to have been recommended by you, since I am in no way inferior to the "super-apostles," even though I am nothing. [12] The signs of an apostle were performed among you in all endurance—not only signs but also wonders and miracles. [13] So in what way were you treated worse than the other churches, except that I personally did not burden you? Forgive me this wrong!

PAUL'S CONCERN FOR THE CORINTHIANS

[14] Look! I am ready to come to you this third time. I will not burden you, for I am not seeking what is yours, but you. For children are not obligated to save up for their parents, but parents for their children. [15] I will most gladly spend and be spent for you.[c] If I love you more, am I to be loved less? [16] Now granted, I have not burdened you; yet sly as I am, I took you in by deceit!

---

[a]12:7 Or *angel*
[b]12:9 Other mss read *My power*
[c]12:15 Lit *for your souls*, or *for your lives*

WORD STUDY

Greek word: *apokalupsis*
[ah pah KAH loop sihss]

Translation: *revelation*

Uses in 2 Corinthians: **2**

Uses in Paul's writings: **13**

Uses in the NT: **18**

Key passage: **2 Corinthians 12:7**

The Greek noun *apokalupsis* is a compound word from the preposition *apo*, meaning *away from*, and *kalumma*, meaning *veil*; thus, an unveiling. *Kalumma* comes from the verb *kalupto*, which means *to hide*; thus the verb *apokalupto* means *to expose that which was hidden* or *to reveal*, and the noun *apokalupsis* can mean not only *an unveiling* but also *a revelation*.

In the NT, *apokalupsis* always refers to God's revelation of Himself in some way. In Luke 2:32, this revelation comes in the person of Christ, while in Romans 8:19 it is in His sons. God often revealed Himself through supernatural means to apostles and prophets such as Paul (Rm 16:25; 2 Co 12:1,7; Gl 1:12; 2:2; Eph 3:3). In the end times, God's judgment will be revealed (Rm 2:5), as will Christ (1 Co 1:7; 2 Th 1:7; 1 Pt 1:7,13; 4:13). In 1 Corinthians, *apokalupsis* is listed as a spiritual gift, though nothing specific is stated about the nature of this gift (14:6,26; see Eph 1:17).

The last occurrence of *apokalupsis* in the NT is in Revelation 1:1. The first word of the Greek text, it eventually became the name of the book. Only here does *apokalupsis* refer to written *revelation*, that is, Scripture. Revelation 1:1 uses *apokalupsis* in its noblest sense, for it introduces the main theme of the book: "The revelation of Jesus Christ."

WORD STUDY

Greek word: **histemi**
[HIHSS tay mee]

Translation: **confirm**

Uses in 2 Corinthians: **2**

Uses in Paul's writings: **16**

Uses in the NT: **155**

Key passage: **2 Corinthians 13:1**

The Greek verb *histemi* means *to stand* and has 47 related words that occur in the NT, such as *anistemi* (*to raise* or *stand up*) and *anastasis* (*resurrection*). In the narrative portions of the NT (Matthew to Acts), *histemi* usually means to stand in a literal sense, but it can also mean *to stand firm* or *to endure*. The meaning to stand gave rise to several figurative meanings referring to that which is firm, confirmed, established, appointed, or ordained. These ideas are the most common ones for *histemi* in the Epistles and Revelation.

For Paul, *histemi* most often served as a term for standing by faith (Rm 5:2; 11:20; 14:4; 1 Co 10:12; 15:1; 2 Co 1:24; Eph 6:11, 13-14; Col 4:12). In discussing the nature of the law, Paul used *histemi* in teaching that righteousness by faith "upholds" [*histemi*], rather than cancels the law, since the law also teaches salvation by faith and not works (Rm 3:31; see 4:1-8). Similarly, Paul used *histemi* in reference to those who "establish their own righteousness" as opposed to those who submit to God's righteousness (Rm 10:3)—another contrast between faith and works as the basis of salvation. Paul also used *histemi* in quoting the Greek OT to establish a principle for church discipline that he would apply on his next visit: "On the testimony of two or three witnesses every word will be confirmed [*histemi*]" (2 Co 13:1; see Dt 19:15).

---

[17] Did I take advantage of you by anyone I sent you? [18] I urged Titus ⌊to come⌋, and I sent the brother with him. Did Titus take advantage of you? Didn't we •walk in the same spirit and in the same footsteps?

[19] You have thought all along that we were defending ourselves to you.[a] ⌊No⌋, in the sight of God we are speaking in Christ, and everything, dear friends, is for building you up. [20] For I fear that perhaps when I come I will not find you to be what I want, and I may not be found by you to be what you want;[b] there may be quarreling, jealousy, outbursts of anger, selfish ambitions, slander, gossip, arrogance, and disorder. [21] I fear that when I come my God will again[c] humiliate me in your presence, and I will grieve for many who sinned before and have not repented of the uncleanness, sexual immorality, and promiscuity they practiced.

FINAL WARNINGS AND EXHORTATIONS

13 This is the third time I am coming to you. On the testimony[d] of two or three witnesses every word will be confirmed.[e] [2] I gave warning, and I give warning—as when I was present the second time, so now while I am absent—to those who sinned before and to all the rest: if I come again, I will not be lenient, [3] since you seek proof of Christ speaking in me. He is not weak toward you, but powerful among you. [4] In fact, He was crucified in weakness, but He lives by God's power. For we also are weak in Him, yet toward you we will live with Him by God's power.

[5] Test yourselves ⌊to see⌋ if you are in the faith. Examine yourselves. Or do you not recognize for yourselves that Jesus Christ is in you?—unless you fail the test.[f] [6] And I hope you will recognize that we are not failing the test. [7] Now we pray to God that you do nothing wrong, not that we may appear to pass the test, but that you may do what is right, even though we ⌊may appear⌋ to fail. [8] For we are not able to do anything against the truth, but only for the truth. [9] In fact, we rejoice when

---

[a]**12:19** Or *Have you thought ... to you?*
[b]**12:20** Lit *be as you want*
[c]**12:21** Or *come again my God will*
[d]**13:1** Lit *mouth*

[e]**13:1** Dt 17:6; 19:15
[f]**13:5** Or *you are disqualified*, or *you are counterfeit*

we are weak and you are strong. We also pray for this: your maturity.ᵃ ¹⁰ This is why I am writing these things while absent, that when I am there I will not use severity, in keeping with the authority the Lord gave me for building up and not for tearing down.

¹¹ Finally, brothers, rejoice. Be restored, be encouraged, be of the same mind, be at peace, and the God of love and peace will be with you. ¹² Greet one another with a holy kiss. All the saints greet you.

¹³ The grace of the Lord Jesus Christ, and the love of God, and the fellowship of the Holy Spirit be with all of you.ᵇ

Make Yourself a Hard Person to Sin Around

Are you a friend of such integrity that you would risk wounding your friends in order to deter them from their sin?

I gave warning, and I give warning—as when I was present the second time, so now while I am absent—to those who sinned before and to all the rest: if I come again, I will not be lenient.

—2 Corinthians 13:2

Make Me a Blessing to Someone Today

God's desire is to fill His people with His Spirit so that others recognize His powerful presence in them. The presence of the Lord in a believer's life ought to be obvious.

You seek proof of Christ speaking in me. He is not weak toward you, but powerful among you.

—2 Corinthians 13:3

ᵃ13:9 Or *completion*, or *restoration*
ᵇ13:12-13 Some translations divide these 2 vv. into 3 vv. so that v. 13 begins with *All the saints* ... and v. 14 begins with *The grace of* ...

GALATIANS

GREETING

1 Paul, an apostle—not from men or by man, but by Jesus Christ and God the Father who raised Him from the dead— [2] and all the brothers who are with me:

To the churches of Galatia.[a]

[3] Grace to you and peace from God the Father and our Lord[b] Jesus Christ, [4] who gave Himself for our sins to rescue us from this present evil age, according to the will of our God and Father, [5] to whom be the glory forever and ever. •Amen.

NO OTHER GOSPEL

[6] I am amazed that you are so quickly turning away from Him who called you by the grace of Christ, ₗand are turningⱼ to a different gospel— [7] not that there is another ₗgospelⱼ, but there are some who are troubling you and want to change the gospel of Christ. [8] But even if we or an angel from heaven should preach to you a gospel other than what we have preached to you, a curse be on him![c] [9] As we have said before, I now say again: if anyone preaches to you a gospel contrary to what you received, a curse be on him![d]

[10] For am I now trying to win the favor of people, or God? Or am I striving to please people? If I were still trying to please people, I would not be a slave of Christ.

---

[a]1:2 A Roman province in what is now Turkey
[b]1:3 Other mss read *God our Father and the Lord*
[c]1:8 Or *you, let him be condemned,* or *you, let him be condemned to hell;* Gk *anathema*
[d]1:9 Or *received, let him be condemned,* or *received, let him be condemned to hell;* Gk *anathema*

PAUL DEFENDS HIS APOSTLESHIP

[11] Now I want you to know, brothers, that the gospel preached by me is not based on a human point of view.[a] [12] For I did not receive it from a human source and I was not taught it, but it came by a revelation from Jesus Christ.

[13] For you have heard about my former way of life in Judaism: I persecuted God's church to an extreme degree and tried to destroy it; [14] and I advanced in Judaism beyond many contemporaries among my people, because I was extremely zealous for the traditions of my ancestors. [15] But when God, who from my mother's womb set me apart and called me by His grace, was pleased [16] to reveal His Son in me, so that I could preach Him among the Gentiles, I did not immediately consult with anyone.[b] [17] I did not go up to Jerusalem to those who had become apostles before me; instead I went to Arabia and came back to Damascus.

[18] Then after three years I did go up to Jerusalem to get to know •Cephas,[c] and I stayed with him 15 days. [19] But I didn't see any of the other apostles except James, the Lord's brother. [20] Now in what I write to you, I'm not lying. God is my witness.[d]

[21] Afterwards, I went to the regions of Syria and Cilicia. [22] I remained personally unknown to the Judean churches in Christ; [23] they simply kept hearing: "He who formerly persecuted us now preaches the faith he once tried to destroy." [24] And they glorified God because of me.

PAUL DEFENDS HIS GOSPEL AT JERUSALEM

2 Then after 14 years I went up again to Jerusalem with Barnabas, taking Titus along also. [2] I went up because of a revelation and presented to them the gospel I preach among the Gentiles—but privately to those recognized ⌊as leaders⌋—so that I might not be running, or have run, in vain. [3] But not even Titus who was with me, though he was a Greek, was compelled to be circumcised. [4] ⌊This issue arose⌋ because of false

You've Been in God's Plans for a Long Time

God was working in your life long before you began working with Him. He knew you before time began, and He knew what He wanted to do with your life.

When God, who from my mother's womb set me apart and called me by His grace, was pleased to reveal His Son in me, so that I could preach Him among the Gentiles, I did not immediately consult with anyone.

—Galatians 1:15-16

Always Be Awaiting Your Next Orders

God's revelation is His invitation for you to join Him in His redemptive work. If your spiritual eyes are pure and alert, you will be overwhelmed by all that you see God doing around you.

I went up because of a revelation and presented to them the gospel I preach among the Gentiles—but privately to those recognized as leaders.

—Galatians 2:2a

---

[a]1:11 Lit *not according to man*
[b]1:16 Lit *flesh and blood*
[c]1:18 Other mss read *Peter*
[d]1:20 Lit *Behold, before God*

Greek word: **peritome**
[peh ree tah MAY]
Translation: **circumcision**
Uses in Galatians: **7**
Uses in Paul's writings: **31**
Uses in the NT: **36**
Key passage: **Galatians 2:7-21**

The Greek noun *peritome* means *circumcision* and comes from two words that literally mean *a cutting around*. The related verb *peritemno* means *to circumcise* and occurs 17 times in the NT, nine times in Paul's writings with six of these in Galatians. These two terms refer to the practice of cutting off the foreskin of a male, normally at birth. God chose circumcision as a special sign of the relationship between Himself and the covenant people of Israel, starting with Abraham (Gn 17:9-14,22-27).

A few times in the NT *peritome* refers simply to the ritual of circumcision that the Hebrew people had been practicing for two thousand years (Jn 7:22,23; Ac 7:8). In Paul's writings, however, *peritome* is prominently used in relation to salvation. Some Jewish believers claimed that Gentiles must be circumcised and follow the law of Moses to be saved (see Ac 15:1-35). Paul explained that this was not true of their father Abraham, for he lived before the law of Moses and was declared righteous before he was circumcised. Circumcision made no contribution to Abraham's relationship with God; that relationship was based on faith (Rm 4:9-25). Both the circumcised and the uncircumcised are saved by faith (Rm 3:30; see Gl 5:6,11; 6:15).

brothers smuggled in, who came in secretly to spy on our freedom that we have in Christ Jesus, in order to enslave us. ⁵ But we did not yield in submission to these people for even an hour, so that the truth of the gospel would remain for you.

⁶ But from those recognized as important (what they really were makes no difference to me; God does not show favoritism[a])—those recognized as important added nothing to me. ⁷ On the contrary, they saw that I had been entrusted with the gospel for the uncircumcised, just as Peter was for the circumcised. ⁸ For He who was at work with Peter in the apostleship to the circumcised was also at work with me among the Gentiles. ⁹ When James, •Cephas, and John, recognized as pillars, acknowledged the grace that had been given to me, they gave the right hand of fellowship to me and Barnabas, ⌊agreeing⌋ that we should go to the Gentiles and they to the circumcised. ¹⁰ ⌊They asked⌋ only that we would remember the poor, which I made every effort to do.

FREEDOM FROM THE LAW

¹¹ But when Cephas[b] came to Antioch, I opposed him to his face because he stood condemned.[c] ¹² For he used to eat with the Gentiles before certain men came from James. However, when they came, he withdrew and separated himself, because he feared those from the circumcision party. ¹³ Then the rest of the Jews joined his hypocrisy, so that even Barnabas was carried away by their hypocrisy. ¹⁴ But when I saw that they were deviating from the truth of the gospel, I told Cephas[b] in front of everyone, "If you, who are a Jew, live like a Gentile and not like a Jew, how can you compel Gentiles to live like Jews?"[d]

¹⁵ We are Jews by birth and not "Gentile sinners"; ¹⁶ yet we know that no one is justified by the works of the law but by faith in Jesus Christ.[e] And we have believed in Christ Jesus, so that we might be justified by faith in Christ[f] and not by the works of the law, because

---

[a]2:6 Or *God is not a respecter of persons*; lit *God does not receive the face of man*
[b]2:11,14 Other mss read *Peter*
[c]2:11 Or *he was in the wrong*

[d]2:14 Some translations continue the quotation through v. 16 or v. 21.
[e]2:16 Or *by the faithfulness of Jesus Christ*
[f]2:16 Or *by the faithfulness of Christ*

by the works of the law no human being will[a] be justi-fied. [17] But if, while seeking to be justified by Christ, we ourselves are also found to be sinners, is Christ then a promoter[b] of sin? Absolutely not! [18] If I rebuild those things that I tore down, I show myself to be a lawbreak-er. [19] For through the law I have died to the law, that I might live to God. I have been crucified with Christ; [20] and I no longer live, but Christ lives in me. The life I now live in the flesh,[c] I live by faith in the Son of God, who loved me and gave Himself for me. [21] I do not set aside the grace of God; for if righteousness comes through the law, then Christ died for nothing.

JUSTIFICATION THROUGH FAITH

3 You foolish Galatians! Who has hypnotized you,[d] before whose eyes Jesus Christ was vividly por-trayed[e] as crucified? [2] I only want to learn this from you: Did you receive the Spirit by the works of the law or by hearing with faith?[f] [3] Are you so foolish? After be-ginning with the Spirit, are you now going to be made complete by the flesh?[g] [4] Did you suffer so much for nothing—if in fact it was for nothing? [5] So then, does God[h] supply you with the Spirit and work miracles among you by the works of the law or by hearing with faith?[f]

[6] Just as Abraham **believed God, and it was cred-ited to him for righteousness,**[i] [7] so understand that those who have faith are Abraham's sons. [8] Now the Scripture foresaw that God would justify the Gentiles by faith and foretold the good news to Abraham, saying, **All the nations will be blessed in you.**[j] [9] So those who have faith are blessed with Abraham, who had faith.[k]

LAW AND PROMISE

[10] For all who ⌊rely on⌋ the works of the law are un-der a curse, because it is written: **Cursed is everyone**

You Haven't Lived Until Christ Has Lived in You

The Christian life is an exchanged life—Jesus' life for your life. Rather than constantly worrying about how you can handle things, you should be continually releasing every area of your life to God's control.

I have been crucified with Christ; and I no longer live, but Christ lives in me. The life I now live in the flesh, I live by faith in the Son of God, who loved me and gave Himself for me.
—Galatians 2:19b-20

God's Love Goes Deeper than His Laws

Christianity is an intimate, growing relationship with the person of Jesus Christ, not a set of doctrines to believe, habits to practice, or sins to avoid. Every activity God com-mands is intended to enhance His love relationship with His people.

Are you so foolish? After beginning with the Spirit, are you now going to be made complete by the flesh?
—Galatians 3:3

---

[a]2:16 Lit *law all flesh will not*
[b]2:17 Or *servant*
[c]2:20 The physical body
[d]3:1 Other mss add *not to obey the truth*
[e]3:1 Other mss add *among you*
[f]3:2,5 Lit *by law works or faith hearing* or *hearing the message*
[g]3:3 By human effort
[h]3:5 Lit *He*
[i]3:6 Gn 15:6
[j]3:8 Gn 12:3; 18:18
[k]3:9 Or *with believing Abraham*

WORD STUDY

Greek word: ***nomos***
[NAH mahss]

Translation: ***law***

Uses in Galatians: **32**

Uses in Paul's writings: **121**

Uses in the NT: **194**

Key passage: **Galatians 3:2-26**

The Greek noun *nomos* means *custom, ordinance, or law.* In the Greek OT *nomos* is used to translate the Hebrew term *torah* 247 times, where it normally refers to the law of Moses in general or to specific laws. In the NT *nomos* most often refers to the OT in some way, such as a specific passage (Mt 12:5), the law of Moses (Mt 23:23), a large portion of the OT (for example, the Pentateuch; Lk 24:44), or the entire OT (Mt 5:18). Paul was particularly fond of *nomos,* and over half of its occurrences in the NT are in Paul's writings.

Paul used *nomos* 96 times in Romans and Galatians alone, for it is mainly in these two books that Paul fought the battle over law and grace in relation to salvation. Paul's phrase "the works of the law" (or something similar) refers to the idea of a salvation based on keeping the law. Paul denied that a law-based righteousness, which is dependent on human effort instead of God's grace and faith in Christ's work, can save or sustain anyone. Performing works of law cannot justify anyone (Rm 3:20,27-28). The law does not save anyone; rather, it brings the knowledge of sin and makes everyone accountable to God (Rm 3:19-20; Gl 3:15-22). By showing unbelievers their sinfulness, the law acts as their guardian until they trust in Christ through faith and become sons of God (Gl 3:23-26).

who does not continue doing everything written in the book of the law.[a] [11] Now it is clear that no one is justified before God by the law, because **the righteous will live by faith.**[b] [12] But the law is not based on faith; instead, **the one who does these things will live by them.**[c] [13] Christ has redeemed us from the curse of the law by becoming a curse for us, because it is written: **Cursed is everyone who is hung on a tree.**[d] [14] The purpose was that the blessing of Abraham would come to the Gentiles in Christ Jesus, so that we could receive the promise of the Spirit through faith.

[15] Brothers, I'm using a human illustration.[e] No one sets aside even a human covenant that has been ratified, or makes additions to it. [16] Now the promises were spoken to Abraham and to his seed. He does not say "and to seeds," as though referring to many, but **and to your seed,**[f] referring to one, who is Christ. [17] And I say this: the law, which came 430 years later, does not revoke a covenant that was previously ratified by God,[g] so as to cancel the promise. [18] For if the inheritance is from the law, it is no longer from the promise; but God granted it to Abraham through the promise.

THE PURPOSE OF THE LAW

[19] Why the law then? It was added because of transgressions until the Seed to whom the promise was made would come. ₍The law₎ was ordered through angels by means of a mediator. [20] Now a mediator is not for just one person, but God is one. [21] Is the law therefore contrary to God's promises? Absolutely not! For if a law had been given that was able to give life, then righteousness would certainly be by the law. [22] But the Scripture has imprisoned everything under sin's power,[h] so that the promise by faith in Jesus Christ might be given to those who believe. [23] Before this faith came, we were confined under the law, imprisoned until the coming faith was revealed. [24] The law, then, was our guardian[i] until Christ, so that we could be justified

---

[a]**3:10** Dt 27:26
[b]**3:11** Hab 2:4
[c]**3:12** Lv 18:5
[d]**3:13** Dt 21:23
[e]**3:15** Lit *I speak according to man*
[f]**3:16** Gn 12:7; 13:15; 17:8; 24:7
[g]**3:17** Other mss add *in Christ*
[h]**3:22** Lit *under sin*

[i]**3:24** The word translated *guardian* in vv. 24-25 is different from the word in Gl 4:2. In our culture, we do not have a slave who takes a child to and from school, protecting the child from harm or corruption. In Gk the word *paidogogos* described such a slave. This slave was not a teacher.

by faith. ²⁵ But since that faith has come, we are no longer under a guardian,ᵃ ²⁶ for you are all sons of God through faith in Christ Jesus.

SONS AND HEIRS

²⁷ For as many of you as have been baptized into Christ have put on Christ. ²⁸ There is no Jew or Greek, slave or free, male or female; for you are all one in Christ Jesus. ²⁹ And if you are Christ's, then you are Abraham's seed, heirs according to the promise.

4 ¹ Now I say that as long as the heir is a child, he differs in no way from a slave, though he is the owner of everything. ² Instead, he is under guardians and stewards until the time set by his father. ³ In the same way we also, when we were children, were in slavery under the elemental forces of the world. ⁴ But when the completion of the time came, God sent His Son, born of a woman, born under the law, ⁵ to redeem those under the law, so that we might receive adoption as sons. ⁶ And because you are sons, God has sent the Spirit of His Son into ourᵇ hearts, crying, "•*Abba*, Father!" ⁷ So you are no longer a slave, but a son; and if a son, then an heir through God.

PAUL'S CONCERN FOR THE GALATIANS

⁸ But in the past, when you didn't know God, you were enslaved to thingsᶜ that by nature are not gods. ⁹ But now, since you know God, or rather have become known by God, how can you turn back again to the weak and bankrupt elemental forces? Do you want to be enslaved to them all over again? ¹⁰ You observe ʟspecialʟ days, months, seasons, and years. ¹¹ I am fearful for you, that perhaps my labor for you has been wasted.

¹² I beg you, brothers: become like me, for I also became like you. You have not wronged me; ¹³ you know that previously I preached the gospel to you in physical weakness, ¹⁴ and though my physical condition was a

---

ᵃ3:25 The word translated *guardian* in vv. 24-25 is different from the word in Gl 4:2. In our culture, we do not have a slave who takes a child to and from school, protecting the child from harm or corruption. In Gk the word *paidogogos* described such a slave. This slave was not a teacher. ᵇ4:6 Other mss read *your* ᶜ4:8 Or *beings*

WORD STUDY

Greek word: ***huios***
[hwee AHSS]

Translation: ***Son, son***

Uses in Galatians: **13**

Uses in Paul's writings: **41**

Uses in the NT: **377**

Key passage: **Galatians 4:4-7**

The Greek noun *huios* means *son,* referring literally to male offspring (Mt 1:21; 20:20).

The two most common uses of *huios* in the NT are in titles for Christ and designations for believers. The expressions "Son" and "Son of God" refer to Christ in His unique and eternal relationship with the Father (Mt 3:17; 8:29; 11:27; Jn 3:16-18,35-36; 5:19-27; 8:36; 14:13; 17:1; Rm 1:3-4; 8:29,32; Heb 1:2,5,8). However, "Son of God" is also used many times as a Messianic title (Mt 14:33; 16:16; 26:63; Mk 1:1; Jn 1:34,49; 11:27; 20:31), as is "Son of David" (Mt 9:27; 12:23; 15:22; 20:30-31; 21:9,15; 22:42, 45). Jesus' self-designation "Son of Man" is a Messianic title taken from Daniel 7:13-14 (Mt 8:20; 12:8; 19:28; 24:47; 25:31; 26:64; Jn 1:51). On the basis of Jesus' Son-ship, believers are called "sons" (Gl 4:6-7) and "sons of God" (Mt 5:9; Rm 8:14,19; Gl 3:26). Their adoption (Gk *huiothesia,* literally *a son placing*) into God's family places them in a special relationship to God so that they can call Him '*Abba*, Father' and enjoy an inheritance (Gl 4:4-7).

The term was commonly used figuratively for the idea of being *characterized by* or *in special relation to.* Once *huios* is used to refer to a spiritual son (1 Pt 5:13; compare "child" in 1 Tm 1:2,8; 2 Tm 1:2; 2:1; Ti 1:4; Phm 1:10), and several times it is used to refer to national identity (Mt 27:9; Lk 1:16; Ac 5:21; 2 Co 3:7; Rv 2:14).

trial for you,[a] you did not despise or reject me. On the contrary, you received me as an angel of God, as Christ Jesus ⌊Himself⌋.

15 What happened to this blessedness of yours? For I testify to you that, if possible, you would have torn out your eyes and given them to me. 16 Have I now become your enemy by telling you the truth? 17 They[b] are enthusiastic about you, but not for any good. Instead, they want to isolate you so you will be enthusiastic about them. 18 Now it is always good to be enthusiastic about good—and not just when I am with you. 19 My children, again I am in the pains of childbirth for you until Christ is formed in you. 20 I'd like to be with you right now and change my tone of voice, because I don't know what to do about you.

SARAH AND HAGAR: TWO COVENANTS

21 Tell me, you who want to be under the law, don't you hear the law? 22 For it is written that Abraham had two sons, one by a slave and the other by a free woman. 23 But the one by the slave was born according to the flesh, while the one by the free woman was born as the result of a promise. 24 These things are illustrations,[c] for the women represent the two covenants. One is from Mount Sinai and bears children into slavery—this is Hagar. 25 Now Hagar is Mount Sinai in Arabia and corresponds to the present Jerusalem, for she is in slavery with her children. 26 But the Jerusalem above is free, and she is our mother. 27 For it is written:

> **Rejoice, O barren woman**
> **who does not give birth.**
> **Break forth and shout,**
> **you who are not in labor,**
> **for the children of the desolate are many,**
> **more numerous than those**
> **of the woman who has a husband.**[d]

28 Now you, brothers, like Isaac, are children of promise. 29 But just as then the child born according to the flesh persecuted the one born according to the Spirit, so also now. 30 But what does the Scripture say?

Expect True Honesty to Invite Opposition

If you have done what you know God has asked you to do, trust Him to see you through the antagonism that comes from those who are not walking with Him.

Have I now become your enemy by telling you the truth?
—Galatians 4:16

Be Patient with Those Who Are Struggling

It can be tempting at times to give up on God's people, but don't lose your patience with them. Keep in mind that God loves them as much as He loves you.

My children, again I am in the pains of childbirth for you until Christ is formed in you.
—Galatians 4:19

---

[a]4:14 Other mss read *me*
[b]4:17 The false teachers
[c]4:24 Typology or allegory
[d]4:27 Is 54:1

Throw out the slave and her son, for the son of the slave will never inherit with the son of the free woman.[a]

31 Therefore, brothers, we are not children of the slave but of the free woman.

FREEDOM OF THE CHRISTIAN

5 Christ has liberated us into freedom. Therefore stand firm and don't submit again to a yoke of slavery. 2 Take note! I, Paul, tell you that if you get circumcised, Christ will not benefit you at all. 3 Again I testify to every man who gets circumcised that he is obligated to keep the entire law. 4 You who are trying to be justified by the law are alienated from Christ; you have fallen from grace! 5 For by the Spirit we eagerly wait for the hope of righteousness from faith. 6 For in Christ Jesus neither circumcision nor uncircumcision accomplishes anything; what matters is faith working through love.

7 You were running well. Who prevented you from obeying the truth? 8 This persuasion did not come from Him who called you. 9 A little yeast leavens the whole lump of dough. 10 In the Lord I have confidence in you that you will not accept any other view. But whoever it is who is troubling you will pay the penalty. 11 Now brothers, if I still preach circumcision, why am I still persecuted? In that case the offense of the cross has been abolished. 12 I wish those who are disturbing you might also get themselves castrated!

13 For you are called to freedom, brothers; only don't use this freedom as an opportunity for the flesh, but serve one another through love. 14 For the entire law is fulfilled in one statement: **Love your neighbor as yourself.**[b] 15 But if you bite and devour one another, watch out, or you will be consumed by one another.

THE SPIRIT VERSUS THE FLESH

16 I say then, •walk by the Spirit and you will not carry out the desire of the flesh. 17 For the flesh desires what is against the Spirit, and the Spirit desires what is

Trust in God, Not in Your Godliness

Obedience without love is legalism. Obedience for its own sake can be nothing more than perfectionism, which only leads to pride.

In Christ Jesus neither circumcision nor uncircumcision accomplishes anything; what matters is faith working through love.
—Galatians 5:6

Love Takes Priority over Your Freedom

The Christian life gives a tremendous freedom, but it also brings a pervasive sense of our accountability to God and to others.

You are called to freedom, brothers; only don't use this freedom as an opportunity for the flesh, but serve one another through love.
—Galatians 5:13

---

a4:30 Gn 21:10   b5:14 Lv 19:18

WORD STUDY

Greek word: **pneuma**
[NYOO mah]

Translation: **Spirit, spirit**

Uses in Galatians: **18**

Uses in Paul's writings: **146**

Uses in the NT: **379**

Key passage: **Galatians 5:16-25**

The Greek noun *pneuma* comes from the related verb *pneo*, meaning *to blow*, and thus can mean *breath, wind, air, ghost,* or *spirit*. In the NT, *pneuma* is almost always used to mean *spirit* in reference to living beings—humans (Mt 26:41; Lk 1:47; 23:46; Ac 7:59; 17:16; 18:25; Rm 1:9; 1 Co 5:5; 14:14; 1 Th 5:23; Heb 12:23; Jms 2:26; Rv 22:6), angels (Heb 1:14), demons (Mt 8:16; 10:1; Ac 19:12-16; Rv 16:13-14), and especially the Holy Spirit (about 240 times).

Three NT writers emphasized the work of the Holy Spirit: Luke (Luke and Acts), John (particularly in John's Gospel and Revelation), and Paul (particularly Romans to Ephesians). Luke referred to the filling of the Spirit 14 times (four in Luke's Gospel; ten in Acts), and each case involves a special work of the Spirit for a specific task, usually proclamation (Lk 1:15-17, 41-45, 67-79; 4:1-15; Ac 4:8-12; 7:55-60; 13:9-11). John the Baptist (Mt 3:11; Jn 1:33) and Jesus (Ac 1:4-8) promised that the Spirit would come to baptize believers, and this was fulfilled on the Day of Pentecost (Ac 2:1-4). Paul explained that the Spirit teaches believers to live by faith according to God's grace and thus to overcome the power of sin (Rm 8:1-26; Gl 5:16-26). Paul's expressions *walking in/according to the Spirit* (Rm 8:4; Gl 5:16,25) and *being led by the Spirit* (Rm 8:14; Gl 5:18) refer to this sanctifying work of the Spirit in the life of the believer.

against the flesh; these are opposed to each other, so that you don't do what you want. [18] But if you are led by the Spirit, you are not under the law.

[19] Now the works of the flesh are obvious:[a] [b] sexual immorality, moral impurity, promiscuity, [20] idolatry, sorcery, hatreds, strife, jealousy, outbursts of anger, selfish ambitions, dissensions, factions, [21] envy,[c] drunkenness, carousing, and anything similar, about which I tell you in advance—as I told you before—that those who practice such things will not inherit the kingdom of God.

[22] But the fruit of the Spirit is love, joy, peace, patience, kindness, goodness, faith,[d] [23] gentleness, self-control. Against such things there is no law. [24] Now those who belong to Christ Jesus have crucified the flesh with its passions and desires. [25] If we live by the Spirit, we must also follow the Spirit. [26] We must not become conceited, provoking one another, envying one another.

CARRY ONE ANOTHER'S BURDENS

6 Brothers, if someone is caught in any wrongdoing, you who are spiritual should restore such a person with a gentle spirit, watching out for yourselves so you won't be tempted also. [2] Carry one another's burdens; in this way you will fulfill the law of Christ. [3] For if anyone considers himself to be something when he is nothing, he is deceiving himself. [4] But each person should examine his own work, and then he will have a reason for boasting in himself alone, and not in respect to someone else. [5] For each person will have to carry his own load.

[6] The one who is taught the message must share his goods with the teacher. [7] Don't be deceived: God is not mocked. For whatever a man sows he will also reap, [8] because the one who sows to his flesh will reap corruption from the flesh, but the one who sows to the Spirit will reap eternal life from the Spirit. [9] So we must not get tired of doing good, for we will reap at the proper time if we don't give up. [10] Therefore, as we

---

[a]**5:19** Other mss add *adultery*
[b]**5:19** Lit *obvious, which are:*

[c]**5:21** Other mss add *murders*
[d]**5:22** Or *faithfulness*

have opportunity, we must work for the good of all, especially for those who belong to the household of faith.

CONCLUDING EXHORTATION

[11] Look at what large letters I have written to you in my own handwriting. [12] Those who want to make a good showing in the flesh are the ones who would compel you to be circumcised—but only to avoid being persecuted for the cross of Christ. [13] For even the circumcised don't keep the law themselves; however, they want you to be circumcised in order to boast about your flesh. [14] But as for me, I will never boast about anything except the cross of our Lord Jesus Christ, through whom[a] the world has been crucified to me, and I to the world. [15] For[b] both circumcision and uncircumcision mean nothing; ⌊what matters⌋ instead is a new creation. [16] May peace be on all those who follow this standard, and mercy also be on the Israel of God!

[17] From now on, let no one cause me trouble, because I carry the marks of Jesus on my body. [18] Brothers, the grace of our Lord Jesus Christ be with your spirit. •Amen.

Others' Needs Are Invitations from God

When a need surfaces around you, immediately go to the Father and say, "You put me here for a reason. You knew this was going to happen. What did You intend to do through me that would help this person become closer to You?"

Carry one another's burdens; in this way you will fulfill the law of Christ.

—Galatians 6:2

You Get What You Pay For

Some people never connect what is happening to them with how they are living. The sooner we understand that today's choices determine tomorrow's rewards, the better off we'll be.

The one who sows to his flesh will reap corruption from the flesh, but the one who sows to the Spirit will reap eternal life from the Spirit.

—Galatians 6:8

---

[a]6:14 Or *which*   [b]6:15 Other mss add *in Christ Jesus*

EPHESIANS

GREETING

1 Paul, an apostle of Christ Jesus by God's will:
To the saints and believers in Christ Jesus at Ephesus.ᵃ

² Grace to you and peace from God our Father and the Lord Jesus Christ.

GOD'S RICH BLESSINGS

³ Blessed be the God and Father of our Lord Jesus Christ, who has blessed us with every spiritual blessing in the heavens, in Christ; ⁴ for He chose us in Him, before the foundation of the world, to be holy and blameless in His sight.ᵇ In loveᶜ ⁵ He predestined us to be adopted through Jesus Christ for Himself, according to His favor and will, ⁶ to the praise of His glorious grace that He favored us with in the Beloved.

⁷ In Him we have redemption through His blood, the forgiveness of our trespasses, according to the riches of His grace ⁸ that He lavished on us with all wisdom and understanding. ⁹ He made known to us the •mystery of His will, according to His good pleasure that He planned in Him ¹⁰ for the administrationᵈ of the days of fulfillmentᵉ —to bring everything together in the •Messiah, both things in heaven and things on earth in Him.

¹¹ In Him we were also made His inheritance,ᶠ predestined according to the purpose of the One who works out everything in agreement with the decision of His

---

ᵃ**1:1** Other mss omit *at Ephesus*
ᵇ**1:4** Vv. 3-14 are 1 sentence in Gk.
ᶜ**1:4** Or *In His sight in love*
ᵈ**1:10** Or *dispensation*; lit *house law* (Gk *oikonomia*)
ᵉ**1:10** Lit *the fulfillment of times*
ᶠ**1:11** Or *we also were chosen as an inheritance*, or *we also received an inheritance*

will, ¹² so that we who had already put our hope in the Messiah might bring praise to His glory.

¹³ In Him you also, when you heard the word of truth, the gospel of your salvation—in Him when you believed—were sealed with the promised Holy Spirit. ¹⁴ He is the down payment of our inheritance, for the redemption of the possession,ᵃ to the praise of His glory.

PRAYER FOR SPIRITUAL INSIGHT

¹⁵ This is why, since I heard about your faith in the Lord Jesus and your love for all the saints, ¹⁶ I never stop giving thanks for you as I remember you in my prayers. ¹⁷ ⌊I pray⌋ that the God of our Lord Jesus Christ, the glorious Father,ᵇ would give you a spirit of wisdom and revelation in the knowledge of Him. ¹⁸ ⌊I pray⌋ that the eyes of your heart may be enlightened so you may know what is the hope of His calling, what are the glorious riches of His inheritance among the saints, ¹⁹ and what is the immeasurable greatness of His power to us who believe, according to the working of His vast strength.

GOD'S POWER IN CHRIST

²⁰ He demonstrated ⌊this power⌋ in the Messiah by raising Him from the dead and seating Him at His right hand in the heavens— ²¹ far above every ruler and authority, power and dominion, and every title given,ᶜ not only in this age but also in the one to come. ²² And **He put everything under His feet**ᵈ and appointed Him as head over everything for the church, ²³ which is His body, the fullness of the One who fills all things in every way.

FROM DEATH TO LIFE

2 And you were dead in your trespasses and sins ² in which you previously •walked according to this worldly age, according to the ruler of the atmospheric

WORD STUDY

Greek word: **_proorizo_**
[prah ah RID zoh]

HCSB translation: **_predestine_**

Uses in Ephesians: **2**

Uses in Paul's writings: **5**

Uses in the NT: **6**

Key passage: **Ephesians 1:5,11**

Proorizo (predestine, predetermine) first appears in Greek literature in the writings of Paul, who may have coined the term. In the NT, this verb consistently refers to God's predetermined plan to culminate salvation history in the person of Jesus Christ. For this reason, God the Father is always the subject of this verb in the NT. The early church saw Jesus' sufferings as the _predetermined_ plan of God in accordance with OT Scriptures (Ac 4:28). The whole of the Christian salvation experience has been predestined by God. Christians have received both their calling and adoption into the rights of Christian sonship because of God's loving _predetermination_ (Rm 8:30; Eph 1:5,11). God has _predetermined_ those whom He foreknew (see _proginosko_; Rm 11:2) to be ultimately conformed to the image of His Son Jesus (Rm 8:29). Finally, God predetermined before the ages His mysterious plan of salvation (1 Co 2:7).

ᵃ1:14 _the possession_ could be either man's or God's
ᵇ1:17 Or _the Father of glory_
ᶜ1:21 Lit _every name named_
ᵈ1:22 Ps 8:6

WORD STUDY

Greek word: **ergon**
[EHR gahn]
HCSB translation: **work**
Uses in Ephesians: **4**
Uses in Paul's writings: **68**
Uses in the NT: **169**
Key passage: **Ephesians 2:9-10**

Ergon (*work*) is related to the verbs *energeo* and *ergazomai*, both meaning *to work* or *accomplish*. Other related terms include *katergazomai* (*to effect* or *achieve*) and *energeia* (*working, action*, or *activity*). *Ergon* appears several hundred times in the Greek OT and is found in every NT book except Philemon. Paul used *ergon* in two primary ways in relation to salvation: to deny that works or human effort contribute to salvation (Rm 3:20,27-28; 4:2,6; 11:6; Gl 2:16; 3:2,5,10; 2 Tm 1:9) and to affirm that those who are saved will manifest good works (1 Co 15:58; 2 Co 9:8; Col 1:10; 2 Th 2:17; 1 Tm 2:10; 6:18; 2 Tm 2:21; 3:17; Ti 2:7,14). Salvation is "not from *works*, so that no one can boast," but God created us "in Christ Jesus for good *works*, which God prepared ahead of time so that we should walk in them" (Eph 2:9-10).

domain,[a] the spirit now working in the disobedient.[b] ³ We too all previously lived among them in our fleshly desires, carrying out the inclinations of our flesh and thoughts, and by nature we were children under wrath, as the others were also. ⁴ But God, who is abundant in mercy, because of His great love that He had for us,[c] ⁵ made us alive with the •Messiah even though we were dead in trespasses. By grace you are saved! ⁶ He also raised us up with Him and seated us with Him in the heavens, in Christ Jesus, ⁷ so that in the coming ages He might display the immeasurable riches of His grace in ⌊His⌋ kindness to us in Christ Jesus. ⁸ For by grace you are saved through faith, and this is not from yourselves; it is God's gift— ⁹ not from works, so that no one can boast. ¹⁰ For we are His creation—created in Christ Jesus for good works, which God prepared ahead of time so that we should walk in them.

UNITY IN CHRIST

¹¹ So then, remember that at one time you were Gentiles in the flesh—called "the uncircumcised" by those called "the circumcised," done by hand in the flesh. ¹² At that time you were without the Messiah, excluded from the citizenship of Israel, and foreigners to the covenants of the promise, with no hope and without God in the world. ¹³ But now in Christ Jesus, you who were far away have been brought near by the blood of the Messiah. ¹⁴ For He is our peace, who made both groups one and tore down the dividing wall of hostility. In His flesh, ¹⁵ He did away with the law of the commandments in regulations, so that He might create in Himself one new man from the two, resulting in peace. ¹⁶ ⌊He did this so⌋ that He might reconcile both to God in one body through the cross and put the hostility to death by it.[d] ¹⁷ When ⌊Christ⌋ came, He proclaimed the good news of peace to you who were far away and peace to those who were near. ¹⁸ For through Him we both have access by one Spirit to the Father. ¹⁹ So then you are no longer foreigners and strangers, but fellow citizens with the saints, and members of God's household, ²⁰ built on the foundation of the apostles and

---

[a]**2:2** Lit *ruler of the authority of the air*
[b]**2:2** Lit *sons of disobedience*
[c]**2:4** Lit *love with which He loved us*
[d]**2:16** Or *death in Himself*

prophets, with Christ Jesus Himself as the cornerstone. [21] The whole building is being fitted together in Him and is growing into a holy sanctuary in the Lord, [22] in whom you also are being built together for God's dwelling in the Spirit.

PAUL'S MINISTRY TO THE GENTILES

3 For this reason, I, Paul, the prisoner of Christ Jesus on behalf of you Gentiles— [2] you have heard, haven't you, about the administration of God's grace that He gave to me for you? [3] The •mystery was made known to me by revelation, as I have briefly written above. [4] By reading this you are able to understand my insight about the mystery of the •Messiah. [5] This was not made known to people[a] in other generations as it is now revealed to His holy apostles and prophets by the Spirit: [6] the Gentiles are co-heirs, members of the same body, and partners of the promise in Christ Jesus through the gospel. [7] I was made a servant of this ⌊gospel⌋ by the gift of God's grace that was given to me by the working of His power.

[8] This grace was given to me—the least of all the saints!—to proclaim to the Gentiles the incalculable riches of the Messiah, [9] and to shed light for all about the administration of the mystery hidden for ages in God who created all things. [10] This is so that God's multi-faceted wisdom may now be made known through the church to the rulers and authorities in the heavens. [11] This is according to the purpose of the ages, which He made in the Messiah, Jesus our Lord, [12] in whom we have boldness, access, and confidence through faith in Him.[b] [13] So then I ask you not to be discouraged over my afflictions on your behalf, for they are your glory.

PRAYER FOR SPIRITUAL POWER

[14] For this reason I bow my knees before the Father[c] [15] from whom every family in heaven and on earth is named. [16] ⌊I pray⌋ that He may grant you, according to the riches of His glory, to be strengthened with power through His Spirit in the inner man, [17] and that the

What a Fellowship, What a Joy Divine

You have just as much of God's powerful presence available to you as the greatest saint in Christian history.

You are no longer foreigners and strangers, but fellow citizens with the saints, and members of God's household,

—Ephesians 2:19

God's Love Goes Back a Long Way

God's plan involves you, just as it has included people throughout the centuries. God wants you to participate in His continuing work to redeem a lost world.

This is according to the purpose of the ages, which He made in the Messiah, Jesus our Lord.

—Ephesians 3:11

---

[a]3:5 Lit *to the sons of men*
[b]3:12 Or *through His faithfulness*
[c]3:14 Other mss add *of our Lord Jesus Christ*

Messiah may dwell in your hearts through faith. ₎I pray that₎ you, being rooted and firmly established in love, ¹⁸ may be able to comprehend with all the saints what is the length and width, height and depth ₎of God's love₎, ¹⁹ and to know the Messiah's love that surpasses knowledge, so you may be filled with all the fullness of God.

²⁰ Now to Him who is able to do above and beyond all that we ask or think—according to the power that works in you— ²¹ to Him be glory in the church and in Christ Jesus to all generations, forever and ever. •Amen.

UNITY AND DIVERSITY IN THE BODY OF CHRIST

4 I, therefore, the prisoner in the Lord, urge you to •walk worthy of the calling you have received, ² with all humility and gentleness, with patience, accepting[a] one another in love, ³ diligently keeping the unity of the Spirit with the peace that binds ₎us₎. ⁴ There is one body and one Spirit, just as you were called to one hope[b] at your calling; ⁵ one Lord, one faith, one baptism, ⁶ one God and Father of all, who is above all and through all and in all.

⁷ Now grace was given to each one of us according to the measure of the •Messiah's gift. ⁸ For it says:

> **When He ascended on high,**
> **He took prisoners into captivity;**[c]
> **He gave gifts to people.**[d]

⁹ But what does "He ascended" mean except that He[e] descended to the lower parts of the earth?[f] ¹⁰ The One who descended is the same as the One who ascended far above all the heavens, that He might fill[g] all things. ¹¹ And He personally gave some to be apostles, some prophets, some evangelists, some pastors and teachers, ¹² for the training of the saints in the work of ministry, to build up the body of Christ, ¹³ until we all reach unity in the faith and in the knowledge of God's Son, ₎growing₎ into a mature man with a stature measured by Christ's fullness. ¹⁴ Then we will no longer be little chil-

God Makes You Strong from the Inside Out

We cannot make ourselves holy. We can become holy only through the power of Christ and the working of the Holy Spirit in our lives.

I pray that He may grant you, according to the riches of His glory, to be strengthened with power through His Spirit in the inner man.

—Ephesians 3:16

God's Plans for You Are Greater Than Yours

You will never set a goal so big or attempt a task so significant that God does not have something far greater that He could do in and through your life.

To Him who is able to do above and beyond all that we ask or think—according to the power that works in you—to Him be glory.

—Ephesians 3:20-21a

---

[a]4:2 Or *tolerating*
[b]4:4 Lit *called in one hope*
[c]4:8 Or *He led the captives*
[d]4:8 Ps 68:18
[e]4:9 Other mss add *first*
[f]4:9 Or *the lower parts, namely, the earth*
[g]4:10 Or *fulfill*; see Eph 1:23

dren, tossed by the waves and blown around by every wind of teaching, by human cunning with cleverness in the techniques of deceit. ¹⁵ But speaking the truth in love, let us grow in every way into Him who is the head—Christ. ¹⁶ From Him the whole body, fitted and knit together by every supporting ligament, promotes the growth of the body for building up itself in love by the proper working of each individual part.

LIVING THE NEW LIFE

¹⁷ Therefore, I say this and testify in the Lord: You should no longer walk as the Gentiles walk, in the futility of their thoughts. ¹⁸ They are darkened in their understanding, excluded from the life of God, because of the ignorance that is in them and because of the hardness of their hearts. ¹⁹ They became callous and gave themselves over to promiscuity for the practice of every kind of impurity with a desire for more and more.ᵃ

²⁰ But that is not how you learned about the Messiah, ²¹ assuming you heard Him and were taught by Him, because the truth is in Jesus: ²² you took offᵇ your former way of life, the old man that is corrupted by deceitful desires; ²³ you are being renewedᶜ in the spirit of your minds; ²⁴ you put onᵈ the new man, the one created according to God's ⌊likeness⌋ in righteousness and purity of the truth.

²⁵ Since you put away lying, **Speak the truth, each one to his neighbor,**ᵉ because we are members of one another. ²⁶ **Be angry and do not sin.**ᶠ Don't let the sun go down on your anger, ²⁷ and don't give the Devil an opportunity. ²⁸ The thief must no longer steal. Instead, he must do honest work with his own hands, so that he has something to share with anyone in need. ²⁹ No rotten talk should come from your mouth, but only what is good for the building up of someone in need,ᵍ in order to give grace to those who hear. ³⁰ And don't grieve God's Holy Spirit, who sealed youʰ for the day of

Nothing Satisfies Like a Godly Life

An abiding security comes from living a blameless life. It is exhilarating to be set apart by God, knowing that He observes your devoted life and is pleased by what He sees.

I, therefore, the prisoner in the Lord, urge you to walk worthy of the calling you have received.

—Ephesians 4:1

You Are Gifted in Order to Give

God does not add you to a church body to be an observer. The Spirit has an assignment for you within the body, and He will equip you by His presence for that work.

He personally gave some to be apostles, some prophets, some evangelists, some pastors and teachers, for the training of the saints in the work of ministry, to build up the body of Christ.

—Ephesians 4:11-12

ᵃ**4:19** Lit *with greediness*
ᵇ**4:21-22** Or *Jesus. This means: take off* (as a command)
ᶜ**4:22-23** Or *desires; renew* (as a command)
ᵈ**4:23-24** Or *minds; and put on* (as a command)
ᵉ**4:25** Zch 8:16
ᶠ**4:26** Ps 4:4
ᵍ**4:29** Lit *for the building up of the need*
ʰ**4:30** Or *Spirit, by whom you were sealed*

WORD STUDY

Greek word: **apolutrosis**
[ah pah LEW troh sihs]

Translation: **redemption**

Uses in Ephesians: **3**

Uses in Paul's writings: **7**

Uses in the NT: **10**

Key passage: **Ephesians 1:7, 14; 4:30**

In the NT, *apolutrosis* may refer to present or future *redemption*. When referring to future redemption, the term looks to the salvation of the Christian's physical body from the distresses of this world. The Son of Man's return will usher in release from suffering and persecution (Lk 21:28). In Paul's theology, the future *redemption* of our physical bodies will be accompanied both by the church's full adoption into divine sonship and by the creation being set free from decay (Rm 8:18-23). Presently, the Holy Spirit is the down payment guaranteeing the future "*redemption* of the possession" (meaning God will fully redeem His church and/or the church will posses its full inheritance; Eph 1:14; 4:30). Christians have *redemption*, described as the forgiveness of sins (Eph 1:7; Col 1:14). Thus the work of God in Christ ensures both present and future redemption for His people.

redemption. [31] All bitterness, anger and wrath, insult and slander must be removed from you, along with all wickedness. [32] And be kind and compassionate to one another, forgiving one another, just as God also forgave you[a] in Christ.

5 Therefore, be imitators of God, as dearly loved children. [2] And •walk in love, as the •Messiah also loved us and gave Himself for us, a sacrificial and fragrant offering to God. [3] But sexual immorality and any impurity or greed should not even be heard of[b] among you, as is proper for saints. [4] And coarse and foolish talking or crude joking are not suitable, but rather giving thanks. [5] For know and recognize this: no sexually immoral or impure or greedy person, who is an idolater, has an inheritance in the kingdom of the Messiah and of God.

LIGHT VERSUS DARKNESS

[6] Let no one deceive you with empty arguments, for because of these things God's wrath is coming on the disobedient.[c] [7] Therefore, do not become their partners. [8] For you were once darkness, but now ˌyou areˌ light in the Lord. Walk as children of light— [9] for the fruit of the light[d] ˌresultsˌ in all goodness, righteousness, and truth— [10] discerning what is pleasing to the Lord. [11] Don't participate in the fruitless works of darkness, but instead, expose them. [12] For it is shameful even to mention what is done by them in secret. [13] Everything exposed by the light is made clear, [14] for what makes everything clear is light. Therefore it is said:

Get up, sleeper, and rise up from the dead,
and the Messiah will shine on you.[e]

CONSISTENCY IN THE CHRISTIAN LIFE

[15] Pay careful attention, then, to how you walk—not as unwise people but as wise— [16] making the most of the time,[f] because the days are evil. [17] So don't be fool-

---

[a]4:32 Other mss read *us*
[b]5:3 Or *be named*
[c]5:6 Lit *sons of disobedience*
[d]5:9 Other mss read *fruit of the Spirit*; see Gl 5:22, but compare Eph 5:11-14

[e]5:14 This poem may have been an early Christian hymn based on several passages in Isaiah; see Is 9:2; 26:19; 40:1; 51:17; 52:1; 60:1.
[f]5:16 Lit *buying back the time*

ish, but understand what the Lord's will is. ¹⁸ And don't get drunk with wine, which ⌊leads to⌋ reckless actions, but be filled with the Spirit:

¹⁹ speaking to one another in psalms, hymns,
and spiritual songs,
singing and making music to the Lord
in your heart,
²⁰ giving thanks always for everything
to God the Father in the name
of our Lord Jesus Christ,
²¹ submitting to one another in the fear
of Christ.

WIVES AND HUSBANDS

²² Wives, submit[a] to your own husbands as to the Lord, ²³ for the husband is head of the wife as also Christ is head of the church. He is the Savior of the body. ²⁴ Now as the church submits to Christ, so wives should ⌊submit⌋ to their husbands in everything. ²⁵ Husbands, love your wives, just as also Christ loved the church and gave Himself for her, ²⁶ to make her holy, cleansing[b] her in the washing of water by the word. ²⁷ He did this to present the church to Himself in splendor, without spot or wrinkle or any such thing, but holy and blameless. ²⁸ In the same way, husbands should love their wives as their own bodies. He who loves his wife loves himself. ²⁹ For no one ever hates his own flesh, but provides and cares for it, just as Christ does for the church, ³⁰ since we are members of His body.[c]

³¹ **For this reason a man will leave his father
and mother
and be joined to his wife,
and the two will become one flesh.**[d]

³² This •mystery is profound, but I am talking about Christ and the church. ³³ To sum up, each one of you is to love his wife as himself, and the wife is to respect her husband.

Sin Dies If You Give It Too Much Light

We free ourselves from sin's bondage when we recognize it for the evil it is. If we simply call our sin a mistake, a bad habit, or a weakness, we will never escape its grasp.

Don't participate in the fruitless works of darkness, but instead, expose them.
—Ephesians 5:11

God's Will Is Clear When We Watch for It

Don't be content merely seeing with physical eyes and hearing with natural ears but not sensing what God is doing. Ask God to sensitize you to His activity that's all around you.

Don't be foolish, but understand what the Lord's will is.
—Ephesians 5:17

---

[a]5:22 Other mss omit *submit*
[b]5:26 Or *having cleansed*
[c]5:30 Other mss add *and of His flesh and of His bones*
[d]5:31 Gn 2:24

WORD STUDY

Greek word: **hrema**
[HRAY mah]

Translation: **word**

Uses in Ephesians: **2**

Uses in Paul's writings: **8**

Uses in the NT: **68**

Key passage: **Ephesians 6:17**

Hrema most frequently appears in the narrative literature of the four Gospels and Acts (a total of 52 times). In the NT, *hrema* (*word*) is used with two different senses. The term is first used with the sense of *that which is said or expressed*. Here the word focuses on what has been communicated. For example, Jesus speaks of men having to give account for every careless *word* they speak (Mt 12:36). In this sense, *hrema* may also refer to any one of many different types of communication. For example, *hrema* can refer to a *prophecy* or *prediction* (e.g., Mk 9:32), to a *speech* or *sermon* (e.g., Rm 10:18), to the *gospel* or a *confessional statement* (e.g., 1 Pt 1:25), or to a *commandment* or *order* (e.g., Heb 11:3). However, *hrema* does not always focus on what has been communicated. It may refer simply to a *thing, object, matter,* or *event.* For example, Paul speaks of every *word* (i.e., *matter* or *event*) being confirmed on the testimony of two or three witnesses (2 Co 13:1), and the angel Gabriel reminds Mary that nothing is impossible with God (Lk 1:37).

CHILDREN AND PARENTS

6 Children, obey your parents in the Lord, because this is right. ² **Honor your father and mother—** which is the first commandment[a] with a promise— ³ **that it may go well with you and that you may have a long life in the land.**[b] [c] ⁴ And fathers, don't stir up anger in your children, but bring them up in the training and instruction of the Lord.

SLAVES AND MASTERS

⁵ Slaves, obey your human[d] masters with fear and trembling, in the sincerity of your heart, as to Christ. ⁶ Don't ⌊work only⌋ while being watched, in order to please men, but as slaves of Christ, do God's will from your heart.[e] ⁷ Render service with a good attitude, as to the Lord and not to men, ⁸ knowing that whatever good each one does, slave or free, he will receive this back from the Lord. ⁹ And masters, treat them the same way, without threatening them, because you know that both their and your Master is in heaven, and there is no favoritism with Him.

CHRISTIAN WARFARE

¹⁰ Finally, be strengthened by the Lord and by His vast strength. ¹¹ Put on the full armor of God so that you can stand against the tactics[f] of the Devil. ¹² For our battle is not against flesh and blood, but against the rulers, against the authorities, against the world powers of this darkness, against the spiritual forces of evil in the heavens. ¹³ This is why you must take up the full armor of God, so that you may be able to resist in the evil day, and having prepared everything, to take your stand. ¹⁴ Stand, therefore,

with truth like a belt around your waist,
righteousness like armor on your chest,
¹⁵ and your feet sandaled with readiness
for the gospel of peace.[g]

---

[a]**6:2** Or *is a preeminent commandment*
[b]**6:3** Or *life on the earth*
[c]**6:2-3** Ex 20:12
[d]**6:5** Lit *according to the flesh*
[e]**6:6** Lit *from soul*
[f]**6:11** Or *schemes,* or *tricks*
[g]**6:15** Ready to go tell others about the gospel

16 In every situation take the shield of faith,
    and with it you will be able to extinguish
    the flaming arrows of the evil one.
17 Take the helmet of salvation,
    and the sword of the Spirit, which is God's word.

18 With every prayer and request, pray at all times in the Spirit, and stay alert in this, with all perseverance and intercession for all the saints. 19 Pray also for me, that the message may be given to me when I open my mouth to make known with boldness the •mystery of the gospel. 20 For this I am an ambassador in chains. Pray that I might be bold enough in Him to speak as I should.

PAUL'S FAREWELL

21 Tychicus, our dearly loved brother and faithful servant[a] in the Lord, will tell you everything so that you also may know how I am and what I'm doing. 22 I am sending him to you for this very reason, to let you know how we are and to encourage your hearts.

23 Peace to the brothers, and love with faith, from God the Father and the Lord Jesus Christ. 24 Grace be with all who have undying love for our Lord Jesus Christ.[b] [c]

Faith in God Is Your Greatest Weapon

Those who let God accomplish mighty things through them do so because they believe He can.

In every situation take the shield of faith, and with it you will be able to extinguish the flaming arrows of the evil one.
—Ephesians 6:16

You'd Be Surprised How Bold You Can Be

God could send fire from heaven or shout the good news with claps of thunder, but that is not His way. His plan is for people like you to be witnesses to His love.

Pray also for me, that the message may be given to me when I open my mouth to make known with boldness the mystery of the gospel.
—Ephesians 6:19

---

[a]6:21 Or *deacon*
[b]6:24 Other mss add *Amen.*
[c]6:24 Lit *all who love our Lord Jesus Christ in incorruption*

PHILIPPIANS

GREETING

1 Paul and Timothy, slaves of Christ Jesus:
To all the saints in Christ Jesus who are in Philippi, including the •overseers and deacons. ² Grace to you and peace from God our Father and the Lord Jesus Christ.

THANKSGIVING AND PRAYER

³ I give thanks to my God for every remembrance of you,[a] ⁴ always praying with joy for all of you in my every prayer, ⁵ because of your partnership in the gospel from the first day until now. ⁶ I am sure of this, that He who started a good work in you[b] will carry it on to completion until the day of Christ Jesus. ⁷ It is right for me to think this way about all of you, because I have you in my heart,[c] and you are all partners with me in grace, both in my imprisonment and in the defense and establishment of the gospel. ⁸ For God is my witness, how I deeply miss all of you with the affection of Christ Jesus. ⁹ And I pray this: that your love will keep on growing in knowledge and every kind of discernment, ¹⁰ so that you can determine what really matters and can be pure and blameless in[d] the day of Christ, ¹¹ filled with the fruit of righteousness that ₍comes₎ through Jesus Christ, to the glory and praise of God.

ADVANCE OF THE GOSPEL

¹² Now I want you to know, brothers, that what has happened to me has actually resulted in the advance-

---

[a]1:3 Or *for your every remembrance of me*
[b]1:6 Or *work among you*
[c]1:7 Or *because you have me in your heart*
[d]1:10 Or *until*

ment of the gospel, [13] so that it has become known throughout the whole imperial guard,[a] and to everyone else, that my imprisonment is for Christ.[b] [14] Most of the brothers in the Lord have gained confidence from my imprisonment and dare even more to speak the message[c] fearlessly. [15] Some, to be sure, preach Christ out of envy and strife, but others out of good will.[d] [16] These do so out of love, knowing that I am appointed for the defense of the gospel; [17] the others proclaim Christ out of rivalry, not sincerely, seeking to cause ⌊me⌋ trouble in my imprisonment.[e] [18] What does it matter? Just that in every way, whether out of false motives or true, Christ is proclaimed. And in this I rejoice. Yes, and I will rejoice [19] because I know this will lead to my deliverance[f] through your prayers and help from the Spirit of Jesus Christ. [20] My eager expectation and hope is that I will not be ashamed about anything, but that now as always, with all boldness, Christ will be highly honored in my body, whether by life or by death.

LIVING IS CHRIST

[21] For me, living is Christ and dying is gain. [22] Now if I live on in the flesh, this means fruitful work for me; and I don't know which one I should choose. [23] I am pressured by both. I have the desire to depart and be with Christ—which is far better— [24] but to remain in the flesh is more necessary for you. [25] Since I am persuaded of this, I know that I will remain and continue with all of you for your advancement and joy in the faith, [26] so that, because of me, your confidence may grow in Christ Jesus when I come to you again.

[27] Just one thing: live your life in a manner worthy of the gospel of Christ. Then, whether I come and see you or am absent, I will hear about you that you are standing firm in one spirit, with one mind,[g] working side by side for the faith of the gospel, [28] not being frightened in any way by your opponents. This is evidence of their destruction, but of your deliverance—and this is from

[a]**1:13** Lit *praetorium*, a Lat word that can also refer to a military headquarters, to the governor's palace, or to Herod's palace
[b]**1:13** Lit *in Christ*
[c]**1:14** Other mss add *of God*
[d]**1:15** The good will of men, or God's good will or favor
[e]**1:17** Lit *sincerely, intending to raise tribulation to my bonds*
[f]**1:19** Or *salvation*, or *vindication*
[g]**1:27** Lit *soul*

WORD STUDY

Greek word: ***euangelion*** [yoo ahn GEHL ee ahn]

Translation: ***gospel, good news***

Uses in Philippians: **12**

Uses in Paul's writings: **60**

Uses in the NT: **76**

Key passage: **Philippians 1:27**

The Christian *euangelion* (*gospel*) is the universal message of God's saving grace through faith in Christ, and the message of His kingdom over which Jesus reigns. Jesus preached the *good news* of God's coming kingdom (Mt 4:23), and substantiated His message by miracles (Mt 9:35). This *good news* of the kingdom's arrival will be preached to the world (Mk 13:10) and is worthy of sacrificial labor (Mk 8:35). Paul believed the *gospel* was an extension of OT promises, where it lay hidden in mystery form (Rm 1:1-3; 16:25-26). Paul's *gospel* encompasses Jesus' entire life: His incarnation, sacrificial death, burial, resurrection, post-resurrection appearances, and ascension (Rm 1:1-6; 1 Co 15:1-8; Php 2:9). It is the Spirit-empowered message (1 Th 1:5) by which God calls the elect (2 Th 2:13-14) and reconciles people to Himself (2 Co 5:18-21). Men will one day be judged by it (Rm 2:16; 2 Th 1:8).

God. ²⁹ For it has been given to you on Christ's behalf not only to believe in Him, but also to suffer for Him, ³⁰ having the same struggle that you saw I had and now hear about me.

CHRISTIAN HUMILITY

2 If then there is any encouragement in Christ, if any consolation of love, if any fellowship with the Spirit, if any affection and mercy, ² fulfill my joy by thinking the same way, having the same love, sharing the same feelings, focusing on one goal. ³ Do nothing out of rivalry or conceit, but in humility consider others as more important than yourselves. ⁴ Everyone should look out not ₗonlyₗ for his own interests, but also for the interests of others.

CHRIST'S HUMILITY AND EXALTATION

⁵ Make your own attitude that of Christ Jesus,

⁶ who, existing in the form of God,
did not consider equality with God
as something to be used for His own advantage.ᵃ
⁷ Instead He emptied Himself by assuming
the form of a slave,
taking on the likeness of men.
And when He had come as a man
in His external form,
⁸ He humbled Himself by becoming obedient
to the point of death—even to death on a cross.
⁹ For this reason God also highly exalted Him
and gave Him the name that is above every name,
¹⁰ so that at the name of Jesus
every knee should bow—
of those who are in heaven and on earth
and under the earth—
¹¹ and every tongue should confess
that Jesus Christ is Lord,
to the glory of God the Father.

LIGHTS IN THE WORLD

¹² So then, my dear friends, just as you have always

Discipleship Always Comes at a Cost

If we are going to take up our cross and follow Jesus, we must be prepared to go with Him to the place of suffering if that's what it takes to bring salvation to those around us.

For it has been given to you on Christ's behalf not only to believe in Him, but also to suffer for Him.
—Philippians 1:29

Pour Yourself Out— God Will Fill You Up

If you find yourself resisting every time God seeks to adjust your life to His will, ask the Holy Spirit to give you the same selfless attitude that Jesus demonstrated.

Make your own attitude that of Christ Jesus, who, existing in the form of God, did not consider equality with God as something to be used for His own advantage.
—Philippians 2:5-6

ᵃ2:6 Or *to be grasped*, or *to be held on to*

obeyed, not only in my presence, but now even more in my absence, work out your own salvation with fear and trembling. [13] For it is God who is working in you, ⌊enabling you⌋ both to will and to act for His good purpose. [14] Do everything without grumbling and arguing, [15] so that you may be blameless and pure, children of God who are faultless in a crooked and perverted generation, among whom you shine like stars in the world. [16] Hold firmly[a] the message of life. Then I can boast in the day of Christ that I didn't run in vain or labor for nothing. [17] But even if I am poured out as a drink offering on the sacrifice and service of your faith, I am glad and rejoice with all of you. [18] In the same way you also should rejoice and share your joy with me.

TIMOTHY AND EPAPHRODITUS

[19] Now I hope in the Lord Jesus to send Timothy to you soon so that I also may be encouraged when I hear news about you. [20] For I have no one else like-minded who will genuinely care about your interests; [21] all seek their own interests, not those of Jesus Christ. [22] But you know his proven character, because he has served with me in the gospel ministry like a son with a father. [23] Therefore, I hope to send him as soon as I see how things go with me. [24] And I am convinced in the Lord that I myself will also come quickly.

[25] But I considered it necessary to send you Epaphroditus—my brother, co-worker, and fellow soldier, as well as your messenger and minister to my need— [26] since he has been longing for all of you and was distressed because you heard that he was sick. [27] Indeed, he was so sick that he nearly died. However, God had mercy on him, and not only on him but also on me, so that I would not have one grief on top of another. [28] For this reason, I am very eager to send him so that you may rejoice when you see him again and I may be less anxious. [29] Therefore, welcome him in the Lord with all joy and hold men like him in honor, [30] because he came close to death for the work of Christ, risking his life to make up what was lacking in your ministry to me.

Salvation Is a One-time Gift, a Lifetime Lifestyle

When you were converted, God made everything available to you. How you implement what He has given you depends on how fully you submit your life to Him each day.

Work out your own salvation with fear and trembling. For it is God who is working in you, enabling you both to will and to act for His good purpose.

—Philippians 2:12b-13

Light Your World

If the world is becoming darker, the problem is not with the darkness. The problem is with the light. When you allow God's light to shine unhindered in your life, the darkness around you will be dispelled.

Be blameless and pure, children of God who are faultless in a crooked and perverted generation, among whom you shine like stars in the world.

—Philippians 2:15

[a]2:16 Or *Offer*, or *Hold out*

KNOWING CHRIST

3 Finally, my brothers, rejoice in the Lord. To write to you again about this is no trouble for me and is a protection for you.

² Watch out for "dogs,"ᵃ watch out for evil workers, watch out for those who mutilate the flesh. ³ For we are the circumcision, the ones who serve by the Spirit of God, boast in Christ Jesus, and do not put confidence in the flesh— ⁴ although I once had confidence in the flesh too. If anyone else thinks he has grounds for confidence in the flesh, I have more: ⁵ circumcised the eighth day; of the nation of Israel, of the tribe of Benjamin, a Hebrew born of Hebrews; as to the law, a •Pharisee; ⁶ as to zeal, persecuting the church; as to the righteousness that is in the law, blameless.

⁷ But everything that was a gain to me, I have considered to be a loss because of Christ. ⁸ More than that, I also consider everything to be a loss in view of the surpassing value of knowing Christ Jesus my Lord. Because of Him I have suffered the loss of all things and consider them filth, so that I may gain Christ ⁹ and be found in Him, not having a righteousness of my own from the law, but one that is through faith in Christᵇ —the righteousness from God based on faith. ¹⁰ ⌊My goal⌋ is to know Him and the power of His resurrection and the fellowship of His sufferings, being conformed to His death, ¹¹ assuming that I will somehow reach the resurrection from among the dead.

REACHING FORWARD TO GOD'S GOAL

¹² Not that I have already reached ⌊the goal⌋ or am already fully mature, but I make every effort to take hold of it because I also have been taken hold of by Christ Jesus. ¹³ Brothers, I do notᶜ consider myself to have taken hold of it. But one thing I do: forgetting what is behind and reaching forward to what is ahead, ¹⁴ I pursue as my goal the prize promised by God's heavenlyᵈ call in Christ Jesus. ¹⁵ Therefore, all who are mature should think this way. And if you think differently about

---

Have You Seen What That God of Yours Can Do?

Don't discount the power of God as described in Scripture simply because you haven't experienced it. Instead, bring your experience up to the standard of Scripture.

My goal is to know Him and the power of His resurrection and the fellowship of His sufferings, being conformed to His death.

—Philippians 3:10

Do What You Know, and Learn as You Go

As you learn to trust God more deeply, He will develop your character to match bigger tests, and with the greater test will come a greater love for God and knowledge of His ways.

In any case, we should live up to whatever truth we have attained.

—Philippians 3:16

ᵃ3:2 An expression of contempt for the unclean, those outside the people of God
ᵇ3:9 Or *through the faithfulness of Christ*
ᶜ3:13 Other mss read *not yet.*
ᵈ3:14 Or *upward*

anything, God will reveal this to you also. [16] In any case, we should live up to whatever ⌊truth⌋ we have attained. [17] Join in imitating me, brothers, and observe those who live according to the example you have in us. [18] For I have often told you, and now say again with tears, that many live as enemies of the cross of Christ. [19] Their end is destruction; their god is their stomach; their glory is in their shame. They are focused on earthly things, [20] but our citizenship is in heaven, from which we also eagerly wait for a Savior, the Lord Jesus Christ. [21] He will transform the body of our humble condition into the likeness of His glorious body, by the power that enables Him to subject everything to Himself.

PRACTICAL COUNSEL

4 So then, in this way, my dearly loved brothers, my joy and crown, stand firm in the Lord, dear friends. [2] I urge Euodia and I urge Syntyche to agree in the Lord. [3] Yes, I also ask you, true partner,[a] to help these women who have contended for the gospel at my side, along with Clement and the rest of my co-workers whose names are in the book of life. [4] Rejoice in the Lord always. I will say it again: Rejoice! [5] Let your graciousness be known to everyone. The Lord is near. [6] Don't worry about anything, but in everything, through prayer and petition with thanksgiving, let your requests be made known to God. [7] And the peace of God, which surpasses every thought, will guard your hearts and your minds in Christ Jesus.

[8] Finally brothers, whatever is true, whatever is honorable, whatever is just, whatever is pure, whatever is lovely, whatever is commendable—if there is any moral excellence and if there is any praise—dwell on these things. [9] Do what you have learned and received and heard and seen in me, and the God of peace will be with you.

APPRECIATION OF SUPPORT

[10] I rejoiced in the Lord greatly that now at last you have renewed your care for me. You were, in fact,

---

[a]4:3 Or *true Syzygus*, possibly a person's name

WORD STUDY

Greek word: ***chairo***
[KIGH roh]

Translation: ***rejoice***

Uses in Philippians: **9**

Uses in Paul's writings: **29**

Uses in the NT: **74**

Key passage: **Philippians 4:4**

Chairo means *to enjoy a state of gladness, happiness,* or *well-being.* Scripture records numerous events that result in this joyful state: finding something formerly lost (Mt 18:13; Lk 15:5,32); the hope of reward from God (Mt 5:12 = Lk 6:23; Lk 10:20); Jesus' miracles (Lk 13:17; 19:37); His birth (Lk 1:14); His post-resurrection appearances (Jn 20:20); suffering (Ac 5:41, Col 1:24); the repentance of others (2 Co 7:9); the faith of others (Col 2:5); the preaching about Christ (Php 1:18); and many other occasions. This state of rejoicing in God is commanded for Christians (2 Co 13:11; 1 Th 5:16, Php 3:1; 4:4). *Chairo* also appears as part of a greeting expressing the wish for a person's happiness (Mt 26:49) and commonly appearing in the introduction to a letter (Ac 15:23; 23:26; Jms 1:1). In the context of miraculous encounters with the divine, *chairo* may mean: *Rejoice* (Mt 28:9; Lk 1:28).

concerned about me, but lacked the opportunity ⌞to show it⌟. [11] I don't say this out of need, for I have learned to be content in whatever circumstances I am. [12] I know both how to have a little, and I know how to have a lot. In any and all circumstances I have learned the secret ⌞of being content⌟—whether well-fed or hungry, whether in abundance or in need. [13] I am able to do all things through Him[a] who strengthens me. [14] Still, you did well by sharing with me in my hardship.

[15] And you, Philippians, know that in the early days of the gospel, when I left Macedonia, no church shared with me in the matter of giving and receiving except you alone. [16] For even in Thessalonica you sent ⌞gifts⌟ for my need several times. [17] Not that I seek the gift, but I seek the fruit that is increasing to your account. [18] But I have received everything in full, and I have an abundance. I am fully supplied, having received from Epaphroditus what you provided—a fragrant offering, a welcome sacrifice, pleasing to God. [19] And my God will supply all your needs according to His riches in glory in Christ Jesus. [20] Now to our God and Father be glory forever and ever. •Amen.

FINAL GREETINGS

[21] Greet every saint in Christ Jesus. Those brothers who are with me greet you. [22] All the saints greet you, but especially those from Caesar's household. [23] The grace of the Lord Jesus Christ be with your spirit.[b]

Can You Be Happy with What You Have?

Discontentment stems from the sin of ingratitude and a lack of faith that God cares enough to provide for you. Contentment demonstrates your belief that God loves you and has your best interests in mind.

In any and all circumstances I have learned the secret of being content—whether well-fed or hungry, whether in abundance or in need.

—Philippians 4:12b

Aren't You Glad God Is Your Soul Supplier?

Seasons of need are not times to become anxious or to panic. It is at these times that God wants to draw from His unlimited storehouse to meet your need as only He can.

My God will supply all your needs according to His riches in glory in Christ Jesus.

—Philippians 4:19

---

[a]**4:13** Other mss read *Christ*   [b]**4:23** Other mss add *Amen.*

COLOSSIANS

GREETING

1 Paul, an apostle of Christ Jesus by God's will, and Timothy our[a] brother:
² To the saints and faithful brothers in Christ in Colossae.

Grace to you and peace from God our Father.[b]

THANKSGIVING

³ We always thank God, the Father of our Lord Jesus Christ, when we pray for you, ⁴ for we have heard of your faith in Christ Jesus and of the love you have for all the saints ⁵ because of the hope reserved for you in heaven. You have already heard about ⌊this hope⌋ in the message of truth, the gospel ⁶ that has come to you. It is bearing fruit and growing all over the world, just as it has among you since the day you heard it and recognized God's grace in the truth.[c] ⁷ You learned this from Epaphras, our much loved fellow slave. He is a faithful minister of the •Messiah on your[d] behalf, ⁸ and he has told us about your love in the Spirit.

PRAYER FOR SPIRITUAL GROWTH

⁹ For this reason also, since the day we heard this, we haven't stopped praying for you. We are asking that you may be filled with the knowledge of His will in all wisdom and spiritual understanding, ¹⁰ so that you may •walk worthy of the Lord, fully pleasing ⌊to Him⌋, bearing fruit in every good work and growing in the knowledge of God. ¹¹ May you be strengthened with all power,

---

[a]1:1 Lit *the*
[b]1:2 Other mss add *and the Lord Jesus Christ*
[c]1:6 Or *and truly recognized God's grace*
[d]1:7 Other mss read *our*

WORD STUDY

Greek word: ***prototokos***
[proh TAH tah kahs]
Translation: ***firstborn***
Uses in Colossians: **2**
Uses in Paul's writings: **3**
Uses in the NT: **8**
Key passage: **Colossians 1:15**

Prototokos (firstborn), derived from *protos* (first in time/rank) and *-tikto* (give birth to), appears eight times in the NT. All six occurrences in the singular refer to Jesus, and it is possible that *prototokos* was a title for the incarnate Christ (Heb 1:6). With the exceptions of Luke 2:7 and Hebrews 11:28, where *prototokos* clearly refers to first-born children, the force of *-tikto* is lost in the NT. The term thus takes on the sense of "preeminence in rank or time." Jesus' preeminent status over His creation is seen in Col 1:15. As Creator "He is before all things" in supremacy (Col 1:17a) and is "the firstborn from the dead" (Col 1:18; Rv 1:5): the first to be resurrected and the One having authority over the resurrection of the dead. Additionally, Jesus' post-resurrection transfiguration is a preview of the glorious transfiguration of the saints in the future (Rm 8:29).

according to His glorious might, for all endurance and patience, with joy ¹² giving thanks to the Father, who has enabled you[a] to share in the saints'[b] inheritance in the light. ¹³ He has rescued us from the domain of darkness and transferred us into the kingdom of the Son He loves, ¹⁴ in whom we have redemption,[c] the forgiveness of sins.

THE CENTRALITY OF CHRIST

¹⁵ He is the image of the invisible God,
    the firstborn over all creation;[d]
¹⁶ because by Him everything was created,
    in heaven and on earth, the visible
        and the invisible,
    whether thrones or dominions or rulers
        or authorities—
    all things have been created through Him
        and for Him.
¹⁷ He is before all things, and by Him all things
        hold together.
¹⁸ He is also the head of the body, the church;
    He is the beginning, the firstborn
        from the dead,
    so that He might come to have first place
        in everything.
¹⁹ For God was pleased ₌to have₌
    all His fullness dwell in Him,
²⁰ and through Him to reconcile everything
        to Himself
    by making peace through the blood
        of His cross[e] —
    whether things on earth or things
        in heaven.

²¹ And you were once alienated and hostile in mind because of your evil actions. ²² But now He has reconciled you by His physical body[f] through His death, to present you holy, faultless, and blameless before Him— ²³ if indeed you remain grounded and steadfast in the faith, and are not shifted away from the hope of

---

[a]**1:12** Other mss read *us*
[b]**1:12** Or *holy ones'*
[c]**1:14** Other mss add *through His blood*
[d]**1:15** The One who is preeminent over all creation
[e]**1:20** Other mss add *through Him*
[f]**1:22** His body of flesh on the cross

the gospel that you heard. ₍This gospel₎ has been proclaimed in all creation under heaven, and I, Paul, have
become a minister of it.

PAUL'S MINISTRY

²⁴ Now I rejoice in my sufferings for you, and I am
completing in my flesh what is lacking in Christ's afflictions for His body, that is, the church. ²⁵ I have become
its minister, according to God's administration that
was given to me for you, to make God's message fully
known, ²⁶ the •mystery hidden for ages and generations
but now revealed to His saints. ²⁷ God wanted to make
known to those among the Gentiles the glorious wealth
of this mystery, which is Christ in you, the hope of
glory. ²⁸ We proclaim Him, warning and teaching everyone with all wisdom, so that we may present everyone
mature in Christ. ²⁹ I labor for this, striving with His
strength that works powerfully in me.

2 For I want you to know how great a struggle I have
for you, for those in Laodicea, and for all who have
not seen me in person. ² ₍I want₎ their hearts to be encouraged and joined together in love, so that they may
have all the riches of assured understanding, and have
the knowledge of God's •mystery—Christ.ᵃ ³ In Him all
the treasures of wisdom and knowledge are hidden.

CHRIST VERSUS THE COLOSSIAN HERESY

⁴ I am saying this so that no one will deceive you with
persuasive arguments. ⁵ For I may be absent in body,
but I am with you in spirit, rejoicing to see your good
order and the strength of your faith in Christ.

⁶ Therefore as you have received Christ Jesus the
Lord, •walk in Him, ⁷ rooted and built up in Him and
established in the faith, just as you were taught, and
overflowing with thankfulness.

⁸ Be careful that no one takes you captive through
philosophy and empty deceit based on human tradition, based on the elemental forces of the world, and
not based on Christ. ⁹ For in Him the entire fullness of

One Thing We Know: God Is in Control

When we say Christ is Lord,
we must remember that Christ
is Lord over all. His power is
infinite, far exceeding anything
we could even imagine.

*He is before all things, and by
Him all things hold together.*
—Colossians 1:17

Talk Like, Walk Like, Be Like Jesus Christ

You do not simply add Christ to
your busy life and carry on with
business as usual. When Christ is
your Lord, everything changes.

*As you have received Christ
Jesus the Lord, walk in Him.*
—Colossians 2:6

ᵃ2:2 Other mss read *mystery of
God, both of the Father and of* *Christ*; other ms variations exist on
this v.

445

God's nature[a] dwells bodily,[b] 10 and you have been filled by Him, who is the head over every ruler and authority. 11 In Him you were also circumcised with a circumcision not done with hands, by putting off the body of flesh, in the circumcision of the •Messiah. 12 Having been buried with Him in baptism, you were also raised with Him through faith in the working of God, who raised Him from the dead. 13 And when you were dead in trespasses and in the uncircumcision of your flesh, He made you alive with Him and forgave us all our trespasses. 14 He erased the certificate of debt, with its obligations, that was against us and opposed to us, and has taken it out of the way by nailing it to the cross. 15 He disarmed the rulers and authorities and disgraced them publicly; He triumphed over them by Him.[c]

16 Therefore don't let anyone judge you in regard to food and drink or in the matter of a festival or a new moon or a sabbath day.[d] 17 These are a shadow of what was to come; the substance is[e] the Messiah. 18 Let no one disqualify you,[f] insisting on ascetic practices and the worship of angels, claiming access to a visionary realm and inflated without cause by his fleshly mind. 19 He doesn't hold on to the head, from whom the whole body, nourished and held together by its ligaments and tendons, develops with growth from God.

20 If you died with Christ to the elemental forces of this world, why do you live as if you still belonged to the world? Why do you submit to regulations: 21 "Don't handle, don't taste, don't touch"? 22 All these ⌊regulations⌋ refer to what is destroyed by being used up; they are human commands and doctrines. 23 Although these have a reputation of wisdom by promoting ascetic practices, humility, and severe treatment of the body, they are not of any value against fleshly indulgence.

THE LIFE OF THE NEW MAN

3 So if you have been raised with the •Messiah, seek what is above, where the Messiah is, seated at the

---

Stick a Fork in the Devil—He's Done

When you resist Satan, you are acknowledging that Jesus has totally defeated him on the cross and in His resurrection, and has given you complete victory over his influence.

He disarmed the rulers and authorities and disgraced them publicly; He triumphed over them by Him.

—Colossians 2:15

Why All the Potential and None of the Power?

Too often Christians live in a world that's void of faith, a world limited by their own understanding and power. How sad to have so much available to them, yet to access so little of it.

If you died with Christ to the elemental forces of this world, why do you live as if you still belonged to the world?

—Colossians 2:20a

---

[a]2:9 Or *the deity*
[b]2:9 Or *nature lives in a human body*
[c]2:15 Or *them through it*; that is, through the cross
[d]2:16 Or *or sabbaths*
[e]2:17 Or *substance belongs to*
[f]2:18 Or *no one cheat us out of your prize*

right hand of God. ² Set your minds on what is above, not on what is on the earth. ³ For you have died, and your life is hidden with the Messiah in God. ⁴ When the Messiah, who is yourᵃ life, is revealed, then you also will be revealed with Him in glory.

⁵ Therefore, put to death whatever in you is worldly:ᵇ sexual immorality, impurity, lust, evil desire, and greed, which is idolatry. ⁶ Because of these, God's wrath comes on the disobedient,ᶜ ⁷ and you once •walked in these things when you were living in them. ⁸ But now you must also put away all the following: anger, wrath, malice, slander, and filthy language from your mouth. ⁹ Do not lie to one another, since you have put off the old man with his practices ¹⁰ and have put on the new man, who is being renewed in knowledge according to the image of his Creator. ¹¹ Here there is not Greek and Jew, circumcision and uncircumcision, barbarian, Scythian,ᵈ slave and free; but Christ is all and in all.

THE CHRISTIAN LIFE

¹² Therefore, God's chosen ones, holy and loved, put on heartfelt compassion, kindness, humility, gentleness, and patience, ¹³ accepting one another and forgiving one another if anyone has a complaint against another. Just as the Lord has forgiven you, so also you must ₍forgive₎. ¹⁴ Above all, ₍put on₎ love—the perfect bond of unity. ¹⁵ And let the peace of the Messiah, to which you were also called in one body, control your hearts. Be thankful. ¹⁶ Let the message about the Messiah dwell richly among you, teaching and admonishing one another in all wisdom, and singing psalms, hymns, and spiritual songs, with gratitude in your hearts to God. ¹⁷ And whatever you do, in word or in deed, do everything in the name of the Lord Jesus, giving thanks to God the Father through Him.

CHRIST IN YOUR HOME

¹⁸ Wives, be submissive to your husbands, as is fitting in the Lord.

Always Keep One Foot in Eternity

The imminence of Christ's coming provides the backdrop for everything the Christian does.

If you have been raised with the Messiah, seek what is above, where the Messiah is, seated at the right hand of God.
—Colossians 3:1

Talk It Up, Live It Out

It is God's desire that anywhere there is a Christian, God has a way for people to learn of His salvation. Our lives ought to be a highway of holiness, providing easy access to God for anyone around us who seeks Him.

Let the message about the Messiah dwell richly among you, teaching and admonishing one another in all wisdom, and singing psalms, hymns, and spiritual songs, with gratitude in your hearts to God.
—Colossians 3:16

ᵃ3:4 Other mss read *our*
ᵇ3:5 Lit *death, the members on the earth*
ᶜ3:6 Other mss omit *on the disobedient*
ᵈ3:11 A term for a savage

WORD STUDY

Greek word: ***kleronomia***
[klay rah nah MEE ah]

Translation: ***inheritance***

Uses in Colossians: **1**

Uses in Paul's writings: **5**

Uses in the NT: **14**

Key passage: **Colossians 3:24**

Kleronomia (*inheritance*) occasionally refers to promised possessions (Ac 7:5) or to the inheritance legally due an heir (Lk 12:13). More frequently, however, NT authors employ the term *inheritance* in a religious, spiritual sense to refer to the future, heavenly, imperishable, eternal salvation of which the saints will one day partake in the kingdom of God (Col 3:24; Eph 1:14; Heb 9:15; 1 Pt 1:4). Jesus, in His "Parable of the Wicked Tenants" (Mt 21:38 = Mk 12:7 = Lk 20:14), loads the term with this deeper, spiritual referent, interpreting the *inheritance* as the kingdom of God (Mt 21:43). Paul speaks of *inheritance* only in this religious sense. Christians, as heirs of God through faith (Gl 3:26), have sole rights to this future *inheritance* (Eph 5:5). The sealing of the Holy Spirit upon believers is the Father's guarantee that He will grant His children their promised *inheritance* (Eph 1:13-14,18).

19 Husbands, love your wives and don't become bitter against them.

20 Children, obey your parents in everything, for this is pleasing in the Lord.

21 Fathers, do not exasperate your children, so they won't become discouraged.

22 Slaves, obey your human masters in everything; don't work only while being watched, in order to please men, but ⌊work⌋ wholeheartedly, fearing the Lord.

23 Whatever you do, do it enthusiastically,[a] as something done for the Lord and not for men, 24 knowing that you will receive the reward of an inheritance from the Lord—you serve the Lord Christ. 25 For the wrongdoer will be paid back for whatever wrong he has done, and there is no favoritism.

4 Masters, supply your slaves with what is right and fair, since you know that you too have a Master in heaven.

SPEAKING TO GOD AND OTHERS

2 Devote yourselves to prayer; stay alert in it with thanksgiving. 3 At the same time, pray also for us that God may open a door to us for the message, to speak the •mystery of the •Messiah—for which I am in prison— 4 so that I may reveal it as I am required to speak. 5 •Walk in wisdom toward outsiders, making the most of the time. 6 Your speech should always be gracious, seasoned with salt, so that you may know how you should answer each person.

CHRISTIAN GREETINGS

7 Tychicus, a loved brother, a faithful servant, and a fellow slave in the Lord, will tell you all the news about me. 8 I have sent him to you for this very purpose, so that you may know how we are,[b] and so that he may encourage your hearts. 9 He is with Onesimus, a faithful and loved brother, who is one of you. They will tell you about everything here.

---

[a]3:23 Lit *do it from the soul*   [b]4:8 Other mss read *that he may know how you are*

[10] Aristarchus, my fellow prisoner, greets you, as does Mark, Barnabas' cousin (concerning whom you have received instructions: if he comes to you, welcome him), [11] and so does Jesus who is called Justus. These alone of the circumcision are my co-workers for the kingdom of God, and they have been a comfort to me. [12] Epaphras, who is one of you, a slave of Christ Jesus, greets you. He is always contending for you in his prayers, so that you can stand mature and fully assured[a] in everything God wills. [13] For I testify about him that he works hard[b] for you, for those in Laodicea, and for those in Hierapolis. [14] Luke, the loved physician, and Demas greet you. [15] Give my greetings to the brothers in Laodicea, and to Nympha and the church in her house. [16] And when this letter has been read among you, have it read also in the church of the Laodiceans; and see that you also read the letter from Laodicea. [17] And tell Archippus, "Pay attention to the ministry you have received in the Lord, so that you can accomplish it."

[18] This greeting is in my own hand—Paul. Remember my imprisonment. Grace be with you.[c]

See Prayer for More Than You Think It Is

Prayer is not difficult to understand. It is difficult to do. Don't allow yourself to become satisfied with shallow, self-centered praying. Stay with God in prayer until He leads you to pray at the level He wants.

Devote yourselves to prayer; stay alert in it with thanksgiving.

—Colossians 4:2

Your Words Say a Lot About Whose You Are

A sanctified mouth is a wonderful instrument for the Lord. Ask Him to discipline your mouth so that every word you speak is used by God to encourage and edify others.

Your speech should always be gracious, seasoned with salt, so that you may know how you should answer each person.

—Colossians 4:6

---

[a]4:12 Other mss read *and complete*
[b]4:13 Other mss read *he has a great zeal*
[c]4:18 Other mss add *Amen,*

THESSALONIANS

GREETING

1 Paul, Silvanus,[a] and Timothy:
To the church of the Thessalonians in God the Father and the Lord Jesus Christ.
Grace to you and peace.[b]

THANKSGIVING

[2] We always thank God for all of you, remembering you constantly in our prayers. [3] We recall, in the presence of our God and Father, your work of faith, labor of love, and endurance of hope in our Lord Jesus Christ, [4] knowing your election, brothers loved by God. [5] For our gospel did not come to you in word only, but also in power, in the Holy Spirit, and with much assurance. You know what kind of men we were among you for your benefit, [6] and you became imitators of us and of the Lord when, in spite of severe persecution, you welcomed the message with the joy from the Holy Spirit. [7] As a result, you became an example to all the believers in Macedonia and Achaia. [8] For the Lord's message rang out from you, not only in Macedonia and Achaia, but in every place that your faith[c] in God has gone out, so we don't need to say anything. [9] For they themselves report about us what kind of reception we had from you: how you turned to God from idols to serve the living and true God, [10] and to wait for His Son from heaven, whom He raised from the dead—Jesus, who rescues us from the coming wrath.

---

[a]**1:1** Or *Silas*; see Ac 15:22-32; 16:19-40; 17:1-16
[b]**1:1** Other mss add *from God our Father and the Lord Jesus Christ*
[c]**1:8** Or *in every place news of your faith*

PAUL'S CONDUCT

2 For you yourselves know, brothers, that our visit with you was not without result. ² On the contrary, after we had previously suffered and been outrageously treated in Philippi, as you know, we were emboldened by our God to speak the gospel of God to you in spite of great opposition. ³ For our exhortation didn't come from error or impurity or an intent to deceive. ⁴ Instead, just as we have been approved by God to be entrusted with the gospel, so we speak, not to please men, but rather God, who examines our hearts. ⁵ For we never used flattering speech, as you know, or had greedy motives—God is our witness— ⁶ and we didn't seek glory from people, either from you or from others. ⁷ Although we could have been a burden as Christ's apostles, instead we were gentleª among you, as a nursing mother nurtures her own children. ⁸ We cared so much for you that we were pleased to share with you not only the gospel of God but also our own lives, because you had become dear to us. ⁹ For you remember our labor and hardship, brothers. Working night and day so that we would not burden any of you, we preached God's gospel to you. ¹⁰ You are witnesses, and so is God, of how devoutly, righteously, and blamelessly we conducted ourselves with you believers. ¹¹ As you know, like a father with his own children, ¹² we encouraged, comforted, and implored each one of you to •walk worthy of God, who calls you into His own kingdom and glory.

RECEPTION AND OPPOSITION TO THE MESSAGE

¹³ Also, this is why we constantly thank God, because when you received the message about God that you heard from us, you welcomed it not as a human message, but as it truly is, the message of God, which also works effectively in you believers. ¹⁴ For you, brothers, became imitators of God's churches in Christ Jesus that are in Judea, since you have also suffered the same things from people of your own country, just as they did from the Jews. ¹⁵ They killed both the Lord Jesus

ª2:7 Other mss read *infants*

Stick to Your Calling Even When It's Hard

We never hear Paul complaining about his commission from God. He accepted his role in the kingdom, even with all its risks and challenges.

After we had previously suffered and been outrageously treated in Philippi, as you know, we were emboldened by our God to speak the gospel of God to you in spite of great opposition.

—1 Thessalonians 2:2

You Are a Constant Expression of Christ

Our world hungers for an expression of Christ as He really is, living out His life through His people. We represent God to those who see us.

We cared so much for you that we were pleased to share with you not only the gospel of God but also our own lives, because you had become dear to us.

—1 Thessalonians 2:8

WORD STUDY

Greek word: ***stephanos***
[STEH fah nahs]

Translation: ***crown***

Uses in 1 Thessalonians: 1

Uses in Paul's writings: 4

Uses in the NT: 18

Key passage: **1 Thessalonians 2:19**

In the Gospels, *stephanos* (*crown*) refers exclusively to the thorny crown worn by Jesus during His Passion (Mt 27:29; Mk 15:17; Jn 19:2,5). Paul consistently exhorts the saints by using the promise of a crown as their future reward. Believers should run the Christian race to obtain an imperishable crown, even as athletes run for a perishable *wreath* (1 Co 9:25; cf. Rv 3:11), and a *crown* of righteousness belongs to all who love the Lord's appearing (2 Tm 4:8). Certain congregations are the *crown* with which Paul will appear before the Lord at His return (1 Th 2:19; Php 4:1). James speaks of a *crown* of life given to those who, despite persecution, maintain their love for God (Jms 1:12; cf. Rv 2:10), and an unfading *crown* of glory awaits elders who lovingly shepherd their congregations (1 Pt 5:4). *Crown* appears frequently in the apocalyptic imagery of Revelation. There it is usually associated with pictures of authority, rule, dominion, power, and/or enablement for a task.

and the prophets, and persecuted us; they displease God, and are hostile to everyone, [16] hindering us from speaking to the Gentiles so that they may be saved. As a result, they are always adding to the number of their sins, and wrath has overtaken them completely.[a]

PAUL'S DESIRE TO SEE THEM

[17] But as for us, brothers, after we were forced to leave you for a short time (in person, not in heart), we greatly desired and made every effort to return and see you face to face. [18] So we wanted to come to you—even I, Paul, time and again—but Satan hindered us. [19] For who is our hope, or joy, or crown of boasting in the presence of our Lord Jesus at His coming? Is it not you? [20] For you are our glory and joy!

ANXIETY IN ATHENS

3 Therefore, when we could no longer stand it, we thought it was better to be left alone in Athens. [2] And we sent Timothy, our brother and God's co-worker[b] in the gospel of Christ, to strengthen and encourage you concerning your faith, [3] so that no one will be shaken by these persecutions. For you yourselves know that we are appointed to[c] this. [4] In fact, when we were with you, we told you previously that we were going to suffer persecution, and as you know, it happened. [5] For this reason, when I could no longer stand it, I also sent to find out about your faith, fearing that the tempter had tempted you and that our labor might be for nothing.

ENCOURAGED BY TIMOTHY

[6] But now Timothy has come to us from you and brought us good news about your faith and love, and that you always have good memories of us, wanting to see us, as we also want to see you. [7] Therefore, brothers, in all our distress and persecution, we were encouraged about you through your faith. [8] For now we live, if you stand firm in the Lord. [9] How can we thank God for you in return for all the joy we experience

---

[a]2:16 Or *to the end*
[b]3:2 Other mss read *servant*
[c]3:3 Or *we are destined for*

because of you before our God, ¹⁰ as we pray earnestly night and day to see you face to face and to complete what is lacking in your faith?

PRAYER FOR THE CHURCH

¹¹ Now may our God and Father Himself, and our Lord Jesus, direct our way to you. ¹² And may the Lord cause you to increase and overflow with love for one another and for everyone, just as we also do for you. ¹³ May He make your hearts blameless in holiness before our God and Father at the coming of our Lord Jesus with all His saints. •Amen.ᵃ

THE CALL TO SANCTIFICATION

4 Finally then, brothers, we ask and encourage you in the Lord Jesus, that as you have received from us how you must •walk and please God—as you are doingᵇ —do so even more. ² For you know what commands we gave you through the Lord Jesus.

³ For this is God's will, your sanctification: that you abstain from sexual immorality, ⁴ so that each of you knows how to possess his own vesselᶜ in sanctification and honor, ⁵ not with lustful desires, like the Gentiles who don't know God. ⁶ This means one must not transgress against and defraud his brother in this matter, because the Lord is an avenger of all these offenses,ᵈ as we also previously told and warned you. ⁷ For God has not called us to impurity, but to sanctification. ⁸ Therefore, the person who rejects this does not reject man, but God, who also gives you His Holy Spirit.

LOVING AND WORKING

⁹ About brotherly love: you don't need me to write you because you yourselves are taught by God to love one another. ¹⁰ In fact, you are doing this toward all the brothers in the entire region of Macedonia. But we encourage you, brothers, to do so even more, ¹¹ to seek to lead a quiet life, to mind your own business,ᵉ and

How Invested Are You in the Lives of Others?

We ought to be so devoted to strengthening one another's faith that we pursue this goal relentlessly.

How can we thank God for you in return for all the joy we experience because of you before our God, as we pray earnestly night and day to see you face to face and to complete what is lacking in your faith?

—1 Thessalonians 3:9-10

Obedience Is an Order, Not an Option

Righteous living is not an option for a Christian. Nor is it something we must try to do over time. It is an obligation, mandatory for every child of God.

You know what commands we gave you through the Lord Jesus. For this is God's will, your sanctification.

—1 Thessalonians 4:2-3a

ᵃ3:13 Other mss omit *Amen.*
ᵇ4:1 Lit *walking*
ᶜ4:4 Or *to control his own body,* or *to acquire his own wife*
ᵈ4:6 Lit *things*
ᵉ4:11 Lit *to practice one's own things*

453

WORD STUDY

Greek word: **harpazo**
[hahr PAH zoh]

Translation: **caught up**

Uses in 1 Thessalonians: **1**

Uses in Paul's writings: **3**

Uses in the NT: **14**

Key passage: **1 Thessalonians 4:17**

Harpazo (*catch up*, *snatch up*) is often invested with the idea of force. In this sense, *harpazo* refers to an arrest (Ac 23:10) and to the near forceful capture of Jesus by a crowd (Jn 6:15). The term is not limited to the physical realm. The Evil One *snatches away* the message of the kingdom sown upon men's hearts (Mt 13:19), Jude exhorts believers to *snatch* some men from the fire (Jd 23), and no one is able to forcefully carry off the sheep belonging to the Good Shepherd (Jn 10:11,28-29). Elsewhere, the term is used of supernatural phenomena and does not carry the concept of force. Paul received glorious revelation after being *caught up* into Paradise (2 Co 12:2,4). The Holy Spirit *carries* Philip away and transports him to Azotus (Ac 8:39). Believers will one day be *caught up* to meet their returning Lord (1 Th 4:17).

to work with your own hands, as we commanded you, [12] so that you may walk properly[a] in the presence of outsiders[b] and not be dependent on anyone.[c]

THE COMFORT OF CHRIST'S COMING

[13] We do not want you to be uninformed, brothers, concerning those who are •asleep, so that you will not grieve like the rest, who have no hope. [14] Since we believe that Jesus died and rose again, in the same way God will bring with Him those who have fallen asleep through[d] Jesus.[e] [15] For we say this to you by a revelation from the Lord:[f] We who are still alive at the Lord's coming will certainly have no advantage over[g] those who have fallen asleep. [16] For the Lord Himself will descend from heaven with a shout,[h] with the archangel's voice, and with the trumpet of God, and the dead in Christ will rise first. [17] Then we who are still alive will be caught up together with them in the clouds to meet the Lord in the air; and so we will always be with the Lord. [18] Therefore encourage[i] one another with these words.

THE DAY OF THE LORD

5 About the times and the seasons: brothers, you do not need anything to be written to you. [2] For you yourselves know very well that the Day of the Lord will come just like a thief in the night. [3] When they say, "Peace and security," then sudden destruction comes on them, like labor pains on a pregnant woman, and they will not escape. [4] But you, brothers, are not in the dark, so that this day would overtake you like a thief. [5] For you are all sons of light and sons of the day. We're not of the night or of darkness. [6] So then, we must not sleep, like the rest, but we must stay awake and be sober. [7] For those who sleep, sleep at night, and those who get drunk are drunk at night. [8] But since we are of the day, we must be sober and put the armor of faith and love on our chests, and put on a helmet of the hope of salvation. [9] For God did not appoint

---

[a]**4:12** Or *may live respectably*
[b]**4:12** Non-Christians
[c]**4:12** Or *not need anything*, or *not be in need*
[d]**4:14** Or *asleep in*
[e]**4:14** *those who have fallen asleep*

through Jesus = Christians who have died
[f]**4:15** Or *a word of the Lord*
[g]**4:15** Or *certainly not precede*
[h]**4:16** Or *command*
[i]**4:18** Or *comfort*

us to wrath, but to obtain salvation through our Lord Jesus Christ, [10] who died for us, so that whether we are awake or •asleep, we will live together with Him. [11] Therefore encourage one another and build each other up as you are already doing.

EXHORTATIONS AND BLESSINGS

[12] Now we ask you, brothers, to give recognition to those who labor among you and lead you in the Lord and admonish you, [13] and to esteem them very highly in love because of their work. Be at peace among yourselves. [14] And we exhort you, brothers: warn those who are lazy,[a] comfort the discouraged, help the weak, be patient with everyone. [15] See to it that no one repays evil for evil to anyone, but always pursue what is good for one another and for all.

[16] Rejoice always!
[17] Pray constantly.
[18] Give thanks in everything,
    for this is God's will for you in Christ Jesus.
[19] Don't stifle the Spirit.
[20] Don't despise prophecies,
[21] but test all things.
    Hold on to what is good.
[22] Stay away from every form of evil.

[23] Now may the God of peace Himself sanctify you completely. And may your spirit, soul, and body be kept sound and blameless for the coming of our Lord Jesus Christ. [24] He who calls you is faithful, who also will do it. [25] Brothers, pray for us also. [26] Greet all the brothers with a holy kiss. [27] I charge you by the Lord that this letter be read to all the brothers. [28] May the grace of our Lord Jesus Christ be with you!

The Way of Peace Is the Will of God

Which is more important to you—to win an argument or to win a friend? As Christians, we are called to bring peace with us wherever we go.

See to it that no one repays evil for evil to anyone, but always pursue what is good for one another and for all.
—1 Thessalonians 5:15

Make Sure the Holy Spirit Has Your Ear

Be wary of resisting the voice of the Holy Spirit in your life. You may not always be comfortable with what the Spirit is saying, but His words will guide you to abundant life.

Don't stifle the Spirit.
—1 Thessalonians 5:19

---

[a]5:14 Or *who are disorderly,* or *who are undisciplined*

THESSALONIANS

GREETING

1 Paul, Silvanus,[a] and Timothy:
To the church of the Thessalonians in God our
Father and the Lord Jesus Christ.

² Grace to you and peace from God our Father and
the Lord Jesus Christ.

GOD'S JUDGMENT AND GLORY

³ We must always thank God for you, brothers, which
is fitting, since your faith is flourishing, and the love
of every one of you for one another is increasing.
⁴ Therefore we ourselves boast about you among God's
churches—about your endurance and faith in all the
persecutions and afflictions you endure. ⁵ It is a clear
evidence of God's righteous judgment that you will be
counted worthy of God's kingdom, for which you also
are suffering, ⁶ since it is righteous for God to repay
with affliction those who afflict you, ⁷ and ⌊to reward⌋
with rest you who are afflicted, along with us. ⌊This
will take place⌋ at the revelation of the Lord Jesus from
heaven with His powerful angels, ⁸ taking vengeance
with flaming fire on those who don't know God and
on those who don't obey the gospel of our Lord Jesus.
⁹ These will pay the penalty of everlasting destruction,
away from the Lord's presence and from His glorious
strength, ¹⁰ in that day when He comes to be glorified by
His saints and to be admired by all those who have believed, because our testimony among you was believed.
¹¹ And in view of this, we always pray for you that our
God will consider you worthy of His calling, and will,
by His power, fulfill every desire for goodness and the

---

[a]1:1 Or *Silas*; see Ac 15:22-32; 16:19-40; 17:1-16

work of faith, [12] so that the name of our Lord Jesus will be glorified by you, and you by Him, according to the grace of our God and the Lord Jesus Christ.

THE MAN OF LAWLESSNESS

2 Now concerning the coming of our Lord Jesus Christ and our being gathered to Him: we ask you, brothers, [2] not to be easily upset in mind or troubled, either by a spirit or by a message or by a letter as if from us, alleging that the Day of the Lord[a] has come. [3] Don't let anyone deceive you in any way. For ⌊that day⌋ will not come unless the apostasy[b] comes first and the man of lawlessness[c] is revealed, the son of destruction. [4] He opposes and exalts himself above every so-called god or object of worship, so that he sits[d] in God's sanctuary,[e] publicizing that he himself is God. [5] Don't you remember that when I was still with you I told you about this? [6] And you know what currently restrains ⌊him⌋, so that he will be revealed in his time. [7] For the •mystery of lawlessness is already at work; but the one now restraining will do so until he is out of the way, [8] and then the lawless one will be revealed. The Lord Jesus will destroy him with the breath of His mouth and will bring him to nothing with the brightness of His coming. [9] The coming ⌊of the lawless one⌋ is based on Satan's working, with all kinds of false miracles, signs, and wonders, [10] and with every unrighteous deception among those who are perishing. ⌊They perish⌋ because they did not accept the love of the truth in order to be saved. [11] For this reason God sends them a strong delusion so that they will believe what is false, [12] so that all will be condemned—those who did not believe the truth but enjoyed unrighteousness.

STAND FIRM

[13] But we must always thank God for you, brothers loved by the Lord, because from the beginning[f] God has chosen you for salvation through sanctification by the Spirit and through belief in the truth. [14] He called you

---

[a]2:2 Other mss read *Christ*
[b]2:3 Or *rebellion*
[c]2:3 Other mss read *man of sin*
[d]2:4 Other mss add *as God*
[e]2:4 Or *temple*
[f]2:13 Other mss read *because as a firstfruit*

WORD STUDY

Greek word: **parousia**
[pah roo SEE ah]

Translation: **coming, presence**

Uses in 2 Thessalonians: **3**

Uses in Paul's writings: **14**

Uses in the NT: **24**

Key passage: **2 Thessalonians 2:8**

Parousia means *presence* or *coming*. In the sense of *presence*, it refers to physical proximity. Paul speaks of the obedience of the Philippian church during both his *presence* and absence (Php 2:12) and of the *presence* of his fellow laborers (1 Co 16:17). Elsewhere, *parousia* refers to the *coming* or *arrival* of men or events. Paul mentions the *coming* of Titus (2 Co 7:6-7), and he hopes to *come* again to the Philippians (Php 1:26). *Parousia* occurs most often in relation to the *coming* of the Lord Jesus as human history moves to closure. His *coming* will be preceded by the *coming* of the "lawless one," the Antichrist (2 Th 2:8-9). The glorious *coming* of Jesus will be accompanied by the destruction of all His enemies, a resurrection of the dead in Christ, and a gathering of the saints still living (1 Co 15:23-25; 1 Th 4:15-16; 2 Th 2:1).

to this through our gospel, so that you might obtain the glory of our Lord Jesus Christ. [15] Therefore, brothers, stand firm and hold to the traditions you were taught, either by our message or by our letter.

[16] May our Lord Jesus Christ Himself and God our Father, who has loved us and given us eternal encouragement and good hope by grace, [17] encourage your hearts and strengthen you in every good work and word.

PRAY FOR US

3 Finally, pray for us, brothers, that the Lord's message may spread rapidly and be honored, just as it was with you, [2] and that we may be delivered from wicked and evil men, for not all have faith. [3] But the Lord is faithful; He will strengthen and guard you from the evil one. [4] We have confidence in the Lord about you, that you are doing and will do what we command. [5] May the Lord direct your hearts to God's love and Christ's endurance.

WARNING AGAINST IRRESPONSIBLE BEHAVIOR

[6] Now we command you, brothers, in the name of our Lord Jesus Christ, to keep away from every brother who •walks irresponsibly and not according to the tradition received from us. [7] For you yourselves know how you must imitate us: we were not irresponsible among you; [8] we did not eat anyone's bread free of charge; instead, we labored and toiled, working night and day, so that we would not be a burden to any of you. [9] It is not that we don't have the right ₍to support₎, but we did it to make ourselves an example to you so that you would imitate us. [10] In fact, when we were with you, this is what we commanded you: "If anyone isn't willing to work, he should not eat." [11] For we hear that there are some among you who walk irresponsibly, not working at all, but interfering with the work ₍of others₎. [12] Now we command and exhort such people, by the Lord Jesus Christ, that quietly working, they may eat their own bread.[a] [13] Brothers, do not grow weary in doing good.

[14] And if anyone does not obey our instruction in this

Stay on Your Knees for Those Who Need Jesus

If we truly have God's love within us, we will feel compelled to plead with God on behalf of those who face His imminent judgment.

Pray for us, brothers, that the Lord's message may spread rapidly and be honored, just as it was with you.

—2 Thessalonians 3:1

God's Help Is Strong Enough to Do the Job

God's will for you may involve hardship, but He loves you and will not allow you to face more than you are able to handle.

The Lord is faithful; He will strengthen and guard you from the evil one.

—2 Thessalonians 3:3

[a]3:12 Or *food*

letter, take note of that person; don't associate with him, so that he may be ashamed. ¹⁵ Yet don't treat him as an enemy, but warn him as a brother.

FINAL GREETINGS

¹⁶ May the Lord of peace Himself give you peace always in every way. The Lord be with all of you. ¹⁷ This greeting is in my own hand—Paul. This is a sign in every letter; this is how I write. ¹⁸ The grace of our Lord Jesus Christ be with all of you.

Love Others Enough to Hold Them Accountable

Don't ever try to protect those you love by disobeying God or glossing over their sins. The cost of disobedience is always greater.

If anyone does not obey our instruction in this letter, take note of that person; don't associate with him, so that he may be ashamed. Yet don't treat him as an enemy, but warn him as a brother.
—2 Thessalonians 3:14-15

TIMOTHY

GREETING

1 Paul, an apostle of Christ Jesus according to the command of God our Savior and of Christ Jesus, our hope:

² To Timothy, my true child in the faith.

Grace, mercy, and peace from God the[a] Father and Christ Jesus our Lord.

FALSE DOCTRINE AND MISUSE OF THE LAW

³ As I urged you when I went to Macedonia, remain in Ephesus so that you may command certain people not to teach other doctrine ⁴ or to pay attention to myths and endless genealogies. These promote empty speculations rather than God's plan, which operates by faith. ⁵ Now the goal of our instruction is love from a pure heart, a good conscience, and a sincere faith. ⁶ Some have deviated from these and turned aside to fruitless discussion. ⁷ They want to be teachers of the law, although they don't understand what they are saying or what they are insisting on. ⁸ Now we know that the law is good, provided one uses it legitimately. ⁹ We know that the law is not meant for a righteous person, but for the lawless and rebellious, for the ungodly and sinful, for the unholy and irreverent, for those who kill their fathers and mothers, for murderers, ¹⁰ for the sexually immoral and homosexuals, for kidnappers, liars, perjurers, and for whatever else is contrary to the sound teaching ¹¹ based on the glorious gospel of the blessed God that was entrusted to me.

---

[a]1:2 Other mss read *our*

PAUL'S TESTIMONY

¹² I give thanks to Christ Jesus our Lord, who has strengthened me, because He considered me faithful, appointing me to the ministry— ¹³ one who was formerly a blasphemer, a persecutor, and an arrogant man. Since it was out of ignorance that I had acted in unbelief, I received mercy, ¹⁴ and the grace of our Lord overflowed, along with the faith and love that are in Christ Jesus. ¹⁵ This saying is trustworthy and deserving of full acceptance: "Christ Jesus came into the world to save sinners"—and I am the worst of them. ¹⁶ But I received mercy because of this, so that in me, the worst ₗof themₗ, Christ Jesus might demonstrate the utmost patience as an example to those who would believe in Him for eternal life. ¹⁷ Now to the King eternal, immortal, invisible, the onlyª God, be honor and glory forever and ever. •Amen.

ENGAGE IN BATTLE

¹⁸ Timothy, my child, I am giving you this instruction in keeping with the prophecies previously made about you, so that by them you may strongly engage in battle, ¹⁹ having faith and a good conscience. Some have rejected these and have suffered the shipwreck of their faith. ²⁰ Hymenaeus and Alexander are among them, and I have delivered them to Satan, so that they may be taught not to blaspheme.

INSTRUCTIONS ON PRAYER

2 First of all, then, I urge that petitions, prayers, intercessions, and thanksgivings be made for everyone, ² for kings and all those who are in authority, so that we may lead a tranquil and quiet life in all godliness and dignity. ³ This is good, and it pleases God our Savior, ⁴ who wants everyone to be saved and to come to the knowledge of the truth.

⁵ For there is one God
and one mediator between God and man,
a man, Christ Jesus,

It Is God in You That Makes You Qualified

If you are willing to obey God in whatever He asks of you, He will see to it that you have all the strength and ability you need to succeed in it.

I give thanks to Christ Jesus our Lord, who has strengthened me, because He considered me faithful, appointing me to the ministry.

—1 Timothy 1:12

Your Nation Is in Need of Your Prayers

Intercessors can sometimes be the only ones standing between a family and God's judgment, between an individual or nation and God's wrath.

I urge that petitions, prayers, intercessions, and thanksgivings be made for everyone, for kings and all those who are in authority, so that we may lead a tranquil and quiet life in all godliness and dignity.

—1 Timothy 2:1-2

ª**1:17** Other mss add *wise*

WORD STUDY

Greek word: **diakonos**
[dee AH kah nahs]

Translation: **deacon, servant**

Uses in 1 Timothy: **3**

Uses in Paul's writings: **21**

Uses in the NT: **29**

Key passage: **1 Timothy 3:8,12**

Diakonos frequently refers to a *servant* who attends to other's needs. Those responsible for serving a meal (Jn 2:5,9) and the attendants of a king are *servants* (Mt 22:13). The person desiring a position of greatness must become a *servant* (Mk 10:43). One can also serve a spiritual power. False apostles are called *servants* of Satan (2 Co 11:15), and Paul is a *servant* of the gospel (Eph 3:7). Governing authorities are *servants* of God, for they dispense justice (Rm 13:4). Elsewhere, *diakonos* retains the idea of service, while adopting the more technical sense of a church leadership position (i.e., *deacon*). Paul may use this technical sense when he calls Phoebe a *servant/deaconess* of the church in Cenchrea (Rm 16:1). In 1 Timothy 3:8-13, Paul delineates the qualifications for holding the diaconate. Lastly, *diakonos* may refer to a *promoter*. Paul rhetorically asks if Christ is one who *promotes* sin (Gl 2:17).

⁶ who gave Himself—a ransom for all,
a testimony at the proper time.

⁷ For this I was appointed a herald, an apostle (I am telling the truth;ᵃ I am not lying), and a teacher of the Gentiles in faith and truth.

INSTRUCTIONS TO MEN AND WOMEN

⁸ Therefore I want the men in every place to pray, lifting up holy hands without anger or argument. ⁹ Also, the women are to dress themselves in modest clothing, with decency and good sense; not with elaborate hairstyles, gold, pearls, or expensive apparel, ¹⁰ but with good works, as is proper for women who affirm that they worship God. ¹¹ A woman should learn in silence with full submission. ¹² I do not allow a woman to teach or to have authority over a man; instead, she is to be silent. ¹³ For Adam was created first, then Eve. ¹⁴ And Adam was not deceived, but the woman was deceived and transgressed. ¹⁵ But she will be saved through childbearing, if she continuesᵇ in faith, love, and holiness, with good sense.

QUALIFICATIONS OF CHURCH LEADERS

3 This saying is trustworthy:ᶜ "If anyone aspires to be an •overseer, he desires a noble work." ² An overseer, therefore, must be above reproach, the husband of one wife, self-controlled, sensible, respectable, hospitable, an able teacher,ᵈ ³ not addicted to wine, not a bully but gentle, not quarrelsome, not greedy— ⁴ one who manages his own household competently, having his children under control with all dignity. ⁵ (If anyone does not know how to manage his own household, how will he take care of God's church?) ⁶ He must not be a new convert, or he might become conceited and fall into the condemnation of the Devil. ⁷ Furthermore, he must have a good reputation among outsiders, so that he does not fall into disgrace and the Devil's trap.

⁸ Deacons, likewise, should be worthy of respect, not hypocritical, not drinking a lot of wine, not greedy for

---

ᵃ**2:7** Other mss add *in Christ*
ᵇ**2:15** Lit *if they continue*
ᶜ**3:1** *This saying is trustworthy* could refer to 1 Tm 2:15.

ᵈ**3:2** Or *hospitable, skillful in teaching*

money, 9 holding the •mystery of the faith with a clear conscience. 10 And they must also be tested first; if they prove blameless, then they can serve as deacons. 11 Wives, too, must be worthy of respect, not slanderers, self-controlled, faithful in everything. 12 Deacons must be husbands of one wife, managing their children and their own households competently. 13 For those who have served well as deacons acquire a good standing for themselves, and great boldness in the faith that is in Christ Jesus.

THE MYSTERY OF GODLINESS

14 I write these things to you, hoping to come to you soon. 15 But if I should be delayed, ⌊I have written⌋ so that you will know how people ought to act in God's household, which is the church of the living God, the pillar and foundation of the truth. 16 And most certainly, the mystery of godliness is great:

> Hea was manifested in the flesh,
> justified in the Spirit,
> seen by angels,
> preached among the Gentiles,
> believed on in the world,
> taken up in glory.

DEMONIC INFLUENCE

4 Now the Spirit explicitly says that in the latter times some will depart from the faith, paying attention to deceitful spirits and the teachings of demons, 2 through the hypocrisy of liars whose consciences are seared. 3 They forbid marriage and demand abstinence from foods that God created to be received with gratitude by those who believe and know the truth. 4 For everything created by God is good, and nothing should be rejected if it is received with thanksgiving, 5 since it is sanctified by the word of God and by prayer.

A GOOD SERVANT OF JESUS CHRIST

6 If you point these things out to the brothers, you will be a good servant of Christ Jesus, nourished by the

a3:16 Other mss read God

Deal with Sin the Second You Spot It

Being blameless does not mean being perfect. It means that in every situation you do the right thing—that when you become aware of a transgression in your life, you are blameless in the way you deal with it.

They must also be tested first; if they prove blameless, then they can serve as deacons.
—1 Timothy 3:10

A Life Without Secrets Is a Life Worth Living

The road to peace, contentment, and happiness is paved with truth, honesty, and integrity—the humble, warm realization that your life can stand the scrutiny of God.

Those who have served well as deacons acquire a good standing for themselves, and great boldness in the faith that is in Christ Jesus.
—1 Timothy 3:13

WORD STUDY

Greek word: **soter**
[soh TAYR]
Translation: **Savior**
Uses in 1 Timothy: **3**
Uses in Paul's writings: **12**
Uses in the NT: **24**
Key passage: **1 Timothy 4:10**

Outside the NT, the title *soter* (*savior, deliverer*) was applied to deserving men, leading officials, rulers, or deities (e.g., of Roman emperors Julius Caesar, Nero, and Vespasian). The term had connotations of "protector," "deliverer," "preserver," or "savior." In the NT, *soter* refers exclusively to Jesus Christ and to God the Father, with a focus on their saving, delivering character as expressed through their actions. The term occurs 8 times in reference to God and 16 times in reference to Jesus Christ. As *Savior,* Christ grants repentance and forgiveness of sin (Ac 5:31), protects and saves the church (Eph 5:23), will come again to deliver His people from this world (Php 3:20), has made possible the outpouring of the Spirit (Ti 3:6), has abolished death (2 Tm 1:10), and has authority in His kingdom (2 Pt 1:11). God is "the *Savior* of everyone, especially of those who believe" (1 Tm 4:10), and "wants everyone to be saved" (1 Tm 2:3). He manifested His love in His saving acts toward the church (Ti 3:4), He poured out the Holy Spirit (Ti 3:6), and He deserves praise and adoration (Jd 25).

words of the faith and of the good teaching that you have followed. ⁷ But have nothing to do with irreverent and silly myths. Rather, train yourself in godliness, ⁸ for,

> the training of the body has a limited benefit,
> but godliness is beneficial in every way,
> since it holds promise for the present life
> and also for the life to come.

⁹ This saying is trustworthy and deserves full acceptance. ¹⁰ In fact, we labor and strive[a] for this, because we have put our hope in the living God, who is the Savior of everyone, especially of those who believe.

INSTRUCTIONS FOR MINISTRY

¹¹ Command and teach these things. ¹² No one should despise your youth; instead, you should be an example to the believers in speech, in conduct, in love,[b] in faith, in purity. ¹³ Until I come, give your attention to public reading, exhortation, and teaching. ¹⁴ Do not neglect the gift that is in you; it was given to you through prophecy, with the laying on of hands by the council of elders. ¹⁵ Practice these things; be committed to them, so that your progress may be evident to all. ¹⁶ Be conscientious about yourself and your teaching; persevere in these things, for by doing this you will save both yourself and your hearers.

5 Do not rebuke an older man, but exhort him as a father, younger men as brothers, ² older women as mothers, and with all propriety, the younger women as sisters.

THE SUPPORT OF WIDOWS

³ Support[c] widows who are genuinely widows. ⁴ But if any widow has children or grandchildren, they should learn to practice their religion toward their own family first and to repay their parents, for this pleases God. ⁵ The real widow, left all alone, has put her hope in God and continues night and day in her petitions and prayers; ⁶ however, she who is self-indulgent is dead

---

[a]**4:10** Other mss read *and suffer reproach*
[b]**4:12** Other mss add *in spirit*
[c]**5:3** Lit *Honor*

even while she lives. [7] Command this, so that they won't be blamed. [8] Now if anyone does not provide for his own relatives, and especially for his household, he has denied the faith and is worse than an unbeliever.

[9] No widow should be placed on the official support list[a] unless she is at least 60 years old, has been the wife of one husband, [10] and is well known for good works—that is, if she has brought up children, shown hospitality, washed the saints' feet, helped the afflicted, and devoted herself to every good work. [11] But refuse to enroll younger widows; for when they are drawn away from Christ by desire, they want to marry, [12] and will therefore receive condemnation because they have renounced their original pledge. [13] At the same time, they also learn to be idle, going from house to house; they are not only idle, but are also gossips and busybodies, saying things they shouldn't say. [14] Therefore, I want younger women to marry, have children, manage their households, and give the adversary no opportunity to accuse us. [15] For some have already turned away to follow Satan. [16] If any[b] believing woman has widows, she should help them, and the church should not be burdened, so that it can help those who are genuinely widows.

HONORING THE ELDERS

[17] The elders who are good leaders should be considered worthy of an ample honorarium,[c] especially those who work hard at preaching and teaching. [18] For the Scripture says:

> **You must not muzzle an ox**
> **that is threshing grain,**[d] and,
> The laborer is worthy of his wages.

[19] Don't accept an accusation against an elder unless it is supported by two or three witnesses. [20] Publicly rebuke[e] those who sin, so that the rest will also be afraid. [21] I solemnly charge you, before God and Christ Jesus and the elect angels, to observe these things without prejudice, doing nothing out of favoritism. [22] Don't be

You Don't Have to Be a Star, Just a Light

Perhaps some things about you seem to disqualify you from serving the Lord effectively. But will you allow God to demonstrate His call upon you by transforming your life into a model of godliness?

No one should despise your youth; instead, you should be an example to the believers in speech, in conduct, in love, in faith, in purity.
—1 Timothy 4:12

Your Chief Ministry Should Be to Those In Your Own Tribe

Sometimes, the people we overlook the most in fulfilling our Christian duties are those closest to us. Ask God to make you especially sensitive to the needs in your own family.

If any widow has children or grandchildren, they should learn to practice their religion toward their own family first and to repay their parents, for this pleases God.
—1 Timothy 5:4

---

[a]5:9 Lit *be enrolled*
[b]5:16 Other mss add *believing man or*
[c]5:17 Lit *of double honor*, or possibly *of respect and remuneration*
[d]5:18 Dt 25:4
[e]5:20 Before the congregation

too quick to lay hands on[a] anyone, and don't share in the sins of others. Keep yourself pure. 23 Don't continue drinking only water, but use a little wine because of your stomach and your frequent illnesses. 24 Some people's sins are evident, going before them to judgment, but ˌthe sinsˌ of others follow them. 25 Likewise, good works are obvious, and those that are not ˌobviousˌ cannot remain hidden.

HONORING MASTERS

6 All who are under the yoke as slaves must regard their own masters to be worthy of all respect, so that God's name and His teaching will not be blasphemed. 2 And those who have believing masters should not be disrespectful to them because they are brothers, but should serve them better, since those who benefit from their service are believers and dearly loved.

FALSE DOCTRINE AND HUMAN GREED

Teach and encourage these things. 3 If anyone teaches other doctrine and does not agree with the sound teaching of our Lord Jesus Christ and with the teaching that promotes godliness, 4 he is conceited, understanding nothing, but having a sick interest in disputes and arguments over words. From these come envy, quarreling, slanders, evil suspicions, 5 and constant disagreement among men whose minds are depraved and deprived of the truth, who imagine that godliness[b] is a way to material gain.[c] 6 But godliness with contentment is a great gain.

> 7 For we brought nothing into the world,
> and[d] we can take nothing out.
> 8 But if we have food and clothing,[e]
> we will be content with these.

9 But those who want to be rich fall into temptation, a trap, and many foolish and harmful desires, which plunge people into ruin and destruction. 10 For the love

---

Great Character Won't Stay Hidden Forever

Have you been performing good deeds but feeling a little hurt that no one seems to notice? A time will come when every good thing you've done will be duly recognized.

Good works are obvious, and those that are not obvious cannot remain hidden.

—1 Timothy 5:25

It's a Fight to the Finish

The Christian life is not for the fainthearted. You must be prepared to stand against any force that tries to dissuade you from following Christ.

Fight the good fight for the faith; take hold of eternal life, to which you were called and have made a good confession before many witnesses.

—1 Timothy 6:12

---

[a]5:22 To ordain
[b]6:5 Referring to religion as a means of financial gain
[c]6:5 Other mss add *From such people withdraw yourself.*
[d]6:7 Other mss add *it is clear that*
[e]6:8 Or *food and shelter*

of money is a root[a] of all kinds of evil, and by craving it, some have wandered away from the faith and pierced themselves with many pains.

COMPETE FOR THE FAITH

11 Now you, man of God, run
    from these things;
  but pursue righteousness, godliness, faith,
  love, endurance, and gentleness.
12 Fight the good fight for the faith;
  take hold of eternal life,
  to which you were called
  and have made a good confession
  before many witnesses.

13 In the presence of God, who gives life to all, and before Christ Jesus, who gave a good confession before Pontius •Pilate, I charge you 14 to keep the commandment without spot or blame until the appearing of our Lord Jesus Christ, 15 which God[b] will bring about in His own time. ⌊He is⌋

  the blessed and only Sovereign,
  the King of kings,
  and the Lord of lords,
16 the only One who has immortality,
  dwelling in unapproachable light,
  whom none of mankind has seen
      or can see,
  to whom be honor and eternal might.
  •Amen.

INSTRUCTIONS TO THE RICH

17 Instruct those who are rich in the present age not to be arrogant or to set their hope on the uncertainty of wealth, but on God,[c] who richly provides us with all things to enjoy. 18 ⌊Instruct them⌋ to do good, to be rich in good works, to be generous, willing to share, 19 storing up for themselves a good foundation for the age to come, so that they may take hold of life that is real.

---

[a]6:10 Or *is the root*
[b]6:15 Lit *He*

[c]6:17 Other mss read *on the living God*

WORD STUDY

Greek word: **epiphaneia**
[epih FAH nay ah]
Translation: **appearing**
Uses in 1 Timothy: **1**
Uses in Paul's writings: **6**
Uses in the NT: **6**
Key passage: **1 Timothy 6:14**

Outside of the NT, the term *epiphaneia (appearing, manifestation)* was often used as a religious technical term to denote the visible manifestation of a deity. This divine manifestation occurred either in the form of a personal appearance or by some work of power. Within the NT, *epiphaneia* appears exclusively in Pauline literature. Paul employs this religious technical sense of the word to refer to the *appearing* or *manifestation* of Jesus Christ. This *appearing* of Jesus can refer to His first coming to earth (2 Tm 1:10). More frequently, however, Paul refers to the second *appearing* of Jesus, at which time He will come to destroy the antichrist and dispense righteous judgment (2 Th 2:8; 2 Tm 4:1,8). It is this second *appearing* of the Lord Jesus that is the "blessed hope" of the believer (Ti 2:13).

GUARD THE HERITAGE

[20] Timothy, guard what has been entrusted to you, avoiding irreverent, empty speech and contradictions from the "knowledge" that falsely bears that name. [21] By professing it, some people have deviated from the faith.

Grace be with all of you.

Recognize Your Gifts and Use Them Wisely

Don't waste the blessings God has given you. Many Christians who had incredible potential for serving the Lord got sidetracked by the very abilities they could have used for God's kingdom.

Timothy, guard what has been entrusted to you, avoiding irreverent, empty speech and contradictions from the "knowledge" that falsely bears that name. By professing it, some people have deviated from the faith.

—1 Timothy 6:20-21

TIMOTHY

GREETING

1 Paul, an apostle of Christ Jesus by God's will, for the promise of life in Christ Jesus:
² To Timothy, my dearly loved child.
Grace, mercy, and peace from God the Father and Christ Jesus our Lord.

THANKSGIVING

³ I thank God, whom I serve with a clear conscience as my forefathers did, when I constantly remember you in my prayers night and day. ⁴ Remembering your tears, I long to see you so that I may be filled with joy, ⁵ clearly recalling your sincere faith that first lived in your grandmother Lois, then in your mother Eunice, and that I am convinced is in you also.

⁶ Therefore, I remind you to keep ablaze the gift of God that is in you through the laying on of my hands. ⁷ For God has not given us a spirit[a] of fearfulness, but one of power, love, and sound judgment.

NOT ASHAMED OF THE GOSPEL

⁸ So don't be ashamed of the testimony about our Lord, or of me His prisoner. Instead, share in suffering for the gospel, relying on the power of God,

⁹ who has saved us and called us
with a holy calling,
not according to our works,
but according to His own purpose and grace,
which was given to us in Christ Jesus
before time began.

---

[a]1:7 Or *Spirit*

WORD STUDY

Greek word: ***aphtharsia***
[ahf thahr SEE ah]

Translation: ***immortality***

Uses in 2 Timothy: **1**

Uses in Paul's writings: **7**

Uses in the NT: **7**

Key passage: **2 Timothy 1:10**

The apostle Paul uses *aphtharsia* (*incorruption, immortality*) in reference to two concepts: physical state and temporal aspect. With respect to physical state, *aphtharsia* refers to the state of not being subject to perishing or decay (i.e., *incorruption*). For example, in 1 Corinthians 15, Paul uses *aphtharsia* four times to refer to the resurrection body. So, the Christian's corruptible, earthly body will be changed to *incorruption* (i.e., the state of being imperishable) through resurrection from the dead (1 Co 15:42,50,53-54). Naturally, that which is incorruptible is also immortal. The relationship of these two concepts provides the bridge to the temporal aspect of *aphtharsia*, in which the term refers to a continuous state or process (*immortality*). Christ Jesus abolished death and brought life and *immortality* (i.e., continuous life) to light through the gospel (2 Tm 1:10).

¹⁰ This has now been made evident
through the appearing of our Savior Christ Jesus,
who has abolished death
and has brought life and immortality to light
through the gospel.

¹¹ For this ⌊gospel⌋ I was appointed a herald, apostle, and teacher,ᵃ ¹² and that is why I suffer these things. But I am not ashamed, because I know whom I have believed and am persuaded that He is able to guard what has been entrusted to meᵇ until that day.

BE LOYAL TO THE FAITH

¹³ Hold on to the pattern of sound teaching that you have heard from me, in the faith and love that are in Christ Jesus. ¹⁴ Guard, through the Holy Spirit who lives in us, that good thing entrusted to you. ¹⁵ This you know: all those in Asia have turned away from me, including Phygelus and Hermogenes. ¹⁶ May the Lord grant mercy to the household of Onesiphorus, because he often refreshed me and was not ashamed of my chains. ¹⁷ On the contrary, when he was in Rome, he diligently searched for me and found me. ¹⁸ May the Lord grant that he obtain mercy from the Lord on that day. And you know how much he ministered at Ephesus.

BE STRONG IN GRACE

2 You, therefore, my child, be strong in the grace that is in Christ Jesus. ² And what you have heard from me in the presence of many witnesses, commit to faithful men who will be able to teach others also.

³ Share in suffering as a good soldier of Christ Jesus. ⁴ To please the recruiter, no one serving as a soldier gets entangled in the concerns of everyday life. ⁵ Also, if anyone competes as an athlete, he is not crowned unless he competes according to the rules. ⁶ It is the hardworking farmer who ought to be the first to get a share of the crops. ⁷ Consider what I say, for the Lord will give you understanding in everything.

ᵃ**1:11** Other mss add *of the Gentiles* ᵇ**1:12** Or *guard what I have entrusted to Him*, or *guard my deposit*

8 Keep in mind Jesus Christ, risen from the dead, descended from David, according to my gospel. 9 For this I suffer, to the point of being bound like a criminal; but God's message is not bound. 10 This is why I endure all things for the elect: so that they also may obtain salvation, which is in Christ Jesus, with eternal glory. 11 This saying is trustworthy:

> For if we have died with Him,
> we will also live with Him;
> 12 if we endure, we will also reign with Him;
> if we deny Him, He will also deny us;
> 13 if we are faithless, He remains faithful,
> for He cannot deny Himself.

AN APPROVED WORKER

14 Remind them of these things, charging them before God[a] not to fight about words; this is in no way profitable and leads to the ruin of the hearers. 15 Be diligent to present yourself approved to God, a worker who doesn't need to be ashamed, correctly teaching the word of truth. 16 But avoid irreverent, empty speech, for this will produce an even greater measure of godlessness. 17 And their word will spread like gangrene, among whom are Hymenaeus and Philetus. 18 They have deviated from the truth, saying that the resurrection has already taken place, and are overturning the faith of some. 19 Nevertheless, God's solid foundation stands firm, having this inscription:

> **The Lord knows those who are His,**[b] and
> Everyone who names the name of the Lord
> must turn away from unrighteousness.

20 Now in a large house there are not only gold and silver bowls, but also those of wood and earthenware, some for special[c] use, some for ordinary. 21 So if anyone purifies himself from these things, he will be a special[d] instrument, set apart, useful to the Master, prepared for every good work.
22 Flee from youthful passions, and pursue righteousness, faith, love, and peace, along with those who call

In God We Trust

Our hope is not mere speculation about what God *might* do. His Word tells us what He *will* do. We can live with confidence because our hope is in One who is faithful.

I am not ashamed, because I know whom I have believed and am persuaded that He is able to guard what has been entrusted to me until that day.

—2 Timothy 1:12b

Is Your Conversation Nothing but Small Talk?

Rarely do we regret taking the time to think before we speak, but how often do we long to take back something we said on the spur of the moment?

Avoid irreverent, empty speech, for this will produce an even greater measure of godlessness.

—2 Timothy 2:16

---

a2:14 Other mss read *before the Lord*   c2:20 Or *honorable*
b2:19 Nm 16:5   d2:21 Or *an honorable*

on the Lord from a pure heart. 23 But reject foolish and ignorant disputes, knowing that they breed quarrels. 24 The Lord's slave must not quarrel, but must be gentle to everyone, able to teach,[a] and patient, 25 instructing his opponents with gentleness. Perhaps God will grant them repentance to know the truth. 26 Then they may come to their senses and escape the Devil's trap, having been captured by him to do his will.

DIFFICULT TIMES AHEAD

3 But know this: difficult times will come in the last days. 2 For people will be lovers of self, lovers of money, boastful, proud, blasphemers, disobedient to parents, ungrateful, unholy, 3 unloving, irreconcilable, slanderers, without self-control, brutal, without love for what is good, 4 traitors, reckless, conceited, lovers of pleasure rather than lovers of God, 5 holding to the form of religion but denying its power. Avoid these people!

6 For among them are those who worm their way into households and capture idle women burdened down with sins, led along by a variety of passions, 7 always learning and never able to come to a knowledge of the truth. 8 Just as Jannes and Jambres resisted Moses, so these also resist the truth, men who are corrupt in mind, worthless in regard to the faith. 9 But they will not make further progress, for their lack of understanding will be clear to all, as theirs[b] was also.

THE SACRED SCRIPTURES

10 But you have followed my teaching, conduct, purpose, faith, patience, love, and endurance, 11 along with the persecutions and sufferings that came to me in Antioch, Iconium, and Lystra. What persecutions I endured! Yet the Lord rescued me from them all. 12 In fact, all those who want to live a godly life in Christ Jesus will be persecuted. 13 Evil people and imposters will become worse, deceiving and being deceived. 14 But as for you, continue in what you have learned and firmly believed, knowing those from whom you learned, 15 and that from childhood you have known the sacred

---

Stand Your Ground, but Do It with a Smile

We often encounter people who have differing viewpoints or perspectives that may not be biblical, but God's Word says we must temper our responses with care and concern.

The Lord's slave must not quarrel, but must be gentle to everyone, able to teach, and patient, instructing his opponents with gentleness. Perhaps God will grant them repentance to know the truth.

—2 Timothy 2:24-25

Friends of God Invite Enemies

Persecution may the best evidence that your life is like that of Christ.

All those who want to live a godly life in Christ Jesus will be persecuted.

—2 Timothy 3:12

---

[a]2:24 Or *everyone, skillful in teaching*

[b]3:9 Referring to Jannes and Jambres

Scriptures, which are able to instruct you for salvation through faith in Christ Jesus. ¹⁶ All Scripture is inspired by God[a] and is profitable for teaching, for rebuking, for correcting, for training in righteousness, ¹⁷ so that the man of God may be complete, equipped for every good work.

FULFILL YOUR MINISTRY

4 Before God and Christ Jesus, who is going to judge the living and the dead, and by His appearing and His kingdom, I solemnly charge you: ² proclaim the message; persist in it whether convenient or not; rebuke, correct, and encourage with great patience and teaching. ³ For the time will come when they will not tolerate sound doctrine, but according to their own desires, will accumulate teachers for themselves because they have an itch to hear something new.[b] ⁴ They will turn away from hearing the truth and will turn aside to myths. ⁵ But as for you, keep a clear head about everything, endure hardship, do the work of an evangelist, fulfill your ministry.

⁶ For I am already being poured out as a drink offering, and the time for my departure is close. ⁷ I have fought the good fight, I have finished the race, I have kept the faith. ⁸ In the future, there is reserved for me the crown of righteousness, which the Lord, the righteous Judge, will give me on that day, and not only to me, but to all those who have loved His appearing.

FINAL INSTRUCTIONS

⁹ Make every effort to come to me soon, ¹⁰ for Demas has deserted me, because he loved this present world, and has gone to Thessalonica. Crescens has gone to Galatia, Titus to Dalmatia. ¹¹ Only Luke is with me. Bring Mark with you, for he is useful to me in the ministry. ¹² I have sent Tychicus to Ephesus. ¹³ When you come, bring the cloak I left in Troas with Carpus, as well as the scrolls, especially the parchments. ¹⁴ Alexander the coppersmith did great harm to me. The Lord will repay

And Always Let the Bible Be Your Guide

The wisdom found in God's Word has been tested and proven true. It is critical that you measure everything you hear against the Scriptures.

Continue in what you have learned and firmly believed, knowing those from whom you learned, and that from childhood you have known the sacred Scriptures, which are able to instruct you for salvation through faith in Christ Jesus.

—2 Timothy 3:14-15

Clear Heads Recognize God's Clear Directions

God has many ways He wants to involve you in what He is doing. He knows what you will face today, and He wants to prepare you. Are you alert? Are you ready?

As for you, keep a clear head about everything, endure hardship, do the work of an evangelist, fulfill your ministry.

—2 Timothy 4:5

---

[a]**3:16** Lit *breathed out by God*; the Scripture is the product of God's Spirit working through men; see 2 Pt 1:20-21.

[b]**4:3** Or *to hear what they want to hear*; lit *themselves, itching in the hearing*

473

WORD STUDY

Greek word: **epitimao**
[eh pee tih MAH oh]
Translation: **rebuke, warn**
Uses in 2 Timothy: **1**
Uses in Paul's writings: **1**
Uses in the NT: **29**
Key passage: **2 Timothy 4:2**

Epitimao (*to rebuke*) appears almost exclusively in the Gospels (27 times) and typically refers to a threatening command or rebuke with negative implications for the one rebuked. Jesus *rebuked* the wind and sea (Mt 8:26), a fever (Lk 4:39), and demons (Mt 17:18 = Mk 9:25; Lk 4:35,41). He *rebuked* James, John (Lk 9:55), and Peter (Mk 8:33). However, *epitimao* may have positive implications for the one rebuked when that rebuke is intended to prevent improper behavior. In such cases, it may be translated *to rebuke*, *warn*, or *correct*. Jesus commanded His disciples to *rebuke* a sinning brother (Lk 17:3), and *warned* them to keep His identity secret (Mt 12:16; Lk 9:21). Peter inappropriately *rebuked* Jesus (Mt 16:22 = Mk 8:32). The disciples *rebuked* those bringing their children to obtain Jesus' blessing (Mt 19:13 = Mk 10:13 = Lk 18:15). Outside the Gospels, *rebuking* is part of the pastoral role (2 Tm 4:2).

him according to his works. ¹⁵ Watch out for him yourself, because he strongly opposed our words.

¹⁶ At my first defense, no one came to my assistance, but everyone deserted me. May it not be counted against them. ¹⁷ But the Lord stood with me and strengthened me, so that the proclamation might be fully made through me, and all the Gentiles might hear. So I was rescued from the lion's mouth. ¹⁸ The Lord will rescue me from every evil work and will bring me safely into His heavenly kingdom. To Him be the glory forever and ever! •Amen.

BENEDICTION

¹⁹ Greet Prisca and Aquila, and the household of Onesiphorus. ²⁰ Erastus has remained at Corinth; Trophimus I left sick at Miletus. ²¹ Make every effort to come before winter. Eubulus greets you, as do Pudens, Linus, Claudia, and all the brothers.

²² The Lord be with your spirit. Grace be with you!

TITUS

GREETING

1 Paul, a slave of God, and an apostle of Jesus Christ for the faith of God's elect and the knowledge of the truth that leads[a] to godliness, [2] in the hope of eternal life that God, who cannot lie, promised before time began, [3] and has in His own time revealed His message in the proclamation that I was entrusted with by the command of God our Savior:

[4] To Titus, my true child in our common faith.

Grace and peace from God the Father and Christ Jesus our Savior.

TITUS' MINISTRY IN CRETE

[5] The reason I left you in Crete was to set right what was left undone and, as I directed you, to appoint elders in every town: [6] someone who is blameless, the husband of one wife, having faithful[b] children not accused of wildness or rebellion. [7] For an •overseer, as God's manager, must be blameless, not arrogant, not quick tempered, not addicted to wine, not a bully, not greedy for money, [8] but hospitable, loving what is good, sensible, righteous, holy, self-controlled, [9] holding to the faithful message as taught, so that he will be able both to encourage with sound teaching and to refute those who contradict it.

[10] For there are also many rebellious people, idle talkers and deceivers, especially those from Judaism.[c] [11] It is necessary to silence them; they overthrow whole households by teaching for dishonest gain what they should not. [12] One of their very own prophets said,

---

[a]1:1 Or *corresponds*
[b]1:6 Or *believing*

[c]1:10 Lit *the circumcision*

WORD STUDY

Greek word: **episkopos**
[eh PIHS kah pahs]

Translation: **overseer**

Uses in Titus: 1

Uses in Paul's writings: 3

Uses in the NT: 5

Key passage: **Titus 1:7**

By the time of the NT, *episkopos* already enjoyed a long history of usage, referring to deities or community officials, rulers, or leaders. In the NT, however, the term takes on a clearly religious overtone, appearing as a title meaning an *Overseer* (apparently synonymous with *presbuteros* [*elder*]; Ti 1:7; Ac 20:28). In the early church, the Holy Spirit commissioned each overseer through apostolic selection and appointment (Ac 14:23, 20:28; Ti 1:7). The overseer held a vital service role within the congregation (1 Tm 3:1). This necessitated high moral standards and management skills (1 Tm 3:2-7; Ti 1:7-9). Several overseers were responsible for shepherding and managing the affairs of their local congregation (Ac 20:28; Php 1:1; Ti 1:7). Jesus, to whom belongs the Church, is the "shepherd and guardian" *par excellence* (1 Pt 2:25).

Cretans are always liars, evil beasts,
lazy gluttons.[a]

13 This testimony is true. So, rebuke them sharply, that they may be sound in the faith 14 and may not pay attention to Jewish myths and the commandments of men who reject the truth.

15 To the pure, everything is pure, but to those who are defiled and unbelieving nothing is pure; in fact, both their mind and conscience are defiled. 16 They profess to know God, but they deny Him by their works. They are detestable, disobedient, and disqualified for any good work.

SOUND TEACHING

2 But you must speak what is consistent with sound teaching. 2 Older men are to be self-controlled, worthy of respect, sensible, and sound in faith, love, and endurance. 3 In the same way, older women are to be reverent in behavior, not slanderers, not addicted to much wine. ⌊They are⌋ to teach what is good, 4 so that they may encourage the young women to love their husbands and children, 5 to be sensible, pure, good homemakers, and submissive to their husbands, so that God's message will not be slandered.

6 Likewise, encourage the young men to be sensible 7 about everything. Set an example of good works yourself, with integrity and dignity[b] in your teaching. 8 Your message is to be sound beyond reproach, so that the opponent will be ashamed, having nothing bad to say about us.

9 Slaves are to be submissive to their masters in everything, and to be well-pleasing, not talking back 10 or stealing, but demonstrating utter faithfulness, so that they may adorn the teaching of God our Savior in everything.

11 For the grace of God has appeared, with salvation[c] for all people, 12 instructing us to deny godlessness and worldly lusts and to live in a sensible, righteous, and godly way in the present age, 13 while we wait for the blessed hope and the appearing of the glory of our

---

[a]1:12 This saying is from the Cretan poet Epimenides (6th century B.C.).
[b]2:7 Other mss add *incorruptibility*

[c]2:11 Or *appeared, bringing salvation*

great God and Savior, Jesus Christ. [14] He gave Himself for us to redeem us from all lawlessness and to cleanse for Himself a special people, eager to do good works.

[15] Say these things, and encourage and rebuke with all authority. Let no one disregard[a] you.

THE IMPORTANCE OF GOOD WORKS

3 Remind them to be submissive to rulers and authorities, to obey, to be ready for every good work, [2] to slander no one, to avoid fighting, and to be kind, always showing gentleness to all people. [3] For we too were once foolish, disobedient, deceived, captives of various passions and pleasures, living in malice and envy, hateful, detesting one another.

> [4] But when the goodness and love for man
> appeared from God our Savior,
> [5] He saved us—
> not by works of righteousness that we had done,
> but according to His mercy,
> through the washing of regeneration
> and renewal by the Holy Spirit.
> [6] This ₍Spirit₎ He poured out on us abundantly
> through Jesus Christ our Savior,
> [7] so that having been justified by His grace,
> we may become heirs with the hope
> of eternal life.

[8] This saying is trustworthy. I want you to insist on these things, so that those who have believed God might be careful to devote themselves to good works. These are good and profitable for everyone. [9] But avoid foolish debates, genealogies, quarrels, and disputes about the law, for they are unprofitable and worthless. [10] Reject a divisive person after a first and second warning, [11] knowing that such a person is perverted and sins, being self-condemned.

FINAL INSTRUCTIONS AND CLOSING

[12] When I send Artemas to you, or Tychicus, make every effort to come to me in Nicopolis, for I have decided to spend the winter there. [13] Diligently help Zenas

---

God's Grace Should Motivate Godly Living

The way you live your life ought to be a tribute to the matchless grace that your Lord and Savior, Jesus Christ, has bestowed upon you.

The grace of God has appeared, with salvation for all people, instructing us to deny godlessness and worldly lusts and to live in a sensible, righteous, and godly way in the present age.
—Titus 2:11-12

God Loves You More Than You Can Believe

The greatest truth in all of Scripture is this: God is love. Understanding this in its fullest dimensions will set you free to enjoy all that is yours as a Christian.

When the goodness and love for man appeared from God our Savior, He saved us—not by works of righteousness that we had done, but according to His mercy.
—Titus 3:4-5a

---

[a]2:15 Or *despise*

the lawyer and Apollos on their journey, so that they will lack nothing.

¹⁴ And our people must also learn to devote themselves to good works for cases of urgent need, so that they will not be unfruitful. ¹⁵ All those who are with me greet you. Greet those who love us in the faith. Grace be with all of you.

God Wants Us to Go Where the Needs Are

Wherever God's people are, they bring with them the power of God to change lives and circumstances.

Our people must also learn to devote themselves to good works for cases of urgent need, so that they will not be unfruitful.

—Titus 3:14

PHILEMON

GREETING

Paul, a prisoner of Christ Jesus, and Timothy, our brother:

To Philemon, our dear friend and co-worker, ² to Apphia our sister,ᵃ to Archippus our fellow soldier, and to the church that meets in your house.

³ Grace to you and peace from God our Father and the Lord Jesus Christ.

PHILEMON'S LOVE AND FAITH

⁴ I always thank my God when I mention you in my prayers, ⁵ because I hear of your love and faith towardᵇ the Lord Jesus and for all the saints. ⁶ ˌI prayˌ that your participation in the faith may become effective through knowing every good thing that is in usᶜ for ˌthe glory ofˌ Christ. ⁷ For I have great joy and encouragement from your love, because the hearts of the saints have been refreshed through you, brother.

AN APPEAL FOR ONESIMUS

⁸ For this reason, although I have great boldness in Christ to command you to do what is right, ⁹ I appeal, instead, on the basis of love. I, Paul, as an elderly manᵈ and now also as a prisoner of Christ Jesus, ¹⁰ appeal to you for my child, whom I fatheredᵉ while in chains— Onesimus.ᶠ ¹¹ Once he was useless to you, but now he is useful to both you and me. ¹² I am sending him—a

---

ᵃ2 Other mss read *our beloved*
ᵇ5 Lit *faith that you have toward*
ᶜ6 Other mss read *in you*
ᵈ9 Or *an ambassador*

ᵉ10 Referring to the fact that Paul led him to Christ; see 1 Co 4:15
ᶠ10 The name *Onesimus* in Gk means "useful."

part of myself [a] —back to you.[b] [13] I wanted to keep him with me, so that in my imprisonment for the gospel he might serve me in your place. [14] But I didn't want to do anything without your consent, so that your good deed might not be out of obligation, but of your own free will. [15] For perhaps this is why he was separated ⌊from you⌋ for a brief time, so that you might get him back permanently, [16] no longer as a slave, but more than a slave—as a dearly loved brother. This is especially so to me, but even more to you, both in the flesh and in the Lord.[c]

[17] So if you consider me a partner, accept him as you would me. [18] And if he has wronged you in any way, or owes you anything, charge that to my account. [19] I, Paul, write this with my own hand: I will repay it—not to mention to you that you owe me even your own self. [20] Yes, brother, may I have joy from you in the Lord; refresh my heart in Christ. [21] Since I am confident of your obedience, I am writing to you, knowing that you will do even more than I say. [22] But meanwhile, also prepare a guest room for me, for I hope that through your prayers I will be restored to you.

FINAL GREETINGS

[23] Epaphras, my fellow prisoner in Christ Jesus, greets you, and so do [24] Mark, Aristarchus, Demas, and Luke, my co-workers.

[25] The grace of the Lord[d] Jesus Christ be with your spirit.

Expect God to Exceed Your Expectations

Rarely does God do something exactly as we think He will. Watch with anticipation and witness His power at work.

Perhaps this is why he was separated from you for a brief time, so that you might get him back permanently, no longer as a slave, but more than a slave—as a dearly loved brother.

—Philemon 15-16a

Place No Conditions on Your Obedience

Only total obedience will accomplish in our lives what God has intended.

Since I am confident of your obedience, I am writing to you, knowing that you will do even more than I say.

—Philemon 21

[a]12 Lit *him—that is, my inward parts*
[b]12 Other mss read *him back. Receive him as a part of myself.*
[c]16 Both physically and spiritually
[d]25 Other mss read *our Lord*

HEBREWS

THE NATURE OF THE SON

1 Long ago God spoke to the fathers by the prophets at different times and in different ways. ² In these last days, He has spoken to us by ⌊His⌋ Son, whom He has appointed heir of all things and through whom He made the universe.ᵃ ³ He is the radianceᵇ of His glory, the exact expressionᶜ of His nature, and He sustains all things by His powerful word. After making purification for sins,ᵈ He sat down at the right hand of the Majesty on high.ᵉ ⁴ So He became higher in rank than the angels, just as the name He inherited is superior to theirs.

THE SON SUPERIOR TO ANGELS

⁵ For to which of the angels did He ever say, **You are My Son; today I have become Your Father,**ᶠ ᵍ or again, **I will be His Father, and He will be My Son?**ʰ ⁶ When He again brings His firstborn into the world,ⁱ He says, **And all God's angels must worship Him.**ʲ ⁷ And about the angels He says:

> **He makes His angels winds,**ᵏ
> **and His servants**ˡ **a fiery flame;**ᵐ

⁸ but about the Son:

> **Your throne, O God, is forever and ever,**

ᵃ**1:2** Lit *ages*
ᵇ**1:3** Or *reflection*
ᶜ**1:3** Or *representation*, or *copy*, or *reproduction*
ᵈ**1:3** Other mss read *for our sins by Himself*
ᵉ**1:3** Or *He sat down on high at the right hand of the Majesty*
ᶠ**1:5** Or *have begotten You*

ᵍ**1:5** Ps 2:7
ʰ**1:5** 2 Sm 7:14; 1 Ch 17:13
ⁱ**1:6** Or *And again, when He brings His firstborn into the world*
ʲ**1:6** Dt 32:43 LXX; Ps 97:7
ᵏ**1:7** Or *spirits*
ˡ**1:7** Or *ministers*
ᵐ**1:7** Ps 104:4

and the scepter of Your kingdom
  is a scepter of justice.
9 You have loved righteousness and hated
  lawlessness;
this is why God, Your God,
  has anointed You,
  rather than Your companions,[a] [b] with the oil
  of joy.

10 And:

In the beginning, Lord, You established
  the earth,
and the heavens are the works
  of Your hands;
11 they will perish, but You remain.
  They will all wear out like clothing;
12 You will roll them up like a cloak,[c]
  and they will be changed like a robe.
But You are the same,
  and Your years will never end.[d]

13 Now to which of the angels has He ever said:

Sit at My right hand
until I make Your enemies
  Your footstool?[e] [f]

14 Are they not all ministering spirits sent out to serve those who are going to inherit salvation?

WARNING AGAINST NEGLECT

2 We must therefore pay even more attention to what we have heard, so that we will not drift away. 2 For if the message spoken through angels was legally binding,[g] and every transgression and disobedience received a just punishment, 3 how will we escape if we neglect such a great salvation? It was first spoken by the Lord and was confirmed to us by those who heard Him. 4 At the same time, God also testified by signs and wonders, various miracles, and distributions ˌof giftsˌ from the Holy Spirit according to His will.

Jesus Paid It All—
All to Him I Owe

How tragic for people to receive the riches of the gospel and then live as spiritual paupers, to accept such great love from Christ and then resent what He asks in return.

How will we escape if we neglect such a great salvation? It was first spoken by the Lord and was confirmed to us by those who heard Him.

—Hebrews 2:3

The Power of God
Is on Your Side

You will no longer fear the future when you understand the awesome Lord who walks with you.

As it is, we do not yet see everything subjected to him. But we do see Jesus.

—Hebrews 2:8b-9a

---

[a]**1:9** Or *associates*
[b]**1:8-9** Ps 45:6-7
[c]**1:12** Other mss omit *like a cloak*
[d]**1:10-12** Ps 102:25-27

[e]**1:13** Or *enemies a footstool for Your feet*
[f]**1:13** Ps 110:1
[g]**2:2** Or *valid*, or *reliable*

JESUS AND HUMANITY

⁵ For He has not subjected to angels the world to come that we are talking about. ⁶ But one has somewhere testified:

> What is man, that You remember him,
> or the son of man, that You care for him?
> ⁷ You made him lower than the angels
>   for a short time;
> You crowned him with glory and honor[a]
> ⁸ and subjected everything under his feet.[b]

For in **subjecting everything** to him, He left nothing not subject to him. As it is, we do not yet see **everything subjected** to him. ⁹ But we do see Jesus—**made lower than the angels for a short time** so that by God's grace He might taste death for everyone—crowned with glory and honor because of the suffering of death.

¹⁰ For it was fitting, in bringing many sons to glory, that He, for whom and through whom all things exist, should make the source[c] of their salvation perfect through sufferings. ¹¹ For the One who sanctifies and those who are sanctified all have one Father.[d] That is why He is not ashamed to call them brothers, ¹² saying:

> I will proclaim Your name to My brothers;
> I will sing hymns to You
>   in the congregation.[e]

¹³ Again, **I will trust in Him.**[f] And again, **Here I am with the children God gave Me.**[g]

¹⁴ Now since the children have flesh and blood in common, He also shared in these, so that through His death He might destroy the one holding the power of death—that is, the Devil— ¹⁵ and free those who were held in slavery all their lives by the fear of death. ¹⁶ For it is clear that He does not reach out to help angels, but to help Abraham's offspring. ¹⁷ Therefore He had to be like His brothers in every way, so that He could become a merciful and faithful high priest in service[h] to God,

---

[a]2:7 Other mss add *and set him over the works of your hands*
[b]2:6-8 Ps 8:5-7 LXX
[c]2:10 Or *pioneer*, or *leader*
[d]2:11 Or *father*, or *origin*, or *all are of one*

[e]2:12 Ps 22:22
[f]2:13 Is 8:17 LXX; 12:2 LXX; 2 Sm 22:3 LXX
[g]2:13 Is 8:18 LXX
[h]2:17 Lit *things*

WORD STUDY

Greek word: *teleioo*
[teh lay AH oh]
Translation: *perfect*
Uses in Hebrews: **9**
Uses in the NT: **23**
Key passage: **Hebrews 2:10**

The verb *teleioo* (*perfect*) has several meanings in the NT. In certain texts, *teleioo* sometimes means *to complete, finish,* or *accomplish* in the sense of fulfilling a task by bringing it to a desired end. In this sense, Jesus was sent *to finish* the works of His Father (Jn 4:34), a task He faithfully *completed* (Jn 17:4). Paul, in his speech to the Ephesian elders, expressed a desire *to accomplish* the ministry he had received from God (Ac 20:24). In other texts, *teleioo* speaks of *bringing something to an end* or *perfecting something*. In this sense, *teleioo* refers to the process or action of overcoming an imperfect or incomplete state with a more perfect or complete one. By virtue of His earthly sufferings, Jesus *has been perfected* (*qualified, brought to His goal*) to minister as high priest forever (Heb 2:10; 5:9; 7:28). Abraham's faith *was perfected* by means of his works (Jms 2:22). The old covenant law could never *perfect* the worshipers who continually offered sacrifices (Heb 7:19; 10:1). Jesus prays that the Father will make His disciples *completely* one (lit., *complete into one*), that is, attaining perfect unity. John speaks of Christians *being perfected* in the love of God (1 Jn 2:5; 4:12,17). Additionally, *teleioo* may refer to a prophecy or promise *being fulfilled* by being brought to completion or being satisfied through its fulfillment (Jn 19:28).

483

to make propitiation[a] for the sins of the people. ¹⁸ For since He Himself was tested and has suffered, He is able to help those who are tested.

OUR APOSTLE AND HIGH PRIEST

3 Therefore, holy brothers and companions in a heavenly calling, consider Jesus, the apostle and high priest of our confession; ² He was faithful to the One who appointed Him, just as Moses was in all God's[b] household. ³ For Jesus[c] is considered worthy of more glory than Moses, just as the builder has more honor than the house. ⁴ Now every house is built by someone, but the One who built everything is God. ⁵ Moses was faithful as a servant in all God's[b] household, as a testimony to what would be said ⌊in the future⌋. ⁶ But Christ was faithful as a Son over His household, whose household we are if we hold on to the courage and the confidence of our hope.[d]

WARNING AGAINST UNBELIEF

⁷ Therefore, as the Holy Spirit says:

> **Today, if you hear His voice,**
> ⁸ **do not harden your hearts**
> **as in the rebellion,**
> **on the day of testing in the desert,**
> ⁹ **where your fathers tested Me, tried ⌊Me⌋,**
> **and saw My works** ¹⁰ **for 40 years.**
> **Therefore I was provoked**
> **with this generation**
> **and said, "They always go astray**
> **in their hearts,**
> **and they have not known My ways."**
> ¹¹ **So I swore in My anger,**
> **"They will not enter My rest."[e]**

¹² Watch out, brothers, so that there won't be in any of you an evil, unbelieving heart that departs from the living God. ¹³ But encourage each other daily, while it

---

Check Your Freedom by Your Responsibility

Christians do not live in isolation. We must do everything with our fellow believers in mind.

Encourage each other daily, while it is still called today, so that none of you is hardened by sin's deception.

—Hebrews 3:13

---

[a]2:17 The word *propitiation* has to do with the removal of divine wrath. Jesus' death is the means that turns God's wrath from the sinner; see 2 Co 5:21.

[b]3:2,5 Lit *His*
[c]3:3 Lit *He*
[d]3:6 Other mss add *firm to the end*
[e]3:7-11 Ps 95:7-11

is still called **today**, so that none of you is hardened by sin's deception. ¹⁴ For we have become companions of the •Messiah if we hold firmly until the end the reality^a that we had at the start. ¹⁵ As it is said:

> **Today, if you hear His voice,**
> **do not harden your hearts**
> **as in the rebellion.**^b

¹⁶ For who heard and rebelled? Wasn't it really all who came out of Egypt under Moses? ¹⁷ And with whom was He "provoked for 40 years"? Was it not with those who sinned, whose bodies fell in the desert? ¹⁸ And to whom did He "swear that they would not enter His rest," if not those who disobeyed? ¹⁹ So we see that they were unable to enter because of unbelief.

THE PROMISED REST

4 Therefore, while the promise remains of entering His rest, let us fear so that none of you should miss it.^c ² For we also have received the good news just as they did; but the message they heard did not benefit them, since they were not united with those who heard it in faith^d ³ (for we who have believed enter the rest), in keeping with what^e He has said:

> **So I swore in My anger,**
> **they will not enter My rest.**^f

And yet His works have been finished since the foundation of the world, ⁴ for somewhere He has spoken about the seventh day in this way:

> **And on the seventh day**
> **God rested from all His works.**^g

⁵ Again, in that passage ₗHe says₎, **They will never enter My rest.**^f ⁶ Since it remains for some to enter it, and those who formerly received the good news did not enter because of disobedience, ⁷ again, He specifies a certain day—**today**—speaking through David after such a long time, as previously stated:

---

^a3:14 Or *confidence*
^b3:15 Ps 95:7-8
^c4:1 Or *should seem to miss it*
^d4:2 Other mss read *since it was not united by faith in those who heard*
^e4:3 Or *rest), just as*
^f4:3,5 Ps 95:11
^g4:4 Gn 2:2

WORD STUDY

Greek word: ***katapausis***
[kah TAH pow sis]
Translation: ***rest***
Uses in Hebrews: **8**
Uses in the NT: **9**
Key passage: **Hebrews 4:1, 3,5,10,11**

In the NT, *katapausis* (*rest*) has multiple referents. Luke makes reference to a temple for God, the place where He would *rest* and live (Ac 7:49). Hebrews refers to *rest* as the Christian's future destination, the place of God's blessing. That *rest* is available to every generation of saints, but its realization comes only through obedience (Heb 4:2,6,11). God's *rest* at creation (Heb 4:4) points past Joshua and David (4:7-8) to this final *rest* for believers (Heb 4:9). For Moses and his generation, that *rest* was the Promised Land, the place of God's blessing (Heb 3:11,16-19). Unfortunately, that generation missed it (Heb 3:19). For the Christian, *rest* is the final place of God's heavenly blessing, which they will receive if they hold fast their faith (Heb 4:11). The author of Hebrews strongly exhorts his audience to strive in obedience and perseverance to ensure they attain that future *rest* (Heb 4:1,11).

WORD STUDY

Greek word: **archiereus**
[ahr kee eh ROOS]

Translation: **high priest**

Uses in Hebrews: **17**

Uses in the NT: **122**

Key passage: **Hebrews 5:10**

In the Gospels and Acts, *archiereus* refers to the Jewish *high priest*, who served as president of the Sanhedrin, the Jewish supreme court (Mt 26:3,57; Ac 24:1). The plural (*chief priests*) indicates members of the priestly aristocracy from which the high priest was chosen. These priests were key figures in the Sanhedrin and belonged to the Sadducean party (Mk 14:55; Ac 5:17). In Hebrews, *archiereus* refers primarily to Christ's priestly ministry, which came from God (Heb 5:5,10) and was superior to that of any earthly *priest* (Heb 7:27-28). Christ is *high priest* of a new covenant, having accomplished the ultimate sacrifice (Heb 8:1-6). He passed through the heavens, entered the true sanctuary, offered Himself as the one final sacrifice, and sat down at God's right hand (Heb 4:14; 6:20; 7:27; 8:1-2; 9:12). Jesus is able to deal mercifully with His people because He was fully human (Heb 2:17; 4:15; 5:1-10).

**Today if you hear His voice,
do not harden your hearts.**[a]

8 For if Joshua had given them rest, He would not have spoken later about another day. 9 A Sabbath rest remains, therefore, for God's people. 10 For the person who has entered His rest has rested from his own works, just as God did from His. 11 Let us then make every effort to enter that rest, so that no one will fall into the same pattern of disobedience.

12 For the word of God is living and effective and sharper than any two-edged sword, penetrating as far as to divide soul, spirit, joints, and marrow; it is a judge of the ideas and thoughts of the heart. 13 No creature is hidden from Him, but all things are naked and exposed to the eyes of Him to whom we must give an account.

OUR GREAT HIGH PRIEST

14 Therefore since we have a great high priest who has passed through the heavens—Jesus the Son of God—let us hold fast to the confession. 15 For we do not have a high priest who is unable to sympathize with our weaknesses, but One who has been tested in every way as we are, yet without sin. 16 Therefore let us approach the throne of grace with boldness, so that we may receive mercy and find grace to help us at the proper time.

THE MESSIAH, A HIGH PRIEST

5 For every high priest taken from men is appointed in service[b] to God for the people, to offer both gifts and sacrifices for sins. 2 He is able to deal gently with those who are ignorant and are going astray, since he himself is also subject to weakness. 3 Because of this, he must make a sin offering for himself as well as for the people. 4 No one takes this honor on himself; instead, a person is called by God, just as Aaron was. 5 In the same way, the •Messiah did not exalt Himself to become a high priest, but the One who said to Him, **You are My Son; today I have become Your Father,**[c]

---

[a] 4:7 Ps 95:7-8
[b] 5:1 Lit *things*

[c] 5:5 Ps 2:7

⁶ also said in another passage, **You are a priest forever in the order of Melchizedek.**ᵃ

⁷ During His earthly life,ᵇ He offered prayers and appeals, with loud cries and tears, to the One who was able to save Him from death, and He was heard because of His reverence. ⁸ Though a Son, He learned obedience through what He suffered. ⁹ After He was perfected, He became the source of eternal salvation to all who obey Him, ¹⁰ and He was declared by God a high priest "in the order of Melchizedek."

THE PROBLEM OF IMMATURITY

¹¹ We have a great deal to say about this, and it's difficult to explain, since you have become slow to understand. ¹² For though by this time you ought to be teachers, you need someone to teach you again the basic principles of God's revelation. You need milk, not solid food. ¹³ Now everyone who lives on milk is inexperienced with the message about righteousness, because he is an infant. ¹⁴ But solid food is for the mature—for those whose senses have been trained to distinguish between good and evil.

WARNING AGAINST REGRESSION

6 Therefore, leaving the elementary message about the •Messiah, let us go on to maturity, not laying again the foundation of repentance from dead works, faith in God, ² teaching about ritual washings,ᶜ laying on of hands, the resurrection of the dead, and eternal judgment. ³ And we will do this if God permits.

⁴ For it is impossible to renew to repentance those who were once enlightened, who tasted the heavenly gift, became companions with the Holy Spirit, ⁵ tasted God's good word and the powers of the coming age, ⁶ and who have fallen away, because,ᵈ to their own harm, they are recrucifying the Son of God and holding Him up to contempt. ⁷ For ground that has drunk the rain that has often fallen on it, and that produces vegetation useful to those it is cultivated for, receives a blessing from God. ⁸ But if it produces thorns and

Hear God Out—He Has Your Life at Heart

The Word of God is alive and can read your thoughts and judge your intentions. Never try to escape the discomfort of conviction by avoiding what God is saying to you.

The word of God is living and effective and sharper than any two-edged sword, penetrating as far as to divide soul, spirit, joints, and marrow; it is a judge of the ideas and thoughts of the heart.
—Hebrews 4:12

Live Your Life on Purpose

You must be determined to experience the fullness of God in every area of your life and never to settle for a shallow, lackadaisical relationship with Almighty God.

Everyone who lives on milk is inexperienced with the message about righteousness, because he is an infant. But solid food is for the mature—for those whose senses have been trained to distinguish between good and evil.
—Hebrews 5:13-14

ᵃ5:6 Ps 110:4; Gn 14:18-20
ᵇ5:7 Lit *In the days of His flesh*
ᶜ6:2 Or *about baptisms*
ᵈ6:6 Or *while*

thistles, it is worthless and about to be cursed, and will be burned at the end.

9 Even though we are speaking this way, dear friends, in your case we are confident of the better things connected with salvation. 10 For God is not unjust; He will not forget your work and the love[a] you showed for His name when you served the saints—and you continue to serve them. 11 Now we want each of you to demonstrate the same diligence for the final realization of your hope, 12 so that you won't become lazy, but imitators of those who inherit the promises through faith and perseverance.

INHERITING THE PROMISE

13 For when God made a promise to Abraham, since He had no one greater to swear by, He swore by Himself:

14 **I will most certainly bless you,**
and I will greatly multiply you.[b]

15 And so, after waiting patiently, Abraham[c] obtained the promise. 16 For men swear by something greater than themselves, and for them a confirming oath ends every dispute. 17 Because God wanted to show His unchangeable purpose even more clearly to the heirs of the promise, He guaranteed it with an oath, 18 so that through two unchangeable things, in which it is impossible for God to lie, we who have fled for refuge might have strong encouragement to seize the hope set before us. 19 We have this ⌊hope⌋—like a sure and firm anchor of the soul—that enters the inner sanctuary behind the curtain. 20 Jesus has entered there on our behalf as a forerunner, because He has become a "high priest forever in the order of Melchizedek."

THE GREATNESS OF MELCHIZEDEK

7 For this Melchizedek—

King of Salem, priest of the Most High God,
who met Abraham and blessed him
as he returned from defeating the kings,

Your Life Will Come Out in God's Favor

When you obey God, no matter the cost, you already have your victory assured.

We want each of you to demonstrate the same diligence for the final realization of your hope, so that you won't become lazy, but imitators of those who inherit the promises through faith and perseverance.

—Hebrews 6:11-12

God's Word Will Prove Itself True

God doesn't make suggestions. He speaks with the full determination that what He has said will come to fruition.

When God made a promise to Abraham, since He had no one greater to swear by, He swore by Himself . . . And so, after waiting patiently, Abraham obtained the promise.

—Hebrews 6:13,15

[a]**6:10** Other mss read *labor of love*   [c]**6:15** Lit *he*
[b]**6:14** Gn 22:17

² and Abraham gave him a tenth of everything;
first, his name means "king of righteousness,"
then also, "king of Salem,"
    meaning "king of peace";
³ without father, mother, or genealogy,
having neither beginning of days
    nor end of life,
but resembling the Son of God—

remains a priest forever.

⁴ Now consider how great this man was, to whom even Abraham the patriarch gave a tenth of the plunder! ⁵ The sons of Levi who receive the priestly office have a commandment according to the law to collect a tenth from the people—that is, from their brothers—though they have ⌊also⌋ descended from Abraham.ᵃ ⁶ But one without thisᵇ lineage collected tithes from Abraham and blessed the one who had the promises. ⁷ Without a doubt,ᶜ the inferior is blessed by the superior. ⁸ In the one case, men who will die receive tithes; but in the other case, ⌊Scripture⌋ testifies that he lives. ⁹ And in a sense Levi himself, who receives tithes, has paid tithes through Abraham, ¹⁰ for he was still within his forefatherᵈ when Melchizedek met him.

A SUPERIOR PRIESTHOOD

¹¹ If, then, perfection came through the Levitical priesthood (for under it the people received the law), what further need was there for another priest to arise in the order of Melchizedek, and not to be described as being in the order of Aaron? ¹² For when there is a change of the priesthood, there must be a change of law as well. ¹³ For the One about whom these things are said belonged to a different tribe, from which no one has served at the altar. ¹⁴ Now it is evident that our Lord came from Judah, and about that tribe Moses said nothing concerning priests.

¹⁵ And this becomes clearer if another priest like Melchizedek arises, ¹⁶ who doesn't become a ⌊priest⌋ based on a legal command concerning physicalᵉ

WORD STUDY

Greek word: ***apator***
[ah PAH tohr]

Translation: ***without father***

Uses in Hebrews: **1**

Uses in the NT: **1**

Key passage: **Hebrews 7:3**

Apator means *without father* and appears once in the NT (Heb 7:3), in reference to the genealogy of Melchizedek, Salem's king. In Classical Greek, *apator* generally meant one without a father. It could refer to a deity who had no father (Orphicha, *Hymni* 10.10), the *fatherless* or *orphans* as those separated from a father (Sophocles, *Trachiniae* 300), or one who is disowned by a father (Plato, *Leges* 929a). Elsewhere, *apator* referred to a person of unknown father (Plutarchus, *Moralia* 2.288e) or of illegitimate birth. In the latter case, *apator* was followed by the mother's name (e.g., "the illegitimate (*apator*) daughter of Tanephremmis"). In Hebrews, *apator* is followed by *ametor* (*without mother*), highlighting that Melchizedek was not born illegitimately but that he had no traceable genealogical origin! The OT lists no genealogy for Melchizedek (Gn 14:18-20; Ps 110:4), who, as a type of Christ, remains a priest forever (Heb 7:3).

ᵃ7:5 Lit *have come out of Abraham's loins*
ᵇ7:6 Lit *their*
ᶜ7:7 Or *Beyond any dispute*
ᵈ7:10 Lit *still in his father's loins*
ᵉ7:16 Or *fleshly*

descent but based on the power of an indestructible life. [17] For it has been testified:

> **You are a priest forever in the order of Melchizedek.**[a]

[18] So the previous commandment is annulled because it was weak and unprofitable [19] (for the law perfected nothing), but a better hope is introduced, through which we draw near to God.

[20] None of this ⌊happened⌋ without an oath. For others became priests without an oath, [21] but He with an oath made by the One who said to Him:

> **The Lord has sworn, and He will not change His mind,**
> **You are a priest forever.**[a]

[22] So Jesus has also become the guarantee of a better covenant.

[23] Now many have become ⌊Levitical⌋ priests, since they are prevented by death from remaining in office. [24] But because He remains forever, He holds His priesthood permanently. [25] Therefore He is always able to save[b] those who come to God through Him, since He always lives to intercede for them.

[26] For this is the kind of high priest we need: holy, innocent, undefiled, separated from sinners, and exalted above the heavens. [27] He doesn't need to offer sacrifices every day, as high priests do—first for their own sins, then for those of the people. He did this once for all when He offered Himself. [28] For the law appoints as high priests men who are weak, but the promise of the oath, which came after the law, ⌊appoints⌋ a Son, who has been perfected forever.

A HEAVENLY PRIESTHOOD

8 Now the main point of what is being said is this: we have this kind of high priest, who sat down at the right hand of the throne of the Majesty in the heavens, [2] a minister of the sanctuary and the true tabernacle, which the Lord set up, and not man. [3] For every high priest is appointed to offer gifts and sacrifices;

God Wants to Be with His People

The heavenly Father's plan from the beginning of time was to place His eternal Son in His people, to draw them into relationship with Him.

The law perfected nothing, but a better hope is introduced, through which we draw near to God.

—Hebrews 7:19

Remember the Price— It Cost Him His Life

How abhorrent was it for the sinless Son of God to have every sin of humanity placed upon Him? What love was required for the Father to watch His only Son bear the excruciating pain of our sin upon the cross?

He doesn't need to offer sacrifices every day, as high priests do—first for their own sins, then for those of the people. He did this once for all when He offered Himself.

—Hebrews 7:27

---

[a]7:17,21 Ps 110:4

[b]7:25 Or *He is able to save completely*

therefore it was necessary for this ⌞priest⌟ also to have something to offer. 4 Now if He were on earth, He wouldn't be a priest, since there are those[a] offering the gifts prescribed by the law. 5 These serve as a copy and shadow of the heavenly things, as Moses was warned when he was about to complete the tabernacle. For He said, **Be careful that you make everything according to the pattern that was shown to you on the mountain.**[b] 6 But Jesus[c] has now obtained a superior ministry, and to that degree He is the mediator of a better covenant, which has been legally enacted on better promises.

A SUPERIOR COVENANT

7 For if that first ⌞covenant⌟ had been faultless, no opportunity would have been sought for a second one. 8 But finding fault with His people,[d] He says:[e]

> "Look, the days are coming," says the Lord,
> "when I will make a new covenant
> with the house of Israel
> and with the house of Judah—
> 9 not like the covenant
> that I made with their fathers
> on the day I took them by their hand
> to lead them out of the land of Egypt.
> Because they did not continue
>   in My covenant,
> I disregarded them," says the Lord.
> 10 "But this is the covenant that I will make
>   with the house of Israel
> after those days," says the Lord:
> "I will put My laws into their minds,
> and I will write them on their hearts,
> and I will be their God,
> and they will be My people.
> 11 And each person will not teach
>   his fellow citizen,[f]
> and each his brother, saying,
>   'Know the Lord,'
> because they will all know Me,

Is Your Heart a Clean Slate for God's Word?

We must meditate on the Word of God until it enters deep into our minds and hearts, preparing ourselves daily for the things He has to say to us.

"I will put My laws into their minds, and I will write them on their hearts, and I will be their God, and they will be My people."

—Hebrews 8:10b

---

[a]8:4 Other mss read *priests*
[b]8:5 Ex 25:40
[c]8:6 Lit *He*
[d]8:8 Lit *with them*
[e]8:8 Other mss read *finding fault, He says to them*
[f]8:11 Other mss read *neighbor*

WORD STUDY

Greek word: *diatheke*
[dee ah THAY kay]

Translation: **covenant**

Uses in Hebrews: **17**

Uses in the NT: **33**

Key passage: **Hebrews 9:4**

___

A *covenant* (*diatheke*) is a legal arrangement between two parties (Gl 3:15) or a document transferring property from the deceased to an heir (Heb 9:16). The use of *diatheke* in the NT is influenced by the Greek OT, where the *covenant* was an agreement by which God's people related to Him. The NT frequently mentions three OT covenants: the Abrahamic covenant (Gn 12:1-3; 15:1-21; 17:1-27), Mosaic covenant (Ex 20–24:8) and new covenant (Jr 31:31-34), and it often focuses on the relationship between the Mosaic and new covenants (e.g., 2 Co 3:6,14). Over half of the occurrences of *diatheke* occur in Hebrews, where Jesus is portrayed as mediator of the new covenant, a covenant superior to the Mosaic covenant (Heb 7:22; 8:6,8-10; 9:15). As the Mosaic covenant was inaugurated with blood, so the new covenant was inaugurated with Jesus' blood (Heb 10:18-28; 13:20; cf. Mt 26:28; 1 Co 11:25).

from the least to the greatest of them.
[12] **For I will be merciful to their wrongdoing, and I will never again remember their sins."[a] [b]**

[13] By saying, **a new** ₍covenant₎, He has declared that the first is old. And what is old and aging is about to disappear.

OLD COVENANT MINISTRY

9 Now the first ₍covenant₎ also had regulations for ministry and an earthly sanctuary. [2] For a tabernacle was set up; and in the first room, which is called "the holy place," were the lampstand, the table, and the presentation loaves. [3] Behind the second curtain, the tabernacle was called "the holy of holies." [4] It contained the gold altar of incense and the ark of the covenant, covered with gold on all sides, in which there was a gold jar containing the manna, Aaron's rod that budded, and the tablets of the covenant. [5] The cherubim of glory were above it overshadowing the mercy seat. It is not possible to speak about these things in detail right now.

[6] These things having been set up this way, the priests enter the first room repeatedly, performing their ministry. [7] But the high priest alone enters the second room, and that only once a year, and never without blood, which he offers for himself and for the sins of the people committed in ignorance. [8] The Holy Spirit was making it clear that the way into the holy of holies had not yet been disclosed while the first tabernacle was still standing. [9] This is a symbol for the present time, during which gifts and sacrifices are offered that cannot perfect the worshiper's conscience. [10] They are physical regulations and only deal with food, drink, and various washings imposed until the time of restoration.

NEW COVENANT MINISTRY

[11] Now the •Messiah has appeared, high priest of the good things that have come.[c] In the greater and more

___

[a]**8:12** Other mss add *and their lawless deeds*
[b]**8:8-12** Jr 31:31-34

[c]**9:11** Other mss read *that are to come*

perfect tabernacle not made with hands (that is, not of this creation), [12] He entered the holy of holies once for all, not by the blood of goats and calves, but by His own blood, having obtained eternal redemption. [13] For if the blood of goats and bulls and the ashes of a heifer sprinkling those who are defiled, sanctify for the purification of the flesh, [14] how much more will the blood of the Messiah, who through the eternal Spirit offered Himself without blemish to God, cleanse our[a] consciences from dead works to serve the living God?

[15] Therefore He is the mediator of a new covenant,[b] so that those who are called might receive the promise of the eternal inheritance, because a death has taken place for redemption from the transgressions ⌊committed⌋ under the first covenant. [16] Where a will exists, the death of the testator must be established. [17] For a will is valid only when people die, since it is never in force while the testator is living. [18] That is why even the first covenant was inaugurated with blood. [19] For when every commandment had been proclaimed by Moses to all the people according to the law, he took the blood of calves and goats, along with water, scarlet wool, and hyssop, and sprinkled the scroll itself and all the people, [20] saying, **This is the blood of the covenant that God has commanded for you.**[c] [21] In the same way, he sprinkled the tabernacle and all the vessels of worship with blood. [22] According to the law almost everything is purified with blood, and without the shedding of blood there is no forgiveness.

[23] Therefore it was necessary for the copies of the things in the heavens to be purified with these ⌊sacrifices⌋, but the heavenly things themselves ⌊to be purified⌋ with better sacrifices than these. [24] For the Messiah did not enter a sanctuary made with hands (only a model[d] of the true one) but into heaven itself, that He might now appear in the presence of God for us. [25] He did not do this to offer Himself many times, as the high priest enters the sanctuary yearly with the blood of another. [26] Otherwise, He would have had to suffer many times since the foundation of the world.

When Grace Found You, Sin Lost Forever

The wonder of salvation is that God has completely dealt with sin. He takes a life devastated by sin and makes it whole.

If the blood of goats and bulls and the ashes of a heifer sprinkling those who are defiled, sanctify for the purification of the flesh, how much more will the blood of the Messiah, who through the eternal Spirit offered Himself without blemish to God, cleanse our consciences from dead works to serve the living God?

—Hebrews 9:13-14

---

[a]9:14 Other mss read *your*
[b]9:15 The Gk word used here and in vv. 15-18 can be translated *covenant*, *will*, or *testament*.
[c]9:20 Ex 24:8
[d]9:24 Or *antitype*, or *figure*

But now He has appeared one time, at the end of the ages, for the removal of sin by the sacrifice of Himself. [27] And just as it is appointed for people to die once— and after this, judgment— [28] so also the Messiah, having been offered once to bear the sins of many, will appear a second time, not to bear sin, but[a] to bring salvation to those who are waiting for Him.

THE PERFECT SACRIFICE

10 Since the law has ⌊only⌋ a shadow of the good things to come, and not the actual form of those realities, it can never perfect the worshipers by the same sacrifices they continually offer year after year. [2] Otherwise, wouldn't they have stopped being offered, since the worshipers, once purified, would no longer have any consciousness of sins? [3] But in the sacrifices[b] there is a reminder of sins every year. [4] For it is impossible for the blood of bulls and goats to take away sins.

[5] Therefore, as He was coming into the world, He said:

> **You did not want sacrifice and offering,**
> **but You prepared a body for Me.**
> [6] **You did not delight**
> **in whole burnt offerings and sin offerings.**
> [7] **Then I said, "See, I have come—**
> **it is written about Me**
> **in the volume of the scroll—**
> **to do Your will, O God!"**[c]

[8] After He says above, **You did not desire or delight in sacrifices and offerings, whole burnt offerings and sin offerings,** (which are offered according to the law), [9] He then says, **See, I have come to do Your will.**[d] He takes away the first to establish the second. [10] By this will, we have been sanctified through the offering of the body of Jesus Christ once and for all.

[11] Now every priest stands day after day ministering and offering time after time the same sacrifices, which can never take away sins. [12] But this man, after offering one sacrifice for sins forever, sat down at the right hand

---

Are You Looking Forward to Forever?

Be constantly encouraged by the reality of the prize that awaits you and by the coming of the Lord who loves you.

The Messiah, having been offered once to bear the sins of many, will appear a second time, not to bear sin, but to bring salvation to those who are waiting for Him.

—Hebrews 9:28

God Gives Us Good Reason to Be Hopeful

The Christian is personally related to the Lord of the universe, who is sovereign not only over all creation, but over every circumstance we experience.

Let us hold on to the confession of our hope without wavering, for He who promised is faithful.

—Hebrews 10:23

---

[a]**9:28** Lit *time, apart from sin,*
[b]**10:3** Lit *in them*
[c]**10:5-7** Ps 40:6-8
[d]**10:9** Other mss add *O God*

of God. ¹³ He is now waiting until His enemies are made His footstool. ¹⁴ For by one offering He has perfected forever those who are sanctified. ¹⁵ The Holy Spirit also testifies to us about this. For after He had said:

¹⁶ **This is the covenant that I will make**
with them
after those days, says the Lord:
I will put My laws on their hearts,
and I will write them on their minds,

¹⁷ ₗHe adds₎:

I will never again remember
their sins and their lawless acts.ᵃ

¹⁸ Now where there is forgiveness of these, there is no longer an offering for sin.

EXHORTATIONS TO GODLINESS

¹⁹ Therefore, brothers, since we have boldness to enter the sanctuary through the blood of Jesus, ²⁰ by the new and living way that He has inaugurated for us, through the curtain (that is, His flesh); ²¹ and since we have a great high priest over the house of God, ²² let us draw near with a true heart in full assurance of faith, our hearts sprinkled ₗclean₎ from an evil conscience and our bodies washed in pure water. ²³ Let us hold on to the confession of our hope without wavering, for He who promised is faithful. ²⁴ And let us be concerned about one another in order to promote love and good works, ²⁵ not staying away from our meetings, as some habitually do, but encouraging each other, and all the more as you see the day drawing near.

WARNING AGAINST WILLFUL SIN

²⁶ For if we deliberately sin after receiving the knowledge of the truth, there no longer remains a sacrifice for sins, ²⁷ but a terrifying expectation of judgment, and the fury of a fire about to consume the adversaries. ²⁸ If anyone disregards Moses' law, he dies without mercy, based on the testimony of two or three witnesses. ²⁹ How much worse punishment, do you think one will

ᵃ10:16-17 Jr 31:33-34

WORD STUDY

Greek word: *hagiazo*
[hah gee AH dzoh]

Translation: *to sanctify*

Uses in Hebrews: **7**

Uses in the NT: **28**

Key passage: **Hebrews 10:10, 14,29**

In the NT, *hagiazo* has three distinct shades of meaning. First, it may indicate the action of dedicating something to the service of God (*consecrate, set aside as holy*). This may involve the consecration of objects (Mt 23:19; 1 Tm 4:5) or persons (Ac 20:32; 26:18; 1 Co 6:11; 7:14; Eph 5:26; Heb 9:13; 10:14) for holy service unto God. Second, *hagiazo* may mean *to treat as holy*. Jesus prays that the Father's name *be honored* as holy (Mt 6:9), and Peter urges believers *to set apart* Messiah as Lord in their hearts (1 Pt 3:15). Third, *hagiazo* may mean *to purify* or *make someone holy*, in the sense of causing someone to have the quality of holiness. Paul prays that God would *sanctify* the Thessalonian believers (1 Th 5:23), and John closes his apocalypse with the heavenly exhortation that the holy should go on *being made holy* (Rv 22:11).

deserve who has trampled on the Son of God, regarded as profane[a] the blood of the covenant by which he was sanctified, and insulted the Spirit of grace? [30] For we know the One who has said, **Vengeance belongs to Me, I will repay,**[b] [c] and again, **The Lord will judge His people.**[d] [31] It is a terrifying thing to fall into the hands of the living God!

[32] Remember the earlier days when, after you had been enlightened, you endured a hard struggle with sufferings. [33] Sometimes you were publicly exposed to taunts and afflictions, and at other times you were companions of those who were treated that way. [34] For you sympathized with the prisoners[e] and accepted with joy the confiscation of your possessions, knowing that you yourselves have a better and enduring possession.[f] [35] So don't throw away your confidence, which has a great reward. [36] For you need endurance, so that after you have done God's will, you may receive what was promised.

[37] For in yet **a very little while,**
the Coming One will come and not delay.
[38] **But My righteous one**[g] **will live by faith;**
and if he draws back,
My soul has no pleasure in him.[h]

[39] But we are not those who draw back and are destroyed, but those who have faith and obtain life.

HEROES OF FAITH

11 Now faith is the reality[i] of what is hoped for, the proof[j] of what is not seen. [2] For by it our ancestors were approved.

[3] By faith we understand that the universe was[k] created by the word[l] of God, so that what is seen has been made from things that are not visible.

[4] By faith Abel offered to God a better sacrifice than Cain ₗdidₗ. By this he was approved as a righteous man,

---

Everyone Has Trouble but We Have Hope

You cannot escape life's sorrows— even though you are a Christian. But you can temper your grief with the hope that Christ is risen, for He is your hope and comfort.

You sympathized with the prisoners and accepted with joy the confiscation of your possessions, knowing that you yourselves have a better and enduring possession.

—Hebrews 10:34

Serving God Costs, but It Really Pays

Spiritual strength doesn't come without exercise. There is a price to pay for having an intimate walk with God.

You need endurance, so that after you have done God's will, you may receive what was promised.

—Hebrews 10:36

---

[a]**10:29** Or *ordinary*
[b]**10:30** Other mss add *says the Lord*
[c]**10:30** Dt 32:35
[d]**10:30** Dt 32:36
[e]**10:34** Other mss read *sympathized with my imprisonment*
[f]**10:34** Other mss add *in heaven*
[g]**10:38** Other mss read *the righteous one*
[h]**10:37-38** Is 26:20 LXX; Hab 2:3-4
[i]**11:1** Or *assurance*
[j]**11:1** Or *conviction*
[k]**11:3** Or *the worlds were*, or *the ages were*
[l]**11:3** Or *voice*, or *utterance*

because God approved his gifts, and even though he is dead, he still speaks through this.

⁵ By faith, Enoch was taken away so that he did not experience death, and **he was not to be found because God took him away.**ᵃ For prior to his transformation he was approved, having pleased God. ⁶ Now without faith it is impossible to please God, for the one who draws near to Him must believe that He exists and rewards those who seek Him.

⁷ By faith Noah, after being warned about what was not yet seen, in reverence built an ark to deliver his family. By this he condemned the world and became an heir of the righteousness that comes by faith.

⁸ By faith Abraham, when he was called, obeyed and went out to a place he was going to receive as an inheritance; he went out, not knowing where he was going. ⁹ By faith he stayed as a foreigner in the land of promise, living in tents with Isaac and Jacob, co-heirs of the same promise. ¹⁰ For he was looking forward to the city that has foundations, whose architect and builder is God.

¹¹ By faith even Sarah herself, when she was barren, received power to conceive offspring, even though she was past the age, since sheᵇ considered that the One who had promised was faithful. ¹² And therefore from one man—in fact, from one as good as dead—came offspring as numerous as the stars of heaven and as innumerable as the grains of sand by the seashore.

¹³ These all died in faith without having received the promises, but they saw them from a distance, greeted them, and confessed that they were foreigners and temporary residents on the earth. ¹⁴ Now those who say such things make it clear that they are seeking a homeland. ¹⁵ If they had been remembering that land they came from, they would have had opportunity to return. ¹⁶ But they now aspire to a better land—a heavenly one. Therefore God is not ashamed to be called their God, for He has prepared a city for them.

¹⁷ By faith Abraham, when he was tested, offered up Isaac; he who had received the promises was offering up his unique son, ¹⁸ about whom it had been said, **In**

WORD STUDY

Greek word: *pistis*
[PIS tis]

Translation: *faith*

Uses in Hebrews: **32**
(24 in Hebrews 11)

Uses in the NT: **243**

Key passage: **Hebrews 11:6**

Pistis carries a spectrum of meaning in the NT. It can refer to something completely trustworthy. Christ's resurrection is the *proof* (i.e., *trustworthy evidence*) that God will one day judge the world (Ac 17:31). *Pistis* may also refer to a solemn promise (1 Tm 5:12). It sometimes means the state of being faithful or trustworthy. God's *faithfulness* ensures He will fulfill His promises (Rm 3:3). *Pistis* may express belief with complete trust. The NT refers to the *faith* of OT characters (Rm 4:9,11-13,16; Heb 11:4-33,39) and of Christians (Heb 6:1; 10:39). In the Gospels, *faith* is often expressed as reliance on the Lord's power over nature, illness, and spiritual powers (Mt 8:10; Mk 2:5; Lk 8:25). Christian piety involves *faith* accompanied by works (Jms 2:14,17,etc.). Finally, *pistis* may refer to the doctrine one believes. Christians should contend for the *faith* (i.e., the body of apostolic doctrine) delivered to them (Jd 3,20).

ᵃ11:5 Gn 5:21-24
ᵇ11:11 Or *By faith Abraham, even though he was past age—and Sar-ah herself was barren—received the ability to procreate because he*

Isaac your seed will be called.[a] 19 He considered God to be able even to raise someone from the dead, from which he also got him back as an illustration.[b]

20 By faith Isaac blessed Jacob and Esau concerning things to come. 21 By faith Jacob, when he was dying, blessed each of the sons of Joseph, and, **he worshiped, leaning on the top of his staff.**[c] 22 By faith Joseph, as he was nearing the end of his life, mentioned the exodus of the sons of Israel and gave instructions concerning his bones.

23 By faith Moses, after he was born, was hidden by his parents for three months, because they saw that the child was beautiful, and they didn't fear the king's edict. 24 By faith Moses, when he had grown up, refused to be called the son of Pharaoh's daughter 25 and chose to suffer with the people of God rather than to enjoy the short-lived pleasure of sin. 26 For he considered reproach for the sake of the •Messiah to be greater wealth than the treasures of Egypt, since his attention was on the reward.

27 By faith he left Egypt behind, not being afraid of the king's anger, for he persevered, as one who sees Him who is invisible. 28 By faith he instituted the •Passover and the sprinkling of the blood, so that the destroyer of the firstborn might not touch them. 29 By faith they crossed the Red Sea as though they were on dry land. When the Egyptians attempted to do this, they were drowned.

30 By faith the walls of Jericho fell down after being encircled for seven days. 31 By faith Rahab the prostitute received the spies in peace and didn't perish with those who disobeyed.

32 And what more can I say? Time is too short for me to tell about Gideon, Barak, Samson, Jephthah, of David and Samuel and the prophets, 33 who by faith conquered kingdoms, administered justice, obtained promises, shut the mouths of lions, 34 quenched the raging of fire, escaped the edge of the sword, gained strength after being weak, became mighty in battle, and put foreign armies to flight. 35 Women received their

God Has Big Jobs for His People to Do

God looks for those who are willing to have their lives radically adjusted away from their self-centered activities and placed into the center of God's activity around the world.

By faith Moses, when he had grown up, refused to be called the son of Pharaoh's daughter and chose to suffer with the people of God rather than to enjoy the short-lived pleasure of sin.

—Hebrews 11:24-25

---

[a]**11:18** Gn 21:12
[b]**11:19** Or *foreshadowing*, or *parable*, or *type*

[c]**11:21** Gn 47:31

dead raised to life again. Some men were tortured, not accepting release, so that they might gain a better resurrection, [36] and others experienced mockings and scourgings, as well as bonds and imprisonment. [37] They were stoned,[a] they were sawed in two, they died by the sword, they wandered about in sheepskins, in goatskins, destitute, afflicted, and mistreated. [38] The world was not worthy of them. They wandered in deserts, mountains, caves, and holes in the ground.

[39] All these were approved through their faith, but they did not receive what was promised, [40] since God had provided something better for us, so that they would not be made perfect without us.

THE CALL TO ENDURANCE

12 Therefore since we also have such a large cloud of witnesses surrounding us, let us lay aside every weight and the sin that so easily ensnares us, and run with endurance the race that lies before us, [2] keeping our eyes on Jesus,[b] the source and perfecter[c] of our faith, who for the joy that lay before Him[d] endured a cross and despised the shame, and has sat down at the right hand of God's throne.

FATHERLY DISCIPLINE

[3] For consider Him who endured such hostility from sinners against Himself, so that you won't grow weary and lose heart. [4] In struggling against sin, you have not yet resisted to the point of shedding your blood. [5] And you have forgotten the exhortation that addresses you as sons:

> **My son, do not take the Lord's discipline lightly,**
> **or faint when you are reproved by Him;**
> [6] **for the Lord disciplines the one He loves,**
> **and punishes every son whom He receives.**[e]

[7] Endure it as discipline: God is dealing with you as sons. For what son is there whom a father does not discipline?

Sin Can't Harm When It's Been Disarmed

Sin subtly robs us of the spiritual power and victory that could be ours. Yet there is no extent to which sin can entangle us that God's grace does not abound still more to free us.

Since we also have such a large cloud of witnesses surrounding us, let us lay aside every weight and the sin that so easily ensnares us, and run with endurance the race that lies before us.
—Hebrews 12:1

God's Discipline Is a Blessing, Not a Curse

It may appear far more glorious to explain away our hardships as Satan's attacks, rather than admitting that we are reaping what we have sown and are being disciplined by our Heavenly Father.

The Lord disciplines the one He loves, and punishes every son whom He receives.
—Hebrews 12:6

---

[a]**11:37** Other mss add *they were tempted*
[b]**12:2** Or *looking to Jesus*
[c]**12:2** Or *the founder and completer*
[d]**12:2** Or *who instead of the joy lying before Him*; that is, the joy of heaven
[e]**12:6** Pr 3:11-12

⁸ But if you are without discipline—which all[a] receive[b] —then you are illegitimate children and not sons. ⁹ Furthermore, we had natural fathers discipline us, and we respected them. Shouldn't we submit even more to the Father of spirits and live? ¹⁰ For they disciplined us for a short time based on what seemed good to them, but He does it for our benefit, so that we can share His holiness. ¹¹ No discipline seems enjoyable at the time, but painful. Later on, however, it yields the fruit of peace and righteousness to those who have been trained by it.

¹² Therefore strengthen your tired hands and weakened knees, ¹³ and make straight paths for your feet, so that what is lame may not be dislocated,[c] but healed instead.

WARNING AGAINST REJECTING GOD'S GRACE

¹⁴ Pursue peace with everyone, and holiness—without it no one will see the Lord. ¹⁵ See to it that no one falls short of the grace of God and that no root of bitterness springs up, causing trouble and by it, defiling many. ¹⁶ And see that there isn't any immoral or irreverent person like Esau, who sold his birthright in exchange for one meal. ¹⁷ For you know that later, when he wanted to inherit the blessing, he was rejected because he didn't find any opportunity for repentance, though he sought it with tears.

¹⁸ For you have not come to what could be touched, to a blazing fire, to darkness, gloom, and storm, ¹⁹ to the blast of a trumpet, and the sound of words. (Those who heard it begged that not another word be spoken to them, ²⁰ for they could not bear what was commanded: **And if even an animal touches the mountain, it must be stoned!**[d] ²¹ And the appearance was so terrifying that Moses said, **I am terrified and trembling.**[e]) ²² Instead, you have come to Mount Zion, to the city of the living God (the heavenly Jerusalem), to myriads of angels in festive gathering, ²³ to the assembly of the firstborn whose names have been written[f] in heaven, to

Give Bitterness Instant Release, Not Instant Replay

No area in your life is so painful that God's grace cannot bring healing, no offense committed against you is so heinous that His love cannot enable you to forgive.

See to it that no one falls short of the grace of God and that no root of bitterness springs up, causing trouble and by it, defiling many.

—Hebrews 12:15

Stay Under Authority and Accountability

By submitting to godly authority and cultivating supportive friendships, we find strength in the encouragement of those who care about us and who model holy lives before us.

Remember your leaders who have spoken God's word to you. As you carefully observe the outcome of their lives, imitate their faith.

—Hebrews 13:7

---

[a]**12:8** In context *all* refers to Christians.
[b]**12:8** Lit *discipline, of which all have become participants*
[c]**12:13** Or *so that the lame will not be turned aside*
[d]**12:20** Ex 19:12
[e]**12:21** Dt 9:19
[f]**12:23** Or *registered*

God who is the judge of all, to the spirits of righteous people made perfect, 24 to Jesus (mediator of a new covenant), and to the sprinkled blood, which says better things than the ⌊blood⌋ of Abel.

25 See that you do not reject the One who speaks; for if they did not escape when they rejected Him who warned them on earth, even less will we if we turn away from Him who warns us from heaven. 26 His voice shook the earth at that time, but now He has promised, **Yet once more I will shake not only the earth but also heaven.**a 27 Now this expression, "Yet once more," indicates the removal of what can be shaken—that is, created things—so that what is not shaken might remain. 28 Therefore, since we are receiving a kingdom that cannot be shaken, let us hold on to grace.b By it, we may serve God acceptably, with reverence and awe; 29 for our God is a consuming fire.

FINAL EXHORTATIONS

13 Let brotherly love continue. 2 Don't neglect to show hospitality, for by doing this some have welcomed angels as guests without knowing it. 3 Remember the prisoners, as though you were in prison with them, and the mistreated, as though you yourselves were suffering bodily.c 4 Marriage must be respected by all, and the marriage bed kept undefiled, because God will judge immoral people and adulterers. 5 Your life should be free from the love of money. Be satisfied with what you have, for He Himself has said, **I will never leave you or forsake you.**d 6 Therefore, we may boldly say:

The Lord is my helper;
I will not be afraid.
What can man do to me?e

7 Remember your leaders who have spoken God's word to you. As you carefully observe the outcome of their lives, imitate their faith. 8 Jesus Christ is the same yesterday, today, and forever. 9 Don't be led astray by

WORD STUDY

Greek word: **epouranios**
[eh poo RAH nee ahs]

Translation: **heavenly**

Uses in Hebrews: **6**

Uses in the NT: **19**

Key passage: **Hebrews 12:22**

Epouranios (*heavenly*) can refer to objects in the sky. Paul speaks of *heavenly* bodies like the sun, moon, and stars (1 Co 15:40-41). *Epouranios* also refers to things related to or located in the spiritual realm. God dwells in the *heavenly* Jerusalem (Heb 12:22), and Christ is seated at God's right hand in *the heavens* (Eph 1:20). Other spiritual beings are located in *the heavens* (Eph 3:10). Paul mentions spiritual forces of evil that battle in *the heavens* (Eph 6:12). All spiritual forces *in heaven* will pay homage to Jesus (Php 2:10). Positionally, believers are seated in *the heavens* with Jesus (Eph 2:6). Hebrews speaks of *heavenly* realities, after which the earthly sacrificial system was modeled (Heb 8:5; 9:23). The saints of old aspired to a *heavenly* homeland (Heb 11:16). Additionally, *epouranios* may refer to things originating from God. Thus, Christians share in a *heavenly* calling (Heb 3:1).

---

a12:26 Hg 2:6
b12:28 Or *let us give thanks*, or *let us have grace*
c13:3 Or *mistreated, since you are also in a body*
d13:5 Dt 31:6
e13:6 Ps 118:6

WORD STUDY

Greek word: *thusia*
[thew SEE ah]

Translation: **sacrifice**

Uses in Hebrews: **15**

Uses in the NT: **28**

Key passage: **Hebrews 13:15**

Thusia (*sacrifice*) refers to what is sacrificially offered up on an altar to God. As prescribed under the Law, Joseph and Mary offered a *sacrifice* to dedicate their first-born son Jesus (Lk 2:24). Under the Old Testament sacrificial system, God was not impressed with outward *sacrifice* when such acts excluded inward obedience (Mt 9:13; 12:7; Mk 12:33). Christ offered Himself on a cross to God as the perfect and final *sacrifice* for sin (Eph 5:2; Heb 9:26; 10:12). In a figurative sense, *thusia* refers to the spiritual act of offering something unto God. Paul speaks of himself as a drink offering being poured out upon the *sacrifice* of the faith of the Philippians (Php 2:17). The financial gifts of the Philippian church to Paul are called a *sacrifice* (Php 4:18). Both verbal confession of praise to God and Christian acts of kindness are referred to as *sacrifices* (Heb 13:15-16).

various kinds of strange teachings; for it is good for the heart to be established by grace and not by foods, since those involved in them have not benefited. ¹⁰ We have an altar from which those who serve the tabernacle do not have a right to eat. ¹¹ For the bodies of those animals whose blood is brought into the holy of holies by the high priest as a sin offering are burned outside the camp. ¹² Therefore Jesus also suffered outside the gate, so that He might sanctify[a] the people by His own blood. ¹³ Let us then go to Him outside the camp, bearing His disgrace. ¹⁴ For here we do not have an enduring city; instead, we seek the one to come. ¹⁵ Therefore, through Him let us continually offer up to God a sacrifice of praise, that is, the fruit of our lips that confess His name. ¹⁶ Don't neglect to do good and to share, for God is pleased with such sacrifices. ¹⁷ Obey your leaders[b] and submit to them, for they keep watch over your souls as those who will give an account, so that they can do this with joy and not with grief, for that would be unprofitable for you. ¹⁸ Pray for us; for we are convinced that we have a clear conscience, wanting to conduct ourselves honorably in everything. ¹⁹ And I especially urge you to pray[c] that I may be restored to you very soon.

BENEDICTION AND FAREWELL

²⁰ Now may the God of peace, who brought up from the dead our Lord Jesus—the great Shepherd of the sheep—with the blood of the everlasting covenant, ²¹ equip[d] you with all that is good to do His will, working in us what is pleasing in His sight, through Jesus Christ, to whom be glory forever and ever.[e] •Amen.

²² Brothers, I urge you to receive this word of exhortation, for I have written to you in few words. ²³ Be aware that our brother Timothy has been released. If he comes soon enough, he will be with me when I see you. ²⁴ Greet all your leaders and all the saints. Those who are from Italy greet you. ²⁵ Grace be with all of you.

---

[a]**13:12** Or *set apart*, or *consecrate*
[b]**13:17** Or *rulers*
[c]**13:19** Lit *to do this*

[d]**13:21** Or *perfect*
[e]**13:21** *Other* mss omit *and ever*

JAMES

GREETING

1 James, a slave of God and of the Lord Jesus Christ:
To the 12 tribes in the Dispersion.
Greetings.

TRIALS AND MATURITY

2 Consider it a great joy, my brothers, whenever you experience various trials, 3 knowing that the testing of your faith produces endurance. 4 But endurance must do its complete work, so that you may be mature and complete, lacking nothing.

5 Now if any of you lacks wisdom, he should ask God, who gives to all generously and without criticizing, and it will be given to him. 6 But let him ask in faith without doubting. For the doubter is like the surging sea, driven and tossed by the wind. 7 That person should not expect to receive anything from the Lord. 8 An indecisive man is unstable in all his ways.

9 The brother of humble circumstances should boast in his exaltation; 10 but the one who is rich ⌊should boast⌋ in his humiliation, because he will pass away like a flower of the field. 11 For the sun rises with its scorching heat and dries up the grass; its flower falls off, and its beautiful appearance is destroyed. In the same way, the rich man will wither away while pursuing his activities.

12 Blessed is a man who endures trials,a because when he passes the test he will receive the crown of life that Heb has promised to those who love Him.

13 No one undergoing a trial should say, "I am being tempted by God." For God is not tempted by evil,c and

---

a1:12 Lit *trial*, used as a collective
b1:12 Other mss read *that the Lord*
c1:13 Or *evil persons*, or *evil things*

He Himself doesn't tempt anyone. [14] But each person is tempted when he is drawn away and enticed by his own evil desires. [15] Then after desire has conceived, it gives birth to sin, and when sin is fully grown, it gives birth to death.

[16] Don't be deceived, my dearly loved brothers. [17] Every generous act and every perfect gift is from above, coming down from the Father of lights; with Him there is no variation or shadow cast by turning. [18] By His own choice, He gave us a new birth by the message of truth[a] so that we would be the •firstfruits of His creatures.

HEARING AND DOING THE WORD

[19] My dearly loved brothers, understand this: everyone must be quick to hear, slow to speak, and slow to anger, [20] for man's anger does not accomplish God's righteousness. [21] Therefore, ridding yourselves of all moral filth and evil excess, humbly receive the implanted word, which is able to save you.[b]

[22] But be doers of the word and not hearers only, deceiving yourselves. [23] Because if anyone is a hearer of the word and not a doer, he is like a man looking at his own face[c] in a mirror; [24] for he looks at himself, goes away, and right away forgets what kind of man he was. [25] But the one who looks intently into the perfect law of freedom and perseveres in it, and is not a forgetful hearer but a doer who acts—this person will be blessed in what he does.

[26] If anyone[d] thinks he is religious, without controlling his tongue but deceiving his heart, his religion is useless. [27] Pure and undefiled religion before our[e] God and Father is this: to look after orphans and widows in their distress and to keep oneself unstained by the world.

THE SIN OF FAVORITISM

2 My brothers, hold your faith in our glorious Lord Jesus Christ without showing favoritism. [2] For suppose a man comes into your meeting wearing a gold ring, dressed in fine clothes, and a poor man dressed

Open Up, and Let the Scriptures Move You

When you allow the Scripture to touch the deepest corner of your soul, the Holy Spirit will transform its truth from your head to your heart— and you into the image of Christ.

Ridding yourselves of all moral filth and evil excess, humbly receive the implanted word, which is able to save you.

—James 1:21

Let Obedience Catch Up to Your Knowledge

Many times what we need is not another conference teaching us more things. We simply need to put into practice what we've already learned.

But be doers of the word and not hearers only, deceiving yourselves.

—James 1:22

---

[a]**1:18** *message of truth* = the gospel
[b]**1:21** Lit *save your souls*
[c]**1:23** Lit *at the face of his birth*
[d]**1:26** Other mss add *among you*
[e]**1:27** Or *before the*

in dirty clothes also comes in. ³ If you look with favor on the man wearing the fine clothes so that you say, "Sit here in a good place," and yet you say to the poor man, "Stand over there," or, "Sit here on the floor by my footstool," ⁴ haven't you discriminated among yourselves and become judges with evil thoughts?

⁵ Listen, my dear brothers: Didn't God choose the poor in this world to be rich in faith and heirs of the kingdom that He has promised to those who love Him? ⁶ Yet you dishonored that poor man. Don't the rich oppress you and drag you into the courts? ⁷ Don't they blaspheme the noble name that you bear?

⁸ If you really carry out the royal law prescribed in Scripture, **Love your neighbor as yourself**,ᵃ you are doing well. ⁹ But if you show favoritism, you commit sin and are convicted by the law as transgressors. ¹⁰ For whoever keeps the entire law, yet fails in one point, is guilty of ⌊breaking it⌋ all. ¹¹ For He who said, **Do not commit adultery**,ᵇ also said, **Do not murder.**ᶜ So if you do not commit adultery, but you do murder, you are a lawbreaker.

¹² Speak and act as those who will be judged by the law of freedom. ¹³ For judgment is without mercy to the one who hasn't shown mercy. Mercy triumphs over judgment.

FAITH AND WORKS

¹⁴ What good is it, my brothers, if someone says he has faith, but does not have works? Can his faithᵈ save him?

¹⁵ If a brother or sister is without clothes and lacks daily food, ¹⁶ and one of you says to them, "Go in peace, keep warm, and eat well," but you don't give them what the body needs, what good is it? ¹⁷ In the same way faith, if it doesn't have works, is dead by itself.

¹⁸ But someone will say, "You have faith, and I have works."ᵉ Show me your faith without works, and I will show you faith from my works.ᶠ ¹⁹ You believe that God

Watch as Your Life Confirms the Word

God does not want you merely to gain intellectual knowledge of truth. He wants you to experience life in His kingdom.

If a brother or sister is without clothes and lacks daily food, and one of you says to them, "Go in peace, keep warm, and eat well," but you don't give them what the body needs, what good is it? In the same way faith, if it doesn't have works, is dead by itself.

—James 2:15-17

It Takes More Than Brains to Believe God

You can know certain facts about God to be true, but you can never really know God until you actually trust Him and experience Him in your life.

You believe that God is one; you do well. The demons also believe—and they shudder.

—James 2:19

ᵃ2:8 Lv 19:18
ᵇ2:11 Ex 20:14; Dt 5:18
ᶜ2:11 Ex 20:13; Dt 5:17
ᵈ2:14 Or *Can faith*, or *Can that faith*, or *Can such faith*

ᵉ2:18 The quotation may end here or after v. 18b or v. 19.
ᶠ2:18 Other mss read *Show me your faith from your works, and from my works I will show you my faith.*

WORD STUDY

Greek word: ***prautes***
[prah OO tays]

Translation: ***gentleness***

Uses in James: **2**

Uses in the NT: **11**

Key passage: **James 3:13**

Prautes (*gentleness*, *humility*) always appears as a positive quality in the NT. Christians are encouraged to receive with *submission* (*a humble attitude toward*) the implanted word able to save their lives (Jms 1:21). This inward attitude of *gentleness* always manifests itself outwardly. There is no such thing as a gentle attitude that does not express itself in gentleness with relation to others! Therefore, good conduct should operate in the *gentleness* that wisdom requires (Jms 3:13). *Gentleness* is a fruit of the Spirit (Gl 5:23). Christians are to clothe themselves with *gentleness* not only towards one another (Col 3:12) but also towards all people (Ti 3:2). Sinners are to be restored in a spirit of *gentleness* (Gl 6:1). The servant of God is not to quarrel even with his opponents. Rather, he is to instruct them in *gentleness* with a view to their repentance (2 Tm 2:24-25; cf. 1 Pt 3:16).

is one; you do well. The demons also believe—and they shudder.

²⁰ Foolish man! Are you willing to learn that faith without works is useless? ²¹ Wasn't Abraham our father justified by works when he offered Isaac his son on the altar? ²² You see that faith was active together with his works, and by works, faith was perfected. ²³ So the Scripture was fulfilled that says, **Abraham believed God, and it was credited to him for righteousness,**ᵃ and he was called God's friend. ²⁴ You see that a man is justified by works and not by faith alone. ²⁵ And in the same way, wasn't Rahab the prostitute also justified by works when she received the messengers and sent them out by a different route? ²⁶ For just as the body without the spirit is dead, so also faith without works is dead.

CONTROLLING THE TONGUE

3 Not many should become teachers, my brothers, knowing that we will receive a stricter judgment; ² for we all stumble in many ways. If anyone does not stumble in what he says,ᵇ he is a mature man who is also able to control his whole body.ᶜ

³ Now when we put bits into the mouths of horses to make them obey us, we also guide the whole animal.ᵈ ⁴ And consider ships: though very large and driven by fierce winds, they are guided by a very small rudder wherever the will of the pilot directs. ⁵ So too, though the tongue is a small part ⌊of the body⌋, it boasts great things. Consider how large a forest a small fire ignites. ⁶ And the tongue is a fire. The tongue, a world of unrighteousness, is placed among the parts of our ⌊bodies⌋; it pollutes the whole body, sets the course of life on fire, and is set on fire by •hell.

⁷ For every creature—animal or bird, reptile or fish—is tamed and has been tamed by man, ⁸ but no man can tame the tongue. It is a restless evil, full of deadly poison. ⁹ With it we bless ourᵉ Lord and Father, and with it we curse men who are made in God's likeness. ¹⁰ Out of the same mouth come blessing and cursing. My brothers, these things should not be this way. ¹¹ Does a spring pour out sweet and bitter water from

---

ᵃ2:23 Gn 15:6
ᵇ3:2 Lit *in word*
ᶜ3:2 Lit *to bridle the whole body*

ᵈ3:3 Lit *whole body*
ᵉ3:9 Or *bless the*

the same opening? [12] Can a fig tree produce olives, my brothers, or a grapevine ⌊produce⌋ figs? Neither can a saltwater spring yield fresh water.

THE WISDOM FROM ABOVE

[13] Who is wise and understanding among you? He should show his works by good conduct with wisdom's gentleness. [14] But if you have bitter envy and selfish ambition in your heart, don't brag and lie in defiance of the truth. [15] Such wisdom does not come down from above, but is earthly, sensual, demonic. [16] For where envy and selfish ambition exist, there is disorder and every kind of evil. [17] But the wisdom from above is first pure, then peace-loving, gentle, compliant, full of mercy and good fruits, without favoritism and hypocrisy. [18] And the fruit of righteousness is sown in peace by those who make peace.

PROUD OR HUMBLE

4 What is the source of the wars and the fights among you? Don't they come from the cravings that are at war within you?[a] [2] You desire and do not have. You murder and covet and cannot obtain. You fight and war. You do not have because you do not ask. [3] You ask and don't receive because you ask wrongly, so that you may spend it on your desires for pleasure.

[4] Adulteresses![b] Do you not know that friendship with the world is hostility toward God? So whoever wants to be the world's friend becomes God's enemy. [5] Or do you think it's without reason the Scripture says that the Spirit He has caused to live in us yearns jealously?[c]

[6] But He gives greater grace. Therefore He says:

> **God resists the proud,**
> **but gives grace to the humble.[d]**

[7] Therefore, submit to God. But resist the Devil, and he will flee from you. [8] Draw near to God, and He will draw near to you. Cleanse your hands, sinners, and

---

WORD STUDY

Greek word: **huperephanos**
[hoo pehr AY fah nahs]

Translation: **proud**

Uses in James: **1**

Uses in the NT: **5**

Key passage: **James 4:6**

In the NT, *huperephanos* appears exclusively in an unfavorable sense, referring to one who is *haughty* or *arrogant*, always in relation to other people. Thus, men show their pride by foolishly refusing to submit to God and authorities. Consequently, God opposes them (Lk 1:51; Jms 4:6). God is opposed to the *proud* believer who resists those in authority and acts arrogantly towards his fellow brothers and sisters (1 Pt 5:5). Thus, *huperephanos* represents a pride of heart which manifests itself through a state of demeaning others. Paul's use of *huperephanos* supports this conclusion. Twice he lists the term in a vice-list (Rm 1:30; 2 Tm 3:2). From the list in Rm 1:30, the range of meaning of *huperephanos* appears to overlap with that of *hubristas* (a violent, insolent man) and *alazones* (an empty boaster) such that the term appears to be a link between empty verbal boasting and violent action.

---

[a]4:1 Lit *war in your members*
[b]4:4 Other mss read *Adulterers and adulteresses*
[c]4:5 Or *He who caused the Spirit to live in us yearns jealously,* or *the spirit He caused to live in us yearns jealously,* or *He jealously yearns for the Spirit He made to live in us*
[d]4:6 Pr 3:34

purify your hearts, double-minded people! ⁹ Be miserable and mourn and weep. Your laughter must change to mourning and your joy to sorrow. ¹⁰ Humble yourselves before the Lord, and He will exalt you.

¹¹ Don't criticize one another, brothers. He who criticizes a brother or judges his brother criticizes the law and judges the law. But if you judge the law, you are not a doer of the law but a judge. ¹² There is one lawgiver and judgeª who is able to save and to destroy. But who are you to judge your neighbor?

OUR WILL AND HIS WILL

¹³ Come now, you who say, "Today or tomorrow we will travel to such and such a city and spend a year there and do business and make a profit." ¹⁴ You don't even know what tomorrow will bring—what your life will be! For you are a bit of smoke that appears for a little while, then vanishes.

¹⁵ Instead, you should say, "If the Lord wills, we will live and do this or that." ¹⁶ But as it is, you boast in your arrogance. All such boasting is evil. ¹⁷ So, for the person who knows to do good and doesn't do it, it is a sin.

WARNING TO THE RICH

5 Come now, you rich people! Weep and wail over the miseries that are coming on you. ² Your wealth is ruined: your clothes are moth-eaten; ³ your silver and gold are corroded, and their corrosion will be a witness against you and will eat your flesh like fire. You stored up treasure in the last days! ⁴ Look! The pay that you withheld from the workers who reaped your fields cries out, and the outcry of the harvesters has reached the ears of the Lord of Hosts.ᵇ ⁵ You have lived luxuriously on the land and have indulged yourselves. You have fattened your hearts forᶜ the day of slaughter. ⁶ You have condemned—you have murdered—the righteous man; he does not resist you.

WAITING FOR THE LORD

⁷ Therefore, brothers, be patient until the Lord's coming. See how the farmer waits for the precious

Better a Do-Gooder Than a Do-Nothing

It's usually not what we don't know that causes us problems. More often, what troubles us are the things we already do know about God but haven't applied in our lives.

For the person who knows to do good and doesn't do it, it is a sin.

—James 4:17

ª**4:12** Other mss omit *and judge*
ᵇ**5:4** Gk *Sabaoth*; this word is a transliteration of the Hb word for *Hosts*, or *Armies*.
ᶜ**5:5** Or *hearts in*

fruit of the earth and is patient with it until it receives the early and the late rains. ⁸ You also must be patient. Strengthen your hearts, because the Lord's coming is near.

⁹ Brothers, do not complain about one another, so that you will not be judged. Look, the judge stands at the door!

¹⁰ Brothers, take the prophets who spoke in the Lord's name as an example of suffering and patience. ¹¹ See, we count as blessed those who have endured.ᵃ You have heard of Job's endurance and have seen the outcome from the Lord: the Lord is very compassionate and merciful.

TRUTHFUL SPEECH

¹² Now above all, my brothers, do not swear, either by heaven or by earth or with any other oath. Your "yes" must be "yes," and your "no" must be "no," so that you won't fall under judgment.ᵇ

EFFECTIVE PRAYER

¹³ Is anyone among you suffering? He should pray. Is anyone cheerful? He should sing praises. ¹⁴ Is anyone among you sick? He should call for the elders of the church, and they should pray over him after anointing him with olive oil in the name of the Lord. ¹⁵ The prayer of faith will save the sick person, and the Lord will raise him up; and if he has committed sins, he will be forgiven. ¹⁶ Therefore, confess your sins to one another and pray for one another, so that you may be healed. The intense prayer of the righteous is very powerful. ¹⁷ Elijah was a man with a nature like ours; yet he prayed earnestly that it would not rain, and for three years and six months it did not rain on the land. ¹⁸ Then he prayed again, and the sky gave rain and the land produced its fruit.

¹⁹ My brothers, if any among you strays from the truth, and someone turns him back, ²⁰ he should know that whoever turns a sinner from the error of his way will save his •life from death and cover a multitude of sins.

Have You Prepared Yourself for Prayer?

If nothing happens when you pray, the problem is not with God. When you adhere to what God requires through confession and obedience, He will lead you to pray for things that align with His purposes.

Confess your sins to one another and pray for one another, so that you may be healed. The intense prayer of the righteous is very powerful.

—James 5:16

God Works in Ordinary People—Just Like Us

Faith is not based on intelligence or ability, but on our willingness to trust what God says.

Elijah was a man with a nature like ours; yet he prayed earnestly that it would not rain, and for three years and six months it did not rain on the land.

—James 5:17

ᵃ5:11 Or *have persevered* ᵇ5:12 Other mss read *fall into hypocrisy*

PETER

GREETING

1 Peter, an apostle of Jesus Christ:
To the temporary residents of the Dispersion in the provinces of Pontus, Galatia, Cappadocia, Asia, and Bithynia, chosen ² according to the foreknowledge of God the Father and set apart by the Spirit for obedience and ₍for the₎ sprinkling with the blood of Jesus Christ.
May grace and peace be multiplied to you.

A LIVING HOPE

³ Blessed be the God and Father of our Lord Jesus Christ. According to His great mercy, He has given us a new birth into a living hope through the resurrection of Jesus Christ from the dead, ⁴ and into an inheritance that is imperishable, uncorrupted, and unfading, kept in heaven for you, ⁵ who are being protected by God's power through faith for a salvation that is ready to be revealed in the last time. ⁶ You rejoice in this,ᵃ though now for a short time you have had to be distressed by various trials ⁷ so that the genuineness of your faith—more valuable than gold, which perishes though refined by fire—may result inᵇ praise, glory, and honor at the revelation of Jesus Christ. ⁸ You love Him, though you have not seen Him. And though not seeing Him now, you believe in Him and rejoice with inexpressible and glorious joy, ⁹ because you are receiving the goal of yourᶜ faith, the salvation of your souls.ᵈ

¹⁰ Concerning this salvation, the prophets who prophesied about the grace that would come to you

---

ᵃ1:6 Or *In this (fact) rejoice*
ᵇ1:7 Lit *may be found for*

ᶜ1:9 Other mss read *our*, or they omit the possessive pronoun
ᵈ1:9 Or *your lives*

searched and carefully investigated. [11] They inquired into what time or what circumstances[a] the Spirit of Christ within them was indicating when He testified in advance to the messianic sufferings[b] and the glories that would follow.[c] [12] It was revealed to them that they were not serving themselves but you concerning things that have now been announced to you through those who preached the gospel to you by the Holy Spirit sent from heaven. Angels desire to look into these things.

A CALL TO HOLY LIVING

[13] Therefore, get your minds ready for action,[d] being self-disciplined, and set your hope completely on the grace to be brought to you at the revelation of Jesus Christ. [14] As obedient children, do not be conformed to the desires of your former ignorance [15] but, as the One who called you is holy, you also are to be holy in all your conduct; [16] for it is written, **Be holy, because I am holy.**[e]

[17] And if you address as Father the One who judges impartially based on each one's work, you are to conduct yourselves in reverence during this time of temporary residence. [18] For you know that you were redeemed from your empty way of life inherited from the fathers, not with perishable things, like silver or gold, [19] but with the precious blood of Christ, like that of a lamb without defect or blemish. [20] He was destined[f] before the foundation of the world, but was revealed at the end of the times for you [21] who through Him are believers in God, who raised Him from the dead and gave Him glory, so that your faith and hope are in God.

[22] By obedience to the truth,[g] having purified yourselves[h] for sincere love of the brothers, love one another earnestly from a pure[i] heart, [23] since you have been born again—not of perishable seed but of

Keep Your Mind on the Main Thing

Many Christians do not exercise their minds to be of service to God. They allow others to do their spiritual thinking for them. Use your mind in a way that brings glory to God.

Get your minds ready for action, being self-disciplined, and set your hope completely on the grace to be brought to you at the revelation of Jesus Christ.

—1 Peter 1:13

Live Every Day in the Light of His Holiness

There is no easy access to God for those with unclean hands or an impure heart. The closer you get to God, the more obvious even your smallest sins will become.

As the One who called you is holy, you also are to be holy in all your conduct.

—1 Peter 1:15

---

[a]**1:11** Or *inquired about the person or time*
[b]**1:11** Or *the sufferings of Christ*
[c]**1:11** Lit *the glories after that*
[d]**1:13** Lit *Therefore, gird the loins of your minds*
[e]**1:16** Lv 11:44-45; 19:2; 20:7
[f]**1:20** Or *was chosen*, or *was known*
[g]**1:22** Other mss add *through the Spirit*
[h]**1:22** Or *purified your souls*
[i]**1:22** Other mss omit *pure*

WORD STUDY

Greek word: *hierateuma*
[hee eh RAH tyoo mah]

Translation: *priesthood*

Uses in 1 Peter: **2**

Uses in the NT: **2**

Key passage: **1 Peter 2:5,9**

Hierateuma (*priesthood*) first appears in written literature in the Greek OT (Ex 19:6; 23:22), where it was evidently coined by the translators of that document. If Israel obeyed God, she would be His treasured possession (Ex 23:22) and would function as a royal *priesthood* through which God would dispense His blessing to the whole earth (Ex 19:5-6, 23:22). In the NT, Peter makes direct reference to Exodus 19:6 and 23:22 and applies the fulfillment of this OT concept of *royal priesthood* to the church (1 Pt 2:9), which now exists to serve God through the worship of her words and deeds. She is being built into a spiritual temple where believers perform the role of a holy *priesthood* by offering "spiritual sacrifices acceptable to God through Jesus Christ" (1 Pt 2:5). The church also serves God through the proclamation of the praises that belong to Him (1 Pt 2:9).

imperishable—through the living and enduring word of God. ²⁴ For

> All flesh is like grass,
> and all its glory like a flower of the grass.
> The grass withers, and the flower
>   drops off,
> ²⁵ but the word of the Lord endures forever.ᵃ

And this is the word that was preached as the gospel to you.

THE LIVING STONE AND A HOLY PEOPLE

2 So rid yourselves of all wickedness, all deceit, hypocrisy, envy, and all slander. ² Like newborn infants, desire the unadulterated spiritual milk, so that you may grow by it in ₗyourₗ salvation,ᵇ ³ since **you have tasted that the Lord is good.**ᶜ ⁴ Coming to Him, a living stone—rejected by men but chosen and valuable to God— ⁵ you yourselves, as living stones, are being built into a spiritual house for a holy priesthood to offer spiritual sacrifices acceptable to God through Jesus Christ. ⁶ For it stands in Scripture:

> **Look! I lay a stone in Zion,**
> **a chosen and valuable cornerstone,**
> **and the one who believes in Him**
> **will never be put to shame!**ᵈ ᵉ

⁷ So the honor is for you who believe; but for the unbelieving,

> **The stone that the builders rejected—**
> **this One has become the cornerstone,**ᶠ

and

> ⁸ **A stone that causes men to stumble,**ᵍ
> **and a rock that trips them up.**ʰ ⁱ

They stumble by disobeying the message; they were destined for this.

ᵃ**1:24-25** Is 40:6-8
ᵇ**2:2** Other mss omit *in your salvation*
ᶜ**2:3** Ps 34:8
ᵈ**2:6** Or *be disappointed*

ᵉ**2:6** Is 28:16 LXX
ᶠ**2:7** Ps 118:22
ᵍ**2:8** Or *a stone causing stumbling*
ʰ**2:8** Or *a rock to trip over*
ⁱ**2:8** Is 8:14

9 But you are **a chosen race,**[a] [b]
    a royal priesthood,[c]
a holy nation,[d] **a people
    for His possession,**[e]
so that you may proclaim the praises[f] [g]
of the One who called you out of darkness
into His marvelous light.
10 Once you were not a people,
    but now you are God's people;
you had not received mercy,
    but now you have received mercy.

A CALL TO GOOD WORKS

11 Dear friends, I urge you as aliens and temporary residents to abstain from fleshly desires that war
against you.[h] 12 Conduct yourselves honorably among
the Gentiles,[i] so that in a case where they speak against
you as those who do evil, they may, by observing your
good works, glorify God in a day of visitation.[j]

13 Submit to every human institution because of the
Lord, whether to the Emperor[k] as the supreme authority, 14 or to governors as those sent out by him to punish those who do evil and to praise those who do good.
15 For it is God's will that you, by doing good, silence
the ignorance of foolish people. 16 As God's slaves, ⌊live⌋
as free people, but don't use your freedom as a way to
conceal evil. 17 Honor everyone. Love the brotherhood.
Fear God. Honor the Emperor.[k]

SUBMISSION OF SLAVES TO MASTERS

18 Household slaves, submit yourselves to your masters with all respect, not only to the good and gentle
but also to the cruel.[l] 19 For it ⌊brings⌋ favor[m] if, because
of conscience toward God,[n] someone endures grief

Let Others See You for Whose You Are

When you are following Jesus'
lordship, others may misunder-
stand or even oppose you, but
your obedience to God reflects
your identity as His child.

*Conduct yourselves honor-
ably among the Gentiles, so
that in a case where they speak
against you as those who do
evil, they may, by observing your good works, glorify
God in a day of visitation.*
—1 Peter 2:12

Never Grow Lax in Living for Jesus

Our freedom in Christ is not
freedom to do anything we want.
It is freedom to live righteously,
something we could not do when
we were in bondage to sin.

*As God's slaves, live as free
people, but don't use your
freedom as a way to conceal evil.*
—1 Peter 2:16

---

[a]**2:9** Or *chosen generation*, or *cho-sen nation*
[b]**2:9** Is 43:20 LXX; Dt 7:6; 10:15
[c]**2:9** Ex 19:6; 23:22 LXX; Is 61:6
[d]**2:9** Ex 19:6; 23:22 LXX
[e]**2:9** Ex 19:5; 23:22 LXX; Dt 4:20; 7:6; Is 43:21 LXX
[f]**2:9** Or *the mighty deeds*
[g]**2:9** Is 42:12; 43:21
[h]**2:11** Lit *against the soul*

[i]**2:12** Or *among the nations*, or *among the pagans*
[j]**2:12** A day when God intervenes in human history, either in grace or in judgment
[k]**2:13,17** Lit *king*
[l]**2:18** Lit *crooked*, or *unscrupulous*
[m]**2:19** Other mss add *with God*
[n]**2:19** Other mss read *because of a good conscience*

from suffering unjustly. 20 For what credit is there if you endure when you sin and are beaten? But when you do good and suffer, if you endure, it brings favor with God.

21 For you were called to this,
　　because Christ also suffered for you,
　　leaving you an example,
　　so that you should follow in His steps.
22 He **did not commit sin,**
　　and no deceit was found in His mouth;ᵃ
23 when reviled, He did not revile in return;
　　when suffering, He did not threaten,
　　but committed Himself to the One
　　　　who judges justly.
24 He Himself bore our sins
　　in His body on the tree,
　　so that, having died to sins,
　　we might live for righteousness;
　　by **His wounding you have been healed.**ᵇ
25 For you **were like sheep going astray,**ᶜ
　　but you have now returned
　　to the shepherd and guardianᵈ
　　of your souls.

WIVES AND HUSBANDS

3 Wives, in the same way, submit yourselves to your own husbands so that, even if some disobey the ⌊Christian⌋ message, they may be won overᵉ without a message by the way their wives live, 2 when they observe your pure, reverent lives. 3 Your beauty should not consist of outward things ⌊like⌋ elaborate hairstyles and the wearing of gold ornamentsᶠ or fine clothes; 4 instead, ⌊it should consist of⌋ the hidden person of the heart with the imperishable quality of a gentle and quiet spirit, which is very valuable in God's eyes. 5 For in the past, the holy women who hoped in God also beautified themselves in this way, submitting to their own husbands, 6 just as Sarah obeyed Abraham, calling him lord. You have become her children when you do good and aren't frightened by anything alarming.

With Faith, You Can Stand Up to Anybody

There will be conflict and opposition in the process of walking with the Lord, but the Holy Spirit will empower you to be strong in every circumstance.

Who will harm you if you are passionate for what is good?
　　—1 Peter 3:13

ᵃ2:22 Is 53:9
ᵇ2:24 Is 53:5
ᶜ2:25 Is 53:6
ᵈ2:25 Or *overseer*

ᵉ3:1 Lit *may be gained*
ᶠ3:3 Lit *and of putting around of gold items*

7 Husbands, in the same way, live with your wives with understanding of their weaker nature[a] yet showing them honor as co-heirs of the grace of life, so that your prayers will not be hindered.

DO NO EVIL

8 Now finally, all of you should be like-minded and sympathetic, should love believers,[b] and be compassionate and humble,[c] 9 not paying back evil for evil or insult for insult but, on the contrary, giving a blessing, since you were called for this, so that you can inherit a blessing.

10 For **the one who wants to love life**
   and to see good days
   must keep his tongue from evil
   and his lips from speaking deceit,
11 **and he must turn away from evil**
   and do good.
He must seek peace and pursue it,
12 **because the eyes of the Lord**
   are on the righteous
   and His ears are open to their request.
But the face of the Lord is against those
   who do evil.[d]

UNDESERVED SUFFERING

13 And who will harm[e] you if you are passionate for what is good?[f] 14 But even if you should suffer for righteousness, you are blessed. **Do not fear what they fear or be disturbed,**[g] 15 but set apart the •Messiah[h] as Lord in your hearts, and always be ready to give a defense to anyone who asks you for a reason[i] for the hope that is in you. 16 However, do this with gentleness and respect, keeping your conscience clear,[j] so that when you are accused,[k] those who denounce your Christian life will be

Are You on the Lookout for the Lost?

Whenever an unbeliever meets a Christian, the unbeliever ought to be face-to-face with everything he needs to know in order to follow Christ.

Always be ready to give a defense to anyone who asks you for a reason for the hope that is in you.

—1 Peter 3:15b

---

[a]3:7 Lit *understanding as the weaker vessel*
[b]3:8 Lit *brotherly-loving*
[c]3:8 Other mss read *courteous*
[d]3:10-12 Ps 34:12-16
[e]3:13 Or *will mistreat*, or *will do evil to*
[f]3:13 Lit *you are zealots*, or *you are partisans for the good*, or *you are eager to do good*

[g]3:14 Is 8:12
[h]3:15 Other mss read *set God*
[i]3:15 Or *who demands of you an accounting*
[j]3:16 Lit *good*; or *keeping a clear conscience*
[k]3:16 Other mss read *when they speak against you as evildoers*

WORD STUDY

Greek word: ***makrothumia***
[ma krah thew MEE ah]

Translation: ***patience***

Uses in 1 Peter: **1**

Uses in the NT: **14**

Key passage: **1 Peter 3:20**

Makrothumia refers to *patient perseverance* in withstanding a difficult situation. The *patience* of the faithful witnesses and martyrs of old is an example for present day believers (Heb 6:12, Jms 5:10). Paul prayed that the Colossian church would be strengthened for all *patience* (Col 1:11). Elsewhere, *makrothumia* speaks of *patience* within the context of personal relationships, referring to the *patience* of people toward one another or of God toward humanity. Paul exhorts Timothy to encourage his congregation with *patience* (2 Tm 4:2), and believers should demonstrate *patience* toward each other (Col 3:12). In reference to God, *makrothumia* always indicates His slowness in bringing about judgment. God's *patience* waited while Noah prepared an ark (1 Pt 3:20), and God's *patience* in bringing judgment provides present opportunity for repentance (Rm 2:4). Similarly, the *patience* of Jesus in bringing judgment should be considered as a present opportunity for salvation (2 Pt 3:15).

put to shame. [17] For it is better to suffer for doing good, if that should be God's will,[a] than for doing evil.

[18] For Christ also suffered for sins
   once for all,[b]
the righteous for the unrighteous,[c]
that He might bring you[d] to God,
after being put to death in the fleshly realm[e]
but made alive in the spiritual realm.[f]

[19] In that state[g] He also went and made a proclamation to the spirits in prison[h] [20] who in the past were disobedient, when God patiently waited in the days of Noah while an ark was being prepared; in it, a few—that is, eight people[i] —were saved through water. [21] Baptism, which corresponds to this, now saves you (not the removal of the filth of the flesh, but the pledge[j] of a good conscience toward God) through the resurrection of Jesus Christ. [22] Now that He has gone into heaven, He is at God's right hand, with angels, authorities, and powers subjected to Him.

FOLLOWING CHRIST

4 Therefore, since Christ suffered[k] in the flesh,[l] arm yourselves also with the same resolve[m] —because the One who suffered in the flesh[l] has finished with sin[n] — [2] in order to live the remaining time in the flesh,[l] no longer for human desires,[o] but for God's will. [3] For there has already been enough time spent in doing the will of the pagans[p] carrying on in unrestrained behavior, evil desires, drunkenness, orgies, carousing, and lawless idolatry. [4] In regard to this, they are surprised that you don't plunge with them into the same

---

[a]**3:17** Lit *if the will of God should will*
[b]**3:18** Other mss read *died for sins on our behalf*; other mss read *died for our sins*; other mss read *died for sins on your behalf*
[c]**3:18** Or *the Righteous One in the place of the unrighteous many*
[d]**3:18** Other mss read *us*
[e]**3:18** Or *in the flesh*
[f]**3:18** Or *in the spirit*, or *in the Spirit*
[g]**3:19** Or *In whom*, or *At that time*, or *In which*
[h]**3:19** The *spirits in prison* are most

likely fallen supernatural beings or angels; see 2 Pt 2:4; Jd 6.
[i]**3:20** Lit *souls*
[j]**3:21** Or *the appeal*
[k]**4:1** Other mss read *suffered for us*
[l]**4:1,2** *In the flesh* probably means "in human existence"; see 1 Pt 3:18.
[m]**4:1** Or *perspective*, or *attitude*
[n]**4:1** Or *the one who has suffered in the flesh has ceased from sin*
[o]**4:2** Lit *for desires of human beings*
[p]**4:3** Or *Gentiles*

flood[a] of dissipation—and they slander you. ⁵ They will give an account to the One who stands ready to judge the living and the dead. ⁶ For this reason the gospel was also preached to ˻those who are now˼ dead, so that, although they might be judged by men in the fleshly realm,[b] they might live by God in the spiritual realm.[c]

END-TIME ETHICS

⁷ Now the end of all things is near; therefore, be clear-headed and disciplined for prayer. ⁸ Above all, keep your love for one another at full strength, since **love covers a multitude of sins.**[d] ⁹ Be hospitable to one another without complaining. ¹⁰ Based on the gift they have received, everyone should use it to serve others, as good managers of the varied grace of God. ¹¹ If anyone speaks, ˻his speech should be˼ like the oracles of God; if anyone serves, ˻his service should be˼ from the strength God provides, so that in everything God may be glorified through Jesus Christ. To Him belong the glory and the power forever and ever. •Amen.

CHRISTIAN SUFFERING

¹² Dear friends, when the fiery ordeal[e] arises among you to test you, don't be surprised by it, as if something unusual were happening to you. ¹³ Instead, as you share in the sufferings of the •Messiah rejoice, so that you may also rejoice with great joy at the revelation of His glory. ¹⁴ If you are ridiculed for the name of Christ, you are blessed, because the Spirit of glory and of God rests on you.[f] ¹⁵ None of you, however, should suffer as a murderer, a thief, an evildoer, or as a meddler.[g] ¹⁶ But if ˻anyone suffers˼ as a Christian, he should not be ashamed, but should glorify God with that name. ¹⁷ For the time has come for judgment to begin with God's household; and if it begins with us, what will the outcome be for those who disobey the gospel of God?

Hasn't Sin Already Damaged Us Enough?

Don't become satisfied with a relationship with God that is broken by sin and void of the power of the Holy Spirit. If you have drifted from God, He calls you to return to Him.

There has already been enough time spent in doing the will of the pagans. . . . Now the end of all things is near; therefore, be clear-headed and disciplined for prayer.

—1 Peter 4:3a,7

Love Sets Us Apart and Knits Us Together

When the Lord measures our motives, He looks for one thing: love. All that we do should proceed from our love for God and for others.

Above all, keep your love for one another at full strength, since love covers a multitude of sins.

—1 Peter 4:8

---

[a]4:4 Lit *you don't run with them into the same pouring out*
[b]4:6 Or *in the flesh*
[c]4:6 Or *in the spirit*
[d]4:8 Pr 10:12

[e]4:12 Lit *the burning*
[f]4:14 Other mss add *He is blasphemed because of them, but He is glorified because of you.*
[g]4:15 Or *as one who defrauds others*

WORD STUDY

Greek word: **hupsoo**
[hoo PSAH oh]
Translation: **exalt, lift up**
Uses in 1 Peter: **1**
Uses in the NT: **20**
Key passage: **1 Peter 5:6**

Hupsoo refers to lifting something to a higher location. As Moses *lifted up* the serpent in the wilderness, Christ was *lifted up* on the cross (Jn 3:14). This concept of *lifting up* is figuratively extended to mean *to exalt* or *honor* (raising something to a position of higher status). In the example above, the *lifting up* of Jesus referred to His crucifixion (cf. Jn 8:28) but also to His exaltation (cf. Jn 12:32). Any real exaltation to a higher status must be done by one who possesses higher authority. Hence, God is often the one who exalts others (Lk 1:52; Ac 2:33; Jms 4:10; 1 Pt 5:6). He *exalted* (*made great* in number and power) the people of Israel in Egypt (Ac 13:17), and He *exalts* the humble (Mt 23:12 = Lk 14:11; Lk 18:14). Elsewhere, Paul humbled himself so that those in the Corinthian church might be *honored* (2 Co 11:7).

18 And **if the righteous is saved with difficulty, what will become of the ungodly and the sinner?**[a]

19 So those who suffer according to God's will should, in doing good, entrust themselves to a faithful Creator.

ABOUT THE ELDERS

5 Therefore, as a fellow elder and witness to the sufferings of the •Messiah, and also a participant in the glory about to be revealed, I exhort the elders among you: 2 shepherd God's flock among you, not overseeing[b] out of compulsion but freely, according to God's ⌊will⌋;[c] not for the money but eagerly; 3 not lording it over those entrusted to you, but being examples to the flock. 4 And when the chief Shepherd appears, you will receive the unfading crown of glory.

5 Likewise, you younger men, be subject to the elders. And all of you clothe yourselves with[d] humility toward one another, because

God resists the proud, but gives grace to the humble.[e]

6 Humble yourselves therefore under the mighty hand of God, so that He may exalt you in due time,[f] 7 casting all your care upon Him, because He cares about you.

CONCLUSION

8 Be sober! Be on the alert! Your adversary the Devil is prowling around like a roaring lion, looking for anyone he can devour. 9 Resist him, firm in the faith, knowing that the same sufferings are being experienced by your brothers in the world.

10 Now the God of all grace, who called you to His eternal glory in Christ Jesus, will personally[g] restore, establish, strengthen, and support you after you have

---

[a]**4:18** Pr 11:31 LXX
[b]**5:2** Other mss omit *overseeing*
[c]**5:2** Other mss omit *according to God's will*
[d]**5:5** Lit *you tie around yourselves*
[e]**5:5** Pr 3:34 LXX
[f]**5:6** Lit *in time*
[g]**5:10** Lit *Himself*

suffered a little[a] [11] To Him be the dominion[b] forever.[c] •Amen.

[12] Through Silvanus,[d] whom I consider a faithful brother, I have written briefly, encouraging you and testifying that this is the true grace of God. Take your stand in it! [13] She who is in Babylon, also chosen, sends you greetings, as does Mark, my son. [14] Greet one another with a kiss of love. Peace to all of you who are in Christ[e]

Needing God's Help Is a Strength, Not a Weakness

One of our greatest errors is to assume we can deal with something ourselves, only to discover that we really can't.

Humble yourselves therefore under the mighty hand of God, so that He may exalt you in due time, casting all your care upon Him, because He cares about you.

—1 Peter 5:6-7

We're Here by Orders of the King

What a comfort to know that we are not out on our own trying to make a difference in the world, but that we have been chosen, appointed, and sent by a Christ who cares for us.

The God of all grace, who called you to His eternal glory in Christ Jesus, will personally restore, establish, strengthen, and support you after you have suffered a little.

—1 Peter 5:10

---

[a]**5:10** Or *a little while,* or *to a small extent*
[b]**5:11** Other mss read *dominion and glory*; other mss read *glory and dominion*
[c]**5:11** Other mss read *forever and ever*

[d]**5:12** Or *Silas*; Ac 15:22-32; 16:19-40; 17:1-16
[e]**5:14** Other mss read *Christ Jesus. Amen.*

PETER

GREETING

1 Simeon[a] Peter, a slave and an apostle of Jesus Christ:

To those who have obtained a faith of equal privilege with ours[b] through the righteousness of our God and Savior Jesus Christ.

2 May grace and peace be multiplied to you through the knowledge of God and of Jesus our Lord.

GROWTH IN THE FAITH

3 For His[c] divine power has given us everything required for life and godliness, through the knowledge of Him who called us by[d] His own glory and goodness. 4 By these He has given us very great and precious promises, so that through them you may share in the divine nature, escaping the corruption that is in the world because of evil desires. 5 For this very reason, make every effort to supplement your faith with goodness, goodness with knowledge, 6 knowledge with self-control, self-control with endurance, endurance with godliness, 7 godliness with brotherly affection, and brotherly affection with love. 8 For if these qualities are yours and are increasing, they will keep you from being useless or unfruitful in the knowledge of our Lord Jesus Christ. 9 The person who lacks these things is blind and shortsighted, and has forgotten the cleansing from his past sins. 10 Therefore, brothers, make every effort to confirm your calling and election, because if you do these things you will never stumble. 11 For in this way, entry into the eternal kingdom

---

[a]1:1 Simon
[b]1:1 Or *obtained a faith of the same kind as ours*
[c]1:3 Lit *As His*
[d]1:3 Or *to*

of our Lord and Savior Jesus Christ will be richly supplied to you.

¹² Therefore I will always remind you about these things, even though you know them and are established in the truth you have. ¹³ I consider it right, as long as I am in this tent,ª to wake you up with a reminder, ¹⁴ knowing that I will soon lay aside my tent, as our Lord Jesus Christ has also shown me. ¹⁵ And I will also make every effort that after my departureᵇ you may be able to recall these things at any time.

THE TRUSTWORTHY PROPHETIC WORD

¹⁶ For we did not follow cleverly contrived myths when we made known to you the power and coming of our Lord Jesus Christ; instead, we were eyewitnesses of His majesty. ¹⁷ For when He received honor and glory from God the Father, a voice came to Him from the Majestic Glory:

> This is My beloved Son.ᶜ
> I take delight in Him!ᵈ

¹⁸ And we heard this voice when it came from heaven while we were with Him on the holy mountain. ¹⁹ So we have the prophetic word strongly confirmed. You will do well to pay attention to it, as to a lamp shining in a dismal place, until the day dawns and the morning star arises in your hearts. ²⁰ First of all, you should know this: no prophecy of Scripture comes from one's own interpretation, ²¹ because no prophecy ever came by the will of man; instead, moved by the Holy Spirit, men spoke from God.

THE JUDGMENT OF FALSE TEACHERS

2 But there were also false prophets among the people, just as there will be false teachers among you. They will secretly bring in destructive heresies, even denying the Master who bought them, and will bring swift destruction on themselves. ² Many will follow their unrestrained ways, and because of them the way

The Christian Walk Is a Whole New Way to Travel

You now have the resources of heaven at your disposal. The success of your endeavors will no longer depend on the way you use your own resources but on how you obey the Spirit of God.

His divine power has given us everything required for life and godliness, through the knowledge of Him who called us by His own glory and goodness.
—2 Peter 1:3

Search the Scriptures for Daily Direction

We should not claim verses we like and ignore those that convict us. We must allow every Scripture to speak to us and teach us what God wants us to learn.

We have the prophetic word strongly confirmed. You will do well to pay attention to it, as to a lamp shining in a dismal place, until the day dawns and the morning star arises in your hearts.
—2 Peter 1:19-21

ª**1:13** A euphemism for Peter's body
ᵇ**1:15** Or *my death*
ᶜ**1:17** Other mss read *My Son, My Beloved*
ᵈ**1:17** A reference to the transfiguration; see Mt 17:5

WORD STUDY

Greek word: **tartaroo**
[tahr tah RAH oh]

Translation: **throw down into
Tartarus**

Uses in 2 Peter: **1**

Uses in the NT: **1**

Key passage: **2 Peter 2:4**

The verb *tartaroo* means *to
throw down into Tartarus*. Its
only NT occurrence (2 Pt 2:4)
refers to God casting disobedient angels into *Tartarus*, an idea
with a Homeric parallel. Well before NT times, Homer (8th c. B.C.)
spoke of Tartarus as a subterranean place of punishment where
Zeus banished the Titans (a family
of ruling gods; Hom. Il. 14.279).
Hesiod (8th c. B.C.) remarked
that "a brazen anvil falling from
earth nine nights and days would
reach Tartarus upon the tenth"
(Hes. *Theog.* 724-5). It is a dark,
dank place "under misty gloom,"
surrounded by a bronze fence—a
place "which even the gods abhor"
(Hes. *Theog.* 730, 739). Eventually,
tartaroo made its way into Jewish apocalyptic literature, retaining
the idea of a place of punishment.
It appears closely equivalent to
Jewish *gehenna* [*hell*] (Syb. Or.
4:186), which supplies the Jewish
background alluded to by Peter in
2 Peter 2:4.

of truth will be blasphemed. ³ In their greed they will
exploit you with deceptive words. Their condemnation,
⌊pronounced⌋ long ago, is not idle, and their destruction does not sleep.

⁴ For if God didn't spare the angels who sinned, but
threw them down into Tartarusᵃ and delivered them to
be kept in chainsᵇ of darkness until judgment; ⁵ and if
He didn't spare the ancient world, but protected Noah,
a preacher of righteousness, and seven others,ᶜ when
He brought a flood on the world of the ungodly; ⁶ and if
He reduced the cities of Sodom and Gomorrah to ashes
and condemned them to ruin,ᵈ making them an example to those who were going to be ungodly;ᵉ ⁷ and if He
rescued righteous Lot, distressed by the unrestrained
behavior of the immoral ⁸ (for as he lived among them,
that righteous man tormented himself day by day with
the lawless deeds he saw and heard)— ⁹ then the Lord
knows how to rescue the godly from trials and to keep
the unrighteous under punishment until the day of
judgment, ¹⁰ especially those who follow the polluting
desires of the flesh and despise authority.

Bold, arrogant people! They do not tremble when
they blaspheme the glorious ones; ¹¹ however, angels,
who are greater in might and power, do not bring
a slanderous charge against them before the Lord.ᶠ
¹² But these people, like irrational animals—creatures
of instinct born to be caught and destroyed—speak
blasphemies about things they don't understand, and
in their destruction they too will be destroyed, ¹³ suffering harm as the payment for unrighteousness. They
consider it a pleasure to carouse in the daytime. They
are blots and blemishes, delighting in their deceptionsᵍ
as they feast with you, ¹⁴ having eyes full of adultery
and always looking for sin, seducing unstable people,
and with hearts trained in greed. Accursed children!
¹⁵ By abandoning the straight path, they have gone
astray and have followed the path of Balaam, the son of
Bosor,ʰ who loved the wages of unrighteousness, ¹⁶ but

ᵃ**2:4** *Tartarus* is a Gk name for a
subterranean place of divine punishment lower than Hades.
ᵇ**2:4** Other mss read *in pits*
ᶜ**2:5** Lit *righteousness, as the eighth*
ᵈ**2:6** Other mss omit *to ruin*
ᵉ**2:6** Other mss read *an example*

*of what is going to happen to the
ungodly*
ᶠ**2:11** Other mss read *them from
the Lord*
ᵍ**2:13** Other mss read *delighting in
the love feasts*
ʰ**2:15** Other mss read *Beor*

received a rebuke for his transgression: a speechless donkey spoke with a human voice and restrained the prophet's madness.

¹⁷ These people are springs without water, mists driven by a whirlwind. The gloom of darkness has been reserved for them. ¹⁸ For uttering bombastic, empty words, they seduce, by fleshly desires and debauchery, people who have barely escaped[a] from those who live in error. ¹⁹ They promise them freedom, but they themselves are slaves of corruption, since people are enslaved to whatever defeats them. ²⁰ For if, having escaped the world's impurity through the knowledge of our Lord and Savior Jesus Christ, they are again entangled in these things and defeated, the last state is worse for them than the first. ²¹ For it would have been better for them not to have known the way of righteousness than, after knowing it, to turn back from the holy commandment delivered to them. ²² It has happened to them according to the true proverb: **A dog returns to its own vomit,**[b] and, "a sow, after washing itself, wallows in the mud."

THE DAY OF THE LORD

3 Dear friends, this is now the second letter I've written you; in both, I awaken your pure understanding with a reminder, ² so that you can remember the words previously spoken by the holy prophets, and the commandment of our Lord and Savior ₍given₎ through your apostles. ³ First, be aware of this: scoffers will come in the last days to scoff, following their own lusts, ⁴ saying, "Where is the promise of His coming? For ever since the fathers fell •asleep, all things continue as they have been since the beginning of creation." ⁵ They willfully ignore this: long ago the heavens and the earth existed out of water and through water by the word of God. ⁶ Through these the world of that time perished when it was flooded by water. ⁷ But by the same word the present heavens and earth are held in store for fire, being kept until the day of judgment and destruction of ungodly men.

⁸ Dear friends, don't let this one thing escape you:

God Can Help Keep You on an Even Keel

If your trust is in God's provision, He will provide you with ways to stay calm and at rest in the midst of life's challenges and difficulties.

The Lord knows how to rescue the godly from trials.
—2 Peter 2:9a

If Sin Keeps Winning, Who Are You Kidding?

If you find yourself falling into sinful habits or not grieving over your sin as you once did, this indicates that you are not abiding in Christ.

People are enslaved to whatever defeats them.
—2 Peter 2:19b

---

[a] **2:18** Or *people who are barely escaping*   [b] **2:22** Pr 26:11

with the Lord one day is like 1,000 years, and 1,000 years like one day. ⁹ The Lord does not delay His promise, as some understand delay, but is patient with you, not wanting any to perish, but all to come to repentance.

¹⁰ But the Day of the Lord will come like a thief;ᵃ on that ₗdayⱼ the heavens will pass away with a loud noise, the elements will burn and be dissolved, and the earth and the works on it will be disclosed.ᵇ ¹¹ Since all these things are to be destroyed in this way, ₗit is clearⱼ what sort of people you should be in holy conduct and godliness ¹² as you wait for and earnestly desire the coming of the day of God, because of which the heavens will be on fire and be dissolved, and the elements will melt with the heat. ¹³ But based on His promise, we wait for new heavens and a new earth, where righteousness will dwell.

CONCLUSION

¹⁴ Therefore, dear friends, while you wait for these things, make every effort to be found in peace without spot or blemish before Him. ¹⁵ Also, regard the patience of our Lord as ₗan opportunity forⱼ salvation, just as our dear brother Paul, according to the wisdom given to him, has written to you. ¹⁶ He speaks about these things in all his letters, in which there are some matters that are hard to understand. The untaught and unstable twist them to their own destruction, as they also do with the rest of the Scriptures.

¹⁷ Therefore, dear friends, since you have been forewarned, be on your guard, so that you are not led away by the error of the immoral and fall from your own stability. ¹⁸ But grow in the grace and knowledge of our Lord and Savior Jesus Christ. To Him be the glory both now and to the day of eternity.ᶜ •Amen.ᵈ

Is Eternity Affecting You Every Day?

Knowing that God is preparing judgment should bring a sobering reality to Christians, helping us recognize what is eternally significant and what is not.

Since all these things are to be destroyed in this way, it is clear what sort of people you should be in holy conduct and godliness.

—2 Peter 3:11

Hold On to God for All He's Worth

Never take the good in your life for granted. If you do not hold on to it firmly, it may be lost in moments of laziness and temptation.

Dear friends, since you have been forewarned, be on your guard, so that you are not led away by the error of the immoral and fall from your own stability.

—2 Peter 3:17

ᵃ**3:10** Other mss add *in the night*
ᵇ**3:10** Other mss read *will be burned up*
ᶜ**3:18** Or *now and forever*
ᵈ**3:18** Other mss omit *Amen.*

JOHN

PROLOGUE

1 What was from the beginning,
what we have heard,
what we have seen with our eyes,
what we have observed,
and have touched with our hands,
concerning the Word of life—
2 that life was revealed,
and we have seen it
and we testify and declare to you
the eternal life that was with the Father
and was revealed to us—
3 what we have seen and heard
we also declare to you,
so that you may have fellowship along with us;
and indeed our fellowship is with the Father
and with His Son Jesus Christ.
4 We are writing these things[a]
so that our[b] joy may be complete.

FELLOWSHIP WITH GOD

5 Now this is the message we have heard from Him and declare to you: God is light, and there is absolutely no darkness in Him. 6 If we say, "We have fellowship with Him," and •walk in darkness, we are lying and are not practicing[c] the truth. 7 But if we walk in the light as He Himself is in the light, we have fellowship with one another, and the blood of Jesus His Son cleanses us from all sin. 8 If we say, "We have no sin," we are deceiving ourselves, and the truth is not in us. 9 If we

---

[a]1:4 Other mss add *to you*
[b]1:4 Other mss read *your*
[c]1:6 Or *not living according to*

WORD STUDY

Greek word: **koinonia**
[koy noh NEE ah]
Translation: **fellowship**
Uses in 1 John: **4**
Uses in John's writings: **4**
Uses in the NT: **19**
Key passage: **1 John 1:3,6,7**

Koinonia most often carries the sense of *communion* or *fellowship*, referring to an association involving close mutual relations. This idea of mutual involvement is seen in extra-biblical usage, where *koinonia* can refer to *marriage* (3 Macc 4:6). Because of a common Spirit, Christians have *fellowship* with God and one another (1 Jn 1:3,6,7). This kind of intimate *fellowship* was displayed among the sharing community of the early church (Ac 2:42). *Koinonia* may also refer to the way in which this fellowship is portrayed, namely, through *sharing, generosity*, or *participatory-feeling*. Paul speaks of the Corinthian church's generosity in *sharing* a financial gift (2 Co 9:13). By extension, *koinonia* may refer to the financial *contribution* itself (Rm 15:26). It may also express *participation* or *common fellowship* in a task or cause. Thus, believers have a common *participation* in the faith (Phm 6) and in Christ's body and blood (1 Co 10:16).

confess our sins, He is faithful and righteous to forgive us our sins and to cleanse us from all unrighteousness. ¹⁰ If we say, "We have not sinned," we make Him a liar, and His word is not in us.

2 My little children, I am writing you these things so that you may not sin. But if anyone does sin, we have an •advocate with the Father—Jesus Christ the righteous One. ² He Himself is the propitiation[a] for our sins, and not only for ours, but also for those of the whole world.

GOD'S COMMANDS

³ This is how we are sure that we have come to know Him: by keeping His commands. ⁴ The one who says, "I have come to know Him," without keeping His commands, is a liar, and the truth is not in him. ⁵ But whoever keeps His word, truly in him the love of God is perfected.[b] This is how we know we are in Him: ⁶ the one who says he remains in Him should •walk just as He walked.

⁷ Dear friends, I am not writing you a new command, but an old command that you have had from the beginning. The old command is the message you have heard. ⁸ Yet I am writing you a new command, which is true in Him and in you, because the darkness is passing away and the true light is already shining.

⁹ The one who says he is in the light but hates his brother is in the darkness until now. ¹⁰ The one who loves his brother remains in the light, and there is no cause for stumbling in him.[c] ¹¹ But the one who hates his brother is in the darkness, walks in the darkness, and doesn't know where he's going, because the darkness has blinded his eyes.

REASONS FOR WRITING

¹² I am writing to you, little children,
 because your sins have been forgiven
 on account of His name.
¹³ I am writing to you, fathers,

---

[a]**2:2** The word *propitiation* has to do with the removal of divine wrath. Jesus' death is the means that turns God's wrath from the sinner; see 2 Co 5:21.
[b]**2:5** Or *truly completed*
[c]**2:10** Or *in it*

because you have come to know the One who is
from the beginning.
I am writing to you, young men,
because you have had victory over the evil one.
14 I have written to you, children,
because you have come to know the Father.
I have written to you, fathers,
because you have come to know the One who is
from the beginning.
I have written to you, young men,
because you are strong,
God's word remains in you,
and you have had victory over the evil one.

A WARNING ABOUT THE WORLD

15 Do not love the world or the things that belong to[a]
the world. If anyone loves the world, love for the Father is not in him. 16 For everything that belongs to[b] the
world—the lust of the flesh, the lust of the eyes, and the
pride in one's lifestyle—is not from the Father, but is
from the world. 17 And the world with its lust is passing
away, but the one who does God's will remains forever.

THE LAST HOUR

18 Children, it is the last hour. And as you have heard,
"Antichrist is coming," even now many antichrists have
come. We know from this that it is the last hour. 19 They
went out from us, but they did not belong to us; for
if they had belonged to us, they would have remained
with us. However, they went out so that it might be
made clear that none of them belongs to us.
20 But you have an anointing from the Holy One, and
you all have knowledge.[c] 21 I have not written to you
because you don't know the truth, but because you
do know it, and because no lie comes from the truth.
22 Who is the liar, if not the one who denies that Jesus is
the •Messiah? He is the antichrist, the one who denies
the Father and the Son. 23 No one who denies the Son
can have the Father; he who confesses the Son has the
Father as well.

Can People Tell You Have Been with Jesus?

It is not necessary for those who have been truly transformed by Christ to convince others of the difference. The change will be obvious.

This is how we know we are in Him: the one who says he remains in Him should walk just as He walked.

—1 John 2:5b-6

Christian Love Is Seen in Loving Christians

A church cannot be on mission with the Father if its members are waging war with one another. A test of your love for God is to examine your love for others.

The one who says he is in the light but hates his brother is in the darkness until now. The one who loves his brother remains in the light, and there is no cause for stumbling in him.

—1 John 2:9-10

---

[a]2:15 Lit things in
[b]2:16 Lit that is in

[c]2:20 Other mss read and you
know all things

REMAINING WITH GOD

²⁴ What you have heard from the beginning must remain in you. If what you have heard from the beginning remains in you, then you will remain in the Son and in the Father. ²⁵ And this is the promise that He Himself made to us: eternal life. ²⁶ I have written these things to you about those who are trying to deceive you.

²⁷ The anointing you received from Him remains in you, and you don't need anyone to teach you. Instead, His anointing teaches you about all things, and is true and is not a lie; just as it has taught you, remain in Him.

GOD'S CHILDREN

²⁸ So now, little children, remain in Him, so that when He appears we may have boldness and not be ashamed before Him at His coming. ²⁹ If you know that He is righteous, you know this as well: everyone who does what is right has been born of Him. ¹ Look at how great a love[a] the Father has given us, that we should be called God's children. And we are! The reason the world does not know us is that it didn't know Him. ² Dear friends, we are God's children now, and what we will be has not yet been revealed. We know that when He appears, we will be like Him, because we will see Him as He is. ³ And everyone who has this hope in Him purifies himself just as He is pure.

⁴ Everyone who commits sin also breaks the law;[b] sin is the breaking of law. ⁵ You know that He was revealed so that He might take away sins,[c] and there is no sin in Him. ⁶ Everyone who remains in Him does not sin; everyone who sins has not seen Him or known Him.

⁷ Little children, let no one deceive you! The one who does what is right is righteous, just as He is righteous. ⁸ The one who commits sin is of the Devil, for the Devil has sinned from the beginning. The Son of God was revealed for this purpose: to destroy the Devil's works. ⁹ Everyone who has been born of God does not sin, because His[d] seed remains in him; he is not able to sin, because he has been born of God. ¹⁰ This is how God's children—and the Devil's children—are made evident.

When Confused, Consult the Scriptures

If you seek your counsel from ungodly people, you will always find yourself moving away from the direction God's Word commands. Hold fast to what you know to be true.

What you have heard from the beginning must remain in you. If what you have heard from the beginning remains in you, then you will remain in the Son and in the Father.

—1 John 2:24

Sin Was Out to Kill You, God to Save You

God established absolute moral and spiritual laws that we are free to ignore, but we do so at our own peril. His desire is to see us turn from our sins and walk in His freedom.

Everyone who commits sin also breaks the law; sin is the breaking of law. You know that He was revealed so that He might take away sins, and there is no sin in Him.

1 John 3:4-5

---

[a]**3:1** Or *at what sort of love*
[b]**3:4** Or *also commits iniquity*
[c]**3:5** Other mss read *our sins*
[d]**3:9** God's

LOVE'S IMPERATIVE

Whoever does not do what is right is not of God, especially the one who does not love his brother. ¹¹ For this is the message you have heard from the beginning: we should love one another, ¹² unlike Cain, who was of the evil one and murdered[a] his brother. And why did he murder him? Because his works were evil, and his brother's were righteous. ¹³ Do not be surprised, brothers, if the world hates you. ¹⁴ We know that we have passed from death to life because we love our brothers. The one who does not love remains in death. ¹⁵ Everyone who hates his brother is a murderer, and you know that no murderer has eternal life residing in him.

LOVE IN ACTION

¹⁶ This is how we have come to know love: He laid down His life for us. We should also lay down our lives for our brothers. ¹⁷ If anyone has this world's goods and sees his brother in need but shuts off his compassion from him—how can God's love reside in him?

¹⁸ Little children, we must not love in word or speech, but in deed and truth; ¹⁹ that is how we will know we are of the truth, and will convince our hearts in His presence, ²⁰ because if our hearts condemn us, God is greater than our hearts and knows all things.

²¹ Dear friends, if our hearts do not condemn ⌊us⌋ we have confidence before God, ²² and can receive whatever we ask from Him because we keep His commands and do what is pleasing in His sight. ²³ Now this is His command: that we believe in the name of His Son Jesus Christ, and love one another as He commanded us. ²⁴ The one who keeps His commands remains in Him, and He in him. And the way we know that He remains in us is from the Spirit He has given us.

THE SPIRIT OF TRUTH AND THE SPIRIT OF ERROR

4 Dear friends, do not believe every spirit, but test the spirits to determine if they are from God, because many false prophets have gone out into the world.

---

[a]3:12 Or *slaughtered*

Real Faith Rubs Some People the Wrong Way

The more your life illuminates the presence of Christ, the more you should expect opposition from others.

Do not be surprised, brothers, if the world hates you.

—1 John 3:13

There's No Freedom Like Christ's Freedom

Being assured of God's love for you sets you free to enjoy the numerous expressions of love He showers upon you each day.

Dear friends, if our hearts do not condemn us we have confidence before God, and can receive whatever we ask from Him because we keep His commands and do what is pleasing in His sight.

—1 John 3:21-22

WORD STUDY

Greek word: ***homologeo***
[hah mah lah GEH oh]

Translation: ***confess***

Uses in 1 John: **5**

Uses in John's writings: **10**

Uses in the NT: **26**

Key passage: **1 John 4:2-3, 15**

Homologeo (to confess) functions in a number of ways in the NT, and it plays an important part in John's theology (nearly 40 percent of its occurrences appear in John's writings). Most often, *homologeo* means *to assert, confess* or *declare publicly* (Mt 7:23; Mt 10:32 = Lk 12:8; Jn 9:22; 12:42; Ac 23:8). This outward confession is viewed as a window into the person's actual beliefs (Rm 10:10). In this sense, *homologeo* may refer to a public declaration of agreement with some religious confession or set of doctrines (Jn 1:20; Ac 24:14; Rm 10:9,10; 1 Tm 6:12; Ti 1:16). The *confession* spoken of in 1 John 1:9 appears to be private but does not exclude public confession. Elsewhere, *homologeo* stresses the idea of *agreement* or *acknowledgment* about something (Heb 11:13), and it may mean *to assure* or *promise* (Mt 14:7; Ac 7:17) and also *to praise* (Heb 13:15).

2 This is how you know the Spirit of God: Every spirit who confesses that Jesus Christ has come in the flesh[a] is from God. 3 But every spirit who does not confess Jesus[b] is not from God. This is the spirit of the antichrist; you have heard that he is coming, and he is already in the world now.

4 You are from God, little children, and you have conquered them, because the One who is in you is greater than the one who is in the world. 5 They are from the world. Therefore what they say is from the world, and the world listens to them. 6 We are from God. Anyone who knows God listens to us; anyone who is not from God does not listen to us. From this we know the Spirit of truth and the spirit of deception.

KNOWING GOD THROUGH LOVE

7 Dear friends, let us love one another, because love is from God, and everyone who loves has been born of God and knows God. 8 The one who does not love does not know God, because God is love. 9 God's love was revealed among us in this way:[c] God sent His •One and Only Son into the world so that we might live through Him. 10 Love consists in this: not that we loved God, but that He loved us and sent His Son to be the[d] propitiation[e] for our sins. 11 Dear friends, if God loved us in this way, we also must love one another. 12 No one has ever seen God.[f] If we love one another, God remains in[g] us and His love is perfected in us.

13 This is how we know that we remain in Him and He in us: He has given to us from His Spirit. 14 And we have seen and we testify that the Father has sent the Son as Savior of the world. 15 Whoever confesses[h] that Jesus is the Son of God—God remains in him and he in God. 16 And we have come to know and to believe the love that God has for us. God is love, and the one who remains in love remains in God, and God remains in him.

---

[a]**4:2** Or *confesses Jesus to be the Christ come in the flesh*
[b]**4:3** Other mss read *confess that Jesus has come in the flesh*
[c]**4:9** Or *revealed in us*
[d]**4:10** Or *a*
[e]**4:10** The word *propitiation* has to do with the removal of divine wrath. Jesus' death is the means that turns God's wrath from the sinner; see 2 Co 5:21.
[f]**4:12** Since God is an infinite being, no one can see Him in His absolute essential nature; see Ex 33:18-23.
[g]**4:12** Or *remains among*
[h]**4:15** Or *acknowledges*

¹⁷ In this, love is perfected with us so that we may have confidence in the day of judgment; for we are as He is in this world. ¹⁸ There is no fear in love; instead, perfect love drives out fear, because fear involves punishment.ᵃ So the one who fears has not reached perfection in love. ¹⁹ We loveᵇ because He first loved us.

KEEPING GOD'S COMMANDS

²⁰ If anyone says, "I love God," yet hates his brother, he is a liar. For the person who does not love his brother whom he has seen cannot love God whom he has not seen.ᶜ ²¹ And we have this command from Him: the one who loves God must also love his brother.

5 Everyone who believes that Jesus is the •Messiah has been born of God, and everyone who loves the parent also loves his child. ² This is how we know that we love God's children when we love God and obeyᵈ His commands. ³ For this is what love for God is: to keep His commands. Now His commands are not a burden, ⁴ because whatever has been born of God conquers the world. This is the victory that has conquered the world: our faith. ⁵ And who is the one who conquers the world but the one who believes that Jesus is the Son of God?

THE SURENESS OF GOD'S TESTIMONY

⁶ Jesus Christ—He is the One who came by water and blood; not by water only, but by water and by blood. And the Spirit is the One who testifies, because the Spirit is the truth. ⁷ For there are three that testify:ᵉ ⁸ the Spirit, the water, and the blood—and these three are in agreement. ⁹ If we accept the testimony of men, God's testimony is greater, because it is God's testimony that He has given about His Son. ¹⁰ (The one who believes in the Son of God has the testimony in himself. The one who does not believe God has made Him a liar,

People See God in Us When We Get Along

Your life will not convince those around you of the reality of Jesus if you cannot live in unity with your fellow Christians.

No one has ever seen God. If we love one another, God remains in us and His love is perfected in us.

—1 John 4:12

God Has Made the Way to Him Simple

Confessing Christ doesn't require eloquent speeches or theological training. We simply declare Him to be who He says He is—the Son of God—even the Lord of our lives.

Whoever confesses that Jesus is the Son of God—God remains in him and he in God.

—1 John 4:15

ᵃ**4:18** Or *fear has its own punishment* or *torment*
ᵇ**4:19** Other mss add *Him*
ᶜ**4:20** Other mss read *seen, how is he able to love ... seen?* (as a question)
ᵈ**5:2** Other mss read *keep*

ᵉ**5:7-8** Other mss (the Lat Vg and a few late Gk mss) read *testify in heaven, the Father, the Word, and the Holy Spirit, and these three are One.* ⁸ *And there are three who bear witness on earth:*

WORD STUDY

Greek word: **eidolon**
[AY doh lahn]
TYranslation: **idol**
Uses in 1 John: **1**
Uses in John's writings: **7**
Uses in the NT: **11**
Key passage: **1 John 5:21**

In the Greek OT, *eidolon* (*idol*) refers to the physical representation of a god (Ex 20:4, Dt 5:8). By extension, it points not only to that physical representation but to the god lying behind that form. This is evidenced by the fact that *idols* were worshipped (Ex 20:5, Nm 25:2, Dt 5:9) and were even understood to have demonic powers (Dt 32:17). This usage provides the background for the NT use of *eidolon*. Paul regards *idols* as false gods, powerless compared to the true God (1 Th 1:9). He acknowledges the existence of demonic powers behind *idols* but understands them to have no real power over the Christian, who knows that *idols* are but false gods (1 Co 8:4-7; 10:19-21). Christians are exhorted to abstain from association with *idols* and the false gods they represent (Ac 15:20; 1 Jn 5:21), for there is only one God (1 Co 8:7).

because he has not believed in the testimony that God has given about His Son.) [11] And this is the testimony: God has given us eternal life, and this life is in His Son.

[12] The one who has the Son has life. The one who doesn't have the Son of God does not have life. [13] I have written these things to you who believe in the name of the Son of God, so that you may know that you have eternal life.

EFFECTIVE PRAYER

[14] Now this is the confidence we have before Him: whenever we ask anything according to His will, He hears us. [15] And if we know that He hears whatever we ask, we know that we have what we have asked Him for.

[16] If anyone sees his brother committing a sin that does not bring death, he should ask, and God[a] will give life to him—to those who commit sin that doesn't bring death. There is sin[b] that brings death. I am not saying he should pray about that. [17] All unrighteousness is sin, and there is sin that does not bring death.

CONCLUSION

[18] We know that everyone who has been born of God does not sin, but the One[c] who is born of God keeps him,[d] [e] and the evil one does not touch him.

[19] We know that we are of God, and the whole world is under the sway of the evil one.

[20] And we know that the Son of God has come and has given us understanding so that we may know the true One.[f] We are in the true One—that is, in His Son Jesus Christ. He is the true God and eternal life.

[21] Little children, guard yourselves from idols.

[a]**5:16** Lit *He*
[b]**5:16** Or *is a sin*
[c]**5:18** Jesus Christ
[d]**5:18** Other mss read *himself*
[e]**5:18** Or *the one who is born of God keeps himself*
[f]**5:20** Other mss read *the true God*

JOHN

GREETING

T he Elder:[a]
    To the elect lady[b] and her children, whom I love
in truth—and not only I, but also all who have come to
know the truth— 2 because of the truth that remains in
us and will be with us forever.

3 Grace, mercy, and peace will be with us from God
the Father and from Jesus Christ, the Son of the Father,
in truth and love.

TRUTH AND DECEPTION

4 I was very glad to find some of your children •walk-
ing in truth, in keeping with a command we have received from the Father. 5 So now I urge you, lady—not
as if I were writing you a new command, but one we
have had from the beginning—that we love one another. 6 And this is love: that we walk according to His
commands. This is the command as you have heard it
from the beginning: you must walk in love.[c]

7 Many deceivers have gone out into the world; they
do not confess the coming of Jesus Christ in the flesh.[d]
This is the deceiver and the antichrist. 8 Watch yourselves so that you don't lose what we[e] have worked
for, but you may receive a full reward. 9 Anyone who
does not remain in the teaching about Christ, but goes
beyond it, does not have God. The one who remains
in that teaching, this one has both the Father and the
Son. 10 If anyone comes to you and does not bring this

---

[a]1 Or *Presbyter*
[b]1 Or *Kyria*, a proper name; probably a literary figure for a local
church known to John; the *children*
would be its members.

[c]6 Lit *in it*
[d]7 Or *confess Jesus Christ as coming in the flesh*
[e]8 Other mss read *you*

teaching, do not receive him into your home, and don't say, "Welcome," to him; [11] for the one who says, "Welcome," to him shares in his evil works.

FAREWELL

[12] Though I have many things to write to you, I don't want to do so with paper and ink. Instead, I hope to be with you and talk face to face[a] so that our joy may be complete.

[13] The children of your elect sister send you greetings.

Grow Up to Be Like Your Heavenly Father

God is pleased whenever He finds someone striving to live a righteous life and bring glory to Him. The world may not accord any special status to you, but you will know that you are cherished by God.

I was very glad to find some of your children walking in truth, in keeping with a command we have received from the Father.

—2 John 4

It's Always Better To Walk Together

It's easy in today's world to live in isolation from our fellow believers, but sharing our lives with others in the church is one of the most important keys to growth and maturity.

Though I have many things to write to you, I don't want to do so with paper and ink. Instead, I hope to be with you and talk face to face so that our joy may be complete.

—2 John 12

---

[a]12 Lit *mouth to mouth*

JOHN

GREETING

T he Elder:
    To my dear friend[a] Gaius, whom I love in truth.
² Dear friend,[b] I pray that you may prosper in every
way and be in good health, just as your soul prospers.
³ For I was very glad when some brothers came and
testified to your ⌞faithfulness⌟ to the truth—how you are
•walking in the truth. ⁴ I have no greater joy than this:
to hear that my children are walking in the truth.

GAIUS COMMENDED

⁵ Dear friend,[b] you are showing your faith[c] by whatever you do for the brothers, and this ⌞you are doing⌟
for strangers; ⁶ they have testified to your love before
the church. You will do well to send them on their journey in a manner worthy of God, ⁷ since they set out for
the sake of the name, accepting nothing from pagans.
⁸ Therefore, we ought to support such men, so that we
can be co-workers with[d] the truth.

DIOTREPHES AND DEMETRIUS

⁹ I wrote something to the church, but Diotrephes,
who loves to have first place among them, does not
receive us. ¹⁰ This is why, if I come, I will remind him
of the works he is doing, slandering us with malicious
words. And he is not satisfied with that! He not only
refuses to welcome the brothers himself, but he even
stops those who want to do so and expels them from
the church.

---

[a]1 Or *my beloved*
[b]2,5 Or *Beloved*

[c]5 Lit *are doing faith*
[d]8 Or *co-workers for*

[11] Dear friend,[a] do not imitate what is evil, but what is good. The one who does good is of God; the one who does evil has not seen God. [12] Demetrius has a ⌊good⌋ testimony from everyone, and from the truth itself. And we also testify for him, and you know that our testimony is true.

FAREWELL

[13] I have many things to write you, but I don't want to write to you with pen and ink. [14] I hope to see you soon, and we will talk face to face.[b]

Peace be with you. The friends send you greetings. Greet the friends by name.

Is Your Witness More Than Just Talk?

It is much easier to talk about the victorious Christian life than it is to live it. Are your words being backed up by the love and power of God in your life?

Dear friend, you are showing your faith by whatever you do for the brothers, and this you are doing for strangers; they have testified to your love before the church.

—3 John 5-6a

Let Nothing Distract You from God's Will

The decisions and disobedience of others will not cancel God's will for you. Other people's actions will affect you, but no one can prevent what He wants to do through you.

Dear friend, do not imitate what is evil, but what is good. The one who does good is of God; the one who does evil has not seen God.

—3 John 11

[b]11 Or *Beloved*   [c]14 Lit *mouth to mouth*

JUDE

GREETING

J ude, a slave of Jesus Christ, and a brother of James:
To those who are the called, loved[a] by God the Father and kept by Jesus Christ.
² May mercy, peace, and love be multiplied to you.

JUDE'S PURPOSE IN WRITING

³ Dear friends, although I was eager to write you about our common salvation, I found it necessary to write and exhort you to contend for the faith that was delivered to the saints once for all. ⁴ For certain men, who were designated for this judgment long ago, have come in by stealth; they are ungodly, turning the grace of our God into promiscuity and denying our only Master and Lord, Jesus Christ.

APOSTATES: PAST AND PRESENT

⁵ Now I want to remind you, though you know all these things: the Lord, having first of all[b] saved a people out of Egypt, later destroyed those who did not believe; ⁶ and He has kept, with eternal chains in darkness for the judgment of the great day, angels who did not keep their own position but deserted their proper dwelling. ⁷ In the same way, Sodom and Gomorrah and the cities around them committed sexual immorality and practiced perversions,[c] just as they did, and serve as an example by undergoing the punishment of eternal fire.

⁸ Nevertheless, these dreamers likewise defile their flesh, despise authority, and blaspheme glorious beings.

---

[a]1 Other mss read *sanctified*
[b]5 Other mss place *first of all* after *remind you*

[c]7 Lit *and went after other flesh*

WORD STUDY

Greek word: *despotes*[dehs
PAH tays]
Translation: **Master**
Uses in Jude: **1**
Uses in the NT: **10**
Key passage: **Jude 4**

Despotes (*Master*) refers to one who holds authority and power over the life and affairs of another person. Most frequently, *despotes* appears as a title for God or Christ. The term emphasizes God's sovereignty, variously highlighting His right to create, judge, or save. Three times the saints use *despotes* when prayerfully entreating their Sovereign (Lk 2:29; Ac 4:24; Rv 6:10). Paul emphasizes God's sovereign right as *Master* to use His people as He chooses (2 Tm 2:21). Likewise, Christ is Sovereign and Lord over salvation, worthy of the saints' obedience (Jd 4), and He is the *Master* who purchased men with His own blood (2 Pt 2:1). Elsewhere, *despotes* may refer to an earthly *master* with a slave in the service of his household. In Christian ethic, slaves are exhorted to respect their *masters* (1 Tm 6:1-2) and to submit to them in everything (Ti 2:9; 1 Pt 2:18).

9 Yet Michael the archangel, when he was disputing with the Devil in a debate about Moses' body, did not dare bring an abusive condemnation against him, but said, "The Lord rebuke you!" 10 But these people blaspheme anything they don't understand, and what they know by instinct, like unreasoning animals—they destroy themselves with these things. 11 Woe to them! For they have traveled in the way of Cain, have abandoned themselves to the error of Balaam for profit, and have perished in Korah's rebellion.

THE APOSTATES' DOOM

12 These are the ones who are like dangerous reefs[a] at your love feasts. They feast with you, nurturing only themselves without fear. They are waterless clouds carried along by winds; trees in late autumn—fruitless, twice dead, pulled out by the roots; 13 wild waves of the sea, foaming up their shameful deeds; wandering stars for whom is reserved the blackness of darkness forever!

14 And Enoch, in the seventh ⌊generation⌋ from Adam, prophesied about them:

> Look! The Lord comes[b] with thousands
>   of His holy ones
> 15 to execute judgment on all,
>   and to convict them[c]
> of all their ungodly deeds that they have done
>   in an ungodly way,
> and of all the harsh things ungodly sinners
>   have said against Him.

16 These people are discontented grumblers, •walking according to their desires; their mouths utter arrogant words, flattering people for their own advantage.

17 But you, dear friends, remember the words foretold by the apostles of our Lord Jesus Christ; 18 they told you, "In the end time there will be scoffers walking according to their own ungodly desires." 19 These people create divisions and are merely natural, not having the Spirit.

---

[a]12 Or *like spots*
[b]14 Or *came*
[c]15 Lit *convict all*

EXHORTATION AND BENEDICTION

20 But you, dear friends, building yourselves up in your most holy faith and praying in the Holy Spirit, 21 keep yourselves in the love of God, expecting the mercy of our Lord Jesus Christ for eternal life. 22 Have mercy on some who doubt; 23 save others by snatching ⌊them⌋ from the fire; on others have mercy in fear, hating even the garment defiled by the flesh.

24 Now to Him who is able to protect you from stumbling and to make you stand in the presence of His glory, blameless and with great joy, 25 to the only God our Savior, through Jesus Christ our Lord,ᵃ be glory, majesty, power, and authority before all time,ᵇ now, and forever. •Amen.

Avoid Sin Like the Plague

The devil is subtle and can easily deceive you into adopting the world's way of thinking. But keep God's Word always before you, wanting nothing to do with your "old man."

On others have mercy in fear, hating even the garment defiled by the flesh.
—Jude 23b

How Do You Love Him? Try Counting the Ways

You should never have difficulty thinking of reasons why God deserves your praise. There is no end to the reasons for worshiping God.

Now to Him who is able to protect you from stumbling and to make you stand in the presence of His glory, blameless and with great joy, to the only God our Savior, through Jesus Christ our Lord, be glory, majesty, power, and authority before all time, now, and forever. Amen.
—Jude 24-25

ᵃ25 Other mss omit *through Jesus Christ our Lord*   ᵇ25 Other mss omit *before all time*

THE

REVELATION

OF JESUS CHRIST

PROLOGUE

1 The revelation of[a] Jesus Christ that God gave Him to show His •slaves what must quickly[b] take place. He sent it and signified it[c] through His angel to His slave John, [2] who testified to God's word and to the testimony[d] about Jesus Christ, in all he saw.[e] [3] Blessed is the one who reads and blessed are those who hear the words of this prophecy and keep[f] what is written in it, because the time is near!

[4] John:

To the seven churches in the province of Asia.[g]

Grace and peace to you from[h] the One who is, who was, and who is coming; from the seven spirits[i] before His throne; [5] and from Jesus Christ, the faithful witness, the firstborn from the dead and the ruler of the kings of the earth.

To Him who loves us and has set us free[j] from our sins by His blood, [6] and made us a kingdom,[k] priests[l] to His God and Father—to Him be the glory and dominion forever and ever. •Amen.

[7] **Look! He is coming with the clouds,**
and every eye will see Him,
including those who pierced[m] Him.
And all the families of the earth[n] [o]

---

[a]**1:1** Or *Revelation of*, or *A revelation of*
[b]**1:1** Or *soon*
[c]**1:1** Made it known through symbols
[d]**1:2** Or *witness*
[e]**1:2** Lit *as many as he saw*
[f]**1:3** Or *follow*, or *obey*
[g]**1:4** Lit *churches in Asia*; that is, the Roman province that is now a part of modern Turkey

[h]**1:4** Other mss add *God*
[i]**1:4** Or *the sevenfold Spirit*
[j]**1:5** Other mss read *has washed us*
[k]**1:6** Other mss read *kings and*
[l]**1:6** Or *made us into* (or *to be*) *a kingdom of priests*; see Ex 19:6
[m]**1:7** Or *impaled*
[n]**1:7** Or *All the tribes of the land*
[o]**1:7** Gn 12:3; 28:14; Zch 14:17

will mourn over Him.[a] [b]
This is certain. Amen.

[8] "I am the •Alpha and the Omega," says the Lord God, "the One who is, who was, and who is coming, the Almighty."

JOHN'S VISION OF THE RISEN LORD

[9] I, John, your brother and partner in the tribulation, kingdom, and perseverance in Jesus, was on the island called Patmos because of God's word and the testimony about Jesus.[c] [10] I was in the Spirit[d] [e] on the Lord's day,[f] and I heard behind me a loud voice like a trumpet [11] saying, "Write on a scroll[g] what you see and send it to the seven churches: Ephesus, Smyrna, Pergamum, Thyatira, Sardis, Philadelphia, and Laodicea."

[12] I turned to see the voice that was speaking to me. When I turned I saw seven gold lampstands, [13] and among the lampstands was One like the •Son of Man,[h] dressed in a long robe, and with a gold sash wrapped around His chest. [14] His head and hair were white like wool—white as snow, His eyes like a fiery flame, [15] His feet like fine bronze fired in a furnace, and His voice like the sound of cascading[i] waters. [16] In His right hand He had seven stars; from His mouth came a sharp two-edged sword; and His face was shining like the sun at midday.[j]

[17] When I saw Him, I fell at His feet like a dead man. He laid His right hand on me, and said, "Don't be afraid! I am the First and the Last, [18] and the Living One. I was dead, but look—I am alive forever and ever, and I hold the keys of death and •Hades. [19] Therefore write what you have seen, what is, and what will take place after this. [20] The secret[k] of the seven stars you saw in My right hand, and of the seven gold lampstands, is this: the seven stars are the angels[l] of the seven churches, and the seven lampstands[m] are the seven churches.

WORD STUDY

Greek word: **pantokrator**
[pahn tah KRAH tohr]

Translation: **Almighty**

Uses in Revelation: **9**

Uses in John's writings: **9**

Uses in the NT: **10**

Key passage: **Revelation 1:8**

Pantokrator means *almighty, omnipotent, all-powerful.* In the Greek OT, the word frequently translates the Hb *Yahweh tseva'ot* (LORD of Hosts), which stresses God's power over forces opposed to Him and His people. *Pantokrator* also translates Hb *Shaddai* (*the Almighty*), a term emphasizing God's power and authority over all things. In every instance in the OT, the one true God is in view.

In the NT, every occurrence of *pantokrator* refers to God the Father. In the book of Revelation, it occurs with the expressions *Lord God* (1:8; 4:8; 11:17; 15:3; 16:7; 19:6; 21:22), *God* (16:14; 19:15), and variations of the phrase "the One who is, who was, and who is coming" (1:8; 4:8; 11:17). John uses these epithets (along with many others) to describe the supremacy of God over all things including human history. God Almighty is actively working to bring everything into conformity with His will.

---

[a]**1:7** Or *will wail because of Him*
[b]**1:7** Dn 7:13; Zch 12:10
[c]**1:9** Lit *the witness of Jesus*
[d]**1:10** Lit *I became in the Spirit* or *in spirit*
[e]**1:10** John was brought by God's Spirit into a realm of spiritual vision.
[f]**1:10** Sunday

[g]**1:11** Or *book*
[h]**1:13** Or *like a son of man*
[i]**1:15** Lit *many*
[j]**1:16** Lit *like the sun shines in its power*
[k]**1:20** Or *mystery*
[l]**1:20** Or *messengers*
[m]**1:20** Other mss add *that you saw*

THE LETTERS TO THE SEVEN CHURCHES

THE LETTER TO EPHESUS

2 "To the angel[a] of the church in Ephesus write:
"The One who holds the seven stars in His right hand and who walks among the seven gold lampstands says: 2 I know your works, your labor, and your endurance, and that you cannot tolerate evil. You have tested those who call themselves apostles and are not, and you have found them to be liars. 3 You also possess endurance and have tolerated ⌊many things⌋ because of My name, and have not grown weary. 4 But I have this against you: you have abandoned the love ⌊you had⌋ at first. 5 Remember then how far you have fallen; repent, and do the works you did at first. Otherwise, I will come to you[b] and remove your lampstand from its place—unless you repent. 6 Yet you do have this: you hate the practices of the Nicolaitans, which I also hate.

7 "Anyone who has an ear should listen to what the Spirit says to the churches. I will give the victor the right to eat from the tree of life, which is in[c] the paradise of God.

THE LETTER TO SMYRNA

8 "To the angel of the church in Smyrna write:
"The First and the Last, the One who was dead and came to life, says: 9 I know your[d] tribulation and poverty, yet you are rich. ⌊I know⌋ the slander of those who say they are Jews and are not, but are a •synagogue of Satan. 10 Don't be afraid of what you are about to suffer. Look, the Devil is about to throw some of you into prison to test you, and you will have tribulation for 10 days. Be faithful until death, and I will give you the crown[e] of life.

11 "Anyone who has an ear should listen to what the Spirit says to the churches. The victor will never be harmed by the second death.

Love Will Keep You Going the Right Way

It is impossible for a Christian to be filled with love *for* God and not to be on mission *with* God.

"I have this against you: you have abandoned the love you had at first."

—Revelation 2:4

---

[a]2:1 Or *messenger* here and elsewhere
[b]2:5 Other mss add *quickly*
[c]2:7 Other mss read *in the midst of*
[d]2:9 Other mss add *works and*
[e]2:10 Or *wreath*

THE LETTER TO PERGAMUM

¹² "To the angel of the church in Pergamum write:

"The One who has the sharp, two-edged sword says:
¹³ I know ª where you live—where Satan's throne is!
And you are holding on to My name and did not deny
your faith in Me,ᵇ even in the days of Antipas, My faithful witness, who was killed among you, where Satan
lives. ¹⁴ But I have a few things against you. You have
some there who hold to the teaching of Balaam, who
taught Balak to place a stumbling blockᶜ in front of the
sons of Israel: to eat meat sacrificed to idols and to
commit sexual immorality.ᵈ ¹⁵ In the same way, you also
have those who hold to the teaching of the Nicolaitans.ᵉ
¹⁶ Therefore repent! Otherwise, I will come to you
quickly and fight against them with the sword of My
mouth.

¹⁷ "Anyone who has an ear should listen to what the
Spirit says to the churches. I will give the victor some
of the hidden manna.ᶠ I will also give him a white stone,
and on the stone a new name is inscribed that no one
knows except the one who receives it.

THE LETTER TO THYATIRA

¹⁸ "To the angel of the church in Thyatira write:

"The Son of God, the One whose eyes are like a fiery
flame, and whose feet are like fine bronze says: ¹⁹ I
know your works—your love, faithfulness,ᵍ service,
and endurance. Your last works are greater than the
first. ²⁰ But I have this against you: you tolerate the
woman Jezebel, who calls herself a prophetess, and
teaches and deceives My slaves to commit sexual immo-
ralityᵈ and to eat meat sacrificed to idols. ²¹ I gave her
time to repent, but she does not want to repent of her
sexual immorality.ʰ ²² Look! I will throw her into a sick-
bed, and those who commit adultery with her into great
tribulation, unless they repent of herⁱ practices. ²³ I will
kill her children with the plague.ʲ Then all the churches

WORD STUDY

Greek word: **nikao**
[nih KAH oh]

Translation: **be victorious,
conquer**

Uses in Revelation: **17**

Uses in John's writings: **24**

Uses in the NT: **28**

Key passage: **Revelation 2:7**

Nikao means *to be victorious* or
to conquer, and the related noun
nike means *victory*, usually in a
military sense but also in a judicial context (Rm 3:4). Outside
of John's writings, *nikao* occurs
only four times (Lk 11:22; Rm 3:4;
12:21). In John's theology, Christ
has already conquered the forces
of evil (Jn 16:33; Rv 5:5). Even
though these forces may gain
temporary, provisional victories
over the saints (Rv 11:7; 13:7), it
is Christ who has won the defini-
tive victory over evil, and those
whom He has enlisted in the fight
will conquer with Him (Rv 3:21;
15:2; 17:14). Each of the messages
to the Asia Minor churches ends
with a promise to *the victor* (Rv
2:7,11,17,26-27;3:5,12,21), to those
who overcome evil not through
human effort but through solidar-
ity with Christ (Jn 5:4-5; 1 Jn 4:4;
5:5; Rv 12:11). These *victors* will
inherit the new heaven and new
earth (Rv 21:7).

ª**2:13** Other mss add *your works
and*
ᵇ**2:13** Or *deny My faith*
ᶜ**2:14** Or *to place a trap*
ᵈ**2:14,20** Or *commit fornication*
ᵉ**2:15** Other mss add *which I hate*
ᶠ**2:17** Other mss add *to eat*
ᵍ**2:19** Or *faith*
ʰ**2:21** Or *her fornication*
ⁱ**2:22** Other mss read *their*
ʲ**2:23** Or *I will surely kill her children*

will know that I am the One who examines minds[a] and hearts, and I will give to each of you according to your works. [24] I say to the rest of you in Thyatira, who do not hold this teaching, who haven't known the deep things[b] of Satan—as they say—I do not put any other burden on you. [25] But hold on to what you have until I come. [26] The victor and the one who keeps My works to the end: I will give him authority over the nations—

> [27] **and He will shepherd[c] them**
> **with an iron scepter;**
> **He will shatter them like pottery[d]** —

just as I have received ⌊this⌋ from My Father. [28] I will also give him the morning star.

[29] "Anyone who has an ear should listen to what the Spirit says to the churches.

THE LETTER TO SARDIS

3 "To the angel of the church in Sardis write:
"The One who has the seven spirits of God and the seven stars says: I know your works; you have a reputation[e] for being alive, but you are dead. [2] Be alert and strengthen[f] what remains, which is about to die, for I have not found your works complete before My God. [3] Remember therefore what you have received and heard; keep it, and repent. But if you are not alert, I will come[g] like a thief, and you have no idea at what hour I will come against you.[h] [4] But you have a few people[i] in Sardis who have not defiled[j] their clothes, and they will walk with Me in white, because they are worthy. [5] In the same way, the victor will be dressed in white clothes, and I will never erase his name from the book of life, but will acknowledge his name before My Father and before His angels.

[6] "Anyone who has an ear should listen to what the Spirit says to the churches.

THE LETTER TO PHILADELPHIA

[7] "To the angel of the church in Philadelphia write:

The Right Response to God's Word Is to Obey

When you hear from the Father, you have an immediate agenda for your life—obedience.

"Anyone who has an ear should listen to what the Spirit says to the churches."

—Revelation 2:29

What Is God's View of Your Life?

If we only compare our personal holiness to those around us, we may be deceived into believing that we are living a consecrated life.

"Be alert and strengthen what remains, which is about to die, for I have not found your works complete before My God."

—Revelation 3:2

---

[a]2:23 Lit *kidneys*
[b]2:24 Or *the secret things*
[c]2:27 Or *rule*; see 19:15
[d]2:27 Ps 2:9
[e]3:1 Lit *have a name*

[f]3:2 Other mss read *guard*
[g]3:3 Other mss add *upon you*
[h]3:3 Or *upon you*
[i]3:4 Lit *few names*
[j]3:4 Or *soiled*

"The Holy One, the True One, the One who has the key of David, who opens and no one will close, and closes and no one opens says: [8] I know your works. Because you have limited strength, have kept My word, and have not denied My name, look, I have placed before you an open door that no one is able to close. [9] Take note! I will make those from the •synagogue of Satan, who claim to be Jews and are not, but are lying—note this—I will make them come and bow down at your feet, and they will know that I have loved you. [10] Because you have kept My command to endure,[a] I will also keep you from the hour of testing that is going to come over the whole world to test those who live on the earth. [11] I am coming quickly. Hold on to what you have, so that no one takes your crown. [12] The victor: I will make him a pillar in the sanctuary of My God, and he will never go out again. I will write on him the name of My God, and the name of the city of My God—the new Jerusalem, which comes down out of heaven from My God—and My new name.

[13] "Anyone who has an ear should listen to what the Spirit says to the churches.

THE LETTER TO LAODICEA

[14] "To the angel of the church in Laodicea write:

"The •Amen, the faithful and true Witness, the Originator[b] of God's creation says: [15] I know your works, that you are neither cold nor hot. I wish that you were cold or hot. [16] So, because you are lukewarm, and neither hot nor cold, I am going to vomit[c] you out of My mouth. [17] Because you say, 'I'm rich; I have become wealthy, and need nothing,' and you don't know that you are wretched, pitiful, poor, blind, and naked, [18] I advise you to buy from Me gold refined in the fire so that you may be rich, and white clothes so that you may be dressed and your shameful nakedness not be exposed, and ointment to spread on your eyes so that you may see. [19] As many as I love, I rebuke and discipline. So be committed[d] and repent. [20] Listen! I stand at the door and knock. If anyone hears My voice and opens

WORD STUDY

Greek word: **arche**
[ahr KAY]

Translation: **Originator, beginning**

Uses in Revelation: **3**

Uses in John's writings: **21**

Uses in the NT: **55**

Key passage: **Revelation 3:14**

Arche indicates the chief position, either in time (*beginning, commencement*), rank/position (*ruler, governor, originator*), or location (*corner*; Ac 10:11). It can also refer to the domain of someone's authority (i.e., their *rule*; Lk 20:20; 1 Co 15:24). Other related terms include the verb *archo* (to rule), *archomai* (to begin), and the noun *archon* (ruler). In John's writings, *arche* always refers to sequential priority, such as the *beginning* of the world (Jn 1:1,2; 1 Jn 1:1; 2:13-14), of some aspect of Jesus' ministry (Jn 2:11; 6:64; 8:25; 15:27; 16:4), of Satan's rebellion against God (Jn 8:44; 1 Jn 3:8), and of Christian witness (1 Jn 2:7,24; 3:11; 2 Jn 5,6). In Revelation, Jesus is called the "*Originator* of God's creation" (3:14) as well as "the *Beginning* and the End" (Rv 22:13), a title shared by God the Father (Rv 21:6), indicating that God started everything and will end everything.

---

[a]**3:10** Lit *My word of endurance*
[b]**3:14** Or *Ruler*, or *Source*, or *Beginning*
[c]**3:16** Or *spit*
[d]**3:19** Or *be zealous*

WORD STUDY

Greek word: *hagios*
[HAH gee ahss]
Translation: *holy*
Uses in Revelation: **25**
Uses in John's writings: **31**
Uses in the NT: **233**
Key passage: **Revelation 4:8**

Hagios (*holy*) frequently refers to that which is dedicated or set apart to God's service, describing things that have a derived holiness. This includes the church (1 Co 3:17; Eph 5:26; 1 Pt 2:9), as well as individual Christians (Rm 12:1). Indeed, *hagios* may be translated "saints" in reference to believers, who are set apart by God for His service (Mt 27:52; Ac 9:13; Rm 1:7; 1 Co 1:2; Rv 5:8). The word also describes Jerusalem (Mt 4:5; Rv 21:2,10; 22:19), the various parts of the sanctuary (Mt 24:15; Heb 9:1-3), angels (Mk 8:38), OT prophets (Lk 1:70), Christian apostles and prophets (Eph 3:5), divine revelation (Rm 1:2; 2 Pt 2:21), and various geographical locations (Ac 7:33; 2 Pt 1:18). Additionally, *hagios* may describe what is *holy* by nature, namely, God the Father (Jn 17:11; 1 Pt 1:15; Rv 4:8), Jesus Christ (Mk 1:24; Ac 3:14), and the Spirit (Mt 3:11; Ac 1:5).

the door, I will come in to him and have dinner with him, and he with Me. 21 The victor: I will give him the right to sit with Me on My throne, just as I also won the victory and sat down with My Father on His throne.

22 "Anyone who has an ear should listen to what the Spirit says to the churches."

THE THRONE ROOM OF HEAVEN

4 After this I looked, and there in heaven was an open door. The first voice that I had heard speaking to me like a trumpet said, "Come up here, and I will show you what must take place after this."

2 Immediately I was in the Spirit,[a] and there in heaven a throne was set. One was seated on the throne, 3 and the One seated[b] looked like jasper[c] and carnelian[d] stone. A rainbow that looked like an emerald surrounded the throne. 4 Around that throne were 24 thrones, and on the thrones sat 24 elders dressed in white clothes, with gold crowns on their heads. 5 From the throne came flashes of lightning, rumblings, and thunder. Burning before the throne were seven fiery torches, which are the seven spirits of God. 6 Also before the throne was something like a sea of glass, similar to crystal. In the middle[e] and around the throne were four living creatures covered with eyes in front and in back. 7 The first living creature was like a lion; the second living creature was like a calf; the third living creature had a face like a man; and the fourth living creature was like a flying eagle. 8 Each of the four living creatures had six wings; they were covered with eyes around and inside. Day and night they never stop,[f] saying:

Holy, holy, holy,[g]
Lord God, the Almighty,
who was, who is, and who is coming.

9 Whenever the living creatures give glory, honor, and thanks to the One seated on the throne, the One who lives forever and ever, 10 the 24 elders fall down before

---

a4:2 Lit *I became in the Spirit* or *in spirit*
b4:3 Other mss omit *and the One seated*
c4:3 A precious stone
d4:3 A translucent red gem
e4:6 Lit *In the middle of the throne*
f4:8 Or *they never rest*
g4:8 Other mss read *holy* 9 times

the One seated on the throne, worship the One who lives forever and ever, cast their crowns before the throne, and say:

> [11] Our Lord and God,[a]
> You are worthy to receive
> glory and honor and power,
> because You have created all things,
> and because of Your will
> they exist and were created.

THE LAMB TAKES THE SCROLL

5 Then I saw in the right hand of the One seated on the throne a scroll with writing on the inside and on the back, sealed with seven seals. [2] I also saw a mighty angel proclaiming in a loud voice, "Who is worthy to open the scroll and break its seals?" [3] But no one in heaven or on earth or under the earth was able to open the scroll or even to look in it. [4] And I cried and cried because no one was found worthy to open[b] the scroll or even to look in it.

[5] Then one of the elders said to me, "Stop crying. Look! The Lion from the tribe of Judah, the Root of David, has been victorious so that He may open the scroll and[c] its seven seals." [6] Then I saw one like a slaughtered lamb standing between[d] the throne and the four living creatures and among the elders. He had seven horns and seven eyes, which are the seven spirits of God sent into all the earth. [7] He came and took the scroll[e] out of the right hand of the One seated on the throne.

THE LAMB IS WORTHY

[8] When He took the scroll, the four living creatures and the 24 elders fell down before the Lamb. Each one had a harp and gold bowls filled with incense, which are the prayers of the saints. [9] And they sang a new song:

> You are worthy to take the scroll
> and to open its seals;

WORD STUDY

Greek word: **biblion**
[bih BLEE ahn]

Translation: **scroll, book**

Uses in Revelation: **23**

Uses in John's writings: **25**

Uses in the NT: **34**

Key passage: **Revelation 5:1**

Biblion means *scroll* but is commonly translated *book*, a term more familiar to modern readers. In the NT, however, *biblion* probably nowhere refers to the codex (the modern folding-book form), since this first-century A.D. invention does not appear to receive common currency in Christian circles until the 2nd century.

Ancient documents were made from papyrus (usually from Egypt) or parchment (processed animals skins). Strips of papyrus pith were laid next to each other, with a second set of strips placed at right angles to these. The resulting sheet was pressed then dried. For longer documents, sheets were glued end-on-end and rolled into a scroll, which could be very long (the Qumran Isaiah scroll measures about 24 feet long). Scrolls were normally written on one side but could be written on both (Rv 5:1). Scrolls containing sensitive documents were sealed with wax along the outer edge to keep them from unrolling, tearing, or being read by an unauthorized person.

---

[a]4:11 Other mss add *the Holy One*; other mss read *O Lord*
[b]5:4 Other mss add *and read*
[c]5:5 Other mss add *loose*
[d]5:6 Or *standing in the middle of*
[e]5:7 Other mss include *the scroll*

WORD STUDY

Greek word: **sphragis**
[sfrah GIHSS]

Translation: **seal**

Uses in Revelation: **13**

Uses in John's writings: **13**

Uses in the NT: **16**

Key passage: **Revelation 6:1**

Sphragis (seal) could refer to an instrument used to apply a seal (Rv 7:2) or to the *seal* (Rv 5:1,2,5) or *inscription* (2 Tm 2:19) itself. The related verb *sphragizo* means *to mark with a seal*, in order to secure (Mt 27:66; Rv 20:3) or hide something (Rv 10:4; 22:10). The person who owns the stamp enjoys authority over what is sealed. This authority indicates ownership, protection, and approval, themes which predominate in Revelation (Rv 7:3-5,8; 9:4). The seven-sealed scroll belongs to God, and only the Lamb is worthy to break the seals to reveal the scroll's contents (Rv 5–6; 8:1).

Metaphorically, a seal could indicate official authentication or confirmation of a truth, and in this sense Paul speaks of circumcision as the *seal* (i.e., *authentication*, Rm 4:11) of Abraham's faith-based righteousness. Similarly, the Corinthian church was the *seal* (i.e., *confirmation*; 1 Co 9:2) of Paul's apostleship.

because You were slaughtered,
and You redeemed[a] ₍people₎[b] for God
by Your blood
from every tribe and language and people
and nation.
¹⁰ You made them a kingdom[c] and priests
to our God,
and they will reign on the earth.

¹¹ Then I looked, and heard the voice of many angels around the throne, and also of the living creatures, and of the elders. Their number was countless thousands, plus thousands of thousands. ¹² They said with a loud voice:

The Lamb who was slaughtered is worthy
to receive power and riches
and wisdom and strength
and honor and glory and blessing!

¹³ I heard every creature in heaven, on earth, under the earth, on the sea, and everything in them say:

Blessing and honor and glory and dominion
to the One seated on the throne,
and to the Lamb, forever and ever!

¹⁴ The four living creatures said, "•Amen," and the elders fell down and worshiped.

THE FIRST SEAL ON THE SCROLL

6 Then I saw[d] the Lamb open one of the seven[e] seals, and I heard one of the four living creatures say with a voice like thunder, "Come!"[f] [g] ² I looked, and there was a white horse. The horseman on it had a bow; a crown was given to him, and he went out as a victor to conquer.[h]

THE SECOND SEAL

³ When He opened the second seal, I heard the second living creature say, "Come!"[f] [g] ⁴ Then another

---

[a]5:9 Or *purchased*
[b]5:9 Other mss read *us*
[c]5:10 Other mss read *them kings*
[d]6:1 Lit *saw when*
[e]6:1 Other mss omit *seven*
[f]6:1,3 Other mss add *and see*
[g]6:1,3 Or *Go!*
[h]6:2 Lit *went out conquering and in order to conquer*

horse went out, a fiery red one, and its horseman was empowered[a] to take peace from the earth, so that people would slaughter one another. And a large sword was given to him.

THE THIRD SEAL

5 When He opened the third seal, I heard the third living creature say, "Come!"[b] [c] And I looked, and there was a black horse. The horseman on it had a balance scale in his hand. 6 Then I heard something like a voice among the four living creatures say, "A quart of wheat for a •denarius, and three quarts of barley for a denarius—but do not harm the olive oil and the wine."

THE FOURTH SEAL

7 When He opened the fourth seal, I heard the voice of the fourth living creature say, "Come!"[b] [c] 8 And I looked, and there was a pale green[d] horse. The horseman on it was named Death, and •Hades was following after him. Authority was given to them[e] over a fourth of the earth, to kill by the sword, by famine, by plague, and by the wild animals of the earth.

THE FIFTH SEAL

9 When He opened the fifth seal, I saw under the altar the souls of those slaughtered because of God's word and the testimony they had.[f] 10 They cried out with a loud voice: "O Lord,[g] holy and true, how long until You judge and avenge our blood from those who live on the earth?" 11 So a white robe was given to each of them, and they were told to rest a little while longer until the number of their fellow slaves and their brothers, who were going to be killed just as they had been, would be completed.

THE SIXTH SEAL

12 Then I saw Him open[h] the sixth seal. A violent earthquake occurred; the sun turned black like

Always Take God's Will over Your Way

Are you willing for God to deny your pleadings, so that even in the midst of your tears you are able to say, "Nevertheless, not my will, but Yours, be done"?

They cried out with a loud voice: "O Lord, holy and true, how long until You judge and avenge our blood from those who live on the earth?"

—Revelation 6:10

---

[a]6:4 Or *was granted*; lit *was given*
[b]6:5,7 Other mss add *and see*
[c]6:5,7 Or *Go!*
[d]6:8 Or *a greenish gray*
[e]6:8 Other mss read *him*
[f]6:9 Other mss add *about the Lamb*
[g]6:10 Or *Master*
[h]6:12 Lit *I saw when He opened*

WORD STUDY

Greek word: *phule*
[foo LAY]
Translation: *tribe*
Uses in Revelation: **21**
Uses in John's writings: **21**
Uses in the NT: **31**
Key passage: **Revelation 7:4-9**

Phule can refer to a group of people united along socio-political lines (i.e., a *nation*) or to a subgroup within a nation, characterized by a distinctive bloodline (i.e., a *tribe*). Outside of the book of Revelation, *phule* normally refers to one or more of Israel's twelve *tribes* (Mt 19:28; Lk 2:36; 22:30; Ac 13:21; Rm 11:1; Php 3:5; Heb 7:13-14), a usage less frequently attested in the book of Revelation (5:5; 7:4-8; 21:12). *Phule* occurs 21 times in Revelation, where John speaks of *tribes* among the Gentile nations (Rv 1:7; 5:9; 7:9; 11:9; 13:7; 14:6; this broader sphere of *tribes* may also be in view in Mt 24:30 and Jms 1:1). In this latter sense, *phule* has some semantic overlap with the Gk terms *genos* (*nation*, *race*) and *ethnos* (*foreigners*, *nations*).

sackcloth made of goat hair; the entire moon[a] became like blood; 13 the stars[b] of heaven fell to the earth as a fig tree drops its unripe figs when shaken by a high wind; 14 the sky separated like a scroll being rolled up; and every mountain and island was moved from its place.

15 Then the kings of the earth, the nobles, the military commanders, the rich, the powerful, and every slave and free person hid in the caves and among the rocks of the mountains. 16 And they said to the mountains and to the rocks, "Fall on us and hide us from the face of the One seated on the throne and from the wrath of the Lamb, 17 because the great day of Their[c] wrath has come! And who is able to stand?"

THE SEALED OF ISRAEL

7 After this I saw four angels standing at the four corners of the earth, restraining the four winds of the earth so that no wind could blow on the earth or on the sea or on any tree. 2 Then I saw another angel rise up from the east, who had the seal of the living God. He cried out in a loud voice to the four angels who were empowered[d] to harm the earth and the sea: 3 "Don't harm the earth or the sea or the trees until we seal the slaves of our God on their foreheads." 4 And I heard the number of those who were sealed:

144,000 sealed from every tribe of the sons of Israel:
5 12,000 sealed from the tribe of Judah,
12,000[e] from the tribe of Reuben,
12,000 from the tribe of Gad,
6 12,000 from the tribe of Asher,
12,000 from the tribe of Naphtali,
12,000 from the tribe of Manasseh,
7 12,000 from the tribe of Simeon,
12,000 from the tribe of Levi,
12,000 from the tribe of Issachar,
8 12,000 from the tribe of Zebulun,
12,000 from the tribe of Joseph,
12,000 sealed from the tribe of Benjamin.

---

[a]6:12 Or *the full moon*
[b]6:13 Perhaps meteors
[c]6:17 Other mss read *His*

[d]7:2 Lit *angels to whom it was given*
[e]7:5-8 Other mss add *sealed* after each number

A MULTITUDE FROM THE GREAT TRIBULATION

⁹ After this I looked, and there was a vast multitude from every nation, tribe, people, and language, which no one could number, standing before the throne and before the Lamb. They were robed in white with palm branches in their hands. ¹⁰ And they cried out in a loud voice:

> Salvation belongs to our God,
> who is seated on the throne,
> and to the Lamb!

¹¹ All the angels stood around the throne, the elders, and the four living creatures, and they fell on their faces before the throne and worshiped God, ¹² saying:

> •Amen! Blessing and glory and wisdom
> and thanksgiving and honor
> and power and strength,
> be to our God forever and ever. Amen.

¹³ Then one of the elders asked me, "Who are these people robed in white, and where did they come from?" ¹⁴ I said to him, "Sir,ᵃ you know."
Then he told me:

> These are the ones coming out
> of the great tribulation.
> They washed their robes and made them white
> in the blood of the Lamb.
> ¹⁵ For this reason they are before the throne
> of God,
> and they serve Him day and night
> in His sanctuary.
> The One seated on the throne
> will shelterᵇ them:
> ¹⁶ no longer will they hunger; no longer
> will they thirst;
> no longer will the sun strike them, or any heat.
> ¹⁷ Because the Lamb who is at the center
> of the throne will shepherd them;
> He will guide them to springs of living waters,
> and God will wipe away every tear
> from their eyes.

You're in Good Hands with God

There is no better place to be than safely in the hands of God. This is not just a theological concept, but a promise you can cling to in the midst of a hostile, menacing world.

The One seated on the throne will shelter them.
—Revelation 7:15b

The Shepherd Takes Care of His Sheep

Your Shepherd knows your every need. He will not always replenish you in the same way, but His response to you will always perfectly correspond to your present need.

"The Lamb who is at the center of the throne will shepherd them; He will guide them to springs of living waters, and God will wipe away every tear from their eyes."
—Revelation 7:17

ᵃ7:14 Lit *My lord*   ᵇ7:15 Or *will spread His tent over*

WORD STUDY

Greek word: **katoikeo**
[kah toi KEH oh]

Translation: **live, dwell**

Uses in Revelation: **13**

Uses in John's writings: **13**

Uses in the NT: **44**

Key passage: **Revelation 8:13**

___

Outside of the book of Revelation, *katoikeo* (*to live, dwell*) mainly refers to residing in a city (Mt 2:23; Lk 13:4;Ac 2:5,14; 9:22,32; 19:17) or a region (Ac 2:9; 11:29; 19:10), though the term is used on occasion to describe spiritual realities: unclean spirits residing in a man (Mt 12:45 = Lk 11:26); God dwelling in His sanctuary (Mt 23:21; cf. Ac 7:48; 17:24); Christ living in believers' hearts (Eph 3:17); God's fullness dwelling in Christ (Col 1:19; 2:9); and righteousness dwelling in the new heavens and new earth (2 Pt 3:11).

In Revelation, *katoikeo* always appears in a negative sense.Twelve of its thirteen occurrences (2:13 being the exception), appear in the phrase "those who live on the earth" (3:10; 6:10; 8:13; 11:10; 13:8,12,14; 17:2,8). This phrase always focuses upon unbelievers, envisioned as those who serve the beast and persecute believers, thus constituting themselves as God's enemies.

THE SEVENTH SEAL

8 When He opened the seventh seal, there was silence in heaven for about half an hour. ² Then I saw the seven angels who stand in the presence of God; seven trumpets were given to them. ³ Another angel, with a gold incense burner, came and stood at the altar. He was given a large amount of incense to offer with the prayers of all the saints on the gold altar in front of the throne. ⁴ The smoke of the incense, with the prayers of the saints, went up in the presence of God from the angel's hand. ⁵ The angel took the incense burner, filled it with fire from the altar, and hurled it to the earth; there were thunders, rumblings, lightnings, and an earthquake. ⁶ And the seven angels who had the seven trumpets prepared to blow them.

THE FIRST TRUMPET

⁷ The first ₗangelₗᵃ blew his trumpet, and hail and fire, mixed with blood, were hurled to the earth. So a third of the earth was burned up, a third of the trees were burned up, and all the green grass was burned up.

THE SECOND TRUMPET

⁸ The second angel blew his trumpet, and something like a great mountain ablaze with fire was hurled into the sea. So a third of the sea became blood, ⁹ a third of the living creatures in the sea died, and a third of the ships were destroyed.

THE THIRD TRUMPET

¹⁰ The third angel blew his trumpet, and a great star, blazing like a torch, fell from heaven. It fell on a third of the rivers and springs of water. ¹¹ The name of the star is Wormwood,ᵇ and a third of the waters became wormwood. So, many of the people died from the waters, because they had been made bitter.

THE FOURTH TRUMPET

¹² The fourth angel blew his trumpet, and a third of

___

ᵃ**8:7** Other mss include *angel*   ᵇ**8:11** *Wormwood* is absinthe, a bitter herb.

the sun was struck, a third of the moon, and a third of the stars, so that a third of them were darkened. A third of the day was without light, and the night as well.

13 I looked, and I heard an eagle,[a] flying in mid-heaven,[b] saying in a loud voice, "Woe! Woe! Woe to those who live on the earth, because of the remaining trumpet blasts that the three angels are about to sound!"

THE FIFTH TRUMPET

9 The fifth angel blew his trumpet, and I saw a star that had fallen from heaven to earth. The key to the shaft of the •abyss was given to him. 2 He opened the shaft of the abyss, and smoke came up out of the shaft like smoke from a great[c] furnace so that the sun and the air were darkened by the smoke from the shaft. 3 Then out of the smoke locusts came to the earth, and power[d] was given to them like the power that scorpions have on the earth. 4 They were told not to harm the grass of the earth, or any green plant, or any tree, but only people who do not have God's seal on their foreheads. 5 They were not permitted to kill them, but were to torment ⌊them⌋ for five months; their torment is like the torment caused by a scorpion when it strikes a man. 6 In those days people will seek death and will not find it; they will long to die, but death will flee from them.

7 The appearance of the locusts was like horses equipped for battle. On their heads were something like gold crowns; their faces were like men's faces; 8 they had hair like women's hair; their teeth were like lions' teeth; 9 they had chests like iron breastplates; the sound of their wings was like the sound of chariots with many horses rushing into battle; 10 and they had tails with stingers, like scorpions, so that with their tails they had the power[d] to harm people for five months. 11 They had as their king[e] the angel of the abyss; his name in Hebrew is Abaddon,[f] and in Greek he has the name Apollyon.[g] 12 The first woe has passed. There are still two more woes to come after this.

---

a8:13 Other mss read *angel*
b8:13 Very high
c9:2 Other mss omit *great*
d9:3,10 Or *authority*

e9:11 Or *as king over them*
f9:11 Or *destruction*
g9:11 Or *destroyer*

WORD STUDY

Greek word: **abussos**
[AH boos sahss]
Translation: **abyss**
Uses in Revelation: **7**
Uses in the NT: **9**
Key passage: **Revelation 9:11**

Abussos (*abyss*) was originally an adjective describing something unfathomable with no apparent depth or bottom. In the Greek OT, *abussos* envisions the fathomless ocean depths (*watery depths*, Gn 1:2; 7:11; 8:2; Is 51:10) and possibly the realm of the dead (*depths* of the earth; Ps 63:9; 71:20). In the few centuries preceding Christ, *abussos* evolved to refer to the place of imprisonment for disobedient angelic spirits. This highly developed meaning carries into the NT, where *abussos* typically refers to the place of punishment in which demonic spirits (including the devil) are held (Lk 8:31; Rv 9:1-2,11; 20:3), and the place from which the beast originates (Rv 11:7-8). *Abussos* may also refer to the present realm of the dead (Rm 10:7), a concept similar to that of the Greek term *hades* and the Hebrew term *sheol* (cf. Ps 16:10; Ac 2:27).

THE SIXTH TRUMPET

[13] The sixth angel blew his trumpet. From the four[a] horns of the gold altar that is before God, I heard a voice [14] say to the sixth angel who had the trumpet, "Release the four angels bound at the great river Euphrates." [15] So the four angels who were prepared for the hour, day, month, and year were released to kill a third of the human race. [16] The number of mounted troops was 200 million;[b] I heard their number. [17] This is how I saw the horses in my vision: The horsemen had breastplates that were fiery red, hyacinth blue, and sulfur yellow. The heads of the horses were like lions' heads, and from their mouths came fire, smoke, and sulfur. [18] A third of the human race was killed by these three plagues—by the fire, the smoke, and the sulfur that came from their mouths. [19] For the power of the horses is in their mouths and in their tails, because their tails, like snakes, have heads, and they inflict injury with them.

[20] The rest of the people, who were not killed by these plagues, did not repent of the works of their hands to stop worshiping demons and idols of gold, silver, bronze, stone, and wood, which are not able to see, hear, or walk. [21] And they did not repent of their murders, their sorceries,[c] their sexual immorality, or their thefts.

THE MIGHTY ANGEL AND THE SMALL SCROLL

10 Then I saw another mighty angel coming down from heaven, surrounded by a cloud, with a rainbow over his head.[d] His face was like the sun, his legs[e] were like fiery pillars, [2] and he had a little scroll opened in his hand. He put his right foot on the sea, his left on the land, [3] and he cried out with a loud voice like a roaring lion. When he cried out, the seven thunders spoke with their voices. [4] And when the seven thunders spoke, I was about to write. Then I heard

---

Make the Hard Choices of Repentance

As destructive as our sinful habits may be, we may prefer living with the familiar rather than being freed to experience the unknown. Do you fear change more than you fear God?

They did not repent of their murders, their sorceries, their sexual immorality, or their thefts.

—Revelation 9:21

---

[a]9:13 Other mss omit *four*
[b]9:16 Other mss read *100 million*
[c]9:21 Or *magic potions*, or *drugs*; Gk *pharmakon*

[d]10:1 Or *a halo on his head*
[e]10:1 Or *feet*

a voice from heaven, saying, "Seal up what the seven thunders said, and do not write it down!"

⁵ Then the angel that I had seen standing on the sea and on the land raised his right hand to heaven. ⁶ He swore an oath by the One who lives forever and ever, who created heaven and what is in it, the earth and what is in it, and the sea and what is in it: "There will no longer be an interval of time,ᵃ ⁷ but in the days of the sound of the seventh angel, when he will blow his trumpet, then God's hidden planᵇ will be completed, as He announced to His servantsᶜ the prophets."

⁸ Now the voice that I heard from heaven spoke to me again and said, "Go, take the scroll that lies open in the hand of the angel who is standing on the sea and on the land."

⁹ So I went to the angel and asked him to give me the little scroll. He said to me, "Take and eat it; it will be bitter in your stomach, but it will be as sweet as honey in your mouth."

¹⁰ Then I took the little scroll from the angel's hand and ate it. It was as sweet as honey in my mouth, but when I ate it, my stomach became bitter. ¹¹ And I was told,ᵈ "You must prophesy again aboutᵉ many peoples, nations, languages, and kings."

THE TWO WITNESSES

11 Then I was given a measuring reed like a rod,ᶠ with these words: "Goᵍ and measure God's sanctuary and the altar, and ₗcountⱼ those who worship there. ² But exclude the courtyard outside the sanctuary. Don't measure it, because it is given to the nations,ʰ and they will trample the holy city for 42 months. ³ I will empowerⁱ my two witnesses, and they will prophesy for 1,260 days,ʲ dressed in sackcloth."ᵏ ⁴ These are the two olive trees and the two lampstands that stand before the Lordˡ of the earth. ⁵ If anyone wants to harm them, fire comes from their mouths and

WORD STUDY

Greek word: **phone**
[foh NAY]

Translation: **voice, sound**

Uses in Revelation: **55**

Uses in John's writings: **70**

Uses in the NT: **139**

Key passage: **Revelation 10:3-4,7-8**

In classical Gk, *phone* normally refers to verbal sounds, including a battle cry, the noise of an animal, or a human language or dialect. Similarly, the related verb *phoneo* means *to produce a sound* or *tone*. In the NT, *phoneo* occurs forty-three times, forty-two in the Gospels and Acts, with the dominant meanings *to call, call out*, or *summon*, but it also refers to a rooster's crowing (e.g., Mt 26:34,74-75). *Phone* most commonly refers to *the voice* (Mt 2:18; Jn 1:23; Rv 10:3-4,7-8), but it also has other uses, such as the *sound* of the wind (Jn 3:8; Ac 2:6), the *sound* of musical instruments (1 Co 14:7-8; Heb 12:19; Rv 8:13; 18:22), and human *language* (1 Co 14:10-11). In Revelation, *phone* sometimes refers to the *rumblings* of thunder, signifying God's presence and power (4:5; 8:5; 11:19; 14:2; 16:18; 19:6).

ᵃ10:6 Or *be a delay*
ᵇ10:7 Or *God's secret* or *mystery*; see Rv 1:20; 17:5,7
ᶜ10:7 Or *slaves*
ᵈ10:11 Lit *And they said to me*
ᵉ10:11 Or *prophesy again against*
ᶠ11:1 Other mss add *and the angel stood up*

ᵍ11:2 Lit *Arise*
ʰ11:2 Or *Gentiles*
ⁱ11:3 Lit *I will give to*
ʲ11:3 Three and a half years of thirty-day months
ᵏ11:3 Mourning garment of coarse, often black, material
ˡ11:4 Other mss read *God*

WORD STUDY

Greek word: *therion*
[thay REE ahn]
Translation: *beast*
Uses in Revelation: **39**
Uses in John's writings: **39**
Uses in the NT: **46**
Key passage: **Revelation 11:7**

Therion (*beast, animal*) was used to refer to any living creature excluding man, but usually wild, undomesticated animals. In mythological imagery, *therion* could describe supernatural creatures such as the griffin, the hydra, or a huge dragon.

In the NT, *therion* normally refers to undomesticated animals in general (Mk 1:13; Ac 11:6; Ti 1:12; Jms 3:7; Heb 12:20), including a snake (Ac 28:4-5) and particularly dangerous animals (Rv 6:8). However, Daniel 7 and most of the occurrences of *therion* in Revelation (6:8; 18:2 excepted) reflect the more metaphorical, mythological imagery. *Therion* occurs ten times in the Greek OT of Daniel 7, where four creatures arise from the sea, understood as four Gentile empires (7:17). Similarly, Revelation uses *therion* as (1) a vivid personification of an ungodly Gentile empire (17:3-5), (2) the antichrist (11:7,17; 13:1-4; 17:7-8; 19:19), or (3) the false prophet (13:11).

consumes their enemies; if anyone wants to harm them, he must be killed in this way. ⁶ These men have the power to close the sky so that it does not rain during the days of their prophecy. They also have power over the waters to turn them into blood, and to strike the earth with any plague whenever they want.

THE WITNESSES MARTYRED

⁷ When they finish their testimony, the beastᵃ that comes up out of the •abyss will make war with them, conquer them, and kill them. ⁸ Their dead bodiesᵇ will lie in the public squareᶜ of the great city, which is called, prophetically,ᵈ Sodom and Egypt, where also their Lord was crucified. ⁹ And representatives fromᵉ the peoples, tribes, languages, and nations will view their bodies for three and a half days and not permit their bodies to be put into a tomb. ¹⁰ Those who live on the earth will gloat over them and celebrate and send gifts to one another, because these two prophets tormented those who live on the earth.

THE WITNESSES RESURRECTED

¹¹ But after the three and a half days, the breathᶠ of life from God entered them, and they stood on their feet. So great fear fell on those who saw them. ¹² Then they heardᵍ a loud voice from heaven saying to them, "Come up here." They went up to heaven in a cloud, while their enemies watched them. ¹³ At that moment a violent earthquake took place, a tenth of the city fell, and 7,000 people were killed in the earthquake. The survivors were terrified and gave glory to the God of heaven. ¹⁴ The second woe has passed. Take note: the third woe is coming quickly!

THE SEVENTH TRUMPET

¹⁵ The seventh angel blew his trumpet, and there were loud voices in heaven saying:

The kingdom of the world has become
the ⌊kingdom⌋

ᵃ11:7 Or *wild animal*
ᵇ11:8 Lit *Their corpse*
ᶜ11:8 Or *lie on the broad street*
ᵈ11:8 Or *spiritually,* or *symbolically*
ᵉ11:9 Lit *And from*
ᶠ11:11 Or *spirit*
ᵍ11:12 Other mss read *Then I heard*

of our Lord and of His •Messiah,
and He will reign forever and ever!

16 The 24 elders, who were seated before God on their thrones, fell on their faces and worshiped God, 17 saying:

We thank You, Lord God, the Almighty, who is
and who was,[a]
because You have taken Your great power
and have begun to reign.
18 The nations were angry, but Your wrath
has come.
The time has come for the dead to be judged,
and to give the reward to Your servants
the prophets,
to the saints, and to those who fear Your name,
both small and great,
and the time has come to destroy those
who destroy the earth.

19 God's sanctuary in heaven was opened, and the ark of His covenant[b] appeared in His sanctuary. There were lightnings, rumblings, thunders, an earthquake,[c] and severe hail.

THE WOMAN, THE CHILD, AND THE DRAGON

12 A great sign[d] appeared in heaven: a woman clothed with the sun, with the moon under her feet, and a crown of 12 stars on her head. 2 She was pregnant and cried out in labor and agony to give birth. 3 Then another sign[e] appeared in heaven: There was a great fiery red dragon having seven heads and 10 horns, and on his heads were seven diadems.[f] 4 His tail swept away a third of the stars in heaven and hurled them to the earth. And the dragon stood in front of the woman who was about to give birth, so that when she did give birth he might devour her child. 5 But she gave birth to a Son—a male who is going to shepherd[g]

Worship God for Who He Really Is

Choose to concentrate on the magnificent truths of God, and they will create in you a noble character that brings glory to God.

We thank You, Lord God, the Almighty, who is and who was, because You have taken Your great power and have begun to reign.
—Revelation 11:17

Does God Have Your Heart This Minute?

We often act as if we have all the time in the world to obey God, but history doesn't wait on our good intentions.

The nations were angry, but Your wrath has come. The time has come for the dead to be judged, and to give the reward to Your servants the prophets, to the saints, and to those who fear Your name, both small and great, and the time has come to destroy those who destroy the earth.
—Revelation 11:18

[a]11:17 Other mss add *and who is to come*
[b]11:19 Other mss read *ark of the covenant of the Lord*
[c]11:19 Other mss omit *an earthquake*
[d]12:1 Or *great symbolic display;* see Rv 12:3
[e]12:3 Or *another symbolic display*
[f]12:3 Or *crowns*
[g]12:5 Or *rule*

all nations with an iron scepter—and her child was caught up to God and to His throne. [6] The woman fled into the wilderness, where she had a place prepared by God, to be fed there[a] for 1,260 days.

THE DRAGON THROWN OUT OF HEAVEN

[7] Then war broke out in heaven: Michael and his angels fought against the dragon. The dragon and his angels also fought, [8] but he could not prevail, and there was no place for them in heaven any longer. [9] So the great dragon was thrown out—the ancient serpent, who is called the Devil[b] and Satan,[c] the one who deceives the whole world. He was thrown to earth, and his angels with him.

[10] Then I heard a loud voice in heaven say:

The salvation and the power and the kingdom
  of our God
and the authority of His •Messiah
  have now come,
because the accuser of our brothers
  has been thrown out:
the one who accuses them before our God
  day and night.
[11] They conquered him by the blood of the Lamb
  and by the word of their testimony,
for they did not love their lives in the face
  of death.
[12] Therefore rejoice, O heavens, and you who dwell
  in them!
Woe to the earth and the sea,
for the Devil has come down to you
  with great fury,
because he knows he has a short time.

THE WOMAN PERSECUTED

[13] When the dragon saw that he had been thrown to earth, he persecuted the woman who gave birth to the male. [14] The woman was given two wings of a great eagle, so that she could fly from the serpent's presence

---

In God We Trust

Our hope is not mere speculation about what God might do. His Word tells us what He will do. We can live with confidence because our hope is in the One who is faithful.

The salvation and the power and the kingdom of our God and the authority of His Messiah have now come, because the accuser of our brothers has been thrown out: the one who accuses them before our God day and night.

—Revelation 12:10

---

[a]**12:6** Lit *God, that they might feed her there*
[b]**12:9** Gk *diabolos*, meaning slanderer
[c]**12:9** Hb word meaning adversary

to her place in the wilderness, where she was fed for a time, times, and half a time.[a] 15 From his mouth the serpent spewed water like a river after the woman, to sweep her away in a torrent. 16 But the earth helped the woman: the earth opened its mouth and swallowed up the river that the dragon had spewed from his mouth. 17 So the dragon was furious with the woman and left to wage war against the rest of her offspring[b] —those who keep the commandments of God and have the testimony about Jesus. 18 He[c] stood on the sand of the sea.[d]

THE BEAST FROM THE SEA

13 And I saw a beast coming up out of the sea. He[e] had 10 horns and seven heads. On his horns were 10 diadems, and on his heads were blasphemous names.[f] 2 The beast I saw was like a leopard, his feet were like a bear's, and his mouth was like a lion's mouth. The dragon gave him his power, his throne, and great authority. 3 One of his heads appeared to be fatally wounded,[g] but his fatal wound was healed. The whole earth was amazed and followed the beast.[h] 4 They worshiped the dragon because he gave authority to the beast. And they worshiped the beast, saying, "Who is like the beast? Who is able to wage war against him?"

5 A mouth was given to him to speak boasts and blasphemies. He was also given authority to act[i] [j] for 42 months. 6 He began to speak[k] blasphemies against God: to blaspheme His name and His dwelling—those who dwell in heaven. 7 And he was permitted to wage war against the saints and to conquer them. He was also given authority over every tribe, people, language, and nation. 8 All those who live on the earth will worship him, everyone whose name was not written from the

Struggles Can Be Part of God's Plan

Spiritual assaults and attacks by the ungodly are not always signs that you are out of the will of God. They may even indicate that you are in the very center of His will.

He was permitted to wage war against the saints and to conquer them. He was also given authority over every tribe, people, language, and nation.
—Revelation 13:7

---

[a]12:14 An expression occurring in Dn 7:25; 12:7 that means 3½ years or 42 months (Rv 11:2; 13:5) or 1,260 days (Rv 11:3)
[b]12:17 Or *seed*
[c]12:18 Other mss read *I.* "He" is apparently a reference to the dragon.
[d]12:18 Some translations put Rv 12:18 either in Rv 12:17 or Rv 13:1.
[e]13:1 The beasts in Rv 13:1,11 are customarily referred to as "he" or "him" rather than "it." The Gk word for a beast (*therion*) is grammatically neuter.
[f]13:1 Other mss read *heads was a blasphemous name*
[g]13:3 Lit *be slain to death*
[h]13:3 Lit *amazed after the beast*
[i]13:5 Other mss read *wage war*
[j]13:5 Or *to rule*
[k]13:6 Lit *He opened his mouth in*

foundation of the world in the book[a] of life of the Lamb who was slaughtered.[b]

⁹ If anyone has an ear, he should listen:

> ¹⁰ If anyone is destined for captivity,
>   into captivity he goes.
>   If anyone is to be killed[c] with a sword,
>   with a sword he will be killed.

Here is the endurance and the faith of the saints.[d]

THE BEAST FROM THE EARTH

¹¹ Then I saw another beast coming up out of the earth; he had two horns like a lamb,[e] but he sounded like a dragon. ¹² He exercises all the authority of the first beast on his behalf and compels the earth and those who live on it to worship the first beast, whose fatal wound was healed. ¹³ He also performs great signs, even causing fire to come down from heaven to earth before people. ¹⁴ He deceives those who live on the earth because of the signs that he is permitted to perform on behalf of the beast, telling those who live on the earth to make an image[f] of the beast who had the sword wound yet lived. ¹⁵ He was permitted to give a spirit[g] to the image of the beast, so that the image of the beast could both speak and cause whoever would not worship the image of the beast to be killed. ¹⁶ And he requires everyone—small and great, rich and poor, free and slave—to be given a mark[h] on his[i] right hand or on his[i] forehead, ¹⁷ so that no one can buy or sell unless he has the mark: the beast's name or the number of his name. ¹⁸ Here is wisdom:[j] The one who has understanding must calculate[k] the number of the beast, because it is the number of a man.[l] His number is 666.[m]

THE LAMB AND THE 144,000

14 Then I looked, and there on Mount Zion stood the Lamb, and with Him were 144,000 who

---

Don't Resent the Call to Suffer

Don't make all your decisions and invest everything you have into avoiding hardship. God didn't spare His own Son. Why should we expect Him to spare us?

If anyone is destined for captivity, into captivity he goes. If anyone is to be killed with a sword, with a sword he will be killed. Here is the endurance and the faith of the saints.

—Revelation 13:10

---

[a]**13:8** Or *scroll*
[b]**13:8** Or *written in the book of life of the Lamb who was slaughtered from the foundation of the world*
[c]**13:10** Other mss read *anyone kills*
[d]**13:10** Or *This calls for the endurance and faith of the saints.*
[e]**13:11** Or *ram*
[f]**13:14** Or *statue,* or *likeness*
[g]**13:15** Or *give breath,* or *give life*
[h]**13:16** Or *stamp,* or *brand*
[i]**13:16** Lit *their*
[j]**13:18** Or *This calls for wisdom*
[k]**13:18** Or *count,* or *figure out*
[l]**13:18** Or *is a man's number,* or *is the number of a person*
[m]**13:18** One Gk ms plus other ancient evidence read *616*

had His name and His Father's name written on their foreheads. [2] I heard a sound[a] from heaven like the sound of cascading waters and like the rumbling of loud thunder. The sound I heard was also like harpists playing on their harps. [3] They sang[b] a new song before the throne and before the four living creatures and the elders, but no one could learn the song except the 144,000 who had been redeemed[c] from the earth. [4] These are the ones not defiled with women, for they have kept their virginity. These are the ones who follow the Lamb wherever He goes. They were redeemed[c] [d] from the human race as the •firstfruits for God and the Lamb. [5] No lie was found in their mouths; they are blameless.

THE PROCLAMATION OF THREE ANGELS

[6] Then I saw another angel flying in mid-heaven, having the eternal gospel to announce to the inhabitants of the earth—to every nation, tribe, language, and people. [7] He spoke with a loud voice: "Fear God and give Him glory, because the hour of His judgment has come. Worship the Maker of heaven and earth, the sea and springs of water."

[8] A second angel[e] followed, saying: "It has fallen, Babylon the Great has fallen,[f] who made all nations drink the wine of her sexual immorality,[g] which brings wrath."

[9] And a third angel[h] followed them and spoke with a loud voice: "If anyone worships the beast and his image and receives a mark on his forehead or on his hand, [10] he will also drink the wine of God's wrath, which is mixed full strength in the cup of His anger. He will be tormented with fire and sulfur in the sight of the holy angels and in the sight of the Lamb, [11] and the smoke of their torment will go up forever and ever. There is no rest[i] day or night for those who worship the beast and his image, or anyone who receives the mark of

WORD STUDY

Greek word: *hexakosioi hexekonta hex*

[heks uh KAH see oi heks AY kahn tah HEX]

Translation: **666**

Uses in Revelation: **1**

Uses in John's writings: **1**

Uses in the NT: **1**

Key passage: **Revelation 13:18**

No biblical number has received as much attention as 666. Much that is said about this mysterious number in popular literature is misleading, but reasonable explanations exist. One explanation applies Gematria. This practice of representing words by numerical equivalents was found in extra-biblical religious sources and was based upon the fact that Hebrew and Greek attached a numerical value to each alphabetical letter. Thus every word could be assigned a numerical value by summing the values of its letters. Thus the beast's name could be deduced from his number (Rv 13:18; 15:2). Others believe 666 is one example of John's normal figurative use of numbers (cf. Rv 5:11; 7:4,9; 9:15; 20:8), none of which were ever intended to be calculated. In this view, the number six indicates incompleteness and serves as a contrastive counterpart to the occurrences of seven (signifying completeness) in the book of Revelation. Triple repetition of six would indicate the absolute sinful imperfection of the beast.

---

[a]14:2 Or *voice*
[b]14:3 Other mss add *as it were*
[c]14:3,4 Or *purchased*
[d]14:4 Other mss add *by Jesus*
[e]14:8 Lit *Another angel, a second*
[f]14:8 Other mss omit the second *has fallen*
[g]14:8 Or *wine of her passionate immorality*
[h]14:9 Lit *Another angel, a third*
[i]14:11 Lit *They have no rest*

WORD STUDY

Greek word: **ouranos**
[oo rah NAHSS]

Translation: **heaven, sky**

Uses in Revelation: **52**

Uses in John's writings: **70**

Uses in the NT: **273**

Key passage: **Revelation 14:13**

In ancient Hb cosmology, *ouranos* was the cosmic sphere located directly above the earth, which was located at the lower end of the cosmos. This sphere included the atmosphere (*sky*; Gn 1:8,20; Dt 11:17; Mt 6:26; 8:20), the universe, as the place above the earth where the stars are located (*heavens, space, celestial sky*; Gn 1:1; Dt 4:32; Ps 19:1; Mt 24:29 = Lk 21:26; Eph 4:10), and God's transcendent dwelling-place, located at the upper end of this cosmic sphere (*heaven*; Ps 2:4; Mt 5:34; 6:9; Rv 4:2). From this highest level, God would dispense His acts of salvation and judgment (Ps 57:3; 78:24; Rv 3:12; 14:13; 18:1; 20:1; 21:2). By NT times, some Jewish groups had expanded this basic three-level cosmology to include more levels, and it is possible that Paul (2 Co 12:2; Eph 4:10) and the author of Hebrews (4:14) believed in such a multi-tiered heavenly sphere.

his name. [12] Here is the endurance[a] [b] of the saints, who keep the commandments of God and the faith in Jesus."[c]

[13] Then I heard a voice from heaven saying, "Write: Blessed are the dead who die in the Lord from now on."

"Yes," says the Spirit, "let them rest from their labors, for their works follow them!"

REAPING THE EARTH'S HARVEST

[14] Then I looked, and there was a white cloud, and One like the Son of Man[d] was seated on the cloud, with a gold crown on His head and a sharp sickle in His hand. [15] Another angel came out of the sanctuary, crying out in a loud voice to the One who was seated on the cloud, "Use your sickle and reap, for the time to reap has come, since the harvest of the earth is ripe." [16] So the One seated on the cloud swung His sickle over the earth, and the earth was harvested.

[17] Then another angel who also had a sharp sickle came out of the sanctuary in heaven. [18] Yet another angel, who had authority over fire, came from the altar, and he called with a loud voice to the one who had the sharp sickle, "Use your sharp sickle and gather the clusters of grapes from earth's vineyard, because its grapes have ripened." [19] So the angel swung his sickle toward earth and gathered the grapes from earth's vineyard, and he threw them into the great winepress of God's wrath. [20] Then the press was trampled outside the city, and blood flowed out of the press up to the horses' bridles for about 180 miles.[e]

PREPARATION FOR THE BOWL JUDGMENTS

15 Then I saw another great and awe-inspiring sign[f] in heaven: seven angels with the seven last plagues, for with them, God's wrath will be completed. [2] I also saw something like a sea of glass mixed

---

[a]**14:12** Or *This calls for the endurance of the saints*
[b]**14:12** This is what the endurance of the saints means
[c]**14:12** Or *and faith in Jesus*, or *their faith in*, or *faithfulness to Jesus*

[d]**14:14** Or *like a son of man*
[e]**14:20** Lit *1,600 stadia*
[f]**15:1** Or *and awesome symbolic display*

with fire, and those who had won the victory from the beast, his image,[a] and the number of his name, were standing on the sea of glass with harps from God.[b] ³ They sang the song of God's servant Moses, and the song of the Lamb:

> Great and awe-inspiring are Your works,
> Lord God, the Almighty;
> righteous and true are Your ways,
> King of the Nations.
> ⁴ Lord, who will not fear and glorify Your name?
> Because You alone are holy,
> because all the nations will come and worship before You,
> because Your righteous acts have been revealed.

⁵ After this I looked, and the heavenly sanctuary—the tabernacle of testimony—was opened. ⁶ Out of the sanctuary came the seven angels with the seven plagues, dressed in clean, bright linen, with gold sashes wrapped around their chests. ⁷ One of the four living creatures gave the seven angels seven gold bowls filled with the wrath of God who lives forever and ever. ⁸ Then the sanctuary was filled with smoke from God's glory and from His power, and no one could enter the sanctuary until the seven plagues of the seven angels were completed.

THE FIRST BOWL

16 Then I heard a loud voice from the sanctuary saying to the seven angels, "Go and pour out the seven[c] bowls of God's wrath on the earth." ² The first went and poured out his bowl on the earth, and severely painful sores[d] broke out on the people who had the mark of the beast and who worshiped his image.

THE SECOND BOWL

³ The second[e] poured out his bowl into the sea. It turned to blood like a dead man's, and all life[f] in the sea died.

---

[a]15:2 Other mss add *his mark*
[b]15:2 Or *harps of God*; that is, harps belonging to the service of God
[c]16:1 Other mss omit *seven*
[d]16:2 Lit *and a severely painful sore*
[e]16:3 Other mss add *angel*
[f]16:3 Lit *and every soul of life*

WORD STUDY

Greek word: ***naos***
[NAH ahss]

Translation: ***sanctuary***

Uses in Revelation: **16**

Uses in John's writings: **19**

Uses in the NT: **45**

Key passage: **Revelation 15:5-6,8**

While *naos* can possibly refer to a temple and its surrounding precincts (i.e., *temple complex*; Mt 27:5,40), it usually refers to the temple structure itself (i.e., *temple, sanctuary*; Mt 23:16-17,21,35; 27:51). Figuratively, *naos* is used as a metaphor for God's special presence with His Son (Mt 26:61; Jn 2:19-21) and with His people—both individual and corporate. Paul refers to the Corinthian church as God's *sanctuary* (1 Co 3:16-17; 2 Co 6:16), a figure that extends to the entire Christian church (Eph 2:21). *Naos* appears most often in Revelation, where a heavenly *sanctuary* is in view (Rv 11:2 excepted), a prominent early Christian image (Heb 8:5; 9:1,24; cf. Ex 25:40; Ac 7:44). This heavenly *naos* is the place of divine habitation, from which God blesses and protects His people (Rv 3:12; 7:15) and administers judgment on His enemies (11:19; 14:15,17; 15:5-6,8; 16:1,17).

Greek word: **axios**
[AH ksee ahss]

Translation: **deserve**

Uses in Revelation: **7**

Uses in John's writings: **8**

Uses in the NT: **41**

Key passage: **Revelation 16:6**

The adjective *axios* describes something that is of comparable value or worth to something else (*comparable, worthy*), or something that is appropriate to a particular person or activity (*corresponding to, deserving of*). In the NT, *axios* occurs several times in reference to those receiving a punishment of death (i.e., the punishment corresponds to the crime; Lk 23:15,41; Ac 23:29; 25:11,25; 26:31; Rm 1:32). In the Gospels, *axios* occasionally describes truths about salvation and discipleship (Mt 3:8; 10:37-38; Lk 12:48), and Paul does the same in Rm 8:18 (the related verb *axioo* occurs in 2 Th 1:11; 1 Tm 5:17, and the adverb *axios* occurs in Eph 4:1; Php 1:27; Col 1:10; 1 Th 2:12). In Revelation, the redeemed are found *worthy* of their reward (3:4); God is *worthy* of glory, honor, and power (4:11); and the Lamb is *worthy* to break the seals of the scroll (5:2,4,9,12).

THE THIRD BOWL

4 The third[a] poured out his bowl into the rivers and the springs of water, and they became blood. 5 I heard the angel of the waters say:

> You are righteous, who is and who was,
>   the Holy One,
> for You have decided these things.
> 6 Because they poured out the blood of the saints
>   and the prophets,
> You also gave them blood to drink;
>   they deserve it!

7 Then I heard someone from the altar say:

> Yes, Lord God, the Almighty,
> true and righteous are Your judgments.

THE FOURTH BOWL

8 The fourth[a] poured out his bowl on the sun. He[b] was given the power[c] to burn people with fire, 9 and people were burned by the intense heat. So they blasphemed the name of God who had the power[c] over these plagues, and they did not repent and give Him glory.

THE FIFTH BOWL

10 The fifth[a] poured out his bowl on the throne of the beast, and his kingdom was plunged into darkness. People[d] gnawed their tongues from pain 11 and blasphemed the God of heaven because of their pains and their sores, yet they did not repent of their actions.

THE SIXTH BOWL

12 The sixth[a] poured out his bowl on the great river Euphrates, and its water was dried up to prepare the way for the kings from the east. 13 Then I saw three unclean spirits like frogs ⌊coming⌋ from the dragon's mouth, from the beast's mouth, and from the mouth of the false prophet. 14 For they are spirits of demons performing signs, who travel to the kings of the whole

---

[a]16:4,8,10,12 Other mss add *angel*
[b]16:8 Or *It*
[c]16:8,9 Or *authority*
[d]16:10 Lit *They*

world to assemble them for the battle of the great day of God, the Almighty.

[15] "Look, I am coming like a thief. Blessed is the one who is alert and remains clothed[a] so that he may not go naked, and they see his shame."

[16] So they assembled them at the place called in Hebrew Armagedon.[b] [c]

THE SEVENTH BOWL

[17] Then the seventh[d] poured out his bowl into the air,[e] and a loud voice came out of the sanctuary,[f] from the throne, saying, "It is done!" [18] There were lightnings, rumblings, and thunders. And a severe earthquake occurred like no other since man has been on the earth—so great was the quake. [19] The great city split into three parts, and the cities of the nations[g] fell. Babylon the Great was remembered in God's presence; He gave her the cup filled with the wine of His fierce anger. [20] Every island fled, and the mountains disappeared.[h] [21] Enormous hailstones, each weighing about 100 pounds,[i] fell from heaven on the people, and they[j] blasphemed God for the plague of hail because that plague was extremely severe.

THE WOMAN AND THE SCARLET BEAST

17 Then one of the seven angels who had the seven bowls came and spoke with me: "Come, I will show you the judgment of the notorious prostitute[k] who sits on many[l] waters. [2] The kings of the earth committed sexual immorality with her, and those who live on the earth became drunk on the wine of her sexual immorality." [3] So he carried me away in the Spirit[m] to a desert. I saw a woman sitting on a scarlet beast that was covered[n] with blasphemous

Realize the Peril That the Unsaved Are In

God is absolutely just. He loves, yes, and He forgives, but He does not compromise His righteousness. And those who reject Him will have destructive consequences to pay.

People gnawed their tongues from pain and blasphemed the God of heaven because of their pains and their sores, yet they did not repent of their actions.

—Revelation 16:10b-11

Be Watching for Christ's Appearing

Strive to be attentive to every word that comes to you from God. Your diligence will benefit you and those around you as you heed His warnings, share His Word, and follow His commands.

"Look, I am coming like a thief. Blessed is the one who is alert and remains clothed so that he may not go naked, and they see his shame."

—Revelation 16:15

---

[a]16:15 Or *and guards his clothes*
[b]16:16 Other mss read *Armageddon*; other mss read *Harmegedon*; other mss read *Mageddon*; other mss read *Magedon*
[c]16:16 Traditionally *the hill of Megiddo*, a great city that guarded the pass between the coast and the valley of Jezreel or Esdraelon; see Jdg 5:19; 2 Kg 9:27
[d]16:17 Other mss add *angel*
[e]16:17 Or *on the air*
[f]16:17 Other mss add *of heaven*
[g]16:19 Or *the Gentile cities*
[h]16:20 Lit *mountains were not found*
[i]16:21 Lit *about a talent*; talents varied in weight upwards from 75 pounds
[j]16:21 Lit *people*
[k]17:1 Traditionally, *the great whore*
[l]17:1 Or *by many*
[m]17:3 Or *in spirit*
[n]17:3 Lit *was filled*

WORD STUDY

Greek word: **bdelugma**
[BDEHL oog mah]
Translation: **vile**
Uses in Revelation: **3**
Uses in the NT: **6**
Key passage: **Revelation 17:4-5**

The noun *bdelugma* (*abomination, vile thing*), the adjective *bdeluktos* (*detestable, vile*) and the verb *bdelusso* (*to make detestable*; Ex 5:21; *bdelussomai, to abhor, detest*, or *be detested*) occur only rarely in the NT (*bdelugma*; 6 times; *bdeluktos*; 1 time; *bdelusso*; 2 times), though they appear frequently in the Greek OT. In the Mosaic law and the Prophets, *bdelugma* describes things which are ceremonially unclean (Lv 5:2; 7:21; 11:10-13,20,23,41-42), as well as pagan idolatrous practices abhorrent to God (Dt 7:25-26; Jr 4:1; 7:10; Ezk 5:11), including human sacrifice (Dt 12:31), homosexuality (Lv 18:22; 20:13), and occultic rites (Dt 18:9-12). In the NT, Jesus used *bdelugma* to describe the antichrist, who will establish himself in God's sanctuary ("*abomination* that causes desolation"; Mt 24:15 = Mk 13:14; cf. 2 Th 2:4; Dn 9:27; 11:31; 12:11). In Revelation, *bdelugma* describes Babylon (17:4).

names, having seven heads and 10 horns. ⁴ The woman was dressed in purple and scarlet, adorned with gold, precious stones, and pearls. She had a gold cup in her hand filled with everything vile and with the impurities of herᵃ prostitution. ⁵ On her forehead a cryptic name was written:

BABYLON THE GREAT
THE MOTHER OF PROSTITUTES
AND OF THE VILE THINGS OF THE EARTH.

⁶ Then I saw that the woman was drunk on the blood of the saints and on the blood of the witnesses to Jesus. When I saw her, I was utterly astounded.

THE MEANING OF THE WOMAN AND OF THE BEAST

⁷ Then the angel said to me, "Why are you astounded? I will tell you the secret meaningᵇ of the woman and of the beast, with the seven heads and the 10 horns, that carries her. ⁸ The beast that you saw was, and is not, and is about to come up from the •abyss and go to destruction. Those who live on the earth whose names were not written in the book of life from the foundation of the world will be astounded when they see the beast that was, and is not, and will be present ₗagainⱼ.

⁹ "Here is the mind with wisdom:ᶜ the seven heads are seven mountains on which the woman is seated. ¹⁰ They are also seven kings:ᵈ five have fallen, one is, the other has not yet come, and when he comes, he must remain for a little while. ¹¹ The beast that was and is not, is himself the eighth, yet is of the seven and goes to destruction. ¹² The 10 horns you saw are 10 kings who have not yet received a kingdom, but they will receive authority as kings with the beast for one hour. ¹³ These have one purpose, and they give their power and authority to the beast. ¹⁴ These will make war against the Lamb, but the Lamb will conquer them because He is Lord of lords and King of kings. Those with Him are called and elect and faithful."

ᵃ**17:4** Other mss read *of earth's*
ᵇ**17:7** Lit *the mystery*
ᶜ**17:9** Or *This calls for the mind with wisdom*

ᵈ**17:10** Some editors or translators put *They are also seven kings:* in v. 9.

¹⁵ He also said to me, "The waters you saw, where the prostitute was seated, are peoples, multitudes, nations, and languages. ¹⁶ The 10 horns you saw, and the beast, will hate the prostitute. They will make her desolate and naked, devour her flesh, and burn her up with fire. ¹⁷ For God has put it into their hearts to carry out His plan by having one purpose, and to give their kingdom[a] to the beast until God's words are accomplished. ¹⁸ And the woman you saw is the great city that has an empire[b] over the kings of the earth."

THE FALL OF BABYLON THE GREAT

18 After this I saw another angel with great authority coming down from heaven, and the earth was illuminated by his splendor. ² He cried in a mighty voice:

It has fallen,[c] Babylon the Great has fallen!
She has become a dwelling for demons,
a haunt[d] for every unclean spirit,
a haunt[d] for every unclean bird,
and a haunt[d] for every unclean
and despicable beast.[e]
³ For all the nations have drunk[f]
the wine of her sexual immorality,
which brings wrath.
The kings of the earth have committed
sexual immorality with her,
and the merchants of the earth
have grown wealthy
from her excessive luxury.

⁴ Then I heard another voice from heaven:

Come out of her, My people,
so that you will not share in her sins,
or receive any of her plagues.
⁵ For her sins are piled up[g] to heaven,
and God has remembered her crimes.
⁶ Pay her back the way she also paid,

Ask God to Help You See Sin for What It Is

Do not lose your abhorrence of sin. You will not be able to walk closely with God unless you see sin the way He sees it.

He cried in a mighty voice: It has fallen, Babylon the Great has fallen! She has become a dwelling for demons, a haunt for every unclean spirit, a haunt for every unclean bird, and a haunt for every unclean and despicable beast.
—Revelation 18:2

Don't Play Around with Temptation

Treating evil lightly shows a foolish disregard for God's redemptive work. An honest evaluation of your life will reveal temptations that you should remove.

I heard another voice from heaven: Come out of her, My people, so that you will not share in her sins, or receive any of her plagues.
—Revelation 18:4

---

[a]17:17 Or *sovereignty*
[b]17:18 Or *has sovereignty* or *rulership*
[c]18:2 Other mss omit *It has fallen*
[d]18:2 Or *prison*
[e]18:2 Other mss omit the words *and a haunt for every unclean beast.* The words *and despicable* then refer to the *bird* of the previous line.
[f]18:3 Other mss read *have collapsed*; other mss read *have fallen*
[g]18:5 Or *sins have reached up*

and double it according to her works.
In the cup in which she mixed,
mix a double portion for her.
7 As much as she glorified herself
and lived luxuriously,
give her that much torment and grief.
Because she says in her heart, 'I sit as queen;
I am not a widow, and I will never see grief,'
8 therefore her plagues will come in one day[a] —
death, and grief, and famine.
She will be burned up with fire,
because the Lord God who judges her is mighty.

THE WORLD MOURNS BABYLON'S FALL

9 The kings of the earth who have committed sexual immorality and lived luxuriously with her will weep and mourn over her when they see the smoke of her burning. 10 They stand far off in fear of her torment, saying:

Woe, woe, the great city,
Babylon, the mighty city!
For in a single hour[a]
your judgment has come.

11 The merchants of the earth will also weep and mourn over her, because no one buys their merchandise any longer— 12 merchandise of gold, silver, precious stones, and pearls; fine fabrics of linen, purple, silk, and scarlet; all kinds of fragrant wood products; objects of ivory; objects of expensive wood, brass,[b] iron, and marble; 13 cinnamon, spice,[c] [d] incense, myrrh,[e] and frankincense; wine, olive oil, fine wheat flour, and grain; cattle and sheep; horses and carriages; and human bodies and souls.[f] [g]

14 The fruit you craved has left you.
All your splendid and glamorous things
are gone;
they will never find them again.

Faithfulness Comes from Not Fearing God

An exalted view of God brings a clear view of sin and a realistic view of self. A diminished view of God brings a reduced concern for sin and an inflated view of self.

As much as she glorified herself and lived luxuriously, give her that much torment and grief. Because she says in her heart, 'I sit as queen; I am not a widow, and I will never see grief.'

—Revelation 18:7

Are You Ready for the Judgment Day?

One day God will hold us accountable for all that He has done for us. He will ask us to show Him the fruit of all His bountiful provision for our lives. What will He find?

The fruit you craved has left you. All your splendid and glamorous things are gone; they will never find them again.

—Revelation 18:14

[a]18:8,10 Suddenly
[b]18:12 Or *bronze*, or *copper*
[c]18:13 Other mss omit *spice*
[d]18:13 Or *amomum*, an aromatic plant
[e]18:13 Or *perfume*
[f]18:13 Or *carriages; and slaves, namely, human beings*
[g]18:13 Slaves;"bodies" was the Gk way of referring to slaves;"souls of men" was the Hb way.

¹⁵ The merchants of these things, who became rich from her, will stand far off in fear of her torment, weeping and mourning, ¹⁶ saying:

> Woe, woe, the great city,
> clothed in fine linen, purple, and scarlet,
> adorned with gold, precious stones, and pearls;
> ¹⁷ because in a single hourᵃ such fabulous wealth
>   was destroyed!

And every shipmaster, seafarer, the sailors, and all who do business by sea, stood far off ¹⁸ as they watched the smoke from her burning and kept crying out: "Who is like the great city?" ¹⁹ They threw dust on their heads and kept crying out, weeping, and mourning:

> Woe, woe, the great city,
> where all those who have ships on the sea
> became rich from her wealth;
> because in a single hourᵃ she was destroyed.
> ²⁰ Rejoice over her, heaven, and you saints,
>   apostles, and prophets,
> because God has executed your judgment
>   on her!ᵇ

THE FINALITY OF BABYLON'S FALL

²¹ Then a mighty angel picked up a stone like a large millstone and threw it into the sea, saying:

> In this way, Babylon the great city
>   will be thrown down violently
> and never be found again.
> ²² The sound of harpists, musicians, flutists,
>   and trumpeters
> will never be heard in you again;
> no craftsman of any trade
> will ever be found in you again;
> the sound of a mill
> will never be heard in you again;
> ²³ the light of a lamp will never shine in you again;
> and the voice of a groom and bride
> will never be heard in you again.
> ₍All this will happen₎

ᵃ18:17,19 Suddenly
ᵇ18:20 Or *God pronounced on her*

the judgment she passed on you;
see Rv 18:6

WORD STUDY

Greek word: *planao*
[plah NAH oh]

Translation: *deceive*

Uses in Revelation: **8**

Uses in John's writings: **13**

Uses in the NT: **39**

Key passage: **Revelation 18:23**

Planao literally means *to wander about* (Heb 11:38). This connotation of wandering can be seen in the related nouns *planes/planetes* (*wanderer*), from which English *planet* ultimately derives. Indeed, the planets often appeared to the ancients as "wandering" across the sky among the seemingly fixed stars. By figurative extension, *planao* could also mean *to go astray* (Mt 18:12-13; Heb 3:10; 5:2; Jms 5:19) or *to be deceived* or *misled* (Mt 22:29 = Mk 12:24; Jn 7:12,47; 1 Co 6:9; 2 Tm 3:13; Gl 6:7; Jms 1:16; 1 Jn 1:8; 2:26; 3:7). *Planao* may also mean *to mislead someone* (Mt 24:4-5 = Mk 13:5-6; Jn 7:12) and this is how the word tends to function in Revelation, where John warns about the deceivers "Jezebel" (2:20), the false prophet (13:14; 19:20), Babylon (18:23), and Satan—the archdeceiver (12:9; 20:3,8,10).

because your merchants were the nobility
of the earth,
because all the nations were deceived
by your sorcery,[a]
24 and the blood of prophets and saints,
and all those slaughtered on earth, was found
in you.[b]

HEAVEN EXULTS OVER BABYLON

19 After this I heard something like the loud voice
of a vast multitude in heaven,
saying:

Hallelujah![c]
Salvation, glory, and power belong to our God,
2 because His judgments are true[d] and righteous,
because He has judged the notorious prostitute
who corrupted the earth
with her sexual immorality;
and He has avenged the blood of His servants
that was on her hands.

3 A second time they said:

Hallelujah![e]
Her smoke ascends forever and ever!

4 Then the 24 elders and the four living creatures fell
down and worshiped God, who is seated on the throne,
saying:

•Amen! Hallelujah![e]

5 A voice came from the throne, saying:

Praise our God,
all you His servants, you who fear Him,
both small and great!

MARRIAGE OF THE LAMB ANNOUNCED

6 Then I heard something like the voice of a vast mul-

[a]18:23 Ancient sorcery or witchcraft often used spells and drugs. Here the term may be non-literal, that is, Babylon drugged the nations with her beauty and power.
[b]18:24 Lit *in her*
[c]19:1 Lit *Praise Yahweh*; the Gk word is transliterated *hallelujah* from a Hb expression of praise and is used in many places in the OT, such as Ps 106:1.
[d]19:2 Valid; see Jn 8:16; 19:35
[e]19:3,4 See note at Rv 19:1

titude, like the sound of cascading waters, and like the rumbling of loud thunder, saying:

> Hallelujah[a] —because our Lord God,
>   the Almighty,
> has begun to reign!

7 Let us be glad, rejoice, and give Him glory,
  because the marriage of the Lamb has come,
  and His wife has prepared herself.
8 She was permitted to wear fine linen, bright
    and pure.

For the fine linen represents the righteous acts of the saints.

9 Then he[b] said to me, "Write: Blessed are those invited to the marriage feast of the Lamb!" He also said to me, "These words of God are true." 10 Then I fell at his feet to worship him, but he said to me, "Don't do that! I am a fellow •slave with you and your brothers who have the testimony about[c] Jesus. Worship God, because the testimony about[c] Jesus is the spirit of prophecy."

THE RIDER ON A WHITE HORSE

11 Then I saw heaven opened, and there was a white horse! Its rider is called Faithful and True, and in righteousness He judges and makes war. 12 His eyes were like a fiery flame, and on His head were many crowns. He had a name written that no one knows except Himself. 13 He wore a robe stained with blood,[d] and His name is called the Word of God. 14 The armies that were in heaven followed Him on white horses, wearing pure white linen. 15 From His mouth came a sharp[e] sword, so that with it He might strike the nations. He will shepherd[f] them with an iron scepter. He will also trample the winepress of the fierce anger of God, the Almighty. 16 And on His robe and on His thigh He has a name written:

KING OF KINGS
AND LORD OF LORDS.

WORD STUDY

Greek word: **poimaino**
[poy MIGH noh]
Translation: **shepherd**
Uses in Revelation: **4**
Uses in John's writings: **5**
Uses in the NT: **11**
Key passage: **Revelation 19:15**

Poimaino (*to shepherd*) basically means *to tend* or *nurture* sheep (Lk 17:7), and the related noun *poimen* was the common term for *shepherd*. However, *poimaino* was typically used in the more metaphorical sense of *to rule* or *govern*, typically with positive results but occasionally with negative ones (Rv 2:27; 12:5; 19:15). These last three references contain an allusion to Psalm 2:9, which indicates that the Lord's anointed will *rule* or *govern* (*poimaino* in the Greek OT) the nations "with a rod of iron." In the NT, *poimaino* typically retains the literal image of a shepherd tending sheep, while applying this metaphorically to those who take care of the Father's "flock" (Mt 2:6; Jn 21:16; Ac 20:28; 1 Pt 5:2; Rev 7:17). Revelation 7:17 involves a mixed metaphor, in that "the Lamb" is going to "*shepherd*" the redeemed.

---

[a]**19:6** See note at Rv 19:1
[b]**19:9** Probably an angel; see Rv 17:1; 22:8-9
[c]**19:10** Or *testimony to*
[d]**19:13** Or *a robe dipped in*
[e]**19:15** Other mss add *double-edged*
[f]**19:15** Or *rule*

THE BEAST AND HIS ARMIES DEFEATED

¹⁷ Then I saw an angel standing in the sun, and he cried out in a loud voice, saying to all the birds flying in mid-heaven, "Come, gather together for the great supper of God, ¹⁸ so that you may eat the flesh of kings, the flesh of commanders, the flesh of mighty men, the flesh of horses and of their riders, and the flesh of everyone, both free and •slave, small and great."

¹⁹ Then I saw the beast, the kings of the earth, and their armies gathered together to wage war against the rider on the horse and against His army. ²⁰ But the beast was taken prisoner, and along with him the false prophet, who had performed signs on his authority,ᵃ by which he deceived those who accepted the mark of the beast and those who worshiped his image. Both of them were thrown alive into the lake of fire that burns with sulfur. ²¹ The rest were killed with the sword that came from the mouth of the rider on the horse, and all the birds were filled with their flesh.

SATAN BOUND

20 Then I saw an angel coming down from heaven with the key to the •abyss and a great chain in his hand. ² He seized the dragon, that ancient serpent who is the Devil and Satan,ᵇ and bound him for 1,000 years. ³ He threw him into the abyss, closed it, and put a seal on it so that he would no longer deceive the nations until the 1,000 years were completed. After that, he must be released for a short time.

THE SAINTS REIGN WITH THE MESSIAH

⁴ Then I saw thrones, and people seated on them who were given authority to judge. ⌊I⌋ also ⌊saw⌋ the souls of those who had been beheadedᶜ because of their testimony about Jesus and because of God's word, who had not worshiped the beast or his image, and who had not accepted the mark on their foreheads or their hands. They came to life and reigned with the •Messiah for

Be a Long Story with a Happy Ending

What joy there is, not only in *beginning* well in our Christian faith, but also in *ending* faithfully.

I also saw the souls of those who had been beheaded because of their testimony about Jesus and because of God's word, who had not worshiped the beast or his image, and who had not accepted the mark on their foreheads or their hands. They came to life and reigned with the Messiah for 1,000 years.

—Revelation 20:4b

ᵃ**19:20** Lit *signs before him*
ᵇ**20:2** Other mss add *who deceives the whole world*

ᶜ**20:4** All who had given their lives for their faith in Christ

1,000 years. ⁵ The rest of the dead did not come to life until the 1,000 years were completed. This is the first resurrection. ⁶ Blessed and holy is the one who shares in the first resurrection! The second death has no powerᵃ over these, but they will be priests of God and the Messiah, and they will reign with Him for 1,000 years.

SATANIC REBELLION CRUSHED

⁷ When the 1,000 years are completed, Satan will be released from his prison ⁸ and will go out to deceive the nations at the four corners of the earth, Gog and Magog, to gather them for battle. Their number is like the sand of the sea. ⁹ They came up over the surface of the earth and surrounded the encampment of the saints, the beloved city. Then fire came down from heavenᵇ and consumed them. ¹⁰ The Devil who deceived them was thrown into the lake of fire and sulfur where the beast and the false prophet are, and they will be tormented day and night forever and ever.

THE GREAT WHITE THRONE JUDGMENT

¹¹ Then I saw a great white throne and One seated on it. Earth and heaven fled from His presence, and no place was found for them. ¹² I also saw the dead, the great and the small, standing before the throne, and books were opened. Another book was opened, which is the book of life, and the dead were judged according to their works by what was written in the books.

¹³ Then the sea gave up its dead, and Death and •Hades gave up their dead; allᶜ were judged according to their works. ¹⁴ Death and Hades were thrown into the lake of fire. This is the second death, the lake of fire.ᵈ ¹⁵ And anyone not found written in the book of life was thrown into the lake of fire.

THE NEW CREATION

21 Then I saw a new heaven and a new earth, for the first heaven and the first earth had passed away, and the sea existed no longer. ² I also saw the

---

ᵃ**20:6** Or *authority*
ᵇ**20:9** Other mss add *from God*
ᶜ**20:13** Lit *each*

ᵈ**20:14** Other mss omit *the lake of fire*

WORD STUDY

Greek word: *hades*
[hah DAYSS]

Translation: **Hades**

Uses in Revelation: **4**

Uses in the NT: **10**

Key passage: **Revelation 20:13-14**

In the Greek OT, *hades* almost always translates Hb *she'ol* (*She-ol*), the realm of the dead, where both righteous and unrighteous (Gn 37:35; Nm 16:30) live in shadowy, prison-like existence (2 Sm 22:6; Ezk 32:18-30). It was a place of no return (Jb 7:9-10; 16:22; Ec 12:5), though the righteous hoped to be delivered from there through divine intervention (Ps 16:10; 49:15; Is 26:19). By NT times, *Hades* was understood as the temporary abode of the dead, a place of peace for the believer and torment for the unbeliever (Lk 16:23-25). After Christ's resurrection, believers do not descend to *Hades* upon death but go immediately into Christ's presence (2 Co 5:8; Php 1:23). At the final resurrection, unbelievers will be raised from *Hades*, judged, and thrown along with *Hades* (Rv 20:14) into Hell (*geenna*), where they will suffer forever (Mt 25:41; Rv 20:15; 21:8). Christians know that *Hades* holds no power over them (Mt 16:18), since Christ rules over Hades (Rv 1:18).

WORD STUDY

Greek word: **alpha**
[AL fah]

Translation: **Alpha**

Uses in Revelation: **3**

Uses in the NT: **3**

Key passage: **Revelation 21:6**

Alpha is the first letter in the Greek alphabet, and *omega* is the last. In the NT, these two letters occur together three times in the phrase "the Alpha and the Omega," twice of God the Father (Rv 1:8; 21:6) and once of God the Son (22:13), indicating the close mutual unity between the Father and Son (cf. Jn 10:38; 14:10-11). "The Alpha and the Omega" appears in juxtaposition to "the One who is, who was, and who is coming" (Rv 1:8; cf. 1:4), as well as to "the Beginning and the End" (21:6) and "the First and the Last" (22:13). The phrase sums up the entirety of God's sovereign power over all things, specifically His control over all human history. "The Alpha and the Omega" has the power to begin and end all things in accordance with His decree, and the phrase provides strong affirmation of Jesus' deity and messianic lordship.

Holy City, new Jerusalem, coming down out of heaven from God, prepared like a bride adorned for her husband. ³ Then I heard a loud voice from the throne:[a]

> Look! God's dwelling[b] is with men,
> and He will live with them.
> They will be His people,
> and God Himself will be with them
> and be their God.[c]
> ⁴ He will wipe away every tear from their eyes.
> Death will exist no longer;
> grief, crying, and pain will exist no longer,
> because the previous things[d] have passed away.

⁵ Then the One seated on the throne said, "Look! I am making everything new." He also said, "Write, because these words[e] are faithful and true." ⁶ And He said to me, "It is done! I am the •Alpha and the Omega, the Beginning and the End. I will give to the thirsty from the spring of living water as a gift. ⁷ The victor will inherit these things, and I will be his God, and he will be My son. ⁸ But the cowards, unbelievers,[f] vile, murderers, sexually immoral, sorcerers, idolaters, and all liars—their share will be in the lake that burns with fire and sulfur, which is the second death."

THE NEW JERUSALEM

⁹ Then one of the seven angels, who had held the seven bowls filled with the seven last plagues, came and spoke with me: "Come, I will show you the bride, the wife of the Lamb." ¹⁰ He then carried me away in the Spirit[g] to a great and high mountain and showed me the holy city, Jerusalem, coming down out of heaven from God, ¹¹ arrayed with God's glory. Her radiance was like a very precious stone, like a jasper stone, bright as crystal. ¹² ⌊The city⌋ had a massive high wall, with 12 gates. Twelve angels were at the gates; ⌊on the gates⌋, names were inscribed, the names of the 12 tribes of the sons of Israel. ¹³ There were three gates on the east,

---

[a]**21:3** Other mss read *from heaven*
[b]**21:3** Or *tent*, or *tabernacle*
[c]**21:3** Other mss omit *and be their God*
[d]**21:4** Or *the first things*
[e]**21:5** Other mss add *of God*
[f]**21:8** Other mss add *the sinful*
[g]**21:10** Or *in spirit*

three gates on the north, three gates on the south, and three gates on the west. [14] The city wall had 12 foundations, and on them were the 12 names of the Lamb's 12 apostles.

[15] The one who spoke with me had a gold measuring rod to measure the city, its gates, and its wall. [16] The city is laid out in a square; its length and width are the same. He measured the city with the rod at 12,000 stadia.[a] Its length, width, and height are equal. [17] Then he measured its wall, 144 •cubits according to human measurement, which the angel used. [18] The building material of its wall was jasper, and the city was pure gold like clear glass.

[19] The foundations of the city wall were adorned with every kind of precious stone:

> the first foundation jasper,
> the second sapphire,
> the third chalcedony,
> the fourth emerald,
> [20] the fifth sardonyx,
> the sixth carnelian,
> the seventh chrysolite,
> the eighth beryl,
> the ninth topaz,
> the tenth chrysoprase,
> the eleventh jacinth,
> the twelfth amethyst.

[21] The 12 gates are 12 pearls; each individual gate was made of a single pearl. The broad street[b] of the city was pure gold, like transparent glass.

[22] I did not see a sanctuary in it, because the Lord God the Almighty and the Lamb are its sanctuary. [23] The city does not need the sun or the moon to shine on it, because God's glory illuminates it, and its lamp is the Lamb. [24] The nations[c] will walk in its light, and the kings of the earth will bring their glory into it.[d] [25] Each day its gates will never close because it will never be night there. [26] They will bring the glory and honor of the nations into it.[e] [27] Nothing profane will ever enter

God's Word Helps Us Keep Eternity in Mind

When God speaks, it is always in the context of eternity. We don't have to know all the implications of what He is asking. We just have to know it is a word from Almighty God.

Then the One seated on the throne said, "Look! I am making everything new." He also said, "Write, because these words are faithful and true." And He said to me, "It is done! I am the Alpha and the Omega, the Beginning and the End."

—Revelation 21:5-6a

---

[a]21:16 A *stadion* (sg) equals about 600 feet; the total is about 1,400 miles.
[b]21:21 Or *The public square*
[c]21:24 Other mss add *of those who are saved*
[d]21:24 Other mss read *will bring to Him the nations' glory and honor*
[e]21:26 Other mss add *in order that they might go in*

WORD STUDY

Greek word: **metopon**
[MEH toh pahn]

Translation: **forehead**

Uses in Revelation: **8**

Uses in the NT: **8**

Key passage: **Revelation 22:4**

___

In the ancient world, a mark on the *forehead* (*metopon*) normally involved a master/slave relationship (cf. word study on *seal* [*sphragis*]). Such markings were used to signify (1) tribal identity, (2) ownership, or (3) loyalty to a deity (closely related to ownership), as well as (4) to punish runaway slaves.

In the NT, *metopon* occurs in Revelation, where a mark on the *forehead* is always in view. On four occasions God claims ownership of His slaves by applying His name to their *foreheads*, protecting them from His judgment (7:3; 9:4; 14:1; 22:4). Three times God's enemies receive the mark of the beast (perhaps his name or 666) on their right hand or *forehead* (13:16; 14:9; 20:4). This represents a Satanic counterpart to God's sealing. Elsewhere, the prostitute riding the scarlet beast bears a cryptic name on her *forehead* (17:5), perhaps an allusion to the ancient practice of Roman prostitutes placing their names on headbands.

it: no one who does what is vile or false, but only those written in the Lamb's book of life.

THE SOURCE OF LIFE

22 Then he showed me the river[a] of living water, sparkling like crystal, flowing from the throne of God and of the Lamb [2] down the middle of the broad street ˌof the cityˌ. On both sides of the river was the tree of life[b] bearing 12 kinds of fruit, producing its fruit every month. The leaves of the tree are for healing the nations, [3] and there will no longer be any curse. The throne of God and of the Lamb will be in the city,[c] and His servants will serve Him. [4] They will see His face, and His name will be on their foreheads. [5] Night will no longer exist, and people will not need lamplight or sunlight, because the Lord God will give them light. And they will reign forever and ever.

THE TIME IS NEAR

[6] Then he said to me, "These words are faithful and true. And the Lord, the God of the spirits of the prophets,[d] has sent His angel to show His servants what must quickly take place."[e]

[7] "Look, I am coming quickly! Blessed is the one who keeps the prophetic words of this book."

[8] I, John, am the one who heard and saw these things. When I heard and saw them, I fell down to worship at the feet of the angel who had shown them to me. [9] But he said to me, "Don't do that! I am a fellow •slave with you, your brothers the prophets, and those who keep the words of this book. Worship God." [10] He also said to me, "Don't seal the prophetic words of this book, because the time is near. [11] Let the unrighteous go on in unrighteousness; let the filthy go on being made filthy; let the righteous go on in righteousness; and let the holy go on being made holy."

[12] "Look! I am coming quickly, and My reward is with Me to repay each person according to what he has

___

[a]**22:1** Other mss read *pure river*
[b]**22:2** Or *was a tree of life*, or *was a tree that gives life*
[c]**22:3** Lit *in it*

[d]**22:6** Other mss read *God of the holy prophets*
[e]**22:6** Or *soon*

done. ¹³ I am the •Alpha and the Omega, the First and the Last, the Beginning and the End.

¹⁴ "Blessed are those who wash their robes,ᵃ so that they may have the right to the tree of life and may enter the city by the gates. ¹⁵ Outside are the dogs, the sorcerers, the sexually immoral, the murderers, the idolaters, and everyone who loves and practices lying.

¹⁶ "I, Jesus, have sent My angel to attest these things to youᵇ for the churches. I am the Root and the Offspring of David, the Bright Morning Star."

¹⁷ Both the Spirit and the bride say, "Come!" Anyone who hears should say, "Come!" And the one who is thirsty should come. Whoever desires should take the living water as a gift.

¹⁸ I testify to everyone who hears the prophetic words of this book: If anyone adds to them, God will add to him the plagues that are written in this book. ¹⁹ And if anyone takes away from the words of this prophetic book, God will take away his share of the tree of life and the holy city, written in this book.

²⁰ He who testifies about these things says, "Yes, I am coming quickly."

•Amen! Come, Lord Jesus!

²¹ The grace of the Lord Jesusᶜ be with all the saints.ᵈ Amen.ᵉ

Just Share What He's Been Showing You

There is nothing more appealing or convincing to a watching world than to hear the testimony of someone who has just been with Jesus.

I, John, am the one who heard and saw these things. When I heard and saw them, I fell down to worship at the feet of the angel who had shown them to me.

—Revelation 22:8

You'll Be So Glad You Served Your Lord

You will never do anything more practical than to place your trust in the Lord. Nothing is more secure or certain than that which you entrust to God.

"Look! I am coming quickly, and My reward is with Me to repay each person according to what he has done."

—Revelation 22:12

ᵃ22:14 Other mss read *who keep His commandments*
ᵇ22:16 *you* (pl in Gk)
ᶜ22:21 Other mss add *Christ*
ᵈ22:21 Other mss omit *the saints*
ᵉ22:21 Other mss omit *Amen.*

Holman CSB Bullet Notes

Holman CSB Bullet Notes are one of the unique features of the Holman Christian Standard Bible. These notes explain frequently used biblical words or terms. These "bullet" words (for example: •abyss) are normally marked with a bullet only on their first occurrence in a chapter of the biblical text. However, certain important or easily misunderstood terms, such as •Jews or •slaves, will have more than one bullet per chapter. Other frequently used words, like •walk, are marked with bullets only where the use of the word fits the definitions given below. A few words in footnotes, like •stumble, also have a bullet.

Abba	Aram word for "father"
abyss	Or *the bottomless pit*, or *the depths* (of the sea); the prison for Satan and the demons
advocate	(see "Counselor/advocate")
Alpha and Omega	First and last letters of the Gk alphabet; used to refer to God the Father in Rv 1:8 and 21:6, and to Jesus, God the Son in Rv 22:13
Amen	Transliteration of a Hb word signifying that something is certain, valid, truthful, or faithful; often used at the end of biblical songs, hymns, and prayers
asleep	Term used in reference to believers who have died
Beelzebul	Term of slander, variously interpreted "lord of flies," "lord of dung," or "ruler of demons"; Mk 3:22
cause the downfall of/ causes to sin	The Greek word *skandalizo* has a root meaning of "snare" or "trap," but no real English counterpart.
centurion	A Roman officer who commanded about 100 soldiers
Cephas	Aram word for *rock* parallel to Gk *petros* from which the Eng name Peter is derived; Jn 1:42; 1 Co 1:12
chief priest(s)	In Judaism a group of temple officers that included the high priest, captain of the temple, temple overseers, and treasurers

company/ regiment	Or *cohort*, a Roman military unit that numbered as many as 600 men
convert/ proselyte	A person from another race/religion who went through a prescribed ritual to become a Jew
Counselor/advocate	Gk *parakletos;* one called alongside to help, counsel, or protect; used of the Holy Spirit in Jn and in 1 Jn
cubit	An OT measurement of distance; about 18 inches.
Decapolis	Originally a federation of 10 Gentile towns east of the Jordan River
denarius	Small silver Roman coin equal to a day's wages for a common laborer
engaged	Jewish engagement was a binding agreement that could only be broken by divorce
firstfruits	The first products of agriculture given to God as an offering; also used to mean the first of more to come
Hades	The Gk word for the place of the dead, corresponding to the Hb word *Sheol*
headquarters/palace	Lat *Praetorium* used by Gk writers for the residence of the Roman governor; may also refer to military headquarters, the imperial court, or the emperor's guard
hell/hellfire	Gk *gehenna;* Aram for Valley of Hinnom on the south side of Jerusalem; formerly a place of human sacrifice, and in NT times, a place for the burning of garbage; place of final judgment for those rejecting Christ
Herod	Name of the Idumean family ruling Palestine from 37 B.C. to A.D. 95; the main rulers from this family mentioned in the NT are:
Herod I	(37 B.C.–4 B.C.) also known as Herod the Great; built the great temple in Jerusalem and massacred the male babies in Bethlehem

Herod Antipas	(4 B.C.–A.D. 39) son of Herod the Great; ruled one-fourth of his father's kingdom (Galilee and Perea); killed John the Baptist and mocked Jesus
Agrippa I	(A.D. 37–44) grandson of Herod the Great; beheaded James the apostle and imprisoned Peter
Agrippa II	(A.D. 52–c. 95) great-grandson of Herod the Great; tried Paul
Herodians	Political supporters of Herod the Great and his family
horn	A symbol of power based on the strength of animal horns
Hosanna	A term of praise derived from the Hb word for save
I assure you	In Mt, Mk, and Lk, a translation of lit *Amen, I say to you,* and in Jn, a translation of lit *Amen, amen, I say to you;* a phrase used only by Jesus to testify to the certainty and importance of His words.
Jew(s)	In Jn the term *Jews* usually indicates those in Israel who were opposed to Jesus, particularly the Jewish authorities in Jerusalem who led the nation.
life/soul	The same Gk word (*psyche*) can be translated *life* or *soul.*
Mary Magdalene	Or *Mary of Magdala;* Magdala was most likely a town on the western shore of the Sea of Galilee and north of Tiberias.
Messiah	Or *the Christ;* Gk *Christos,* meaning "the anointed one"
Mount of Olives	A mountain east of Jerusalem across the Kidron valley
mystery	Transliteration of Gk *mysterion,* a secret hidden in the past but now revealed
Nazarene	A person from Nazareth; growing up in Nazareth was an aspect of the Messiah's humble beginnings; see Jn 1:46.
offspring/seed	This term is used literally or metaphorically to refer to plants or grain, sowing or harvest, male reproductive seed, human children or physical descendants, and also to spiritual children or to Christ (Gl 3:16).

One and Only	Or *only begotten,* or *one of a kind,* or *incomparable;* the Gk word could refer to someone's only child; see Lk 7:12; 8:42; 9:38. It could also refer to someone's special child; see Heb 11:17.
overseer(s)	Or *elder(s),* or *bishop(s)*
palace	(see "headquarters/palace")
Passover	The Jewish ritual meal celebrating Israel's deliverance from slavery in Egypt
Pharisee(s)	In Judaism a religious sect that followed the whole written and oral law
Pilate	Pontius Pilate was governor of the province of Judea A.D. 26–36.
proconsul	Chief Roman government official in a senatorial province who presided over Roman court hearings.
proselyte	(see "convert/proselyte")
Rabbi	*Rabbi = my great one* in Hb, used of a recognized teacher of the Scriptures
regiment	(see "company/regiment")
sacred bread	Lit *bread of presentation;* 12 loaves, representing the 12 tribes of Israel, put on the table in the holy place in the tabernacle, and later in the temple. The priests ate the previous week's loaves.
Sadducee(s)	In Judaism a religious sect that followed primarily the first five books of the OT (Torah or Pentateuch)
Samaritan(s)	People of mixed, Gentile/Jewish ancestry who lived between Galilee and Judea and were hated by the Jews
Sanhedrin	The seventy-member supreme council of Judaism, patterned after Moses' 70 elders
scribe(s)	A professional group in Judaism that copied the law of Moses and interpreted it, especially in legal cases

slave	The strong Greek word *doulos* cannot be accurately translated in English by "servant" or "bond servant"; the HCSB translates this word as "slave," not out of insensitivity to the legitimate concerns of modern English speakers, but out of a commitment to accurately convey the brutal reality of the Roman empire's inhumane institution as well as the ownership called for by Christ.
Son of Man	Most frequent title Jesus used for Himself
stumble	(see "cause the downfall of/cause to sin")
synagogue	A place where the Jewish people met for prayer, worship and teaching of the Scriptures
tabernacle	Or *tent,* or *shelter,* terms used for temporary housing
tassel	Fringes that devout Jews wore on their clothing to remind them to keep the law
temple complex	In the Jerusalem temple, the sanctuary (the holy place and the holy of holies), at least four courtyards (for priests, Jews, women, and Gentiles), numerous gates, and several covered walkways.
Unleavened Bread	A seven-day festival celebrated in conjunction with the Passover
walk	Term often used in a figurative way to mean "way of life" or "behavior"
wise men	Gk *magoi;* "magi," based on Persian word; eastern sages who observed the heavens for signs and omens
woman	When used in direct address, "Woman" was not a term of disrespect but of honor.